THE FLAWED ARCHITECT

The Flawed Architect

HENRY KISSINGER
AND AMERICAN
FOREIGN POLICY

Jussi Hanhimäki

OXFORD
UNIVERSITY PRESS
2004

OXFORD
UNIVERSITY PRESS
Oxford   New York

Auckland   Bangkok   Buenos Aires   Cape Town   Chennai
Dar es Salaam   Delhi   Hong Kong   Istanbul   Karachi   Kolkata
Kuala Lumpur   Madrid   Melbourne   Mexico City   Mumbai   Nairobi
São Paulo   Shanghai   Taipei   Tokyo   Toronto

Copyright © 2004 by Jussi Hanhimäki

Published by Oxford University Press, Inc.
198 Madison Avenue, New York, New York, 10016
www.oup.com

Library of Congress Cataloging-in-Publication Data
Hanhimäki, Jussi M., 1965–
The flawed architect : Henry Kissinger and American
foreign policy / by Jussi Hanhimäki.
p.   cm.   Includes bibiliographical references and index.
ISBN 0-19-517221-3
1. Kissinger, Henry, 1923–   2. Statesmen—United States—Bibliography.
3. Cabinet officers—United States—Bibliography.   4. United States—Foreign relations—
1969–1974.   5. United States—Politics and government—1969–1974.   I. Title.
E840.8.K58H36   2004
973.924′092—dc22   2004008371

1 3 5 7 9 8 6 4 2
Printed in the United States of America
on acid-free paper

To my son Jari

Contents

Acknowledgments

Every book has its own history and *The Flawed Architect* is no exception. My initial interest in writing about Henry Kissinger goes back to 1995, when the London School of Economics hired me as a lecturer in international history. Upon discussing my first year's teaching assignments, the chair (or "convenor") of my new department told me about a popular course that he hoped (insisted would have been the correct word) I would take on. Eager to please my new boss I accepted, although the title of the course gave me some pause. Yet, for the next three years I taught "Henry Kissinger and the Crisis of American Foreign Policy."

During those three years, several things happened. First, I discovered, largely due to the enthusiasm of my students and certainly to my own surprise, that I had stumbled on an exciting topic. Second, after the first year of teaching the course, I realized that while the reading list I had inherited was massive, the literature on Henry Kissinger was stale and influenced heavily by the preconceptions of Kissinger's defenders and detractors. Gradually, the idea of writing a brief reassessment of the Kissinger years began to form in my mind. As soon as I set my mind on that task, however, yet another development occurred. The record of the Nixon and Ford years began to be declassified. Starting in the late 1990s, the Nixon Presidential Materials Project released massive amounts of the administration's National Security Council materials that included records of Kissinger's negotiations with the Soviets, the Chinese, the Vietnamese, and others. Similar documents were opened in the Gerald Ford Library. There were the Nixon tapes that, even as much of them remain classified, provided a revealing window into the Kissinger–

Nixon relationship. And there was a trickle of documents from Soviet, Chinese, Vietnamese, and other relevant archives.

Thus, instead of a brief textbook-like reassessment, I chose to utilize the newly released materials and undertake a fuller reevaluation of Henry Kissinger and American foreign policy. The end result—*The Flawed Architect*—took somewhat longer to complete than originally planned. But the excitement of working with previously unseen documents, eavesdropping on Nixon and Kissinger's conversations, and interviewing Kissinger and other members of the Nixon and Ford administrations was certainly worth the procrastination.

*   *   *

Over the years I accumulated an increasing number of debts to institutions and individuals. In addition to my many students in HY 306 (that "popular" course), I would like to acknowledge my former colleagues at the London School of Economics. A special thanks goes to Antony Best, MacGregor Knox (who persuaded me to teach HY 306), Piers Ludlow, Kirsten Schultze, David Stevenson, and Odd Arne Westad. Similarly, I would like to acknowledge the encouragement of a number of my colleagues at the Graduate Institute of International Studies in Geneva, Switzerland, particularly: Bruno Arcidiacono, Gopalan Balachandran, Philippe Burrin, Pierre Dubois, Keith Krause, Andre Liebich, David Sylvan, Danny Warner, and Lanxin Xiang. My students in Geneva did not have to endure a year-long course on Kissinger. But they patiently tolerated my numerous references and anecdotes that touched upon the subject matter of this book. Merci.

At the Norwegian Nobel Institute in Oslo, where I was fortunate to spend several months in the spring of 2001, I would like to thank Geir Lundestad and Olav Njolstad for their encouragement and good-humored criticism as well as everyone in the staff—especially Grete Haram, Sigrid Langebrekke, Torill Johansen, Anne Kjelling, Inger-Guri Flogstad, and Bjorn Vangen—for making my stay a great success in all possible ways. Tack. I would further like to acknowledge the camaraderie that developed between the other fellows in residence at Drammensveien during my stay: John Macmillan, John Mueller, and Patrick Salmon.

The Woodrow Wilson International Center for Scholars provided a wonderful setting for completing the bulk of this manuscript. The Center's director, Lee Hamilton, was gracious with his time and even helped me with securing an interview with Henry Kissinger. Christian Osterman, the director of the Cold War International History Project at the Wilson Center and Rob Litwak, the director of the International Studies Program, were particularly helpful. Others who helped make my year at the Wilson Center a truly memorable one included: Joe Brinley, Arlyn Charles, Kim Conner, Dagne Gizaw, Bob Hathaway, Michelle Kutler, Nancy Meyers, Mircea Munteanu, Janet Spikes, Don Wolfensberger, Joseph Tulchin, and Sam Wells. My interns at the Wilson Center, Rodolfo Neirotti and Jonathan White, offered exemplary research assistance. And, I particularly wish to acknowledge my buddy on the third floor, Lindsay Collins.

The archivists at the National Archives and the Gerald R. Ford Library deserve a special thank you for their patience with my often naïve questions. I would also like to acknowledge the financial assistance of the Ford Library that enabled me to travel to Ann Arbor for an extended period of time.

For a historian, there is nothing like meeting those who were "present at the creation." I am grateful to those who agreed to be interviewed. In addition to Henry Kissinger, among these were: Lee Hamilton, Winston Lord, Peter Rodman, William Rogers, Brent Scowcroft, Richard Solomon, and Helmut Sonnenfeldt. Others preferred to remain anonymous.

A special mention, as always, goes to two men I consider as my mentors. Arnold Offner who, aside from serving as my Ph.D. adviser during the (first) Bush administration has been, over the years, a great supporter and friend. Keith Olson was instrumental in getting me started on the study of American history. In the past five–six years Keith not only read many draft chapters of this work in their earlier phases but he and Marilyn Olson were incredibly generous with their hospitality during my many research trips to Washington.

I was extremely fortunate to have Timothy Bartlett as my editor at Oxford University Press. His close attention to the details of this book improved its final shape immeasurably. I would also like to acknowledge the other members of the OUP team who bore some of the burden of getting this book into its final form: Barbara Fillon, Woody Gilmartin, Peter Harper, Helen Mules, Matthew Sollars, Rob Tempio and others. For a thorough job of copyediting I would like to acknowledge Maria E. denBoer and Carol Bifulco.

There are many others who have offered their suggestions and encouragement in a number of ways. I would like to thank Avis Bohlen, William Burr, David Calleo, Saki Dockrill, John Gaddis, Bill Keylor, Jeffrey Kimball, Denis Kux, Klaus Larres, Vojtech Mastny, David Mayers, Andrew Preston, Robert Schulzinger, Thomas Schwartz, Jeremi Suri, Tapani Vaahtoranta, and Tom Zeiler. I may have missed someone—do forgive me!

Last, but assuredly not least, I would like to acknowledge my family. My parents, Hilkka Uuskallio and Jussi K. Hanhimäki, whom I see far too seldom, but who have never ceased to be supportive of their errant son's foolish efforts. Kiitos. My in-laws, Marian and Alan Schauber, for their encouragement (yes, it's finally finished). Most importantly my wife, Holli Schauber, was, yet again, supportive in all possible ways. I can never thank her enough. But I've tried.

The book is dedicated to my son, Jari Albin Hanhimäki. To the shock of some of my colleagues and to the delight of others, Jari's first three-syllable word was Kissinger. That, alone, made all the work worthwhile.

Needless to say, the responsibility for any mistakes and shortcomings in this book is solely mine.

J.M.H.
Geneva, Switzerland
March 2004

Introduction

A Prize-Winning Performance?

It was late afternoon on December 10, 1973. At the town hall of Oslo, Norway, everyone was getting ready for the ritual that each year briefly focuses the world's attention on this Scandinavian capital: the awarding of the Nobel Peace Prize. There was
just one problem: the recipient of the prize, U.S. Secretary of State Henry Alfred
Kissinger, was nowhere in sight.

Two months earlier, the Norwegian Nobel Committee had, in fact, announced
two winners. Le Duc Tho, Kissinger's principal North Vietnamese counterpart in
the Paris peace talks, angrily refused to accept the prize, denouncing South Vietnamese violations of the January 1973 agreements. Kissinger had accepted but cited
a NATO foreign ministers' conference in Brussels as the reason for his absence from
the ceremonies. Many observers, though, assumed that he simply did not wish to
be subjected to the wrath of the demonstrators who would surely protest his winning the award. Others wondered whether Kissinger decided to bypass the ceremonies in order not to further inflame his tense relationship with his boss, Richard
Nixon, who resented his high-profile secretary of state for stealing the limelight
while the president himself was being attacked for his role in the Watergate scandal. Whatever the reason for Kissinger's absence from Oslo, however, the U.S.
ambassador to Norway, Thomas Byrne, ended up reading Kissinger's brief acceptance speech to an audience, which in keeping with the uniqueness of that year's
ceremony, had not filled the auditorium. In the United States Edwin Reischauer, a
renowned scholar of Japan, tapped into the popular mood when he quipped that
the choice of Kissinger "shows either that the people of Norway have a very poor

understanding of what happened out there [in Vietnam] or a good sense of humor." He implied that the former was the case.[1]

Aase Lionës, the chair of the Norwegian Nobel Committee, showed that she could also partake in the controversy that the announcement had so obviously provoked. In her speech during the ceremonies, Lionës provided a selective overview of the Vietnam War. She mentioned that the South Vietnamese government had refused to hold elections in 1956 because they "maintained that free elections could not be carried out under the Communist regime" in the North; she did not describe the United States' role in supporting that decision. Nor did Lionës assess the various stages of escalation and carnage that had followed. Although acknowledging that hostilities still continued, Lionës asserted that the January 1973 Paris Agreements constituted a "tremendously important step on the road to full peace." As a carrot of sorts, Lionës said that Le Duc Tho had until October 1, 1974, to accept the prize. Tho, or "Ducky" as Kissinger and his staff members liked to call him, was not interested. In due course, at the end of April 1975, North Vietnamese troops overran South Vietnam and unified the country under communist rule.

There was another, little noticed, aspect to Lionës's speech. She emphasized that the prize was not given simply for Kissinger's efforts in Vietnam but for his entire "experiment" (Lionës's word) since 1969. With due attention to Kissinger's "realism" Lionës particularly applauded his efforts to promote the triangular framework: Kissinger's policy of enlisting China and the Soviet Union as "equal partners" in pursuing peace. Lionës also acknowledged Kissinger's increasingly central role in the Middle East peace process that had commenced in the aftermath of the 1973 (Yom Kippur) War.[2]

In announcing one of the most controversial of the Nobel Peace Prizes, Aase Lionës thus made it clear that the honor was not just for the hours Kissinger had spent with Le Duc Tho in negotiating the Paris Agreements that ended the American involvement in Vietnam. Instead, Kissinger was receiving the Nobel Peace Prize for his overall performance as a statesman and diplomat who had helped launch a new era in American foreign policy and international relations. Vietnam, by implication, was but a sideshow when compared to Kissinger's broader achievements. No matter what happened in Vietnam, the Nobel Committee's chairperson asserted, Kissinger deserved the prize for his efforts in reshaping the nature of international relations. But the absence of the guest of honor, the hundreds of demonstrators camping outside the town hall in the cold Norwegian winter, and the quips of observers like Reischauer were all indications of the controversy surrounding the man who had just been awarded one of the most sought-after prizes a statesman of any nationality could ever achieve.

What should have been one of the highpoints of Henry Kissinger's career was thus symbolic of how divisive the record of the United States' fifty-sixth secretary of state had already become. Many considered him the foremost statesman of his era. Polls had shown him to be the most admired man in America. Kissinger had dazzled the world with his globetrotting diplomacy that had produced, by 1973, the historic opening to China, the first nuclear arms treaty between the United States and the Soviet Union, and the extrication of American forces from the country's longest war. Early in 1974, Kissinger would be at the center of yet another breakthrough, as Israel and Egypt signed a disengagement agreement that launched a decades-long peace process in the Middle East. Many even thought that as Kissinger's boss battled his Watergate ghosts, it was only the aura of Kissinger that kept Nixon in office.

Yet, there was the other side. Already by December 1973, Kissinger was shrouded in controversy. His penchant to operate secretly and abilities at bureaucratic maneuvering made many consider Kissinger more a schemer and a stuntman than a miracle-worker. Others wondered whether Kissinger (and Nixon) had missed a chance to conclude the Vietnam War when they first came into office, choosing to prolong the war by another four years at the cost of some 20,000 additional American (and countless Vietnamese) lives. While the opening to China was heralded as a major breakthrough, the abandonment of Taiwan seemed to some, particularly those on the right, to be a shameful act. The SALT I agreement of 1972 had done little to curb the arms race, many argued, while others complained that it had given the Soviets an unfair advantage to develop their nuclear arsenal. In subsequent years further controversies—over Kissinger's role in the overthrow of Salvador Allende in Chile, his links to the CIA, his apparent disregard for human rights, and his wiretapping of his own staff members—further inflamed those unwilling to regard Henry Kissinger in a positive light.

Three decades after he was awarded the Nobel Peace Prize, the controversy continues.

To many, Henry Kissinger is the quintessential American icon, a great American success story. Kissinger is, after all, a Jewish-German immigrant who narrowly escaped the Holocaust to serve at the highest levels of U.S. government. A quarter century after he left office, the former secretary of state and national security adviser to Presidents Nixon and Ford commands the attention of scholars, policy makers, and the general public. Kissinger continues to yield influence through his links to Republican policy makers and his frequent, and always noted, media appearances. At the age of eighty, the German-born scholar-diplomat-entrepreneur remains a household name around the globe. When compared to his successors, Henry Alfred Kissinger—the Harvard professor, national security adviser, secretary of state, Nobel Peace Prize winner, best-selling author, opinion maker, chairman of a multimillion-dollar consulting company, and media celebrity—remains, clearly, in a class of his own. As Ronald Reagan's Secretary of State George P. Shultz, once remarked: "There's only one Henry Kissinger. They broke the mold after they made him."[3]

"Thank god," some would immediately respond. After the 2001 publication of Christopher Hitchens's vitriolic *Trial of Henry Kissinger* and the 2002 release of BBC's eighty-minute documentary based on that work, Kissinger suddenly reemerged as the central character in a controversy usually reserved for such dictators as the former Yugoslav President Slobodan Milosevic or the former Chilean head of state Augusto Pinochet. As Hitchens and many others contend, Henry Kissinger may have opened China and negotiated the first major nuclear arms limitations treaty, but he also pushed for the secret bombing and subsequent invasion of Cambodia in 1969–70, has been implicated in the overthrow and assassination of Chile's President Salvador Allende, and may have given the green light to the Indonesian crackdown on East Timor in late 1975. Kissinger himself has countered such charges in his recent publications that include the 1999 third volume of his memoirs, *The Years of Renewal*, his 2001 book *Does America Need a Foreign Policy?* and the 2003 works *Ending the Vietnam War* and *Crisis*.[4] In December 2002, amid controversy regarding his business contacts, Kissinger chose to resign as the chairman of a high-profile committee set up to investigate the terrorist attacks of September 11, 2001.

Indeed, the debate over "Dr. Kissinger"—the prince of realpolitik who put his remarkable insights to the service of a nation in deep trouble—and "Mr. Henry"—the immoral, power-hungry, and secretive bureaucratic schemer bent on self-aggrandizement—will forever cloud the assessments and reassessments of Kissinger's career.[5]

In essence, the central question still remains: Was his a prize winning performance? By carefully analyzing the mass of newly declassified documents from Kissinger's years in office, this book will endeavor to answer that question.

The main thrust of the argument in *The Flawed Architect* runs as follows. When he joined the Nixon administration as the new president's key foreign policy adviser, Kissinger hoped to reclaim for the United States its position as the dominant player in world affairs that it had, arguably, lost as a result of the Vietnam War. He was initially successful. Stressing private diplomacy and operating out of the public eye through a series of back channels and secret negotiations, Kissinger orchestrated the era of détente with the Soviet Union and the opening to China in 1971. He managed to negotiate the American exit from (if not a durable peace in) Vietnam by early 1973. And, after the October 1973 War, Kissinger played an instrumental role in securing for the United States a dominant position in the Middle East.

At this point (in 1973–74), however, Kissinger's foreign policy began to disintegrate. The Sino-American rapprochement did not proceed toward a full normalization of diplomatic relations until after Kissinger left office. Détente with the Soviet Union became such a dirty word, as a result of growing domestic criticism from the left and the right, that Gerald Ford banned the use of the word in his unsuccessful 1976 presidential campaign. Meanwhile, many of Kissinger's other diplomatic achievements, including the Vietnam peace agreements, began to fall apart at the seams. "Super-K" (as *Newsweek* dubbed Kissinger in 1974) left office in early 1977 both widely admired and bitterly criticized. Yet, one fact appeared clear: even as Kissinger had become a household name, he had not managed to build a sustainable foreign policy structure.

Whereas the architect had soared to public consciousness, the architecture itself was collapsing.

The big question, of course, is why Kissinger was unable to build and sustain a new foreign policy structure even as he managed to negotiate a seemingly endless series of breakthroughs with the Soviets, the Chinese, and the leaders in the Middle East.

Part of the answer has to do with the incompatibility of Kissinger's operating style and U.S. domestic politics. The Kissinger years were, after all, as much the era of Watergate as they were an era of détente and triangular diplomacy. At the time of the Watergate scandal and revelations of other Nixon-era abuses of power, Kissinger's operating methods were bound to arouse intense scrutiny and criticism. In the early 1970s, back channels may have been justified as a means of launching détente. Secrecy may have been necessary to secure the opening to China. But such clandestine activity had no place in an America suffering from the hangover of Nixon's ignoble and self-inflicted political destruction. Moreover, there was always the lingering question about Kissinger's own role in fostering the climate that produced the "White House Horrors" of the Nixon years. He had, after all, ordered the wiretapping of several of his own staff members as early as 1969. In this regard, Kissinger's personal flaws—his susceptibility to worrying about leaks of information and bureaucratic conspiracies—eventually undermined the substance of his foreign policy.

Perhaps more important—a point Kissinger himself has repeatedly stressed— the Watergate era, together with the lingering trauma of the Vietnam War, produced an adversarial relationship between the executive and the legislative branches of government. In the mid-1970s, the U.S. Congress constantly scrutinized and often strenuously opposed various foreign policy initiatives. Détente with the Soviet Union, for example, was dealt a severe blow when the Congress insisted on a linkage between freedom of emigration from and the granting of Most Favored Nation (MFN) status to the USSR. Having been largely cut off from major foreign policy decisions in past decades, congressional leaders, particularly those with aspirations for higher office, wanted to get their piece of the action. By 1976, moreover, Kissinger's policies became campaign fodder in the mills of Republican and Democratic political machines.

Kissinger may have been an effective negotiator and a capable architect of a strategic vision. He may have understood the limits and capabilities of American power more clearly than many of his contemporaries. He may have stunned the world and emerged as the first diplomatic superstar of the modern era. But Kissinger was a poor salesman, incapable of articulating a foreign policy vision in a way that would have secured broad support from domestic audiences. This lack of rapport with the American public—the heartland that he tried to reach during a series of speeches in 1976— was another central shortcoming that made Kissinger a flawed architect.

But there was something else. In addition to Kissinger's secretive operating style and his inability to relate to domestic policy concerns, one must look elsewhere to fathom fully why his architecture failed to take hold. One key point, explored in detail throughout the book, warrants some elucidation at the outset.

Simply put, the architecture itself was flawed. While Kissinger was undoubtedly correct in stressing the limits of American power in the context of the Vietnam War and the need to emphasize diplomacy as an instrument of fighting the Cold War, he was unable to break with some of the persistent paradigms of the Cold War. He operated, essentially, in the same bilateral framework as his predecessors had, taking it as a given that containing Soviet power—if not communist ideology—should be the central goal of American foreign policy. Almost every initiative he pursued— the opening to China, the search for a negotiated settlement in Vietnam, shuttle diplomacy in the Middle East, the efforts to renew the transatlantic alliance—was aimed at serving this goal. Given the context of his times there was, of course, nothing surprising in Kissinger's preoccupation with the Soviet Union. Moreover, his effort to deal with the Soviet Union in a creative manner by employing China as a counterweight to the USSR was commendable.

Yet, Kissinger's approach was also limiting and, ultimately, counterproductive.

The Flawed Architect illustrates this central flaw in Kissinger's policies by emphasizing the relationship between his overall strategic vision—triangular diplomacy and détente—and the need to deal with specific but often complex, sudden, and geographically disparate regional conflicts. While Kissinger engaged the Chinese and the Soviets in a serious process of negotiation, limited wars continued (Vietnam, 1969–75), exploded onto the scene (Angola, 1974–76) or were reignited due to specific local circumstances (the 1971 Indo-Pakistani and the 1973 Middle East Wars). Without exception, I argue, Kissinger viewed the regional crises as inherently linked to triangular diplomacy. His approach to the settlement in Vietnam, for example, relied heavily on engaging the Soviets and Chinese in the peace process. But Vietnam was not the only example. Kissinger was concerned about the Indo-Pakistani crisis of 1971 mainly because of its potential impact on the simultaneous opening to China. Kissinger justified his intense involvement in the Middle East negotiations after October 1973 as a way of limiting the considerable Soviet influence in the region. In 1975, Kissinger's failed efforts to prevent the Soviet-backed Movimento Popular de Libertacao de Angola, or the Popular Movement for the Liberation of Angola (MPLA) from gaining power in Angola were based on a similar logic: the Soviets needed to be prevented from gaining a foothold in southwest Africa. Whether it was tilting toward Pakistan in its conflict with India, shuttle diplomacy in the Middle East, or covert aid to the Frente Nacional de Libertacao de Angola, or the National Front for the Liberation of Angola (FNLA) in Angola, the justification remained the same: containing enhanced Soviet influence. In a sense, Kissinger was not reacting to the crises themselves, but treating them as part of his predetermined agenda, as extensions of the big game of triangular diplomacy. As a result, the complex regional and local causes of these conflicts were largely ignored and remained unresolved during Kissinger's period in office. Many of these regional conflicts continue to haunt American policy makers today.

With the possible exception of the Middle East, American policy in these regional conflicts yielded few positive results. One needs only to cite the fall of Saigon and the unification of Vietnam in the spring of 1975 or the foundation of the People's Republic of Angola in early 1976 to underline this point. In short, whatever his early successes in launching triangular diplomacy, Kissinger espoused a policy toward regional conflicts—and the so-called third world in general—that failed to introduce stability in the most volatile areas of the world. Moreover, the tension created by the regional conflicts, particularly the Middle East War and the Angolan conflict, would undermine Soviet-American détente and erode the very basis of Kissinger's diplomacy. While there were some enduring legacies—there was no turning back the clock on the opening to China, for example—Kissinger's architecture was inherently flawed. Realpolitik proved a poor match with the realities of the third world.

*   *   *

The structure of *The Flawed Architect* reflects the rise and fall of Kissinger's grand strategy. It begins with a discussion of Kissinger's life and career—from his childhood in Nazi Germany to his gradual rise within the American foreign policy establishment—prior to his coming into office in early 1969, followed by a brief analysis of the Nixon–Kissinger relationship in 1968 and the centralization of foreign policy decision making in the first Nixon administration. In contrast, the last chapter of the book charts out Kissinger's career after he left office in early 1977: his memoirs, his role as the chairman of Kissinger Associates, an international consulting firm that did a brisk multimillion-dollar business, and his influence on subsequent administrations' foreign policy.

The bulk of the work, though, is devoted to Kissinger's time in office. Chapters 3 through 12 examine Kissinger's diplomacy from January 1969 to the summer of 1973. These chapters focus heavily on the emergence of détente and triangular diplomacy and their links to the Vietnam War. Chapter 8 focuses on one of the key regional crises of this period—the Indo-Pakistani War of 1971—and the ways in which the emergence of triangular diplomacy affected American policy toward the South Asian subcontinent.

Chapter 13 begins with Kissinger becoming secretary of state in September 1973. This added responsibility (Kissinger also maintained his post as the national security adviser for another two years) marked the zenith of his career, as Kissinger—in part due to Nixon's Watergate troubles, in part due to Gerald Ford's inexperience— had virtually total control over the foreign policy making machinery. As subsequent chapters show, such control coincided by declining support for the Nixon– Kissinger foreign policy at home and a series of grave crises abroad. In October 1973 the Middle East War commenced, demanding much of Kissinger's attention and resulting in a growing distrust between the United States and the Soviet Union. In other words, while Kissinger was successful in placing the United States at the center of the Middle East peace process, the price for this achievement was a gradual increase in Soviet-American tensions. These were evident during Nixon's second trip to the Soviet Union in July 1974 and were only tentatively healed at the Vladivostok summit in November 1974. Meanwhile, the Sino-American relationship was in a standstill as a result of a deadlock over Taiwan and internal power struggles within the PRC. By 1975 a series of events—the fall of Saigon, the signing of the Helsinki Accords, the failure to negotiate a SALT II agreement, and the Angolan conflict—caused a virtual breakdown of détente. By 1976 both conservative Republicans and liberal Democrats attacked Kissinger's policies and the former miracle-worker became a political liability to President Ford (who released Kissinger from his national security adviser's portfolio in the fall of 1975). In January 1977 Kissinger's reputation as an effective negotiator remained untarnished, but his foreign policy program had been rejected by most of the electorate. Kissinger left office with his policies under attack and his historical reputation insecure.

*   *   *

In the end, *The Flawed Architect* will not attempt to exonerate Kissinger for any possible crimes or misdemeanors. It will not purport to present a conclusive case for either the prosecution or the defense. Rather, my goal is to scrutinize the Kissinger record in detail and to break through the heavy polemics that has tended to mar most previous accounts and certainly colors the current debate of his place in history. *The Flawed Architect* will aim at a balanced view of its subject, criticizing Kissinger when such critique is called for, but awarding credit when it is due. It will do so with the benefit of a massive amount of previously classified archival materials. It may not be the last word on its subject. But it is the first comprehensive reassessment of the career of one of the most enduring figures in American public life.

The worst nightmare of a scholar writing a book based on newly available documents is that even newer materials arrive when the book is going to publication. In my case, this happened on May 26, 2004, when 20,000 pages of transcripts of Kissinger's telephone conversations in 1969–74 were released. Fortunately, I discovered that I was already familiar with much of the material (having already tuned into Kissinger's conversations with Nixon that were available in the White House Tapes) and that the other transcripts tended to support my conclusions. The newly released transcripts did, though, bring wonderful color to many parts of the book. There was, for example, Nixon's inability to play a major role in decision-making during the October War in 1973 because of his heavy drinking (he was "loaded" Kissinger told his deputy Brent Scowcroft at one point). And there was confirmation, if such was needed, that the Nixon administration had "created the conditions"—that is engaged in economic warfare against Chile—for the coup against Salvador Allende. And there was even evidence that it tended to be Nixon, rather than Kissinger, who was far more eager to use massive bombing in Cambodia. "The whole goddamn Air Force over there farting around doing nothing," Nixon complained in December 1970. Indeed, on many occasions, Kissinger actually comes off rather better—and certainly as more rational—than his boss. On one occasion, former secretary of defense Robert McNamara, who many still hold responsible for getting the United States bogged down in Vietnam, even credits Kissinger for the American exit from Southeast Asia.

Ultimately, the most difficult task when assessing Henry Kissinger from the perspective of the twenty-first century, however, is not the reconstruction of events. The documentary evidence is, after all, by and large available; if anything, the problem today is the sheer magnitude of materials at the scholar's disposal. Similarly, it is hardly an impossible task to judge the long-term significance of Kissinger's policies. Three decades after the events described in this book took place may not be an adequate time span for a full rendition of the opening of Sino-American relations, for example. But it seems that a sufficient amount of time has passed to allow for a cool-headed analysis of Kissinger's relative significance on, say, the subsequent course of Soviet-American relations or the rise of the United States' role in the Middle East.

What is infinitely more difficult—yet absolutely essential for any analysis of Kissinger's role—is to consider the relationship between morality and foreign policy. "Is Kissinger a moral man?" was a question I was confronted with while writing this book on more occasions than I care to remember. "Oh, he's a war criminal," others helpfully opined. Indeed, the general consensus has always been that Kissinger was the arch realist, a man whose conception of the American national interest left no room for idealism. It seems that Kissinger's record proves the point. How else could he have justified his policies toward the Soviet Union and China or conspired in the secret bombing of Cambodia? What else but an unsentimental attitude could account for his ability to countenance the human costs of some of his policies in the various regional crises, such as the Indo-Pakistani conflict of 1971 or the Angolan civil war? What else could have been behind his seemingly inexplicable ability to negotiate with both the Israelis and the many Arab leaders than a cool, calculating mind that did not let his personal background interfere?

The Flawed Architect argues that Kissinger's thinking was not as rigid as a superficial analysis might suggest. He was critical of moral crusaders (whether on the left or the right of the political spectrum) not because they were wrong, but because moral absolutes, when used as guidelines for foreign policy, rarely offered anything but, as he would put it, "disillusionment." For someone who took office at the height of the American involvement in Vietnam, which many still view as having been caused by crusading anticommunist idealism, this was hardly an unreasonable assumption. In a sense, there was something inherently moral about choosing to fight the Cold War primarily through diplomacy and negotiations, rather than military interventions and nation building. Moreover, it is important to recognize that the Nixon administration—and Kissinger as its foreign policy czar—faced strict limits to the use of force as an instrument of American foreign policy. Instead of being able to send the marines to, say, the Dominican Republic (as Lyndon Johnson had done in 1965) or pump up the numbers of Americans in Vietnam (as both Kennedy and Johnson had ordered), the Nixon administration had to do find ways of limiting direct American military presence abroad. This was not, to use modern terminology, a time for unilateral military action. America was no hyperpower. It was in retreat.

This is not to say that Kissinger should be excused for mistakes or deceit. His overall approach to foreign policy as a game in which only the great powers (the United States, the Soviet Union, and China) mattered often blinded Kissinger to the suffering of real people in real places. As we will see, in South Asia during the Indo-Pakistani conflict of 1970–71 and in Southeast Asia (from Vietnam and Cambodia to East Timor) throughout Kissinger's period in office, his limited worldview resulted in mistaken policies that contributed to immense human suffering. Similarly, Kissinger's penchant for employing covert action as a replacement for open military intervention in such places as Chile or Angola cannot be categorized as anything but a series of immoral undertakings that resulted in far too many innocent casualties. Even if Kissinger's realism was qualified, it was costly in terms of innocent lives lost and often counterproductive in its end results. Kissinger's realism, much like the idealism he criticized, ultimately led to disillusionment.

But what seems crucial—if not almost elemental—is to place Kissinger in his historical context. For while it is relatively easy to find shocking revelations about wrongdoing from the mass of documentary material now available, it is equally easy to ignore the various pressures and contingencies, domestic and international, that limited the options available at the time when what may seem like shocking decisions in retrospect were taken. For ultimately the historian's task is not merely to judge but to understand.

The story that follows is, then, an account of American foreign policy making during a period when dramatic challenges in the international arena coincided with the most severe domestic and constitutional crisis within the United States since the Civil War. It is told from the perspective of a unique man, a man who not only personified the American dream but, due to his own intellectual upbringing and the circumstances of time, appeared ideally suited for meeting the challenges facing the United States around the globe in the late 1960s and 1970s. That he often successfully met such challenges is a large part of the story, a part that has recently been ignored in the heated debates over Kissinger's less than honorable conduct toward an elected government of Chile or the lengthy Vietnam endgame. This is not to say that the book is anything like a hagiography: Kissinger was extremely capable, but he was far from perfect. He made many wrong decisions and he occasionally allowed personal ambition to cloud his judgment. And yet, the ultimate question that this book tackles is not whether Kissinger's flaws outweighed his virtues, or whether he is a war criminal or not.

Rather, the ultimate question is: Did he make a difference?

1

The Aspiring Statesman

The announcement on December 2, 1968, was a surprise.

A forty-five-year-old Harvard professor who had arrived in the United States as a refugee from Nazi Germany some thirty years earlier and risen to a highly coveted position within the American academia seemed, to many, an unlikely choice as Richard Nixon's national security adviser. This selection seemed to indicate a suspiciously broad mind on Nixon's part. For one thing, Kissinger had served previously as foreign policy adviser to New York governor and presidential hopeful (and Nixon antagonist) Nelson Rockefeller. Further, Kissinger was representative of an Ivy League establishment the new president-elect had grown to hate. Moreover, few could have expected that the appointment would have as far-reaching consequences as it did: Kissinger and Nixon would soon be running foreign policy as their private reserve; they would launch initiatives that, in some ways, revolutionized postwar U.S. foreign policy; and Kissinger himself would, in five years' time, hold two key posts as the mantle of the secretary of state was added to his National Security Council (NSC) position. Fewer yet could have anticipated that it would be Kissinger, rather than Nixon, that would stay in Washington for the next eight years.

By then, Kissinger's life would be an open book. In fact, the interest in a Harvard professor joining Nixon's team was high from the very start. Already in February 1969, his picture would be featured in the first of numerous *Time* magazine cover articles. "Bonn, London, and Paris, may disagree on a score of issues, but they are in happy unanimity in their respect for him; even Moscow is not displeased," the article commented. It went on to describe how Kissinger, the Harvard professor and occasional consultant to the two previous administrations, "knows more foreign leaders than many State Department careerists." Although there was a hint that Kissinger had already at this point—February 1969—amassed an enormous amount of influence, *Time* did not forecast the extraordinary powers that he would eventually accrue. Yet, the article ended presciently with a quote from the nineteenth-century Austrian statesman, Prince Metternich, whom Kissinger had cited in his Harvard Ph.D. dissertation: "I was born to make history, not to write novels."[1]

In time, Kissinger would also make history. In early 1969, however, he was "just" a Harvard professor, who had received some critical acclaim for his writings, and had worked briefly as a consultant for the two previous administrations. His main connection to the Republican Party had been as an adviser to Rockefeller. Indeed, unlike the case with Prince Metternich, Kissinger's rise to the pinnacles of power was hardly a matter of family heritage. If anything, Kissinger's family background—that of a German-born Jew—should have hindered his career prospects. It certainly was not a hearty recommendation for membership in the inner circle of Richard Nixon, where anti-Semitic comments could be heard on a regular basis.

So what did Kissinger have to offer to the new president? To understand the policies Kissinger pursued while in office, it is crucial to take a brief look at his writings and career prior to the commencement of the partnership with Nixon. In doing this, one must ask a number of questions that bear upon our understanding of the man who shaped American foreign policy and international relations during his eight years in the White House, at the State Department, and, perhaps most of all, in top-level negotiations across the globe with friend and foe alike.

Was Kissinger a brilliant analyst of international relations? An original thinker? A European mind in an American setting?[2] A man whose writing, teaching, and other duties had prepared him in a unique way to take up the task he himself characterized as nothing less than a complete reshaping of American foreign policy?

Or was Kissinger perhaps a mediocre scholar but a good political animal? Was he a man who wrote—and still does—books with few lasting insights but managed to muscle himself into the right place at the right time? An individual equipped with a remarkable set of courtier's instincts? Was he a man who did not have time for serious scholarly pursuits but was more keen on personal aggrandizement, on making friends in high places that later allowed him to claim a place in the history books that, given his personal background, was as improbable as almost any other "from rags to riches" story in American history?

To answer these questions even partially one needs to consider in some detail Henry Kissinger's life and career prior to December 1968. Taken in isolation it is a remarkable story on a human level and speaks highly of the possibilities that the American system can offer to someone as driven to achieve as Henry Kissinger. He was a man who made his own luck. For that one must admire the refugee from Germany who attained positions unthinkable and unattainable to anyone that came before him.

Kissinger's spectacular rise to the corridors of power also offers an opportunity to examine the baggage that he brought with him to Washington. There had been, as in any great American success story, casualties along the way. Perhaps more important, examining Kissinger the scholar offers clues to his intellectual parameters, the prejudices and stereotypes he inherited or developed along the way, and the blind spots of his particular interpretation of international relations. After all, in choosing Kissinger over other possible candidates in 1968, Nixon chose more than an academic from Harvard; he chose a particular type of a thinker who was soon to have the opportunity to put his ideas into practice in ways that had global implications.

FROM BAVARIA TO HARVARD

Heinz Alfred Kissinger was born on May 27, 1923, in Fürth, a small town in Bavaria, Germany. The time and the place could hardly have been less fortunate for a middle-class Jewish family. This was the year when Adolf Hitler launched an unsuccessful putsch in nearby Munich—the so-called Beer Hall Putsch—and began writing *Mein Kampf* (to be published in 1925). With Nazism on the rise, the Bavarian Jews, like other German Jews, were gradually being ostracized within a country that had, in the century preceding Kissinger's birth, apparently become more accepting of religious minority groups. Indeed, at the time of Kissinger's birth his father Louis was a respected schoolmaster in Fürth. But by the time young Heinz turned ten years old, Hitler was in power. By his twelfth birthday the Nazi government's Nüremberg Laws denied Jews citizenship, forbade marriages between Jews and gentiles, and banned Jewish teachers, including Louis Kissinger, from holding jobs in state-run schools. After a few years of agonizing, Louis and his wife Paula finally made the painful decision to leave their native country. In August 1938 the Kissingers—Louis, Paula, Heinz, and his younger (by one year) brother Walter—left Germany for England. They stayed in London for two weeks before setting sail to the United States. During this move Heinz became Henry.

The move from Germany to the United States not only, in all likelihood, saved Kissinger's life, but it also freed him from the oppressive surroundings of 1930s Nazi Germany. In Manhattan, where the family settled in 1938, Kissinger found a society he wanted to become a part of and thrive in, a society that was not free of prejudices or discrimination, but at least in theory espoused the ideal of equal opportunity. Most important, the opportunities matched Kissinger's ambition and intellectual talent. Despite his linguistic handicap, Kissinger quickly established himself as a straight A student even though, after his first year at high school, he worked by day at a shaving-brush manufacturer and attended school by night.

After graduating from New York's George Washington High School, he completed a year of undergraduate studies in accounting at the City College of New York.

Kissinger's life took yet another turn in February 1943, when, along with numerous other young Americans, he enlisted in the army and was sent to a military training camp in South Carolina. The following month, he was naturalized. The four-year stint in the army that included a trip back to Germany, where he stayed as part of the occupation forces until 1947, transformed the young German immigrant into an assimilated (and hyphenated) American. In many ways this was a natural outcome: if one chooses to overlook the fact that the U.S. Army was still racially segregated during World War II—and most of Kissinger's contemporaries did choose to ignore it—the military was the ultimate melting pot. For Kissinger, who, despite his continental moves, had never ventured far beyond his German-Jewish-American milieu, the experience was doubly challenging and exciting. The army also brought Kissinger in contact with his first mentor, Fritz Kraemer.

In May 1944 Kraemer was a thirty-five-year-old U.S. Army private with an unusual background. Born into a wealthy Prussian family that intensely disliked the Nazis, Kraemer had a degree from the London School of Economics and doctorates from the Goethe University in Frankfurt and the University of Rome. In 1939, working in Rome for the League of Nations, he decided to stay abroad and eventually moved to the United States and enlisted in the army. After he impressed General Alexander Bolling of the 84th Infantry Division, Kraemer's abilities were put to good use giving pep talks to soldiers, explaining to them the horrors of Nazi philosophy. It was on one of these occasions that the young private Kissinger happened to be in the audience. The future secretary of state was impressed. He wrote Kraemer a brief note: "Dear Pvt. Kraemer. I heard you speak yesterday. This is how it should be done. Can I help you in any way? Pvt. Kissinger."

Kraemer, who would later become a strategist at the Pentagon, was struck by "this little Jewish refugee." Over the next three years, Kraemer secured Kissinger an appointment as a translator for General Bolling, helped him to become an administrator in occupied Germany (1945–47), and eased Kissinger's way into the Counter-Intelligence Corps. And Kraemer encouraged Kissinger to study history and philosophy, a vocation that has stayed with the "little Jewish refugee" ever since. Although they would later clash—neither man was equipped with a small ego— Fritz Gustav Anton Kraemer was undoubtedly a seminal influence in Kissinger's life. "I have a very high regard for him," Kissinger would reminisce some sixty years after the two men's initial encounter. Sven Kraemer, Fritz's son, would later join Kissinger's NSC staff.[3]

Having experienced World War II and bonded with men from a variety of backgrounds, Kissinger was occupied with the same question as many returning GIs: what to do with the remainder of his life. Already twenty-four years of age, Kissinger, despite his obvious academic talent, did not even have an undergraduate degree. But the army experience had changed him. The shy boy who had grown up in a climate of fear returned to his adopted land a conqueror, whose innate intellectual abilities had begun to awaken. "Living as a Jew under the Nazis, then as a refugee in America, and then as a private in the army isn't exactly an experience that builds confidence," he would later comment.[4] But it seems that as he returned to the United States from Germany, Kissinger no longer felt like an outsider. Henry Kissinger had become Americanized.

Yet, he had no master plan. The prewar path of becoming an accountant held little appeal in 1947. "I know nothing," he complained to Kraemer. "Go to a fine college," Kissinger's mentor replied, adding, "A gentleman does not go to the College of the City of New York."

Kissinger's growing ambition, so effectively stroked by Fritz Kraemer, made him apply to a rather different set of colleges: Columbia, Princeton, and Harvard. But it was already the summer of 1947, very late in the year to gain admission to an elite university. In the end, Harvard, which was making a special effort to accommodate returning war veterans, accepted Kissinger and even offered him a scholarship.

The experience would, yet again, change his life forever.

THE YOUNG SCHOLAR BECOMES A BEST-SELLER

In the fall of 1947 Kissinger entered Harvard University's Class of 1950 as a second-year undergraduate; ten years later he published two books, *Nuclear Weapons and Foreign Policy* and *A World Restored: Metternich, Castlereagh, and the Problems of Peace, 1812–22*. The books secured him an appointment at Harvard's International Affairs Department. They were also representations of the fact that Kissinger had, by the mid-1950s, become an adept student in a number of fields that would later make him uniquely qualified for membership in the country's foreign policy elite: the young man who had worked in a shaving brush factory in the early 1940s emerged, during the Eisenhower administration, as an acknowledged analyst of nuclear weapons and international relations.

His record at Harvard after 1947 was nothing but remarkable. A mature undergraduate student, Kissinger devoted his time to his studies with the vigor of someone who, due to circumstances beyond his control, had been kept from pursuing his dreams and ambitions for too long. Starting off as a philosophy major, Kissinger soon moved—after receiving his one and only B in a philosophy course—into the Government Department. There he made Harvard history by writing the longest senior thesis (353 pages) on a topic no less demanding than "The Meaning of History." In practice, the senior thesis was slightly more limited in scope: it compared the thinking of Immanuel Kant with that of Arnold Toynbee and Oswald Spengler. Kissinger's main goal was commendable: to argue that free will mattered, that historical determinism went too far, and that individuals were the responsible agents of history. Indeed, "The Meaning of History" was a surprisingly optimistic work from a young man who had narrowly escaped the horrors of Nazi Germany. It stressed the significance of individual choice within a context of circumstances beyond one's control. As he wrote:

> The generation of Buchenwald and the Siberian labor-camps cannot talk with the same optimism as its fathers . . . But this merely describes a fact of decline and not its necessity . . . The experience of freedom enables us to rise beyond the suffering of the past and the frustration of history. In this spirit resides human-ity's essence, the unique which each man imparts to the necessity of his life, the self-transcendence which gives peace.[5]

Kissinger, at twenty-seven years of age, clearly did not shy away from making over-arching, if at times almost impenetrable, statements that would later become a trademark of his writing.

Kissinger's undergraduate thesis and overall performance during his first three years at Harvard had earned him summa cum laude (placing him at the top one percent of the class of 1950) and a ticket to a bright future. He now enrolled in the Ph.D. program in the Government Department under the tutorship of William Yandel Elliott, who had already guided him during his undergraduate years.

By the early 1950s, Elliott, a former all-American tackle at Vanderbilt and Rhodes Scholar at Oxford, was past his academic prime. Before World War II, the Ten-nesseean had published on European politics in the 1920s but was, by the time Kissinger came to Harvard, apparently keen on writing novels. "A glorious ruin," Arthur Schlesinger Jr. would later describe Elliott. Yet, while Elliott was no longer academically productive, he still retained a great deal of institutional clout within the confines of Harvard Yard and commuted to Washington on a weekly basis as a consultant to the House Committee on Foreign Affairs. Unlike many Harvard pro-fessors, Elliott was also committed to his students and displayed little jealousy when some of them, such as Kissinger, surpassed his intellectual achievements.

The personal patronage of such an influential professor as Elliott proved invalu-able for Kissinger's future by providing him with the necessary support when it came down to acquiring key experience and contacts. Thus, while Kissinger prob-ably did not rely on Elliott too deeply for intellectual guidance, the professor helped pave Kissinger's career in important ways. Among these, one of the most signifi-cant was the launch of the Harvard International Seminar in 1951, which Kissinger would direct throughout his subsequent years at Harvard. The program, which received funding from the Ford and the Rockefeller Foundations, as well as—unknown to Kissinger at the time—the CIA, fit nicely into the broader aims of American foreign policy. Its task was to bring together every summer a group of young leaders—mostly politicians, journalists, or civil servants—from countries allied with the United States. While at Harvard the visitors were treated to a pro-gram that Kissinger, as the leader of the seminar, had always designed with great

care. The participants, also carefully selected by Kissinger, were addressed by eminent Americans (one of the speakers was Eleanor Roosevelt), took classes in
humanities and politics from Harvard scholars, and socialized with each other. In
short, the Harvard International Seminar was like a fast-track, elite, and miniature
version of the famed Fulbright exchange program, aimed at passing on the benefits of American education and values to a generation of carefully selected European, Latin American, and Asian leaders. In the process, Kissinger built an elaborate
network of international contacts that included, among others, future French president Valery Giscard d'Estaing, future Japanese Prime Minister Yasuhiro Nakasone,
and future Turkish Prime Minister Bulent Ecevit.

In 1952 Kissinger also became the founding editor of a foreign affairs journal
called *Confluence*, which featured a modest readership but numerous high-profile
contributors, including John Kenneth Galbraith, Raymond Aron, Walt Rostow,
Reinhold Niebuhr, Hans Morgenthau, and Hannah Arendt. Much like the International Seminar, *Confluence* helped Kissinger establish contacts with prominent
figures, many of them outside academia, in a way that was not possible for the average Ph.D. candidate even at Harvard.

But Kissinger's graduate school career was not just about building contacts with
future leaders or prominent figures of the time. He also distinguished himself by
the quality of his academic work and, in particular, by the choice of his dissertation topic. In a department where most worked on current topics—something to
do with post–World War II international relations—Kissinger wrote about the
Concert of Europe in the early nineteenth century. *A World Restored: Metternich,
Castlereagh and the Problems of Peace, 1812–1822* was in a class of its own; some less
than impressed colleagues even suggested that Kissinger might want to transfer to
the History Department. However, Kissinger insisted (and most others had to
admit) that his dissertation had specific relevance to the Cold War world. Much
like in the early nineteenth century, when Napoleon's France had presented a challenge to the stability of the European state system, so did the Soviet Union (and its
then ally China) represent the twentieth-century revolutionary menace to a stable
world order. If Napoleon's challenge had provided the great threat to stability in
the Europe of the early nineteenth century, the Sino-Soviet challenge provided a
similar threat to global stability in the mid-twentieth century. By implication, then,
if the conservative statesmen Metternich and Castlereagh had restored peace and
stability through their diplomatic efforts, a similar solution could certainly be
arrived at by Western statesmen a century and a half later.

Kissinger's dissertation, which gained him a Ph.D. in May 1954, was also a statement of the author's worldview. He was, and would remain, a firm believer in
realpolitik, in the primacy of geopolitics and the balance of power as key ingredients to providing international stability, and in the ability of a select number of
diplomats to shape (or reshape) international relations. If anything, *A World
Restored* stresses the importance of the individual statesman as the one that can

shape events—or restore order—that otherwise might lead to a catastrophe. As Kissinger put it: "The test of a statesman is his ability to recognize the real relationship of forces and to make this knowledge serve his ends."[6]

Yet, there was also a sense of the limits that even such eminently skillful statesmen as Castlereagh and Metternich had been forced to accept. While the title of the dissertation leads one to suggest an overtly laudatory account of the statesmanship of two early nineteenth-century Europeans, Kissinger ended his account by stressing the shortcomings rather than the achievements of the two. Neither was, in the end, Kissinger's hero (nor was the German statesman Bismarck, whose statesmanship he was to applaud in some writings later on), but rather provided examples of the extent to which accident and circumstance could undermine the work of even the most eminent and skillful leaders. Or, as the historian John Lewis Gaddis puts it, Kissinger's guide to the statesmen—and presumably to himself—was that they needed to "rescue choice from circumstance."[7] While Kissinger's later conduct may not have been an example of such apparent humility, it is obvious that at least in the early 1950s, the Harvard Ph.D. student had a healthy appreciation of the limits that each and every national or international leader faced.

When *A World Restored* was published in 1957, however, Kissinger had moved from being a slightly eccentric graduate student at Harvard to being a recognized expert on the role of nuclear weapons in American foreign policy. When he completed his Ph.D. in 1954, Kissinger had faced, yet again, the question of what to do with the rest of his life. He was initially disappointed that Harvard did not elect him to its Society of Fellows, a group of scholars with generous funding and limited teaching responsibilities that had earlier included, among others, such notables as McGeorge Bundy and Arthur M. Schlesinger Jr., but merely granted him an open-ended appointment as an instructor. By early 1955, however, he faced an "embarrassment of riches," with good offers from the University of Chicago and the University of Pennsylvania. He rejected both and opted for a three-year position as a director of a study group analyzing the impact of nuclear weapons at the Council on Foreign Relations, a high-powered foreign policy institution in New York.[8] In the next three years Kissinger, whose appointment coincided with the publication of his first major article on U.S. national security in the council's prestigious journal *Foreign Affairs*,[9] moved closer to the corridors of power.

* * *

Kissinger's three-year appointment at the council had a number of significant outcomes. For one, it brought him in contact with many of the most powerful men in the nation, who were either permanent members of the group or addressed it on occasion. These included Hamilton Fish Armstrong (editor of *Foreign Affairs*), Robert Bowie (director of the Policy Planning Staff at the State Department), McGeorge Bundy (dean of faculty at Harvard and later Kennedy's and Johnson's adviser on national security affairs), Paul Nitze (former holder of Bowie's post at the State in the early 1950s), David Rockefeller (soon to head both the council and the powerful Chase Bank), and General Walter Bedell Smith (former undersecretary of state). Gordon Dean, previously head of the Atomic Energy Commission, headed the group. During his time at the council, Kissinger also made contact with Nelson Rockefeller, the man whose patronage in the 1950s and 1960s was to further Kissinger's career in numerable ways. Aside from linking up with some of the most brilliant, powerful, and, in the case of the Rockefellers, richest men in the country, Kissinger's stint at the council resulted in his first breakthrough into the high-level debate about American national security and foreign policy.

That came in 1957, when Kissinger published *Nuclear Weapons and Foreign Policy*, a book authored by him but based on the discussions in the nuclear study group. Almost four months on the best-seller list, the book won critical praise from most reviewers—Paul Nitze was a characteristic exception—and was discussed in the pages of major American newspapers. Chalmers Roberts, the *Washington Post*'s diplomatic correspondent at the time, called *Nuclear Weapons and Foreign Policy* "the most important book of 1957, perhaps even of the past several years."

Nuclear Weapons and Foreign Policy was a breakthrough. Kissinger received the Woodrow Wilson Prize and a citation from the Overseas Press Club. The book set the basis for Kissinger's future reputation as a capable synthesizer—and at times original thinker—of major foreign policy issues. If he wasn't yet a household name, Kissinger had by the age of thirty-four earned the respect of most of his colleagues and, more significantly for him, many of the decision makers in or about to gain power. He had, in effect, joined the elite club of defense intellectuals.

The arguments presented in *Nuclear Weapons and Foreign Policy* were not, however, entirely unique to Kissinger. This was hardly a surprise. After all, the book was based on the monthly discussions at the council and, given the participants, thus often reflected dominant views about the problems and role of nuclear weapons. Above all, Kissinger was interested in the dilemma of the nuclear age, which he defined as the fact that "the enormity of modern weapons makes the thought of war repugnant, but the refusal to run any risks would amount to giving the Soviet rulers a blank check."[10]

This was, indeed, the dilemma that the Eisenhower administration's massive retaliation doctrine—the idea that Washington could effectively deter war by threatening to use U.S. nuclear weapons—faced as the Soviet nuclear arsenal grew. It was largely one of credibility: massive retaliation implied the willingness to use nuclear weapons while their sheer destructive power raised serious doubts about the feasibility of such a proposition. "Maximum development of power is not enough," Kissinger argued, because "with modern technology such a course must paralyze the will." What was needed, Kissinger maintained, was a "strategic doctrine which gives our diplomacy the greatest freedom of action and which addresses itself to the question of whether the nuclear age presents only risks or whether it does not also offer opportunities."[11]

For Kissinger the latter was more the case. The most distinguishing (and most frequently discussed) characteristic of Kissinger's book was his argument that while an all-out nuclear war was an unlikely possibility because it would be too destructive, a war between the United States and the Soviet Union might well evolve into a limited nuclear war. As he wrote: "Limited nuclear war represents our most effective strategy against nuclear powers or against a major power which is capable of substituting manpower for technology."[12]

The problem for Kissinger was actually not so much one of technology but of political will and psychology. Americans had for some time—and particularly due to World War II—considered total victory (or unconditional surrender) the only kind of victory. Since the Soviets developed their bomb in 1949, however, this will had become hampered by the fear of prompt and utter destruction. What was therefore needed in large part was a redefinition of the meaning of victory. Since there could not be an all-out war, there could not be all-out victory, at least not over a nation, such as the Soviet Union, which possessed thermonuclear weapons.

Kissinger went on to argue that American diplomacy needed to develop a "framework within which the question of national survival is not involved in every military decision. But equally, we must leave no doubt about our determination ... to resist by force any Soviet military move." If that were the task for diplomacy, then the challenge for U.S. military policy was "to develop a doctrine and a capability for the graduated employment of force" that would support these diplomatic efforts. The United States, in other words, would need to develop the capability of responding to different forms of aggression in the appropriate manner. A Soviet-inspired guerrilla war in a remote corner of the globe, for example, hardly called for a nuclear strike against Moscow. In this way, Kissinger further maintained, the dilemma of nuclear weapons and foreign policy could be successfully addressed by "seeking to avoid the horrors of all-out war by outlining an alternative, in developing a concept of limitation that combines firmness with moderation, diplomacy can once more establish a relationship with force, even in the nuclear age."[13] In terms of geopolitics this essentially implied that while the possession of nuclear weapons made the United States and the Soviet Union virtually immune to direct nuclear attack from each other, this should not allow the United States to shrink from contemplating the possibility that local nuclear war might well erupt.

Much of Kissinger's book thus implied the obvious: the United States needed to embrace a military doctrine with an array of choices. In this regard, he was simply advocating what many others were arguing for: that the United States should adopt a strategy of flexible response to meet the increasingly complex challenges posed by such developments as the decolonization of European empires. The United States could simply not rely on nuclear weapons alone as a means of projecting its military power abroad. When the Kennedy administration took office in 1961, it quickly adopted flexible response and began to build up U.S. conventional and nonconventional military capabilities (in addition to retaining and constantly upgrading a strong nuclear arsenal).

But critics also pointed out that Kissinger's rationale did carry some disturbing implications. He did not, after all, reject the possibility of using nuclear weapons. According to Kissinger's rationale in *Nuclear Weapons and Foreign Policy*, Europe and the third world were, in theory at least, fair game for a limited nuclear war. No wonder he later earned the nickname "Dr. Strangelove, East" (Edward Teller, a nuclear physicist, was his Western counterpart).[14]

Of course, Kissinger did not advocate this stand purely, or even primarily, because he believed that the United States should be engaging in limited nuclear wars around the globe. His point was more nuanced: only by embracing a strategic doctrine that assumed a limited nuclear war as a realistic option could the United States derive the necessary diplomatic leverage from its military arsenal. Kissinger's arguments were essentially meant to correct the shortcomings of the doctrine of massive retaliation with a limited nuclear war corollary. They amounted ultimately to theoretical postulations rather than practical guidance.

The two books that Kissinger published in 1957 had an important similarity when it came down to the making of foreign policy: both were concerned with the limits imposed upon statesmen by their domestic constituencies. Of course, the domestic constituencies facing Castlereagh and Metternich were far different from the one American foreign policy elite had to contend with in the 1950s. (Yet, even in *A World Restored* Kissinger argued that the "acid test of a policy is its ability to obtain domestic support."[15]) In both books, moreover, Kissinger maintained that the greatest threat to truly great statesmanship, statesmanship that could yield significant long-term positive consequences, came from within, from "bureaucratic inertia"[16] or from the "inherent tension between the mode of action of a bureaucracy and the pattern of statesmanship."[17]

This argument, which Kissinger came back to in his next major work, *Necessity for Choice* (1961), was to remain the key to his foreign policy making. In the end, when looking at Kissinger's modus operandi once he was in a position of power, it is this disdain for bureaucracies that strikes a chord. For while Metternich and Castlereagh may not have been his heroes, Kissinger certainly displayed a need to distill the prerequisites and obstacles to great statesmanship. Hence, bureaucracies became an obvious target of his antipathy, likely to provide the greatest obstacle for statesmen wishing to move toward new territory—toward, that is, new policies that were radically different from familiar traditions. For, in his eyes, true statesmen were visionaries; they were the ones who needed to act while the rest of the society slept; they were the ones who set the course of policy without the benefit of knowing what that policy might yield. As he wrote in *Nuclear Weapons*:

> The inclination of a bureaucracy is to deny the possibility of great conception by classifying it as "unsound," "risky," or other terms which testify to a preference for

equilibrium over exceptional performance. It is no accident that most great statesmen were opposed by the "experts" in their foreign offices, for the very greatness of the statesman's conception tends to make it inaccessible to those whose primary concern is with safety and minimum risk.[18]

These words in large part explain the care that Kissinger took, once in power, to insulate himself from the influence—and at times advice—of the bureaucracy most closely involved in making American foreign policy: the State Department. Kissinger was, after all, if not modeling himself after Metternich, Castlereagh, or Bismarck, obsessed with the pursuit and prerequisites of greatness. In 1957, however, while he had suddenly become a nuclear celebrity, Kissinger was still more than a decade away from assuming the role of a statesman. For now, it was back to Harvard yard.

ALMOST THERE

In the late 1950s and 1960s, Henry Kissinger's career took on a new mixture of theory and practice. On the one hand, he became a tenured Harvard professor who wrote about current issues in U.S. foreign policy with particular emphasis on NATO. On the other, he was itching to be a policy maker and was constantly at the fringes of power during the Kennedy and Johnson administrations. In the end, fortunately for him, he did not gain a major position within the inner circles of the Democratic administrations, perhaps because of his close association with Rockefeller. Hence, by 1968, Kissinger was in the enviable position of being an academic whose reputation had not been tarnished by being one of the "best and the brightest" who had been in charge of American foreign policy during the country's increasing involvement in the Vietnam War. If not completely apolitical, Kissinger was at least relatively nonpartisan in his quest for power, and found himself ready to take advantage of the changes that rocked American politics during the last year of Lyndon B. Johnson's presidency.

The publication of *A World Restored* and *Nuclear Weapons* in 1957 catapulted Kissinger back to his alma mater as a promising young scholar with a national reputation. However, the world of academia, in which he thrived, had its drawbacks. It was—and still is, as the author himself has learned—a world filled with petty squabbles and tug-of-wars over issues that were incomprehensible (at times laughable) to those operating in the real world. Kissinger, as is well known, liked to quip that in academia "the disputes are so bitter because the stakes are so small."[19] To Kissinger, as to most of those who get somewhat disillusioned with the pettiness of academia, such statements could only come after he had secured his position as a permanent member within one of the world's finest centers of higher learning.

This he did with remarkable speed. In 1957 the dean of Harvard's faculty, McGeorge Bundy, recommended Kissinger to Robert Bowie, who was about to leave the State Department and become the director of a newly founded Center for International Affairs (CIFA). Bowie, probably impressed by Kissinger's growing reputation and his latest article in *Foreign Affairs* ("Strategy and Organization") offered Kissinger the deputy directorship of the CFIA, which was coupled with a post as lecturer. Two years later, he had become a tenured associate professor. Full professorship followed in 1962.

By today's standards such a rapid rise seems unprecedented. Yet, in the world of the late 1950s and early 1960s, Kissinger was hardly the only one on the fast track. At such a well-endowed institution as Harvard University, which lost many of its best and brightest to the Kennedy administration (including McGeorge Bundy and Arthur Schlesinger), it was a feat, but not a unique one.

Kissinger's intellectual productivity made this rapid, if not unprecedented, rise in academic circles possible. He published constantly in such journals as *Foreign Affairs*, *Daedalus*, and *The Reporter*, while writing occasional pieces for the *New York Times*.[20] Most important for Kissinger's tenure, though, he published, in 1960, his third book *The Necessity for Choice: Prospects of American Foreign Policy*. Based largely on his earlier articles, this work was, as Walter Isaacson puts it, "packaged as a coherent approach to foreign policy—and as a job application in case the new president decided to seek some fresh thinking from Cambridge."[21] Dividing the book into chapters on deterrence, limited war, the United States and Europe, negotiations, arms control, the role of emerging nations, and the relationship between the policy maker and the intellectual, Kissinger clearly, as so many of his class at Harvard, wanted to be picked as one of the "best and the brightest" in 1961.

So why did Kissinger not become, in the early 1960s, an instrumental figure among a cast of characters that included a number of his earlier benefactors and many of his Harvard colleagues (such as McGeorge Bundy)?

The answer lay in part in Kissinger's own writings and personality that seemed to clash with that of such "action intellectuals" as Bundy, Robert McNamara, and Walt Rostow. His writings had, for one, displayed a strong penchant for realpolitik and a keen interest in diplomacy as it was traditionally practiced: through negotiations at the highest levels. Moreover, Kissinger was interested in subject matters that did not necessarily draw the attention of the Kennedy team. Kissinger had little interest in economics, he was not an adept number cruncher, and he focused excessively on the Soviet Union and Europe. In contrast, the Kennedy foreign policy team's key members—Rostow, McNamara, and Bundy—stressed the role of economic aid in countering communist threats (witness the Alliance for Progress for Latin America) and appeared convinced that the third world (particularly Southeast Asia, but also the Middle East and Africa) was the main arena where the Soviet-American confrontation was to be fought in the future. In this sense, Kissinger was simply not a good fit for the Kennedy administration, and, although he acted as a consultant to Bundy's NSC staff in 1961–62, he felt frustrated in "offering unwanted advice and inflicting on President Kennedy learned disquisitions about which he could have done nothing even in the unlikely event that they aroused his interest."[22]

Following the disappointment of his year as an outside consultant to the Kennedy White House, Kissinger continued to publish. His major work focused still, though, on the Atlantic partnership and the need to rethink the American-West European relationship. In 1965, *The Troubled Partnership: A Reappraisal of the Atlantic Alliance* and an edited work *Problems of National Strategy* hit the bookstores, just before French President Charles De Gaulle withdrew French troops from NATO's unified military command and expelled NATO's headquarters from Paris. Not surprisingly, Kissinger called for improving the consultative networks within NATO in order to allay some of the complaints of U.S. unilateralism that led to De Gaulle's withdrawal and the biggest crisis for NATO's unity to date. And yet, Kissinger was characteristically skeptical about sharing real power with allies. To him consultation would work best if there were a consensus over alliance goals and policy; this not being the case, consultation was unlikely to resolve the differences on other than peripheral issues. As he put it in typically Kissingerian prose: "consultation is least effective when it is most needed: when there exist basic differences of assessment or of interest. It works in implementing a consensus rather than creating it."[23] To Kissinger, the lack of consensus that became so evident when France left NATO was a hindrance to effective and unified Western policy, but it was not one that could necessarily be solved through consultation. Moreover, Kissinger stressed the need for the United States not to allow its allies to minimize Washington's freedom of action. During his years in power, Kissinger's penchant for working unilaterally to set the framework for détente with the Soviet Union surely was based in part on these beliefs in the poverty of multilateral consultation and the need to retain maximum freedom of action for the United States.

Without discounting his ideas about the Atlantic alliance, the key to Kissinger's future lay not in his intellectual productivity in the 1960s. Luckily for him, Kissinger was able to remain at the fringes of power throughout the 1960s by, in effect, being connected to both sides of the political spectrum. His lack of interest in domestic political issues made it easier for him to be available for both Democrats and Republicans. Thus, throughout the 1960s, although Kissinger was unable to gain access to the inner circles of either the Democratic Kennedy and Johnson administrations, he remained connected to both. In April 1965, for example, Kissinger wrote letters to McGeorge Bundy supporting Johnson's decision to send troops to Vietnam—on this one he was likely to be, as Bundy noted in his reply, "somewhat lonely among all our friends at Harvard."[24] From October 1965 onward, Kissinger served as a consultant to the Johnson government on its Vietnam policy, participating, among other things, in the secret "Pennsylvania Negotiations" in Paris in 1967. While these talks eventually collapsed due to North Vietnamese insistence on a complete U.S. bombing halt, Kissinger had had his first touch of secret diplomacy for which his appetite would later prove insatiable.

While the contacts with the Kennedy and Johnson administrations kept Kissinger at the outer fringes of power throughout the 1960s, he had also secured his place as the chief foreign policy adviser to one of the richest politicians in America.

Nelson Rockefeller was, undoubtedly, Kissinger's favored choice as a future president of the United States, a man, who, Kissinger maintains in his memoirs, "I am certain would have made a great President."[25] When Rockefeller died in 1979, Kissinger dedicated the first volume of his memoirs, *White House Years,* to the memory of his former mentor. And yet, it must have been clear to Kissinger by 1968 that the governor of New York was unlikely ever to claim the highest prize. Having worked for him in the campaigns of 1964 and 1968, Kissinger had certainly come to respect the man whom he would later be able to work with, as "Rocky" became Gerald Ford's vice president. But there was also the realization that as a national campaigner Rockefeller was no match for his competitors, be they Republican or Democrat. While he had the financial resources to match any Kennedy campaign, Rockefeller was, unfortunately for him, too liberal to ever gain the respect of the Republican right and thus have a realistic chance of gaining his party's nomination.

The man who claimed the Republican nomination at the Miami Beach convention in August 1968 and went on to win the November elections held, according to Kissinger, a "dangerous misunderstanding" of foreign policy. As Kissinger told Rockefeller's speech writer Emmett Hughes soon after the Republican convention, Richard Nixon was "of course, a disaster. Now the Republican Party is a disaster. Fortunately, he can't be elected—or the whole country would be a disaster."[26]

Three months later Kissinger would join Richard Nixon's team.

AT THE PORTAL OF POWER

The long road from Bavaria to America's foreign policy elite is undoubtedly one of the great success stories of modern times. It was, however, only the beginning. What lay ahead for Kissinger, aside from the task of bureaucratic maneuvering in which he proved to be remarkably adept, was the awesome challenge of rescuing American foreign policy from a deep morass. For, in 1969, the United States, the once almost omnipotent power, was in deep trouble. This was hardly news for Kissinger. Already in his 1961 book *Necessity for Choice,* he had opened with the rather astonishing statement that United States' influence had been in constant decline since World War II. If not halted, Kissinger had predicted, such deterioration would, in a matter of fifteen years, render the United States irrelevant.[27] Eight years later, given the situation in Vietnam, where more than half a million U.S. troops were bogged down in a war with no end in sight, American decline appeared to have accelerated further. Thus, if one were to take Kissinger's 1961 insights seriously, any administration that would take over in January 1969 was under a pressing deadline to halt the further descent of the United States toward irrelevancy.

Kissinger appeared in many ways a perfectly qualified person to participate in an effort to find a renewed meaning and a fresh approach for U.S. foreign policy. He had written extensively on the role of nuclear weapons and had probably a more clear-cut understanding of the political limitations of possessing such incredible destructive power than most. He was well versed in the problems facing the Atlantic Alliance, the Soviet-American relationship, and had been involved in the Vietnam peace negotiations. As Nelson Rockefeller's foreign policy adviser he had exhibited more than a passing interest in the China problem.

But while Kissinger could offer a realist reappraisal of American foreign policy in 1968, there was no guarantee that he would either become important as the new administration's foreign policy czar or be able to achieve such significant foreign policy coups as the opening to China a few years later. All of that ultimately depended on the man Kissinger had just called a "disaster."

2

Kissinger, Nixon, and the Challenges of '69

The Oval Office, 7:50 A.M., January 21, 1969.

This was Richard Nixon's first full day in office. The new president, having been sworn in the day before, had slept only four hours. But it hardly mattered. If nothing else, adrenalin would pull him through. He was, after all, finally the president of the United States. And there was so much to do, particularly in the area Nixon hoped to make his mark as president: foreign policy. The man sitting across the large oak desk in the Oval Office that Tuesday morning would help Nixon—or so he hoped—solve or deal with the many problems the thirty-seventh president faced abroad: the Vietnam War, the Soviet Union, the uncertainty regarding the People's Republic of China (PRC), the explosive situation in the Middle East.

The man sitting across the table was Henry Kissinger. He was, already in January 1969, slated to become the foreign policy czar of the new administration. The previous day, while the inaugural parade had been under way, Kissinger had been hard at work, perfecting the bureaucratic machinery that placed the White House at the center of foreign policy making. Most important, three National Security Decision Memorandums (NSDM 1, 2, and 3) had been delivered to key officials, establishing a structure that assured that Kissinger's NSC would have more than the purely analytical role the agency usually played. On that day, January 20, 1969, as Secretary of State Rogers watched the inaugural parade, Kissinger had completed a series of private letters from Nixon to the most important foreign leaders (such as Leonid Brezhnev and Charles de Gaulle). They were delivered directly to the respective countries' embassies without informing the State Department. There was nothing illegal in that, but the act was symbolic. On the very first day of the Nixon administration, the State Department had, in effect, been relegated to a secondary role. That the new president's first appointment was with his NSC adviser, symbolized Kissinger's emerging power base within the Byzantine confines of the Nixon administration.[1]

Over the five and a half years that Kissinger served Nixon as the national security adviser (and as of September 1973, secretary of state), the two men developed a relationship that has been the subject of numerous articles, chapters, and books. Many have analyzed the seemingly different backgrounds of the two men: one a German-born Jewish immigrant, who rose to a coveted position within the American academia; the other a son of a Quaker farmer from California who, despite humble beginnings, burst onto the American political scene in the immediate aftermath of World War II, becoming Dwight D. Eisenhower's vice president before losing to John F. Kennedy in the 1960 presidential race. They were, as Nixon himself liked to say, "the odd couple."

But was the partnership as odd and seemingly accidental as Nixon and many others—Kissinger among them—implied? Given the amount of pages already devoted to analyzing the Nixon–Kissinger relationship over the past three decades, it seems unnecessary to repeat all the curious aspects of their interaction. Yet, a few central issues are worth some exploration. First, it is important to focus on the rationale behind Nixon's choice of Kissinger. Was it a major leap from Nixon's perspective, or a logical decision based on what the new president hoped to achieve in the area of foreign policy? Second, it is crucial to look at the various elements that made Kissinger indispensable to Nixon (and conversely made others, such as Secretary of State William Rogers, dispensable). Was the partnership based purely on a shared desire for power and secrecy? Or was it fundamentally a result of a similar view of the world and the American role in it?

Yet, personalities offer only a partial explanation. Thus, it is important to preview the challenges the new administration faced when it came into office in January 1969. In the end, it is in those challenges—and the ways in which Nixon and Kissinger answered them—that the odd couple's relationship found its ultimate glue.

RICHARD NIXON

The post–World War II era has been called an "age of Nixon." And while few would like to think that the chief villain of the Watergate scandal merits such a high position, there is little doubt that Nixon was one of the most visible American politicians during his three decades in public life. Elected to the House of Representatives in 1946 and the Senate in 1950, he was one of the most prominent of the newcomers in Washington. When Dwight D. Eisenhower selected Nixon as his running mate in 1952, the future president was not yet forty (he was born in January 1913). Having spent two terms as Ike's vice president, Nixon was the obvious candidate to lead the Republican Party in the 1960 elections. But then he suffered two defeats. John F. Kennedy won a narrow victory in November 1960; in 1962 Nixon was humiliated in the California gubernatorial election by the incumbent, Edmund G. Brown. After sixteen years in the political arena, Nixon announced the day after his defeat that he had had it. "This is my last press conference," Nixon told the startled reporters who had come to hear him out. Everyone thought he was finished.

Of course, Nixon had not retired from politics. Over the next few years he did, however, take some time off and worked in a law firm in New York City alongside his future secretary of state William Rogers. Political animal that he was, Nixon retained his links to the Republican Party's leadership but sat out the 1964 presidential campaign, where the Republican Barry Goldwater was soundly defeated by Lyndon Johnson. Soon thereafter, Nixon started positioning himself for a run in the 1968 elections. He built links to the moderate wing of his party dominated by Kissinger's mentor Nelson Rockefeller. By late 1967 Nixon appeared to be the most electable of those senior Republicans in contention for the nomination (in addition to Rockefeller, these included California Governor Ronald Reagan). And, as an experienced campaigner, Nixon had the best political machinery within his own party. By the summer of 1968 his nomination was a virtual certainty, confirmed at the Miami Beach Republican convention in August, where Kissinger made those legendary disparaging comments about his future boss. Three months later Nixon finally won the ultimate prize of his political career as voters narrowly chose him, rather than Vice President Hubert Humphrey.

Richard Nixon may have been the consummate American politician but he also had something that his predecessor, Lyndon B. Johnson, and his successor, Gerald R. Ford, lacked. Nixon was experienced and knowledgeable in foreign affairs and, once elected, intended to become a foreign policy president. Over his years as Eisenhower's vice president Nixon had spent more time on foreign policy than any previous holder of that post. He had traveled the world, both as vice president and later as a private citizen, and had met most of the prominent world leaders in office. He had shown an ability to hold his ground in debates with powerful adversaries (most famously with Soviet leader Nikita Khrushchev in the famous "kitchen debate" of 1958). Although Nixon had deserved a reputation as the right-wing Republican leader due to his merciless attacks on a number of Democratic opponents as soft on communism, this did not, in the end, place him in a unique category among American political leaders of the early Cold War. During the 1960 election against John F. Kennedy, Nixon's rhetoric had actually been less ideologically driven than that of his rival. Nixon was, in short, a pragmatist, someone that used rhetoric when it fit his needs. He believed, of course, that Soviet communism was the chief nemesis of the United States and that American democracy was superior to Soviet communism. But he was not dogmatic about the East-West rivalry.

Although Nixon had not advertised his foreign policy views, he had dropped hints about some of the issues that would dominate his and Kissinger's agenda after January 1969. He had, by and large, supported the escalation of the Vietnam War and offered, in 1968, only a nonspecified "plan" on how to end the war. He had published, in 1967, what many would consider a remarkably prophetic essay on China, arguing, in essence, that in the long run the United States would have to come to terms with the world's most populous nation, regardless of the political philosophy of its leaders. And he made numerous references in various speeches during the presidential campaign about "a new era of negotiation" with the Soviet Union. There was a hint of change, but hardly anything approaching an opening commitment to détente.

Nixon's personality was, as almost every observer has noted, full of contradictions. He was the consummate American politician but he was also shy in personal contact with people. He could deliver a good speech but found it difficult to make chitchat. He had few friends and could apparently only relax in the company of men that had no obvious connection to politics, such as the Miami businessman Bebe Rebozo. Even as the president of the United States, Nixon appeared insecure, unable to confront people face-to-face, yet craving public approval. He claimed to hate the press, but was seriously concerned about what they wrote. He was, in short, a complex man. As one of his biographers puts it, Nixon "was devious, manipulative, driven by unseen and unknowable forces, quick as a summer storm to blame and slow as a glacier melt to forgive, passionate in his hatreds, self-centered, untruthful, untrusting, and at times so despicable that one wants to avert one's eyes in shame and embarrassment." Yet, the same Nixon "could be considerate, straightforward, sympathetic, and helpful" and "was blessed with great talent, superb intellect, an awesome memory, and a remarkable ability to see things whole, especially on a global scale and with regard to the world balance of power."[2]

He was, in many ways, not unlike Henry Kissinger.

CHOOSING KISSINGER

The 1968 election finally catapulted Kissinger to the corridors of power. Having returned to Cambridge after the Republican convention in August 1968, Kissinger, after some hesitation, refused to establish an open connection with Richard Nixon's foreign policy team, at the time headed by Richard Allen, a thirty-two-year-old staunch anticommunist who had studied in Munich and Stanford (but had not, although others addressed him as "Dr. Allen," actually finished his doctorate). According to Allen, and journalist-author Seymour Hersh, Kissinger did, however, offer his help behind the scenes. At the same time, Kissinger maintained connections with the Democratic camp and in mid-September spent a few days in Paris, where an American delegation, headed by Averell Harriman, was engaged in peace talks with the North Vietnamese. Upon his return from Paris, Kissinger—while he had no specifics to offer—informed the Nixon camp that the Johnson administration was working hard to get a bombing halt prior to the early November elections. It was the first of many Kissinger back channels.[3]

Kissinger's links to the Nixon camp have spawned numerous conspiracy theories not only about Kissinger's conduct but also about the possibility that Nixon may have sabotaged the Paris peace talks in order to secure his victory in November 1968. The strongest case to this effect has been made recently by William Bundy. In his 1998 book, *A Tangled Web*, Bundy—while dismissing any information that Kissinger may have provided about Washington and Hanoi's willingness to establish a bombing halt in November as nothing but common sense ("Almost any experienced Hanoi watcher might have come to the same conclusion")—implies a clandestine effort on Nixon's part to destroy any possibility of a peace agreement. Through his contacts via Anna Chennault (a member of Nixon's campaign staff and strong supporter of the cause of Nationalist China) and South Vietnam's Ambassador Bui Diem, Nixon had apparently, since July 1968, encouraged South Vietnamese President Nguyen Thieu not to rush into accepting any agreement with Hanoi during the Johnson presidency.[4]

Bundy, whose account is undoubtedly colored by his particular partisan leanings (Bundy was assistant secretary of state for the Far East during the Johnson administration; his brother McGeorge had been Kennedy and Johnson's NSC adviser), does make a fairly persuasive case that Nixon was playing politics with the war in the months preceding the 1968 election. Yet, this was hardly a singularly Nixonian trait at the time. The same could of course be said of Johnson and Vice President Hubert Humphrey, who had secured the Democratic nomination the previous summer. Indeed, Johnson's bombing halt was undoubtedly timed so as to affect the election result to Humphrey's favor. And, as the close popular vote (Nixon got 43 percent, Humphrey 42 percent, and the third party candidate George Wallace 15 percent) indicated, the Democrats nearly managed to catch what had seemed, a few weeks prior to the November elections, a decisive victory for the Republicans. Yet, one might also speculate that in the absence of the Wallace campaign, Nixon's victory might have been far more decisive.[5]

While there is no doubt that both major candidates played politics with the war in 1968, it seems equally clear that Kissinger engaged both sides during the last months of the presidential campaign. If he gave some information about the peace talks to the Nixon camp, Kissinger also made vague promises to the Democrats. After the Republican convention, he offered, but never delivered, the Rockefeller camp's extensive "Nixon files" to the Humphrey camp. Despite efforts by such Harvard colleagues as the future National Security Adviser Zbigniew Brzezinski, Kissinger never handed over any useful information; perhaps he did not have the access to it or, as many would later suspect, he was already clearly tilting toward the Nixon camp due to poll numbers that in September indicated a convincing Republican victory. There is, however, no question that Kissinger was covering his bases and setting himself up for a job offer no matter which side was eventually successful in November.[6]

The job offer—certainly in the form it came—from Nixon was not a given. The only known meeting between the two men before November 1968 had been a five-minute talk at a Christmas party in 1967 that had apparently not left lasting impressions on either man. And yet, when Henry Cabot Lodge, who had worked with Kissinger while an ambassador to Vietnam and had been Nixon's running mate in 1960, recommended Kissinger to the president-elect as a potential national security adviser, Nixon indicated that he was already seriously considering such an appointment. On Friday, November 22, 1968, then, Kissinger received a call from Dwight Chapin, Nixon's appointments secretary. Kissinger, who was, ironically, at the time having lunch with Nelson Rockefeller and his advisers, was invited for an interview at the Hotel Pierre in New York, where Nixon had set up his transition headquarters, the following Monday. A week later, after a successful meeting with Nixon in the interim, Kissinger accepted the job. The public announcement followed on Monday December 2, 1968. Nixon said he wanted a "fresh approach"— which was true enough—but then assured that "Dr. Kissinger is keenly aware of the necessity not to set himself up as a wall between the secretary of state." This, later events would bear out, was simply untrue.

But why had Nixon chosen Kissinger?

The NSC adviser-elect Kissinger had many qualities that—aside from his manipulative behavior during the last months of the 1968 campaign—made him an appealing choice to Nixon. He was a Harvard academic with connections to the eastern establishment that provided links to the parts of American elite that Nixon had grown to hate—but whose approval he seemed to crave—during his political career. There was also the Rockefeller connection; by appointing Kissinger, Nixon may have hoped to heal some of the wounds within the Republican Party that had opened up during the 1968 primaries. Alternatively, as the historian Joan Hoff suspects, Nixon may have wanted to "strike a blow at Rockefeller by 'stealing' someone close to him."[7]

Such motivations aside, what about the possibility that Nixon simply considered Kissinger the best man for the job? As Kissinger's young aide Peter Rodman divulged in an interview in 1994, Nixon had actually made queries about having Kissinger join his staff immediately after he had secured the Republican nomination. In Rodman's words: "Nixon, I think, largely realized that Kissinger was really the outstanding person on the Republican side." The call that eventually came could not have been a complete surprise.[8]

To some extent, Rodman was probably correct: while there was no shortage of supplicants, Kissinger had made a name for himself as Rockefeller's adviser and thus as one of the few Republican foreign policy intellectuals. Within the Republican field, moreover, there were few other obvious contenders. Certainly Richard Allen was never considered a serious possibility for such a high post: Nixon had not even bothered to take the thirty-two-year-old with him when he received the first major foreign policy briefing as president-elect from Johnson's major foreign policy advisers.

In the end, the initial choice of Kissinger was probably the result of many calculations, ranging from political motivations and Nixon's personal quirks to serious foreign policy considerations. It certainly had the immediate impact of causing a collective sigh of relief among the many observers who remembered Nixon mainly as an unrepentant and rather shallow red-baiter. James Reston of the *New York Times* (not a paper that would frequently endorse Nixon), for example, considered it "significant" that Kissinger "has the respect of most of the foreign policy experts" in the country. The conservative columnist William F. Buckley summed up the press's reaction when he later wrote to Kissinger: "Not since Florence Nightingale has any public figure received such public acclamation."[9]

Being selected was one thing. Becoming a central actor in the making of the Nixon administration's foreign policy was something else. That would take more than opportunism.

THE BOND

In early 1969, few expected that Kissinger would become such a global figure as he eventually did. For example, according to Nixon's White House chief of staff, Bob Haldeman, the outgoing president Lyndon Johnson had no inclinations that the NSC adviser was one of the best and the brightest of the Nixon administration. Although Johnson politely told Billy Graham on January 17 that the Nixon cabinet was "the best in history," he identified, ironically, Secretary of State William Rogers as one of "the stars."[10]

Johnson could hardly have been more off the mark regarding Rogers. For William Rogers was not destined to stardom in the area of foreign policy. The former attorney general and Nixon's law partner was constantly undermined by Kissinger and rarely supported by the president. Already in February 1969, *Time* magazine cited a close Nixon aide as saying, "Kissinger is seen as tremendously talented, energetic and hard-working . . . But there is a certain weariness about him and the whole empire he is building." Indeed, while Nixon would repeatedly assure in public that the secretary of state was the principal officer in matters of foreign policy, only one of the major issues on Nixon's agenda fell under Rogers' purview: the Middle East. And even there, the secretary of state's control of events—largely a result of Nixon's concern that Kissinger's Jewish background would cloud his judgment regarding the Arab-Israeli conflict—did not last. Rogers lost control of Middle East policy by the fall of 1970. For all intents and purposes, as Kissinger clearly gained the upper hand in his bureaucratic rivalry with Rogers, the secretary of state became more a figurehead than an effective decision maker.[11]

Above all there was the necessity that both saw for centralizing foreign policy decision making. Nixon made this clear at their November meeting at the Hotel Pierre in New York, when he displayed open contempt—a legacy of his service as Eisenhower's vice president—for the State Department and its large bureaucracy. He wanted to be his own secretary of state. Kissinger responded by suggesting that the way around the State Department was to put together a strong NSC staff that would be located in the White House. The Departments of State and Defense, the other two agencies that normally played a decisive role in shaping foreign policy, would be kept occupied by demanding detailed studies of various foreign policy aspects. The true planning and decision making would take place in the NSC staff and, ultimately, in lengthy meetings between Nixon and Kissinger.

Kissinger began to plan this "quiet coup," as Walter Isaacson calls it, in December 1968 at Nixon's orders and with the help of a young Pentagon foreign policy expert, Morton Halperin. The plan, outlined by Halperin, was twofold. First, the Nixon administration would have a National Security Review Group that, unlike its predecessor during the Johnson administration, was to be chaired by the national security adviser. This would give Kissinger effective control of both the NSC agenda and all the policy papers going to the president. Second, Kissinger was to have the power to ask for National Security Study Memoranda (NSSMs), which were a series of extensive studies on various foreign policy topics done by the bureaucracies at the State, Defense, Treasury, and other departments. By being able to order such studies, Kissinger gained control over what the various departments were actually working on, while his chairmanship of the review group minimized the number of independent initiatives that could arise. Nixon approved the plan as one of the first orders of his presidency, hence guaranteeing Kissinger's position as the foreign policy czar.[12]

In addition to the revamping of the NSC system, however, Kissinger managed to take control over a number of other committees that enhanced his power base within the administration. Among the most significant were the Washington Special Action Group (WSAG), which handled rapid responses to breaking events and crises, and the Forty Committee, a panel that was in charge of authorizing the Nixon administration's covert actions conducted by the CIA and other agencies. Both were interagency committees, yet as the chair of these bodies Kissinger would control the agenda and be in a prominent position to shape the outcomes of the meetings. Both the WSAG and the Forty Committee would be in action throughout Kissinger's time in office and be used regularly during such crises as Chile in 1970, the October 1973 War in the Middle East, and the Angolan conflict in 1975.[13]

*   *   *

No plans or bureaucratic moves, though, guaranteed the end result. Kissinger did not enter the West Wing Basement of the White House guaranteed to emerge as the foreign policy czar of the new administration. It depended most of all on Nixon, who had the power, as the president, to fashion foreign policy in the way he wanted. The emergence of Kissinger as the prime foreign policy maker in the Nixon administration was ultimately, as Peter Rodman later put it, "Nixon's doing." Yet, Rodman wryly added, "Henry didn't object, obviously."

The point to stress is that the consolidation of power took time and constant effort. It was hardly possible that a former Harvard professor—even one with extended experience working as a consultant for the two previous administrations—would arrive in Washington with a staff of a few dozen and sweep aside the entire State Department and its thousands of well-connected and experienced personnel. As Kissinger later put it in an interview with the author, "The idea that I went in there to take it away from Nixon's best friend [Secretary of State William Rogers], as a Rockefeller disciple, it's preposterous. I didn't know anybody in the Nixon entourage." That Kissinger managed to establish such a prominent position for himself was ultimately dependent not just on his own bureaucratic skills—although these naturally helped—but first and foremost on the president's desire to run foreign policy and Kissinger's ability to provide the type of advice that he was seeking.[14]

Again, Nixon's personal quirks—his dislike of open confrontation and large meetings—undoubtedly helped Kissinger in his gradual consolidation of power. There was, after all, the sheer physical proximity that allowed the two to spend inordinate—some say "unhealthy"—amounts of time together. Based in the West Wing of the White House, Kissinger, unlike his colleagues at Foggy Bottom or Pentagon, had easy access to the president, who seems to have enjoyed the long rambling conversations they engaged in, sometimes for two hours at a time. Nor did Kissinger have to work too hard to keep others from gaining access to Nixon: the president made it very clear to his chief of staff, Bob Haldeman, that he wished to "build a wall" against unsolicited advice. Very few men—Haldeman, Kissinger, and Nixon's chief domestic policy adviser, John Ehrlichman—would have anything resembling open access.[15]

And Kissinger, even as he sometimes privately loathed and complained about the president, knew how to take advantage of Nixon's two principal insecurities: his amazing difficulty in confronting people directly and his need for constant praise. The former characteristic increased the appeal of back channels, almost without fault controlled by Kissinger, as a way of conducting the White House's foreign policy. In the first Nixon administration, such secret avenues of diplomacy proliferated as Kissinger established private links to the Soviet Union, China, North Vietnam, West Germany, Japan, and elsewhere. With each new back channel, Kissinger's influence as a foreign policy maker increased while the State Department was left further in the dark.

Kissinger was also an expert at flattering Nixon. Whenever the president gave a major speech, the NSC adviser would be the first to congratulate him on the impressive performance just rendered. Nixon, who believed in the power of the bully pulpit and in the decisive significance of grand oratory, undoubtedly appreciated such praise.

One example serves to illustrate this point. At 9:00 P.M. on April 7, 1971, Nixon gave one of his many live radio/television addresses on the situation in Vietnam. On this occasion the major topics were the South Vietnamese incursion into Laos earlier in the year, which Nixon—with some creative argumentation—portrayed as a success story indicating that his policy of Vietnamization (the gradual withdrawal of American forces from the region coupled with intensive training and enhanced military aid to South Vietnam) "has succeeded." At 9:31 P.M. the president was on the phone with Kissinger. "This was the best speech you've given since you've been in office," Kissinger said, repeating the mantra from previous such occasions. It had been "movingly delivered," he added. Everyone in his staff agreed, Kissinger said. After eight minutes they got off the phone and Nixon called around to get similar confirmations of his oratorical skills from elsewhere. But Kissinger was back on line by 10:21 P.M. Then again at 10:35 and 11:13. And on it went, all the way into the next evening, with Kissinger (and others) stroking the president's ego. The scenario was not an isolated incident. Nixon, a man uncomfortable with face-to-face contact, was also a man with an excessive need for reassurance.

The Nixon–Kissinger conversations in April 1971 are also indicative of some other central features in the relationship. For one, there was Nixon's pathological hatred of the press that was exceeded only by his desire to know exactly what the press was saying about him. "Of course I didn't look at the [postspeech] commentary," he told Kissinger. "I don't care what the bastards say," he added. "I never look at that shit," Nixon said when Kissinger offered to call his friend, the journalist Joseph Alsop, for a preview of next day's press reactions. Eight minutes later, after Kissinger reported that Alsop had called the speech Nixon's "greatest," the president wondered whether he should call the influential columnist right away. "Not tonight," Kissinger (who may or may not have been reporting Alsop's exact words) replied. Nixon agreed.

But the president clearly cared about "that shit."[16]

Kissinger's relationship with the press was almost diametrically opposite to that of Nixon. If the president loathed most reporters and newscasters, Kissinger loved talking to them. Although he had had limited experience with the media prior to 1969, Kissinger developed fairly close relationships with many of the most influential newsmen of the early 1970s. In addition to Alsop, Kissinger developed relationships with such notables of the Washington media circuit as Joseph Kraft and Katharine Graham; later on Kissinger would also become expert in courting such television notables as Ted Koppel of ABC and Marvin Kalb of CBS. As the NSC adviser he gave them "backgrounders": briefings on various foreign policy matters that could not be directly attributed to Kissinger (but simply to a "senior White House official"). Given that Kissinger kept a tight lid on his own staff, he became the major source of inside information and, hence, the man who effectively controlled the official news. As one *Washington Post* editor remarked: "Kissinger was important to us." Indeed, as Roger Morris writes, the Washington press corps quickly understood that Kissinger was "the most authoritative source on American diplomacy, the man who obviously had the President's ear in Washington."[17]

In other words, Kissinger became the Nixon administration's supreme spin doctor on matters of foreign policy.

The problem from Nixon's perspective was that while he generally approved of Kissinger's contacts with the press, the president noticed a peculiar kind of spin in the reporting: over time, and particularly after Kissinger's secret trip to China in July 1971, journalistic commentary tended to attribute an increasing amount of praise to the administration's foreign policy successes to the 'wrong' man, Henry Kissinger. Already in the first year of the administration, however, Nixon would fire off repeated memos and comments to Kissinger about the need to build up the president's image. As he put it in a memo on August 7, 1969, Kissinger needed to use his background briefings to "point out that the President was in constant charge" and "effective." And he wanted to hear and read such commentary from "the wire service, a major weekly news magazine, a thoughtful television commentator." To punctuate the point, Nixon stressed: "This is the top priority project."[18]

Image was not everything. But guarding their public image was crucial to Nixon and, as we will see, over time he increasingly (and not without cause) worried more and more that the NSC adviser was overshadowing the boss.

While Nixon and Kissinger shared an appetite for foreign policy and used each other for their specific ends, while they spent numerous hours together, one aspect of the relationship was curiously absent. There was little, if any, personalized, human contact. "We never knew each other very well humanly," Kissinger would later comment in an interview, adding, "I mean, we had very few dinners together. We never went to baseball games together." Not only did the two never go to a baseball game together, they hardly ever socialized. Nixon, of course, was not a man who could relax—lest it was drinking with his old friend Bebe Rebozo. Talking shop was his hobby, Haldeman once remarked. Kissinger, for his part, could be socially charming, but probably found the president's manners awkward. Nixon's often blatantly anti-Semitic comments (usually with reference to the news media that, Nixon would rant and rave, was controlled by Jews and treated him unfairly) could not have touched some chord. Indeed, instead of his co-workers or his boss, Kissinger found social fulfillment elsewhere: among the journalists, the intellectuals, and, increasingly, what Nixon derisively called "the Hollywood crowd." Bound together for many years, Kissinger and Nixon remained ultimately as distant as their personal backgrounds suggested.

The Nixon–Kissinger relationship that developed over the years was, in short, multifaceted. At one level, it reflected Nixon's deep need for praise, for the proximity and approval of someone with the stature and intelligence of Kissinger. While they never became close and can hardly be considered to have been friends, there was a strange bond.[19] Perhaps it was both men's understanding that they were never full members of the establishment; that Nixon had alienated much of the intellectual and political elite due to his anticommunist crusades, his persecution—justified or not—of one of the brightest members of that elite, Alger Hiss, in the late 1940s. Meanwhile, Kissinger, as a Jew among elite dominated by WASPs, was, undoubtedly, a target of latent anti-Semitism. Perhaps the bond had to with the fact that both men embodied, to their considerable credit, the American dream: neither had gained his position as birthright but had, in effect, made his own luck. And, in order to get to their respective positions, both Kissinger and Nixon had shown an ability to be opportunists. To Nixon, it had meant reinventing himself and his image after the defeat in the 1962 California gubernatorial race; to Kissinger it had translated into a willingness to join the crew of a man he had privately denigrated as a "disaster." But whatever the specific ingredients of the relationship, Nixon and Kissinger were thrown together and bonded, in their special way and with dramatic consequences, over the next five and a half years.

Richard Reeves provides an astute analysis of the Nixon–Kissinger relationship in his 2001 book *President Nixon*: "Two strange men linked. Kissinger could not exist without President Nixon. President Nixon could not do what he wanted—build what he called a structure of peace—without Kissinger."[20]

As Reeves implies, there was a more substantial reason than sheer personal aggrandizement behind the revamping of the foreign policy decision-making process at the start of the Nixon administration that explains Kissinger's role as the foreign policy czar.

Simply put: in January 1969 American foreign policy was in serious trouble.

CHALLENGES OF '69

At the center of American difficulties lay the Vietnam War. The Tet Offensive of February 1968 had exposed the hollow nature of Lyndon Johnson's assurances of late 1967 that the enemy's breaking point was about to be reached and that the war was coming to an end. Instead, the commander of U.S. forces in Vietnam, General William Westmoreland, had asked for another 200,000 troops to top up the half million already stationed in South Vietnam. That had been too much for Johnson, who had refused the request and announced, in late March, his decision not to seek a continuation of his presidency. And, although he had ordered a bombing halt in late October, the Vietnam War presented mostly problems and few promising opportunities for the incoming administration in early 1969.

Aside from Vietnam, however, Kissinger and Nixon faced a whole host of other challenges and uncertainties. The relationship with the Soviet Union was at a crossroads, as the Soviets approached nuclear parity. While their resources were far from equal with those of the United States when it came down to other "types" of power, the Kremlin's confidence appeared to have been boosted by the crackdown on Czechoslovakia in August 1968. The moderate response of the United States and its West European allies to the arrival of thousands of Warsaw Pact troops in Prague could only have indicated to the Soviets that their sphere of influence in East-Central Europe was secure. The inherent right of the USSR and its allies to defend socialism in East European countries by force if necessary—often referred to as the Brezhnev Doctrine—had apparently been accepted in Washington. In addition, the Soviets continued to support militarily a number of Arab states, particularly Egypt and Syria, in their quest for retribution after Israeli victories in the 1967 Six Days War. The Soviet Union, it seemed, was casting its quest for influence far beyond East-Central Europe.

The PRC remained a major question mark, particularly after it had turned increasingly inward with the commencement of Mao's Cultural Revolution in 1966. While Beijing had severed its ties with Moscow, there was no obvious indication in 1969 that the Chinese were looking for rapprochement with Washington. The PRC continued to support North Vietnam and castigate the United States for its support of South Vietnam.

Throughout the 1960s the Americans also had had troubles with their friends. The European allies were far from happy with America's continued involvement in Vietnam, something Charles de Gaulle would take issue with during Nixon's first trip abroad as president. While de Gaulle's furor at the Americans appeared to diminish after France left NATO's integrated military structure in 1966 (it remained formally a member of the alliance), there was also the troublesome nature of West Germany's so-called *Ostpolitik*. When the Social Democrat leader Willy Brandt became chancellor in September 1969 (after serving as foreign minister in a coalition government), his government moved quickly to improve relations with the Soviet bloc. This, in turn, would threaten to make it impossible to have a unified NATO policy vis-à-vis the USSR, or at least the type of unified policy that left Washington firmly in the driver's seat. Added to these political woes were the economic challenges presented by European integration and the Japanese economic miracle; for the first time in the postwar years, the United States faced a serious economic challenge to its dominance of the international marketplace.

Beyond all that, there existed a volatile "rest of the world." After the 1967 Six Days War in the Middle East, the Arab-Israeli conflict had been left unresolved. Decolonization in Africa was creating civil wars from which the Soviets (or even the Chinese) could possibly benefit. In Latin America, the Alliance for Progress of the 1960s had not produced more reliable allies but an upsurge in anti-Americanism. In South Asia, old hostilities between India and Pakistan were adding to regional instability already provoked by the Sino-Indian War of 1962 and the Indo-Pakistani War of 1965.

It was, indeed, an unstable world full of challenges, a world that may have resembled, if on a much larger scale and through a particularly selective set of glasses, the Europe that had faced Prince Metternich in the early nineteenth century. Kissinger could hardly have entered high public office at a time when American foreign policy was under greater siege at home and abroad. In 1968 it seemed that few of the certainties of American Cold War policy remained intact. And yet, even with a half million American forces bogged down in Vietnam, Washington's nuclear superiority in jeopardy, America's influence over its allies in decline, and the impact of decolonization on international relations unresolved, the United States was still the most powerful nation on earth. Its military might was still unsurpassed, its economic power unequalled, and its human potential enormous.

The real question thus was: how could the United States redeem itself and reestablish trust in American leadership? How could the administration accomplish this in a manner that would be acceptable and respectable to friend and foe at home and abroad? To Kissinger, the task meant a search for a new global equilibrium that would reflect the changing nature of power without jeopardizing the United States' preponderant influence in international affairs. It meant creative diplomacy and the application of his understanding of the nature of power in the modern world to American foreign policy. It meant reinventing the ground rules for American diplomacy in order to restore the United States' role in the world while extricating it from its most disastrous military engagement yet. Ultimately, it also meant finding a way out of Vietnam and looking for new ways of dealing with its major Cold War adversary, of taking advantage of existing opportunities.

Kissinger and Nixon wanted to assure that, as in previous decades, the United States played a central role in international affairs. However, given that this role was, at the time, being challenged from numerous directions—America's troubles in the Vietnam War, a growing domestic criticism of the principles of containment that had led to that involvement, a Soviet Union approaching parity in nuclear weapons—new strategies were needed. As Kissinger himself later put it, the task facing the new administration was vast: "Simultaneously we had to end a war, manage a global rivalry with the Soviet Union in the shadow of nuclear weapons, reinvigorate our alliance with industrial democracies, and integrate the new nations into a new world equilibrium."[21]

Written, as it was, after he left office, the statement may well have been meant to build up Kissinger's reputation by arguing that the odds were, in effect, against him (and Nixon) in 1969. But the point is worth stressing that there was more than a grain of truth in Kissinger's assertion. The United States desperately needed a new foreign policy design.

AN ARCHITECT IN SEARCH OF A DESIGN

Kissinger's theoretical disposition and background seemed to make him an ideal man to meet this challenge. Although an embodiment of the American dream, he was not deeply ideological. He was steeped in the realist tradition of international relations. Thus, Kissinger would have little problem in treating his future Soviet or Chinese interlocutors as leaders of countries with specific national interests rather than proponents of world revolution. This understanding coincided with the obvious limits that the new administration faced when it came down to using American military power abroad. Diplomacy, Kissinger's specific field of expertise, would thus command the central position in implementing the new administration's grand design.

A shared taste for realpolitik was, indeed, one of the factors that brought Nixon and Kissinger closer together (and undermined Rogers' influence). It was to serve them well when it came to negotiating with the Soviets or the Chinese, in implementing the notions of détente and triangular diplomacy. Of course, there were other shared interests as well. There was the often mistaken assumption that toughness was a key to success; that a show of force, properly used, could yield significant diplomatic gains. This shared belief would later become evident in Kissinger and Nixon's strategy for ending the Vietnam War. It would also, in modified form, find itself into the so-called Nixon Doctrine.

Détente, triangular diplomacy, and the Nixon Doctrine would, eventually, be some of the central elements of Kissinger's foreign policy. On the morning of January 21, 1969—when he discussed the shape of the world with Nixon at the Oval Office—they were yet to be formulated. Kissinger faced problems, none of them less pressing than Vietnam. But he had not yet come up with clear-cut solutions. He, and Nixon, may have had an overall framework in mind. But theories would not always survive the pressure of contingency. Kissinger would find that out soon.

3

Bombs and Back Channels

February 17, 1969, stands out as one of the defining moments of Soviet-American relations. Not that there was anything too unusual about a meeting between the new president of the United States and the Soviet ambassador to Washington, which was simply good diplomatic practice. But the meeting was unique in two respects. First, it set in motion the policy of détente that would later be hailed as one of the Nixon administration's, and Henry Kissinger's, great foreign policy feats. Second, the meeting established the venue in which the most important discussions would take place: the Kissinger–Dobrynin back channel. That the deputy assistant secretary for European affairs, Malcolm Toon, rather than Secretary of State William Rogers, represented the State Department at the meeting symbolized the influential position that Kissinger had acquired less than a month into Nixon's first term. In the months and years to come, he would clearly emerge as the key American arbiter of détente through numerous meetings with the Soviet ambassador.

Although he was clearly enthusiastic about becoming the Nixon administration's major link to Moscow, Kissinger was far less impressed with one of the president's other pet projects—the opening to China. Alexander Haig, Kissinger's deputy and future secretary of state under Ronald Reagan, later recalled his boss's amusement when Nixon tried to press the new national security adviser to explore the possibility of establishing a relationship with the PRC. "He has just ordered me to make this flight of fancy come true," Kissinger sighed, according to Haig, after one of his meetings with Nixon in early February. Nevertheless, if only to please his new boss, on February 1, 1969, Kissinger ordered an internal review of U.S. China policy. At the time, however, Nixon's order required Kissinger merely to create "an impression of activity" rather than to come up with any clear-cut plans.[1]

Kissinger's less than enthusiastic attitude about China during the early stages of the administration was quite understandable. Not only was China not among his fields of expertise, but most important, in early 1969, it seemed rather unimportant when compared to urgent issues such as a dialogue over nuclear weapons with the Soviet Union or trying to find an acceptable way of ending the Vietnam War. In January and early February Kissinger was focused on establishing his relationship with Soviet Ambassador Anatoly Dobrynin as a way of improving the prospects for a Soviet-American dialogue. Soon after that, Kissinger joined Nixon and other key officials for a weeklong tour of Europe, making stops in Brussels, London, Bonn, Berlin, Rome, and Paris between February 23 and March 2. While China popped up from time to time during the trip—during Nixon's meeting with Charles de Gaulle, for example, the French president argued that it was time for the United States to seriously reconsider its nonrecognition policy vis-à-vis the PRC—there was little to indicate that the Europeans, many of whom already dealt with the Chinese on a normal diplomatic level, pressed the Nixon administration in any direction. The Europeans remained more concerned with the prospects of détente and the American attitude toward the further expansion of the European Economic Community (EEC).[2]

Then there was—there always was—Vietnam. In the spring of 1969, no other foreign policy issue occupied Nixon and Kissinger's time more than the Vietnam War. It was, at least at the start of his presidency, the issue on which everything else seemed to hinge. As Nixon had asked Lyndon Johnson back in July 1968: "Can we do anything until Vietnam is off the burner?"[3] During the spring of 1969, Kissinger was more concerned with the secret bombing of Cambodia and Defense Secretary Mel Laird's Vietnamization, the policy of gradually removing U.S. troops from Vietnam while increasing aid to the South Vietnamese Army (the Army of the Republic of Vietnam, ARVN), proposals than with any other issues. That these decisions on Cambodia and Vietnam coincided with Sino-Soviet border clashes in early March 1969 undoubtedly distracted the administration's immediate attention from the significance of the events along the Ussuri River.

But not for long. Already by the summer of 1969 Kissinger was beginning to hint to the Soviet ambassador, Anatoly Dobrynin, that a qualitative change in Sino-American relations was in the offing. As the Chinese leadership simultaneously agonized over the possibility of an escalated military conflict with the Soviets and about the incremental, but noticeable, North Vietnamese gravitation toward the USSR and away from China, Beijing gave serious thought to a potential rapprochement. By the end of Nixon's first year in office, Sino-American ambassadorial talks were under way in Warsaw and Kissinger began to position himself as America's future emissary to the PRC. He was undoubtedly encouraged by the combination of Soviet anxiety over a possible Sino-American rapprochement and

the apparent reluctance of the Soviets, as well as of the North Vietnamese, to deliver
on the other two major secret channels that were under Kissinger's control.

THE CHANNEL: HENRY AND ANATOLY

In early 1969 Anatoly Dobrynin, a head taller than Kissinger, cut a formidable fig-
ure in Washington's diplomatic circles. With an ego that easily matched Kissinger's,
Dobrynin was the longest-serving Soviet ambassador to the United States. He had
taken up this demanding post in March 1962; Dobrynin's baptism by fire came
seven months later when the Cuban missile crisis erupted. After that ordeal,
Dobrynin faced numerous other challenges, including the gradual escalation of the
Vietnam War, the 1967 Middle East War, and the 1968 Warsaw Pact invasion of
Czechoslovakia. He also had survived the changing of the guard in Moscow in 1964.
In contrast to a relatively little known Harvard professor like Kissinger, Dobrynin
appeared a gigantic figure on the diplomatic scene. By 1969, he probably knew his
way around Washington as well as any foreign diplomat, whether from a friendly
or unfriendly nation. Dobrynin, moreover, was already an experienced back-
channel communicator; one of his first assignments in March 1962 had been to take
over the confidential channel operated by Georgi Bolshakov, an officer in the Soviet
military intelligence and the chief of the local TASS news bureau. By October 1962,
when the Cuban missile crisis erupted, Dobrynin and the confidential channel
played a key role through various meetings with Robert Kennedy.[4]

Back channels—confidential channels of communication between two countries' leaders—were not, as Dobrynin's experience itself indicated, a novelty as
such. They had been deemed necessary as ways of exchanging views and negotiating deals that would, if discussed openly, be likely to result either in a severe domestic backlash that would make achieving a desired negotiation result impossible, or
would allow third countries to sabotage such negotiations. In the history of American foreign policy, for example, Alexander Hamilton had commenced the practice
of back channels during George Washington's presidency in the late eighteenth
century as a way of bypassing the then secretary of state Thomas Jefferson. Hamilton wanted to work toward a rapprochement with Great Britain whereas Jefferson
was avidly pro-French. More recently, various confidential channels had been used
to solve specific crises (such as the Cuban missile crisis).

But while there was nothing new to secret channels in times of crisis, the back
channel established in February 1969 was unique. For one thing, over time the scope
of the subject matter became virtually unlimited, ranging from Vietnam and the
Middle East to nuclear arms limitations and Soviet-American trade. The Kissinger–
Dobrynin back channel was not, in other words, a venue for crisis management
(although it could be used for that purpose as well). It was, ultimately, *the* medium
for negotiating on *all* the important issues affecting the superpower relationship.

The back channel made Kissinger the prime mover of U.S. policy toward the Soviet Union. However, it should also be noted that largely due to the establishment of the channel, Dobrynin—an astute interpreter of the international scene and a keen observer of American domestic politics—became an increasingly important member of the Soviet foreign policy-making elite in 1969–71. Yet, the Soviet ambassador faced his own complications at home. Dobrynin was, clearly, a proponent of détente. So was, it became clear, the general secretary of the Soviet Communist Party, Leonid Brezhnev, and the foreign minister, Andrei Gromyko. Yet, this hardly meant that the entire Soviet leadership—many of whom lacked even the basic knowledge of American society and politics—was united. As in the United States, powerful forces inside the USSR objected to the relaxation of tensions and the curbing of the arms race that détente implied. To the defense minister, Marshall Andrei Grechko, for example, reducing the nuclear arms race translated into restrictions in his department's budgets and, hence, his power base. To the chief ideologue of the Politburo and the second secretary of the Soviet Communist Party, Mikhail Suslov (the "gray cardinal"), improvements in relations with the United States were anathema. In other words, the onset of détente in 1969–71 had an internal subtext in the Kremlin that complicated Soviet-American negotiations in the first Nixon administration.

In contrast to Dobrynin, Kissinger had limited experience in high-level diplomacy. He had engaged in a few ad hoc missions for the Johnson administration. For all intents and purposes, however, Kissinger was a novice. But, he was a fast learner and could take heart in the fact that the United States was hardly devoid of negotiating assets. The Americans were still ahead in the missile race (in 1969 the United States had an estimated 4,200 nuclear warheads, while the USSR had only about 1,900), their economic power far exceeded that of any other country (in 1970, for example, the United States' share of gross world product was 23 percent compared to the USSR's 12.4 percent), and Washington's overall influence was felt around the globe in a way that the Soviet Union's was not. There was a downside to this as well: because its influence was so widespread, Washington's interests could also be challenged in far more areas and regions than those of the USSR.

*   *   *

Enter linkage. As Nixon explained in a memorandum, prepared by Kissinger's NSC staff, to key cabinet members at the start of his administration: "I do believe that crisis or confrontation in one place and real co-operation in another cannot long be sustained simultaneously." The basic point was, he added, that "on the crucial issues of our day, I believe we must seek to advance on a front at least broad enough to make clear that we see some relationship between political and military issues." In short, part of the agenda was that the Soviet leaders "should be brought to understand that they cannot expect to reap the benefits of co-operation in one area while seeking to take advantage of tension or confrontation elsewhere." The potential drawback was that Soviet-American diplomacy would be hampered by constant delays. As Nixon's memo recognized, "there may be no talks at all." Indeed, the notion of linkage—the assumption that all issues were interconnected—raised Soviet complaints early on. In late January 1969, the Soviet charge d'affaires in Washington, Yuri Chernyakov, warned Assistant Secretary of State Robert Ellsworth that "his government was highly sensitive to any suggestion that one subject matter was being used to blackmail the Soviet government on another subject."[5]

What was unique about the Dobrynin–Kissinger back channel, however, was not the strategic concept of linkage. After all, it would be foolish to assume that Soviet-American diplomacy had been neatly compartmentalized prior to Kissinger's tenure in office. Linkages had always existed. Carrots and sticks were the usual fare of almost any bilateral relationship. What distinguished the back channel was not the conceptual approach that either side took in terms of the great issues of the day, but the remarkable amount of latitude (and power) that Kissinger gained in the process of his meetings with the Soviet ambassador. The sheer existence of the channel built up the former Harvard professor's stature inside Washington and also within the Soviet leadership to an unprecedented (many would argue unnecessary) degree. Meanwhile the channel clearly minimized, almost to the point of being insulting, the significance of the State Department and the impact that the Congress could have on U.S.-Soviet relations. Eventually this "coup" would backfire, providing ammunition to Nixon and Kissinger's critics who would argue that the centralization of policy making sidelined the experts of the Foreign Service but was profoundly undemocratic.

In the early stages of Soviet-American détente, however, the creation of the back channel was as clear an indication to the Soviets as it was to those within the Nixon administration that there were, ultimately, only two men who had the power to shape policy. Others were and would remain outsiders. Clearly it was Nixon and Kissinger's foreign policy, not Secretary of State Rogers'. As time went by, Dobrynin and Kissinger ended up developing a relationship that was shielded from the general public and, unquestionably, yielded important results. But the main advantage (or disadvantage) was, in Dobrynin's words, that "the White House not only shaped American foreign policy, but also directly carried it out without the intrusion of Congress and the public, which were totally unaware of this secret channel of diplomacy."[6] Checks and balances were consciously limited.

Nixon's chief of staff, Bob Haldeman, who was given the unpleasant task of informing Secretary of State Rogers that he was to be excluded from the meetings that established the back channel, had a slightly more cynical attitude. "K[issinger] feels very important," Haldeman recorded in his diaries.[7]

In fact, Kissinger had been important prior to officially assuming his new post. He had begun preparing the ground for the launch of détente already during the transition period. As the NSC adviser-elect, Kissinger met with Boris Sedov, the Soviet embassy's highest-ranking KGB official, on several occasions in December

1968 and in January 1969. In these talks, Kissinger prepared the ground for the broad-based détente he would later practice. On December 18, 1968, for example, Kissinger emphasized to Sedov that Nixon meant business when he called for negotiations to replace confrontation. At the same time, he warned that any call for a summit before inauguration would be viewed as propaganda from the U.S. side and would make holding serious talks difficult. In early January 1969, he used another meeting to make essentially the same points.[8]

At the time, the Soviets were still debating how best to take advantage of the new American administration's apparent interest in détente during the first weeks after Nixon took office on January 20, 1969. Ambassador Dobrynin was in the Soviet Union in late January, ostensibly visiting a sanitarium near Moscow. The fact that Brezhnev, Kosygin, and Podgorny were staying in the same sanitarium, however, was convenient and hardly an accident: it undoubtedly allowed for some intense brainstorming and speculation about the future of Soviet-American relations under Richard Nixon's leadership. It is probably fair to assume that the Soviet leadership was uncertain about how exactly to conduct business with Nixon and his inner circle. But they were eager to give it a try.

This was clearly evident upon Dobrynin's return from Moscow. The Soviet ambassador did not immediately seek out Kissinger but Secretary of State Rogers. On February 13, the two met at the State Department. Dobrynin asked Rogers to arrange a meeting with Nixon as soon as possible. He had nothing urgent to relay, Dobrynin maintained, but had been asked to give Nixon the USSR's "current views on the most important international issues." Rogers used the opportunity to raise the issues of Vietnam and Berlin, emphasizing Washington's hope for a positive Soviet attitude on both. The Soviets were also ready to discuss the Middle East, either bilaterally or in a multilateral context. "Discussions," Dobrynin said, "could take place in New York, Moscow and Washington." Finally, just before departing, Dobrynin mentioned SALT. But he warned against linkage. "It would be unfortunate," Dobrynin stated, "if this matter were to be linked with progress on other issues."[9]

The following day Kissinger attended a reception at the Soviet embassy. Dobrynin, suffering from influenza, had his aide bring Kissinger to his apartment. According to Kissinger's memo of the meeting, Dobrynin said that he had a message from the Soviet leadership that he would like to relay to the president. Significantly, Kissinger wrote, Dobrynin "would prefer to deliver" this message to Nixon "without any diplomats present." In the future, Kissinger added, "Dobrynin would like to conduct his conversations in Washington with some person you designate who has your confidence, but who was not part of the diplomatic establishment." In addition, Dobrynin had indicated that "if we wanted simultaneous progress on several fronts at once, they were ready to proceed on the basis of equality." The Soviets were particularly interested in bilateral talks on the Middle East between an American diplomat in Moscow and a high-level official of the Soviet foreign

ministry. Kissinger recommended that Nixon meet with Dobrynin at the earliest
possible opportunity.[10]

A CHAT IN THE FISH ROOM

When Dobrynin arrived at the White House at 11:45 on Monday, February 17, Nixon
greeted him in the Fish Room, so named for its nautical theme, which had been
first established by FDR. They had a brief private chat. Nixon told Dobrynin of the
need for establishing the back channel. After a few minutes, Kissinger and Malcolm
Toon joined the meeting. With reference to Nixon's inaugural address, Dobrynin
then expressed the Soviet leadership's desire to launch an era "of negotiations." He
added that Moscow was curious about "what the President had in mind by negotiations—specifically what issues the President felt should be the subject of negotiations and when, where, and at what level these should take place." Confirming
what he had told Kissinger a few days earlier, Dobrynin assured Nixon that the
USSR was ready for simultaneous negotiations "on various subjects and at various
levels." Such negotiations could eventually lead to a summit meeting. He mentioned the Middle East and SALT as possible subjects for the talks.

Nixon expressed skepticism about the need for an early summit meeting (thus
echoing Dobrynin) and preference for discussions "at lower levels." He went on to
stress that the starting point for any talks was a candid recognition of the "basic differences between us." The task ahead, Nixon added, consisted of making sure that
such differences "do not result in a sharp confrontation." The president agreed that
"an exchange of views" on the Middle East was crucial, since "it would be the height
of folly to let the parties directly involved in the Middle East conflict bring about a
confrontation between Moscow and Washington."

In a roundabout way Nixon went on to stress the need for linkage. "It was not
his view that the initiation of [SALT] talks must be conditioned on the settlement
of larger political issues." But, to confuse the point, Nixon added that he wanted
"parallel" talks on SALT and "critical political situations such as the Middle East
and Vietnam." Dobrynin pressed for further information on "the linkage between
arms talks and negotiations on political issues" and asked for any views on a possible timetable for SALT. Nixon explained that the new director of the Arms Control and Disarmament Agency (ACDA), Gerard Smith, was currently reviewing
"our entire position on arms control issues" and promised to initiate action on the
Middle East front. But, while he refrained from the use of the term *linkage,* Nixon
also stressed "that progress in one area is bound to have an influence on progress
in all other areas."

As expected, Nixon moved on to Vietnam. After outlining his disappointment
over the slow pace of the Paris peace negotiations, Nixon stressed that the United
States was ready "to go 'the extra mile' in Paris." He stressed the administration's

"determination to bring the conflict to an end, one way or another," and his "hope that the Soviets will do what they can to get the Paris talks off dead-center." Dobrynin, fully aware of his government's inability to give outright orders to the North Vietnamese and Hanoi's stubborn refusal to recognize the legitimacy of the South Vietnamese government, was evasive. "If all participants in the Paris talks would face realities and treat each other on an equal basis, then the Soviets might be in a position to play a constructive role." Still, Dobrynin maintained, "it would be wise not to begin with the most difficult issues."[11] Dobrynin made clear, as Toon put it in his account of the meeting, "that we [the United States] must deal with the National Liberation Front (NLF) if there is to be any progress at Paris."[12]

Clearly, linkage was part of the game plan for both sides. While rejecting explicit linkage (i.e., clear cut trade-offs between, say, Berlin and Vietnam), Nixon and Dobrynin acknowledged that issues were interrelated. This, in turn, meant that the impact of positive and negative developments tended to become magnified and have an impact on the overall relationship. This lack of compartmentalization prevented rapid progress. In the spring of 1969, Kissinger and Nixon were not in a strong position. Kissinger (much like Nixon) was convinced that the United States could only achieve its goals vis-à-vis the USSR if it acted—or gave the impression that it was acting—from a position of strength. Kissinger thus advised "continued firmness" on such issues as Vietnam, the Middle East, and nuclear weapons, suggesting that the Soviets were unsure about the general direction of U.S. policy. They worried, for example, about the possibility that the Nixon administration might undertake new nuclear weapons programs. Soviet anxiety, Kissinger thought, was the best asset for the Americans. Keep them guessing. As long as the Soviets remained anxious they would be more likely to make concessions. In Kissinger's own words: "we should seek to utilize this Soviet interest to induce them to come to grips with the real sources of tension, notably in the Middle East, but also in Vietnam."[13]

A week later, before he departed with Nixon for a tour of Europe, Kissinger called Dobrynin to emphasize the issue that would dominate the back-channel discussions for the next few years. Kissinger stressed that Nixon "wanted it to be known in Moscow that if the situation in Vietnam should turn into a general offensive or attack on major population centers, we would have to respond strongly. We would consider it very unfortunate. We would try not to have to take this step, but we would have no choice if it turns into that."

In short, the United States would not allow South Vietnam to be overrun by a northern offensive and, Kissinger implied, the USSR should do what it could to restrain Hanoi. He thus, for the first time, explicitly tied together the emergence of détente with the intricacies of a specific regional crisis. The two then agreed to meet for lunch on March 3, the day after the presidential party would return from Europe. The back channel and the principle of linkage had been established.[14]

Notably absent from these communications in February 1969 was any direct mention of the role that China might play in the future relations between the

United States and the Soviet Union. When Nixon's entourage landed at Andrews Air Force Base on the afternoon of March 2, 1969, events in northeast Asia were about to change that.

USSURI RIVER

On March 2 and 15, 1969, respectively, Zhenbao Island (Damansky Island in Russian) on the Ussuri River, the site of a highly contested border between the USSR and China, became the scene of two military clashes between Chinese and Soviet troops. On both occasions the Chinese, despite inferior weaponry, inflicted significant casualties (up to fifty on March 2 and sixty on the 15th) on the Soviets. Both sides, naturally, blamed each other for what were, to date, the most serious clashes on the highly contested frontier.

They were not the first such incidents to occur between Chinese and Soviet border patrols. The Sino-Soviet alliance had deteriorated severely since its heyday in the early 1950s. In the early 1960s confrontation caused by ideological clashes, personality differences (especially between Khrushchev and Mao), military competition, domestic pressures, and numerous other factors had become the norm. On the Sino-Soviet frontier the tension played itself out in countless minor border incidents. In May 1969, the PRC's official statement claimed the exact number of clashes had been as high as 4,189 between October 1964 and March 1969. While that figure may be inflated, there was no question that the Zhenbao/Damansky Island incidents of March 1969 were part of a pattern that had emerged as the Sino-Soviet conflict escalated in the second half of the 1960s. It was not that a clash in itself was unexpected in March 1969; what surprised and worried outside observers was the sudden escalation in the level of violence. After all, should the Sino-Soviet conflict lead to an open war between the USSR and the PRC, few countries, least of all the United States, could remain untouched or uninterested.[15]

In 1969, though, it was Moscow's reaction that truly mattered. Following the first clash on March 2 and a heated Soviet Politburo debate in which the defense minister, Andrei Grechko, even called for nuclear strikes against China, Brezhnev pressed through a more measured response. The Soviets began to build up their conventional forces on the Chinese border and launched an attack on March 15. After this incident, the Soviets began to search for a diplomatic solution in earnest. On March 21, Kosygin even tried to resume negotiations by telephone. When he rang up Beijing and asked to speak to Chairman Mao or Premier Zhou Enlai, however, the Chinese telephone operator, refused to put through a call from such a renowned revisionist as the Soviet premier. A week later, the frustrated Soviets issued an official statement, warning the Chinese of the possibility of a severe military strike.[16]

Subsequent Soviet activity revealed how deep the anxiety about China was in Moscow. In a report to the East German leadership about the first border clash, for example, the Soviets indicated their heightened concern over "the crime by the Mao Zedong group," and talked about how the Chinese were apparently planning to use the occasion "to establish Mao Zedong's anti-Soviet and chauvinist great power course as the general line of Chinese policy." The Soviet leadership also warned the East Germans about "Beijing's intention to activate the opportunistic political flirtation with the imperialist countries—above all with the United States and West Germany."[17]

* * *

As coercive diplomacy produced limited results, tensions between Beijing and Moscow escalated. On the Chinese side, the government launched a vigorous propaganda campaign calling for intensive preparations for a war with the Soviets; *Red Star*, a journal that published the Soviet military's hardline views, retaliated by threatening the Chinese with a nuclear strike. The Soviets, meanwhile, began to amass additional troops on the Sino-Soviet border. When the Chinese eventually seemed to give in to the relentless Soviet pressure by proposing a resumption of border talks in late May 1969, the Chinese counterbalanced this olive branch with intense criticism of the Soviet Union. Indeed, according to the official Chinese ideological perspective, the USSR had betrayed true Marxist revolutionary principles and acted like a capitalist imperialist power in Eastern Europe. It was China, not the Soviet Union, that represented the anticapitalist forces of the world. In an interesting reversal of the Soviet report to the East Germans a few months earlier, the Chinese thus charged the Soviets with "currying favor with the U.S. imperialists." Such a mixed message only managed to sharpen the division within the Soviet Politburo between hardliners like Grechko (who favored a strong military strike against China) and more dovish leaders like Foreign Minister Andrei Gromyko (who advocated using diplomacy to dissolve the crisis).[18]

While the Zhenbao Island incidents did not suddenly propel China into a major issue on Kissinger's agenda, the continued escalation of tensions between Moscow and Beijing did not go unnoticed. On March 10, Kissinger flew down from Washington to meet Nixon in Key Biscayne, Florida, where the president had established his "Southern White House" as an escape from the pressures of Washington. Prior to seeing Nixon, Kissinger had a chat with White House Chief of Staff Bob Haldeman. Kissinger, always prone to pessimism, was concerned that the Sino-Soviet clashes would make the Soviets act more belligerently in Vietnam in order to upstage Beijing in their competition over influence in Hanoi. Haldeman did not deny the possibility, but also suggested that the border clashes offered Kissinger an opportunity to play upon Soviet anxieties. The chief of staff suggested that Kissinger "turn this to [our] advantage by a maneuver designed [to] totally confuse the Soviets."[19] Haldeman did not elaborate on the type of maneuver he had in mind, yet he was obviously suggesting that Kissinger should begin the triangular game. Notwithstanding the impact that the Ussuri River clashes might have on Soviet policy in Vietnam, a potential rapprochement with China would clearly offer a means of pressuring Moscow.

Musing about the possibilities opening up for complex diplomatic maneuvering, Kissinger returned to Washington. The next evening at 9:00 P.M. he met with Dobrynin at the Soviet embassy. Feeding Kissinger's curiosity, Dobrynin gave a "gory account of Chinese atrocities," adding that "China was everybody's problem." Dobrynin even asked whether the Nixon administration was "going to take advantage of the Soviet Union's difficulties."

Assuring Dobrynin that the United States considered the entire affair a bilateral Sino-Soviet matter, Kissinger rushed back to the White House and called Nixon. "Obviously, this is much on their minds," Kissinger said. The president liked what he heard. "Sometimes events which we could not have foreseen may have some helpful effect," he responded. "Who knows."[20]

It would take time before the "China card" could become an effective tool of Kissinger's diplomacy. Yet, even before the second series of Sino-Soviet clashes on March 15, the potential opportunities such a conflict presented for the United States were all too obvious to be missed. In particular, the Ussuri River clashes provided an entirely new context for dealing with the biggest headache the Nixon administration had inherited: the Vietnam War.

RIDDLE OF VIETNAM

In 1969, the Vietnam War was a central issue to those working closest to Richard Nixon, no one more so than Kissinger. But Vietnam was also an issue on which the two men did not always see eye to eye. When it came to Vietnam, Nixon showed little of the foreign policy talent he may have exhibited elsewhere; for him the war remained primarily an issue of perceptions and image. The consummate politician was, in fact, caught between two opposite pressures. On the one hand, he could not be seen as a loser. He could not be the first president to lose a war. On the other hand, Nixon needed to convince the American public that he was serious about getting out of Vietnam. He had promised as much during the 1968 campaign. Nixon had to show that he really did have a secret plan to end the war. In contrast, Kissinger was more interested in the geopolitical ramifications of Vietnam and the potential impact that any decisions and developments in Indochina had on American credibility (or at least on his perception of how others viewed and measured American credibility). Reaching a peace settlement in Vietnam was important for Kissinger's reputation and, by 1971–72, to Kissinger's own job prospects. But the need to monitor and accommodate public opinion was rarely, as in Nixon's case, a key consideration for Kissinger's Vietnam policy.[21]

In large part because of Nixon's sensitivity to public pressure, Kissinger lost one strategic battle over Vietnam policy early on in the Nixon administration. Although implemented only later in the year, Nixon decided in principle on March 15 to pursue Vietnamization.

Vietnamization was Defense Secretary Mel Laird's pet project. In early March 1969, the former Republican congressman from Wisconsin made an extensive visit to South Vietnam. Laird returned to Washington with a fairly optimistic picture about the situation: it was time to press ahead with increasing the flow of supplies to the ARVN while reducing the combat role of American troops and commencing a gradual American troop withdrawal. The war, and the responsibility for the future of South Vietnam, should be transferred to the Vietnamese.[22]

Laird's plan appealed to Nixon. In particular, Vietnamization would be enormously useful at home in the United States. While the antiwar critics could not charge that Nixon was simply continuing the war effort as before, the fact that the withdrawals were coupled with increased U.S. aid meant that nobody could argue that Nixon was abandoning an ally. After all, was it not only logical to let the Vietnamese themselves to do the fighting? In other words, while fewer body bags were likely to mean fewer moratoriums, more material aid should satisfy the concerns of those who could not stomach the reality that the United States was being gradually smoked out of Vietnam.[23]

While Vietnamization may have made sense to Laird and Nixon, it was a disaster from Kissinger's point of view. It would inevitably weaken the U.S. bargaining position in negotiations with the North Vietnamese, he argued. How could one achieve an honorable peace in a situation where the most important part of U.S. leverage in negotiations—the presence of a large number of American troops—was being removed?[24] As Kissinger put it in his memoirs, he had "great hope for negotiations" but that with Vietnamization—and the slight reduction in the bombing of North Vietnam that preceded it in 1969—U.S. policy

> ran the risk of falling between two stools. With Hanoi we risked throwing away our position in a series of unreciprocated concessions. At home, the more we sought to placate the critics, the more we discouraged those who were willing to support a strategy for victory but who could not understand continued sacrifice for something so elusive as honorable withdrawal.[25]

Kissinger did not explain what "honorable withdrawal" meant. One should note, however, that his public views were not dramatically different from those of Laird. In a book published in 1969, Kissinger maintained that "American objectives should be to (a) bring about a staged withdrawal of external forces, North Vietnamese and American, (b) thereby to create a maximum incentive for the contending forces in South Vietnam to work out a political agreement."[26] The major difference was that Laird's Vietnamization strategy gave no guarantees for simultaneous North Vietnamese and American withdrawals. It could easily mean a simple transfer of the burden of war to the South Vietnamese without any progress toward a military or a political settlement.

One answer to the complexity of Vietnam was the gradual escalation of the war into Cambodia through a series of secret bombings that commenced in mid-March 1969.

Codenamed MENU, the barrage of raids had both a military and a political-diplomatic objective. Militarily, the aim of MENU (which was divided into a series of operations, respectively codenamed BREAKFAST, LUNCH, SNACK, DINNER, DESSERT) was to cause severe damage to the Ho Chi Minh Trail, the enemy's main infiltration route that ran south from North Vietnam through Laos and Cambodia to South Vietnam. In the fourteen months following the commencement of the bombings in March 1969, the United States conducted 3,630 B-52 bombing raids in Cambodian territory. From a pure military perspective, disrupting the route surely improved the prospects of the ARVN and American troops in South Vietnam, and would make it increasingly difficult for Hanoi to build up enough strength in the South to launch yet another Tet Offensive. MENU was also undertaken to destroy the Central Office for South Vietnam (COSVN), the headquarters of the Communists' operation in the South that were, according to U.S. intelligence sources, based in Cambodia.[27] Hanoi's weakness, even if only temporary, would also buy valuable time for Vietnamization: if the enemy were unable to launch major attacks, Americans would be freer to train and then transfer the burden of war to the ARVN.

Politically MENU was aimed at impressing both Vietnamese sides. On the one hand, it was to convince the Saigon government that the Nixon administration was not going soft on the enemy and was even willing to escalate the war if necessary. On the other hand, MENU was designed to impress on the North Vietnamese America's staying power and willingness to escalate. Nixon, for one, liked the idea of cultivating himself as a "madman," ready to launch even nuclear war if necessary. Hence, Kissinger would not be completely robbed from his negotiating cards as the United States was conducting the war with renewed vigor during the Nixon administration. In short, the idea was that MENU would tilt the existing military stalemate against North Vietnam and ensure Hanoi's more forthcoming attitude in the negotiations.[28]

*   *   *

This was what Kissinger and Nixon appear to have agreed upon. It was also clear, however, that any new air strikes needed to be executed in secrecy. This was important for two reasons. First, the domestic body politic was likely to have no appetite for MENU. Most Americans would be outraged if Nixon's secret plan to end the war turned out to be a euphemism for expanding it. Second, the operational effectiveness of the bombing would be reduced with advance notice (and possible leaks to the press). In addition, there was, of course, the love of secrecy that Nixon and Kissinger shared and which created that curious bond between this odd couple of American foreign policy.

The MENU operation's details were originally conceived during a meeting at the Brussels airport aboard Air Force One on February 24, 1969, between Kissinger, Haldeman, and Haig following Nixon's decision during the previous day's transatlantic flight to attack North Vietnamese sanctuaries in Cambodia. Illuminating of the perceived need to keep MENU secret was the fact that Nixon himself did not attend this particular planning group meeting, because "it was felt he could not attend himself without attracting attention." Nixon also continued to waver. As the State Department refused to accept responsibility for the program and Charles de Gaulle urged Nixon to get out of Vietnam, the president seemed to have had second thoughts. To Kissinger's disappointment, on March 1, 1969, Nixon called off MENU while the presidential tour was in Paris.[29]

Nixon was clearly torn and only gave his final approval for the campaign two weeks later. Part of the reason for the delay may be that he received conflicting advice. Mel Laird, for example, was supportive of the bombings but doubtful about the possibility of keeping them secret. Secretary of State Rogers, who was consulted, argued against the raids because he thought they would prevent any possibility for a negotiated settlement. Most important, however, Nixon worried about the public's reaction should something leak to the press.

Nixon's final decision to go ahead represented therefore not only a fateful move regarding the Vietnam War, but also a significant early victory for Kissinger in his campaign to outmaneuver Secretary of State Rogers. But it came at some cost to his mental stability. In fact, the postponement of MENU and Rogers' meeting with Dobrynin on March 8—during which Rogers apparently suggested that the United States was not as committed to South Vietnam as previously—prompted the first of Kissinger's numerous resignation threats. Rogers "can't adequately serve the P[resident] and should have been made Chief Justice," Kissinger fumed at the time to Haldeman. Haldeman, who thought that Kissinger was "basically right," managed to talk Kissinger out of even mentioning his own resignation to Nixon at the time. Eventually, though, Kissinger's relentless pressure—he flew down to Key Biscane (where the president had escaped after returning from Europe) to pledge his case and bombarded Nixon with memos and pressed the matter during lengthy private meetings with the president—and Nixon's own inclination to appear "tough" carried the day.

Yet, even in the days leading to the final decision on March 15, Nixon did not feel entirely comfortable about how to handle his old friend Bill Rogers. Thus, he told Kissinger over the phone that "State is to be notified only after the point of no return ... The order is not appealable." Kissinger, although satisfied with the decision, recommended that Nixon meet with Rogers and Laird on the following day. It happened to be Sunday and the meeting took place soon after church services. Rogers was the only one who argued against the decision. It did no good. "Operation Breakfast" commenced on March 18. The following day Kissinger was, according to Haldeman, "beaming" as early reports showed that the campaign was a success.[30]

Such delight on Kissinger's part would later turn to frustration as the bombing campaigns had seemingly little impact on Hanoi's position. In this sense, the jealously guarded secrecy of the bombings—made possible through an elaborate double bookkeeping system—did not advance the prospects of ending the war.

Instead, the Cambodian bombing campaign caused the first series of wiretappings in the already secretive Nixon White House.

On May 9, 1969, a *New York Times* article reported that American B-52s had been conducting raids in Cambodia. Nixon and Kissinger ordered the FBI to wiretap Kissinger's NSC staffers Morton Halperin, Helmut Sonnenfeldt, and Daniel Davidson to see whether one of them had leaked the story. Kissinger's deputy, Alexander Haig, whose job it was to read all FBI transcripts, later argued that these and other similar wiretaps were authorized to solve "a matter of most grave and serious consequence to national security." Perhaps. The transcripts revealed no leaks. Instead, as the practice later became common knowledge, Kissinger lost some of his brightest aides, including Halperin (who later successfully sued Kissinger). The wiretapping of a group of men so close to the national security adviser and the president had, as historian Christopher Andrew put it, seriously "corrosive effects on the morale and confidence of White House staff."[31]

BEIJING—HANOI—MOSCOW

The deterioration of Sino-Soviet relations and the American MENU bombing campaign had an impact on the relationships of Hanoi with its two major external supporters. On April 20–21, 1969, a COSVN delegation visited Beijing to discuss the new situation. The Chinese premier Zhou Enlai had mixed feelings. On the one hand, Zhou told the visitors that he was "not as optimistic as [the COSVN delegation] about the situation in Cambodia." On the other hand, Zhou was determined to prevent a North Vietnamese tilt toward the Soviet Union. Throughout the spring of 1969 Zhou Enlai constantly warned the North Vietnamese of the "revisionist Soviets." The leaders of the Kremlin were, much like Nixon, "imperialist chieftains." Such language clearly reflected the Chinese concern over the impact that the Ussuri River border clashes could have on the Sino-Vietnamese alliance. Zhou repeatedly warned the Vietnamese not to listen to Soviet advice about negotiating a compromise solution with the United States. This, Zhou stressed, might be in the Soviet Union's interest but would create grave difficulties for the North Vietnamese.[32] A week later, Li Xiannian, a member of the Chinese Communist Party's Politburo, put the point to Kissinger's future negotiating partner, Le Duc Tho, more bluntly:

> The final victory [in Vietnam] depends on fighting. According to our experience, the victory cannot be gained at the negotiating table. We have to be determined to fight the enemy until he has nothing else to resort to. In all, negotiation is of secondary importance with a view to exposing the enemy's schemes and we have to rely on fighting with a view to annihilating the enemy.[33]

The Soviets acted in much the same manner as the Chinese. Starting in February 1969, Nixon and Kissinger had tried to persuade the Soviets that any improvement in Soviet-American relations depended on Moscow's help in bringing about peace to Southeast Asia. After MENU commenced, Kissinger intensified his efforts on the back channel. His threats were often blunt. On April 3, for example, he warned Dobrynin that Nixon "was determined to end the war one way or another." On April 14, Kissinger said that the president had decided to make "one more" peace offer to North Vietnam. If that produced no result, Nixon would "draw the conclusion that the war could only be ended by unilateral means." Dobrynin protested. Moscow had minimal influence in Hanoi, he professed. The whole affair seemed to be a Chinese plot "to produce a clash between the Soviet Union and the United States." Because the PRC was close to North Vietnam, Dobrynin argued, the Soviet Union was in a bind. It was not Vietnam that mattered but the USSR's position as the leader of the socialist camp. "While the Soviet Union might recommend certain steps," he added, "it would never cut off supplies [because] the Soviet Union could not afford to appear at a Communist meeting and find itself accused of having undermined a fellow Socialist country."[34]

With the MENU bombings producing few tangible results, and the attempt to enroll the Soviets in the peace program deadlocked, Nixon and Kissinger made their next move. On May 14, the president gave a nationally televised address, unveiling an eight-point peace initiative that Kissinger's staff had put together. The most significant new offer was the mutual and *simultaneous* withdrawal of North Vietnamese and American troops (since 1966 Americans had offered to withdraw their troops six months *after* Hanoi withdrew its forces). Three weeks later, after meeting with the South Vietnamese president Nguyen Thieu on the Pacific Midway Island, Nixon, while stressing the American commitment to the survival of an independent South Vietnam, announced the first set of U.S. troop withdrawals, hence officially commencing the policy of Vietnamization. The reluctant Thieu also agreed to another proposal: the United States could commence secret peace talks with the North Vietnamese, provided the Americans kept Saigon fully informed.[35]

By June 1969, the key elements of the Nixon administration's Vietnam policy were all present. First, there was the coercive element in the form of the secret bombing campaign of Cambodia. Second, there were the U.S. withdrawals, aimed primarily at pacifying the antiwar movement (and other critics) at home. Third, Nixon and Kissinger had decided to initiate secret peace talks with Hanoi (which would commence in Paris in early August). Fourth, there was the effort to pressure the Soviets into playing a role as Washington's peace advocate with Hanoi. Throughout the remainder of Nixon's first term, these strategies would dominate the quest for the elusive peace with honor Nixon had promised to the American public.

Kissinger agreed with most of the elements of this complex strategy. He had been a key advocate of the bombing campaign in Cambodia and would control the

Paris negotiations. His influence had clearly surged in the first half of 1969. Yet, as the decision to go ahead with Vietnamization indicated, when domestic pressure so demanded, Nixon would not hesitate to go against the advice of his NSC adviser. Kissinger was clearly influential. But in the summer of 1969 he had yet to prove his worth to Nixon.

LINKAGE AND LEVERAGE

Important though Vietnam was, the circumstances of 1969 had also created a favorable context for a more fundamental shift in American foreign policy. Kissinger's back-channel meetings with Dobrynin had clearly indicated that the Soviets were anxious about the future direction of Chinese policy. This fact, if utilized properly, offered opportunities for creative diplomacy. The question was how to make the most of it.

Part of the answer was to drop delicate hints to the Soviets about a possible Sino-American rapprochement in order to throw the Soviets off balance. Accordingly, Nixon, at Kissinger's behest, gave the new U.S. ambassador to Moscow, Jacob Beam, a carefully worded letter to the Soviet premier Alexei Kosygin. The United States had no interest in seeing USSR and PRC in conflict, Nixon assured, "and certainly no intention to exploit their present difficulties." But Beam, under instructions, added a significant caveat. "We do hope over the long run to achieve some normalization in our relations with China." Nixon, via Beam, also pledged that "if contacts eventuate with the Chinese, we will continue, as did the previous administration, to keep the Soviets informed." It was a pledge the Nixon administration would abandon once contacts with the Chinese did eventuate in late 1969.[36]

Still, in the late spring and summer of 1969, the China card was hardly more than a potential tool in Kissinger and Nixon's quest to increase America's leverage with Moscow. There was nothing concrete to indicate that progress would follow. After all, the Chinese had been drifting away from the USSR for a decade (if not more), but they had not come any closer to Washington. If anything, the Chinese had taken an even more antagonistic line toward the United States after launching the Cultural Revolution in 1966. Supporting wars of national liberation remained central to the PRC's foreign policy dogma.[37] Even in the context of the Sino-Soviet border clashes it was hard to conceive how Kissinger could use China, even vicariously, as leverage in Soviet-American relations.

What made it all the more frustrating was the minimal progress that the Kissinger–Dobrynin back channel made in solving the many problems plaguing American-Soviet relations in the late 1960s. The Vietnam War, the continued arming of the adversaries in the Middle East, the issue of Berlin and a possible European security treaty, the nuclear stalemate—all these concerns were continually raised in the Kissinger–Dobrynin back-channel meetings. At the rhetorical level both sides seemed keen on moving ahead with détente. But real progress was slow.

Part of the explanation for the deadlock is simple: the Soviets and the Americans had very different priorities. In general, Kissinger, putting into practice the principles of linkage, wanted to press a broad agenda, while Dobrynin wanted to separate issues and make incremental progress. Nixon was particularly anxious for Soviet help in reaching a settlement in Vietnam. Had there been such assistance on Vietnam, Nixon would likely have been hard pushed—given Vietnam's significance not only for America's external relations but for the domestic fortunes of the new president—*not* to make concessions to the Soviets on other issues.[38]

One problem with the regional issues, as was amply proved in Vietnam and the Middle East, was that they could not, ultimately, be solved merely through bilateral Soviet-American negotiations. Regional players—whether in Indochina, the Middle East, or Europe—had their own interests and carried their own leverage. The need to avoid even an appearance of a Soviet-American condominium, for example, was a central message of the European leaders during Nixon's first trip abroad as president in late February and early March. The Soviets could not, even if they had wished to do so, bully the North Vietnamese into accepting a compromise solution in Indochina. What it all boiled down to was that the relative collapse of the bipolar system—evidenced in part by the Sino-Soviet conflict but also by the rise of the third world and the increasingly competitive nature of U.S. relations with its European and Japanese allies—meant that the back channel was ultimately no place to settle regional conflicts. The major flaw in Kissinger's foreign policy architecture—the relative lack of interest in the intricacies of the local causes of the conflicts and the emphasis he put on the role of Soviet-American relations as a way of finding solutions to such conflicts—would become increasingly clear as the Vietnam War dragged on and Kissinger got more deeply involved in the making of U.S. policy in the Middle East, South Asia, and, eventually, Africa.

* * *

Bilateral issues were another matter. Dobrynin and Kissinger could reasonably be expected to have made quick progress on, say, the SALT negotiations. As the Soviet ambassador later wrote, however, the first back-channel meetings stood out in his mind because "Kissinger ignored our proposal to resume our exchange on limiting strategic arms, which had been suspended for months since the invasion of Czechoslovakia [in August 1968]." Kissinger explains such foot-dragging in large part as a result of bureaucratic divisions and Nixon's lack of interest in the specific details, although not in the broad outlines, of the SALT talks. Hence, Kissinger was left effectively in charge of planning America's SALT strategy in the spring of 1969, a task he embarked upon through a series of studies and position papers from various departments (including State, Defense, and the CIA). The end result was no less than seven packages detailing possible responses to Soviet proposals on various weapons systems and a series of delays. Only in November 1969 did the SALT talks commence in Helsinki, Finland. The first meaningful breakthrough, however, would have to wait until May 1971.[39] The reason for the slow pace of the SALT negotiations lay in large part in the U.S. insistence on pursuing linkage.

By definition, linkage was not supposed to allow the isolation of individual issues or the reaching of limited progress. It held that one should not explore strategic arms separately from, say, the Vietnam War and the Middle East. Nixon had made a special point about the SALT talks already in his February 4 letter to Rogers, Laird, and Helms that established linkage as an official policy. In the message that had been drafted by Kissinger's staff, the new president had stressed that "I believe our decision on when and how to proceed does not depend on our review of the purely military and technical issues. This decision should also be taken in light of the prevailing political context and, in particular, in light of progress toward stabilizing the explosive Middle East situation, and in light of the Paris talks [on Vietnam]." SALT talks, in other words, were not to be treated as their own separate category but were intertwined with regional issues.[40]

Such thinking affected Nixon's decisions on nuclear arms development at the start of his presidency. Importantly, Kissinger and Nixon agreed—despite strong opposition from within and without the administration—to go ahead with the development and deployment of the new systems.

The first issue was the question of antiballistic missiles (ABMs). The ABMs, as the name suggests, were defensive guided missiles to be used in the event of an attack to shoot down incoming missiles before they reached the United States. Developing such systems would make the United States invulnerable to a missile strike. In 1967 Secretary of Defense Robert McNamara had, somewhat reluctantly and under public and congressional pressure, unveiled the American Sentinel ABM program as a counterweight to a Soviet defensive missile system program begun three years earlier. Ironically, by the time Nixon entered the White House, there were increasing calls to discontinue ABM development. In the March 1969 Senate hearings, Democratic politicians such as Ted Kennedy and Hubert Humphrey, as well as a number of distinguished scientists, argued that in practical terms, ABMs would be prohibitively expensive, technologically complicated, likely to speed up the arms race, and, at least as it appeared in 1969, easily defeated by Soviet countermeasures. In short, the ABM program appeared to be a waste of resources and a potential death knell to any hope of serious nuclear arms control negotiations with the Soviets.[41]

Kissinger disagreed, and pressed Nixon to go ahead with ABM development, arguing that it was important for "both military and diplomatic" reasons. Yet, as Kissinger's memoirs indicate, the diplomatic reasons mattered most to him; he needed a full load of trump cards in the forthcoming SALT negotiations. By approving the so-called Safeguard system on March 14, 1969, Nixon thus handed Kissinger and the other future U.S. SALT negotiators a useful, if potentially expensive, bargaining tool.[42]

The second, and in the long run more significant, issue was the future of multiple independently-targetable reentry vehicles (MIRVs). MIRVs were a new technology that allowed for a nuclear delivery vehicle to be loaded with several nuclear warheads, each directed at a different target (i.e., one missile would split into several nuclear warheads, and they would in turn hit their separate targets more or less at the same time). The United States had begun to test MIRVs in 1968 for a simple reason: they were a cost-effective way of increasing American firepower, of providing infinitely "more bang for the buck." Without building new rockets or launchers the United States could, once the technology was perfected, double or triple the number of warheads placed on the existing missile sites. Among other things, the United States could, in this way, flood any Soviet ABMs by firing more missiles than any defensive system could cope with. The downside was that as the Soviets began to develop their own MIRV capability—the first tests of the SS-9 triple warhead missile were conducted in 1969—the arms race was moving to a new level.

Much as in the case of the ABMs, the opposition to MIRVs became a cause célèbre for many American politicians. In the spring of 1969, forty senators and the House Foreign Affairs Committee supported a freeze on MIRV development. Kissinger's academic peers tried to persuade him to oppose an MIRV program during a series of arms control meetings in Washington. They were joined by the members of the President's General Advisory Committee on Arms Control, a group established by President Kennedy in 1961 and headed by such elder statesmen as John J. McCloy (who Kissinger frequently consulted) and former Secretary of State Dean Rusk. Within the administration the most significant anti-MIRV advocate was the new director of the ACDA and the future head of the U.S. SALT negotiation team, Gerard Smith.[43]

Such opposition was all in vain. In May 1969, Nixon decided to go ahead with the MIRV program, siding with Kissinger, Laird, and the Joint Chiefs of Staff. Without a clear commitment, or even a hazy roadmap, toward a SALT agreement, Nixon was easily convinced that he should not freeze any nuclear arms development project, let alone such a promising prospect as the MIRVs. Kissinger's argument, that "unilateral restraint [on the U.S. part] would be an incentive for the Soviets not to settle but to procrastinate, to tilt the balance as much in their favor as possible," surely made sense to the president. Yet, Kissinger proved overly optimistic about the impact that U.S. decisions on ABMs and MIRVs would have on Soviet willingness to negotiate. There would be plenty of Soviet procrastination and the arms race, even when the SALT I agreements were finally signed in 1972, would show little sign of slowing down.[44]

Kissinger and Nixon also hoped to use trade as a major tool for extracting concessions from the Soviets. To be able to do this more effectively, Nixon decided to take firm control over the practical application of the Export Administration Act (EAA) that in December 1969 replaced the twenty-year-old Export Control Act (ECA). On the one hand, the 1969 EAA was a clear victory for the advocates of the relaxation of trade restrictions to the Soviet bloc. On the other hand, the EAA reflected the negative trend in the U.S. balance of payments in the late 1960s.

The arguments that the proponents of the EAA used were primarily economic: by practicing stringent export control policy toward the Soviet bloc, the United States was in danger of losing out to its Western European and Japanese competitors. By 1969 the ECA—adopted at the height of the Cold War (1949) in order to weaken the Soviet bloc's war-making capabilities—had become an anachronism. Most American allies had significantly relaxed their controls by the 1960s, putting the United States at a disadvantage in nonmilitary trade with Eastern Europe. During the intense congressional hearings of April–July 1969, the main issue was not whether but to what extent and on what basis the export controls should be eased.[45]

During the hearings a number of Democratic senators called for a significant liberalization of East-West trade. They argued that the only country suffering from such restrictions was the United States. Their rationale reflected a classical liberal viewpoint: increased trade would not only profit U.S. exporters but would help to change internal political dynamics in the country purchasing American goods. Kissinger disagreed. To him trade was an integral ingredient of linkage. But, he did not share the belief that increased trade with the Soviet bloc would bring these countries closer to the American way of thinking. "Expanding trade without a political quid pro quo was a gift," Kissinger wrote in his memoirs. He added: "it did not seem unreasonable to require Soviet restraint in such trouble spots as the Middle East, Berlin, and Southeast Asia in return" for trade liberalization. Ultimately, Kissinger did not see any point in objecting to the new EAA. Because the EAA gave the executive discretionary authority to liberalize (or not) trade with a given country, its passage was a blessing in disguise: it enhanced the White House's control over policy implementation, in effect giving Nixon the power to use trade more effectively as a tool of linkage. Hence, Kissinger recommended to Nixon that the president approve the relaxation of export controls to bring the United States in line with the western Coordinating Committee (COCOM) list (but hold firm on such items as computers on which the United States effectively had a monopoly).[46]

Once the Congress eventually passed the EAA in December 1969, Nixon, like Kissinger, was not displeased: the new act did declare that the United States favored trade liberalization, but it also left the implementation of such liberalization to the White House. Effectively, this gave Kissinger, whose desk in 1969 was already full of various requests to grant export licenses for items previously banned for export to the Eastern bloc, an added means of control over U.S. policy toward the Soviet Union. As the political scientist Michael Mastanduno puts it, in 1969 "the transition from economic warfare was to trade in the service of politics, that is, tactical linkage."[47]

The moves on trade did not, infuriatingly to Nixon and Kissinger, make the Soviets more inclined to help on Vietnam. If anything, the Sino-Soviet confrontation made supporting the North Vietnamese even more important for the Soviet Union's international prestige. As Soviet aid to North Vietnam increased, moreover, the PRC, concerned over the loss of Vietnam, would move to enhance its aid efforts in 1970.[48]

In the first half of 1969 nothing seemed to suggest that linkage, whether in terms of bilateral Soviet-American détente or the Vietnam War, would work. The result was a deadlock in Soviet-American relations. To break it, something dramatic and substantial was needed. It was with this in mind that Nixon, in mid-June 1969, repeatedly told Kissinger that he needed to "find a way" to increase Soviet anxiety about possible Sino-American collusion.[49]

Kissinger followed the president's advice. After weeks of continued back-and-forth within his staff, Kissinger ordered, on July 3, 1969, an NSSM on Sino-Soviet differences. He asked for, in particular, an analysis of the "choices confronting the United States as a result of the intensifying Sino-Soviet rivalry" and "the broad implications of the Sino-Soviet rivalry on the U.S., Soviet, Communist Chinese triangle." In the same month, as a practical indication of its attempt to take advantage of the situation in Sino-Soviet relations, the United States eased travel restrictions to the PRC.[50]

The germ of triangular diplomacy had been set in motion. Soon thereafter, Nixon announced another foreign policy initiative that would carry his name.

THE NIXON DOCTRINE

On July 23, 1969, Kissinger joined Nixon and the rest of the president's entourage for a trip that took them through a number of Asian countries (including the Philippines, South Vietnam, and Thailand) as well as Romania. They also stopped in London before returning to the United States on August 3.

Aside from the visit to Romania that was calculated to unnerve the Soviets (Romanian leader Nicolae Ceausescu had distanced himself from the USSR), the trip's major highlight was an unexpected one. In an informal press conference in Guam on the evening of July 25, 1969, Nixon articulated what would soon be dubbed the Nixon (sometimes Guam) Doctrine. In essence, he affirmed three points. First, the United States would keep its treaty commitments to allied nations in the Far East (e.g., to those countries that belonged to the Southeast Treaty Organization [SEATO]). Second, the president reaffirmed that the United States would continue to provide a nuclear shield to its allies as well as to governments that were considered necessary to American national security. Third, Nixon said that in the future, when friendly governments were under a military threat, the United States "is going to encourage and has the right to expect that the responsibility" for these countries defense "be handled by Asian nations themselves."

Although the forum where Nixon announced his doctrine was unexpected, the basic idea—that the United States would not get involved in another Vietnam-like situation—was not new. In many of his writings, Kissinger had spoken about the need "to encourage a sense of local responsibility." A week before Nixon's pro-nouncements Kissinger had said during his press briefing ("on background" as was customary) that in the future the United States, while keen "to participate" in the defense of its Asian allies "cannot supply all the conceptions and all the resources." Nixon, for his part, would refer to the Nixon Doctrine in an address to the UN General Assembly in September 1969. Finally, in early November 1969 Nixon would outline the doctrine as "a policy which not only will help end the war in Vietnam, but which is an essential element of our program to prevent future Vietnams." He also further clarified the third point of his Guam briefing as follows: "we shall furnish military and economic assistance when requested in accordance with our treaty commitments. But we shall look to the nation directly threatened to assume the primary responsibility of providing the manpower for its defense." These words would also be found in the administration's first foreign policy report—authored by Kissinger's NSC staff—that was published in February 1970.[51]

The Nixon Doctrine was, at one level, simply the public extension of the policy of Vietnamization. As he planned to do in Vietnam, Nixon would limit direct American involvement in military conflicts and focus American efforts on providing material assistance. Indeed, the announcement coincided with the first troop withdrawals from South Vietnam.

Considered more broadly, however, the Nixon Doctrine had a far-reaching significance. It quickly became considered a global rather than a purely Asian doctrine. And the flip side of the Nixon Doctrine's affirmation of support for friendly governments that were involved in a war (such as South Vietnam) was the presumption that one could, if acting properly, preempt Vietnam-like situations from arising in the first place. In practice this meant that the Nixon administration would provide strong military assistance to regional powers that would act as the guarantors of stability in their specific corners of the globe. Over the next several years this would translate into, for example, American support to the shah of Iran. In short, the Nixon Doctrine was both part of the strategy of ending the Vietnam War and a key ingredient in Kissinger's global architecture of limiting direct American commitments in disparate regions.

In the summer of 1969 the Nixon Doctrine was the final opening move in the administration's foreign policy architecture. Along with the Kissinger–Dobrynin back channel, the effort to pressurize the North Vietnamese via the bombing of Cambodia, and the first halting moves toward China, it set the stage for the policies that would ultimately culminate in 1972–73. But already in late 1969, many of the earlier assumptions on the prospects for détente, the possibilities of a peace in Vietnam, and the chance for a dialogue with China would be tested in earnest.

4

Progress and Promise

On the evening of July 25, 1969—after Nixon had announced his doctrine to the press corps in Guam—the president's entourage had got on board Air Force One. Soon after the long onward flight to the Philippines commenced, Kissinger had a brief chat with Haldeman. Nixon had just told him, Haldeman confided, that "he seriously intends to visit China before the end of the second term." Kissinger smiled. "Fat chance," he quipped.[1]

Kissinger's apparently dismissive attitude about the possibility of visiting Beijing was neither surprising nor an entirely accurate reflection of his growing interest in China policy. As already noted, in early July he had ordered a full-scale study of the implications of the Sino-Soviet border clashes. He was fully aware of Nixon's attempt to initiate contact via the Pakistani and Romanian leadership during the round-the-world tour of late July and early August. Such moves would eventually place Kissinger at the center of Sino-American rapprochement. By September 1969 he was fully engaged in such efforts (although they were still conducted in collaboration with the State Department).

Kissinger's growing interest in an opening to China was largely a result of what he saw as the compensating gains that such a move would bring to the United States. "The effect on Hanoi alone would be traumatic," he later wrote, stressing the interconnected nature of the Vietnam War and America's relations with the two main supporters of North Vietnam.[2] As became clear by the early fall of 1969, moreover, the Kremlin's reaction to an American opening to Beijing would be outright dramatic. And it was this that truly mattered. For ultimately it was the Soviet Union that represented the primary concern of Kissinger's foreign policy against which all other issues were weighed.

Yet, as Kissinger surely knew, his ability to play the triangular game ultimately depended on China's willingness to engage with the United States.

CHINA TANGLE

In Beijing a potential opening to the United States, even as a counterweight to the USSR, was a controversial issue. Even those within the Chinese leadership, such as Premier Zhou Enlai, who saw the realpolitik rationale in an opening to the United States, would find it difficult to openly call for such a shift that effectively translated into a compromise between long-held ideological convictions and a new geopolitical situation. If anything, the commencement of the Cultural Revolution in 1966, together with the growing American involvement in Vietnam, had prompted an intensification of anti-American propaganda during the last years of the Johnson administration.

Throughout early 1969, the Chinese had sent mixed signals to Washington. In January, Mao, in an unprecedented move, had Nixon's inaugural address published in all major Chinese newspapers. The Nixon administration consisted of "jackals of the same lair" as the Johnson administration, the official Chinese communication succinctly put it.

Soon after, however, the Chinese announced that the Sino-American ambassadorial talks in Warsaw, scheduled to commence in February, had been aborted. Indeed, as the Nixon administration was in the process of establishing itself in Washington, the Chinese leadership proceeded cautiously. In early 1969, Zhou began closely observing any changes in U.S. rhetoric about China and feeding Mao information about the Nixon administration's more positive stance toward Beijing. On February 19, 1969, Mao himself ordered four of his veteran military leaders— Marshals Chen Yi, Ye Jianyng, Xu Xiangqian, and Nie Rongzhen—to observe the development of the international situation in light of the aggravated Sino-Soviet relationship.[3]

The border clashes in March tilted the internal balance in Beijing in favor of Zhou's conciliatory diplomacy. Prior to 1969, the United States—with its half million troops in Vietnam and continued presence in Taiwan, South Korea, and Japan—had presented the major threat to the PRC. The armed conflict with the Soviets radically changed Chinese priorities: it was now the Soviet Union that represented the main threat to China's security. Still, Mao wavered. During the Chinese Communist Party's (CCP) Ninth Congress in April 1969, Mao ignored the marshals' study of international developments. At the same conference the defense minister Lin Biao, who believed that an all-out war with the USSR was likely and who advocated a dramatic increase in the defense budget, was effectively made

Mao's heir. Mao stopped short, however, of approving the increase in military spending. As Yang Kuisong has argued, the Chairman either did not share Lin Biao's assumption that an all-out war with the USSR was probable, or simply considered any huge increase in the PRC military spending as a waste of sparse resources (and possibly as a way of giving Lin Biao too much power). Although Mao drummed up anti-Soviet propaganda throughout the spring and summer of 1969, the Chinese military budget remained largely unchanged.[4]

Pressure, meanwhile, continued to build up. In June 1969 the Soviets proposed an Asian collective security system and a regional economic grouping (consisting of Afghanistan, India, Iran, Pakistan, and the USSR) that further widened the gap between Moscow and Beijing.[5] Significantly, such Soviet proposals coincided with Nixon's Vietnamization announcement of June 8. The contrast could hardly have been clearer. While the Soviets were proposing the establishment of explicitly anti-Chinese regional agreements in South and Southeast Asia, the United States was taking steps to limit direct American involvement in the area. Such a geopolitical realignment could only make a possible rapprochement with Washington more appealing to Chinese leaders. It was hardly an accident that Nixon and Kissinger's interest in exploiting the Sino-Soviet confrontation clearly increased exactly at this moment—as evidenced by Kissinger's July 3 demand for a first NSC study on its implications to U.S. policy and the subsequent relaxation of U.S. travel restrictions to China.

Throughout the period, Zhou Enlai, who emerged as the clearest advocate (and architect) of Sino-American rapprochement, urged the group of four marshals to continue their efforts and pay specific attention to the policies of the United States and the Soviet Union. Accordingly the marshals submitted a report to the CCP Central Committee on July 11, 1969. Clothed in carefully designed, "ideologically correct," language, the marshals' report reassured that an attack on the PRC by either the USSR or the United States was unlikely. At the same time, however, the marshals made a point of stressing that it was "the Soviet revisionists" rather than the "U.S. imperialists," who posed "a more serious threat to our security."[6]

In the following months such an attitude appeared to ring true. On August 13, 1969, the Soviets attacked a Chinese border patrol in the Tielieketi area in the northwest, killing thirty Chinese soldiers. In late August the Chinese also learned that the Soviets were inquiring how their Warsaw Pact allies would react to a Soviet nuclear attack on China. Soon afterward, the Chinese began a rapid mobilization program.[7]

China's predicament alerted Washington. Kissinger and Nixon were encouraged by the reports of Mao's growing hostility toward Moscow and weighing its potential usefulness. State Department intelligence notes in July and August stressed the mixture of "implacable hostility and distrust, tinged with fear" that characterized Chinese attitudes toward the USSR. Equally significant, the Chinese were showing growing interest in the Nixon administration's latest Vietnam initiatives. While the Soviets explicitly refrained from playing a constructive role in Vietnam, Chinese officials in

Beijing and elsewhere were making inquiries about the nature and purpose of the Nixon administration's policies in Vietnam (particularly Vietnamization).[8]

To encourage further Chinese initiatives and to unnerve the Soviets, the Nixon administration dropped a series of hints in early August. As part of a round-the-world tour, Nixon made stopovers in Pakistan (August 1–2) and Romania (August 2–3). In both Lahore and Bucharest, the president passed on an encouraging message to the Chinese, suggesting that the United States and China should reopen the Warsaw ambassadorial talks. Nixon and Kissinger thus laid the groundwork for what would in 1970 become two important secret channels to China. A week later, Secretary of State Rogers told an Australian audience in Canberra that the United States was seeking to resume contact with the PRC.[9]

Finally, at an NSC meeting on August 14, 1969, Nixon—in part because of concern over the renewed escalation of tensions on the Sino-Soviet border following the Tielieketi ambush—told his cabinet that in his opinion it was the Soviets, not the Chinese, who were the more aggressive party in this conflict. Even more important, he maintained that the United States should not allow the Soviets to "smash" China. As Kissinger put it in his memoirs, Nixon had effectively "declared that we had a strategic interest in the survival of a major communist country, long an enemy, and with which we had no contact."[10]

The significance of the China initiative was confirmed a few days later. Boris Davydov, a KGB officer placed at the USSR's Washington embassy, and William L. Stearman, a Vietnam specialist from the State Department, had lunch on August 18. The Soviet official dropped a bombshell by asking Stearman the same question other Soviet diplomats were asking in Eastern Europe: how would the United States react to a possible Soviet attack on China's nuclear facilities? Stearman, quite logically, responded that while the United States might not wish to intervene, such preemptive strikes as Davydov seemed to be hinting at would not be condoned. "We would take an extremely grave view of that," Stearman told Davydov. The two did not dwell on the matter further, but after the luncheon Stearman rushed to write a memo on the conversation.[11]

Kissinger and Nixon took Davydov's remarks seriously. American bombers stationed at Beale Air Force Base in California were put on high alert for several weeks. When news arrived from the National Security Agency (NSA) that the Soviet commanders had ordered their air force in the Far East to "stand down," indicating the possibility that a military operation was forthcoming, Kissinger immediately demanded an assessment of the ways in which a Soviet nuclear attack on China could be launched. Suddenly, the United States faced, or so it seems, a potential all-out Sino-Soviet war in which nuclear weapons could be put into practical use.[12]

Not everyone on Kissinger's staff thought that a Soviet attack on China should be prevented. William Hyland, one of the Soviet experts, worried that any overt, or even lukewarm, sympathy toward China could produce "a massive overreaction from the USSR." Given the nonexistent relationship with Beijing, moreover, this might be coupled with continued hostility from China. Hyland even suggested, that "a Sino-Soviet war, for a limited period and if limited in scope, is by no means a disaster for the U.S. [and] might be the way to an early Vietnam settlement (and) a 'solution' to the China nuclear problem."

Kissinger evidently read Hyland's analysis with interest. "First rate paper," he wrote in the margin. But the flip side of Sino-Soviet tensions was also tempting. As a September 8, 1969 intelligence note from the State Department put it: "Peking's private mood seems more receptive to Sino-US discussions than at any time since the cancellation of February's Warsaw meeting." Two days later, an NSC memo concurred: "there is a substantial body of opinion in Beijing which is ready to explore Sino-US relations more rationally than has been done for some time."[13] The specter of a Soviet attack—at least as long as it remained merely a specter—was working to the Americans' favor.

Kissinger and Nixon decided it was time to begin exploring the opportunity in earnest. On September 9, they met in the White House with Walter Stoessel, the U.S. ambassador to Poland. Nixon gave specific instructions: upon his return to Warsaw Stoessel should make contact with his Chinese counterpart and tell him that the president was "interested in concrete discussions."

It may seem inexplicable that it took Stoessel almost three months to deliver the message. Yet, to find the right moment to approach an ambassador of a country with which the United States did not enjoy diplomatic relations was not a straightforward task in Cold War Poland (a member of the Warsaw Pact and hence at least technically on the side of the Soviet Union in the Sino-Soviet confrontation). Moreover, Chinese diplomats were still evidently under instructions to treat the Americans as representatives of a hostile country; thus, they consciously avoided direct contact. In the end, Stoessel did not find the appropriate opportunity to pass on Nixon's offer to open the Warsaw channel until early December. Nixon, meanwhile, continued to drop further hints: at the UN on September 18 he maintained that the United States was "ready" for "frank and serious" talks with the PRC.[14] In the meantime, the Nixon administration made public statements disassociating itself from the Sino-Soviet conflict, and American diplomats were told to "deplore the idea of a Soviet strike against Chinese nuclear facilities or any other major Soviet military action."[15]

At this point, developments in Vietnam further complicated the picture. On September 3, 1969, Ho Chi Minh died. The death took place at a crucial moment in terms of the emergence of triangular diplomacy and the Nixon administration's search for an exit in Vietnam. From Kissinger's perspective the nightmare scenario was that Ho's funeral—which was attended by Soviet Premier Alexei Kosygin and a Chinese delegation headed by Li Xiannian (Zhou Enlai visited Hanoi the day after Ho's death but returned the same day)—would set the stage for a Sino-Soviet rapprochement, which would raise the possibility of the North Vietnamese suddenly backed by a united Sino-Soviet front. The failure of Moscow and Beijing to settle their differences, however, made the impending North Vietnamese tilt toward the USSR a growing concern in China. Conversely, this increased the appeal of an opening to the United States.

Prior to his September 6 trip to Ho Chi Minh's funeral, Soviet Premier Kosygin passed on a message indicating his willingness to stop in China on his return trip. The Chinese kept him waiting, so that Kosygin had already made half of his journey back home when, after a refueling stop in Tajikistan, he turned back east and headed back to Beijing. On September 11, he held a four-hour meeting with Zhou Enlai at Beijing airport.

The two premiers seemed ready to compromise. Zhou said that China was willing to settle border disputes and wished to prevent further military clashes with the USSR. "We have so many domestic problems to deal with," he stressed. Kosygin and Zhou seemingly reached several agreements, such as the return of their respective ambassadors, the expansion of bilateral trade, and the restoration of regular transport networks between China and the Soviet Union. Yet, as soon as the meeting was over, the two sides informed each other that no official notes—as the two premiers had agreed at the end of their long dialogue at Beijing airport—would be exchanged.[16]

The meeting did not signal a true rapprochement. Mao remained suspicious of Soviet motives, and the general sentiment in the CCP Politburo during its meetings in mid-September 1969 was that the Soviets could simply not be trusted. The presence of a million or so Soviet troops near the Chinese border was enough to convince Mao that the Soviets were, at the minimum, trying to intimidate China into submission. There were essentially two ways to ameliorate the situation: through diplomacy and by raising China's military preparedness.

On the diplomatic front, Mao was increasingly convinced that an opening to the United States was a strategic necessity lest China be subjected to a massive Soviet onslaught, including the possible use of nuclear weapons. The four marshals he had previously ignored were thus called upon to provide another report to the Central Committee of the CCP on September 17, 1969. They neatly summarized China's emerging triangular rationale by saying that "we must wage a tit-for-tat struggle against both the United States and the Soviet Union, including using negotiation as a means of fighting against them." In a line that could have been taken from a number of Kissinger's writings, the marshals noted that the Chinese "should be firm on principles and flexible on tactics." Referring to American suggestions, which had reached Beijing via Romania and Pakistan, to reopen ambassadorial talks, the marshals concluded: "we should respond positively when the time is proper [because] such tactical actions may bring about results of strategic significance." As Marshall Chen Yi, one of the authors of the report, explained in an additional memorandum: "because of the strategic need for dealing with the Soviet revisionists, Nixon hopes to win over China. It is necessary for us to utilize the contradiction between the United States and the Soviet Union in a strategic sense and pursue a breakthrough in Sino-American relations."[17] Nixon's message at the UN the following day, emphasizing the United States' readiness for "frank discussions" with the PRC, could only strengthen the hand of the marshals' argument. Yet, a prospective opening to the United States was bound to be a long and arduous affair. It was hardly enough to calm those members of China's elite—such as the defense minister and Mao's designated heir, Lin Biao—who were concerned over a severe Soviet military strike.

For good measure, Mao decided to play some carrot and stick diplomacy with the Soviets.

The stick came first. In late September, the Chinese military conducted two major hydrogen bomb tests in China's western desert, launching radioactive fallout toward the Soviet troops stationed in Kazakhstan and Mongolia, causing yet untold environmental damage. It was hardly a delicate hint. But the tests undoubtedly succeeded in driving home to the Soviets a basic point: China had powerful bombs and was willing to use them if necessary. More to the point: should the Soviets launch a nuclear attack and fail to destroy the entire Chinese nuclear arsenal, Mao could be expected to retaliate in kind.[18]

The carrot followed. On October 7, 1969, the Chinese agreed to hold border negotiations with the Soviets. These were scheduled to commence on October 20. Having made his point with military tests, Mao was, it seemed, ready to find a diplomatic solution.

Even while making such an apparent diplomatic concession, however, the Chinese continued their military preparations. Lin Biao took the lead. On September 30, he had ordered the Chinese armed forces (the People's Liberation Army [PLA]) to be on full alert in anticipation of a potential Soviet surprise attack on October 1, the National Day of the PRC. A few weeks later, Lin, who had left Beijing for Suzhou in the South, issued the so-called Number One Order: a declaration of a national emergency that included full-combat readiness for all PLA forces, extensive anti-airstrike maneuvers, and some evacuations of Chinese cities. According to Chinese sources, close to a million soldiers, 4,000 planes, and 600 ships were moved to new locations following Lin Biao's order. Clearly, war hysteria had seized at least some of China's leadership. (It is important to note that Lin Biao's Number One Order was given without Mao's authorization, a deed that may have played a role in Lin's subsequent downfall.)[19]

Kissinger and Nixon knew little about the details of the Sino-Soviet game. Nor were they deeply focused on it. At the time, the White House's attention focused on its stillborn efforts to end the Vietnam War.

"DIDDLED" IN VIETNAM

In the fall of 1969, the Nixon administration's foreign policy balance sheet looked rather disappointing. Most significantly, the prospect for an early settlement in Vietnam appeared dim. Dobrynin had offered little help in the back-channel talks.

Nixon and Kissinger had been optimistic about Kissinger's secret meeting with the North Vietnamese diplomat Xuan Thuy on August 24, but nothing concrete transpired. The North Vietnamese appeared determined to stand up to American pressures. One of Ho Chi Minh's last acts had been to rebuff Nixon's earlier ultimatum. In a July 15 letter to Ho, Nixon had expressed his interest in furthering the peace process, threatening that unless progress was made by November 1, 1969, he would need to take "measures of great consequence and force."[20]

Following Ho's polite but noncommittal reply, which Nixon received on August 30, the administration moved to accelerate plans for an extensive American military operation. Kissinger, sensing a tough North Vietnamese stand on the diplomatic front, assembled a group of ten advisers to come up with a "military plan designed for maximum impact on the enemy's military capability." With diplomacy seemingly leading nowhere and the Soviet channel producing little, and with pressure for American troop withdrawals increasing at home, Kissinger had concluded that the only option for enhancing the administration's search for a peace with honor was a "savage, decisive blow against North Vietnam." As he famously put it to his aides: "I refuse to believe that a little fourth-rate power like Vietnam does not have a breaking point."[21]

The operation was codenamed Duck Hook. In the planning stages, Kissinger told his staff that everything, with the exception of the use of nuclear weapons (although even these were apparently briefly considered), was fair game. In the end, the two major parts of Duck Hook included a massive four-day bombing campaign against economic and military targets throughout the North and the mining of Haiphong harbor (the major supply route to Hanoi). If the North Vietnamese would not respond by commencing serious negotiations, the plan called for further periodic attacks, including the bombing of Red River dikes (which would cause a massive flood throughout North Vietnam) and even a ground invasion of the North. The target date for the campaign was November 1, 1969, the anniversary of the U.S. bombing halt against the North. It was never implemented.

While Kissinger oversaw the planning of Duck Hook, Nixon found himself under growing domestic pressure to deescalate the war. His September 16 announcement that another 35,000 U.S. troops would be withdrawn from Vietnam by the middle of December had a positive if short-lived impact on public opinion. It certainly did not quiet down the peace movement. On Moratorium Day (October 15), for example, millions of Americans participated in teach-ins, memorial services, and other acts that demonstrated the strength of the antiwar movement. The opposition to aggressive military moves within the administration was also growing. Rogers and Laird, who only learned about Nixon's deadline to Ho in early October, stepped up their opposition to further aggressive military moves. To Kissinger's dismay, Laird was able to use the opinions of some members of the NSC staff (such as Anthony Lake and Roger Morris) to shore up his argument that any major military maneuver would have a short-lived impact, incur high costs, and do little to advance the peace process.[22]

Ultimately, Nixon found himself unable to take strong military measures in the fall of 1969. Instead, he fell back on public relations. In his famous "Silent Majority" speech of November 3, 1969, Nixon pleaded for the country to unite behind his pursuit of peace and rebuke the efforts of the "vocal minority" (i.e., the antiwar movement) to "humiliate the United States." With opinion polls showing that 77 percent of Americans approved of Nixon's message, he had, at least for the moment, pacified the pacifists. Still, ten months after taking office the Nixon administration had moved no closer to ending America's involvement in Vietnam.[23]

Perhaps it was such a state of apparent deadlock that prompted Kissinger, on October 13, 1969, to write Nixon an exceedingly pessimistic memo. The United States was facing a "generally deteriorating strategic position" Kissinger maintained. In contrast, the NSC adviser argued, "the world situation, as viewed from Moscow, provides [no] great cause for communist pessimism."[24] In addition to the continued deadlock in Vietnam, Kissinger and Nixon could hardly expect that the United States was destined to capitalize on the Sino-Soviet conflict anytime in the near future. The attempts to open meaningful channels of communication in August via the Pakistanis and the Romanians had apparently gone nowhere, while Ambassador Stoessel had yet to make contact with his Chinese counterparts in Warsaw.

And yet, there was a glimmer of hope. A week after Kissinger bemoaned the sorry state of the United States' strategic position in his memo to Nixon, Anatoly Dobrynin came to the White House to meet with Nixon and Kissinger. The Soviet ambassador had two messages to deliver. First, he handed Nixon a brief note suggesting November 17 as the opening date for the SALT talks. After some back-and-forth over the respective merits of Helsinki and Vienna as meeting places and the need to have serious discussions rather than "a series of platitudes," the president and Kissinger agreed to the Soviet proposal.

The second message was less specific but more revealing. Moscow warned:

If someone in the United States is tempted to make profit from Soviet-Chinese relations at the Soviet Union[']s expense, and there are some signs of that, then we would like to frankly warn in advance that such a line of conduct, if pursued, can lead to a very grave miscalculation, and is in no way consistent with the goal of better relations between the U.S. and the USSR.

Nixon was furious. He handed Dobrynin a yellow legal pad. "You'd better take some notes," Nixon said. Then he started a thirty-minute monologue. Nixon criticized Soviet conduct in the Middle East, Europe, and, in particular, Vietnam. His point on China was straightforward:

China and the United States cannot tolerate a situation to develop where we are enemies, anymore than we want to be permanent enemies of the Soviet Union.

Therefore, we expect to make moves in trade and exchange of persons and eventually in diplomacy.

Nixon then linked China, the Soviet Union, and Vietnam into one package: "The
only beneficiary of U.S.–Soviet disagreement over Vietnam is China. And, therefore, this is the last opportunity to settle these disputes . . . we [will] not hold still
for being 'diddled' to death in Vietnam."

Although the major concrete outcome of the meeting had been the agreement
to commence SALT talks in November, Dobrynin had made the continued Soviet
anxiety over China and the potential uses of Sino-American rapprochement abundantly clear. More to the point: given the deadlock in Vietnam, the United States
needed additional leverage vis-à-vis the USSR. The conclusion was simple. "We
should not be diverted from our China policy," Kissinger summed it up the day
after the meeting with Dobrynin.[25]

Nixon and Kissinger thus stepped up their efforts to reach out to China. Already
on October 10, Kissinger had asked Pakistani ambassador Hilaly to pass on a message to the Chinese that the United States had decided to withdraw a destroyer
patrol from the Taiwan straits—obviously as a signal to Beijing. By early November the message finally reached Zhou Enlai. There was no immediate response.
Meanwhile, Nixon and Secretary of State Rogers were exploring possibilities of
relaxing trade restrictions toward China. At the minimum they might complicate
the possibilities of a Sino-Soviet rapprochement, which had, soon after the convening of the border negotiations, hit a snag.[26] But nothing seemed to work.

Not, that is, until early December.

WARSAW "OPENING"

Although Kissinger had initiated secret contacts via Pakistan, the initial move
toward rapprochement, unlike the ultimate opening in 1971, was still a combined
White House–State Department effort. In fact, the initial contacts in late 1969 and
early 1970 were still controlled by traditional diplomats, clearly indicating that
Kissinger had yet to take complete control over this aspect of U.S. policy.

On December 3, 1969, Ambassador Walter Stoessel, at a fashion show put on by
the Yugoslav mission in Warsaw, finally approached the PRC's charge d'affaires Lei
Yang. It took some physical effort: Stoessel had to run after Lei and his interpreter
outside the Warsaw Palace of Culture (the setting of the fashion show). Stoessel's
message, delivered in Polish to the Chinese interpreter, was simple: the Nixon
administration wanted to hold serious talks with the Chinese in Warsaw.[27]

The talks commenced quickly. On December 11, Stoessel and Lei Yang met for
over an hour at the Chinese embassy and Stoessel formally restated his proposal
for "serious, concrete talks." At another meeting on January 8, 1970, the countries

agreed to commence formal discussions in Warsaw twelve days later. In the meantime, the Chinese were also sending positive signals via the suddenly active Pakistani channel. On December 19, Pakistani Ambassador Hilaly told Kissinger that the Chinese were most encouraged and had decided to release two imprisoned Americans as a response to the U.S. message regarding destroyers in the Taiwan straits. Kissinger, delighted, passed on another message: if the Chinese wished, the Americans could abandon the fairly exposed Warsaw channel in favor of "channels that are less widely disseminated within the bureaucracy." He thus made his first significant pitch for secret diplomacy.[28] For the time being, however, the China opening remained a collective effort.

The Warsaw meetings in early 1970 were encouraging. On January 20, 1970, Stoessel suggested to Lei that the two countries exchange emissaries. He further expressed "hope" that the United States could reduce troop levels not only in the Taiwan straits but also generally in Southeast Asia. In other words, the Nixon administration was drawing an obvious link between the Vietnam War and the touchy issue of Taiwan by indirectly suggesting that Chinese help in reaching a Vietnam settlement would allow the United States to reduce its troop levels in Taiwan. Stoessel further assured that the United States had no interest in collaborating with the USSR against China. Lei Yang replied with expressions of Chinese willingness to continue along the chosen path. On February 20, 1970, he went even further. Lei Yang indicated that the Chinese side would "in principle" welcome a high-level U.S. emissary to Beijing. The Warsaw channel was looking increasingly promising as a launching pad for triangular diplomacy.[29]

That the Warsaw meetings were publicly announced allowed Nixon and Kissinger to play upon evident Soviet concern over a potential Sino-American rapprochement. In fact, it was far too tempting to do otherwise. Throughout late 1969 and early 1970, Ambassador Dobrynin expressed a heightened interest in Sino-American contacts, prompting Nixon, on December 12, to order that no information should be shared with the Soviets on the actual content of the Warsaw exchanges. The decision had an immediate impact. Ten days later, a puzzled Dobrynin asked Kissinger: "What exactly are you up to? Are you trying to annoy the Soviet Union?" In January 1970, Dobrynin again inquired about the meetings in Warsaw. Kissinger, on both occasions, played the triangular game. He reiterated that while the Americans took no sides in the Sino-Soviet conflict, they did not "accept the proposition that permanent hostility is the iron law of US-Chinese relations." Given that the possibility of an opening was still rather faint, this was not a huge understatement. But Kissinger could only be impressed by such a "neuralgic" concern in Moscow. From a tactical point of view, the less the Soviets knew of the process of such an opening, the better. As Nixon put it in a handwritten comment on one of Kissinger's late 1969 memos: "K-good! Keep Dobrynin guessing."[30]

To Nixon and Kissinger, Dobrynin's obvious concern over the Warsaw meetings could only mean that they were on the right path: an opening, or even a plausible threat of an opening, to China could not but yield tremendous leverage to the United States in its relationship with the Soviets. In the context of the stalemate between Moscow and Washington that became evident during the first series of SALT negotiations in Helsinki in November–December 1969, such leverage was sorely needed.[31]

There was, finally, more than a glimmer of hope in early 1970. Although the Vietnam War dragged on and the North Vietnamese remained as recalcitrant as ever, although there had been no unambiguous sign that the PRC was ready to open a bilateral relationship with the United States, and although the Soviets had yet to make any significant concessions on any issue, the task ahead was increasingly clear. With the Soviets clearly nervous and the Chinese warming up to the idea of rapprochement, Kissinger could view the American position in a cautiously optimistic light.

HIGH POTENTIAL

The Nixon administration's first foreign policy Report (FPR) to the U.S. Congress was published two days prior to the February 20 meeting between Lei Yang and Walter Stoessel. Authored by Kissinger and his staff, the FPR did not provide a full accounting of the administration's maneuvering with Moscow and Beijing (not to mention Hanoi and Saigon). Yet, it clearly stated the basic outlook of the administration's stance toward China and the USSR. The United States did not regard the Soviet Union and China as posing a monolithic threat to the United States and its allies in Europe and the Far East. More important, the FPR restated the importance of encouraging the PRC to come out of its isolation. Although this was hardly news to the Chinese leadership, the signal could not have been stronger: the Nixon administration was ready for an opening.

The FPR summarized the Nixon administration's overall approach to the Soviet Union and China as follows:

> We will regard our Communist adversaries first and foremost as nations pursuing their own interests as they perceive these interests, just as we follow our interests as we see them. We will judge them by their actions as we expect to be judged by our own. Specific agreements, and the structure of peace they help build, will come from a realistic accommodation of conflicting interests.[32]

It was as clear-cut a statement of realpolitik as any American administration had yet put forth publicly. For the first time an American administration maintained that communist ideology was no obstacle to having a fruitful relationship with another nation. Interests, rather than ideals, formed the basis of the Nixon administration's policies toward the USSR and the PRC.

Given the positive signals in the Warsaw channel two days after the publication of the FPR, the document can be seen, at least in part, as an effort to prepare the ground in Congress for the obvious next step: a visit of a high-level American emissary to China in 1970. That Kissinger would be this emissary was, of course, not a fait accompli in early 1970; after all the most significant progress had thus far been reached via traditional diplomatic channels. Still, a visit of a high-level American official to China appeared as a very real possibility in early 1970. Yet, assuming that someone from the State Department had been sent on such a mission in 1970 would undoubtedly have undercut Kissinger's ability to exercise ever growing influence over U.S. China policy.

Although he was not able to include it in the FPR, Kissinger was also making progress—or what seemed like progress—in another set of negotiations. At 10:00 A.M. on February 21, 1970, Kissinger—with NSC staff members W. Richard Smyser and Tony Lake, as well as General Vernon Walters in tow—arrived at a run-down apartment at 11 Darthe Street in the Choisy-le-Roy district of Paris. There he met Le Duc Tho, a member of the North Vietnamese Politburo. The two men, who would eventually share the 1973 Nobel Peace Prize, sat down for the first of their many secret meetings. They would continue to haggle over Vietnam, on and off, for the next three years.[33]

Finally there was progress on several fronts. The SALT negotiations were under way. The Chinese were apparently ready to commence serious talks with Washington. The North Vietnamese had apparently blinked, by sending one of their most seasoned diplomats to meet with Kissinger. To those very few who were aware of all these developments, it must have seemed like a historic moment, a moment when a year's worth of frustration was finally starting to pay off. The opening to China—and the emergence of triangular diplomacy—seemed so close. The Nixon administration seemed to be on the verge of shaking the deadlock in Soviet-American relations and the Vietnam peace process. Along the way, Kissinger had managed to outmaneuver his major bureaucratic competitors and confirm his position as the Nixon administration's foreign policy czar. There was just one problem.

Cambodia.

5

Negotiating in the Shadow of War

The negotiations "have not gone one inch forward," Le Duc Tho told Kissinger on April 4, 1970.[1]

It was a disappointing assessment. Over the past two months, the two men had met three times to negotiate an end to the Vietnam War. On February 21, March 16, and April 4, the North Vietnamese Politburo member, dressed in a black "Mao suit," and the U.S. national security adviser, sporting a suit and tie, had exchanged views and offers at a shabby apartment on 11 rue Darthé in Paris. In January 1973, Kissinger and Tho would eventually initial an accord bringing the American phase of the Vietnam War to an end. But in the spring of 1970 no such agreement was in sight. Instead, more bombing and bloodshed ensued as the United States and South Vietnam invaded Cambodia in May 1970, hence expanding the war that most Americans, given the ongoing process of Vietnamization, thought was being curtailed.

The Cambodian invasion caused a series of negative reactions. College campuses erupted in protest. Members of Kissinger's own staff resigned in disgust. The Chinese responded by closing down the promising Warsaw channel of Sino-American contacts. The Soviets appeared less eager for an early move toward détente, while they simultaneously engaged the West German government of Willy Brandt in a series of negotiations. By the late summer of 1970 it almost seemed as though Kissinger and Nixon were being outmaneuvered by Moscow, Hanoi, and Beijing.

THO AND KISSINGER

When he sat down with Kissinger for the first time on February 21, the fifty-nine-year-old Le Duc Tho was a hardened veteran revolutionary. Born in 1911 in North Vietnam, Tho had joined Ho Chi Minh's movement as a teenager and belonged to the relatively small group of men who organized the Indochina Communist Party in 1930. He had spent ten years in French prisons, had acted as the chief commissioner for South Vietnam before 1954, and supervised military and political campaigns in the South throughout the 1960s. He was also a veteran of "private talks." In June 1968, the gray-haired, five feet eight inches tall Tho had arrived in Paris as a member of the Democratic Republic of Vietnam's (DRV) negotiation team. Throughout the summer and early fall, he and Xuan Thuy met privately—that is without South Vietnamese representatives—at the outskirts of Paris with U.S. negotiators Averell Harriman and Cyrus Vance. But, as described above, the 1968 talks, while producing a bombing halt in October, had eventually ended without an agreement. Le Duc Tho had gone back to Hanoi to wait for the next opportunity to continue his personal diplomatic struggle. In early 1970 that opportunity had arrived.[2]

In the spring of 1970, the first series of Kissinger–Tho talks were a struggle between two diplomats bent on making few, if any, concessions. In February Kissinger, Xuan Thuy, and Tho each gave lengthy exposes of their positions, with Tho stating the rather obvious point that the United States could not win the war. Implementing Vietnamization or using threats were of no use, Tho argued. "We have won and you have failed . . . you cannot change the trend of the war . . . I am convinced we will have victory." It was not mere bravado. In the spring of 1970, the North Vietnamese were not losing the war and held important cards at the negotiating table. Vietnamization, the persistent pressure of the antiwar movement, and the emptiness of Nixon's threats the previous year all served to embolden Le Duc Tho to make such seemingly arrogant and uncompromising statements and demand that the Thieu government in South Vietnam be removed. Kissinger's assistant, Tony Lake, who would later serve as NSC adviser in the Clinton administration, aptly summed up Tho's position in March 1970: "it is almost certain that the North Vietnamese will not agree to mutual withdrawal unless they have a good idea about how the political future looks in South Vietnam."

As a result, Kissinger's hopes for a negotiated settlement were extremely slight. The United States could not fold under pressure from Hanoi, which was what Tho was effectively demanding. To do that would have meant an open betrayal of an ally (South Vietnam) with potential repercussions for American allies throughout the globe. Credibility was at stake. Given that Kissinger thought of the globe as, in essence, a large battlefield of the Cold War, he also worried that losing in Vietnam might embolden the Soviets to act more aggressively in other areas (such as the

Middle East). It would certainly not add any incentive for Moscow to make concessions on other issues and would preempt the use of Vietnam as a form of linkage.

Thus, in March and early April, Tho and Kissinger made no progress, as
Kissinger insisted on separating the political and military solutions from each
other. In practice, his demand boiled down to an immediate end to fighting, followed by a gradual U.S. withdrawal. The political future of South Vietnam could
not, Kissinger maintained, be decided while fighting continued. And the United
States would most certainly not play a role in the ouster of Nguyen Thuy's government. Yet, all the while, Nixon pressured Kissinger to deliver "a breakthrough."[3]

The secret talks over Vietnam were becoming an early example of the difficulties that Kissinger faced in applying his overall theoretical maxims to the making
of foreign policy. Kissinger had never considered Vietnam to have a specific geopolitical significance to the United States and had proceeded from the assumption
that a combination of diplomatic and military pressure would deliver an acceptable outcome. But a year after taking the first steps to apply this strategy, he had
lost some negotiation assets and had, despite opening a secret channel with North
Vietnam, made no headway. Moreover, the president was apparently beginning to
lose his patience and, potentially, his trust in Kissinger's ability to actually deliver.
"It's obvious [that Kissinger] can't negotiate, he makes debating points instead,"
Nixon remarked to Bob Haldeman after reviewing the record of Kissinger's April
1970 meeting with Le Duc Tho.[4]

It was against this background of mounting frustration that Cambodia's head
of state, Prince Sihanouk, was overthrown, spurring the joint U.S.-ARVN invasion
of Cambodia at the end of April 1970. Justifying what the United States called "an
incursion" as, alternatively, a peace enforcement mission, as part of the U.S. military strategy of destroying the base of COSVN, or as a way of forcing Hanoi's hand
at the negotiation table, the Cambodian intervention endangered a number of the
Nixon administration's foreign policy moves. For one, there would be a long halt
in the Kissinger–Tho meetings as the North Vietnamese protested the invasion as
a sign of American duplicity. When secret negotiations did resume in September
1970 the seriousness of the North Vietnamese also remained in doubt. Kissinger
would have to deal with Xuan Thuy alone. Le Duc Tho, whose presence was an indication that the negotiations carried the imprint of the highest levels of Hanoi's
leadership, would only return to Paris in June 1971. For another, the Cambodian
invasion hampered the progress of Sino-American contacts. At home, antiwar
demonstrations closed down hundreds of college campuses.

As predicted by many, the Cambodian invasion of 1970 prevented immediate
advances in the major areas of foreign policy that Kissinger was now treating as his
personal reserve. Yet, despite the many protests of his staff members, Kissinger did
not oppose the invasion. The explanations for this seemingly contradictory behavior have as much to do with the military merits of the invasion as they have with
the less-than-noble concern over personal status and continued influence. The bot-

tom line, though, was that the short-term military advantages of the invasion paled when measured against the counterproductive impact to Kissinger's overall foreign policy agenda as well as the medium-term impact in Indochina. Vietnam, the regional crisis the Nixon administration had inherited, yet again blocked the realization of the grand design.

INCURSION

Since the spring of 1969 Cambodia had suffered from extensive American bombing campaigns that drew the country deeper into the morass of the Vietnam War. In spite of this, Prince Sihanouk still wished to retain a semblance of a relationship with the United States in case he needed external support against the North Vietnamese. In effect, he had, if indirectly, indicated that he would not object to an American pursuit of the North Vietnamese in Cambodia. While that did not mean that he was happy to see, or expected, an intense bombing campaign in 1969–70, his muted attitude toward MENU could only lead Kissinger to conclude that Sihanouk "acquiesced" to the bombing.[5]

Like so many others, Sihanouk engaged in a careful balancing act. After breaking off diplomatic relations with the United States in 1965, the Cambodian ruler had maintained close ties with Beijing. In 1966 he acquiesced to the use of Sihanoukville, a port city in the Gulf of Siam, as a major supply route to the Vietcong (and, eventually, to the Khmer Rouge). Sihanouk's tilt toward China made some sense. After all, from the Cambodian perspective the major threat came not from the United States or the PRC but from Vietnam—something that was later evident as the united Vietnam invaded Cambodia in the late 1970s. As long as Sihanouk—who had established a personal rapport with Zhou Enlai in the 1950s— enjoyed a working relationship with Beijing, he could expect the Chinese to restrain Hanoi's interest in using Cambodian territory as a base for operations against Saigon.[6]

By the spring of 1969 Sihanouk's balancing act became untenable. For one, the MENU operations pushed the North Vietnamese regulars that protected the Ho Chi Minh Trail in eastern Cambodia westward. American bombers followed suit. Along the way, the North Vietnamese came into increasing contact with the Cambodian army. Moreover, in early 1968, the Khmer Rouge (or the Cambodian Communist Party, or the Communist Party of Kampuchea [CPK]) decided to wage armed struggle against Sihanouk's government. Sihanouk responded with air strikes against suspected communist strongholds—Cambodian and North Vietnamese—in Cambodia. But, as befit Sihanouk's longstanding neutralist balancing act, he simultaneously tried to position himself in a noncommittal diplomatic position by reestablishing diplomatic relations with the United States (in June 1969) and allowing the National Liberation Front (NLF) to have an embassy in

Cambodia. All the while, Sihanouk tried to maintain cordial relations with the increasingly suspicious Chinese.[7] Unfortunately for him, the combination of increased military activity in the Cambodian countryside and the failure of Sihanouk's foreign policy created a fertile ground for a military takeover in Phnom Penh. In March 1970, while the prince was out of the country, the prime minister, General Lon Nol, seized control of the government. Sihanouk, who was in Moscow trying to recruit Soviet help in pressing the North Vietnamese to reduce their operations in Cambodia, had few places to turn to for help. Ironically, his next stop was Beijing. A few days later, on March 23, 1970, Sihanouk—in a stunning reversal of fortunes—announced that he was joining forces with the Khmer Rouge to form the National United Front.[8] The civil war that was to last until 1975 (and beyond) thus pitted Sihanouk, the Khmer Rouge, and their supporters (the PRC but also the North Vietnamese and by extension the USSR) against the American-supported Lon Nol.

*   *   *

There is no direct evidence that the Nixon administration or Kissinger was directly involved in the planning for Lon Nol's coup, yet American officials in Vietnam and CIA agents in the region were certainly aware that preparations to this effect were under way. Yet, Kissinger certainly welcomed the change of government, not least because the North Vietnamese appeared "confused" about Sihanouk's ouster. When he met with Le Duc Tho in Paris two weeks after the coup, Kissinger found Tho "completely off balance." Kissinger had, he reported, also told Tho that it was up to the North Vietnamese to come up with "something positive to offer" if they wished to continue the negotiations. Clearly, the overthrow of Sihanouk represented a welcome change to Kissinger.

The administration's actions immediately after the coup also made it clear that Lon Nol was welcomed as an American asset. Nixon was particularly pleased with the new Cambodian leader's plan to expand the nation's army and, on March 19, wrote to Kissinger that he wished CIA Director Richard Helms "to develop and implement a plan for maximum assistance to pro-US elements in Cambodia." In the coming weeks the United States extended recognition to Lon Nol, launched a military and aid program to Cambodia, and even authorized South Vietnamese troops—with U.S. air support—to attack North Vietnamese sanctuaries in Cambodia in late March. As Haldeman summed it up, the coup "was all right with us."[9]

While Lon Nol was more agreeable to Nixon and Kissinger than Sihanouk, the situation in Cambodia complicated the administration's choices. How far should the United States go in supporting the new Cambodian regime? What course of action would have the most beneficial impact on the Paris peace talks? What about American public opinion? Could Nixon count on the support of the silent majority, or would U.S. military action provoke a massive revolt?

An internal debate that culminated in a two-track policy ensued. The first decision was announced on April 20, 1970. The United States was moving "from a period of 'cut and try' to a longer-range program for the replacement of Americans by South Vietnamese troops," Nixon announced in a televised speech from the Western White House in San Clemente. 150,000 Americans would be withdrawn over the subsequent twelve months. The president attempted to give the impression that he was still on course with his peace program and that the continuation of the war rested with Hanoi. "I again remind the leaders of North Vietnam that while we are taking these risks for peace," Nixon warned, "they will be taking grave risks should they attempt to use the occasion to jeopardize the security of our remaining forces in Vietnam by increased military action in Vietnam, in Cambodia, or in Laos."[10]

Although he congratulated Nixon on a fine speech, Kissinger had argued strongly against the withdrawals. On April 17, for example, he had maintained that the announcement would further weaken his hand as he contemplated future negotiations in Paris. He warned: "we are making budget and troop withdrawal decisions today without fully examining the implications of these decisions for the future. We may not know we are in trouble until it is too late to do anything about it." Should the openly pro-American Lon Nol government fall he would be left without an ace. Moreover, in order for the withdrawals not to cause major military setbacks in South Vietnam, the United States and Saigon needed to exhibit their military prowess.[11]

In short, to Kissinger the issue was one of credibility, prestige, and negotiating assets.

Paradoxically, the decision to go ahead with the withdrawals strengthened the case for intervention in Cambodia. The argument was simple: before large numbers of American troops were withdrawn, the United States needed to remove the threat to South Vietnam that emanated from North Vietnamese sanctuaries along the Cambodian-South Vietnamese border. After lengthy deliberations, Nixon decided, on April 28, to intervene in Cambodia. A few days later approximately 75,000 South Vietnamese and American (about 31,000) troops moved into the formerly neutral country. On the evening of April 30, in another televised speech—this time from the White House—Nixon told the American people: "to guarantee the continued success of our withdrawal and Vietnamization programs, I have concluded that the time has come for action." The joint U.S.-ARVN operations would commence that evening.

Nixon then implausibly added: "This is not an invasion of Cambodia." The American troops had no intention of actually occupying Cambodia, Nixon assured the American public. Kissinger, who had reviewed the speech with Nixon and Haldeman in the afternoon before it was delivered, later called it "vainglorious." At the time, though, he had raised few objections.[12]

KISSINGER, NIXON, AND THE "BLEEDING HEARTS"

The decision to invade Cambodia was preceded by weeks of intense debate within the Nixon administration. The proponents maintained that the invasion would, at the minimum, buy time for Vietnamization and possibly even cause the North Vietnamese to make concessions at the negotiation table, while the opponents argued that the drawbacks—domestic uproar, international condemnation, and the prospects of widening the war—were singularly counterproductive.

The big question, though, was ultimately not over the invasion itself but over the use of American ground troops in the operation. On Wednesday, April 22, the NSC discussed three options: (1) no military action (course supported by State and Defense); (2) strikes by South Vietnamese ground troops with U.S. air support (Kissinger's position); (3) a joint action by U.S. and South Vietnamese troops (recommended by the JCS and US commanders on the field). In the meeting Nixon initially backed Kissinger's recommendation. During the next few days, however, Nixon grew increasingly anxious to use the opportunity to deliver a serious blow to North Vietnam's military capabilities. He held long sessions with Kissinger and CIA Director Helms indicating, according to Haldeman, that he could still "get [the war] wound up this year if we keep enough pressure on and don't crumble at home." Given that he had just announced troop withdrawals, Nixon may have thought that he had adequately mollified American public opinion. But the opportunities for using the GIs for offensive moves were bound to decrease as their numbers dwindled. It was, in Nixon's logic, now or never.

Kissinger's attitude was somewhat less confident. While Nixon was increasingly determined about the need to use American troops, Kissinger worried about the backlash that would follow if U.S. troops openly (Americans had conducted small-scale secret counterinsurgency operations in both Cambodia and Laos throughout the past few years) and in large numbers invaded neutral Cambodia. As Bob Haldeman recorded in his diaries on Friday, April 24: "K[issinger] was very worried that [the] P[resident] is moving too rashly without really thinking through the consequences."[13]

Kissinger's concern about the use of American troops and his eventual decision to fall in line with Nixon's tough stand, was partially a reflection of a revolt brewing within his own staff, which, almost uniformly, opposed the invasion. Throughout April several members of the NSC team—what Kissinger dubbed the "bleeding hearts" club—lobbied strongly against widening the war. On April 2, in a lengthy analysis of U.S. options, NSC staffer Winston Lord argued that regardless of North Vietnamese action, "under no circumstances should we put U.S. troops into Cambodia. The present rules of engagement limiting us to protective reaction along the border should apply in all instances." If there was no all-out North Vietnamese/Vietcong offensive against Lon Nol, Lord argued, the United States should "restrain ARVN action . . . while events clarify and we sort out all the policy implications with regard to Paris and Southeast Asia." Even if there were a massive attack, moreover, the United States "should make it clear to the GVN that the ARVN should not overextend itself, and that we would not send in American ground forces to bail them out."[14] A few weeks later, Lord joined with Roger Morris and Tony Lake to warn that

> short of sending US divisions and/or of deep and long-term ARVN penetrations of Cambodia, it does not seem possible to achieve . . . an anti-communist Cambodian government in control of its country and preventing VC/NVN use of its territory against South Vietnam . . . To try to find this "best solution" is unrealistic.

Trying to push the credibility button, the bleeding hearts further argued: "There should be no direct US military involvement in Cambodia. We must assume that any use of US forces in Cambodia . . . would increase our involvement and prestige in a losing cause, limit diplomatic flexibility, and have severe political consequences in the US."

Lord, Lake, and Morris did leave an opening for an invasion: "If we do decide on direct U.S. involvement in Cambodia, we believe it should be a) public and b) in a multilateral context." Yet, their conclusion was prophetic: "In the end, the US must face squarely the basically untenable situation in Cambodia—and that no remedy in proportion to our interests may be available."[15]

The only argument that was adopted from the bleeding hearts' eight-page report—that would never make it to Nixon's desk—was to abandon secrecy and include the ARVN.

On Friday, April 24, as it was clear that Nixon was leaning toward the use of American troops in the invasion, Kissinger again convened the bleeding hearts. In addition to Lord, Lake, and Morris, these included Larry Lynn and Bill Watts. "Ah, here are my bleeding hearts," Kissinger told the group as they entered his office. They all argued against the invasion. Instead of a full-scale invasion, Lake, Morris, and Lord maintained, the United States should work out a private agreement with Lon Nol that would allow intermittent bombings and cross-border raids into Cambodian territory (much like before). Kissinger appeared puzzled. What was "the moral distinction" between cross-border raids and an invasion? he asked. The major difference would be felt by the Cambodians, the three staffers argued: cross-border raids could be contained, but a full-scale invasion would make Cambodia part of the theater of war with all its potential implications for that nation's political future. Moreover, should the United States participate in the invasion, Tony Lake warned, the administration would be "bogged down in a wider war."

"Well, Tony, I knew what you were going to say," Kissinger responded. Lake was incensed. Yet, like the others in the meeting, he refrained from an emotional outburst.

Others piled up additional arguments against the invasion. Lord stressed the domestic outburst that would inevitably follow and destroy much of the support for the administration's policy. Watts accurately predicted that there would be massive protests at home and that an invasion of Cambodia could easily lead to a similar invasion of Laos later on. Lynn pointed out that the invasion was not a cost-effective way of using U.S.–South Vietnamese military resources and that the human costs, particularly to civilian populations, would be far too high in contrast to any potential benefits that might be derived from the invasion.

Kissinger, perhaps sensing that his relationship with his staff was at a crossroads, listened intently, asked questions, and argued. But he knew that there was no changing of Nixon's mind; the meeting with the bleeding hearts was, therefore, in part Kissinger's attempt at damage control within his own staff: he knew they objected to what was about to happen, but he did not wish to lose them as a result. Thus, the former professor listened to his "students" but made it clear that while their arguments were valid, they did not add up to a convincing case against the invasion. In particular, the bleeding hearts were not able to explain how, in an absence of an invasion, Vietnamization could continue without causing a collapse in the South. If the North Vietnamese were allowed to use Cambodia as a staging area for continued infiltration into South Vietnam, Kissinger asked, what would happen as American troops gradually returned home? Cross-border raids, or a limited attack on one or two communist sanctuaries, would merely stir up domestic protest (as Lord and Watts predicted), but would not discourage the North Vietnamese. If one was to attack, there was no point in holding back.

While Kissinger was meeting with the bleeding hearts on the evening of April 24, Nixon was at Camp David having drinks with his friend, the Miami businessman Bebe Rebozo. As was his custom, the president's toughness and determination increased when reinforced by alcohol. He was clearly eager for a show of force. Yet Nixon worried, as did Kissinger and his staff, about potential failure and blame. He remained torn, sensing the weight of the inevitable public outcry. Perhaps because of such concerns, perhaps because they were in a prankish mood, Nixon and Rebozo decided to place a call for Kissinger.

After a few minutes, Nixon passed the phone to Rebozo. "The president wants you to know, Henry, that if it doesn't work, it's your ass." It was not exactly a show of trust.[16]

The next day, when Kissinger arrived at Camp David, Nixon's mood had changed again. Why not use the occasion to deliver a truly decisive blow? Why not implement the Duck Hook plan that had been canceled six months earlier? Why not go for broke, mine Haiphong harbor, and bomb Hanoi? Kissinger, not sure whether Nixon was serious, said that they had "enough on their plates." Yet, the mining and bombing remained as contingency plans to be eventually implemented two years later. But for the time being, as Nixon, Kissinger, and Rebozo headed back to Washington on the afternoon of Saturday, April 25, the major new decision— that is, different from the course apparently adopted during the NSC meeting three days earlier—was to use American ground troops.

*   *   *

The decision clearly brought to the fore the divisions within the administration. Secretary of State Rogers and Defense Secretary Mel Laird, kept in the dark after the April 22 NSC meeting, were bound to disagree with the incursion. The showdown came on Monday and Tuesday, April 27–28.

At 11:00 A.M. on Monday the secretaries of defense and state met with Nixon, Kissinger, and Haldeman in Nixon's hideaway office at the Executive Office Building. As Haldeman records, Rogers strongly opposed the invasion and "tried to hang K[issinger] for [giving] inadequate information to [the] P[resident] about [its] consequences." Rogers felt that the invasion would "cost great United States casualties with little gain. Not significant, not permanent base, not a really crippling blow." Laird, however, was less worried about invasion itself and more concerned about the way in which the Defense Department had been bypassed. When Kissinger produced a report from the commander of U.S. forces in Vietnam, General Creighton Abrams, that strongly supported the decision to intervene, Laird—who knew when to cut his losses—assented. But Rogers remained upset. He was particularly disturbed about a scheduled appearance in front of the Senate Foreign Relations Committee that afternoon. While he could hardly give full information about an upcoming invasion without robbing it of the element of surprise, Rogers insisted he would not lie in public. Nixon, always sensitive to such charges, paused and told Kissinger to suspend orders for twenty-four hours. The situation, he said, "maybe need[s] another look."

There was no such need. Nixon had simply given Rogers a chance to save face. After Rogers' appearance at the Foreign Relations Committee on Monday afternoon, Nixon called another meeting. On Tuesday morning at 10:15 he had Rogers, Laird, and Attorney General Mitchell in the Oval Office "to lay down the law" on Cambodia. The United States would "go ahead with the full plan," the president announced, regardless of the potentially adverse public reaction. Fashioning himself as a truly historical figure, Nixon later tried to place the decision ("The Decision" in Haldeman's diaries) to intervene in its proper historical perspective. Discussing the matter with Kissinger and Haldeman, he reviewed Eisenhower's decision to send the marines to Lebanon in 1958 and Kennedy's actions during the Cuban missile crisis. Nixon, Haldeman recorded in his diary, "decided this was tougher than either of those, especially since it didn't have to be made."[17]

In retrospect, it probably should not have been made. To be sure, the invasion itself began rather smoothly. While the South Vietnamese forces engaged in an operation in the Parrot's Beak area (directly west of Saigon en route to Phnom Penh), the American troops crossed the border about twenty miles farther north in an area called the Fish Hook. Meanwhile, Nixon ordered the resumption of the bombing of North Vietnam, although it was still confined to the areas immediately north of the seventeenth parallel (showing "restraint"). During the operation, which lasted until late June 1970, the ARVN and the U.S. Army managed to capture a virtual mountain of supplies, including ammunition, rockets, antiaircraft equipment, and hand grenades, while destroying large tracts of the famed North Vietnamese bunkers. When General Abrams recorded such "successes" to Nixon, the president was, it seems, elated, thinking that the North Vietnamese were "crippled" for at least a year.[18]

Ultimately the search for the communist headquarters in Cambodia proved elusive. For couple of months, the ARVN and U.S. forces, numbering up to 80,000 at their peak, trekked throughout eastern Cambodia, wrecking havoc on the countryside as they captured enemy supplies. But they rarely made direct contact with the enemy and merely managed to drive the Communists—the North Vietnamese and the Khmer Rouge—farther west. Consequently, the incursion created a large flood of refugees, most of them searching for sanctuary in Phnom Penh. Within a few years, the city's population of 600,000 would more than double. Moreover, the inevitable end result of intensified fighting was increased military and civilian casualties. Although no accurate figures have ever been confirmed, estimates of Cambodian deaths in 1970–73 vary between 100,000 and 300,000. Hence, scholars like William Shawcross are not far off the mark when they claim that Cambodia's subsequent fall to Pol Pot's murderous dictatorship was in some ways an indirect result of the decision to expand the war into (or, rather, escalate the ongoing war within) Vietnam's unhappy neighbor that caused a further destabilization of Cambodia's already fragile political, social, and economic structure.[19]

In addition, Nixon had to face the American public's reaction. The incursion made no sense to college students, who started a wave of protests around the country; as the historian Melvin Small puts it: "No single event so inflamed the college campuses as the Cambodian invasion." The most famous result of the uproar was the May 4 killing of four students at Kent State University; four days later a similar incident occurred at Jackson State University in Mississippi. In the early morning hours of May 9, Nixon—perhaps burdened by guilt, confused after too many martinis, or hoping to score a major PR victory (or, most likely, a combination of the three)—even visited a group of students at the Lincoln memorial, engaging them in a rather banal conversation about football and how Neville Chamberlain disgraced appeasement policies in the 1930s.

It was no wonder that many Americans felt betrayed by a president who had just two weeks earlier announced substantial troop withdrawals and was now saying on TV—with a straight face—that the American and South Vietnamese crossings into Cambodian territory did not constitute an invasion of that country. Arguing that more war was needed in order to guarantee a decreased American involvement in the future was less than convincing. Not surprisingly, one of the results of the invasion of Cambodia was that in late June the Senate passed a resolution (sponsored by Senators Frank Church and John Sherman Cooper) forbidding the use of U.S. troops outside South Vietnam's borders.[20]

For Kissinger, the decision to invade Cambodia had a complex impact. He had, yet again, been on the "right" side of a major decision, siding with Nixon against Rogers' recommendations. This undoubtedly strengthened his relationship with the president. Yet, within Kissinger's NSC staff, the Cambodian decision marked a major turning point. Most of the bleeding hearts decided to resign. Morris, Lake, Watts, and Lynn left, all with the exception of Lynn doing so before the invasion even commenced. Despite his serious reservations about Cambodia, Winston Lord, apparently after serious soul-searching with his wife, Bette Bao Lord, decided to stay on. At thirty-two, the future ambassador to China soon became Kissinger's special assistant (the mantle previously belonging to Tony Lake). Lord, along with Al Haig, would remain a key aide for most of Kissinger's remaining time in office. As disturbing and disappointing as the resignation of some of his brightest aides may have been, the shakeups in Kissinger's staff also served to strengthen his position within the administration. Kissinger's staff was now by and large devoid of men that Nixon might consider too liberal. Cambodia, in short, had been a test of sorts for the reliability of Kissinger's NSC staff.[21]

The resignation of the bleeding hearts did not change the fact that they had been correct about the domestic impact that sending American troops to Cambodia would have. Worst of all from Kissinger's perspective, though, was that many of the other warnings of his staff members proved equally adept. In the near term, one of the most obvious ones was the additional hurdle that the invasion produced to the possibility of Sino-American rapprochement.

"ENORMOUS, UN-CHINESE INTENSITY"

While his bleeding hearts were busy arguing against the invasion of Cambodia, two other senior members of Kissinger's staff worried about the impact that such military action would have on the prospects for an opening to China. On April 15, Helmut Sonnenfeldt and John Holdridge wrote a memorandum to Kissinger (unlike the "doves" memo, Kissinger passed this one to Nixon) regarding the state of Sino-Soviet relations and the possibilities of an American opening to China. They were rather pessimistic. Although maintaining that an invasion of Cambodia would not be enough to deter the Chinese from seeking rapprochement, Sonnenfeldt and Holdridge warned that the pace of the warming would slow down significantly.[22]

They were right. The Chinese reaction to the incursion was immediate. One of the new points of sporadic contact with the PRC, a Paris-based UNESCO worker, Ernst Winters, felt some of it during a lunch on April 30, just hours prior to Nixon's speech that announced the invasion. Upon his arrival in Washington a few days later Winters informed Kissinger of the "enormous, un-Chinese intensity" of his Chinese hosts during that meeting. "Clearly, a nerve had been touched," Winters told Kissinger when the two met to discuss the matter in Kissinger's White House office on May 3. Kissinger, aware of the complications that Cambodia was bound to create for Sino-American rapprochement, responded by asking Winters, who was scheduled to return to Paris that evening, to pass on a message to his Chinese contacts. Winters was to assure that the United States had no "aggressive intentions concerning Communist China." The message, which Winters—not knowing its actual content—passed on in early May added that "Dr. Kissinger is prepared to talk to a person of stature on the Communist China side if this can be done secretly." The Chinese, if they so wished, were simply to contact General Vernon Walters of the U.S. embassy in Paris, who had passed a similar message to the Chinese a few days earlier. Even as Vietnam was clearly a priority on his agenda in April 1970, Kissinger tried to keep the germ of Sino-American rapprochement alive. Yet, he was also doing something else: he was positioning himself as the point man of the Nixon administration's China policy that had, while the Warsaw talks were under way, remained a joint State Department–White House operation.[23]

The Chinese responded to the Cambodian invasion by canceling the prospective (if already twice postponed) May 20, 1970 meeting in Warsaw that had been set up to discuss the possible visit of a high-level American emissary to China. Concerned over the increasingly pro-Soviet tilt of North Vietnam, the Chinese could hardly remain aloof regarding the rapid succession of events in Cambodia. To bolster their regional role the Chinese embarked upon alliance building between the two Cambodian sides that Lon Nol's coup influenced the most: Prince Sihanouk and the Khmer Rouge. This was doubly important given Sihanouk's recent efforts to court Moscow; Premier Kosygin had in fact broken the news about the coup in Phnom Penh to Sihanouk as the prince was about to depart for Beijing from Moscow on March 16. Kosygin's departing words had been discouraging. "You will see how it is with the Chinese. They helped you while you were in power in Phnom Penh but now that you are no longer in power you will see what they will do!" Sihanouk, not perturbed by Kosygin, got on his plane and arrived in Beijing the following day.[24]

Zhou Enlai met Sihanouk at the Beijing airport on March 19. Pledging to uphold the prince's claim that he still was Cambodia's chief executive, the Chinese premier suggested that it was better for Sihanouk to stay in China for the time being. Sihanouk agreed. He had little choice.

While they offered Sihanouk a sanctuary in Beijing, the Chinese remained unsure about how to approach the Cambodian situation. In late March, Zhou Enlai sounded out the North Vietnamese position and was able to convince Premier Pham Van Dong that Sihanouk's popularity in Cambodia was an asset to the anti-American cause. Thus, on March 23, Sihanouk issued a general call for an anti-Lon Nol campaign and announced an alliance with the Khmer Rouge. The North Vietnamese and the NLF responded by withdrawing their diplomats from the Cambodian capital in late March. As evidence of their uncertainty, however, the Chinese retained their ambassador, Kang Maozhao, in Phnom Penh until May 5 (throughout April Kang negotiated with Lon Nol over a possible agreement). Not that this was necessarily unusual: the Soviets were also reluctant to break off diplomatic relations with Lon Nol and even suggested, on April 17, the convening of another Geneva conference. While they soon backtracked on this proposal, the Sino-Soviet rivalry clearly complicated the already patchy local picture in Cambodia.[25]

To counter the Soviets, the Chinese moved to consolidate their position in the Far East. On April 24–25, Zhou Enlai played a key role at a summit of Indochinese peoples near the city of Guangzhou in southern China. Among those attending the conference were Sihanouk, Pham Van Dong, and delegations representing Laos and the PRG. Desperately trying to rescue any possible decline in China's prestige in the area, Zhou pushed the delegates ahead to issue a declaration condemning American imperialism and its local lackeys. It called for the Indochinese people to join forces against this foe, while the Chinese promised "powerful backing" for the revolutionary war. The Chinese thus put their influence behind continued anti-American struggle in Indochina, if only to prevent any further increase in Soviet presence. They would continue to act as the "Great Rear."[26]

* * *

Against such a background it is obvious that the Chinese could hardly overlook the American incursion a few days later. Beijing accordingly promoted the creation of the Royal Government of National Union of Kampuchea (RGNUK) under Sihanouk's leadership on May 5, 1970, the same day as the PRC withdrew its ambassador from Phnom Penh to coordinate the anti-Lon Nol resistance. Still, it took another two weeks for the May 19 announcement that the Warsaw ambassadorial meeting would not take place. Mao himself, through the *Beijing Review*, condemned Nixon's "fascist atrocities." A few days later, on May 25, Beijing and Hanoi signed a supplementary trade agreement that provided additional economic and military aid to the DRV. As a result, over the next few years, Chinese military aid to the DRV significantly increased, even as the course of Sino-American rapprochement was restored. In short, from the Chinese perspective the Cambodian invasion ran contrary to the hopeful signs of a decreased U.S. role in the region, including the Nixon Doctrine, and provided an opportunity to increase Chinese influence with the North Vietnamese. Equally important was the calculation that their possible inactivity might drive the DRV further toward the Soviets and increase Hanoi's influence with the Khmer Rouge.[27]

In the spring of 1970, the Vietnam War thus once again had a major impact on the unfolding of triangular diplomacy. The decision to launch a joint U.S.-South Vietnamese invasion of Cambodia was a severe roadblock to the opening to China. It also highlighted how much control and how many second thoughts the Chinese had over the pace of the opening. For while the possibility of rapprochement with the United States was of increasing importance to the PRC's foreign policy agenda, pushing ahead at full steam was extremely difficult and domestically risky for a

China trying to maintain its position as a key revolutionary power in the Far East. The ongoing internal struggles of the Cultural Revolution, the differences between radical ideologues led by Lin Biao and realpoliticians siding with Zhou Enlai was still unresolved, and the possibility of rapprochement with the USSR—which still was technically China's ally—ensured that the Chinese would, even in the best of circumstances, move cautiously with its emerging diplomatic relationship with the United States. Within the context of the Cambodian events, however, such moves could simply not continue as if nothing had happened.[28]

From Kissinger's perspective there was a bright spot in all this. The death of the State Department's Warsaw contact meant a bureaucratic (if somewhat Pyrrhic) victory for Kissinger. He could now truly coordinate the administration's China policy. As his signals via Paris and Pakistan indicated, Kissinger had positioned himself as the key man in the process that would eventually lead to his dramatic secret trip to China in July 1971. While he had previously been a player engaged in the administration's efforts to devise a new China policy, he had now, in the spring of 1970, emerged as *the* player. Yet, it did not translate into immediate success in the arduous road toward a Sino-American rapprochement. By urging the invasion of Cambodia, Kissinger had also played a major role in adding the latest hurdle to the opening to China.

This was doubly unfortunate because the Nixon administration needed added leverage vis-à-vis the USSR. As peace in Vietnam remained elusive and the chance for an early opening to China had slipped away, Moscow's "intransigence" (a favorite Kissinger word) had reached new levels.

DÉTENTE STALLED

Throughout April, the Soviets complained about U.S. policy in Cambodia. In back-channel meetings on April 7 and 9, Dobrynin warned Kissinger against military escalation. On April 29, 1970, the Soviet Union's charge d'affaires, Yuli Vorontsov, called upon Kissinger at the White House and handed him a formal note of complaint that stressed Moscow's "definitely negative attitude towards the United States interference into internal affairs of Cambodia." Kissinger, well aware of the forthcoming incursion, took a harsh line, asking Vorontsov why the Soviets made no mention of the presence of foreign (i.e., North Vietnamese) troops in Cambodia at the time. When Vorontsov replied that the only foreign troops there he knew about were from South Vietnam, Kissinger closed the brief meeting. "There was no point in continuing the conversation [until Vorontsov] would be better briefed," he said.[29]

The Soviets did not react to the Cambodian incursion in an overtly aggressive manner. Naturally, the Kremlin had to protest. Thus, in early May, Soviet Premier Alexei Kosygin gave a press conference using exceedingly harsh language. Yet,

Kissinger noted to Nixon, Kosygin made no new public commitment to Hanoi but simply gave the United States "a general warning." To be sure, Kosygin linked the incursion to the general development of Soviet-American relations and progress in SALT negotiations.[30]

Even without Cambodia, however, the SALT talks were effectively deadlocked. On April 28, Vorontsov had met with Helmut Sonnenfeldt, Kissinger's chief Soviet aide. The two had discussed the second phase of the SALT talks and concurred that "an agreement was a long way off."[31] Much like the exploratory Helsinki phase of SALT talks, the talks in the Austrian capital were distinctive mostly for the lack of common ground. Questions over on-site inspection and MIRVs still stalled progress. For example, the Soviets rejected an American proposal to ban MIRVs at the outset of the Vienna talks. This was hardly a surprise. The American delegation, led by Ambassador Gerard Smith, had been authorized to deliver a proposal calling for on-site inspections and a ban on the testing and deployment (but not the production) of MIRVs.[32] The Soviets refused on-site inspection outright and responded with a proposal that called for a ban on production and deployment (but not testing) of MIRVs. As Raymond Garthoff, a member of the U.S. delegation, put it, the Soviets found the American proposals unacceptable on MIRVs because it "would have left the United States with the option of producing and storing (merely not deploying) MIRV warheads in unlimited quantities." Oleg Grinevsky, a member of the Soviet delegation, later told Garthoff: "We had been hoping you would make serious MIRV proposal."[33] To the consternation of many, not least Garthoff, the inclusion of MIRVs in a prospective nuclear arms control agreement—and hence the conclusion of a comprehensive arms control agreement—was beginning to look increasingly impossible.

The American delegation also made another proposal in Vienna. This one had to do with the number of strategic nuclear launchers each side was allowed to have. Americans proposed a freeze at the level of 1,710, the combined number of SLBM and ICBM launchers the Americans held at the time. Hidden in the proposal, though, was a clear attempt to maintain American superiority: it omitted several American launchers able to strike the Soviets while including some Soviet missiles unable to hit the United States. In particular, American forward-bases were excluded, while the proposal called for a reduction in land-based missile forces that were a particular strength for the USSR. Moreover, the U.S. proposal called for a limit on Soviet SS-9s that, many thought at the time, had a high potential for being converted to MIRV use. No wonder the Soviets rejected the proposal.[34]

The Vienna SALT meetings dragged on until August 1970 with limited progress. To be sure, the two delegations made some headway on the issue of defensive missiles, as the Soviets accepted an American proposal to limit the ABMs to cover Washington and Moscow. Moreover, in late July and early August the American delegation finally dropped the MIRV bans from its proposal in order to advance the talks on offensive missiles. But questions about what to count continued to plague the talks and made serious progress impossible. Effectively, the Vienna talks thus ended in an impasse. The next stage of talks, scheduled to begin in Helsinki in November 1970, would only confirm the deadlock.[35]

The SALT deadlock was equally evident on the back channel. On February 18, Kissinger suggested to Dobrynin that the two add SALT to their agenda; Dobrynin agreed to the two-channel approach a month later. In subsequent, virtually weekly, meetings, the two men further developed their mutually respectful and cordial relationship. But no substantive progress was made. By June Dobrynin flatly announced that no agreement was possible in Vienna but expressed the Soviets' interest in an agreement that would only cover the ABM systems. Kissinger rejected the offer. The United States would not "split off ABMs as a separate agreement," he told Dobrynin during a back-channel meeting on July 20.[36]

Nixon, eager for some sort of foreign policy success as the 1970 mid-term elections approached, had also instructed Kissinger to press Dobrynin for a high-level summit meeting, preferably to be convened in September or October 1970. But the Soviets stalled. Instead, in July 1970 Dobrynin showed his ability to play the linkage game. Meeting with Kissinger on the presidential yacht *Sequoia* on July 13, the Soviet ambassador hinted that an early summit was, of course, a possibility. But the Americans would have to deliver something first. In particular, Dobrynin stressed that compromises on the Middle East and SALT were needed if a superpower summit were to be held in 1970. Kissinger retorted by indicating that the United States was ready for a "fundamental departure in our relations with the Soviets but that we must move soon."[37]

In the summer of 1970, Kissinger and Dobrynin were engaged in a stalling competition. Linkage trumped linkage. As a precondition to an early summit meeting Kissinger pressed for some meaningful progress on Vietnam. Dobrynin responded by asking for joint action to defuse the tense situation in the Middle East. At one point the Soviet ambassador showed his fairly sophisticated understanding of American domestic politics by asking whether the Nixon administration was thinking that a summit, if held in 1970, should take place before or after the November congressional elections. It was a sparring match in which each side was hoping the other would make an unlikely concession. While the Soviet side probably thought that time was on their side, the Americans could not see that things could get much more difficult. In August, while Kissinger professed to Nixon his belief that "a summit meeting is under active consideration at the highest level" in Moscow and that "something big was stirring" among the Soviet leadership, he could not offer anything concrete. Kissinger also had to concede that "the Soviets [were] not yet ready to commit themselves (to a summit) officially." It was clear that the president would not have a summit before the November 1970 mid-term congressional elections.[38]

In addition to SALT, Vietnam, and the Middle East, there were several other contentious issues and strategies that made the back channel a less than effective medium in the summer of 1970. None of these issues was more central than the unfolding of *Ostpolitik*.

OSTPOLITIK AND ANOTHER BACK CHANNEL

In 1970 European developments lacked the heightened drama of the Vietnam War. Yet, the old continent remained central to American foreign policy. Most obviously, the NATO alliance was a major part of the basic structure of U.S. policy toward the Soviet Union; its cohesiveness was a necessary ingredient in building détente. Conversely, any rupture within the alliance—such as France's partial exit from NATO in 1966 as part of President Charles de Gaulle's search for a more independent French-European policy—was bound to complicate the building of Soviet-American détente. Indeed, a consistent worry throughout the late 1960s and early 1970s was that the Soviet Union would be able to play on any differences within NATO to advance its own agenda. And the country that remained the focus of such concerns during the first Nixon administration was West Germany. The individual who commanded their interest was the 1971 Nobel Peace Prize laureate, Willy Brandt.

Born in 1913, the same year as Nixon, Willy Brandt had a background that bore some interesting similarities to that of Kissinger. Although not Jewish, Brandt escaped Hitler's Germany in the 1930s and, after losing his German citizenship in 1938 (the same year as Kissinger and his family left Germany), Brandt, like Kissinger, became a citizen of another country, Norway. Brandt spent most of 1933–45 in Scandinavia (Norway and Sweden) and his close affinity to Scandinavia was strengthened through two marriages to Norwegian women. His ideas of social democracy were undoubtedly shaped by his experiences in the region that boasted to have perfected a middle way between socialism and capitalism, between the Soviet Union and the United States. Having returned to Germany after the war, Brandt, who had worked as journalist and, in 1947–48, as the Norwegian press attaché in Berlin, decided to enter politics and regained his German citizenship. His political rise was meteoric: Brandt was elected to the *Bundestag* in 1949, became the governing mayor of Berlin in 1957, and was the foreign minister of Kiesinger's Grand Coalition government in 1966. After two failed attempts, in 1961 and 1965, Brandt's Social Democrats finally scored a sufficient victory in 1969 to become the major partner in a coalition government with the Free Democratic Party led by Walter Scheel.[39]

By this time Brandt's *Ostpolitik* (his policy of West German rapprochement with East Germany and its Warsaw Pact allies) was already well publicized as the party line of the Social Democratic Party (SDP). Its basic outline was straightforward. During the Adenauer era and most of the 1960s, the Federal Republic had refused to establish diplomatic relations with any country that recognized East Germany. While such a hard line was meant to eventually bring about German unification by isolating (and thus destroying its chances of independent existence) East Germany, the Halstein Doctrine had not, by the late 1960s, brought the prospect of unification any closer. By 1963 Egon Bahr, Brandt's longtime associate and foreign policy adviser, had coined the notion of change through rapprochement (*Wandel durch Annäherung*), the idea that a policy of engagement would bring about a gradual change in the East German regime. In short, in the late 1960s Brandt and Bahr set out to put in practice their alternative approach to West German foreign policy in the hopes that it would gradually create conditions under which eventual unification would be possible.[40]

Brandt's victory in the September 28, 1969 elections had opened up a new era in the Federal Republic's foreign policy. The time of the Hallstein Doctrine was now firmly in the past and the period of *Ostpolitik*—of rapprochement between West and East Germany, between Bonn and Moscow—was about to begin. In the early 1970s, a number of treaties were signed: a Non-Aggression Pact with the USSR in August 1970, a West German-Polish Treaty recognizing the Oder-Neisse line in December 1970, a Four-Power agreement on the status of Berlin in 1971 and, finally, the Basic Treaty between East and West Germany in 1972. In a span of few years the German question was transformed from being the focal point of East-West tensions to becoming the centrepiece of détente.

Kissinger and Nixon had problems with Brandt's diplomacy and the direction that *Ostpolitik* might take. In particular, Kissinger thought that *Ostpolitik* might, if it proved successful as a unilateral West German policy, become a new form of Gaullism, that is, that it would create similar transatlantic tensions as de Gaulle's search for an independent French role had done during the Kennedy and Johnson presidencies.[41] The problem was that the United States could not, without risking an adverse reaction in West Germany and countries that either supported or condoned Brandt's policy (including Britain), move to block the progress of *Ostpolitik*. Moreover, should they object to the overwhelming desire for détente in Europe, the Nixon administration would have played into Soviet hands by promoting further disunity within NATO. As Kissinger put it in February 1970:

> [there is] a danger that as Brandt pursues the quest for normalization, his advisers and supporters will eventually succeed in leading him to jeopardize Germany's entire international position . . . [while] there is no necessary incompatibility between alliance and integration with the West on the one hand, and some degree of normalization with East, on the other . . . assuming Brandt achieves a degree of normalization, he or his successor may discover before long that the hoped-for benefits fail to develop. Instead of ameliorating the division of Germany, recognition of the G[erman] D[emocratic] R[epublic] may boost its status and strengthen the Communist regime . . . More fundamentally, the Soviets having achieved their first set of objectives may then confront the FRG with the proposition that a real and lasting improvement in the FRG's relations with the GDR and other Eastern countries can only be achieved if Bonn loosens its Western ties.

"[M]en like Brandt, Wehner and Defense Minister Schmidt undoubtedly see themselves as conducting a responsible policy," Kissinger added. But he warned "their problem is to control a process which, if it results in failure could jeopardize their political lives and if it succeeds could create a momentum that may shake Germany's domestic stability and unhinge its international position"[42]

*   *   *

The answer to the puzzle was to work with Brandt in order to push *Ostpolitik* in the right direction. Kissinger and Nixon's European policy focused, in effect, on co-opting Willy Brandt's *Ostpolitik*. As he wrote in 1979 Kissinger "sought to channel [West German foreign policy] in a constructive direction by working closely with Brandt and his colleagues." Indeed, Kissinger saw as his main task the need to coordinate, as much as was possible, U.S.-Soviet détente with the unfolding of Brandt's *Ostpolitik*. There needed to be linkage. In Kissinger's words: "If *Ostpolitik* were to succeed, it had to be related to other issues involving the Alliance as a whole; only in this manner would the Soviet Union have incentives for compromise."[43]

The effort to anchor West Germany's policy to that of the United States had commenced at the start of the Nixon presidency. Already during his February 1969 trip Nixon had warned Brandt (at the time the foreign minister) and Chancellor Kurt Kiesinger that the Soviets' interest in *Ostpolitik* was part of "a major Soviet objective to weaken the [NATO] alliance and especially the FRG."[44] A few months later, at an April 1969 NATO ministerial conference in Washington, Kissinger's concerns became apparent to Brandt. In his memoirs Brandt recalled the public warnings against "selective" détente directed, no doubt, toward the West Germans. Brandt, echoing a persistent German (and European) concern wrote: "this meant that Washington wanted to have the last word."[45]

The West Germans, including Brandt, had no intention of breaking away from NATO; what they wanted to do was find a way of aligning *Ostpolitik* with NATO policy. Brandt was after a new kind of equilibrium between East and West in Europe, an equilibrium in which the United States played a key role by maintaining its presence on the old continent. This was not dramatically different from Kissinger's own ideas or from Nixon's talk of a structure of peace. The problem for Kissinger was not with the Germans. It was that the Soviets could use *Ostpolitik* to their advantage by moving toward Soviet-West European détente that would gradually drive a wedge within the transatlantic relationship. To Kissinger, *Ostpolitik*, if not properly managed, would easily become an asset for the USSR to be used to counter any leverage that the United States might get from improving relations with China.

Brandt also well understood the need to coordinate his policies with those of the United States. Nor did he have any illusions as to who, aside from Nixon, was the prime foreign policy maker in Washington. In October 1969 he sent Bahr to the United States to meet Kissinger, not Rogers, thus creating another Kissinger back channel. In the October discussions Bahr outlined to Kissinger—who would in private call Brandt's envoy a "reptilian" influence[46]—the way that *Ostpolitik* was to unfold in the near future, detailing the planned West German overtures toward the USSR, Poland, and East Germany. In his report to Nixon that was drafted by Helmut Sonnenfeldt, Kissinger's key adviser on Europe, Kissinger warned that the planned German initiatives "could become troublesome if they engender euphoria, affect Germany's contribution to NATO and give ammunition to our own détente-minded people here at home. The Germans may also become so engaged in their Eastern policy that their commitment to West European unity may decline. The Soviets, and with some apparent prodding by Moscow, [East German leader Walter] Ulbricht, seem willing enough to receive Bonn's overtures." Yet, Kissinger's talks with Bahr also implied that the United States held significant leverage that could be used to channel *Ostpolitik* in the right direction: Bahr had expressed concern about unilateral U.S. troop cuts in Germany. Kissinger had promised that this would be done only after consultations, but that there were likely to be some cuts over the next two years. At the end of their meeting Bahr had said that there was likely to be "less of a guilt complex in Bonn under Brandt and hence more self-reliant and not always compliant attitude toward us." Kissinger agreed and promised Bahr that the United States would "deal with Germany as a partner, not a client." According to Bahr, Kissinger added: "your success will be ours."[47]

By the spring of 1970 it was clear that the Brandt–Bahr *Ostpolitik* had claimed the forerunner's role in East-West détente. This increased Kissinger's concern that *Ostpolitik* played into the hands of the Soviet Union and was, therefore, partly responsible for the slow pace of Soviet-American détente. Thus, when Brandt visited the United States in April 1970, in the midst of the Cambodian crisis, hoping to get the Nixon administration's formal endorsement of *Ostpolitik,* Kissinger was distinctly recalcitrant. When his key European adviser, Helmut Sonnenfeldt, informed Kissinger that the State Department considered *Ostpolitik* as beneficial to Western unity because it allowed for more flexibility vis-à-vis the East and reduced fears of a unified Germany, Kissinger's comment was succinct. "Baloney," he responded. Instead, Kissinger specifically warned Nixon against endorsing any specific element of *Ostpolitik* in public.[48]

Nixon, while siding with his national security adviser, decided that confronting Brandt was ultimately futile and potentially counterproductive. During his meeting with the West German leader on April 11, Nixon said that he had confidence in FRG policy but warned, correctly so, that there might be some uncertainty in France and Britain, as well as among the old style cold warriors in the United States. Nixon told Brandt that he understood if the Germans were willing to recognize the Oder-Neisse line (the frontier between Germany and Poland established in 1945) and simply stressed that "the main point was the understanding between us that we would keep in close touch over all East-West questions." Brandt was "greatly relieved" over American reassurances, Kissinger recollects. Yet, as the memorandum of the conversation of April 11 suggests, the difference in the two leaders' emphasis was clear: while Nixon stressed alliance solidarity, Brandt focused on "new paths" to Eastern Europe.[49]

In fact, whatever Nixon had chosen to say would have been unlikely to stop the momentum of *Ostpolitik*. On March 19, almost a month prior to his trip to Washington, Brandt had met with the East German leader Willi Stoph in Erfurt. As the inter-German talks proved unproductive at this stage, Egon Bahr, under instructions from Brandt, pressed ahead with his Soviet diplomacy. Bahr, with whom Kissinger had established another back channel, did, though, keep Kissinger informed of his talks with the Soviets. The key moment came in May 1970, when Bahr went to Moscow for an extensive session of secret talks.

The result was a set of agreements that quickly leaked to the West German press and became the basis for formal treaties to be concluded in subsequent years. West Germany agreed to recognize the postwar border changes (the Oder-Neisse line in particular), Bonn would formally renounce the use of force as a means of changing borders, and the Federal Republic would establish a formal relationship with the German Democratic Republic. Bahr also confirmed that Bonn would throw its support behind the Soviet-inspired proposal for a multilateral Conference on European Security (that would later become the Conference on Security and Cooperation in Europe and climax at a thirty-five-nation meeting in 1975), renounce nuclear weapons, and seek to build a mutually profitable economic relationship with the USSR. Such agreements provided the crux of the Soviet-West German treaty that was signed in Moscow on August 12, 1970, less than a year after Brandt's election as chancellor. Yet, Walter Scheel, Brandt's foreign minister and head of the Free Democrats, had negotiated some important caveats in his July talks with Soviet Foreign Minister Andrei Gromyko. In particular, Gromyko agreed to an accompanying statement expressing support for German unification (through peaceful means). Moreover, the conclusion of a new agreement on Berlin—negotiated between the four occupying powers and the two Germanies—was understood to be a condition for the eventual FRG ratification of the West German-Soviet treaty.[50]

The "Berlin condition" was an indication that despite the apparently bilateral process between Bonn and Moscow, the Soviets were unlikely to succeed in engineering a decisive split between the United States and the Federal Republic of Germany (FRG)—or ultimately between the United States and Western Europe. In fact, it seems that for most of the Kremlin's top brass such an outcome was neither expected nor particularly desirable. As Michael Sodaro writes, prominent Soviet officials, including Brezhnev, Kosygin, Suslov, Podgorny, and Gromyko, all favored détente with West Germany but did not view it as a way station to some sort of a neutralization-unification-pacification solution. An undercurrent of traditional Soviet distrust of Germany resulted in continued Soviet arms buildup despite the unfolding of *Ostpolitik*. The Soviet leadership explicitly refused to link military and political détente, a linkage that was the ultimate goal of Brandt's *Ostpolitik*. As Sodrano writes:

the Brezhnev coalition deeply feared the potential political effects of comprehensive disarmament in Europe . . . While a withdrawal of troops and weaponry
from the continent might well reduce America's role in Europe substantially, it
would also emasculate the Kremlin's controls over Eastern Europe. A West German government that could no longer be portrayed as a serious threat to the
security of the region would only accelerate the East Europeans' desire to free
themselves from Soviet domination. To risk potentially irresistible pressures to
establish a unified and powerful German state, while at the same time risking the
disintegration of Moscow's security buffer in Eastern Europe, would be to jeopardize virtually everything Leonid Brezhnev and his generation of Soviet leaders
had fought for in World War II and immediately afterward.[51]

In other words, *Ostpolitik* did not break down Western unity in large part because
the Soviets resisted pushing strongly for a selective détente in the first place. The
rapid succession of treaties after the Soviet-West German agreement in August 1970
probably had their most profound impact on the German-German level, allowing
the process of engagement to begin its gradual progression.

OUTMANEUVERED?

Although things were apparently not going according to plan in the summer of
1970, Kissinger had retained his sense of humor. "I am sitting here on [the] back
patio thinking about peaceful coexistence," he told Soviet ambassador Anatoly
Dobrynin over the telephone on July 28. "Good for you, Henry," replied Dobrynin.
"I am living with the same thought," he added.[52]

The trouble was that as the second anniversary of Nixon's election and the mid-
term congressional elections of November 1970 approached, the administration
had very little to show for its effort at reshaping American foreign policy. There had
been no obvious breakthroughs—quite the contrary given the incursion of Cambodia—regarding Vietnam, no significant agreements with the Soviets on détente,
and no progress on the China front.

In the fall of 1970 Kissinger found West German *Ostpolitik* particularly worrying. It was bound to play into the Soviets' hands by increasing intra-European suspicions and strengthening Moscow's hand in Soviet-American negotiations. As he
put it in early September 1970, "other European nations will sense a growing FRG
attitude of self-importance and independence and this will be disturbing—particularly for the French." Kissinger added: "as a result of the signature of the German-
Soviet Treaty, European political relationships have turned a corner, and we will be
facing a new period in our relationship with Europe."[53] In October Kissinger further worried about the apparent resurgence of French independent diplomacy with
the USSR. After President Pompidou visited Moscow for eight days in October

1970, Kissinger was concerned that the Soviets were "succeeding in stimulating the competition between Bonn and Paris that they have long wanted."[54]

With the European situation in flux in the summer and fall of 1970—and with Brandt spearheading a general improvement in East-West relations with its uncertain consequences—the need to regain American leadership and initiative was becoming an increasingly pressing concern for the White House. Assuming that the USSR was trying to separate the United States and its allies by practicing independent diplomacy with both, and relating this to the general deadlock in Soviet-American relations, Kissinger could only conclude that the Soviets had become ardent practitioners of linkage. The Soviets were eager to push for European détente, he wrote to Nixon, because they believed that "movement along the lines of a European rapprochement will eventually also increase pressures on the US to move on the Middle East settlement, and perhaps on SALT as well, lest we become isolated on positions which have no support from our principal allies."[55] Were the Soviets outmaneuvering the Americans? In the fall of 1970 this seemed like a worrying possibility.

But Kissinger did not just worry about the Soviets and their maneuvers. What caused him to lose far more sleep was the possibility that Nixon was actually listening to Secretary of State William Rogers. As Haldeman recorded in his diaries, on August 15 Nixon invited Rogers—together with a number of others including Ehrlichman and Haldeman—for a quiet Saturday night at Camp David. What was probably an innocent social occasion turned into a "monumental flap." Kissinger, not invited, spent the night fuming with Al Haig and called Haldeman the following day. He accused Nixon of "playing games" and trying to "cover up" his intentions. On August 17, Kissinger was still "very bitter and uptight," Haldeman noticed. Nixon, learning about the incident, told Haldeman that the incident was worrying because it showed Kissinger's inability to see things clearly and his proclivity for "delusions." Nixon even wondered whether Kissinger had "reached the end of his usefulness."[56]

He had not. Yet, the incident was symptomatic of how insecure Kissinger remained after spending seventeen months in the Nixon White House. And for good reason. For he had yet to prove himself. Despite an elaborate set of back channels and easy access to Nixon, Kissinger had not delivered any major breakthroughs. As a result, the president had good reason to doubt not only Kissinger's mental stability but also his foreign policy acumen. No man was, after all, irreplaceable. Fortunately for Kissinger, a series of opportunities for demonstrating his abilities and securing his role as the foreign policy czar of the Nixon administration lay just around the corner.

6

Crises and Opportunities

Instead of a summit with the Soviets in the fall of 1970, Kissinger and Nixon faced a series of crises in the Middle East and Latin America. The virtually simultaneous developments in Cuba (where the Soviets were apparently building a submarine base), Chile (where the socialist candidate Salvador Allende claimed the presidency despite strenuous U.S. efforts to the contrary), and Jordan (where a Palestinian uprising led to near full-scale regional war) were reminders of the interconnected nature of regional developments and Soviet-American relations.

From the perspective of their maximum goals, Kissinger and Nixon could only view the end results of the three crises as a mixed bag. On the negative side, the administration found itself unable to prevent the confirmation of Allende as the president of Chile in October 1970. Yet, if one considered Chile within the broader context of the unfolding of American foreign policy and the efforts to launch triangular diplomacy, it hardly mattered. It was, as Kissinger so memorably is said to have quipped, "a dagger pointed at the heart of Antarctica." Chile was, at the time, an irritant, a blemish. But it seemed peripheral when set against the overall goal of détente with the Soviet Union.

The Middle East and Cuba were far more central to Kissinger for a simple reason: both involved, rather directly, the interests of the Soviet Union. And in both cases, he could argue, a strong American stance produced a positive result: the Soviets backed down on Cuba and the Soviet-armed Syrians did not launch an all-out attack against Jordan. For Kissinger, the 1970 Middle East crisis had yet another important outcome: it confirmed his role as the key policy maker in an area that

Nixon had initially reserved to Secretary of State Rogers. With increasingly strong hints about a potential opening coming from Beijing at the end of 1970, even the hopeless state of the Vietnam War could not hurt Kissinger's stock in Nixon's eyes. By his tough stands during the three crises of the fall of 1970 and by supporting another escalation of the Vietnam War (the South Vietnamese invasion of Laos in February 1971), Kissinger clearly earned Nixon's trust. Two years after arriving in Washington Kissinger had not only survived, he had confirmed his position as the foreign policy czar. It was a position he would not relinquish.

BLACK SEPTEMBER

The 1970 crisis in Jordan began as a revolt by groups of radical Palestinian refugees against the rule of King Hussein. Although Jordan had provided a home for the roughly million Palestinian refugees (most had come as early as after the 1948 Arab-Israeli War, but another 200,000 had fled Israeli armies during the 1967 Six Days War), Hussein's tentative peace feelers toward Israel after 1967 threatened the radical Palestinian goal of destroying the Jewish state. To many, the young King Hussein was also a symbol of reactionary forces within the Arab world. He had narrowly escaped an assassination attempt in June 1970.

At the time, Hussein's Jordan—a country Winston Churchill had, according to some accounts, dreamed up in the back of a car—was an extremely turbulent piece of real estate. The major cause was the continued unrest among the Palestinian refugee population. Since the 1967 War, the forty-one-year-old Yasser Arafat had effectively established a Palestinian state within Hussein's Jordanian Bedouin state. Arafat set up headquarters in the town of Karameh (about four miles east of the Jordan River). From there, Arafat and his Fatah organization conducted terrorist attacks against Israeli targets in the occupied West Bank. Arafat, who counted among his patrons the Egyptian president Gamal Abdel Nasser, quickly emerged as the symbolic leader of the Palestinian movement, taking over the Palestine Liberation Organization (PLO, an umbrella organization of eight Palestinian groups). Over the years, Arafat, the 5 feet 4 inches tall man who always seemed to wear his headscarf, would become the international symbol of the Palestinian movement and (amid controversy that rivaled the announcement of Kissinger's prize in 1973), would, in 1993, become one of the few self-proclaimed terrorists to be awarded the Nobel Peace Prize.

In 1970, though, it was the Popular Front for the Liberation of Palestine (PFLP), led by a devout Marxist, George Habash, that triggered the crisis. A Palestinian Christian, Habash had left Palestine in 1948 at the age of twenty-three and obtained a medical degree from the American University in Beirut, Lebanon. In the 1950s and 1960s he had become more involved in various Palestinian causes and became increasingly radical after the 1967 War, founding the PFLP in 1968. Although relatively small,

Habash's PFLP gained international notoriety with a bizarre series of hijackings in September 1970: four planes with several hundred passengers were taken over by members of the PFLP, forced to fly to an abandoned military airport near Amman (called Dawson's field), and, after the release of hostages, blown up. No one was hurt and no Palestinian activists were released from Israeli jails (one of the demands of the hijackers). But the world's attention focused, for the first time in a concerted way, on the connection between terrorism and the plight of the Palestinian refugees.

King Hussein, still reeling from the humiliation of the assassination attempt and worried about the impact on Jordan's security of the continued Palestinian raids to the West Bank, decided it was time to act. On the morning of September 17, the Jordanian army moved against various Palestinian strongholds. Although he played a mediating role in the release of a number of hostages, Arafat, along with other PLO leaders, made the removal of Hussein one of the goals of what was quickly building up to a serious crisis for the Jordanian ruler. To make matters worse for Hussein, his northern neighbor Syria, whose support Arafat had actively sought since 1967, appeared ready to take advantage of the situation and support the Palestinian revolt. And behind Syria lurked its major arms supplier, the Soviet Union. A serious international crisis loomed.[1]

* * *

At the time, the Nixon administration's Middle East policy was sorely lacking in direction and woefully uninterested in the Palestinian question. Initially, the Middle East had been the one region in the world where Nixon—in part because he thought that Kissinger as a Jew could not act impartially when the interests of Israel were concerned—had allowed Secretary of State Rogers to play a major policy-making role at the start of the administration. But Rogers was unable to deliver. In the summer of 1970 the region remained even more volatile than it had been at the start of the administration. The Rogers Plan of October 1969 had embodied the search for a comprehensive negotiated peace settlement among the key countries in the region and under the auspices of the United States and the Soviet Union. But it had met with strong objections from all sides. It was effectively sabotaged by Israeli and Egyptian border raids in late 1969 and throughout the first half of 1970. Although both sides did accept—the Israelis reluctantly and with a subsequent shakeup of the government—a standstill ceasefire (called the Rogers Initiative) in July 1970, even this measure appeared poised for collapse in early September as the Egyptians began a deployment of missile sites close to the Suez Canal. As Jordan suddenly erupted, the Arab-Israeli conflict was, yet again, heating up.

The failure of the State Department's Rogers Plan and Rogers Initiative was in part a result of Kissinger's successful effort to tie any progress in the region to progress in other areas, most specifically Vietnam. Already in June 1969 he had told Dobrynin that at the time the State Department was not giving "top level attention to the Middle East," thus intimating that Rogers' involvement did not count as "top level." In the fall of 1969, after he met secretly with North Vietnam's Xuan Thuy in Paris (see chapter 3), Kissinger also managed to convince Nixon that it was important to tie the Middle East settlement to progress on Vietnam. The United States should "not move too fast on the Middle East," Kissinger argued during a telephone conversation with the president on September 27, 1969, until the Soviets used their influence in Hanoi. He wanted a quid pro quo of sorts. Nixon listened attentively and concluded that Kissinger was right. He promised to "cool off Rogers" on the Middle East.[2]

In the first half of 1970 Kissinger assumed an increasingly important role in the Nixon administration's Middle East policy. In February 1970, Kissinger indicated to Dobrynin that Nixon approved the inclusion of the Middle East as an item in the back channel. The next month Dobrynin told Kissinger that the Soviets were ready to press Egypt and Syria, provided the Americans exerted influence on Israel. In a memo to Nixon, Kissinger celebrated this as an indication that his recommendation to hold back on any serious multilateral efforts, such as the Rogers Plan, had been the right thing to do. As he wrote, "our policy of relative firmness has paid off . . . The Soviet Union has made the first move . . . holding firm and offering no concessions was the right course." Of course, this also meant that if Kissinger was correct, then Rogers had been wrong. Nixon, always ready to side with firmness, agreed with Kissinger.[3]

Kissinger's enhanced role in America's Middle East policy resulted in a shift from an effort to find a balanced solution via multilateral negotiations to a policy that relied on Israeli military strength as the key to stability in the region. Underlining this shift was Kissinger and Nixon's belief that this was the only way of minimizing Soviet influence in the region (and stationing the United States as the key country in future regional initiatives and settlements). Perhaps more important in the context of 1970, when the possibility of a regional settlement was minimal, Kissinger, true to his realist instincts, viewed the region as a means to another end.

In 1970 the Middle East emerged as one of Kissinger's major carrots in trying to extract Soviet aid on forging a settlement in Vietnam; the Middle East became another form of linkage. For example, in March and April 1970, when Dobrynin pressed him to lean on the Israelis to stop their continued border raids against Egypt, Kissinger responded, "The key to our attitude in the Middle East would be found in the Soviet attitude toward Vietnam." While Dobrynin did not take the bait on Vietnam, Kissinger offered no movement on the Middle East. By June 1970, however, as Egyptian and Israeli retaliatory strikes continued, Dobrynin charged the United States for deliberate stonewalling that was only making an already volatile situation worse. "It's [the border raids] your problem now, he told Kissinger at the end of their meeting on June 23. Dobrynin was more conciliatory after the Rogers Initiative in July promised at least a temporary ceasefire. Yet, as he was about to leave for consultations in Moscow at the end of July, Dobrynin warned Kissinger against "a unilateral approach" in the Middle East.[4]

Unilateralism was exactly what Kissinger had in mind when the Jordanian crisis suddenly commenced and King Hussein's army moved against Palestinians on September 17, 1970, capturing the PLO headquarters in Amman and shelling several refugee camps. From the U.S.-Israeli perspective a successful Palestinian takeover of Jordan (or even part thereof) would not only depose the most moderate Arab leader in the region but also, due to the Palestinian groups' links to Soviet-supported Syria, create an opportunity for increased Soviet influence. In short, for both the Americans and the Israelis, King Hussein's survival was crucial.

From the outset the crisis in Jordan threatened to escalate. Part of the fighting between the Jordanian army and the Palestinians took place in northern Jordan, prompting Syria to move tanks to their border with Jordan. On September 19, reports indicated that some of these tanks had started to cross into Jordan (with hastily painted Palestinian markings on them). Given Syria's dependency on Soviet military aid, Kissinger interpreted the move as Soviet-inspired.

Over the next few days Kissinger, with Nixon's blessing (and to Rogers' dismay), engineered a series of controversial moves. Already on September 17, while Nixon was campaigning in Chicago, he had ordered an additional (there were already two) aircraft carrier to the eastern Mediterranean to boost American presence in the region. In response to King Hussein's pleas for help he also recruited Israeli assistance; by the morning of September 21, Israeli Ambassador Yitzhak Rabin informed Kissinger that the Israelis were considering both air strikes and a ground attack against the Syrians. The following day, Israeli tanks started moving to the Jordan River and preparing for potential strikes against Syria from the Golan Heights. King Hussein, who may have wanted external support but was at best ambivalent about the prospect of Israeli assistance (and unequivocally rejected any possibility of having Israeli ground troops in Jordan), launched a counterattack against Syrian forces. By September 22 Syrian tanks, possibly suffering from Israeli air attacks,[5] began to retreat. Five days later, Hussein and Arafat met in Cairo under the auspices of Nasser. They agreed to a ceasefire and the withdrawal of Palestinian army and guerrilla forces from major Jordanian cities. The Jordanian crisis gradually withered away.[6]

The end result of the crisis was, more or less, what Kissinger had wanted: King Hussein's position was strengthened, the Syrian invasion blocked, and the Palestinian uprising thwarted. With the sudden death of the Egyptian leader Gamal Abdel Nasser only a day after the Arafat–Hussein ceasefire (Nasser had a stroke soon after seeing his guests off to the airport) he had helped to mediate, the American position in the Middle East suddenly appeared brighter. Consequently, the Soviets' ambitions had suffered a setback, thus "raising by another notch the growing Arab disenchantment with Moscow."[7]

If all this was true then, surely, the time had come for the United States (perhaps Kissinger himself) to play a significant role as the peace-broker of the Middle East. But that had to wait for yet another Arab-Israeli War in October 1973. Instead of reviving a search for a comprehensive settlement, Kissinger, whose position as the key player in U.S.-Middle East policy was now confirmed, relied increasingly on the Israeli military as a key to stability in the region. This was based on a simple lesson: assuming that it was the threat (and possible use) of Israeli military might that had caused the Syrians to withdraw from Jordan, then it was this same military might that could act as a deterrent in the future. It was a classic example of the Nixon Doctrine at work: a strong regional ally policing its tough neighborhood with no actual loss of American lives.

Such an assumption ignored several key aspects of the regional situation. In particular, it overlooked an internal power struggle then going on in Syria. One of the two key players in that tug-of-war, Hafez al-Assad, the commander of the Syrian air force, had during the Jordanian crisis refused to commit the air force. Although this decision may have been in part due to prudence—Assad saw no reason to allow the inferior Syrian air force be obliterated by the Israelis—it was undoubtedly also part of the ongoing struggle for power. Equally significantly, the Syrian tanks had moved to Jordan at the command of Assad's chief rival, Salah Jadid. Two months later, Assad used the ill-fated adventure to discredit his domestic rival and establish his decades-long rule in Syria. Israeli power may have had an impact on the outcome of the Jordanian crisis, but it was hardly the only factor that explains the sudden Syrian withdrawal.[8]

Syrian internal developments notwithstanding, it was clear that Kissinger's enhanced role in Middle East policy translated in 1970 to an overstated emphasis on the need to minimize the Soviet role and maximize Israel's military predominance in the region. Israel, in a sense, was now considered one of the strong regional allies that, according to the principles of the Nixon Doctrine, would maintain regional stability by deterring further Arab adventures through its awesome military might. All the Americans had to do to keep the peace was outclass Soviet military aid to the neighboring Arab countries.

As Kissinger advised Nixon in the midst of Israeli Prime Minister Golda Meir's visit to the United States, which coincided with the Jordanian crisis, the key question in the prime minister's mind was: "What is the US going to do about the USSR?" Kissinger suggested that Nixon approve an immediate antimissile package worth $9.5 million, while in the long-term the United States should boost its deliveries of military aircraft, continue defense cooperation, and enhance its economic assistance. Kissinger maintained that the purpose of such aid was "to provide firm support for Israel's security [and] to keep Israel with us on the peace initiative."

The key to unlocking the Middle East conundrum was to be kept firmly in Washington.[9]

It was a fateful decision, reflecting the persistence of the Cold War framework, which allowed little room for creative diplomacy as a solution to regional conflicts. Both Nixon and Kissinger realized that the Jordanian crisis had done little to boost the chance for a comprehensive regional settlement. But it had been a victory of sorts vis-à-vis the USSR, a boost to the administration's morale and credibility at a time when such a victory was sorely needed. And it was the Soviet Union, the broader Cold War context, that truly mattered. In October 1970, Kissinger reported that Dobrynin had complained bitterly about the United States' facilitation of Israeli aggressiveness and blamed Washington for the failure of peace efforts. Kissinger was not worried. As far as the Middle East was concerned, "the Soviets find themselves overextended and have been engaged in a retreat to a more tenable position while covering their tracks with a tough public position." While there would be "a delicate period of both private and public diplomacy with the Soviets," the Middle East was finally, Kissinger assumed, presenting an advantage for the United States. As such, the Jordanian crisis had come at an opportune moment.[10]

This essential belief in the stability and durability of the American approach to the Middle East would only be shaken in October 1973, when the Egyptians and Syrians unleashed their armies against Israel (see chapter 14).

A SOCCER FIELD IN CIENFUEGOS

In September 1970, Kissinger also took heart in his ability to manage his own "Cuban Missile Crisis." In the summer of 1970, the Soviets appeared to be engaged in feverish military preparations on the Caribbean island. In June 1970, Kissinger worried that growing Soviet activity in Cuba was a reflection of "an apparent strengthening of Soviet-Cuban military relations, and a greater Soviet strategic presence in this area."[11] In subsequent months, American intelligence sources continued to indicate a strong possibility that the Soviets were building a nuclear submarine base at Cienfuegos. This, if true, would have violated the Soviet-American understanding of 1962 that had been reached as part of the solution to the Cuban Missile Crisis. Some of the reports were deliberately leaked to the press and on August 4, the Soviet charge d'affaires Yuli Vorontsov came to see Kissinger with a note confirming the 1962 understandings. Kissinger responded three days later: Nixon was happy to reconfirm that the understanding—a verbal agreement that the Soviets would not place offensive weapons on Cuba and the United States would not attempt to overthrow the Cuban government—was still in force.[12]

The issue did not go away. As reports led him to suspect the worst and because Ambassador Dobrynin was in the Soviet Union (he only returned in mid-September after a seven-week hiatus), Kissinger let the Soviets know of the growing American uneasiness through a public channel. At a press briefing in Chicago on September 16, he touched briefly on this issue by saying "on background" that should the Soviets "start operating strategic forces out of Cuba, say, Polaris-type submarines, and they use that as a depot, that would be a matter we would study very carefully."[13]

Kissinger did much more than just study the matter. On September 18, CIA Director Richard Helms showed Kissinger U-2 photographs that indicated, in a manner eerily reminiscent of similar photographs presented to President Kennedy eight years earlier, that a sizeable facility was under construction. Kissinger immediately sprang into action. He went over to see Nixon and, as a way of persuading Bob Haldeman to grant him an immediate appointment, dramatically slammed down the file of intelligence photos. The pictures, Kissinger announced, "show the Cubans are building soccer fields" in Cienfuegos.

"These soccer fields could mean war, Bob," he told the poker-faced White House chief of staff.

"Why?" Haldeman, reasonably enough, asked.

"Cubans play baseball. Russians play soccer," Kissinger patiently explained.

Initially, though, Kissinger failed to transform the Cuban base into an open show of resolve with the Soviets, as Nixon agreed with Rogers to keep the entire matter out of the public eye. Sporting fields of whatever variety were hardly a sufficient cause for playing nuclear brinksmanship.

But on September 25 C. L. Sulzberger's column in the *New York Times*, based on Kissinger's briefing nine days earlier in Chicago, transformed the issue into a public crisis. On the same day, a few hours before he left for Paris for a secret session with North Vietnam's Xuan Thuy, Kissinger had a face-to-face with Anatoly Dobrynin, lamenting the situation as one of "utmost gravity." But, he added, the United States was ready to allow the Soviets a graceful opportunity to withdraw without a public confrontation.[14]

Kissinger had a hectic program that week. He was still managing the Jordanian crisis and engaged in diplomacy in various fronts in Europe. In late September Kissinger first flew to Paris for separate meetings with the South Vietnamese vice president Nguyen Cao Ky and the North Vietnamese negotiator Xuan Thuy. He then joined Nixon and the rest of the presidential tour in Rome, where the program included an audience with the pope. The presidential party continued on to Yugoslavia, Spain, and Ireland. In the midst of all the traveling and official meetings, Nasser died. When Kissinger finally returned to Washington and met with Dobrynin on October 6, the Soviet ambassador handed him a Soviet statement that denied any departure from the 1962 understandings on Cuba. Three days later they exchanged further clarifying notes.[15]

Although Soviet submarines would visit Cuba on occasion, Kissinger could take heart in the fact that no Soviet missile base would be erected in Cuba on his watch. Whether there ever had been a full-fledged plan to build such bases remains, though, in question; Ambassador Dobrynin, for one, strongly protested the assumption at the time and later suspected that other motivations—such as trying to appear tough as the Republican Party geared up for the November 1970 congressional elections—might have been at play.[16]

For Kissinger the crisis was also important because it confirmed his ever-present suspicion about Soviet tactics. "We could not forget, the deception that had been attempted," Kissinger later wrote. Perhaps most important, however, the handling of the mini-missile crisis confirmed—much like the coinciding Jordanian crisis—that toughness paid off. "Considering Cuba (and) deception in Syria—until we got tough ... (the Soviets) deserve the cold treatment," he told Nixon on September 24. Nixon agreed.[17] Indeed, from the fall of 1970 on the President, when faced with a choice, almost invariably sided with Kissinger rather than Rogers—even when the evidence was something as flimsy as a picture of a soccer field.

As the journalist Seymour Hersh wrote, "Cienfuegos marked a turning point for Kissinger. He had bypassed an indecisive and election-minded President to challenge the Russians and win. Whether it was a victory over what actually did exist, or over what he thought might exist in the future, did not matter."[18]

Kissinger had taken one more step toward marginalizing Secretary of State Rogers and gaining Nixon's full confidence. His overall command of U.S. foreign policy making had, yet again, tightened.

BATTLING ALLENDE

The third crisis that Kissinger faced in September 1970 was least obviously tied to the unfolding of détente and most clearly a sign of how even self-styled realists like Kissinger and Nixon could have an irrational knee-jerk response to a development that made little difference to the overall direction of the administration's foreign policy. Kissinger, in particular, had exhibited little interest in the affairs of South America in the first two years of the Nixon administration. And yet, as fate would have it, his actions in this particular crisis have haunted his reputation for more than three decades. Thanks to the declassification of numerous documents, Kissinger's role in undermining Chilean democracy has recently been damningly accounted in books by, among others, Christopher Hitchens and Peter Kornbluh.[19]

On September 4, Salvador Allende, the socialist candidate, won a narrow plurality of the popular vote in Chile's presidential election. With 36.2 percent he led the three-way race against the conservative Jorge Alessandri (35 percent) and the moderate Radomiro Tomic (27.8 percent). The incumbent president, Eduardo Frei, had been barred by the Chilean Constitution from running again. According to the Constitution, the final decision was passed to the Chilean parliament, which had, in similar situations in the past, always gone along with the candidate who received most of the popular vote. Thus Allende, who had unsuccessfully run for the presidency in 1958 and 1964, appeared poised to assume the post on November 1, 1970, following a parliamentary ratification on October 24.

The prospect of a Socialist in power in Latin America raised alarm bells in Washington. This was particularly the case because already in the 1964 election Allende had received support from various communist organizations with known ties to Moscow; the Johnson administration had countered by providing assistance to a number of conservative and Catholic organizations and newspapers, including the *El Mercurio* newspaper conglomerate. To many, including such key figures as the Santiago CIA station chief Henry Hecksher (who was a clear-cut supporter of the conservative Alessandri) and Ambassador Edward Korry (who preferred the more centrist views of Frei and Tomic), Allende's victory spelled serious trouble. CIA Director Richard Helms, prompted by the dark visions of a potential Allende victory, had tried to convince the so-called Forty Committee—a small committee of high-level officials, chaired by Kissinger as the NSC adviser, that oversaw U.S. covert activities during the Nixon and Ford administrations—to launch a similar anti-Allende effort as in 1964. The Forty Committee, which, in addition to Kissinger and Helms, consisted of Air Force General George Brown (chairman of the Joint Chiefs of Staff), William P. Clements (deputy secretary of defense), and Joseph Sisco (undersecretary of state), had been unwilling to approve significant funds. Helms's direct appeal to Nixon had met a similar fate. In fact, in 1968 U.S. economic grant aid to Chile—a country that had been the largest per capita recipient of U.S. aid under the Alliance for Progress of the 1960s—had ended, and American loans dropped from $57.9 million in 1968 to a mere $18 million in 1970. Only after March 1970 did the Nixon administration begin paying some attention to Chile, where Allende had managed to forge a broad socialist alliance. By then the combination of CIA involvement and private funding from such interested U.S. companies as Anaconda Copper, GET, and Pepsi-Cola could not secure Alessandri's election and Allende's defeat.[20]

Prior to the news of Allende's victory in early September Kissinger had paid scant attention to Chile or Latin America. Indeed, his more memorable comments about the region were legendary dismissives. At one point Kissinger referred to Chile as the "dagger pointed to the heart of Antarctica"; at another occasion he reportedly told a Chilean visitor:

Latin America is not important. Nothing important can come from the South. History has never been produced in the South. The axis of history starts in Moscow, goes to Bonn, crosses over to Washington, and then goes to Tokyo. What happens in the South is of no importance.[21]

But in September 1970 the prospect of a socialist government in Chile did concern Kissinger. Like Nixon, he feared the emergence of "another Cuba" which, however insignificant Chile and Latin America may have appeared in comparison to such issues as détente with the USSR, the prospect of an opening to China, or the Vietnam War, could simply not be tolerated. Hence, in the midst of dealing with the Jordanian crisis, the mini-missile crisis in Cuba, and other pressing issues, the Nixon administration considered various possibilities of avoiding what, in the words of one Italian businessman, would create a "red sandwich" in Latin America.[22] Kissinger, half in jest, summed up the attitude of many in the Nixon administration when he once remarked to the Forty Committee: "I don't see why we have to let a country go Marxist just because its people are irresponsible."[23]

Thus came into being the now infamous Tracks I and II.

Track I, or the "Rube Goldberg gambit," was approved by the Forty Committee on September 14 and translated into persuading the Chilean Congress through a mixture of bribes and threats to defy historical precedent by electing Alessandri, who had already publicly said that if selected he would resign. After his election and resignation Chile could then have a new presidential election in which the incumbent president Eduardo Frei would be eligible to stand as a candidate. The Forty Committee authorized Ambassador Korry to spend $250,000 to buy votes in the Chilean Congress to this effect. In addition, the scheme was supported by an enhanced propaganda effort that was geared at convincing the Chileans that their economy would be ruined under an Allende presidency.[24]

Frei was, Ambassador Korry had argued on September 9, "the one and only hope for Chile." Encouraged by Frei's refusal to immediately recognize Allende as the future president, Korry had encouraged Track I and even titled one telegram, on September 11, 1970, "Some Hope for Chile." A few days later he characterized Frei as follows: "For a mobbled player, he is surprisingly alert and alive; in a long-odds game that will get very rough indeed as those seconds tick off before October 24th (the day of the congressional decision)." After meeting with Frei on September 13, Korry thought that the Chilean was "calm and cool," yet expressed concern that a much "more open challenge to Allende" was necessary in order to prevent his confirmation and inauguration. Frei was, according to Korry, even "thinking of how to worsen the economic situation in Chile quickly without hurting the country over the long-term."[25]

But, even with Frei's apparent (but never open) support, the chief American diplomat in Chile could not subvert the constitutional practices of his designated country. In a series of lengthy cables he ruminated about Frei's true intentions and came to the conclusion, on September 22, that the outgoing president "had not yet decided what it is he will do." By this point Korry had also become discouraged by the apparent pro-Allende sentiments of most of the Chilean media (with the exception of the conservative El Mercurio). "The prospects are not optimistic," Korry ruminated, complaining that Frei "may have what it takes as a transactor but all he may be doing is spending his time showing us that he has it."[26]

Unknown to Korry, the Nixon administration had already written off his efforts as inadequate. Convinced by various other interested parties—including Attorney General John Mitchell, Chilean newspaper publisher Augustin Edwards, and Donald Kendall, the president of Pepsi-Cola—Nixon laid out the basic blueprint of Track II on September 15. In a brief meeting that afternoon with Kissinger, Helms, and Mitchell, Nixon—according to Helms's notes—demanded his advisers come up with a plan "to make the [Chilean] economy scream." In addition to such plans for economic warfare, Nixon also wanted immediate action without the "involvement of [the U.S.] embassy," which was code for covert action by the CIA. He stressed that in preparing such action the CIA should not be "concerned [over the] risks involved." To aid the anti-Allende campaign Nixon promised $10 million—"more if necessary"—for an operation that was to be a "full-time job" with the "best men we have."[27]

Track II—fomenting a military coup in Chile—now became the lynchpin of the anti-Allende effort. On September 16, with the help of Thomas Karamessinis, head of the CIA's covert operations, and William Broe of the Latin American division, Helms set up a top secret Chilean task force. The CIA station in Santiago quickly began to approach members of the Chilean military about blocking Allende's election. This meant, however, removing the chief of staff, General Rene Schneider, a man known for his unwavering support of the Chilean constitution. Hence, the "best men" contacted Generals Roberto Viaux and Camilo Valenzuela, two lesser figures within the Chilean military, and encouraged their plans for kidnapping Schneider. Small shipments of arms were sent via the U.S. military attaché and some payments were made to Viaux and Valenzuela. As a number of other generals apparently worried that a coup might jeopardize U.S. military aid to Chile, Kissinger further instructed Ambassador Korry—although without giving him a full briefing of Track II—to approach Chilean military leaders and tell them not to worry about such adverse consequences.[28]

While U.S. military aid would continue there were plenty of adverse consequences, as the first attempt at realizing Track II turned into a fiasco. To his credit, on October 15 Kissinger did veto Viaux's plan to kidnap General Schneider, because he considered it too unlikely to succeed. "Nothing could be worse than an abortive coup," he wrote to Nixon. Unfortunately, the CIA's Chilean contacts continued their efforts and, after two failed attempts to kidnap General Schneider by another group, Viaux's men succeeded on October 22 in killing, rather than kidnapping, the Chilean chief of staff. Two days later Allende's election was confirmed and, upon taking over the presidency a week later, he now appeared, even to many of his previous Chilean critics, as a force for stability and order in Chile. Tracks I and II had, in other words, succeeded only in strengthening Allende's fragile political base.[29]

Not that this was the end of the story. Track II was not "turned off," as Kissinger later claimed. Instead, he advised Karamessinis to "keep pressure on every Allende weak spot in sight." While Viaux's group had been discouraged, the pursuit of Allende's overthrow remained "firm and continuing policy," Karamessinis thus cabled to his operatives in Chile on October 16, 1970. Aside from this, the Nixon administration decided upon a detailed policy aimed at undermining the new president's ability to hold on to power. At an NSC meeting on November 6, Nixon approved Option C, which summarized the administration's policy as follows: "Maintain an outwardly correct posture, but making clear our opposition to the emergence of a communist government in South America; act positively to retain the initiative vis-à-vis the Allende government." Three days later, in NSDM 93, Kissinger described the policy in somewhat more detail. The administration would try to isolate Chile and seek support for its policy from other countries in the Western Hemisphere, "particularly Brazil and Argentina," and to "establish and maintain close relations with friendly military leaders in the hemisphere." In the economic field, U.S. private investment in Chile was to be discouraged; "existing guarantees and financing arrangements terminated or reduced" whenever possible; and international financial institutions were to be pressured into limiting credits and loans to Chile. In addition, private U.S. businesses were to be informed of the government's "concern" over the implications of Allende's presidency.[30] In short, as of November 1970, Chile had become a pariah state, a subject of relentless American economic warfare.

The policies adopted in November 1970 would eventually help bring down the first democratically elected socialist president in the Western Hemisphere. Over the next few years the United States cultivated various disaffected groups (including a number of military leaders), funneled money to anti-Allende politicians, blocked Chile's credits, and discouraged investment in Chile. Helped by Allende's own disastrous internal policies and an inflation rate that climbed to 400 percent in a few years following his election, the Chilean army finally launched a successful coup against Allende's regime on September 11, 1973.[31] Allende either committed suicide or was murdered, while thousands of his supporters suffered a dismal fate at the hands of the military dictatorship headed by Augusto Pinochet. At that point Kissinger, whose confirmation hearings (he was nominated secretary of state in August 1973) roughly coincided with Allende's downfall, probably had no direct link to the coup planners. In a conversation with Nixon two days after the 1973 coup, Kissinger would acknowledge that while "we didn't do it, . . . we helped them." the US had "created the conditions as great as possible" for the overthrow of Allende. Kissinger was hardly displeased by the eventual outcome. But the human costs, as well as the backlash of anti-Americanism that would be created by Allende's martyrdom, were hardly necessary to bring the "dagger pointed at the heart of Antarctica" back to the fold.[32]

The rationale for such economic warfare and continued support for Allende's opposition was simple. It had little to do with grand. As Kissinger told Nixon's appointments secretary Dwight Chapin: "Chile could end up being the worst failure in our administration—'our Cuba' by 1972."[33]

From the perspective of democracy and human rights, America's Chile policy cannot, however, be considered anything other than a failure. The effort to prevent Allende's confirmation in the fall of 1970 was an ethically reprehensible adventure that was based on an overreaction to a prospect of a socialist president in the southern tip of Latin America. What followed was even worse, considering the rapid U.S. acceptance of the new Pinochet regime in Chile in 1973 that, for all its anticommunist credentials, trampled on Chile's longstanding democratic principles and ruled by repression and intimidation.

Lastly, one should note that even from a realist perspective the policy toward Chile in 1970 was a miserable failure. Simply put, Kissinger and Nixon failed in achieving their stated objectives and, ultimately, managed to create a surge in anti-American sentiments that threatened U.S. national interests in the region at large. When Allende was ousted and killed (or committed suicide) in 1973, he became a martyr for those in Latin America who organized their politics largely on anti-Yankee sentiments. Chile may have seemed like a prospective Cuba-like failure to Kissinger in 1970. One unintended consequence of his and Nixon's policies was assuring that it became one.

Ultimately, the casualties of American covert action in Chile in 1970 were minimal, and the failure to prevent Allende's confirmation represented but a minor wound in the Nixon administration's flesh. Although it hardly makes his actions in September–October 1970 any more defensible—indeed, treating one of the largest countries in South America with obvious disdain is itself revealing of the shortcomings in Kissinger's foreign policy architecture—Chile and Allende were hardly the major issues on the Nixon administration's agenda. The big game was elsewhere.

CHINA'S LUSHAN TURNAROUND

The crises in Jordan, Chile, and Cuba may have briefly diverted Kissinger's attention from the moribund China initiative. At the same time, however, the lack of progress on Vietnam and the continued recalcitrance of the Soviets strengthened the need to push more firmly toward the eventual opening to Beijing. Moreover, the series of crises in September 1970, as well as the earlier shakeups within NSC staff after the invasion of Cambodia, had clearly strengthened Kissinger's position within the Nixon administration by widening his already sizeable responsibilities. If anything, he now controlled the agenda on almost everything that mattered. Even the previously untouchable Middle East had, as a result of the Jordanian crisis, become a part of Kissinger's portfolio. With most of the doves gone from his staff after the invasion of Cambodia and the hard-line General Alexander Haig as Kissinger's key aide, Nixon clearly trusted his NSC adviser more than before. Hence, by the fall of 1970 Kissinger's ability to formulate, control, and execute policy had been greatly enhanced. As Walter Isaacson put it, "the end of 1970 represented a high point in Kissinger's relationship with the president."[34]

But that made it even more important that he perform.

And the one area that begged for a positive result was the administration's policy toward China. With the State Department's Warsaw channel effectively dead, Kissinger had taken charge of implementing and designing the next moves toward Beijing. Yet, he was also reduced, in the summer and early fall of 1970, to trying to entice the Chinese to open a back channel with the United States, while he attempted to send (and interpret) various signals. Neither effort was particularly successful. To the contrary, on July 2, 1970, two Chinese MIGs attacked an American intelligence plane. Although the U.S. C-130 escaped unharmed, the incident hardly inspired confidence within the Nixon White House about a potential opening to China.[35]

Meanwhile, attempts to create a secret channel to the PRC via Paris were unsuccessful. In late August and early September General Vernon Walters, Nixon and Kissinger's confidant at the U.S. embassy in Paris, tried to pass on an invitation for secret talks to his Chinese counterpart, Fang Wen. But no response was forthcoming from the Chinese defense attaché. In late September, when he was in Paris for a secret meeting with the North Vietnamese, Kissinger asked his old friend, the French diplomat Jean Sainteny, to pass a similar message to the Chinese Ambassador Huang Chen. Sainteny promised to do his best but was not able to make contact until December.[36]

Coinciding with these unsuccessful efforts at creating a back channel to China was a series of efforts at making a front channel. In late July, Nixon, upon Kissinger's recommendation, approved a small shipment of U.S-made diesel engines and spare parts to China. The following month, the administration lifted longstanding restrictions that prohibited American oil companies from fueling foreign ships that were carrying goods to the PRC. Finally, in an interview published on October 5, 1970, in *Time* magazine, Nixon made another famous statement that could hardly have been clearer: "If there is anything I want to do before I die, it is to go to China."[37] Still, it was up to the Chinese to invite him, a prospect that appeared no closer at the time than it had a year earlier.

By this point, the debate over an opening to the United States was all but closed in Beijing. And yet, although the United States remained at the top of Zhou Enlai's agenda, it required extreme delicacy and careful preparation. At the Lushan Plenum of the CCP (August 23–September 6, 1970), Zhou was bolder in his advocacy of an opening to the United States than ever before. He had apparently received more than lukewarm support from Mao.[38] Yet, the tricky Soviet-Sino-Vietnamese triangle and the lingering possibility of improving Sino-Soviet relations continued to complicate Zhou's position.

While the details of the Lushan Plenum remain inaccessible to historians, it seems to have marked a significant turning point in Mao's attitude toward the United States and the final ascendancy of Zhou's long career. In contrast, for Lin Biao, the defense minister and Mao's appointed successor, the Lushan Plenum meant that his opposition to the opening to the United States was losing ground. Yet, until his death a year later, the opposition to the Sino-American opening remained a strong strand within the Chinese leadership particularly, it seems, with those affiliated with the People's Liberation Army and Lin Biao. It needs to be stressed that this did not mean that Lin was a promoter of a pro-Soviet policy, as later Chinese claims suggested. Rather, his was the dual adversary position; maintaining, as Mao did in many public speeches, that both the United States and the Soviet Union were China's mortal enemies. While Mao (and Zhou) hardly believed that any genuine friendship was possible with the United States, the apparent danger in Lin's position was, at least to Mao and Zhou that it could easily produce a permanent mobilization of the PLA. This, in turn, would strengthen the position of the defense minister, Lin Biao.[39]

While Zhou Enlai may have emerged from Lushan with a clearer mandate for pursuing an opening with the United States, this course of action had to be balanced with China's Vietnam strategy. In particular, the Chinese leadership remained wary of the potential that any overture to the United States would be interpreted in Hanoi as a violation of the Sino-Vietnamese alliance. With the Soviets eager to capitalize on any such shifts, Mao and Zhou worked hard to maintain their relationship with North Vietnam and to minimize any adverse reaction on the part of the DRV leadership.

The North Vietnamese's continued interest in negotiations with the United States may have made this task easier. On September 17, 1970—the same day as the Provisional Revolutionary Government (PRG) representatives in Paris presented a new eight-point peace plan—Zhou met with North Vietnamese Premier Pham Van Dong in Beijing. Pham said that despite the new proposal and continued secret meetings between Xuan Thuy and Kissinger (the two met on September 7 and 27 in Paris), the North Vietnamese had no illusions. The United States still hoped for a military victory and was not ready to concede defeat. Pham added: "for us and for Nixon, diplomacy is a play of words. Neither we nor he has any illusion about diplomacy." But, Pham continued, the diplomatic front had several advantages for the Vietnamese. First, public diplomacy (such as the new peace proposal) was important in winning South Vietnamese people to the side of the PRG and in influencing American and general world public opinion. The basic idea, Pham Van Dong continued, was to "further corner Nixon by influencing public opinion in the US and the rest of the world." In his response Zhou, without offering specifics, promised continued support from the Great Rear.

Pham Van Dong stayed in Beijing for a week. Finally, on September 23, Mao received him. The Chairman, in his own indirect way, began to prepare the ground for the eventual opening to the United States that was bound to shock the Vietnamese.

Mao played down American power and the abilities of their chief diplomat. During the meeting with Pham Van Dong, Mao wondered out loud why the United States was not making a fuss about Chinese troops helping build Vietnamese railways. To the Great Helmsman, the implication seemed clear: Americans were more interested in trying not to provoke the PRC than they were about the conduct of the war in Vietnam. Mao then continued to talk about the Americans' hopes to make an opening to Beijing and pressed on to ridicule the Nixon administration's effort to negotiate a secret peace with Hanoi. Kissinger was honored with the lowest of estimates. He was "a stinking scholar, a university professor who does not know anything about diplomacy." Mao added: "I think that he is not someone who can compete with Xuan Thuy."[40]

Soon after these conversations with the North Vietnamese Mao and Zhou embarked on a potentially significant symbolic overture. The Chairman invited Edgar Snow, the author of *Red Star over China* (a 1938 book based on Snow's meetings with Mao that had popularized an image of Mao as a Robin Hood like figure) and a longtime admirer of the PRC's leader, to share the podium at the October 1 celebrations that marked the PRC's twenty-first anniversary. The China News Agency dispatched the photo worldwide after Zhou Enlai had made sure that the photo was properly airbrushed (to remove any others than Mao and Snow from the picture) to dramatize the Chairman's gesture of having an American citizen on his side at a time when official relations between the United States and China did not yet exist. Unfortunately, as Kissinger writes in his memoirs, he "completely missed the point" of an American author standing in between Mao and his wife watching the parades on Tiananmen Square.[41]

It was Mao and Zhou's turn to be frustrated by the slowness of the other side's response. Secrecy had become a hindrance to Kissinger's search for an opening to China.

To send an unmistakable signal of their intentions, the Chinese then opened diplomatic relations with Canada on October 13, 1970. While Pierre Trudeau, the flamboyant Canadian prime minister, basked in the limelight of what was the end result of almost two years of secret contacts, Kissinger and Nixon worried lest the apparent condition for the Canadian "opening to China" would be the price the United States might have to pay as well. Ottawa severed its official diplomatic ties with Taiwan, which was something that Nixon could not envisage any American administration could do without facing a momentous debacle at home. Worst, the Canadian shock had come as a complete surprise; Nixon's already evident personal dislike of the Canadian prime minister was thus confirmed.[42]

Within two weeks, Kissinger received promising signals of Chinese interest in opening a new dialogue through the Pakistani and Romanian channels. In late October, the Pakistani president Yahya Khan came to New York for the annual meeting of the UN General Assembly. On the 25th, he met with Nixon and Kissinger in the White House. After promising that the United States would be "as helpful as we can" in the brewing conflict between India and Pakistan (see chapter 8), Nixon turned the conversation to China.

"I understand you are going to Peking," Nixon said. After Yahya had briefly explained the background to his trip to China, Nixon inserted:

> It is essential that we open negotiations with China. Whatever our relations with
> the USSR or what announcements are made I want you to know the following:
> 1) we will make no condominium against China and we want them to know it
> whatever may be put out; 2) we will be glad to . . . establish links secretly.

Kissinger interjected that Nixon had in mind a secret meeting in "some mutually convenient capital such as, for example, Rawalpindi or conceivably Paris." Nixon added that if such a meeting were arranged he might even send Kissinger to represent him.

Yahya promised to deliver the message to Zhou Enlai when he met with the Chinese premier the following month.[43]

Over the next two days, Nixon and Kissinger met with Romanian President Nicolae Ceausescu. Although the bulk of the conversations focused on Vietnam, Nixon stressed the United States' keen interest in establishing contacts with Beijing. As Kissinger put it to Ceausescu: "we have great interest in establishing political and diplomatic communications with the People's Republic of China." As with Yahya, Kissinger stressed that the United States was "prepared to set up channels . . . free from outside pressures." Any communications that Beijing wished to relay via the Romanians, Kissinger assured, "will be confined to the White House." Ceausescu, like Yahya, promised to pass on the message and report any reactions back to Washington.[44]

It was the Pakistani channel that eventually delivered. During his meeting with Zhou on November 12, Yahya Khan cited Nixon's assurance that a U.S. rapprochement with the PRC was "essential" and suggested Nixon's willingness to visit China in the future. On November 23 Yahya received a reply. Yet, due to the distractions caused by a devastating cyclone in East Pakistan and the results of the Pakistani national elections in early December (discussed in more detail in chapter 8), Zhou's answer reached Washington only on December 8. The following evening, Ambassador Hilaly met with Kissinger and delivered the first of the messages that would eventually culminate in the opening to China: the Chinese would gladly welcome a Nixon emissary "to discuss the subject of the vacating of Chinese territories called Taiwan."[45] If one ignored the point about Taiwan, Zhou's message was, unquestionably, a breakthrough. On December 16, Kissinger gave Hilaly a positive American response. On January 11, 1971, a message from the Romanian ambassador Corneliu Bogdan confirmed that the Chinese were serious.[46]

At this point Nixon decided to hold back. "I believe we may appear too eager," he wrote on the memoranda that detailed the January 11 Kissinger–Bogdan meeting. "Let's cool it—Wait for them to respond to our initiative."[47]

They had to wait for more than three months. Just as a breakthrough with China beckoned, another crisis in Southeast Asia intervened.

LAM SON 719

The background to the invasion of Laos in early 1971 coincided with and was closely linked to developments in Cambodia. Although Cambodia and Laos had been recognized as neutrals in the 1954 and 1962 Geneva Agreements, respectively, the Ho Chi Minh Trail ran along the eastern borders of both countries; thus Laos, like

Cambodia, was used as a staging point for the North Vietnamese campaign in the south. Against such similarities, however, one needs to set the different approach that the Laotian and Cambodian governments had taken vis-à-vis the United States. While Prince Sihanouk had broken off diplomatic relations with the United States in the mid-1960s, Laotian Prime Minister Prince Souvanna Phouma had remained a neutral ally of the United States. Yet, compelled to fight a war on two fronts—one in the north against the Communist Pathet Lao and another in the south against the North Vietnamese—did little to increase Phouma's hold on power. If anything, the Laotian prime minister became dependent on the United States as his country was drawn deeper into the Vietnam War. By 1969 Laos, much like Cambodia, was an integral part of the North Vietnamese war effort and, hence, of the Nixon administration's search for a peace with honor.

The similarities between Laos and Cambodia did not stop there. To contain a North Vietnamese offensive that had begun in February 1969, American bombers started hitting enemy targets in Laos. They continued these strikes for three years. Unlike in the case of the Cambodian bombings, though, Kissinger had pressed for and Nixon had agreed to make the Laotian bombings public. Yet, the president did not give full details of the scale of the B-52 strikes ripping the Laotian countryside apart. Nor did he disclose much information about American covert support to Souvanna Phouma and his war against the communist insurgents (Pathet Lao). Although overshadowed by Vietnamization and the Cambodian incursion, American bombers continued to pound communist targets in Laos throughout 1969–70.

By late 1970, though, Nixon and Kissinger were searching for another way of impressing the North Vietnamese to become more forthcoming in the secret negotiations in Paris. Perhaps because he was "no match" against his North Vietnamese counterparts, as Mao suggested, Kissinger had made little progress in the secret meetings in Paris. His meetings with Xuan Thuy on September 7 and 27 produced nothing substantive. Exasperated with the lack of progress and the continued pressure from the Congress and the general American public, Nixon "went to the limit," as the new chief U.S. negotiator in Paris David Bruce put it. Although aware of the negative, even horrified, reaction it would yield from the South Vietnamese, Nixon proposed in a televised speech—drafted by Kissinger's NSC staff and polished by William Safire, one of Nixon's prolific speechwriters—on October 7, 1970, a standstill ceasefire and an American bombing halt throughout Indochina. Nixon also called for a comprehensive peace conference to end the fighting throughout the region, and offered to negotiate a comprehensive U.S. withdrawal from Indochina.

It was, in Kissinger's retrospective view, "a comprehensive program that could well have served as a basis for negotiation except with an opponent bent on total victory." His point is well taken (although one searches in vain for evidence of such skepticism at the time): amid applause at home for what many considered a generous offer, the North Vietnamese refused the latest Nixon proposal on October 10. David Bruce, who formally presented Xuan Thuy with the same offer as Nixon was delivering his speech to the nation, tried to keep the idea alive in subsequent weeks, but without success. Yet, Bruce agreed with Kissinger: the United States could not go further with their concessions. For the North Vietnamese to continue demanding the removal of South Vietnamese President Thieu was "sheer impudence."[48]

There was a minor bright spot in all this. While Nixon had not been able to solicit a positive response from Hanoi, he had momentarily quieted down domestic critics. As Bob Haldeman recorded in his diaries, both hawks and doves in Washington felt that the "ball [was] now in Hanoi's court." Kissinger's view appears more to the point. The speech provided, he later wrote, "some temporary relief from public pressures." William Safire, the man who prepared the final text of the speech, agreed. The speech was "presented primarily for its political impact in the States . . . with little chance of its acceptance by the North Vietnamese."

While the North Vietnamese refused to yield Nixon's frustration increased. By December the president was seething about the ineffectiveness of continued American bombing in Cambodia. In a classic "madman-moment" he told Kissinger to order the Air Force—something Nixon could not bring himself to do—to "really go in (with) everything that can fly and crack the hell out of them." He was tired of "these Mickey Mouse games" and, raising his voice a notch, barked: "what the hell are they doing? The goddamn Air Force over there farting around doing nothing!" Kissinger, as used to Nixon's temper tantrums as he was prone to his own, promised to "get it done immediately." A few minutes later, though, Kissinger and Haig devised a way of 'downgrading' Nixon's demands. After sharing a laugh about "our friend's" (Nixon's) wish to use "anything that flies" to bomb "anything that moves," the two men devised an alternative plan of obliterating 'just' one district.[50]

While not following up on Nixon's orders Kissinger, not for the first time, still clearly believed that it was necessary to continue with military pressure. But the target was changing. Instead of Cambodia, the next show of force came in Laos.

*   *   *

Much like in the Cambodian case, the planning for Lam Son 719 elicited some protest from Kissinger's staff. Winston Lord, sensing that another Cambodia was in the offing, wrote Nixon on November 25 that the search for "dramatic recoups" in Vietnam represented "a dangerous mood apparently flowing strongly enough to justify rehearsing the follies of escalation which one would like to think were self-evident by now." Instead of contemplating further aggressive moves, Lord concluded, the administration should either continue present policy or offer a fixed date for U.S. withdrawal in return for some concessions from the other side.[51]

It was to no avail. Tired with a lack of progress with "impudent" North Vietnamese Nixon leaned for a show of force. Nixon initially authorized the Laos attacks on January 18, 1971, in a meeting with Rogers, Laird, Helms, Kissinger, and Admiral Thomas Moorer, the acting chairman of the Joint Chiefs of Staff. On the same day, he talked with Kissinger and Haldeman about Vietnamization, citing

Thieu's concerns over further U.S. troop withdrawals. The South Vietnamese president, who was facing elections later in the year, had asked the Nixon administration not to cut U.S. troop levels below 200,000 before his reelection was secured in October. Nixon thus decided to hold back on significant troop withdrawals until the election and then "announce the massive withdrawal right after the Vietnamese elections."[52]

As had become customary, Nixon's decisions sparked off internal debate. On January 21 Kissinger barged into Haldeman's office and complained to him about a revolt brewing in the State Department. Kissinger charged that Rogers, Laird, and Undersecretary of State U. Alexis Johnson had met the previous day and decided to send off a cable to Ambassador Bunker in Saigon "as an attempt to try to turn off the planned Laotian operation." Johnson had apparently confessed this to Kissinger and warned that Rogers was going to try and clear the cable with Nixon. Despite Kissinger and Haldeman's efforts, the draft cable made it to Nixon's desk. But the president, to Haldeman's delight, refused to approve it. Nixon passed the whole matter to the WSAG. Rogers had, yet again, suffered a bureaucratic loss over an issue that bore major repercussions on the Vietnam War.[53]

Kissinger had high hopes for the forthcoming operation. On January 26, he met with Nixon and Moorer to discuss Lam Son 719. In apparently high spirits, he briefed Haldeman on the general contents that evening and told him about the planned assault on Laos. Kissinger stressed his belief that the operation was going to be a great success and "would in effect end the war because it would totally demolish the enemy's capability." When Haldeman expressed concern over the domestic reaction, Kissinger tried to assure him. The previous year's incursion into Cambodia, he believed, had "cleared things up so we've got no problem in '71." Sure, a negative reaction now could haunt Nixon in the 1972 elections, Kissinger conceded. An attack on North Vietnam's supply routes in Laos, however, would hamper the North Vietnamese ability to send troops and materials to the South and thus buy more time for Vietnamization. A forceful attack might prevent the possibility of a massive North Vietnamese offensive in 1972 by which time, in any case, the South Vietnamese military (ARVN) should be strong enough to handle the situation on its own. Thus, Lam Son 719 would also yield dividends for Nixon in domestic political terms by reducing the potential need to use U.S. troops in the forthcoming election year. In sum, the "new action in Laos now would set us up so we wouldn't have to worry about problems in '72, and that of course is most important." What if the North Vietnamese anticipated an attack? Kissinger speculated. That would be even better, because the North Vietnamese could be drawn "into a monumental trap." In other words, Lam Son 719 could be called off and the United States could move in to "bomb them, maybe with the same effect as going ahead with the plan." This, he added, "of course would be a much more viable alternative domestically." Either way, Kissinger was fully optimistic that a turning point in Vietnam was finally at hand.[54]

After 36,000 ARVN troops crossed the border into Laos on February 8, 1971, Kissinger's hopes were quickly dashed. Lam Son 719 turned into an utter disaster. Even with substantial American air support (U.S. planes dropped about 48,000 tons of bombs during the operation), the ARVN took a month, rather than five days as General Abrams had predicted, to get to its target Tchepone, a village in southern Laos. Once there, the troops found themselves trapped and President Thieu ordered an immediate withdrawal. This turned into a nightmare as the enemy attacked those troops using the roads; many had to be airlifted by U.S. helicopters. In a panic, the South Vietnamese troops often grabbed onto the skids of helicopters which, when they landed at the U.S. air base in Khe Sanh, provided wonderful material for photographers and journalists. Those who watched an ARVN contingency returning from this ill-fated operation ignored any talk of military success and orderly retreat.

*   *   *

In the end, Lam Son 719 was yet another in a series of misguided efforts to find some sort of a military solution to the war. It did not meet any of its military objectives. It did not substantially enhance the possibilities of Vietnamization being a success. It did not give a boost to the morale in South Vietnam, but instead exposed their weaknesses and did this on the eve of further troop withdrawals. Nor did the operation, in all likelihood, improve Kissinger's hand in the negotiating table. If anything, the failure of the Laotian operation, the American inability to provide ground troop support, and the ARVN's humiliating retreat indicated to the North Vietnamese that another major offensive against the South in the future was likely to be successful. Hanoi was hardly given cause to doubt that their resolve would, eventually, prevail.[55]

Kissinger conceded that Lam Son 719 had not been a wholehearted success. Yet, he, like Nixon, would claim that the South Vietnamese troops and American bombs had achieved important strategic results. In particular, Hanoi would find it impossible to launch a major attack in 1971 and the Spring Offensive of 1972 was thus more limited in scope than Hanoi's leaders had originally hoped and could be repelled with a combination of American airpower and South Vietnamese manpower. In fact, Kissinger maintains, "the incursions into Laos and Cambodia saved us in 1972." This may well have been the case. But it was a far cry from Kissinger's earlier argument that with Lam Son 719, Vietnam would be a nonissue in 1972. And, as Kissinger later admitted, the incursion actually increased the probability "that we would face another major military challenge the next year [1972]."[56]

*   *   *

The rapid retreat of the South Vietnamese forces from Laos did not stop Nixon from portraying Lam Son 719 as proof of the ARVN's much improved fighting capabilities in his nationally televised speech on April 7, 1971. He was pleased to "report that Vietnamization has succeeded." His policy had resulted in "the increased strength of the South Vietnamese" and included "the success of the Cambodian operation" as well as "the achievements of the South Vietnamese operation in Laos." Accordingly, Nixon announced that between May and December 1971 an additional 100,000 Americans would be brought home. Nixon even proudly illustrated the reduction in U.S. military personnel with a chart that showed how, by the end of the year, Nixon would have reduced the number of U.S. forces in Vietnam by two-thirds since he took office (from 540,000 to roughly 180,000). His conclusion was upbeat: "the American involvement in Vietnam is coming to an end."[57]

Nixon could also take heart in the fact that Vietnamization had produced a positive side effect at home. While college campuses had exploded in protest following the incursion of Cambodia in May 1970, the public reaction to the Laotian campaign was muted. Only about 50,000 demonstrators participated in scattered protests on February 10. In the spring of 1971 the antiwar movement suffered further from a well-publicized violent streak that seems to have increased the American public's concern over radicalism. Prior to the Laotian operation six extremists had been indicted for a plan to kidnap Kissinger and bomb several buildings in Washington. In the early morning hours of March 1, 1971, a bomb, planted by a radical left-wing group known as the Weather Underground (or, more popularly the Weathermen), actually exploded in the Capitol Building. Although no one was hurt, the attack popularized the image of the antiwar movement as a group of radicals and resulted in calls for tighter internal security measures. The Weathermen's activities also helped splinter the antiwar movement: when hundreds of thousands of demonstrators showed up in Washington in April, a number of their leaders met with Nixon administration officials, showing that their cause was less than unified. After weeks of protests and some violence the administration removed a group of radicals camping along the Potomac. The public reaction was muted. Nixon sensed that he had the backing of the silent majority. To many other administration figures, including John Ehrlichman, it seemed that the end of mass public demonstrations had finally arrived. After a few thousand demonstrators were arrested on May 4, Nixon was, Haldeman recorded, "very pleased."[58]

KISSINGER IN CHARGE

In the spring of 1971 Kissinger also had reason to be rather pleased with himself. He had weathered the storm of the past two years and clearly enhanced his position as the president's foreign policy czar. Kissinger had, or so it seemed at the time, interpreted the situation in the Middle East correctly in September 1970. He had managed to extract a Soviet concession of sorts on Cuba. And, while Allende remained, for the moment, the president of Chile, there had been positive developments in more significant areas. The negative Chinese reaction to the invasion of Cambodia had been expected, but it did not necessarily prevent the possibility of an opening. Perhaps most important, Kissinger clearly had the upper hand vis-à-vis Secretary of State Rogers.

Kissinger's control of the foreign policy process did concern some members of the American foreign policy elite. Among these was Rogers' predecessor, Dean Rusk. In March 1971 Rusk wrote another former secretary of state, Dean Acheson:

> The impression I get . . . both from reading the press and talking to various people in Washington, is that there is substance to the speculation that Henry Kissinger is gutting the role and responsibilities of Bill Rogers. If so, I am deeply disturbed because I do not believe this is good for the President, for the country or for the office of Secretary of State . . . The purpose of this note is to ask you whether you have the same impression as I and, if so, whether you think it would do any good if one or both of us had a quiet word with Bill Rogers on the subject. I have reason to believe that the morale of the Department of State is being adversely affected by this development and I suspect that it may have some effect on the ability of Bill Rogers to speak effectively to foreign governments.

Acheson agreed with Rusk's impression about the Kissinger–Rogers relationship. Yet, he had little sympathy for the secretary of state. "I do not think it would do any good for either of us—certainly not for me—to speak to Bill Rogers," Acheson wrote back. He added:

> Bill Rogers' difficulties, including his inability to speak effectively to foreign governments which you mention, spring from his own inadequacies and not from Henry Kissinger or anyone else. One conclusion I hold after some experience is that a quiet word with Bill Rogers is not only a waste of time, but is far better left unspoken.[59]

By that point, March 1971, it was too late to rescue Secretary of State Rogers from his growing irrelevancy. Kissinger had already outmaneuvered Rogers, with Nixon's apparent approval, at almost every turn. And while the results of the administration's foreign policy were hardly sensational in March 1971—there had been no resolution to the Vietnam War, no opening to China, no SALT agreement with the Soviets—within the next few months Kissinger would record a series of triumphs that would only strengthen his hold on the making of American foreign policy.

The triumphs began with important news from China.

7

Breakthroughs

At 6:15 P.M. on April 27, 1971, Pakistani Ambassador Agha Hilaly visited Henry Kissinger's office in the White House. Hilaly carried a brief message, from Zhou Enlai, handwritten as usual. The Chinese premier reaffirmed his government's "willingness to receive publicly in Beijing a special envoy of the President of the U.S. (for instance, Mr. Kissinger) or the U.S. Secretary of State or even the President of the U.S. himself for a direct meeting and discussions."

Zhou's message broke a silence that had lasted for more than four months. It could not have been more forthcoming. Ironically, it arrived on the same day as Kissinger and Alexander Haig had launched another attempt to break the ice with China by employing, once again, the help of Kissinger's old friend Jean Sainteny in Paris.[1]

Finally, a breakthrough had arrived. After Hilaly departed, Kissinger rushed to relay the message to Nixon, who was in the Lincoln Sitting Room. All that remained was deciding on who would go and when. Zhou had indicated that Beijing was uninterested in such details because they were "of no substantive significance." He had simply suggested the practical arrangements be made via the Pakistani government. Interestingly, the premier spoke of a "public" meeting, rather than the secret one that would eventually follow in July.

The question, rarely addressed in historical writing about the Nixon administration, is simple: why? Why did Zhou's April 27 message prompt a *secret* Kissinger trip, codenamed Polo I, in early July 1971, rather than an open one by Kissinger (or someone else)?

The answer, it seems, has as much to do with the secretive and Byzantine atmosphere of the Nixon White House, as it does with the expected political benefits of a shock at home and abroad. For the secrecy of Kissinger's trip to China grew from a mixture of domestic political motives, international calculations, and personal ambition.

SHROUD OF SECRECY

Politically, the secrecy made some sense. If Nixon could appear on TV announcing a sudden turnabout in United States–China relations, the president's domestic opponents, many of whom had criticized Nixon for his slow approach to the opening to China, would be stunned. At the same time, those on the right who opposed any warming of relations with Beijing (the pro-Taiwan China lobby) would find themselves swept away by the rapid unfolding of events. Perhaps more important, Kissinger and Nixon assumed that a shock announcement would shake the Soviets from their intransigence, and make them more forthcoming on the unresolved issues of Berlin, SALT, Vietnam, and a Soviet-American summit.

A skeptic might, though, argue that none of the above justified the neurotic guarding of the big secret. Very few men were privy to the secret: initially, in addition to Kissinger and Nixon, only Haldeman, Haig, and Winston Lord knew of Zhou's letter. During the two months of preparations, Lord, in fact, became Kissinger's principal aide, performing the duties of camouflage with great efficiency. Lord even had to keep the trip from his wife, Bette Bao Lord, a Chinese-American novelist born in Saigon and with close ties to Taiwan. As the trip approached and the planning intensified, the circle of knowledge increased. Yet, the secrecy continued even within Kissinger's own staff. For example, when the trip commenced on July 1, 1971, Lord was charged with the "monumental task" of keeping track of the three separate sets of briefing books that had been prepared to the staff members that went along with what was, officially, a tour of various Southeast Asian and South Asian capitals. For, as Kissinger puts it, "there were three separate levels of knowledge. Some knew where I was going and what I would say when I got there. Others knew of my destination but not of my agenda . . . Still others were aware of neither." Indeed, as Kissinger jokes, one of the greatest achievements of the journey was that Lord was able to provide each group with an updated knowledge-appropriate briefing book at each of the many stops during the trip.[2]

If Nixon wished to open China, he didn't need to do it secretly. In fact, a public announcement could have helped prepare the ground with domestic constituencies, such as the so-called China lobby (the pro-Taiwan lawmakers and businessmen who would view any move toward the People's Republic as a threat to Taiwan's independence). Even the majority of Democratic and Republican lawmakers who could be counted upon welcoming an opening to Beijing, would probably have reacted even more positively if they were included in, or at least kept informed of, the process of rapprochement. One could further argue that any shock that the Soviets would feel could not justify the shock that the Japanese (and some other American allies) would have to endure in July.

Whether secrecy was justified in political terms is an open question. However, it was clearly a means to a bureaucratic end for Kissinger. For him to be the chief official on the first U.S. mission to the PRC since 1949 would mean the ultimate coup de grace: it would confirm that China policy was his personal reserve; in subsequent years he would control U.S. China policy even more than he did the Nixon administration's Soviet policy through the back channel. Perhaps unforeseen in April 1971, the secret trip would also make Kissinger a household name around the world: he would be the new Marco Polo, the man who ventured into the unknown and engineered what Kissinger himself would, without a modicum of modesty, call a "geopolitical revolution." He would become the modern Metternich. And, as Kissinger surely knew, celebrity—while perhaps a complication for secret meetings—translated into power. As Winston Lord's wife Bette once remarked of Kissinger: "He realizes that fame can make him powerful."[3]

Nixon, hardly blind to the potential of the situation, was torn. He knew that Kissinger was dying to be the front man. And if secrecy were crucial, then the national security adviser was the man for the job. But Nixon did not want to be left out of the limelight or further inflame the relationship between the White House and the State Department; he worried that sending Kissinger "would break all the china with State." Thus, over the next few days Nixon, Kissinger, and Haldeman discussed a number of potential candidates for the mission.

In a telephone conversation with Kissinger on the evening of the 27th, Nixon identified George H. W. Bush, Nelson Rockefeller, and David Bruce as possible envoys. The president appeared particularly intrigued by the idea of sending Kissinger's old mentor Rockefeller. Kissinger, probably unsure whether Nixon was simply toying with him or seriously considering sharing the limelight with his 1968 rival, admitted that a Rockefeller mission had "possibilities." Yet, Kissinger also warned that Rockefeller was a difficult man to control. Someone from the NSC staff, such as Alexander Haig, would have to go along to keep the former New York governor in check.

In fact, Kissinger had no interest in having someone else be the senior official on the mission to China. He effectively ruled out UN Ambassador George Bush as "too soft and not sophisticated enough" for the job. The veteran diplomat David Bruce was, as Nixon agreed, a risky choice because of his role as the head of the official U.S. delegation to the Vietnam peace negotiations in Paris. Moreover, while Kissinger may have appeared positive about the possibility of sending Nelson Rockefeller, his underlying message was something else: sending Rockefeller, or any other high-profile politician, as the first envoy to China, would translate into a free gift of political capital.[4] Did Nixon really wish to build up a potential rival?

Of course not. Thus, when Kissinger, Haldeman, and Nixon met at the Executive Office Building on the afternoon of the 28th, Kissinger managed to convince the president that he had little choice. As Haldeman recorded, Kissinger "made the point that he was the only one who really could handle this." What Kissinger suggested was an initial secret trip that would "set it up" for a public presidential visit later on. Kissinger's limited public stature and lack of political aspirations meant that he would not steal the political credit that Nixon so badly desired. Continued secrecy would maximize such credit and allow Nixon to shock the rest of the world. And only Kissinger, of course, could be trusted with keeping the secret.

Nixon finally agreed. After sending an interim reply to Zhou, Kissinger took off for a week's vacation in Palm Springs.[5]

Upon his return Kissinger met with Ambassador Hilaly at noon on May 10 and handed the Pakistani envoy a more substantial message from the president to be delivered to Zhou. Nixon designated Kissinger as his envoy and indicated that the NSC adviser could come to China after June 15. The purpose of the trip would be to prepare the ground for Nixon's eventual visit. Lastly, the message emphasized secrecy: the last two sentences were underlined and read as follows: "For secrecy, it is essential that no other [than the Pakistani] channel be used. It is also understood that this first meeting between Dr. Kissinger and high officials of the People's Republic be strictly secret."[6]

Over the next few weeks several messages passed between Washington and Beijing via the Pakistanis. Finally, on June 2, 1971, Kissinger received the full text (he had been handed a quick summary earlier) of Zhou Enlai's response. The same evening he called Bob Haldeman in an ebullient mood. The Chinese premier's response, Kissinger announced, "was even more accommodating than he had thought it would be." Zhou welcomed Nixon to China for "direct conversations in which each side would be free to raise the principal issue of concern to it." In order to prepare for the high-level meeting, Kissinger himself was invited to visit China secretly (although Zhou Enlai made the point that secrecy was at the United States' request)—preferably sometime between June 15 and 20. When the two met with Nixon the following morning Haldeman, after reading the letter, agreed. As the White House chief of staff recorded in his diaries, the Chinese were "leaning over backward to set up a meeting and want [Kissinger] to come practically immediately."[7]

The implications of Zhou's letter were potentially massive. Kissinger was particularly excited that to "have the ball rolling" with China "will put a lot of pressure on North Vietnam to settle with him." According to Haldeman, Kissinger was "extremely optimistic that we may get all of the settlements that we're working toward on all of our initiatives."[8]

The Chinese invitation, which Nixon duly accepted in a letter to Zhou a few days later, seemed perfectly timed. And the care in the planning and execution of the secret trip in July 1971 that followed was an indication of the way in which personal ambition, search for domestic political advantage, and foreign policy blended to produce a clandestine operation that, once revealed to the general public in mid-July 1971, dramatically transformed Kissinger's foreign policy. The secret trip was the big break he had longed for. As he prepared for the trip in May and June 1971, Kissinger could justifiably expect that his visit to China would give him an extra trump card in his negotiations with the North Vietnamese, and put additional pressure on the Soviets to settle the vexing issue of Berlin and agree to a Nixon–Brezhnev summit. If all went well Nixon could then move toward the reelection year as a man who had accomplished a triad of feats in the field of foreign policy.

Much of this, with the characteristic exception of Vietnam, did indeed go according to script. But there was an additional bonus that Kissinger may not have fully appreciated prior to his return from the secret trip. The inevitable publicity that he gained as the practical engineer of the opening to China would quickly make him a worldwide celebrity. This, in turn, strengthened Kissinger's hand within the administration. After more than two years of frustration and lackluster progress, Kissinger was about to become the *Überdiplomat*. No wonder that he would develop, over time, an almost sentimental regard for Zhou Enlai, the man who had sent him the note that ended up transforming Kissinger's personal fortune as much as American foreign policy.

LAM SON TO PING PONG

The significance of Zhou's April message and the subsequent exchanges that lay down the details of Kissinger's secret trip went far beyond the confines of bilateral Sino-American relations. For one, Zhou confirmed Kissinger and Nixon's hopes that in 1971 the Vietnam War no longer prevented a rapprochement between the two countries. Unlike the 1970 invasion of Cambodia, Lam Son 719 had not derailed the process of Sino-American rapprochement. To be sure, the movement of South Vietnamese into Laos in February 1971 had its impact on the Chinese. Much like during the Cambodian incursion, the Chinese publicly attacked Nixon. The *People's Daily*, for example, denounced Nixon for having "fully laid bare his ferocious features and reached the zenith of his arrogance." Still, Nixon's reassurances to China in a news conference on 17 February that the Laotian operation was not directed against PRC but North Vietnam probably helped Zhou Enlai's hand within the PRC. In fact, unlike in the aftermath of the 1970 Cambodian incursion, the Chinese indicated, via Norway's ambassador to China, Ole Ålgård, their continued interest in talks with Washington. Ålgård passed on the message that the PRC was merely "postponing" the talks with Washington as a result of Laos, not "canceling" them.[9]

Perhaps because of China's reluctance to do more than denounce Nixon verbally, Lam Son 719 did have an unfavorable side effect on Sino-Vietnamese relations. In the spring of 1971, the DRV began to tilt increasingly toward Moscow. By

May 1971 at the latest, the Soviet embassy in Hanoi had noted a clear pro-Soviet direction in North Vietnamese policy. One report, by Ambassador I. Scherbakov, noted that "by leaning toward the Soviet Union, the V[ietnamese] W[orkers] P[arty] has endured the crude pressure of the Chinese leaders."[10] Not that the Chinese wished to lose an ally in Southeast Asia by engaging in a highly questionable courtship with Washington. Throughout the spring of 1971 they tried to convince the North Vietnamese of China's continued support, if only to prevent Hanoi from moving even closer to the USSR. Indeed, the triangular Sino-Soviet-Vietnamese relationship was at a crossroads during Lam Son 719 and its immediate aftermath.

This is evident from Zhou Enlai's talks with the North Vietnamese leaders Le Duan and Pham Van Dong in early March. Zhou stressed to the North Vietnamese the dangers inherent in any type of united action with the USSR. "If we take the Soviets' side, they will control us," the Chinese premier warned the Vietnamese leaders. He added that "if we establish a world-wide people's front that includes the Soviets, they will control this front." On their part, Le Duan and Pham Van Dong were concerned over the possibility of a Sino-American rapprochement. To test the waters, Le Duan called upon China to take a leading role in the formation of a people's alliance that would "oppose the Nixon Doctrine, further isolate the US, weaken the US-Japan alliance and shake the Southeast Asian bourgeois class, thus contributing to the defeat of US global strategy." Provocatively he added: "It is only China that has the strength to do this."

Zhou was taken aback. "This is a new issue," he said. "We need more time to think."[11]

The Chinese premier was not completely forthcoming. If anything, he was profoundly uneasy about the Vietnamese pressure on the Chinese that might succeed in derailing the process toward rapprochement with the United States. And, in the spring of 1971, it was that rapprochement and the benefits he expected from it—a counterweight against further Soviet pressures, a break in China's isolated status, a possible undercutting of Taiwan (and the expelling of Taiwan from the United Nations)—that was foremost in his mind. North Vietnam, which had already tilted more clearly toward the Soviet Union in the past two years, was not to be allowed to derail this process. Thus, Zhou evaded making any additional commitments to his Vietnamese visitors.

At the farewell banquet on March 8, 1971, Zhou hinted to his North Vietnamese hosts that their very success made further Chinese efforts unnecessary. "Standing firm as a rock and full of confidence," Zhou said, "you are prepared to face new battles and seize new victories." Ironically, Zhou was implying that the success of the North Vietnamese counterattack, combined with Vietnamization, indicated how strong Hanoi's position now was. They should, he seemed to be saying, stand on their own.[12] The fact that the United States did not get directly involved in Laos, the continued American troop withdrawals, and the relative rapidity of the ARVN withdrawal seemed to indicate that victory was just around the corner.

The North Vietnamese leaders' efforts to probe Zhou Enlai on China's willing-ness to maintain a vigorous anti-American stance were undoubtedly affected by numerous—to Hanoi ominous—signs of an impending Sino-American rap-prochement. There was, for one, the fact that Nixon had made a significant seman-tic break with his predecessors. Unlike Truman, Eisenhower, Kennedy, or Johnson, Nixon referred to mainland China by its official name, "the People's Republic of China," rather than the euphemism "Communist China" (or even the more obnox-ious "Red China"). In his second Foreign Policy Report of February 25 and in a speech in early March, Nixon publicly announced that the United States was "pre-pared to establish a dialogue with Beijing." He promised to "examine what further steps" Washington could take to this effect.[13]

Such steps quickly followed. On March 15 the State Department announced that it was removing restrictions on Americans wishing to travel to China (while still enforcing such restrictions on North Vietnam, North Korea, and Cuba). Charles W. Bray, the State Department's press officer who made the announcement, also took the opportunity to stress the "unilateral steps" Washington had taken since 1969 regarding China (e.g., relaxing restrictions on the purchase of Chinese goods and the removal of certain travel restrictions to the PRC). A month later, on April 14, Nixon announced further liberalization, promising that the United States would expedite visas for prospective Chinese visitors to the United States and that Washington would lift restrictions on U.S. oil companies trading with China. Nixon also revealed that he had "asked for a list of items of non-strategic nature which can be placed under gen-eral license for direct export to the People's Republic of China." The United States was in the process of abandoning its decades-long economic war on the PRC.[14] The Nixon administration's willingness for an opening to China was hardly a secret.

Nothing, however, could capture the American public's imagination in the same way as sports. And no sport was closer to the hearts of the Chinese people than ping-pong.

Nagoya, Japan, was the location of the thirty-first World Table Tennis Champi-onship in early April 1971. For several years the PRC had not participated in inter-national sporting events. This time, though, Mao approved a petition, supported by Zhou, from the National Committee on Sports to send a Chinese team. When the team arrived in Nagoya, it was clear that they had not arrived simply to play ping-pong. While refusing to play against the South Vietnamese and Cambodian teams (considered representing illegitimate governments), they warmed to the Americans. The two teams exchanged gifts and the Americans indicated an interest in visiting the PRC. After initial reluctance Mao decided to invite the Americans.

It was a sensational visit. Although several other teams visited China at the same time, it was the Americans who captured everyone's attention. In the U.S. press the young Americans made headline news throughout April. Nixon was elated and sur-prised as the general public became intoxicated with the spectacle. No doubt, there were votes to be garnered from an opening to China; no doubt the Chinese had invited the American ping-pong team for a visit in order to pass on a message that the times were changing.

Zhou delivered exactly such a message when he met with the U.S. team in the Great Hall of the People on April 14. The visit of the ping-pong players had "opened a new chapter in the relations of the American and Chinese people," the premier announced. "I am confident," he added, "that this beginning will certainly meet with majority support of our two peoples." The Americans were dumbstruck. "Don't you agree?" Zhou asked. How could they not, the athletes implied as they started applauding the Chinese premier.

It is hardly an accident that the visit of the U.S. ping-pong team coincided with Nixon's announcement regarding travel restrictions and the easing of economic sanctions. In fact, Kissinger and Nixon spent several hours in mid-April discussing—and guessing—whether the moment when everything would fit together had finally arrived. Zhou's invitation, Nixon said on April 15, had been "one hell of a move." Kissinger, no less euphoric, speculated, largely erroneously as it turned out, that the Chinese may have decided to make this move because "they know Hanoi is gonna make a peace move and they don't want to be left out." One should not be too surprised if "Vietnam will break suddenly," he added. There was "a better than even chance now that in the next three months something will break."[15]

*　*　*

On Friday evening, April 16, Nixon appeared at the annual convention of the American Society of Newspaper Editors. The panel interview was broadcast live on radio. When asked about recent developments on China, Nixon was positive but cautious. "It is up to the Chinese," he said, maintaining that "we have taken several steps. They have taken one." When the interviews were over Nixon was, as usual, soliciting impressions while Kissinger, as usual, was beside himself with accolades. During a telephone conversation at 10:45 P.M. he said that the president had been "wise" and "tremendously effective." Nixon agreed and took tremendous pride in the fact that, as he put it: "I didn't give away goddamned thing." In between other phone calls, Nixon and Kissinger spoke two more times about the press conference that evening, with the same Nixon who didn't care about "that shit"—the press's reaction—repeatedly asking how it all had "played." Kissinger, the careful courtier, was sure to pander the president's need for reassurance.[16]

The two worried, though, that the promising moves by the Chinese and the opening itself might not materialize. Nixon, in particular, was torn between his enthusiasm to move fast and his worry that appearing too eager would be counterproductive. In a similar vein Kissinger worried "that if we are too eager the Chinese will go back to a shell." For this purpose, he advised Nixon, it was important to crack down on any enthusiasm in the State Department. The best way of doing this, Kissinger insisted, was by keeping the knowledge of any significant developments within as small a circle as possible. On April 18, Nixon agreed. "Our Chinese game should be played exactly as it has been played," he said. Given his desire to maximize the shock effect that any sudden shift could produce—both internationally and domestically—it was no wonder that Nixon was willing to play it close. Yet, he also had an uncomfortable feeling that this was it: do or die. With Vietnam in the doldrums and the Soviets intransigent, with the next presidential election only nineteen months away, Nixon summed up the significance of a potential opening to China: "We're playing for very high stakes now, we have very little time left, and we cannot diddle around".[17]

The following day, April 19, Kissinger, at Nixon's behest, ordered NSSM 124: "Next Steps Toward the People's Republic of China." The study, to be completed by May 15, was to explore "possible diplomatic initiatives which the United States might take toward the PRC with the objective of furthering the improvement of our relations."[18]

NSSM 124 was essentially an academic exercise. On April 27, while the NSC Interdepartmental Group was working on the study, Kissinger received the message from Zhou that set the ball rolling toward his July secret trip to China.

Later that same evening Nixon and Kissinger ruminated with each other about the historic significance of the moment:

> Kissinger: "We set up this whole intricate web. When we talked about linkage everyone was sneering, so we got it all hooked together, Berlin, SALT . . . I think if we get this thing [with China] working, we'll end Vietnam this year."
>
> Nixon: "Yeah, we got a bit more luxury than we used to have. Normally we don't have much to move with, but . . ."
>
> Kissinger: "[This is] one of those occasions where everything is beginning to fit together."[19]

It was, undoubtedly, a triumphant evening. After twenty-seven months of frustration and false starts, the structure—the architecture—that the men had so often discussed was about to be erected.

Yet, to guard the secrecy of Polo I, Kissinger's staff engaged in normal activities throughout May and June that clearly deceived most observers about the events that were about to unfold in July. The most evident substantive progress in U.S. national security policy in the late spring and early summer of 1971 appeared to take place in the field of Soviet-American relations.

THE "CONCEPTUAL BREAKTHROUGH"

As the U.S. ping-pong team was meeting with Zhou Enlai, Kissinger's mind was calculating the global ramifications of such a public display of Sino-American rapprochement. "The current moves on China will help to shake the Soviets up,"

Kissinger told Haldeman and Nixon on April 12, 1971. "Brezhnev's need to make a big peace move of some kind should play in favor for a SALT agreement and a Summit conference," he further speculated. The following evening, April 13, Kissinger reported to Nixon that the Soviet chargé d'affaires Yuli Vorontsov had been particularly forthcoming and suggested that the Soviets would soon be ready for an agreement to hold a high-level summit with the United States. Vorontsov had been "slopping all over me," Kissinger told Nixon. Most significantly, Vorontsov had promised that when Anatoly Dobrynin returned from his trip to Moscow in a few days, he would have new instructions. Kissinger had then called Dobrynin in Moscow, ostensibly to congratulate him for becoming a member of the Soviet Communist Party's Central Committee. Dobrynin had reiterated Vorontsov's statement. There was "definitely something," Kissinger told Nixon.

"With some luck we get some nibble from the Soviet front," Kissinger repeated in another telephone conversation the following evening. "Logically [it] ought to happen," he added.[20]

Kissinger was right. Just over a month later Nixon was able to announce the "first major step in breaking the stalemate on nuclear arms talks."[21] As he prepared to launch his 1972 reelection bid, the president was suddenly sensing a whole series of dramatic changes in U.S. relations with its major communist adversaries.

The Soviets had, in fact, decided to accelerate the détente process months before the advent of ping-pong diplomacy. By late 1970 the Kremlin had grown frustrated over the lack of progress in Soviet-American relations. Thus, at the recommendation of Foreign Minister Andrei Gromyko and KGB Chief Yuri Andropov, the Soviet Politburo decided to engage the Nixon administration more actively. The posture was remarkably similar to that of the other side: while continuing their military buildup the Soviets should engage the Americans. Or, in Soviet terminology: it was important to use Soviet military strength to convince "[the] American ruling circles that it is in the most vital national interest of the United States" to move toward "peaceful coexistence." It was "peace through strength"—in reverse. Lastly the Politburo agreed that it was important "to demonstrate the possibility of a further development of Soviet-American relations."[22] Moscow was ready for the next move.

Thus, while Nixon and Kissinger were considering the pros and cons of Lam Son 719 in 1971, Dobrynin suddenly indicated that the Soviets were willing to move forward on a summit meeting later in the same year. What he asked for, however, was that the administration be willing to discuss a wide range of issues (from the Middle East to SALT and from the European Security Conference to the question of Berlin). In a meeting with Dobrynin on January 9, 1971, Kissinger discussed these issues in detail. He indicated that Nixon was ready to devote full attention to improving Soviet-American relations and focused on Berlin and SALT. Three weeks later Dobrynin went even further, indicating that the Soviets were keen on: (a) holding a summit later in the year; (b) ironing out an agreement on Berlin before the summit; (c) negotiating a SALT agreement. According to Kissinger's memo of the meeting, Dobrynin also "implied strongly that in its present framework Indochina would not be an obstacle to our relations." In Moscow, Dobrynin volunteered, "everybody was quite optimistic" about the prospects of Soviet-American détente. The agenda and chances of progress appeared manageable. After agreeing to meet "regularly and systematically," Dobrynin closed the meeting with some hyperbole. "The future of our relations is in our hands," he told Kissinger. After almost two years of endless sparring, the back channel had at long last, become "operational."[23]

All three issues—Berlin, SALT, and agreement on holding a high-level summit—were subjects of heated negotiation over the next six months. These were not simple issues, yet progress was clear. Indeed, had it not been for Zhou Enlai's invitation in late April, followed by Kissinger and Nixon's decision to postpone agreements with the Soviets until after Kissinger's secret trip to China, it is likely that Nixon and Brezhnev would have held their summit as early as the fall of 1971. By May of that year, however, triangulation—and the additional leverage that the Americans expected to gain from the opening to China—served to postpone the Soviet-American agreements already in sight.

*   *   *

The question of Western access routes to Berlin was a legacy of the division of Germany after World War II that had left Berlin, deep inside East Germany, divided into four occupation zones (American, British, French, and Soviet). In 1948, the Soviets had blocked western land access to Berlin and the United States responded with a massive airlift. In the late 1950s Berlin's status had yet again created heightened tension that climaxed in the 1961 Berlin Crisis and the erection of the Berlin Wall. Although economically supported by West Germany, West Berlin remained in a legal limbo: neither the Western powers nor the Bonn government described it as a part of West Germany but regarded it as an occupied territory. By the time the Nixon administration came to office, however, the Western demand for unhampered access to their respective zones still remained technically unresolved and the West refused to recognize East Germany as a sovereign state. The road, rail, and air links that ran through East German territory to Berlin could easily be cut off by Soviet or East German forces. Thus, what the Western powers and West Germany wanted, in essence, was a Soviet, rather than East German, guarantee of more normal access to West Berlin itself as well as between the eastern and western parts of the city.

Even as Willy Brandt moved towards *Ostpolitik* (see chapter 5), the potential for another Berlin crisis was high and the city remained the most potent symbol of the Cold War division of Europe. Naturally, Berlin also symbolized the struggle for German reunification: the link between West Germany and West Berlin was also a much-valued one for policy makers in Bonn, while taking control of the access routes from the USSR was seen as a goal of asserting East Germany's sovereignty and, hence, the permanent division of Germany. Thus, while the West Germans and their allies demanded some form of recognized economic political presence in West Berlin, the East Germans and Soviets argued that any official West German presence was illegal. Lastly, the Berlin question was so complicated because it could not be solved without the involvement of the four occupying powers (France, Great Britain, the Soviet Union, and the United States) or without German (East and West) approval. And yet, the two German governments could not directly participate in the Four Power talks over Berlin because these were, legally, about the rights of the occupying powers. It was no wonder that the Four Power talks were moving slowly in 1970–71.

Enter back channels. In the spring of 1971, Kissinger employed two back channels to break the deadlock in the Four Power negotiations. In addition to the Dobrynin–Kissinger channel, Kissinger involved Willy Brandt's confidant, Egon Bahr (who had conducted his own secret talks with Moscow in 1970), and the American ambassador to Bonn, Kenneth Rush, in the process. Essentially, the purpose of the latter channel was to make sure that West Germans were coordinating their approach with the Americans. Rush, to Kissinger's great satisfaction, not only kept him apprised of the status of the Four Power talks but managed to keep the rest of the State Department uninformed.

The talks processed slowly until late April. After a meeting with Bahr in Vermont that month, Kissinger suggested that the negotiators drop the legal wrangling that was bound to lead nowhere (since the Western powers would never recognize East Germany and the Soviets kept looking for a formula that would imply such a recognition). Instead, they should focus on the practical issues and responsibilities at stake: to make sure that access to Berlin was guaranteed by the Soviets. Dobrynin had no real problem with that. But he insisted that some sort of consensus needed to be reached.

On April 26 (the day before Kissinger received Zhou Enlai's letter that invited an American emissary to Beijing) Dobrynin told Kissinger that he was bound by instructions from Moscow. A week later the sudden resignation (under Soviet pressure) of Walter Ulbricht and the ascendancy of Erich Hoenecker as the new leader of the East German Communist Party indicated that the Soviets had found a leader more willing to accept a compromise. A week after Ulbricht's resignation a new secret forum between Bahr, Rush, and the Soviet Ambassador to Bonn Valentin Falin began a series of secret meetings in the West German capital.

By early June the outlines of an agreement were ironed out in which the Soviets guaranteed western access to Berlin; West Germans were secured civilian access to West Berlin, but West Berlin itself was not officially recognized as a part of West Germany. Aside from the question of a Soviet consulate in West Berlin, the agreement was basically complete. But, in an ironic twist of fate, it had come too early. Kissinger, by this time busily planning for his forthcoming foray to Beijing, told Rush to hold on until mid-July.

It was a puzzling decision to those, such as Ambassador Rush, who had no idea that Kissinger was packing his bags for a trip to Beijing. Nor did the decision to postpone the agreement—finally signed on September 3, 1971—result in any substantial changes in the text itself. What the postponement did accomplish, though, was an impression that Kissinger's secret trip provided him with additional leverage vis-à-vis the USSR.[24]

*   *   *

By this point Kissinger and Dobrynin had already negotiated a basic agreement on SALT. As on Berlin, Kissinger proposed in January 1971 that he and Dobrynin break the continuing deadlock in the official negotiations—American and Soviet SALT delegations were scheduled to begin their official discussions in Vienna later in the spring—through talks in the back channel. Dobrynin agreed.[25] Between early February and May 1971 Kissinger and Dobrynin met almost on a weekly basis, exchanging proposals and counterproposals, oral notes and written communiqués that, in retrospect may appear as a grand waste of time. Yet, one has to keep in mind that, much as in the case of Berlin, the two were negotiating over one of the most contentious issues of the Cold War.

At stake was, after all, not merely a game of numbers and theoretical advantages, but that concept so dear to most statesmen: credibility. While the ongoing wrangling over whether one should conclude an agreement over defensive missiles before or jointly with a deal on offensive missiles strikes one as a highly theoretical debate suitable best for that odd breed known as defense intellectuals, at the heart of the entire process was a set of difficult political issues. If the Americans gave away too much, how would the Western allies react? What would a sellout mean to Nixon's reelection chances? What propaganda advantages would the Soviets possibly gain from a rushed deal? How would all this influence (or be influenced by) the China initiative?

The SALT negotiations were further complicated by the reinvigorated domestic debate in the United States over nuclear weapons. At the heart of it was the highly publicized and growing opposition to anti-ballistic missiles (ABMs) on the part of leading Democrats like Edward Muskie, Frank Church, and Hubert Humphrey. They, as well as Senator William Fulbright, continued to attack the administration's contention that ABMs were a useful bargaining chip in the talks with the USSR. Criticism over the administration's MIRV program as too expensive further added to the pressure of achieving a breakthrough. The Soviets undoubtedly hoped to use such pressure as well as Nixon's obvious reelection calculations to their advantage.[26] Time, in many ways, seemed to be on their side.

Nevertheless, the Kissinger–Dobrynin SALT negotiations began on a promising note. On February 4, Dobrynin told Kissinger that the Soviets were ready to decouple defensive and offensive missiles. Given the respective strengths and weaknesses of each side, this was a key to any compromise solution. The Americans, for example, continued to maintain a technological edge and a numerical advantage in offensive weapons (weapons designed to strike the USSR, or its allies, either from land-based missile sites in the United States, or from long-range bombers or submarines equipped with nuclear weapons). Meanwhile, the Soviets were leaping ahead in the development of ABMs, networks of missiles built around, say, Moscow and designed to shoot down any incoming American missiles. Once the two sides agreed to discuss these two categories of nuclear weapons separately, it was possible to reach a compromise on each (as would eventually be the case in 1972).

Delighted that the Soviets were finally coming up with serious proposals, Kissinger had a draft agreement ready by the end of February. Then the stalling game began. In their meetings on February 26 and March 5, Dobrynin, perhaps disingenuously, referred to the upcoming Party Congress in the USSR that was preoccupying all Soviet leaders. When he did come back with a counterproposal on March 12, it was unacceptable to Kissinger: although the Soviets decoupled (as agreed) defensive and offensive missiles, they wanted to agree on an ABM treaty first and then continue with negotiations on offensive missiles (ICBMs and SLBMs). As Dobrynin flew to Moscow to participate in the Party Congress that was scheduled to begin on March 30, the issue was unresolved. It would remain so for the next six weeks.[27]

To complicate matters, the public negotiations began in the spring of 1971. While the back channel remained deadlocked on ABMs and ICBMs, the official American SALT delegation arrived in Vienna to begin negotiations with their Soviet counterparts. In the usual fashion Gerard Smith, Paul Nitze, Raymond Garthoff, and the rest of the American delegation had been kept in the dark about the back-channel talks that had already consumed much of Kissinger's time. In all fairness, though, one should note that Kissinger repeatedly complained to Dobrynin about his inability to issue firm directions to the Vienna talks because of Soviet stalling.[28]

In April 1971 KGB chief Yuri Andropov, as well as Dobrynin, reported to the Soviet Communist Party Secretariat that the Americans were still holding on to a rather uncompromising line. Andropov emphasized the primacy of domestic politics in Nixon's thinking and argued that while the president was undoubtedly ready to compromise, he wished to get maximum political credit from SALT by signing an agreement as close to the 1972 elections as possible. Andropov also made reference to Kissinger: the NSC adviser had said at a "private dinner" that for domestic reasons it was better for Nixon to hold out for the summit until the following year. Still, Andropov correctly anticipated a partial SALT agreement, separating offensive and defensive missiles, in the near future.[29] Armed with instructions to accept such a separation of the two groups of nuclear weapons, Dobrynin returned to Washington in mid-April.

In subsequent back channel meetings on April 26 and May 12–13, Kissinger and Dobrynin agreed on the "conceptual breakthrough." In effect, the two sides agreed on a general formula for the SALT I agreements to be signed a year later. There would be an ABM Treaty and a simultaneous, albeit more limited, treaty to limit offensive nuclear weapons. It was still rather vague. As the official statement put it, the United States and the Soviet Union had agreed to "concentrate this year on working out an agreement for the limitation of the deployment of ABMs. They have also agreed that, together with concluding an agreement to limit ABMs, they will agree on certain measures with respect to the limitation of offensive strategic weapons."

There were no specifics. Still, Nixon hailed the announcement as "a major step in breaking the stalemate on nuclear arms talks." As Bob Haldeman records in his diaries, the president was elated. Throughout the following day, he was "cranked up [and] bouncy." Kissinger was equally buoyant. To him, though, the May 20 agreement was as much about nuclear weapons as it was about internal struggle for authority; it essentially confirmed that the NSC, rather than the State Department, was the operational arm of Nixon's foreign policy team. As Kissinger put it in his memoirs, the agreement "was a milestone in confirming White House dominance in foreign affairs. For the first two years [of the Nixon administration] White House control had been confined to the formulation of policy; now it extended to its execution."[30]

Therein lay the cause for much of the criticism about the "conceptual breakthrough." It was less than revolutionary. That the two sides committed themselves to negotiating a separate ABM agreement that would coincide with limits on the building of offensive weapons was a compromise that could have been reached much earlier. It was also a deal that, both Gerard Smith, who headed the U.S. SALT delegation in the official negotiations in Helsinki and his key aide Raymond Garthoff insist, was less advantageous than one reached via the official negotiations.[31] The major criticism about the "conceptual breakthrough" has to do, however, more with the method by which the breakthrough had been reached. The primacy of the back channel to Nixon and Kissinger amply demonstrated to the Soviets the jealousies and rivalries that had by this point become so endemic within U.S. foreign policy making circles. As Garthoff puts it: "What the Soviet leadership learned about Nixon, Kissinger, and the American administration [in May 1971] was worth far more than quibbling over any details."[32] What they learned, of course, was that the back channel was the premium avenue for progress in Soviet-American relations and that, as a result, cultivating Kissinger was well worth the effort.

In retrospect, some of the backbiting and demand for secrecy that preceded the "conceptual breakthrough" seems almost comic. At one point, for example, Kissinger got upset when the issues he and Dobrynin had discussed in the back channel (but had already been abandoned) suddenly surfaced as an official Soviet proposition in Vienna. Such a breach, Kissinger maintained, raised questions about the Soviet good faith—in other words, about the reliability of the Soviet side to keep information to themselves rather than sharing it with the other Americans engaged in what was, presumably, the same general negotiation process.

* * *

As in the case of the opening to China, the other justification for secrecy was polit-ical. Kissinger and Nixon (Kissinger insists mainly the president) were concerned about receiving the appropriate credit for the breakthrough. In particular, they worried that someone else, such as William Rogers or Gerard Smith, would be able to claim some of the limelight. Whether such concerns had to do with sheer per-sonal vanity or domestic political needs, they created another awkward moment for Bob Haldeman. Neither Nixon nor Kissinger wished to be the one breaking the news of a back-channel deal to Rogers. On May 19, once he had finally been filled in on most of the details, the secretary of state vented his anger at Haldeman. "Why had he not been informed about the Kissinger–Dobrynin talks?" Rogers demanded. After all, the secretary of state claimed, "he's fully posted Henry on everything." So why "is he not being posted by Henry?"

Haldeman had no satisfactory answer and Nixon finally spoke directly with Rogers on the telephone. Immediately after the conversation, which was neither the first or the last of its kind, Nixon "heaved a deep sigh, looked out the window, and said: "it would be goddamn easy to run this office if you didn't have to deal with people."[33]

Notwithstanding the criticism and bad blood the back-channel agreement had produced within the administration, the May 20 announcement was the most dra-matic one Nixon had yet made on issues having to do with Soviet-American rela-tions. It was greeted with almost universal public approval. When he told about the breakthrough to a joint meeting of the cabinet and congressional leaders, Nixon received a standing ovation. Press reports were positive and John Scali, a former ABC-TV correspondent who had recently joined the White House staff as a con-sultant on information policy, wrote a memo a week after the announcement about "an avalanche of favorable comment that [had] been unleashed since the SALT announcement." In sum, the president could finally claim to have concluded a practical step on the road to launching détente.[34]

While the announcement was a political triumph for Nixon, the conceptual breakthrough also represented another bureaucratic victory for Kissinger. While he could not take public credit for it, Kissinger had certainly confirmed his central role as the architect of détente. The back channel was where the decisions were clearly made; Kissinger as the operator of that channel thus ran the show. No wonder that William Rogers complained to Haldeman about being made a "laughing stock."[35]

But the conceptual breakthrough was hardly enough. From a political perspec-tive—as Nixon looked ahead toward the 1972 presidential elections—the SALT breakthrough alone would not resonate widely with the general public. In fact, opposition to the SALT agreements was bound to be rampant, with conservatives blaming the Nixon administration for bargaining away America's tactical advan-tage and liberals accusing it for failing to make a serious enough effort to reduce the arms race. Moreover, by the summer of 1971 the Nixon administration had given the American public little hope regarding the Vietnam War. The fruits of Soviet-American détente appeared meager in the summer of 1971.

Fortunately for both Kissinger's reputation and Nixon's reelection bid, the SALT breakthrough was soon overshadowed by something far more dramatic. On June 11 Zhou Enlai accepted the proposed schedule for Kissinger's secret July 9–11 visit to Beijing, while Pakistan's President Yahya Khan—embroiled in a conflict in East Pakistan that would eventually demand Kissinger's full attention—assured that his government would make "absolutely foolproof arrangements" to safeguard the secrecy of the forthcoming trip.[36]

VIETNAM, TRIANGULATION, AND SECRECY

In the weeks between the May 20 announcement and Kissinger's departure for Asia in early July, three issues dominated the NSC adviser's agenda: secret meetings with the North Vietnamese in Paris, back-channel diplomacy with Dobrynin, and careful planning for the China trip. Aside from the assumption that Vietnam, détente, and China were inextricably linked, the key common denominator for all was simple: the need to preserve secrecy in order to guarantee that control for policy making remained in the White House. While Kissinger was successful in this regard, there was no substantive progress on either Vietnam or the emerging détente. This undoubtedly contributed to his apparent belief that everything would change once Kissinger returned from his secret July excursion to the Middle Kingdom.

After a series of exchanges, the secret meetings in Paris resumed on May 31. On the appointed date, at the familiar Rue Darthé apartment, Kissinger tabled another (seven-point) proposal that he had worked on with Lord and Smyser. It was, Kissinger claimed in his memoirs, effectively the plan that would be accepted sixteen months later. The major new element was an offer to set a terminal date for U.S. troop withdrawals. Of course, it was tied to six other points, including withdrawal of all outside forces; a ceasefire (to commence with the start of American troop withdrawals); an end to external infiltration into Indochina; international supervision; reinstatement of the 1954 and 1962 Geneva Accords; and the return of all POWs. Xuan Thuy, not authorized to bargain, reiterated previous points. Yet, Kissinger thought, he had expressed, or at least implied, an interest in continued negotiations.[37]

In Hanoi, the Politburo found the seven-point proposal promising yet ultimately unacceptable. Repeated references to "outside forces" were considered evidence of the American unwillingness to accept North Vietnamese presence in the South. A ceasefire that would coincide with the withdrawal of American troops would mean that the North Vietnamese troops (the People's Army of Vietnam [PAVN]) could not send reinforcements; meanwhile South Vietnamese President Thieu could use the ceasefire to strengthen his position in the South and hence complicate the post–

American unification struggle. The Americans, the Politburo concluded, were moving in the right direction but would have to do better. They would demand a more rapid U.S. withdrawal, coupled with a political solution that would include the removal of Thieu and most of his government. In addition, the North Vietnamese would demand reparations and the end to all attacks on the North.[38]

* * *

To make the North Vietnamese stand more authoritative, Le Duc Tho, who had not attended the secret sessions for fourteen months, arrived in Paris for the next meeting. En route to the French capital he stopped in Beijing and Moscow, hence signaling that a serious negotiation was in the offing. On June 26, when Kissinger and his aides arrived at the secret meeting place in Paris, they found that the North Vietnamese had, for the first time, arranged the meeting room to resemble a formal negotiation room. Previously the negotiators had sat around in easy chairs; this time there was a green, cloth-covered conference table with the North Vietnamese and Americans sitting across from each other. The atmosphere, although hardly friendly, also gave a general impression of a seriousness of purpose. During a brief break in the talks, Tho and Kissinger even walked together in the outside garden.[39]

But appearances did not guarantee substantial progress. Le Duc Tho was not about to give in to any American demands. "Have I made any progress?" Kissinger jokingly asked Tho at one point. "Not one inch," the Vietnamese negotiator responded. He wanted a package deal; military and political problems could not be negotiated separately. More specifically, Tho added, "as long as you maintain the Nguyen Van Thieu administration the problem still remains unresolved." After a lengthy critique of U.S. policy, Xuan Thuy read out Hanoi's nine-point counterproposal. Hanoi demanded that the United States cease supporting the Thieu government and withdraw its forces by the end of 1971. Point 4 of the proposal further stated that Washington "should bear full responsibility and pay damages for the losses caused to the whole of Vietnam." Kissinger, naturally, objected. Yet, the two sides agreed that progress might just be possible and set another meeting date for July 12.[40]

While the North Vietnamese remained intransigent, the Soviets appeared in no hurry to set a date for the prospective superpower summit. During back-channel meetings on June 8, 14, and 21, Kissinger raised the issue, reminding Dobrynin that he had indicated strong Soviet interest in a high-level meeting already in January 1971 but, despite numerous American probes, no date had yet been set. The Nixon administration would prefer to hold the summit in the fall of 1971, Kissinger maintained. On the 21st, after the details for his China trip were set, Kissinger demanded an answer by the end of the month; otherwise, the summit idea might have to be abandoned completely.[41]

Dobrynin's reply came on July 5, four days after Kissinger had left for an extensive tour in the Far East and four days prior to his arrival in Beijing. The note Dobrynin handed to Kissinger's deputy, Alexander Haig, was noncommittal, setting no precise date for a summit. Hence, Haig recommended to Nixon that he advise "Kissinger [to] proceed with the other option [of] seeking an early summit in Peking."

Nixon agreed.[42]

*   *   *

While Kissinger engaged Le Duc Tho and probed Dobrynin, the need for secrecy dominated preparations for the China trip, creating some awkward moments. Nixon had to dissuade both Vice President Agnew and Secretary of Defense Laird from planning stopovers in Taiwan in order not to offend Beijing and risk the impending rapprochement during their Far East tours in June.[43] Most significantly, though, Kissinger continued to insist on the, by now routine, need to keep Rogers in the dark. The justification he used remained the same: the State Department was filled with various vested bureaucratic interests opposed to a sudden opening to China and prone to leaking to the press. Hoping to maximize the shock effect of the China initiative, Nixon generally sympathized with Kissinger's argument. While the president agreed that open debate about the China initiative was likely to "scuttle the whole effort," the publication of the Pentagon Papers, which started to appear in the *New York Times* on June 13, drove him into a fury of accusations about leaks in Kissinger's own staff. Kissinger himself was enraged, but mainly because the papers had been leaked to the *New York Times* by Daniel Ellsberg, a former associate who had worked on NSSM-1, the first NSC study of Vietnam during the Nixon administration. In fact, the *Pentagon Papers*, an approximately 7,000-page history of the decision-making process that dug the United States deeper and deeper into the Vietnam morass in the 1960s, dealt almost exclusively with pre-1969 Vietnam policy. As such, their publication did not substantively reflect on the policies of the Nixon administration. Alexander Haig, for one, thought that the administration should "keep out of it and let the people that are affected cut each other up on it." Kissinger thought otherwise. Because Nixon associated Ellsberg with Kissinger, because his staff had had its previous leaking problems—for example, in the aftermath of the secret bombings of Cambodia in 1969 (discussed in chapter 3)—the publication of the Pentagon Papers was bound to reflect poorly on the NSC adviser. Perhaps overcompensating, Kissinger ranted and railed about Ellsberg in mid-June and supported the activities of the so-called plumbers unit that would use every trick in the book, including raiding Ellsberg's psychiatrist's office, to plug the leaks. But the Kissinger–Ellsberg link also adversely affected Kissinger's argument about the chronic leaks in the State Department. Kissinger's familiar argument—"the State leaks"—was now treated with an irritated reply: "So does your staff."[44]

Whatever the level of his anger at the time, Nixon still accommodated Kissinger's pleas to keep the secretary of state in the dark as long as possible. The last thing either man wanted was to hand the *New York Times* another major scoop.

Eventually, after Kissinger had departed for his mission, Nixon did fill his old friend in, albeit in a manner that spoke volumes about the president's own personal insecurities and character. At 10:30 A.M. on July 8, 1971, Nixon invited Rogers to his office at the Western White House in San Clemente, California. It could hardly be described as a man-to-man talk (or confession); in addition to Haldeman, Nixon asked Kissinger's deputy (and future White House Chief of Staff and Secretary of State) Al Haig to sit in. To top it all off, once Rogers arrived, Nixon followed an intricate script of lies and half-truths.

Haldeman had, upon Nixon's instructions, earlier told Rogers that Pakistani President Yahya Khan had asked for a presidential emissary to pick up a sensitive message from the Chinese. But once Kissinger got to Islamabad to receive this (nonexisting) message, Nixon told Rogers, the situation had changed: "rather than just delivering a message to him, [the Chinese] wanted him to come to Peking for a meeting with Zhou." This is what Kissinger was now doing, Nixon told his secretary of state, then elaborating on plans about a future presidential visit. "Rogers, of course, would be going on the visit," Nixon reassured. "Rogers took it all extremely well," Haldeman jotted down in his diaries, adding that: "the meeting accomplished everything the P[resident] had hoped for, and then some."[45]

Maybe so. But it was also a shining example of Nixon's curious personality that he would avoid telling the entire truth even as he knew that Rogers would learn the truth, sooner rather than later.

EUREKA!

While Nixon was meeting with Rogers in San Clemente, Kissinger was on "the most momentous journey" of his life. On July 1, 1971, he had commenced a tour of South and Southeast Asia. Kissinger took along NSC staffers John H. Holdridge, Winston Lord, Richard Smyser, Harold Saunders, and David Halperin, as well as two NSC secretaries, Diane Matthews and Florence Gwyer, and two secret service agents, Jack Ready and Gary McCleod. The group made stopovers in South Vietnam, Thailand, and India before arriving in Islamabad on July 8. After an evening reception from which Kissinger retired early—"feeling slightly indisposed," the *New York Times* reported—the national security adviser, at 3:30 A.M. the following morning, got up and returned (with Lord, Smyser, Holdridge, and two Secret Service men) to the airport. Waiting there was a Boeing 707, manned by a Pakistani and a Chinese crew[46] and ready for an immediate takeoff to Beijing. By prior arrangement but to the great surprise of the two Secret Service men, who had not been briefed about the destination of the group, four Chinese officials awaited on board: Zhang Wenjin (a longtime associate of Zhou Enlai), Wang Hairon (Mao's mother's grand-niece), Tang Longbin (of the Foreign Ministry's Protocol Department), and Nancy Tang (an American-born interpreter).[47]

As they approached Beijing, the first crisis erupted. Kissinger had asked his special assistant David Halperin, who stayed behind in Pakistan and acted as Kissinger's double over the next few days, to make sure that a few clean shirts were set aside for the China trip. Halperin had done so, with extreme care. Unfortunately, the shirts were so carefully set aside that they never made it onto the plane; Kissinger, who wished to change into a new shirt before the plane touched down in Beijing, flew into a rage (or, as he puts it, "invoked Halperin's name with somewhat less than the affection I actually felt for him"). He ended up borrowing John Holdridge's—"a six foot-two trim former West Pointer whose build did not exactly coincide with my rather more compact physique"—shirts. As a result, on this historic occasion, Kissinger complained to Winston Lord, he looked like a penguin![48]

Over the following two days Kissinger spent, according to his calculations, up to seventeen hours in discussions with Chinese Premier Zhou Enlai (half of this time, he would later note, was spent on translation). During these talks Kissinger did his best to win over the Chinese veteran revolutionary who had been so memorably snubbed by the erstwhile John Foster Dulles during the multilateral talks on Indochina in Geneva in 1954. When they first met at the guesthouse where Kissinger and his entourage stayed during the trip, Kissinger made sure to offer his hand first. Zhou smiled and shook it, thus acknowledging the symbolic significance of the gesture.

It was a handshake worthy of remembering. To Kissinger, in particular, the scene would be etched in memory. As he later wrote, Zhou "was one of the two or three most impressive men I have ever met." On that afternoon of July 9, 1971, as Zhou arrived at Kissinger's guesthouse in the Forbidden City, Kissinger was struck by Zhou's "gaunt, expressive face . . . dominated by piercing eyes, conveying a mixture of intensity and repose, of wariness and calm self-confidence . . . He moved gracefully and with dignity, filling a room not by his physical dominance but by his air of controlled tension, steely discipline, and self-control, as if he were a coiled spring."

In contrast to Kissinger, Zhou's praise or criticism of his American interlocutor remains sparse. Yet, the premier was not entirely untouched during the hours he was to spend with his American visitor. Kissinger was, Zhou would say in March 1972, "very intelligent—indeed a Dr." Zhang Wenjing, who had been Zhou's personal secretary for many years and would later serve as China's ambassador to the United States, described the Chinese view of Kissinger somewhat more elaborately in an interview with Zhou's biographer Han Suyin: "At first we were puzzled by Mr. Kissinger. We thought, quite frankly, that he was being arrogant . . . but then we were not used to his style. He talked much of philosophy, and general principles, but it seemed to us inappropriate, a little like a moral lecture." Zhang Wenjing does support Kissinger's account in one important aspect: "Premier Zhou set the tone and pace, and got to the matters to be discussed." In other words, it was Zhou, not Kissinger, who was in charge during the secret trip.[49]

In July 1971 the two men engaged in long sessions that focused on, in Kissinger's words, ensuring that each side understood "the fundamental purposes of the other." Aside from agreeing on Nixon's future visit and on the text of the communiqué that would announce it, there was hardly anything practical to discuss. After all, the purpose of the trip was to break the ice that had built over the last two decades of hostility.

The best way of doing this was, naturally, by finding compromise solutions on controversial issues such as Taiwan. This was the leadoff topic during Kissinger and Zhou's first meeting on July 9 that stretched almost seven hours, from 4:35 P.M. through dinner until 11:20 P.M. Zhou gave a long presentation, stressing the historical importance of Taiwan to the mainland and the necessity for the United States to remove all its armed forces from the Taiwan straits. This was the "crucial question," Zhou stressed. The United States must recognize the PRC "unreservedly . . . Just as we recognize the U.S. as the sole legitimate government without considering Hawaii, the last state, an exception to your sovereignty."

In response Kissinger, not unlike the way he approached negotiations with the North Vietnamese, wanted to separate the question into political (question of PRC's sovereignty over Taiwan) and military (U.S. presence) matters. He also linked the Taiwan question directly to the Vietnam War. Kissinger assured that the United States had no interest in "advocating a 'two Chinas' or a 'one China, one Taiwan' solution." As a result of the historical process, Taiwan would eventually be part of the PRC, he predicted. Kissinger further stressed that the United States military presence on the Taiwan straits was bound to diminish by "two-thirds . . . within a specified brief period of time after the ending of the war in Indochina."

Zhou responded favorably to part of the argument. Kissinger's assurance that the United States did not adhere to a two-China policy "shows that the prospect for a solution and the establishment of diplomatic relations between our two countries is hopeful." Zhou also volunteered that the Chinese would like to move toward this goal while Nixon was in office. Kissinger agreed. Yet, he thought it unlikely that formal diplomatic recognition could be achieved before the first half of Nixon's second term.[50]

Later on during the trip Kissinger further indicated that the Americans were willing to let Taiwan become marginalized. He and Zhou discussed the PRC's bid for membership in the UN and Kissinger even assured that Washington would be ready to move toward full normalization with Beijing in the first half of Nixon's second term. As James Mann puts it, during Kissinger's secret trip the Nixon administration effectively "made many, though not all, of the concessions China had sought."[51]

The key phrase is "not all." The secret trip—or the Nixon administration's policy in general—hardly translated into a complete abandonment of Taiwan. What Kissinger gave was an assurance that the United States was willing to downgrade its relationship with Taiwan by, for example, not objecting to the PRC becoming a member of the UN Security Council. This, in the end, only brought U.S. policy more in line with the existing reality, recognized by 1971 by most of its allies. The

Chinese, it seems, well understood that Kissinger's admission and subsequent U.S. policy did not translate into a green light to incorporate Taiwan into the PRC by force.

While Taiwan was an important topic in Beijing, Kissinger and Zhou spent even more time discussing Vietnam. It was, in fact, Kissinger's leadoff topic on July 9. This was hardly surprising. After all, a few days earlier Kissinger had met with President Thieu in Saigon and he was scheduled to sit down with Le Duc Tho for another secret meeting in Paris on July 12. The time seemed appropriate for a serious bid for peace.

Thus, Kissinger outlined the U.S. position—the seven-point program he had recently offered to the North Vietnamese in Paris—in some detail. He stressed that Hanoi's demand for reparations was unacceptable, that the United States could not overthrow the Thieu government, and that a withdrawal of U.S. forces could only take place if the North Vietnamese agreed to a complete ceasefire throughout all of Indochina. "What we need," Kissinger said, "is what I told the Prime Minister with relation to Taiwan. The military settlement must be separated from the political settlement."

While establishing that fact, however, Kissinger also indicated that the Nixon administration's strategy in Vietnam was, in effect, one of finding a decent interval between the American military withdrawal and the unification of Vietnam. "When we offer to withdraw from Vietnam, it is not in order to devise some trick to re-enter in some other manner but rather that we want to base our foreign policy on the realities of the present."

Zhou was not convinced but returned to his theme:

As you just mentioned, you would like to make an honorable retreat. We think the best way to do this is forthrightly withdraw and completely withdraw all forces and leave the problems of Indochina to be determined by the people of the three countries of Indochina [Vietnam, Cambodia, and Lao] . . . This is the most honorable and glorious way to withdraw.

Even over dinner, the exchange continued. "There can be no cease fire with those people," Zhou said, referring to the South Vietnamese government. They would have to be removed, he added. When Kissinger suggested that this was a possibility once elections were held in South Vietnam, Zhou made clear that he had no interest in such procedures. "We don't believe in elections in South Vietnam," he told Kissinger.

Such was the man Kissinger thought was one of the two or three most impressive he had ever met.

When the delegations returned to the talks in Kissinger's guesthouse Zhou still refused to change the topic of conversation. Asked why the United States wished to leave a "tail" behind after its ground troops were withdrawn, he referred specifically to American advisers and the Thieu government. Kissinger responded that the

advisers were not going to be military men and that the United States had no interest in maintaining a particular government in Saigon. However, he added,

> We cannot participate in the overthrow of people with whom we have been
> allied, whatever the origins of the alliance. If the government [of South Vietnam]
> is as unpopular as you seem to think, then the quicker our forces are withdrawn
> the quicker it will be overthrown . . . if it is overthrown after we withdraw, we will
> not intervene.

Kissinger further volunteered that the ceasefire in Indochina could have "a time
limit, say 18 months."

On the afternoon of the 10th, Kissinger returned to the Vietnam question. He
told Zhou that "what we require is a transition period between the military withdrawal and the political evolution . . . If after complete American withdrawal, the
Indochinese people change their government, the US will not interfere."[52] It was as
close as Kissinger would come to a description of a decent interval. Upon their
departure U.S. troops could not leave behind a unified, communist-controlled
Vietnam. But once the troops were gone, Kissinger implied, they would not return,
nor would the United States intervene in the political settlement that would follow.
Remarkably, Kissinger was making this point as early as July 1971, a year and a half
before the Paris Peace Agreements were signed and only a few days before he was
going to meet with his North Vietnamese interlocutors in Paris.

At the time, however, the Chinese offered no help on Vietnam. When Zhou
informed Mao about Kissinger's comments on Vietnam, the Chairman's attitude
was straightforward: there would be no Chinese pressure on Hanoi. While China,
Mao said, was "in no hurry on the Taiwan issue because there is no fighting on Taiwan," he insisted that in Vietnam "the United States should make a new start and
let the domino fall." Accordingly, Zhou, after lecturing Kissinger on the dangers to
stability throughout the Far East if the war continued, summed up China's attitude
on Vietnam: "if you are able to solve this question, of course, we will be happy. If
not, we can only continue to give them [the North Vietnamese] support."

"I understand your position," Kissinger responded. "There is no misunderstanding."[53]

*   *   *

Aside from Taiwan and Vietnam, Kissinger and Zhou discussed the Soviet Union,
the timing and substance of Nixon's forthcoming trip, and the general state of
international relations. At the end, they briefly touched upon the conflict between
India and Pakistan (this will be elaborated somewhat in the following chapter).

In discussions about the Soviet Union, Kissinger emphasized that the United
States "will never collude with other countries against the People's Republic of
China." "We will not participate in efforts to lasso you," Kissinger told Zhou on

July 10. He further emphasized Nixon's commitment to Sino-American relations, and promised to keep the Chinese informed of any understandings the Americans would make with the Soviets in the future. In sum, Kissinger was clearly laying down the groundwork for his and Nixon's vision of the PRC as a strategic ally of the United States against the Soviet Union.

Yet, while the Soviet Union was frequently mentioned during the secret trip, substantive discussions about it were limited. Although Chinese antipathy toward the USSR was evident, there were no Chinese requests for American help. Instead, the major discussion that included the Soviet Union had to do with the timing of Nixon's visit to Beijing; in short, whether it should occur *before or after* a prospective Soviet-American summit.

Due to Dobrynin's reluctance in setting a firm date for the Soviet-American summit prior to the secret trip, Kissinger and Nixon had agreed to punish Moscow by going to Beijing first. In other words, the timing of the respective Soviet and Chinese summits was part of triangular diplomacy, if not even the opening shot of the game.

But Zhou had a different idea. He suggested that Nixon should go to Moscow first. Not that the Chinese were "afraid of a big turmoil," if the president came to Beijing first. "But we would not deliberately create tensions," he added. Kissinger waffled. While the Soviets had extended an invitation, they had later attached unacceptable conditions. It was still possible that a summit might take place in the next six months. He then indicated a desire for Nixon's visit to Beijing sometime in March or April 1972. "Fine," said Zhou. "But you do agree in principle that it would be good for the President first to visit Moscow and then China?"

"In all honesty," Kissinger responded, "I cannot promise you it [the Soviet summit] will happen no matter when we set the date."

Later on the same day Kissinger briefly returned to the question of timing. He simply stressed that "there was no fixed plan," but should there be significant agreements on SALT or Berlin, then a summit might take place in the next six months.

The point of recounting this seemingly secondary issue is to stress that, for a number of reasons, Kissinger was very keen on securing a visit to Beijing before the Soviet summit. In effect, it was one of the concrete results of the secret trip. And, as much of Kissinger's China policy at this time, the point was to shake up the Soviets and give Americans an edge in subsequent negotiations. The simple act of going to China before going to the Soviet Union was a key part of the tactics—if not the substance—of triangular diplomacy.[54]

After Zhou had agreed to Nixon's visit in the spring of 1972, the final day of the trip was spent on negotiations regarding the announcement of Nixon's future visit and setting up a reliable channel of communication between the two governments. On the Chinese side this part of the talks was handled mostly by Huang Hua, who was soon to travel to Ottawa as the first Chinese ambassador to Canada. A veteran of the Korean armistice talks of 1953, Hua did not give Kissinger an easy time. His first draft of the announcement was completely unacceptable: the Chinese version basically implied that Nixon was asking for permission to visit Mao in order to discuss the American withdrawal from Taiwan as a preparatory step toward the normalization of U.S.-PRC relations. Presented shortly after midnight on Kissinger's second day in Beijing, the Chinese side was, perhaps, trying to use the pressure Kissinger was under to squeeze some concessions; at 1:40 A.M. on the day of departure Hua suggested a half hour recess. He returned to the talks eight hours later.

To Kissinger and his staff, the delay was nerve-racking. Walking around the grounds of their guesthouse in the middle of the hot July night, Kissinger and John Holdridge pondered whether some internal power struggle had suddenly emerged. Perhaps Chinese military leaders were successfully scuttling Zhou's plans for an opening to America because they wished to restore military cooperation with the Soviet Union? Perhaps Mao's own wife, Jiang Qing, known for her rabid anti-Americanism, had impressed the Chairman of the need to humiliate the American president's secret envoy? Perhaps the Chinese were using Kissinger's approaching departure as a negotiating tactic, trying to get him to agree to a wording that was more favorable to the PRC than to the Americans?

In fact, as the historian Jian Chen points out, the explanation for the delay was probably far less sinister—although perhaps equally disturbing—than any of the above. Mao had simply gone to sleep. Hua needed his approval and did not dare to wake him up.[55]

To his credit, despite the approaching deadline (he was to depart in the early afternoon of July 11) Kissinger did not budge. The Chinese proposed a formula that effectively (with a change of one word) became the announcement that was released a few days later. In three short paragraphs the two sides announced that they had held talks, that the Chinese had invited Nixon to Beijing, and that the president had accepted. The purpose of the visit would be to "seek the normalization of relations between the two countries and also to exchange views on questions of concern to the two sides."[56]

Just before lunchtime on July 11, Kissinger and Zhou held their last meeting of the secret trip. They agreed to set up a secret channel through General Vernon Walters and Ambassador Huang Chen in Paris (the other alternative—Ottawa—was turned down because it would be much more prone to leaks and speculation). Kissinger promised to keep Zhou informed of any Soviet-American agreements. They briefly discussed Japan, the Soviet Union, and Korea. Then they closed the meetings.

"I think we have done some historic work here," said Kissinger.

Zhou was a bit more restrained. "We have gone the first step," he said.[57]

* * *

On the afternoon of July 11, 1971, Kissinger and his group returned to Islamabad, arriving there at 3:00 P.M. local time. With the codeword *Eureka,* Kissinger signaled Nixon in San Clemente that Polo I had been a success.

It is worth noting that during this and all successive encounters with Zhou Enlai over the next two years, Kissinger formed an extraordinarily positive view of the Chinese premier. In contrast to Mao's often unintelligible ramblings, Zhou was the man who provided "continuity and consistency" for the Chinese side. But it was so much more that impressed Kissinger (and a number of his staff members). For example, in the last installment of his memoirs Kissinger described Zhou with such adjectives as "graceful, suave, and elegant." Zhou, of course, had flattered Kissinger by allowing no interruptions, lest it was a call to go and visit Chairman Mao, during their many marathon sessions. Most of all, however, Zhou was eager, much like Kissinger, to focus "on the geopolitical aspects of Sino-American relations" and "to orchestrate parallel contributions to the global, and especially to the Asian, balance of power." With Zhou Kissinger thus engineered—or hoped to engineer—a "Sino-American strategic partnership" that both sides realized had to be based on something less than a formal, public treaty but rather on "tacit understandings regarding the details of the balance of power."[58]

Was Kissinger being taken for a ride by an experienced and duplicitous negotiator? Was he, perhaps, too eager to bring home successful results to see through the Chinese premier's mask? Was the manipulator being manipulated?

Without full access to internal Chinese documents it is difficult to answer such questions with any precision. But two points need to be stressed. First, in all their 1971–73 conversations, Zhou was on his home turf. This enabled him to, in effect, control the pace (if not always the agenda) of the negotiations. While Kissinger had held numerous back-channel sessions with Dobrynin and had met secretly with the North Vietnamese, he was now as far removed from the familiar terrain of Washington and Paris as one could be. In July 1971 the first communication with the outside world was, in fact, Kissinger's brief message to Haig on July 11, after the talks had been completed. Second, Zhou's experience far outweighed Kissinger's. The Chinese premier was a legendary figure, a man who had played a key role in shaping postwar Asia for a quarter century. Kissinger, while quickly learning the trade, was still a relative newcomer to the game of high-level diplomacy. To have written about Metternich, Bismarck, and other great diplomats of the nineteenth century was one thing; to meet face-to-face with one of Asia's most experienced statesmen and discuss issues of potentially monumental significance was quite another.[59]

With this in mind it is hard to escape the conclusion that, while hardly perfect, the visit had been a success. Sure, little concrete had been discussed. Kissinger had not managed to recruit the Chinese behind the peace program in Vietnam and had, in essence, agreed to the diplomatic isolation of Taiwan. Yet, whatever one may think in retrospect of his courting of the Chinese and the attitude he displayed regarding Taiwan and Vietnam, Kissinger had achieved what he had set out to achieve. Nixon's visit was settled, the opening to China a reality. In spite of the pressure of time, the isolation from communication facilities, the limited staff with him, the likelihood that the Chinese were eaves-dropping on the Americans, he and his team had performed well.

But, as they all knew, it was only the start.

"THE SMARTEST GUY AROUND"

Kissinger had a few days to think it over before an agitated and excited Nixon welcomed him at the San Clemente White House. Not that there was time to rest. Still digesting the Chinese food and keen on maintaining the secrecy of their excursion to Beijing, Kissinger and his staff continued their hectic travel schedule. With a stopover in Tehran (and a brief chat with the Iranian foreign minister) they flew thousands of miles to Paris. On July 12, after a few hours' rest, Kissinger held a three-hour secret session with his North Vietnamese negotiating partner, Le Duc Tho. It was, he recalls, "the most hopeful I had had." Kissinger and Winston Lord even speculated about the possibility of a double breakthrough.[60]

Throughout Kissinger's travels, the president demanded absolute secrecy. Drama was what counted and, from Nixon's point of view, it was important that he, not Kissinger, be in the limelight. Kissinger should not talk to any reporters before he arrived in San Clemente on the morning of July 13 (Standard Pacific Time).

Indirectly, though, by the time Kissinger arrived in California he had almost leaked the information. While in Paris he had met David Bruce, the veteran diplomat who was in charge of the public side of the Vietnam peace talks. Kissinger, with the adrenalin still flowing from his historic visit, told Bruce about his recent foray into the Middle Kingdom. Bruce, an exceptional man not only due to his distinguished service as a diplomat but the trust that Kissinger placed on him, was enormously excited. Later the same day he met the *Los Angeles Times* journalist Don Cook, and rambled on about the great benefits that the United States would derive from opening diplomatic relations with China. Although suspicious, Cook did not make a connection but simply alluded to "rumors" that the administration was having secret talks with the Chinese in a short piece that was published in the *L.A. Times* the morning that Kissinger arrived in California.[61]

Two days later Cook realized how close he had been to a major scoop.[62] On July 15, 1971, at 10:30 P.M. Eastern Standard Time Richard Nixon delivered a seven-minute address at NBC studios in Burbank, California. The president, holding court in the nearby San Clemente Western White House, told his audience that Kissinger had recently returned from a round-the-world tour that had included a stopover, on July 9–11, in Beijing. The Chinese government had extended, and Nixon was glad to accept, an invitation to visit the PRC the following spring. After reading the joint announcement Nixon briefly added that the initiative was not "at the expense of our old friends," nor "directed against any other nation." Nixon's trip would be, simply, "a journey of peace."[63]

The moment Nixon made the announcement Kissinger, already well known in Washington's press circles, became a worldwide celebrity. Suddenly his face appeared everywhere. In late July and early August *Time, Newsweek* and the *U.S. News and World Report* ran major stories of the "Modern Metternich," who became popularly known as "Henry the K" and "Superkraut." His "mission to Red China has few parallels in the annals of U.S. diplomacy," one article declared, while another dubbed him, simply, "the smartest guy around."[64]

It was bound to make Nixon squirm, particularly because he had wanted to control the news coverage and use it to enhance his own statesman's image. Indeed, the president had worried about Kissinger grabbing the headlines throughout the preparations and unfolding of the secret trip. During a celebratory dinner with Kissinger, Haldeman, Ehrlichmann, and Press Secretary Ron Ziegler, the president weightily pronounced that "there must be no further discussion with the press about Henry's trip." Kissinger was quick to agree. "You are so right, Mr. President."

In the weeks and months that followed, however, the president's worst fears seemed confirmed. Kissinger, not Nixon, emerged as the man of the moment. Nixon was beside himself with a mixture of frustration and jealousy. He repeatedly ordered Kissinger to build "an absolute wall around himself" against the media. Kissinger did nothing of the sort. He embarked on a briefing frenzy that, as Walter Isaacson puts it, "assured that within a week few publications in the Western world did not have a wealth of colorful details" about the secret trip. Kissinger was reveling in the art form that Nixon never truly learned: he was spinning his way to fame.

Another frustrated man was Secretary of State Rogers. When he arrived to join the July 13, 1971 meeting at Nixon's San Clemente residence, he knew of Kissinger's trip. Rogers could have few doubts that, as far as his job was concerned, he was on his way out. After all, what was the point? Bureaucratically outmaneuvered and outsmarted, he was not a player in the great game unfolding around him. Nobody considered him the smartest guy around. He was not shown the transcripts of Kissinger's meetings with Zhou (which would eventually be declassified in 2001). To add insult to injury he was given the most thankless task: to explain to foreign governments the need for secrecy and significance of the series of shocks that Nixon delivered in July and August 1971.[65]

The reactions abroad to the July 15 announcement varied from shock to delight, often depending on the particular country's geopolitical location and past history with the PRC. Few in Europe could, for example, be unhappy that the United States was opening to China and starting to practice triangular diplomacy. France's President Georges Pompidou considered the opening, albeit much overdue, a welcome development. The British government of Edward Heath echoed such sentiments; the United Kingdom had recognized the PRC as early as 1950. In Bonn, the soon-to-be Nobel laureate, Chancellor Willy Brandt, was also under the somewhat false impression that the opening to China had forced the Soviets to become more accommodating in Europe and would, in turn, be beneficial for the unfolding of FRG's

Ostpolitik. Although the Four Power agreement that guaranteed Western access to Berlin had virtually been completed before the secret trip to China, Kissinger's careful orchestration of its timing—his decision to put it on ice before taking off for the Far East on July 1, 1971—assured an impression that there was a connection. If it had been completed earlier, the Berlin agreement would have appeared a result of multilateral bargaining. But once the Americans, British, French, and Soviets signed the agreement on September 3—six weeks after Nixon's announcement—there appeared to have been a triangular connection. In short, while the Berlin agreement had not substantially changed between June and September 1971, the timing made a difference on popular perceptions. The impression was that the secret trip to China had an immediate impact on European détente by making the Soviets more willing to accommodate on such a symbolically significant issue as Berlin.[66]

* * *

America's Asian allies were quite another matter. Needless to say, the Taiwanese felt betrayed, particularly as Kissinger failed to provide any details of his discussions with Zhou. Still in mid-October 1971, as he was preparing for another visit to Beijing, Kissinger told Taiwan's Ambassador, James Shen that he was fairly optimistic that a lobbying campaign to save Taiwanese membership in the UN—spearheaded by UN Ambassador George Bush Sr.—would be successful. For the Taiwanese, membership in the UN was crucial: it was an international guarantee that the Republic of China was a legitimate nation-state. In reality, however, since the PRC was adamant that Taiwan was but a lost province of the mainland, there was no room for compromise (such as having both Chinas as members of the UN). Kissinger, willing to sacrifice Taiwan's needs for the more significant rewards he anticipated from the developing relationship with Beijing, thus had little interest in safeguarding Taiwan's membership in the UN. In fact, he was seriously upset about the strength of the campaign to save Taiwan's seat and noticeably relieved when the effort ultimately failed. The rules of realpolitik and the logic of Kissinger's foreign policy architecture clearly dictated that Taiwan, like ultimately South Vietnam, was expendable. Or as Kissinger would put it somewhat more antiseptically later on, the loss of Taiwan's UN seat was "a diplomatic setback which had been recognized as inevitable," a necessary price, indeed, for the "new flexibility" that the opening to the PRC had brought to U.S. foreign policy.[67]

But while Taiwan was, by and large, considered a necessary casualty of the opening to China, the most delicate job that Rogers and the State Department faced in mid-July was with Japan. Not that the Japanese had any serious objections to a Sino-American opening. Successive governments in Tokyo had rather begrudgingly followed the U.S. lead on their policy toward the PRC, a country that by virtue of its proximity and size offered a large potential market for Japanese goods. The Japanese were in the process of courting China as well; in January 1971 Prime Minister Eisaku Sato had publicly offered to increase contacts with the PRC and begin intergovernmental talks. Moreover, in the wake of ping-pong diplomacy and other signals in the spring and early summer of 1971, the Japanese would have to have been completely blind not to expect more moves in Sino-American relations. Still, Prime Minister Sato could be excused for not expecting something as dramatic as this to happen as early as July 1971. After all, Secretary of Defense Melvin Laird had told Sato in early July that "no basic change" in U.S. China policy was forthcoming.[68]

It was the manner in which the Japanese were given the news rather than the substance of the opening itself that constituted the rub. Sometime in the course of July 14 Nixon decided against sending U. Alexis Johnson, undersecretary of state for political affairs and a previous ambassador to Japan, to Tokyo so that Prime Minister Sato could be briefed appropriately. Instead, the Japanese, much like others, were not given any advance warning; Rogers was to start working the phones—beginning with a call to the Japanese ambassador Ushiba—about an hour before Nixon's speech. Given that by that time working hours in Washington, D.C., had long since ended, there were delays. Prime Minister Sato eventually found out about the opening three minutes before Nixon went on air. The American ambassador to Japan, Armin Meyer, was even less in the know. He found out about the opening on the radio while having a haircut. What was known in the Japanese foreign office as the "Asakai nightmare" had happened. The United States, as Ambassador Asakai Koichiro is said to have dreamed in the 1950s, had suddenly shifted policy toward China without bothering to inform Tokyo first. The first Nixon shock (*shokku*) and the Sato government's decision not to back the PRC's entry into the UN in October 1971 also played a role in Sato's eventual downfall the following year.[69]

Almost as in revenge for the Asakai nightmare, the Japanese leapfrogged over the United States into normalizing their relations with the PRC. After Sato's resignation in June 1972, Kakuei Tanaka's new cabinet quickly moved to normalize Sino-Japanese relations. In September Tanaka traveled to Beijing and the two countries announced the restoration of normal relations (six years before the United States and the PRC exchanged ambassadors). Moreover, the Japanese side agreed to break off official diplomatic relations with Taiwan—a precedent that Zhou, Mao, and other Chinese officials would repeatedly cite in their future talks with Kissinger.[70]

For most of America's allies in Europe and Japan, with the obvious exception of Taiwan, the opening to China was clearly a beneficial development. But what was its impact on the two countries most obviously targeted: the Soviet Union and North Vietnam?

MOSCOW AND THE CHINA CARD

"No one was more surprised and confused than the Kremlin when it received the news of Nixon's plan to go to China even before he would meet Brezhnev at the summit in Moscow."[71] This was Anatoly Dobrynin's description of the impact of the secret trip announcement on the USSR. By all accounts, the Soviets had been shocked into action. Yet, while reacting in much the way that Kissinger had expected to the July 15 announcement, the Soviets were equally quick to begin realigning their policies to fit with the new reality.

As a clear indication of whom the China initiative was primarily meant to impress and where the priorities of U.S. diplomacy lay, the Soviets, in fact, learned about the China initiative earlier than America's allies.

At 9:00 A.M. on the morning of July 15, Anatoly Dobrynin was called to the White House to speak with Kissinger on a secure telephone line. From San Clemente, Kissinger delivered the bombshell that would be announced on national television later in the day: he had been to China and Nixon would be going there before March 1972. According to Dobrynin, sounding "noticeably pleased" and "clearly implying that our [Soviet] delays in responding to the president's requests about a Soviet-American summit played into the hands of the Chinese," Kissinger asked Dobrynin to pass on an oral message to the Soviet leadership from President Nixon. It stressed the continued American interest in a summit with the Soviet Union. While proclaiming that the opening to China was "not directed against any third country," Kissinger added that the Soviet decision to postpone the Nixon–Brezhnev summit had "made Nixon advance his meeting with the Chinese." The decision did not, however, have any "bearing whatsoever on American-Soviet relations." He then presented Dobrynin with a stark choice: to "advance quickly" on the present course or to "retreat to a painful reassessment of our relations."[72]

Triangular diplomacy had truly been launched.

A few days later Kissinger and Dobrynin met at the White House. "For the first time in my experience with him," Kissinger recalled, "Dobrynin was totally insecure . . . his oily best." After Kissinger criticized the Soviets for their stalling on the summit, Dobrynin "was almost besides himself with protestations of goodwill." The Soviet ambassador "brightened considerably" when Kissinger told him that the Soviet Union had featured very little in the Kissinger–Zhou talks. When Dobrynin inquired whether it was still possible to arrange the Soviet-American summit before Nixon's China trip, Kissinger replied that the president "would go in the order in which announcements were made." Yet, he added, it might be possible to announce the Soviet summit before Nixon actually went to Beijing.[73]

The immediate follow-up to this meeting was much as Kissinger had hoped. Over the next few weeks, the details of the Berlin Four Power Agreement that Kissinger had put on hold a few weeks earlier were finally hammered out and the pact was signed on September 3. On August 10, 1971, the Soviets issued a formal invitation for what eventually became the May 1972 Soviet-American summit in Moscow. A week later Kissinger told Dobrynin that Nixon accepted the invitation; by September 7 the details of the announcement of the Moscow summit had been laid down. In keeping with the cult of secrecy within the Nixon administration, this was the same date that Nixon also told Secretary of State Rogers about the summit.

It was finally announced on October 12, 1971, after Andrei Gromyko's annual visit to the UN General Assembly.[74]

Kissinger's tone with Dobrynin presented a remarkable contrast to his discussions with the Chinese. His first face-to-face meetings with the designated channel of direct Sino-American communications, the Chinese ambassador to Paris, Huang Chen, are illustrative. During their July 26 meeting Huang first invited Kissinger—in Paris ostensibly for the funeral of Charles de Gaulle—for an advance trip to China in October. Kissinger reiterated the promise he had made to Zhou of keeping the Chinese informed of any mentions of China in future contacts with the Soviets.[75] A few weeks later, Kissinger gave Huang a thorough overview of U.S. contacts with the Soviets and plans for a Soviet-American summit. Once again, he assured that the Soviet effort to outmaneuver the Chinese would not work and that he would continue keeping the Chinese informed. It was "a useful session," Kissinger wrote to Nixon. He was particularly pleased that "we are building a solid record of keeping the Chinese informed on all significant subjects of concern to them." This, Kissinger added, "gives them an additional stake in nurturing our new relationship."[76] Kissinger was clearly relishing the balancing act between Moscow and Beijing.

DUCKY'S INTRANSIGENCE

While the Soviets reacted "correctly" in the aftermath of the China announcement, the North Vietnamese remained, in Kissinger's view, as intransigent as ever. To be sure, there had been signs of hope in June and July. On June 26 Le Duc Tho and Xuan Thuy had, for example, agreed in principle to the release of all POWs, one of the points that had presented a severe hurdle in previous meetings. Encouraged by such success and with the China trip on his mind, Kissinger had written to Nixon that "there is nothing we lose by waiting right now."[77]

After the July 12 secret meeting—the first "real negotiating session" with Le Duc Tho (or "Ducky," as the Americans had dubbed the erstwhile North Vietnamese Politburo member)—and the announcement of Kissinger's secret trip to China three days later, the ball should have been rolling. And, sure enough, when they met again two weeks later, the two sides seemed to move ever closer to an agreement on a schedule for American troop withdrawals, on a ceasefire, and on international guarantees for Cambodia and Laos. After a decision in the North Vietnamese Politburo, Le Duc Tho and Xuan Thuy even seemed to drop the impossible demand that Americans agree to pay reparations by changing that offensive term into "U.S. contributions to heal the destruction of war."[78]

But they did not move enough on a basic point: that the United States had to remove Thieu, Ky, and Khiem from office in order to jumpstart the political solution for South Vietnam. According to Kissinger, Le Duc Tho even suggested to him during a break that if the United States could not find a way of replacing Thieu in the forthcoming presidential elections in South Vietnam, "an assassination would do admirably." One of Tho's aides later denied that his superior had made such a blatant suggestion; instead, he had needled Kissinger by saying that since the Americans "have replaced their stooges many times in many places in the world, they have enough imagination to do it again." Either way, the suggestion was clear: if the Americans wanted an agreement they had to get rid of Thieu. How they wanted to accomplish this was up to them. "You must not ask us to do impossible things," Kissinger stressed. Tho also warned Kissinger not to think that the opening to China would make any difference. "You have gone here and there to seek a way out, I wonder whether you have drawn on your experience." He added: "In fact, your efforts are futile and they make things more complicated."

"I do not want to find a solution in any other place than here," Kissinger responded.[79]

Kissinger went to Paris again in mid-August. This time he did not expect much from the meeting, mainly because Le Duc Tho had flown to Hanoi for consultations and Xuan Thuy was, Kissinger had long since concluded, not authorized to engage in serious negotiations. He arrived half an hour late due to his "useful session" with Chinese Ambassador Huang Chen. The meeting focused heavily on the political solution for South Vietnam. Part of Kissinger's eight-point proposal, the political formula he presented stressed the American willingness to remain neutral in the upcoming South Vietnamese elections, to respect the vote, and to establish relations with any government that was formed as a result. Thuy responded by restating the objections to Thieu and hinting that the United States should encourage him to withdraw from the elections. Thuy argued that a mere American pledge of neutrality in the elections meant nothing. He was right. Thieu used his American-backed position to ensure that the October 3 election was uncontested and resulted in Thieu winning 94.3 percent of the vote. While the U.S. embassy pledged neutrality, Thieu's power base and his ability to maneuver other potential candidates to withdraw from the race owed much to his incumbency and American connections.[80]

By the time Thieu clinched his convincing victory the dialogue of the deaf in Paris had seen its last encounter. On September 13 Kissinger once again arrived in Paris to meet with Xuan Thuy. Lasting only two hours, it was "the shortest secret session ever." Neither side offered anything new. In fact, Le Duc Tho had told Thuy the previous week that "in the immediate future, nothing can be solved."[81]

Even so, Kissinger still tried to find a way of reaching a negotiated settlement to the war. He suggested to Nixon another secret effort: a Kissinger–Pham Van Dong meeting in Moscow. Perhaps because Kissinger maintained that such an effort, even if unsuccessful, would be useful on record—to show the general public that the administration had tried every avenue to reach a peace agreement—Nixon did not turn this suggestion down outright. He did, though, order a bombing strike on the Demilitarized Zone on September 17 (it was carried out on the 20th). On the following day, prompted by such apparently mixed signals from the president, Kissinger submitted a long position paper on Vietnam.

He presented two key options. The first one included continued Vietnamization that would result in a withdrawal of all but 40,000 U.S. troops by August 1, 1972. This residual force would be kept in South Vietnam as a bargaining chip while the Americans continued heavy bombing and stepped up economic and military assistance to South Vietnam. To minimize domestic discontent, the administration would simultaneously reveal the record of the secret talks. The other option, one that Kissinger preferred, was for him to fly to Moscow in November for a meeting with Pham Van Dong and offer a new peace proposal that included a political settlement for South Vietnam. This scenario consisted of new elections in South Vietnam in September 1972, preceded by Thieu's voluntary resignation.[82]

Nixon wavered. He rejected the idea of a trip to Moscow. But Nixon gave Kissinger the green light to try the second option; if it did not work, the Americans would resort to the first option (or some modified form of it). By late September Thieu had approved the plan. General Walters presented it to the North Vietnamese in Paris on October 11. On October 25, just as Kissinger was departing Beijing from his second trip to China, Hanoi suggested a meeting on November 20. Both Le Duc Tho and Xuan Thuy would be there. Early in November Kissinger accepted the date.

But there was no meeting. In the first week of November the North Vietnamese Politburo came to the conclusion that it was useless for Le Duc Tho to meet with Kissinger. The only point that would be served with such a meeting, the Politburo concluded on November 11, was to "maintain contact."[83] Six days later they informed the Americans that due to an unspecified illness Le Duc Tho would not be able to travel to Paris. Kissinger drew his own conclusions and rejected the prospect of yet another session with Xuan Thuy. It was too bad that he had fallen ill, but without Ducky there was no point in having another secret session, General Walters was advised to tell the North Vietnamese in Paris.[84] The secret talks that had commenced more than two years earlier had come to an end as preparations for a North Vietnamese military offensive were being accelerated.

It was all so puzzling. While the China opening had shaken the Soviets to agree on numerous, previously unattainable, issues, it seemed to have had a minimal impact on the North Vietnamese. While making some adjustments to their proposals, Xuan Thuy and Le Duc Tho did not give in enough to make it possible for the Nixon administration to conclude an agreement that they could reasonably claim was a peace with honor. Worse yet, the critics of the administration, unaware of the secret meetings, were once again on the attack in the fall of 1971.

Had the opening to China, then, no impact at all in terms of the Vietnam War?

If anything, it seems that the opening accelerated Hanoi's plans for another major military offensive, while prompting further Sino-Soviet competition over North Vietnam. While Kissinger was in Paris meeting with Le Duc Tho on July 12, Zhou was in Hanoi, where the Chinese premier had flown soon after bidding farewell to Kissinger and his staff. At Mao's behest he did not press the North Vietnamese to change their attitude in the Paris talks. Once in Hanoi, Zhou Enlai met with Le Duan and Pham Van Dong in order to assure the North Vietnamese that he had made no deals over their heads. China remained committed to the revolutionary cause, Zhou maintained. Undoubtedly he made much of the Chinese decision in early July to increase military aid to North Vietnam. It was to no avail. As far as the North Vietnamese were concerned, China was beginning to look increasingly untrustworthy. Kissinger's visit, Le Duan told Zhou, had been "designed to forestall the surprises" that lay ahead for the United States in Vietnam. The publicity that was bound to follow would surely render Hanoi's latest peace proposal obsolete. In short, the North Vietnamese could see little good emanating from the forthcoming opening.[85]

Two months later, Le Duc Tho made this point forcefully to Ieng Sary, one of Pol Pot's closest collaborators in the Cambodian Communist Party Politburo. "We will always remember the experience in 1954," Tho told Sary, pressing the need to be wary of both Moscow and Beijing. At the Geneva conference of 1954, Tho said, the North Vietnamese had made the mistake of agreeing to the (supposedly temporary) division of Vietnam along the seventeenth parallel. They had done this, he added, "because both the Soviet Union and China exerted pressure." As a result, "the outcome became what it became" (i.e., a prolonged division of Vietnam and what the North Vietnamese called the "American War"). There was no point in taking sides in the Sino-Soviet conflict, he added. It would only make "the situation more complicated."[86]

Although Tho's anger in early September was more clearly directed at Beijing than Moscow—at this point the Moscow summit had yet to be announced—he neatly summed up the North Vietnamese's worst nightmare: a repetition of 1954 as a result of pressure from Moscow and Beijing. Hints that the Chinese now supported, as the Soviets had done over a year earlier, another Geneva conference did not help.[87] Indeed, if Zhou Enlai had been gravely insulted in 1954 in Geneva by Secretary of State Dulles's refusal to shake his hand, the North Vietnamese carried their own baggage from that conference.

But Le Duc Tho also summed up how Hanoi could avoid reliving that experience: by using the Sino-Soviet split to its advantage, by not taking sides. This was, after all, the major difference between 1954 and the early 1970s; the Chinese and the Soviets, while pressed by the United States to do the same thing, had no interest in coordinating their policies. And, more significantly, both Moscow and Beijing feared the loss of their position as the central supporters of world revolution. If they pressed the North Vietnamese to this direction, they might easily send the wrong message, for example, to the Cambodian Communists.

The Chinese knew as much and acted accordingly. In addition to increasing China's military aid to North Vietnam (which reached record levels in 1972–73), Zhou continued to stroke the Vietnamese. In October 1971 he stressed to Le Duan

in Beijing that the Chinese were in full agreement with the North Vietnamese negotiating stand, hence, perhaps, contributing to the North Vietnamese Politburo's
decision effectively to discontinue the Paris secret talks. At the same time, in October and November, the preparations for the March 1972 Spring Offensive were significantly accelerated.[88]

Of course, there was a limit to how far the Chinese—or the Soviets—would go
to accommodate Hanoi. They would not cancel the prospective summit meetings
with the United States. Mao himself made this clear to North Vietnamese Premier
Pham Van Dong during the latter's stay in Beijing on November 20–25, 1971. And,
as long as Nixon's China trip was on schedule, the Soviets were unwilling to jeopardize the Moscow summit, scheduled for May 1972.

A GEOPOLITICAL REVOLUTION WITHIN LIMITS

Kissinger's secret trip to China was, by far, the most significant foreign policy event
of the Nixon administration. It clearly shook the Soviets. Even if one ignores
Kissinger's possibly exaggerated descriptions of Dobrynin's anxiety after the July 15
announcement, the Soviets did move quickly on a number of fronts. The year 1972
would see two summits and, hence, a vindication of the efforts of previous years.
There was even a Soviet offer to be helpful, finally, on Vietnam: on September 20,
Dobrynin asked whether the Nixon administration wished to relay any message to
Hanoi via Soviet President Nikolai Podgorny, who was going to the North Viet-
namese capital in October. As the historian Robert Schulzinger puts it, even the
many critics of the administration "could only mutter and look embarrassed as
Nixon and Kissinger rewrote the script of post–World War II foreign policy."[89]

Yet, it was not an unmitigated triumph. In October 1971, Podgorny did indeed
go to Hanoi. But the visit, as noted above, did little to advance Kissinger's search
for an honorable peace. Instead, the Soviets increased their military shipments to
North Vietnam and hence encouraged Hanoi's plans for the 1972 Spring Offensive.[90] The opening to China and the launch of triangular diplomacy had therefore
not translated into an obvious American advantage in the Vietnam peace talks. By
going to China Kissinger had heightened and complicated the Sino-Soviet competition in Indochina. In the second half of 1971 both Moscow and Beijing responded
by increasing their military and economic aid to Hanoi, not by pressing for concessions in the Paris negotiations.[91] In the end, this could only encourage the North
Vietnamese to continue fighting while negotiating.

Compared to his dealings with the "suave" Zhou and the suddenly forthcoming
Dobrynin, the Vietnamese negotiation experience thus remained one of excessive
frustration for Kissinger. No wonder he would degrade his North Vietnamese interlocutors repeatedly in his memoirs. They were alternatively "sinuous" or "not
amenable to ordinary mortal intercourse," and possessed an "obsessive drive for

hegemony in Indochina." The use of "Ducky" as a synonym for Le Duc Tho (a man whose "profession was revolution, vocation guerrilla warfare") stands out as the only such nickname Kissinger used in his memoirs. In a characteristic assessment of his fellow Nobel Peace Prize laureate, Kissinger wrote in 1979: "Le Duc Tho undoubtedly was of the stuff of which heroes are made. What we grasped only with reluctance—and many at home never understood—is that heroes are such because of monomaniacal determination. They are rarely pleasant men; their rigidity approaches the fanatic; they do not specialize in the qualities required for negotiated peace."[92]

Vietnamese intransigence notwithstanding, the breakthrough on China was one of the most significant moments in postwar American foreign policy. By making triangular diplomacy into a reality, Kissinger's secret trip to Beijing caused a virtual geopolitical revolution by forging a significant shift in the Soviet attitude toward negotiations with the United States. Moreover, while the impact on Vietnam of the forthcoming Nixon visits to China and the Soviet Union remained to be seen, there was, after July 15, 1971, an entirely new geopolitical framework for working out a solution to America's longest war.

Yet, in spite of Kissinger's efforts and frustrations regarding the Vietnam negotiations in the fall of 1971, Indochina was not the only testing ground of the triangular framework. To a large extent it was not even *the* testing ground in the fall of 1971. That honor belonged to a conflict in South Asia.

8

The First Test

Triangular Diplomacy and the Indo-Pakistani War

If the secret trip to Beijing in July 1971 was one of the highlights of Kissinger's career, then his handling of the Indo-Pakistani crisis of 1971 was one of his worst performances. The crisis—that brought to the fore longstanding Indo-Pakistani hostilities and ultimately resulted in the independence of East Pakistan (what became the nation of Bangladesh)—had little to do with triangular diplomacy. Instead, it was the culmination of the tense relationship between East and West Pakistan. Although both parts of Pakistan were Muslim, they were ethnically different (Punjabis in the West and Bengalis in the East), and the more prosperous West dominated the impoverished East politically and, often, with the aid of the West Pakistanis control of the country's military. In addition, India and Pakistan had fought wars in 1947–48 and 1965. The relations between the two countries remained poor at the time the crisis began to escalate following a natural disaster in East Pakistan that created a mass of refugees fleeing from East Pakistan to eastern India. In the spring of 1971 West Pakistan imposed martial law in the East as a response to growing calls for autonomy, while India supported the Bengalis' calls for independence. By the time Kissinger was in Beijing for the secret trip, therefore, Indo-Pakistani relations had deteriorated to the point where another war looked increasingly likely. If such a conflict did break out, moreover, it was likely that the Chinese (who had fought a war with India in the early 1960s) were likely to sympathize with Pakistan.

Kissinger's response to the Indo-Pakistani-Bengali crisis shows how poorly his grand design—triangular diplomacy and détente—fit with the realities of regional developments in South Asia. Viewing the respective policies of India and Pakistan through the spectacles of Sino-Soviet-American triangulation, Kissinger managed to associate the United States with the eventual loser in the conflict (Pakistan). Between July and December 1971, despite voluminous advice to the contrary from the State Department experts Kissinger, apparently, saw only one reality: India was a friend of the Soviet Union; Pakistan a friend of China's. The United States needed to side with Pakistan in order to safeguard the opening to China without which, it was clear, Kissinger's architecture was bound to collapse. Sadly, all of this amounted to a false reading of South Asian realities in 1971.

Kissinger was, to be sure, under some pressure to side with Pakistan in the conflict. It was, in fact, Zhou Enlai who suggested to Kissinger during the secret meeting the particular approach he would follow throughout the next five months as the Indo-Pakistani crisis unfolded and led to a war. During the farewell banquet on July 11, Zhou Enlai suddenly brought up the ongoing crisis in South Asia. He said to Kissinger: "Please tell [the Pakistani] President Yahya Khan that if India commits aggression, we will support Pakistan." Referring to a potential Indian attack, Zhou then added: "You are also against that."

Kissinger, caught unprepared, replied, "We will oppose that, but we cannot take military measures." Zhou recognized that the United States was "too far away. But you have strength to persuade India. You can speak to both sides."

"We will do our best," Kissinger replied.[1]

Over the next five months Kissinger tried to live up to this promise. To him, the South Asian crisis that resulted in the creation of Bangladesh emerged as the first practical test of triangular diplomacy. It was an infuriating one, pitting the White House against the State Department and Nixon against India's Prime Minister Indira Gandhi. In late 1971 and early 1972 American policy in South Asia produced probably more criticism than any other initiative aside from the Vietnam War. Later on, Kissinger explained the crisis in his memoirs as follows:

> [The Indo-Pakistan War of 1971] was perhaps the most complex issue of Nixon's first term . . . What made the crisis so difficult was that the stakes were so much greater than the common perception of them. The issue burst upon us while Pakistan was our only channel to China; we had no other means of communication with Peking. A major American initiative of fundamental importance to the global balance of power could not have survived if we colluded with the Soviet Union in the public humiliation of China's friend—and our ally . . . Had we acquiesced in such a power play, we would have sent a wrong signal to Moscow and unnerved our allies, China, and the forces for restraint in other volatile areas of the world.[2]

The description is, most observers would claim, at least partially misleading. While Pakistan was a major channel to China and the steppingstone of Kissinger's secret trip to Beijing in July 1971, it had never been the sole channel of communication. After the secret trip, moreover, Kissinger established direct contact with the Chinese ambassador Huang Chen in Paris and, after November, with the PRC's UN representative Huan Hua in New York. Nor is there any clear evidence to suggest that the Soviets encouraged an Indian assault on Pakistan. But tilting toward Pakistan in the fall of 1971 may have encouraged the beleaguered Pakistanis to attack India. In short, American actions may have provoked, rather than prevented, a war in December 1971. Former Deputy Assistant Secretary of State Christopher Van Hollen, whom Kissinger referred to as "the idiot" during the crisis, summarized this opinion as early as 1980: "White House policies [during the Indo-Pakistani War of 1971] were badly flawed and ill served the interests of the United States." It is remarkable that most writers, such as Raymond Garthoff, William Bundy, and Denis Kux, agree with Van Hollen's statement.[3]

Yet, while tilting toward Pakistan was a disastrous policy, there was a clear logic behind it. It was, essentially, a tilt toward China, based on Kissinger and Nixon's perceptions of the Chinese reaction to American policy choices. In the minds of both Kissinger and Nixon, the future of their foreign policy efforts hinged almost entirely on the success of the opening to China. Ultimately, the Indo-Pakistani conflict—a regional dispute based on ethnic divisions and colonial legacies—became the first test case of triangular diplomacy. The point is that while the consequences of U.S. policy were not impressive, there was nothing illogical about the tilt itself. The real tragedy of the tilt lay in the failure of the United States to prevent the war and the bloodshed that, ultimately, was not a result of any particular American policy decision but a product of the series of developments—both man-made and natural—that coincided in 1970–71.

THE SOUTH ASIAN CRISIS

What brought the crisis in Indo-Pakistani relations to a boiling point in the early 1970s was the issue of East Pakistan, which in the process became the independent state of Bangladesh. Since the independence of a divided Pakistan in 1947, the rift between the two parts of the country had increased steadily. Separated by a predominantly Hindu India, Muslim East and West Pakistan were ethnically different (with Punjabis predominant in the West and Bengalis in the East). Although less populous, the West dominated the East politically, economically, and militarily. To complicate the regional picture, the history of Indo-Pakistani hostilities—wars in 1947–48 and 1965—made India a natural ally of the growing independence movement in East Pakistan.[4]

The most populated democracy in the world, India had emerged, unfortunately from the American perspective, in the 1950s as one of the leading nations of the nonaligned movement; a loose grouping of mostly third world countries that opted for a policy of neutralism and rejected the East-West division as the overriding raison d'etre of the post–World War II period. Consisting mostly of former European colonies—in addition to India, some of the key countries included Egypt and Algeria—the nonaligned countries attempted to group their resources together in order to direct global attention away from the Cold War confrontation and toward the economic and political problems of what was, in the West, called the third world. In fact, Nehru's India had exemplified many of the concerns of the nonaligned movement: a former British colony, it was beset by poverty and, while often eager to receive development aid from the richer countries, was manifestly unwilling to respond by committing itself politically to either Cold War bloc. Accordingly, Nehru had played a leading role in the first major gathering of the leaders of the nonaligned movement that had taken place in Bandung, Indonesia, in 1955. Nehru's career, however, also exemplified the need to attract external aid with minimum political commitments, a sentiment that was shared by many leaders of newly independent countries in the 1950s and 1960s. Thus, Nehru, who died in 1964, had, with mixed success and at different periods, tilted toward all the Big Three during his long time in office. In the early 1950s he leaned toward the PRC, in 1956 (during the Suez crisis) he was sympathetic toward the USSR, but in 1962 (when China invaded Tibet) he moved toward the United States. Unfortunately, such zigzags had produced no lasting solutions to the conflict between India and Pakistan. As Rena Fonseca put it: "as a foreign policy for India, nonalignment failed in the critical area of security."[5]

While nonalignment may have failed as a national security policy for India, Nehru's legacy was still alive and well in the years preceding the 1971 Indo-Pakistani War. After Lal Bahadur Shastri's brief rule, Nehru's daughter, Indira Gandhi, became prime minister in 1966. Like her father, she continued to search for ways of safeguarding Indian security while maintaining the country's independent position as a leader of the nonaligned movement. Unlike her father, though, Gandhi faced severe challenges from within her own Congress Party. She had, as a result, often resorted to leftist, at times blatantly anti-American, sloganeering as a means of solidifying popular support for her regime.[6]

As had been the case throughout much of Indian history from 1947 to 1971, two countries represented the greatest security threats to India: Pakistan and China. India had fought wars against both. The fact that the PRC had successfully tested nuclear weapons in 1964 and had routed India in a short border war in 1962 was bad enough; what made things worse was that in the aftermath of their 1965 Indo-Pakistani War China and Pakistan became de facto allies. Ultimately, this meant that in the late 1960s Gandhi tilted toward the USSR, a country that, as a result of American preoccupation with Vietnam, had emerged as a key player in the region. At the Tashkent Conference of January 1966, Soviet Premier Alexei Kosygin had, for example, mediated an end to the 1965 Indo-Pakistani War.[7] Gandhi visited Moscow in July 1966 and to Washington's consternation signed a communiqué that denounced the "imperialists in Southeast Asia."[8] The Johnson administration responded by tightening already faltering regulations on wheat shipments to India at a time when the country suffered from drought-like conditions. In combination with Indian criticism of U.S. policy in Vietnam and New Delhi's apparent pro-Moscow tilt, the American stinginess in helping India at a time of an increasingly acute food crisis left a legacy of tense Indo-American relations for the Nixon administration.[9]

While India had moved toward the Soviet Union, the Pakistani government welcomed Nixon's arrival in the White House and the developments leading to the opening to China. Since the Sino-Indian border conflicts of 1962 and the Indo-Pakistani War of 1965, the Sino-Pakistani relationship had become a key ingredient of Pakistani security policy. However, with the ascent of the Cultural Revolution, China had turned inward in the late 1960s. This, together with the apparent American neglect of South Asia during the last years of the Johnson administration and with India's courting of the USSR, meant that Pakistan had felt increasingly isolated.

But Richard Nixon was an old friend of Pakistan. He had visited the country twice as Eisenhower's vice president and again as a private citizen—and presidential hopeful—in 1967. The same year Nixon had called Pakistan "India's more successful neighbor" in what became a famous "Asia after Vietnam" article in *Foreign Affairs*. While it was clear that Nixon did not consider South Asia a priority when he took office in 1969, his frustrations with India (a huge country that was "both challenging and frustrating" as he wrote in that same *Foreign Affairs* article) meant that the new president, unlike some of his Democratic predecessors, had a pro-Pakistani bent.[10]

Kissinger, whose experience with India and Pakistan was limited to a trip to the region in 1962, came to share Nixon's disposition toward Pakistan. And his disdain for India was later illuminated in his memoirs *White House Years*, where Kissinger referred to the U.S. embassy in New Delhi as "perhaps the most overstaffed of our diplomatic service."[11] By his own admission, South Asia only became a matter of importance to Kissinger because of the opening to China and the link to Beijing that the Pakistanis provided after Nixon's visit to Pakistan in August 1969.[12] In the next two years the cementing of Pakistan's position as a key link between the United States and the PRC had presented Islamabad with a great diplomatic asset at the exact moment that its territorial integrity was under an imminent threat. As a sign of his pro-Pakistani feelings, in October 1970 Nixon approved a $50 million "one-time exception" to the arms embargo that allowed Pakistan to purchase replacement aircraft and armored personnel carriers from the United States.[13]

Although Pakistan emerged as the key link to China in 1969–71, the threat to the country's unity increased. Having lost the 1965 war with India, President Ayub Khan suffered politically in West Pakistan and faced a growing independence movement in East Pakistan. He lost power in 1969. While the new president, General Yahya Khan, was able to raise his stock in Washington by acting as a secret link to China, he faced a rising tide of discontent, particularly in East Pakistan. The ethnic differences and economic inequalities between the two parts of Pakistan were further exacerbated by the West Pakistani Punjabis' dominant position in the political and military elites. The Bengalis of East Pakistan found themselves dominated by an ethnically different political and military establishment that, they felt, treated them almost as a colony. In November 1970, the situation was made worse by a devastating cyclone that hit East Pakistan, killing up to 200,000 and leaving scores of others homeless. On December 7, 1970, the pro-independence Awami League won 98 percent of the vote in the East Pakistani elections. Perhaps most significantly, the first democratic election in Pakistan had produced a paradoxical result: because the East was more populous than the West, the Awami League had won an absolute majority in the country's National Assembly (160 seats out of a total of 300). In response to calls for autonomy and, ultimately, independence, Yahya Khan sent 40,000 troops to the East in March 1971 to crush the Awami League. Sheikh Mujibur Rahman, the head of the Awami League, was arrested. Pakistan was to remain one state, by force if necessary.[14]

The consequences of the political crisis were predictable. As violence and political repression in East Pakistan grew during the spring and summer of 1971, a flood of refugees (up to 10 million by the fall of 1971) headed from East Pakistan to India, threatening to destabilize the already volatile West Bengali region of India. The Indian government, which had maintained a low profile during the months following the December elections, launched a severe and vocal critique of Pakistani policy. In April 1971 Indira Gandhi's government permitted the establishment of a Bangladeshi government in exile in Calcutta and supported the training of liberation forces on Indian soil. As the refugee crisis continued to mount, Gandhi told the Indian parliament in an ominous tone on May 24:

> Conditions must be created to stop any further influx of refugees and to ensure their early return under credible guarantees for their safety and well-being. I say with all sense of responsibility that unless this happens, there can be no lasting stability or peace on this subcontinent. We have pleaded with other powers to recognize this. If the world does not take heed, we shall be constrained to take all measures as may be necessary to ensure our own security.[15]

Five weeks later Kissinger left for a tour of Asia that included the secret trip to China and stopovers in both India and Pakistan.

"LOVE RATHER THAN BRUTALITY"

Although the U.S. Congress partly responded to Gandhi's threat by approving a $250 million aid fund to help India deal with the refugee crisis, Kissinger's secret trip occurred in the shadow of a mounting regional crisis in South Asia that presented a severe dilemma. The last thing he and Nixon wanted was to let the opening to China be derailed by a regional crisis they had paid scant attention to in previous months. But, given the refugee crisis, both the world opinion at large and American public opinion were clearly more sympathetic to India than to the repressive regime of Yahya Khan. This had been reflected in the State Department's—and particularly those serving in Dacca, East Pakistan, at the time—resistance to the policy of "massive inaction" that Kissinger had pushed for since March 1971. This is not surprising. Unaware of the progress of the China initiative, the State Department could hardly be expected to take it into account in formulating its policy toward one of the major humanitarian crises of the 1970s.[16]

Kissinger met with Indira Gandhi on July 7, 1971, in Delhi, only two days prior to his "disappearance" from Islamabad for the secret China trip. Knowing that Kissinger was about to fly to meet with the Pakistani leaders, Gandhi did her best to impress the Indian point of view. During this encounter, Gandhi stressed the pressure of the East Pakistani refugee crisis on India and expressed concern over growing Chinese influence in East Pakistan. Gandhi assured him, though, that India had no desire to use force to solve the problem. Kissinger's response was evasive. "[The] US has no specific ideas of its own at this point on how Pakistan might achieve the kind of political solution necessary to permit the refugees to return home," he told Gandhi. "However," Kissinger added, "the whole point of U.S. policy had been to try to retain enough influence to encourage Pakistan in [a] general way toward a political solution (with the East Pakistani independence movement)." When prompted to put pressure on the Pakistani government, Kissinger doubted that cutting off the "insignificant" amount of aid the United States was giving to Pakistan would have any effect on the situation. He was not convinced by Gandhi's Private Secretary P. N. Haksar's argument of the "psychological" significance of American pressure and gave little heed to the advice that "US make clear [that] aid [to Pakistan was] dependent on well-defined development." Gandhi's point that the history of the U.S.-Pakistani relationship had "led Pakistan to expect U.S. support no matter what its actions" also failed to impress the national security adviser. Kissinger responded that the United States was trying "to preserve [its] position in Islamabad which could contribute [to the] avoidance of war." He concluded: "[the] U.S. fully understands [the] problems created by refugees and importance of political solution in Pakistan which would permit their return."[17]

To be sure, the Indians were not exactly doing their utmost to pacify the situation. When Kissinger, in a conversation with T. N. Kaul, the head of India's foreign office, tried to press the necessity of the Indian government to stop the continued cross-border raids by Bengali guerrilla forces based in West Bengal, Kaul took refuge in the point that the Indian-East Pakistani border was one "without any natural obstructions or barriers." When Kissinger prompted Kaul about the Indian government's future plans, the response was far from reassuring: "We have come reluctantly to the conclusion that international pressure is not going to influence

Yahya Khan's decision." Kaul then issued a thinly veiled warning: "We do not want to rush into a military conflict with Pakistan because we know it would be suicidal for both countries and the only gainer would be outside powers. But we have to solve this problem of refugees."[18]

If anything, the quick visit to New Delhi confirmed the mutual suspicions that Kissinger and Gandhi held of each other's policies. According to Kissinger, whose stopover in India was in large part necessary to cover up his true mission in the region (the secret visit to China), he "left New Delhi with the conviction that India was bent on a showdown with Pakistan." Indian officials—Gandhi, Haksar, Kaul, and Foreign Minister Swaran Singh—had done little to assuage this fear by repeating their concerns about Bengali refugees and the unrepresentative nature of the Pakistani regime that, they maintained, was to blame for the crisis. At the same time, telling the Indians that Washington "would take a grave view of an unprovoked Chinese attack on India," only about a week before his secret trip and Nixon's planned visit to China were publicly announced, could hardly inspire trust among Indian leaders. The secrecy surrounding the China diplomacy, particularly as it soon became clear that the Pakistanis were well apprised of the process of Sino-American rapprochement, could only increase Indian doubts about Kissinger's sincerity. If anything, Kissinger's pre-secret trip conversations in India could only have added to the growing distrust of the United States in New Delhi.[19]

While Kissinger was in China, the crisis in South Asia gathered momentum and became a potential testing ground for triangular diplomacy. Intelligence reports indicated that the Soviets continued to make advances toward Gandhi. On July 9, 1971, Al Haig, manning Kissinger's desk while the NSC adviser was out of reach, wrote a memo to Nixon in which he discussed intelligence reports about Indian foreign minister Swaran Singh's recent trip to Moscow. The Soviets had, Haig summarized, agreed to supply Indian-supported guerrillas in East Pakistan (the Mukhti Bahini) with arms and guaranteed Soviet military protection against any potential Chinese pressure. Such a "radical break in Soviet policy," Haig surmised, was likely to make India "feel much less inhibited about military intervention." Nixon's handwritten comment was clear enough: "warn them [Indians] that if they intervene RN will personally cut off all aid to them."[20]

What warning Haig could (or ever did) possibly have given to the Indian government is unclear. The administration was, however, under increasing pressure to stop all aid to Pakistan, not India. In early July, the World Bank's Pakistan consortium suspended all aid to the country. On July 15, a few hours prior to Nixon's announcement about Kissinger's trip to China, the House Foreign Affairs Committee voted for a resolution to ban assistance to Pakistan; three weeks later a full session of the House supported the vote. State Department officials, including most of the American diplomats in South Asia, generally agreed with such pressure on Pakistan. The Nixon administration grudgingly announced that it was suspending aid pending a "clarification" of the situation in South Asia.[21]

Everyone, Nixon and Kissinger included, agreed on one thing: another Indo-Pakistani War should be avoided. The difference over the ways in which the crisis could be defused, however, was dramatic. The State Department favored using a mixture of diplomatic and economic pressure on Pakistan to accept the division of the country and, in effect, bow to the combined pressure of India and the dissatis-faction in East Pakistan. Nixon and Kissinger considered such a course of action as a clear-cut tilt toward India that could not be implemented without jeopardizing the opening to China. In short, they wanted to prevent a war because of the broader complications it might produce. With reports about Indo-Soviet collusion (how-ever misleading such reports may have been), Kissinger's general pessimism about India's intentions and his recent talks with Zhou Enlai, as well as Nixon's long-term preference for Pakistan, it was almost inevitable that the White House would tilt toward Pakistan. While wanting to prevent a full-scale war in South Asia and being pressed by the State Department to adopt a pro-Indian bent, Kissinger and Nixon were clearly more concerned with safeguarding the emergence of triangular diplo-macy. In practice this meant that the complexities of the regional situation in South Asia, including the hardships of millions of refugees and the repressive practices of the Pakistani army, were of secondary importance when contrasted with the geopolitical benefits that might be lost if the Chinese thought the United States was siding with India. It was realpolitik of the simplest and most cynical form.[22]

The NSC discussed the Indo-Pakistani situation a day after the China announce-ment. Kissinger's analysis was pessimistic. He thought that India was readying itself for a war, that Yahya Khan's government was unlikely to find a successful solution to the crisis in East Pakistan, and that the Pakistani army's ability to control a pop-ulation of 75 million would be short-lived. Kissinger believed that the American objective should be an independent East Pakistan and that the United States might not be able to do anything to prevent an imminent Indian attack. Nixon, always more sensitive to the impact of public opinion than his national security adviser, decided that the United States should convince the Pakistanis to ease the lot of the refugees. Yet, as he had already indicated to Haig, the president also decided to threaten the Indian government with a cut-off of American aid should New Delhi initiate hostilities.[23]

The tilt toward Pakistan produced major problems between the White House and the State Department. Most regional experts disagreed with the pro-Pakistani bent on both objective (Pakistan would be unable to prevent the independence of Bangladesh and was bound to lose in a war against India) and moral grounds (political repression and the plight of the refugees were diametrically opposed to American ideals; association with a repressive regime would only hurt America's image). Instead, they advocated applying strong public pressure on Islamabad. In two Senior Review Group meetings in late July, Kissinger had to pound forcefully the tilt policy to resistant State Department representatives. It was apparently to no avail. "State is driving me to tears," he complained to Ambassador Farland (on a brief visit in Washington from Islamabad) on July 30. "It is better to talk to Yahya 'with love rather than brutality,'" Kissinger said, adding: "we could say anything to Yahya as long as we related it to a refugee settlement and did not describe it as related to 'political accommodation.'" Then Kissinger reiterated: "there will some day be an independent Bangladesh. However, the problem now is to defuse the refugee situation so that India cannot use it as a plausible excuse for going to war." It was crucial, Kissinger continued, that Farland impress on Yahya the need to propose a comprehensive refugee program so that "we would have something to take to the Indians as a basis for squeezing them not to go to war." More specifically, Kissinger contemplated getting the UN in place:

> Kissinger said he would urge Yahya to be "sweeping on refugees." He would urge him to allow the intrusion of UN officials into every village. Then, with the international civil servants on the scene, we could go to the Indians and refute the allegations they were making to keep the refugees from returning. The onus would be on them [the Indians].

During the meeting Kissinger also established another back channel: "Let's make a deal—that if you get some instructions from the State Department that you consider absolutely crazy, you will use the special communications channel with us." Farland, the record indicates, had no problem in becoming one of Kissinger's "special ambassadors."[24]

A few days later, after the House of Representatives approved a bill banning all aid to Pakistan, Nixon—undoubtedly at Kissinger's behest—tried to use the bully pulpit to establish White House control over South Asia policy. In a press conference on August 4, he discussed U.S. efforts to relieve the refugee crisis and promised further steps to help the homeless in India and East Pakistan. Nixon rejected the House vote and emphasized the need to continue economic assistance to Pakistan as the best way of reducing the refugee flow. On the idea that the United States should put public pressure on Pakistan, Nixon was categorical: "These are matters that we will discuss only in private channels." Under the circumstances, public pressure on Yahya's government "would be totally counterproductive." It was an indication of the general public's lack of interest in the matter that no one in the White House pressroom asked any questions.[25]

While the differences between the White House and the State Department continued to sharpen, U.S. South Asian policy was in a bind. Requesting the UN to deflect the crisis was unlikely to bring about a solution because India seemed manifestly unwilling to cooperate. New Delhi refused proposals for UN supervision of the refugee problem in West Bengal and declined to curb guerrilla activity in East Pakistan based on the Indian side of the border. To Kissinger, such intransigence was a sign that Indira Gandhi was bent on an eventual military offensive against Pakistan that might not be confined to East Pakistan but could include Kashmir, a region along the northwestern border of India and West Pakistan that both countries had claimed since the late 1940s.[26]

In early August any remaining doubts Kissinger may have had about this complex web of linkages were erased.

INDO-SOVIET TREATY

On August 9, 1971, India and the Soviet Union signed a twenty-year friendship treaty. The treaty did not establish a formal alliance but provided for bilateral consultations at times of crisis and affirmed that neither Moscow nor New Delhi would support a third country against the other. Indira Gandhi insisted that India had not departed from its nonaligned position; the treaty provided a deterrent against a potential Chinese or Pakistani attack. For the Soviets, the treaty was, in large measure, a reaffirmation of its growing role on the South Asian subcontinent and an opportunity to respond to the opening to China with a geopolitical move of its own.[27]

The Indo-Soviet treaty was an outcome of negotiations that had commenced in 1969. It signaled an end to the USSR's low-key efforts to pressure Pakistan to grant autonomy to East Pakistan in the spring and summer of 1971. The first serious step had been taken in June, when Indian Foreign Minister Swaran Singh visited Moscow. That visit resulted only in a watered down communiqué about a shared interest in preventing the refugee crisis from exploding into a war but no commitment to joint action. The Soviets did, though, express sympathy for India and publicly and privately pressed the Pakistani government to deal with the refugee crisis. The following month, Kissinger's secret trip to China and the American tilt toward Pakistan naturally caused concern in India about a possible Sino-American-Pakistani axis. On July 20, Singh publicly voiced such Indian concerns in a speech anticipating the treaty with Moscow: "I sincerely hope that any Sino-American détente will not be at the expense of other countries . . . We are in touch with the countries concerned and shall see to it that any Sino-American détente does not affect us or the other countries in this region adversely."[28]

Two weeks later Soviet Foreign Minister Andrei Gromyko arrived in New Delhi for a state visit that culminated in the signing of the Indo-Soviet Treaty. As most observers have commented, the initiative was largely Indian: the Soviets may have been keen on signaling their geopolitical prowess, but they remained reluctant to offer full support for India. Not until late September, when Indira Gandhi visited Moscow, did the Soviets endorse India's position by providing additional military supplies and political support. Even then, the joint communiqué issued at the end of Gandhi's visit singled out the refugee crisis (but not the Pakistani actions that had prompted it) as the root cause of tension.[29]

Such relative circumspection on Moscow's part failed to impress the United States. It was viewed, at best, as a result of Soviet interest in continued détente with

Washington. In his memoirs Kissinger described the August 9 treaty as amounting to "a Soviet guarantee against Chinese intervention if India went to war with Pakistan." Gandhi, he maintained, viewed the treaty as a deterrent against China and as a way of isolating Pakistan further, while the Soviets saw the South Asian conflict as "an opportunity to humiliate China and to punish Pakistan for having served as intermediary" between the United States and China. In the months leading to the outbreak of the Indo-Pakistani War, Kissinger and Nixon viewed the South Asian crisis not as a complex regional problem, but as part of a larger geopolitical game. The terms of such a game could be summarized as follows: (1) India was about to use Bangladesh as a pretext for splitting its historic enemy Pakistan; (2) the Soviets were encouraging India; (3) the PRC was ready to come to Pakistan's aid if India attacked; (4) this might lead to Soviet involvement on India's side and a full-blown proxy war. By confirming such assumptions, the Indo-Soviet treaty assured an American tilt toward Pakistan. To Kissinger, still hoping to avert a war, this meant that he needed to send the correct signals and apply the appropriate pressure to prevent further Soviet meddling in the situation. As two of Kissinger's staff members, Hal Sonnenfeldt and Bill Hyland, argued, the Indo-Soviet treaty had transformed the crisis in South Asia into "a sort of Sino-Soviet clash by proxy."[30]

Nixon agreed. On August 11, the president met with Kissinger and members of the Senior Review Group to discuss the South Asian crisis. Nixon was in top form. "Let me be blunt," he said. "The Pakistanis are straightforward—and sometimes extremely stupid. The Indians are more devious, sometimes so smart that we fall for their line." Many people in both countries may think that a war would be a good thing, Nixon added, but the only important issue was that "the interests of the US would not be served by a war. The new China relationship would be imperiled, probably beyond repair, and we would have a 'very sticky problem' with the USSR." He understood the pro-Indian arguments and the criticism of Pakistani actions, Nixon continued, but while "we want to help India we will not be parties to their objective."

The problem was that Nixon and Kissinger had no realistic strategy for solving the East Pakistan problem. They could not press the Pakistanis to accept an independent Bangladesh because that would, in effect, have meant siding with India (and vicariously with the USSR) and thus created problems with China. As Kissinger sarcastically noted, it was virtually impossible even to imagine the possibility of talks between Yahya Khan and the Awami League, the only conceivable alternative to avoiding a military confrontation. It would be "like asking Abraham Lincoln to deal with Jefferson Davis," Kissinger noted. When the Yahya government began a secret trial against Sheikh Mujib later the same day, any hopes for an inter-Pakistani political settlement were virtually extinguished.[31]

In the end, the real issue for Kissinger was neither the fate of the Awami League, the designs of India, nor the unity of Pakistan. What mattered was how the Soviets and, in particular, the Chinese viewed American policy. And, in the aftermath of the August 9 treaty the logic seemed clear: the Soviets had to be restrained from encouraging India to launch a war or, even better, Moscow should be pressed into restraining India. Otherwise, as Nixon had said in the August 11 meeting, the regional crisis might well jeopardize the China initiative and the launch of triangular diplomacy. The timing of the treaty had clearly strengthened Kissinger's perception of South Asia as a testing ground for triangular diplomacy.

In light of such apparent success of the China initiative, however, Kissinger felt able to press Dobrynin for a Soviet commitment in South Asia. At the same August 17 back-channel meeting where he delivered Nixon's positive response to the summit invitation, Kissinger also pressed the Soviets "not [to] encourage Indian pressures for an immediate political solution since that would make the problem [in South Asia] impossible." Dobrynin, while assuring that "the Soviets were doing their best to restrain India," also pointed out the ironies of the South Asian situation "where [the Soviets] were lined up with what looked [the Americans] had always thought was the pillar of democracy [i.e. India] while [the U.S.] were lined up with the Chinese." Kissinger, naturally, denied that the United States was "lined up with anybody" and maintained that it would be best if the United States and the Soviet Union "worked on the refugee and relief problems first and on political accommodation later." When Dobrynin expressed his bewilderment over U.S. policy toward Pakistan that was clearly running against the general public and world opinion, Kissinger simply replied, "we never yield to public pressure."[32] In August 1971, the Kissinger–Dobrynin back channel was of little use when it came down to finding a solution to the South Asian crisis.

PROTECTING THE "TENDER SHOOT"

While Kissinger faced the pressures emanating from the turbulence in South Asia and the respective roles played by the USSR and the PRC in the countdown toward the Indo-Pakistani War, his main concern remained guarding the success of the China initiative. Kissinger thus worked extremely hard to convey to the Chinese that the United States was serious about its new relationship with the PRC and to avoid any misunderstandings about American policy. As Kissinger puts it, he had to "protect the tender shoot of our China policy from being crushed by this combination of Soviet embrace and menace." While rejecting any notion of giving the Chinese a veto over U.S. policy, Kissinger admits that in the months following his secret trip he "took great pains to keep the Chinese informed of all our moves with Moscow and our assessments of Soviet intentions."[33]

In practice this meant that a new secret channel between Kissinger and Zhou Enlai was opened—as agreed during the secret trip—in Paris. On July 19, General Vernon Walters, the U.S. military attaché and a veteran of Kissinger's secret channels with the North Vietnamese, met with the Chinese ambassador Huang Chen. To avoid press scrutiny, they met at Huang's residence. Huang Chen, a veteran of the Long March who, in 1973, would become the first chief of China's liaison office in Washington, was extremely cordial and hospitable. He gave Walters two phone numbers so that he could reach the ambassador "whenever [he] wanted." They would use the codename *Jean* (perhaps because both men were associated with Kissinger's longtime friend Jean Sainteny) and Walters stressed that "no one in the U.S. Embassy in Paris was aware of the existence of this channel." The following day Walters received the first of Kissinger's messages regarding his talks with Anatoly Dobrynin and emphasized "the need to insulate Sino-U.S. relations from U.S. domestic politics."[34]

Kissinger had an opportunity to explain his point a few days later when he came to Paris to meet with Le Duc Tho under the cover of attending President Charles de Gaulle's funeral. The Nixon administration simply wanted to minimize the attacks on its China policy from the Taiwan lobby and its "right-wing" supporters. This would, however, be much easier if the Chinese did not make comments that would "encourage left-wing spokesmen," Kissinger added. He then asked the PRC to show restraint in its public commentary. Huang Chen said that there was no problem with China's restraint but wondered whether the Nixon administration could respond in kind. Of course, Kissinger admitted, it was difficult to avoid speculation about the content of Zhou's and Kissinger's talks in the U.S. press, but he assured, erroneously as it was, that these had not been and would not become based on information leaked by the administration. All articles in the U.S. press were based on mere "speculation," Kissinger maintained. It was an assertion that, given Kissinger's intense personal background briefings after his return from the secret trip in July, was, quite plainly, a lie.

The main point of the meeting, though, had to do with Huang's invitation: Kissinger was welcome to come to China again for the purpose of preparing for Nixon's forthcoming visit in 1972. The caveat was also significant. "Owing to understandable reasons, it would not be appropriate for Mr. [David] Bruce to come to China." Bruce's position as the head of the official U.S. delegation to the Paris peace negotiations on Vietnam obviously made his visit to Beijing too complicated from the standpoint of Sino-Vietnamese relations. In his report to Nixon, Kissinger wrote that he "did not press Bruce's acceptability . . . but hope to get Peking to reconsider him for future assignments." Indeed, in 1973 Bruce would become Huang's American counterpart in Beijing.[35]

During their next meetings in Paris—a week after the Indo-Soviet treaty was signed and just a day before he delivered Nixon's acceptance of the Moscow summit invitation to Dobrynin—Kissinger outlined for Huang U.S. policy in South Asia. On the morning of August 16, he stressed U.S. domestic difficulties in maintaining a pro-Pakistani tilt and Nixon's threat that he would cut all economic aid to India if it launched an offensive. He noted that the United States was trying to "develop a program to make it possible for a maximum number of refugees to return home [to East Pakistan] so as to deprive India of any pretext for intervention." In accordance with the policy of avoiding a war, Kissinger asked the Chinese to do what they could to prevent Pakistan from launching military action. But he contradicted this advice by saying "that we would understand the furnishing of military equipment by the PRC to Pakistan." Huang Chen said little, aside from criticizing India's interference "in the internal affairs of Pakistan."

True to form, Kissinger congratulated himself about this meeting as a masterly example of triangular diplomacy. As he wrote to Nixon:

> We are building a solid record of keeping the Chinese informed on all significant subjects of concern to them, which gives them an additional stake in nurturing our new relationship. We laid out our South Asia policy and made clear that we are not colluding against their ally. We have now foreshadowed the potentially unpleasant combination of a Moscow Summit and visits by the Emperor of Japan and Prime Minister Gandhi in a way that should make these events at the same time palatable and a reminder that we are not so eager with the Chinese that we will shy away from those countries which they dislike.[36]

Notwithstanding the self-congratulatory tone of Kissinger's message to Nixon—the depiction of a carefully planned and successful maneuvering with the Chinese—there was hardly any doubt that as Kissinger began to prepare for his second visit to China and the South Asian situation continued to deteriorate, the tilt toward Pakistan had become a reality, subsumed by the logic of the emerging triangular diplomacy. In no uncertain terms it was, ultimately, a tilt toward China. The "tender shoot" needed to be protected at all costs.

POLO II: CHINA TRIP OCTOBER 1971

In early September, while preparing for his second visit to China and tilting toward Pakistan, Kissinger was struck by curious—in his words: "ominous" and "mystifying"—developments within China. As he writes in his memoirs,

> we suddenly became aware that all of China's leaders had disappeared from public view for five days; all Chinese planes had been grounded for the same time. As the month wore on it became clear that several key leaders had been removed from office, including much of the top leadership of the armed forces. Foremost among the suddenly missing was [Defense Minister] Lin Biao.[37]

What actually happened in China in September 1971 would not be known in any detail until the following year. The Lin Biao incident of September 1971 confused and potentially complicated an already complex situation. Only two-and-a-half years earlier, at the 9th Chinese Communist Party Congress in April 1969, Lin—

who was also the minister of defense and the vice chairman of the CCP Politburo—had emerged as Mao's assumed successor. According to the Chinese official portrait of the Lin Biao affair, the number two position had not been enough and Lin, unsuccessfully, attempted to oust Mao. The Great Helmsman had foiled Lin's plans to take over the number one position during the Lushan conference of 1970 only to have Lin orchestrate plans for a coup in 1971. It all culminated, the story goes, on September 13, 1971, when Lin Biao—after his plan to assassinate Mao was foiled—boarded a plane that then crashed in Mongolia.[38]

Most observers in the West, including most prominent sinologists, agree that a power struggle between Mao and Lin Biao was the cause of the latter's demise; which one of them was playing the more proactive role is another question. Most Western scholars, moreover, see a strong link between the Sino-American opening and the fall of Lin Biao: once Kissinger had been to Beijing and Nixon's visit had been settled, Mao had, the argument goes, effectively sided with Zhou against Lin Biao (and a rapprochement with the Soviet Union). One should note, however, that recent research appears to indicate a far less serious challenge from Lin, who became, effectively, a passive victim of Mao's paranoia. Or, as Frederick C. Teiwes and Warren Sun put it: "Lin Biao was tragically entrapped by his political system and political culture . . . a victim who could not escape Mao's increasingly unpredictable demands."[39] Although the evidence either way is rather scattered, one can presume that the Lin Biao affair, which caused a great deal of confusion in the United States, was not simply the last act in an ongoing struggle over the direction of China's foreign policy, but a phase in the development of elite politics in Mao's China, where the Chairman's paranoia could easily result in a purge of those he, rightly or wrongly, viewed as threats to his dominant position.[40]

Whatever its actual cause, Lin Biao's downfall did have a positive impact on Sino-American rapprochement. "Under these circumstances," writes Chen Jian in *Mao's China and the Cold War*, "Mao was even more in need of a major breakthrough in China's international relations, one that could help boost the chairman's declining reputation and authority while enhancing the Chinese people's support for Mao's Communist state—if not necessarily for Mao's Communist revolution." Moreover, with Mao's reputation staked on the success of the opening to America, Zhou Enlai's position was inevitably enhanced. Due to the fall of Lin, the foremost Chinese architect of the opening to America was at the zenith of his influence as Kissinger and his entourage arrived in Beijing for Polo II (the codename for the October 1971 visit).[41]

In fact, in an interesting coincidence, Kissinger met with Huang Chen in Paris on the same day that Lin Biao's plane crashed in Mongolia. The two discussed preparations for Kissinger's trip to Beijing and broadly outlined the contents of Nixon's subsequent visit. During the "extremely cordial" meeting, the two agreed that Kissinger would arrive in China on October 20 for a four-day visit. There was no discussion about the internal situation in China. Lin Biao was never mentioned.[42]

Even as Kissinger—as well most of the rest of the world—remained unaware of the Lin Biao affair, the preparation for Kissinger's second trip to China took place in an atmosphere mixed with optimism and uncertainty. On the one hand, Kissinger and Nixon remained optimistic because the Paris channel indicated that nothing was about to derail the process now under way. On the other hand, the looming crisis in South Asia, the question of the PRC's UN membership, and the clear lack of progress in the secret meetings with the North Vietnamese—that took place on the same days (August 16 and September 13) as his discussions with Huang Chen—prevented any euphoria in the Nixon White House.

The main purpose of Kissinger's trip to China in October 1971 was to pave the way for Nixon's more public visit four months later. This particular visit, as well as another by Alexander Haig in January 1972, was to lay down the issues and agreements that the president, in his heavily ceremonial excursion, would not have the time to explore in detail. Thus, in the months before the October trip, Kissinger's NSC staff was busily ensconced in planning the practical details and substance of Nixon's visit. Aside from the big issues of the day, such as the USSR and the Vietnam War, the latter included such outstanding matters as the Chinese assets in America that the United States had frozen after 1949 and American-owned properties that the PRC had nationalized after Mao's forces had defeated Chiang Kaishek's nationalist forces.

Given the complex, and often mundane, nature of the issues, Kissinger agreed to include a State Department representative, the director of the Office of Mainland China and Mongolian Affairs Alfred ("Al") Lesesne Jenkins. But, as Chas Freeman, who served as an interpreter during Nixon's February 1972 trip, later reminisced, "Al Jenkins had been essentially co-opted by Kissinger and was working with Kissinger directly, behind the back of Marshall Green and the secretary of state, Bill Rogers." Yet, even in such a situation, the division of labor reflected the NSC's and State's respective positions in the Nixon administration's foreign policy making hierarchy. As John Holdridge later reminisced, Al Jenkins and his staff were to prepare the background material concerning merely "the practical, bilateral issues affecting U.S.-China relations; the NSC staff would prepare the background books on the more politically sensitive issues, particularly those dealing with the Soviet Union and Vietnam." As befitted Kissinger and Nixon's style, the "real stuff" remained within the purview of the White House alone.[43]

Kissinger landed in China for the second time on October 20, 1971. As a simulation of Nixon's February 1972 trip, Kissinger used Air Force One and made stopovers in Hawaii and Guam; for the same purpose, he would visit Shanghai after departing Beijing. On the 20th, though, Beijing appeared to be a city under siege. Traffic had been halted and PLA troops seemed to be in evidence on every street corner in Beijing. And, when Kissinger's party arrived at their guesthouse there was an unwelcome information sheet waiting. In every room was a special issue of the *People's Daily* that called the peoples of the world to overthrow the "American imperialists and their running dogs." Kissinger ordered John Holdridge to collect all of the issues and give them to their Chinese hosts. Holdridge was advised to say that previous guests had apparently left the papers behind.[44]

Over the next five and a half days Kissinger and Zhou held ten meetings lasting a total of roughly twenty-five hours, many of them held with only a few assistants (in six meetings Winston Lord was the only other American present, even as Zhou brought in several advisers). Although the focus of the discussion was on the specifics of Nixon's trip, Kissinger and Zhou covered much of the globe during their talks. Yet, their focus was decisively regional: the key topics were Taiwan, Indochina, Korea, Japan, the Soviet Union, and South Asia. There were also many banquets and sightseeing tours with Marshal Yeh Chien-ying, vice chairman of the Military Affairs Commission of the CCP and Chi Peng-fei, the acting foreign minister. While Kissinger missed some of the sights due to his private meetings with Zhou, he did attend the Beijing Opera, saw the Great Wall and the Ming Tombs, took in a boat trip near the Summer Palace, and accompanied the rest of the group to the Temple of Heaven. And he feasted, as much as possible, on Chinese delicacies. In addition to Kissinger's meetings with Zhou, there were several lower-level meetings about diplomatic contacts, bilateral exchanges, trade, and technical arrangements for Nixon's visit—what Kissinger collectively referred to as "subsidiary issues." The general tone of discussions contained "no surprises," Kissinger noted in his report to Nixon. He summed up the Sino-American relationship as follows:

> Both sides know there are profound differences but recognizing that domestic and international constraints demand a phased resolution of outstanding issues. Meanwhile, the very momentum of our joint initiative carries inherent advantages: for them, the burnishing of their global credentials, a general direction on Taiwan, and the prospect of a lower American profile in Asia; for us, some assistance in reaching and safeguarding an Indochina settlement, and built-in restraint on Chinese activities in Asia; for both of us, less danger of miscalculation, greater exchanges between our peoples, and a counter-weight to the Soviet Union.[45]

As far as preparations for Nixon's trip were concerned, the visit was a success. Although the joint communiqué—what would become known as the Shanghai Communiqué—was not completely ironed out at this point, the basic agreements (or public disagreements) over such issues as Taiwan were dealt with in a way that both parties could accept. That is, on potentially controversial issues Kissinger and Zhou, after much haggling, agreed that they would disagree. On Taiwan, for example, Kissinger promised that the United States would continue to reduce the American military presence and that the American "attempt will be to bring about a solution within a framework of one China by peaceful means." The U.S.-Taiwanese Mutual Defense Treaty was not a "permanent feature of our foreign policy," Kissinger added, and "after unification of China by peaceful negotiation has been achieved we will be prepared to abrogate it formally." Regardless of achieving such a settlement, he further maintained, the United States would "withdraw our military presence in stages." In short, the United States would "Taiwanize" Taiwan's defense.

The real haggling on Taiwan and other matters, though, focused on the exact wording of what would eventually become known as the Shanghai Communiqué after Nixon's visit in February. On the evening of October 23, Zhou presented Kissinger with a harshly phrased Chinese version of the joint communiqué—with blank pages left for the Americans to define their position—that Mao had approved only hours earlier. This commenced the haggling over two communiqués: the one to be released after Kissinger's departure and the draft of the eventual Shanghai Communiqué that would be publicized on the last day of Nixon's February 1972 visit. The draft of the Nixon communiqué was eventually agreed in a meeting that commenced at 5:30 A.M. on Tuesday, October 26, and included the later famous phrase: "the United Sates acknowledges that all Chinese on either side of the Taiwan Strait maintain there is but one China." At 8:10 A.M. the meeting concluded, at 10:30 A.M. Kissinger's group departed from Beijing. They stopped over in Shanghai, had lunch at the airport lounge, and then continued back to the United States with a stopover in Alaska.[46]

* * *

Aside from Taiwan and the communiqué, Vietnam and the Soviet Union were the most frequently mentioned topics. On Vietnam—"an even more urgent question than the Taiwan issue," Zhou said—the two made little progress. On October 22, Zhou complained about the United States reluctance to set a date for the final withdrawal of American troops, while Kissinger reviewed the secret negotiations in Paris and complained about North Vietnam's intransigence. "While I am sure your allies in Vietnam know how to fight, I am not sure they know how to negotiate," he said. Kissinger also tried to enlist Chinese help in convincing the North Vietnamese to negotiate seriously. The United States had no interest in prolonging the war or American presence in Indochina: "Why should we want to maintain bases in one little corner of Asia when the whole trend of our policy is to form a new relationship with the most important country in Asia?" Zhou professed that he knew none of the details of the secret talks and instead blamed the Soviets. "All three horses of the troika [Brezhnev, Podgorny, and Kosygin] are busier than ever," Zhou said. "They are sticking their hands everywhere," he added. But Zhou also criticized American support for the "Lon Nol/Sirik Matak clique," in Cambodia. "If you will give assistance to [them], then we will certainly have to give assistance to Sihanouk," Zhou complained. He made comparisons—often popular in the later literature on the Vietnam War—between the Vietnam War and the American war of independence (with Ho Chi Minh as George Washington). In the end, Zhou offered no real assistance and summed up the situation simply as: "there is a knot in your negotiations that hasn't been untied."

"This is true," Kissinger replied.[47]

In fact, the Soviet Union was the country that Kissinger and Zhou referred to most often. Both Zhou and Kissinger were, though, short on specifics. Aside from blaming the USSR for North Vietnam's intransigence, for conspiring with India against Pakistan, and for creating trouble in the Middle East, however, Zhou was relatively restrained in his comments. At one point he referred to the Soviet Union simply as "one of the five powers." Kissinger, for his part, promised to keep the Chinese fully informed of all contacts with the USSR and said that he always refused to share with the Soviets any details of his discussions with the Chinese. In the end, he wrote Nixon, "the Chinese try to downgrade the Russian factor, but their dislike and concern about the Soviet Union is clear."[48]

One aspect of the October visit truly surprised Kissinger: Zhou Enlai's glaring lack of interest in discussing the Indo-Pakistani conflict. When they did get down to the topic, on October 22, Kissinger was blunt, blaming India and the Soviet Union. "The Indians see in this situation no longer a legal problem of East Pakistan but an opportunity to settle the whole problem of Pakistan . . . and they are encouraged in this tendency by what they believe to be the support of some outside countries," he said. "Quite a big encouragement," Zhou commented. Kissinger continued:

> The United States is . . . the only major western country that has not condemned Pakistan. It is only because of us, and I may say over the opposition of the pro-Indian element of our government, that the consortium hasn't cut off aid to Pakistan. And we will bring about now a $90 million debt relief for Pakistan. And we have in the form of relief made available $250 million of other funds. We are totally opposed to Indian military action against Pakistan . . . I have warned the Indian ambassador on behalf of the president that if there was an attack by India we will cut off all economic aid to India. We have told the Russians our view, and they have told us they are trying to restrain the situation, but I am not sure that I believe them.

Kissinger's prognosis was pessimistic: "We believe there is a good chance that India will either attack or provoke the Pakistanis to attack by driving the Pakistanis into desperate action in the next month or two." Zhou made few comments except to stress "the desire of the Soviet Union to exploit the situation." He then suggested that they discuss South Asia at a later stage during the visit.[49]

Significantly, Zhou did not return to the Indo-Pakistani situation. He did not lobby for a common front or a tough joint warning to India or the Soviet Union. Zhou had—probably under instructions from Mao—decided to cool it. In his assessment of this seeming lack of interest, Kissinger seemed puzzled. "I believe the PRC does not want hostilities to break out, is afraid of giving Moscow a pretext for an attack, and would find itself in an awkward position if this were to happen." Add to this China's delicate internal position in the months subsequent to the Lin Biao incident that, unknown to Kissinger, hardly encouraged risking the active use of the People's Liberation Army against India or, for that matter, the Soviet Union. Indeed, Zhou expressed neither approval nor disapproval of the Nixon administration's tilt toward Pakistan. Despite evident Chinese dislike of India and the Soviet Union, "he did not attempt to contrast their stand with ours as demonstrating greater support for our common friend, Pakistan."[50]

On his return journey Kissinger heard that on Monday evening (shortly after 11:00 EST), October 25, the UN General Assembly had voted to admit the PRC and expel Taiwan. The final vote—in favor of the Albanian resolution that had been introduced every year since the early 1960s—was 76–35 (with seventeen countries abstaining). Secretary of State Rogers' dual representation resolution that would have allowed both Chinas to have a seat, never made it to a formal vote; given that it was rejected by Taiwan and the PRC it would hardly have mattered. The United States had voted—for domestic political reasons Kissinger explained to the Chinese who publicly criticized, as expected, the American vote—with the minority and without any NATO allies on its side (they either abstained or voted for the PRC's entry). After the vote, Taiwan's UN ambassador stood up and walked out of the General Assembly for the last time.[51]

While Rogers and Bush had failed in their effort to save Taiwan's seat, Nixon and Kissinger—as well as the Chinese—had foreseen the outcome for weeks. "I always thought it [the China vote in the UN] was a loser," Kissinger had told Nixon three weeks prior to departing for Beijing. The two had worried, though, about the timing of the vote in relation to Kissinger's trip. "Going [to China] after, immediately after the vote would be worse than your going before the vote," Nixon had told Kissinger on September 30. Kissinger had agreed, and the two had rejected Secretary of State Rogers and Ambassador Bush's efforts to postpone the Kissinger trip.[52]

As it happened, Kissinger was in China when the voting took place (several days earlier than had originally been anticipated). This made him agitated over the reaction at home and any possible accusations of his complicity in the outcome. The China lobby had attacked him ever since the secret trip and Kissinger's presence in Beijing at the time of the UN vote hardly helped Taiwan's cause. Indeed, one of the first things he had to do upon his return was to telephone two of Taiwan's most vocal supporters, California Governor Ronald Reagan and the conservative columnist William F. Buckley. In the end, though, losing the Taiwan vote was hardly a major problem for Kissinger. The idea of dual representation had not been his but Rogers'; its failure only confirmed Kissinger's central position as the czar of U.S. China policy. The coincidence of the vote and Kissinger's second trip to China made him, in effect, the foremost of the new China hands.[53]

Nixon, as Patrick Tyler has observed, could actually have it both ways. On the one hand, his public denunciation of the loud celebration at the General Assembly showed the conservative supporters of Taiwan that Nixon had not sold out Taiwan. On the other hand, the president could claim some credit for the PRC's entry to the UN, made possible in part by the Nixon administration's China policy. The key issue, though, was to minimize the negative fallout among the conservatives. Hence, Nixon, Kissinger, Attorney General John Mitchell, and others spent several days calming down such stalwart Taiwan supporters as Reagan, Buckley, and Arizona Senator (and the 1964 Republican presidential candidate) Barry Goldwater.[54]

The admission of the PRC to the UN had another, operational, outcome. On November 15, Kissinger suggested via Vernon Walters in Paris that China's UN mission be used as another secret channel between the two countries. The Chinese accepted a few days later and Alexander Haig arranged a CIA safe house in New York's Lower East Side (238 East Thirty-sixth Street, Apartment B) to be used as a meeting place. At 10:00 P.M. on Tuesday, November 23, the PRC's first UN ambassador Huang Hua (who had moved to New York after a brief stint as Beijing's envoy to Canada), met there with Kissinger, Haig, Lord, and Bush. Most of the discussion would focus on the increasing likelihood of an Indo-Pakistani War.[55]

CONTAINING INDIRA

Indian Prime Minister Indira Gandhi's visit to Washington in early November 1971 only a week after Kissinger's return from Beijing provided one of the last opportunities to prevent the outbreak of war in South Asia. Unfortunately, the tension—a result of the circumstances that were pitting the two countries on opposite sides of the crisis—in the talks between Gandhi and Nixon was palpable. The meetings turned into, in Kissinger's words, "a dialogue of the deaf." Nixon's private assessment of Gandhi was more brutal: "That bitch, that whore," he ruminated after the Indian prime minister had left the Oval Office on November 4. "He's in kind of a strange mood," Bob Haldeman commented in his diaries about Nixon's behavior that day.[56]

In fact, Nixon and Kissinger were predisposed not to believe Nehru's daughter's assurances of India's peaceful intentions and instead to assume that Gandhi, in concert with Moscow, was planning to use force not only to create an independent Bangladesh but also to take over Kashmir. They had reasonable cause to be suspicious. In the months preceding her visit to Washington, Gandhi and her government continued to support the various liberation forces (most prominently the Mukti Bahiini) based in West Bengal and supported (as well as dominated) the organization of a Bangladeshi coalition government in exile. The Indian government had also done its utmost to gain international support by lobbying various UN organizations. (Given the fact that the Pakistani repression of Bengalis was the chief cause of the refugee crisis this was not exceedingly difficult.) In late September Gandhi had been to Moscow and had, apparently, secured the USSR's support for Indian policy. This was, at least, what the Indian government wanted American officials to believe. Any talk about Soviet restraint on India, the Indian foreign secretary

T. N. Kaul told U.S. Ambassador Kenneth Keating on October 9, was "rubbish." Instead, the "Soviets recognize imperatives of situation from Indian viewpoint, unlike U.S. which is prepared to see situation drag along for one or two years." The Soviets, Kaul added, "expressed solidarity with [the] Indian position." How much solidarity Brezhnev, Podgorny, and Kosygin had expressed is unclear; certainly the public communiqué at the end of Gandhi's visit was more circumspect than Kaul suggested to Keating. Yet, the Indians, perhaps as a way of counseling restraint on the United States and China, felt that it was in their interest at this point to stress Indo-Soviet unity.[57]

The Soviets presented a different picture to Kissinger. At the same time as Gandhi held discussions in Moscow, the Soviet foreign minister Andrei Gromyko visited the United States. After attending the annual UN meetings in New York, Gromyko met with Nixon and Kissinger. Nixon suggested that the United States and the Soviet Union should cooperate to discourage Indian aggression against Pakistan. Gromyko countered by assuring that Moscow was urging restraint on India and that Gandhi had promised that India would "not precipitate a conflict." Gromyko added that the "country that should be restrained first of all was Pakistan." Nixon disagreed with the last point but suggested that Moscow and Washington remain in close touch over South Asia. In subsequent weeks Kissinger and Dobrynin thus discussed the South Asian crisis repeatedly in the back channel. Amid assurances that the Soviets were urging restraint on India, however, Dobrynin professed that Soviet influence had its limits. At one point he even warned: "the Indians were getting extremely difficult."[58]

Gandhi's first meeting with Nixon on the morning of November 4—with only Kissinger and Gandhi's adviser, P. N. Haksar, in attendance—was an indication of how difficult the prime minister could be. The discussion focused almost exclusively on the situation in South Asia. Nixon stressed his interest in finding a peaceful solution. He justified U.S. military assistance and relief aid to Pakistan as being necessitated "by the imperative to retain influence with the Government of Pakistan." Washington had, Nixon continued, successfully pressed Yahya Khan to proclaim a general amnesty to all East Pakistanis that had been jailed by the West Pakistanis, to appoint a civilian governor for East Pakistan, and not to execute Awami League head Mujibur Rahman. While "the U.S. could not urge policies which would be tantamount to overthrowing President Yahya . . . in the long run Pakistan must acquiesce in the direction of greater autonomy for East Pakistan," Nixon added. He also warned Gandhi:

> The consequences of military action were incalculably dangerous. In this regard, India's recent agreement with the Soviet Union was understood by this government but India must recognize it is not popular in the U.S. It must, therefore, have an impact on the general attitude of the U.S. government. Should the situation deteriorate to armed conflict, there is doubt that the conflict could be lim-

ited to just India and Pakistan . . . The American people would not understand if India were to initiate military action.

As the transcript of the meeting indicates, Nixon made little impact on Gandhi. Aside from insisting that the cause of the troubles lay in Pakistan and that India had no aggressive motives, the prime minister went on to deny any accusations of her government's complicity. She drew parallels between U.S. support to anti-Castro Cubans and India's aid to Bengali guerrillas. Gandhi attacked Yahya Khan and the Pakistani army's suppression of East Pakistan, and deplored the refugee crisis in West Bengal that Pakistani policies had provoked. Nixon argued that the United States had done its best to try and avert a serious famine in East Pakistan and was doing what it could to diffuse the crisis. The Americans had pressed the Pakistanis to pull back some of their troops from the Indian border, Nixon added, and had received assurances directly from Yahya Khan that Pakistan was ready to negotiate with the leaders of the Awami League. Gandhi was not impressed. The partition of Pakistan was already, she said, "a reality." Nixon's only response was: "nothing could be served by the disintegration of Pakistan."[59] Adding to Nixon's frustration, Gandhi was not only dismissive of the president's arguments but also rather effective in selling the Indian viewpoint on NBC's *Meet the Press* a few days later. On Sunday, November 7, Gandhi strongly stressed that the refugee crisis had become "a real threat to Indian democracy and Indian stability."[60]

Gandhi's visit had confirmed in Nixon's and Kissinger's minds what they already believed; only a complete capitulation by Yahya Khan over East Pakistan could prevent an Indian attack. By early November, moreover, the Soviets had begun shipping arms to India. In short, while it is hard to prove that India was definitely bent on war—and while there was little indication that Gandhi's plans included, as Kissinger would predict, a major offensive in the disputed Kashmir region—there seems to be no question that New Delhi was ready to support the creation of an independent Bangladesh by force if necessary. Indira Gandhi, Kissinger and Nixon had come to believe, could simply not be contained.

The weeks following Gandhi's visit were clouded by numerous reports of escalated fighting and two brief Indian incursions into East Pakistan. On November 10, Assistant Secretary of State Joseph Sisco met with the Indian and Pakistani ambassadors, urging the two sides to defuse the situation. The following day, Kissinger warned the Indian ambassador Jha about the disastrous consequences a war would entail and asked how the situation could be improved. On November 15, Pakistan's Foreign Secretary Sultan Khan came to Washington and met with Kissinger. They discussed the possibility of a mutual pullback of Indian and Pakistani forces from the Indian-West Pakistan borders and Kissinger raised the possibility of allowing Sheikh Mujib a role in a negotiation process. This, he had come to believe, would be the only way of preventing India from taking its chosen path. To this effect, Kissinger said, "it would be extremely desirable for him to have an authoritative

statement of President Yahya's view on the role of Mujib over the next six months."
Kissinger also tried to press the Soviets to prevent a prospective Indian attack. But
Dobrynin was evasive. On November 18, the Soviet ambassador again assured that
"the Soviet Union was urging restraint on India." Kissinger responded by saying
that Soviet arms shipments to India "was not restraint [and] it would have a bad
impact on our relations if their actions produced a war." Dobrynin "rejoined that
there was no danger of that, although some Indian elements wished war."[61]

Four days later, however, Dobrynin's assurances appeared utterly disingenuous.
At noon on November 22, 1971, Kissinger burst into Bob Haldeman's office. Pakistani Radio and TV were reporting that India had attacked Pakistan, he told the
White House chief of staff. For the rest of the day the situation in South Asia
remained unclear. Late in the evening there was no reliable intelligence report that
would have confirmed an Indian attack. The following day, November 23, the White
House received Yahya Khan's message, reporting that Indian forces had commenced a sustained attack. Yahya charged: "12 Indian divisions have been deployed
around East Pakistan." Although it was not clear to observers in Washington
whether these incursions represented the first stage in a full-fledged assault on East
Pakistan or merely a continuation of earlier cross-border raids, the Pakistani president was clearly getting desperate. "The offensive launched by Indian armed
forces," Yahya said, "must be met by us with all the force at our command." He had
concluded that the war had, in effect, started.[62]

Frenetic activity followed. At 10:00 P.M. on November 23, Kissinger met secretly
with the PRC's newly appointed ambassador to the UN, Huang Hua, in a safe house
on East Thirty-sixth Street in New York. The bulk of the meeting was devoted to
South Asia. With Winston Lord, the UN ambassador George Bush, and Al Haig on
his side, Kissinger assured that the United States would cut off any assistance to
India if the latter "*clearly* launched aggression." He showed maps of presumed
Indian troop movements and offered to send any further information to Hua in "a
sealed envelope." Huang Hua stressed continued Chinese support for Pakistan. Yet,
he also emphasized, reasonably enough, that Beijing was not going to send any
troops to the area and that the PRC wished to leave the matter to the UN Security
Council. "It was out of their hands," Huang told Kissinger, who was clearly frustrated as his "efforts to elicit more precise positions on their part were fruitless."[63]

The journalist-author Patrick Tyler has charged that this memo indicates that
Kissinger tried "to induce China to consider an attack on India's frontier, an act that
certainly would have touched off a general war in the region and driven the superpowers toward a serious confrontation."[64] Such an argument, though, makes little
sense. Lest he was hoping to trade all the gains of the previous year for a military conflict with uncertain end results, Kissinger could not have been trying to expand the
conflict. If anything, the situation in South Asia was an irritant—not dissimilar to
that of the Vietnam War—that was complicating the early application of triangular
diplomacy. The difference was that in the case of the South Asian crisis, Kissinger felt

it was necessary to side with the Pakistanis in large part because of where the Chinese and Soviets stood. In other words, whatever the merits of the tilt, it acted as a useful, if hardly necessary, pretext for winning the confidence of the PRC.

THE BANGLADESH WAR

On December 4 (December 3 in Washington), the full-scale war commenced when the Pakistanis launched the first series of air strikes from West Pakistan against Indian airfields.[65]

Should Nixon and Kissinger be blamed for the outbreak of war in December? Did the obvious tilt toward Pakistan result in a misguided and unfortunate belief in Islamabad that Nixon had given the Yahya government, if not a green light, then at least a yellow one, to launch a sustained attack? Or did the Pakistani attack on India simply represent a desperate move by a beleaguered nation?

Even with the benefit of thirty years of hindsight it is difficult to answer such questions with certainty. Indeed, it is hard to see how, once the crisis in East Pakistan had generated a huge flood of refugees, a military confrontation between two traditional enemies could have been avoided without an outright Pakistani capitulation to the Awami League's demands for independence. How Yahya Khan and his government could have done that without jeopardizing their internal position is equally unfathomable. At the same time the American (and perceived Chinese) support for Pakistan could only strengthen the hand of those favoring military action in the West (where the Pakistani army was the strongest), especially when it could be justified as retaliation for Indian attacks in the East.[66]

Kissinger's activity during the fighting followed the logic of his efforts during the previous months. His main concern was, as it had been since July 1971, to safeguard the opening to China and the emergence of triangular diplomacy. Hence, his major efforts were directed at the USSR and the PRC, rather than India or Pakistan. Even as the brewing crisis climaxed in the outbreak of a war, Kissinger thus remained primarily interested in the impact the fighting would have on the opening to China, a fact that rendered his ability to stop the war as ineffectual as his efforts at containing the conflict had been during the months leading to the outbreak of war.

The public diplomacy of the Indo-Pakistani War was conducted in New York. Both India and Pakistan took their case to the UN. Predictably, both branded the other side as the aggressor but while the Pakistanis asked for UN protection of their country's territorial integrity, the Indian government appealed to the world organization not to intervene. In accordance with American policy, George Bush worked closely with Pakistan's UN ambassador, Agha Shahi, and publicly referred to India as the "major aggressor." As the Soviet Union used its veto to prevent any Security Council Resolution, the issue reverted to the General Assembly (GA). On

December 7, the GA passed a resolution (by 104 to 11), calling for an immediate ceasefire and the creation of conditions that would allow the refugees to return to East Pakistan/Bangladesh. While Pakistan accepted the resolution two days later, India rejected it on December 12, prompting another series of Security Council discussions and American charges that India was responsible for the further deterioration of the situation. As the fighting came to an end a few days later, a heated debate—during which Ali Bhutto, Pakistan's deputy prime minister and foreign minister, dramatically tore up one of the many draft resolutions and stormed out of the meeting room—was still continuing.[67]

While George Bush spent his days debating various resolutions at the UN, Kissinger played triangular diplomacy in secret. He dispatched letters, in Nixon's name, to Brezhnev, warning the secretary general of the adverse effects that Indian aggression were bound to have on the Soviet-American relationship. On December 9, Kissinger and Nixon met with Soviet Agriculture Minister Vladimir Matskevich—who was coincidentally in the United States at the time—to urge the USSR to restrain India. While acknowledging that East Pakistan's independence (and Indian domination) was by now virtually assured, Kissinger advised Nixon to "make clear that India should not turn on West Pakistan." The same day Kissinger also met with the Soviet charge d'affaires Yuli Vorontsov (Dobrynin was in Moscow). He pressed the Soviets to discourage their "ally" (India) from aggression, and warned about the consequences for the planned U.S.-Soviet summit. Kissinger told Vorontsov that the U.S.-Pakistani agreement had a secret protocol dating back to November 1962 assuring American military support against possible Indian aggression. Kissinger further pressed the Soviets by telling Vorontsov that the U.S. military was preparing itself for this eventuality by moving an aircraft carrier to the Bay of Bengal. On the same day the United States backed these threats by moving the aircraft carrier *Enterprise* (along with four escorts) from the Gulf of Tonkin toward Singapore and, by December 14, down the Strait of Malacca to the Bay of Bengal. Thus, at the time that the Pakistani forces surrendered in the East on December 16, the *Enterprise* (or Task Force 74) was located just southeast of Sri Lanka. It remained in the area until January 7, 1972, when the American ships returned to the Gulf of Tonkin to join the rest of the Seventh Fleet. The Soviets responded by moving their Indian Ocean fleet toward the same region but also by pressing the Indian government to accept a ceasefire.[68]

During his meeting with Vorontsov, Kissinger had said that he had no contact with China on the matter and proposed taking the issue to the UN. This was an outright lie. In fact, Kissinger met with Huang Hua in New York on the next day and stressed to his Chinese interlocutor that "we tell you about our conversations with the Soviets; we do not tell the Soviets about our conversations with you." (He added: "In fact, we don't tell our own colleagues that I see you.") Kissinger then outlined how the tilt toward Pakistan had played out in practice: he reviewed U.S. economic and disaster relief aid to Pakistan, and stressed the cancellation of all military and economic aid to India. Then he explained that while the administration could not give direct military aid to Pakistan under existing laws and conditions (imposed by the administration), it had worked out arrangements via such third countries as Saudi Arabia, Jordan, and Iran and was working out a deal with Turkey. The message to these countries, Kissinger conspiratorially added, was that if they wanted to ship American arms to Pakistan the United States was "obliged to protest, but we will understand. We will not protest with great intensity. And we will make up to them in next year's budget whatever difficulties they have." (Shipments were already going from Jordan and would soon commence from Iran.) Kissinger also displayed a map of the area that detailed U.S. (and Soviet) ship movements.

Somewhat perturbed by all this information on the secretive American efforts to aid Pakistan, Huang laughed. "I am no expert," he added.

Kissinger was clearly anxious about the possibility that the opening to China might be in jeopardy. Hence he was willing to bend over backward by offering information that Americans had about the disposition of Soviet forces along the Sino-Soviet border and by promising that if the PRC took action regarding the Indo-Pakistani conflict, the United States would "oppose efforts by others to interfere." By "others" Kissinger meant the USSR. Huang seized the opportunity to argue that the creation of an independent Bangladesh was akin to the creation of the puppet state of Manchukuo (Manchuria) by the Japanese in the 1930s; it was, he stressed, "a step to encircle China." Kissinger agreed with this rather forced historical analogy and promised, directly contradicting the account in his memoirs, that "no matter what you read, no one is authorized to talk to the Bangladeshes. We don't recognize Bangladesh and will not recognize it."[69]

It was a promise he could not keep. The Indo-Pakistani War was brief and decisive. In the East, the badly battered Pakistani forces surrendered unconditionally on December 16; this was followed by a ceasefire in the West the following day. As a result of the war Bangladesh became an independent nation and Zufikar Ali Bhutto replaced Yahya Khan as the president of Pakistan.[70] In July 1972 Bhutto and Gandhi negotiated a postwar settlement at the city of Simla that restored normal (or at least formal) diplomatic relations, led to the return of all of the 93,000 Pakistani prisoners of war, and even spelled out a commitment to resolve all disputes (including Kashmir) peacefully. Months earlier, Sheikh Mujibur had organized the first Bangladeshi government; two years later Pakistan finally recognized the full independence of former East Pakistan (Mujibur was assassinated in 1975).[71]

With such end results it would seem that Kissinger had suffered a major defeat and that the tilt toward Pakistan had been for naught. Yet, in his memoirs Kissinger argues that the most important lessons of the South Asian crisis lay elsewhere: "Peking had learned that we took seriously the requirements of the balance of power; Moscow had seen a sufficiently strong reaction not to be tempted to test us in areas of more central concern." The Indo-Pakistani War and Kissinger's diplomacy surrounding it had, in short, set the stage for "a string of spectacular foreign policy successes."[72]

Maybe so. But the more pertinent question is, probably, were the major successes of 1972—the summits in Beijing and Moscow—possible *because* or *despite*
the tilt? Was the tilt justified by broader foreign policy concerns? Or was the South
Asian crisis essentially irrelevant to the emergence of triangular diplomacy?

THE CRUCIBLE OF TRIANGULAR DIPLOMACY

The central criticism of Nixon and Kissinger's conduct during the South Asian crisis is easily summed up: what they saw as the first test case of triangular diplomacy
was also an example of the potential tragedy that ensues when geopolitical predis-
positions are allowed to determine policy toward a regional conflict in the third
world. That is, not only did the United States tilt openly toward a brutal and non-
democratic regime (Pakistan) and against the world's most populous democracy
(India), Washington actually ended up supporting the losing side.

Of course, as Dennis Kux has argued, "there is little evidence that U.S. pressures
or advice significantly affected either India's or Pakistan's actions."[73] But even if one
accepts the fact that a different U.S. policy would have had little impact on the bilateral Indo-Pakistani confrontation—not to mention the East Pakistani/Bengali
drive for independence—the Nixon administration did not enhance its credibility
and prestige in the third world. If anything, the end result was lost prestige and a
punctured moral authority. Realpolitik postulations and rationalizations did little
to impress anyone outside Nixon and Kissinger's inner circle.

One must, moreover, question the morality of a policy that may well have contributed to the gravity of, even as it did not create the conditions for, the refugee
crisis resulting from the Pakistani crackdown. While the NSC and State Department argued over policy in Washington, many lost sight of the fact that each delay
in aid actually cost real lives. The Nixon administration could hardly have saved all
of the more than half a million (according to some estimates up to three million)
Bengalis that perished in 1970–71. But it could certainly have done more, particularly given the questionable logic of the administration's policy and the expectation that, as Kissinger himself acknowledged as early as July 1971, there would
eventually be an independent Bangladesh.

At the same time one must note that even if they were shortsighted, Nixon and
Kissinger's actions were not illogical. In 1971 their central aim was to safeguard the
opening to China and to use the new relationship with the PRC as a way of influencing Soviet behavior. Kissinger's (and Nixon's) obsession with assuring that the
opening to China not be jeopardized—more than any personal antipathy toward
Indira Gandhi or warm feelings of gratitude for the Pakistanis—in large part
explains the tilt. In the State Department, however, a lingering resentment of having been excluded from the secret contacts and being relegated into a clearly secondary role during the preparation for Nixon's China visit that coincided with the

Indo-Pakistani conflict meant that cooperation between NSC and State was at a low point throughout the fall of 1971. The substantive differences over India and Pakistan thus played out within a context of extreme intergovernmental suspicion pitting, yet again, Kissinger against Rogers, the NSC against the State Department. Given Nixon's pro-Pakistani stand, the Indo-Pakistani crisis, even with its disastrous end result, further strengthened Kissinger's already dominant position as the administration's foreign policy czar.

Soviet Ambassador Dobrynin later assessed the Nixon administration's conduct in much the same way as the many American critics have done. As he writes: "what really mattered was that, after taking Pakistan's side as a payoff for helping open up China, Nixon and Kissinger had to rely on Moscow's word that India would not attack West Pakistan."[74] Indeed, Dobrynin argues that it was really the Soviets who played the key role in solving the conflict and preventing Pakistan's complete dismemberment. He thus faults Kissinger and Nixon for giving the Pakistanis an impression of full-fledged support that, in Dobrynin's words, "led to Pakistan's arrogant behavior at the start of the conflict."[75]

At the time, however, Dobrynin, perhaps unwittingly, gave the impression that the Soviets also viewed the crisis as intricately linked to the emergence of triangular diplomacy. In January 1972, he told Kissinger: "Signs of U.S. favoritism toward China [during the Indo-Pakistani-War] strengthened the hand of anti-U.S. people in the [Soviet] Politburo." Kissinger had an answer ready. "Soviet policy had an extraordinary capacity for bringing about greater U.S.-Chinese cooperation," he responded. In the back channel, at least, triangular diplomacy had become a regular part of Soviet-American dialogue.[76]

Back-channel sparring notwithstanding, it is worth asking whether the Soviets should be credited for the prevention of any further escalation of the Indo-Pakistani War of 1971. Yes and no. Dobrynin's assessment confirms an additional nuance of the story: the Soviets had close contacts with India at the time and communicated messages from India to the United States through the back channel. Yet, nowhere in his memoirs does Dobrynin indicate that there was any significant Soviet pressure on India and no evidence to that effect has, as of yet, materialized from either the Soviet or the Indian archives. Instead, Indira Gandhi's government seems to have used the Soviets as their messengers in order to convince the Americans and Pakistanis that they had no intention of expanding the conflict to Kashmir. This indeed would have been foolish. While the Indians were victorious regarding Bangladesh, they also had a severe crisis in their hands with the refugee problem. While New Delhi could count on international support in addressing the humanitarian crisis, the Gandhi government could not expect much sympathy if it did launch aggressive action in Kashmir. Nor would such action have been worth risking potential Soviet, Chinese, and American involvement and the resulting dependency on Moscow's military assistance. At the minimum, any further collaboration with the USSR would have severely damaged the image of India as the leader of the nonaligned movement.

What about the impact of the American stance during the Indo-Pakistani conflict on the Sino-American relationship?

The tilt unquestionably had an impact in Beijing, albeit not necessarily the kind of impact that Kissinger and Nixon had hoped. Based on the rather meager evidence available from Chinese sources, one can surmise that Mao and Zhou—without committing Chinese forces and without risking a confrontation—had managed to persuade the Nixon administration to do their bidding in South Asia. A broader war was not in China's interest and U.S. actions had at least partially deterred the escalation of the Indo-Pakistani conflict. Moreover, the Americans' tilt was clear evidence that the Nixon administration desperately needed a success with China. As Zhou indicated in his address to the CCP in December 1971, "there are mistakes in the domestic policy of Pakistan, [such as] the massacre in East Pakistan and the lack of policy toward nationalities." Be that as it may, Zhou maintained that it was Nixon who was virtually begging to visit China. This had given China the upper hand, he believed, because Nixon had to have "something in his pocket" when he returned to the United States, while the Chinese side was in a position in which "it is to our advantage if the negotiation succeeds but it constitutes no detriment to us if the negotiation fails."[77]

While this may have been simply brave talk intended to convince skeptical CCP cadres of the wisdom of China's reversal of policy vis-à-vis the United States, Zhou's argument was not far-fetched. Given the tilt, given Kissinger's constant briefing of the Chinese on the situation between India and Pakistan, on American moves, and considering his efforts to coordinate the two countries' policies, it was obvious who was courting whom. Such courting was equally clear as Nixon embarked on his historic trip to China.

9

"The Week That Changed the World"

On February 21, 1972, Henry Kissinger arrived in China for the third time in an eight-month period. He would return again in June 1972, a remarkable statistic considering that no senior American official had been to China in more than two decades prior to Kissinger's secret trip of July 1971. Such frequent forays to Beijing were also an indication of the significance that Kissinger placed on the new relationship with the People's Republic that had, after all, made triangular diplomacy possible and catapulted Henry Kissinger into a global celebrity.

In February 1972, though, the stakes and the setting were different. Kissinger was not the center of attention. The visit was extensively covered by the American media. This was Richard Nixon's show. It was the "journey of peace," or "the week that changed the world." Kissinger and Nixon met with the major Chinese leaders and held discussions over a host of issues, including the Vietnam War, Taiwan, and relationships with the Soviet Union. At the end of the trip the two countries issued the Shanghai Communiqué, a document dealing with—if not solving—most of the major issues in Sino-American relations: Taiwan, Asian security, Vietnam.

Negotiating the communiqué was, in fact, Kissinger's major job during the Nixon trip. Along with Winston Lord and a few other staff members, Kissinger spent much of his time during the February trip—while Nixon toured historic sites or attended to domestic U.S. business—drafting and negotiating the fine points of this communiqué that, for several decades would serve as a guideline for Sino-American relations. The State Department, although represented in large numbers, was cut off from the process. Indeed, Nixon's China trip both highlighted and confirmed Kissinger's role as the administration's indisputable foreign policy czar.[1]

Nixon's visit to China was one of the highlights of an eventful year. At home, 1972 was a reelection year that ended with Nixon winning a majority in forty-nine states over his Democratic challenger, George McGovern. But five months before his electoral routing of the South Dakota senator, the saga that would undo Nixon's presidency had began to unfold, when five men were arrested for a break-in at the Democratic National Committee's headquarters in the Watergate building complex. By the time Nixon commenced his second term, the Watergate crisis was already beginning to erode his ability to govern effectively.[2]

Watergate would, in time, also transform Kissinger's fortunes, albeit in a dramatically different way than Nixon's. In 1972, though, Kissinger's main concerns were securing the launch of triangular diplomacy and using the new framework to bring about a peace in Vietnam. Following the visit to Beijing in February, Kissinger readied for the Moscow summit scheduled for May. But the summit was almost called off due to the North Vietnamese Spring Offensive in March 1972 and despite Kissinger's second secret trip—this time to Moscow—in April 1972. As the Soviets went ahead with the May summit despite the Americans' massive bombing campaign against their allies in North Vietnam, triangular diplomacy was seemingly vindicated. The Soviets, or so the conventional wisdom would later have it, were so concerned about the opening to China that they were willing to ignore the events in Vietnam in order to safeguard détente. Linkage was, it seemed, truly operational. The different pieces of Kissinger and Nixon's grand design had fallen in place.

And yet, as the newly declassified documents indicate, in the midst of the May summit, Kissinger was also busily selling the idea of a "decent interval" in Vietnam to the Soviets and the Chinese. In other words, while the Soviets may have been willing to overlook the American bombing campaign in Vietnam and have Nixon, the man who had decided upon the bombardment of the USSR's erstwhile allies in Southeast Asia, visit Moscow, this did not mean that the Soviets—much less the Chinese—would actually pressure Hanoi to end its offensive in the South. Instead, it was Kissinger who would, in Moscow in May and in Beijing in June (where he went for another visit a month after the summit with the Soviets), plead for help: the Americans, he would effectively explain to the Soviet foreign minister Andrei Gromyko and to the Chinese premier Zhou Enlai, simply wished to withdraw their troops without witnessing an immediate takeover of the South by North Vietnamese forces. But, if a period of time elapsed after the American withdrawal, the United States would not reintervene in Vietnam.

The triangular framework, so spectacularly on display in the first five months of 1972, was, indeed, allowing Kissinger to involve Moscow and Beijing in the Vietnam endgame in 1972. But the impact of that involvement was neither to restrain the North Vietnamese from taking further military action against South Vietnam nor to induce Hanoi into making meaningful concessions to secure a peace agreement with the United States. Instead, the North launched a massive attack against the South and would only negotiate once it was clear that an agreement with the Americans would serve its ultimate goal of uniting Vietnam. Much like during the Indo-Pakistani conflict of 1971, triangular diplomacy produced counterproductive —and morally questionable—end results when integrated with the search for the end of America's longest war in 1972. The high point of triangular diplomacy thus painfully illustrated a central flaw in Kissinger's overall strategy: improved Sino-American and Soviet-American relations did little to solve the problems of third world regional conflicts.

"HENRY NEEDED PSYCHIATRIC CARE"

In the aftermath of the Indo-Pakistani War Nixon contemplated firing Kissinger. The reason for such ruminations, however, had little to do with Kissinger's foreign policy acumen and more with the negative side effects of the secretive and manipulative way the NSC adviser conducted himself. For one, there was Nixon's concern that Kissinger had overshadowed the president in the press ever since the July 1971 secret trip to China. For another, there was the continuing Kissinger–Rogers rivalry that the president was unable to resolve (and in which he had ultimately been Kissinger's most influential co-conspirator). But in late 1971 and early 1972 there was something else: Nixon was concerned about Kissinger's mental stability.

What made Nixon contemplate firing his "secret agent" was the NSC adviser's reaction to the discovery that the Pentagon had been spying on Kissinger and his NSC staff. Just before Christmas 1971, Yeoman Charles Radford, a Navy stenographer who was assigned to the Joint Chiefs of Staff Liaison office to the National Security Council and had access to various top secret documents, was identified as the man who had leaked reports about internal NSC discussions over U.S. policy toward India and Pakistan to the journalist Jack Anderson. But White House investigators also established that Radford had passed numerous other documents—including parts of Kissinger's memoranda of conversations with Zhou Enlai in July 1971—to the chairman of the Joint Chiefs of Staff, Admiral Thomas Moorer. Radford's boss, Admiral Robert Welander, was interrogated by members of John Ehrlichman's staff and calmly told them that such a procedure had been necessary because of the secretive way Kissinger operated. When Ehrlichman told Nixon, the president was not shocked or even surprised. Of course the military would keep an eye on civilians, he told Ehrlichman. His main concern was that the story would not leak to the press. Nixon told Haldeman to cover up the matter; to "sweep it under the rug."

When Ehrlichman told about the spy-ring and Nixon's reaction to Kissinger, the NSC adviser was initially calm. But his attitude soon changed. After brooding over the matter for a few hours on December 23, Kissinger's blood started to boil. "I was beside myself," he would later recall. So, at 10:00 P.M. Kissinger called Ehrlichman, who was at home singing Christmas carols. After listening to Kissinger throw a temper tantrum, Ehrlichman told him to come by the following day.

"He [Nixon] won't fire Moorer!" Kissinger yelled at Ehrlichman on the morning of December 24. "They can spy on me and spy on him and he won't fire them!" An hour after leaving Ehrlichman, Kissinger marched, unannounced, into Nixon's hideaway office in the Executive Office Building. "I tell you, this is very serious. We cannot survive the kinds of internal weaknesses we are seeing," he told the president. Nixon thought otherwise and tried to calm Kissinger. He even tried a jab at humor, wishing Kissinger a merry Christmas. But when Kissinger left the president's office—still muttering to himself—Nixon's chief worry was not Moorer's spying or the possible leaks of secret documents. Sure, he did order a complete review of the security arrangements in Kissinger's staff in late December 1971.

But Nixon also wondered aloud whether "Henry needed psychiatric care."

Unwilling to deal with the issue himself, Nixon refused to see Kissinger or take his phone calls for a few days after their dramatic encounter on Christmas Eve. In shock from a sudden lack of access to the president, Kissinger started talking about resigning. Meanwhile, even as he resumed contact with Kissinger, Nixon wondered with Haldeman whether early 1972 was a good time to fire Kissinger. Haldeman thought not and Nixon agreed. On January 14, while Nixon was at Camp David, Haldeman and Attorney General John Mitchell met with Kissinger and tried to bring him to his senses. Although they did not suggest that Kissinger see a psychiatrist, Mitchell and Haldeman tried to impress on Kissinger the absolute need to project an image of a united administration in advance of Nixon's China trip. The president had not lost trust in him, they told Kissinger, but Nixon could not afford to let infighting and mood swings overshadow his historic journey to Beijing. Kissinger was not convinced. "We ended up not having accomplished a great deal," Haldeman noted in his diaries. Yet, the next morning (January 15, 1972) Kissinger called Haldeman and told him that "he can't leave the government." His decision, Kissinger piously noted, was due to a sense of duty to "the country and the P(resident)." As the China trip approached, the Nixon–Kissinger relationship resumed.

Although Nixon had decided against firing Kissinger in early 1972, he would entertain such thoughts at various points over the subsequent thirteen months, adding an element of uncertainty (over his job prospects) and pressure (to perform) on Kissinger conduct in 1972. By denying Kissinger access, Nixon had effectively made it clear that the NSC adviser was not irreplaceable. In January 1972, though, he did something else. He raised the stakes on Vietnam.[3]

RAISING STAKES

Vietnam was, in fact, high on the agenda in early 1972. In late 1971 Nixon had repeatedly complained to Kissinger about the domestic pressure he was under to end the war. Kissinger had worried—and had said so to Haldeman on New Year's Day—that the president might be getting ready to "bug out" from Vietnam just as all the pieces of his triangular game plan were coming together.

In the end, Nixon did not bug out entirely. Sure, the president did make an announcement of another set of troop withdrawals on January 13, promising that by May 1, 1972, American troops would be down to 69,000 from the high of 540,000 three years earlier. Clearly, Nixon aimed to maintain the illusion that Vietnamization was working.

Ten days later the president went further. At 8:30 P.M. on January 25, Nixon spoke on national TV about his latest plan for peace in Vietnam. He again asserted that Vietnamization had been a success and disclosed that Kissinger had engaged the North Vietnamese in secret peace talks since August 1969. Despite meeting Le Duc Tho and Xuan Thuy twelve times, Hanoi remained intransigent, Nixon stated. He then summarized the American proposals: a complete withdrawal of U.S. and allied forces, an exchange of POWs, a ceasefire throughout Indochina, and a new presidential election in South Vietnam. He added that President Thieu was even ready to resign a month before the new elections were held. "We are ready to negotiate peace immediately," Nixon stated, adding:

> If the enemy rejects our offer to negotiate, we shall continue our program of ending American involvement in the war by withdrawing our remaining forces as the South Vietnamese develop the capacity to defend themselves. If the enemy's answer to our peace offer is to step up their military attacks, I shall fully meet my responsibility as the Commander in Chief of our Armed forces to protect our remaining troops.[4]

In the short term, the speech had mostly a positive impact on its major target audience: public opinion at home. While Kissinger had been worried that the press would jump on the revelations of his secret diplomacy and criticize his inability to secure an agreement after several years of talks, most newspapers praised Nixon for making a serious offer for peace. "War Issue is Deflated," headlined the *Washington Post*. At the end of January, polls showed that the public approved his handling of the war by a margin of 52 percent. The pattern was like the one he had received after similar speeches earlier on (e.g., after the "Silent Majority" speech in November 1969). But critics, many of them presidential hopefuls, did not quiet down. Leading Democratic Senators Ted Kennedy and Edmund Muskie, as well as former Defense Secretary Clark Clifford, publicly complained that the January 25 speech and the lack of any new American proposals were only likely to prolong the war.

There were other headlines as well. On the front page of the *New York Times* one could find a picture of Kissinger leaving a Paris restaurant with Margaret Osmer, a CBS News producer. The text above it read: "A Few Clues from a Super Secret Agent." Over the next weeks Kissinger appeared on the covers of *Newsweek* and

Time as "Nixon's 'Secret Agent.'" *Life* ran a lengthy story about "The Most Important No. 2 Man in History." If the secret trip to China had made Kissinger a worldwide celebrity, news about his secret diplomacy with the North Vietnamese confirmed to the public that it had not been a one-off performance. Once again, it was Kissinger (who readily gave interviews about his diplomatic exploits), not Nixon, who was getting most of the good press.[5]

While he was being lionized in the press, Kissinger met Dobrynin on January 28. He "expressed disappointment with Soviet performance on Vietnam" and repeated the main themes of Nixon's speech. Ending the war in Vietnam was a key to a successful summit in Moscow and "would remove an obstacle to better U.S.-Soviet relations." Kissinger brushed aside Dobrynin's defenses and argued: "the objective consequence of Soviet policy was to encourage the continuation of the war." When Dobrynin said that the Beijing summit and American behavior during the Indo-Pakistani War had strengthened the hand of the opponents of détente in the Kremlin, Kissinger replied that all such distortions in Soviet-American relations could be avoided if the Vietnam War was concluded.[6]

On January 31 the North Vietnamese responded to Nixon's speech by publicizing their nine-point proposal of June 26, 1971, which Xuan Thuy had presented to Kissinger in Paris. It included two points that the United States could never, formally, accept: reparations payments to North Vietnam and an end to U.S. support of President Thieu's government. According to Hanoi, the true procrastinator in the negotiations was the United States. Two days later, on February 2, the Provisional Revolutionary Government issued a similar statement and called for Washington to declare a definite withdrawal date.[7]

As Nixon and Kissinger prepared for their trip to China, there were some indications that they could expect a quick settlement in Vietnam. On February 14, Vernon Walters cabled from Paris that the North Vietnamese had invited Kissinger to a luncheon meeting on March 17. Kissinger was, Haldeman recorded, "ecstatic." The fact that the Vietnamese wanted to share a meal with him, for the first time since negotiations had commenced in 1969, was "significant." It assured that there would be "no major offensive [this spring in Vietnam] as we've been fearing."[8]

Nixon did not quite agree with such a sweeping interpretation based on a luncheon date but, after initial skepticism, agreed that Kissinger should accept the invitation. On February 16, Walters told the North Vietnamese that the White House was ready for a meeting but suggested March 20 and warned Hanoi against "escalating the level of military activity."[9]

In the end, the North Vietnamese would not listen and Kissinger's predictions about North Vietnamese restraint proved mistaken. Hanoi continued to prepare for and eventually launched a massive attack on the South. Even with the intense Sino-Soviet-American summitry of 1972—what amounted to, in effect, two Nixon "journeys of peace"—there would be no relief to the real war being fought in

Indochina. Triangular diplomacy seemed to be of little help in bringing an end to America's longest war.

THE JOURNEY FOR PEACE

The so-called journey for peace was perhaps the most successful public relations event of the Nixon presidency. It played a major role in jumpstarting his reelection campaign. Behind the public façade, though, there were serious problems in China that made the potential implications of the tense Nixon–Kissinger relationship look like a minor tempest in a teacup.

In early 1972, soon after Kissinger's deputy, Al Haig, visited Beijing to iron out the last practical details of Nixon's trip, Mao had almost died. On January 18 he had been diagnosed with severe heart and lung problems. Only intensive medical care and physical therapy, which Mao refused to accept until early February, allowed him to be alert enough to see the American president later in the month.[10] One can only speculate what would have happened to the opening to China if the Great Helmsman had suddenly died as Nixon's party was on its way to—or, worse yet, was already in—Beijing.

By the time Nixon and his entourage arrived in China, Mao's condition had improved. With Zhou Enlai in charge on the Chinese side, the talks proceeded smoothly. This was due, in large part, to the fact that the substantial issues were rather limited; to both sides the meetings were about creating an atmosphere and, most important, about sending a signal to the USSR.

The most memorable encounter of the trip was, undoubtedly, with Mao. Soon after the Americans had arrived on February 21, Zhou came to the Americans' guesthouse with his instructions from the Chairman. Nixon, fresh out of the shower, joined Kissinger and his assistant Winston Lord; the three were then taken to Mao's study, which turned out to be "a medium-sized room [where] manuscripts lined bookshelves along every wall." Mao rose to greet his American visitors.

Although he was bloated by edema and under constant medical supervision, Mao impressed Kissinger in a way no other statesman (with the possible exception of Charles de Gaulle) had ever done. Even at eighty years of age and needing a nurse close by, Mao "dominated the room—not by the pomp that in most states confers a degree of majesty on the leaders, but by exuding in almost tangible form the overwhelming drive to prevail." Obviously, Mao's recent flirtation with death had left few marks on his general presence or charisma. Perhaps it was the Chairman's smile, "both penetrating and slightly mocking," perhaps it was his mysterious way of speaking in "elliptical phrases," or perhaps Kissinger was most taken by Mao's ability to overshadow Zhou, who "seemed a secondary figure" in the room. Whatever the explanation, Kissinger found Mao a "colossus."[11]

While mostly dwelling on generalities, the meeting left Kissinger, in particular, awed by the man whose writings he used to assign to his students at Harvard (Mao dismissed these as having "nothing instructive" in them) and who was now down-playing his revolutionary zeal in a conversation that, while physically challenged, he clearly dominated. With little reservation, Mao even said: "I like rightists. People say you are rightists, that the Republican Party is to the right ... I am comparatively happy when people on the right come into power." Mao did not explain why he felt this way, allowing Nixon to express his hearty approval. The president then explained the strange workings of the American domestic political system. "In America," he said, "those on the right can do what those on the left talk about."

At this point Kissinger pitched in: "There is another point, Mr. President. Those on the left are pro-Soviet and would not encourage a move toward the People's Republic, and in fact criticize you on these grounds."

"Exactly that," Mao agreed.

As he would do in subsequent meetings with Zhou, Nixon tried to impress Mao by referring to the American stand during the recent conflict in South Asia. He "could not let a country, no matter how big, gobble up its neighbor," the president said, adding that he was certain that "history will record that it was the right thing to do." When Mao asked, in a comment obviously aimed at Kissinger's eagerness to talk to the press about his trips to China, that the American side "do a little less briefing," Nixon assured him that secrecy would be followed. "Good," the Chairman replied.

After an hour, the Nixon–Mao meeting ended appropriately. Mao told his American guests: "It is alright to talk well and also alright that if there are no agreements, because what use is there if we stand in deadlock?"[12]

It had been a banal conversation that, nevertheless, set the cordial tone that characterized the rest of Nixon's talks in China. Talking and debating, exchanging views, and gently disagreeing were the modus operandi of the Nixon–Zhou meetings that followed.

*   *   *

There were three separate sets of talks. At the first plenary meeting, the two sides agreed with Zhou's suggestion—in fact, Kissinger had agreed to this already in October and preparations had been made accordingly—to a division of labor. Secretary of State William Rogers, Assistant Secretary of State Marshall Green, and the rest of the State Department team would discuss "bilateral specific matters"—such as the question of Chinese assets in the United States that had been frozen during the Korean War and the American assets in China that the PRC had seized upon taking over in 1949—with the Chinese Foreign Minister Chi Peng-fei and his advisers. But for "basic matters"—such major foreign policy issues as Vietnam, Taiwan, and the formal normalization of Sino-American relations—Zhou added, "we must depend on Mr. President." Moreover, Zhou and Nixon agreed that Kissinger and Qiao Guanhua would handle the drafting of the final communiqué.[13]

Starting on February 22, Nixon (with Kissinger, Lord, and Holdridge on his side) would spend his afternoons with Zhou Enlai, Vice Minister for Foreign Affairs Qiao Guanhua, and other Chinese representatives, while the State Department team was busy in its "counterpart talks" that covered such nitty-gritty issues as trade, travel, consular affairs, property rights, and cultural exchanges.[14] While Nixon was occupied with domestic U.S. matters and touring key sights, Kissinger would spend his spare time ironing out the Shanghai Communiqué. No wonder that, as Bob Haldeman noted in his diaries, by the end of the visit Kissinger "was dead on his feet." But he had also assured his standing among the American press corps: the exclusion of Rogers from the top-level meetings left no doubt that Kissinger was Nixon's key China hand. That it was Kissinger, rather than Rogers, who was assigned to brief the press on the Shanghai Communiqué—widely viewed as the key document resulting from the trip—was another clear indication who was in charge. The way Rogers was treated amounted to "a great big cow turd on his face," Seymour Hersh recalls. The humiliation of the State Department was all but complete.[15]

The four Nixon–Zhou meetings were clearly the heart of the February trip to China and provide a fascinating example of Nixon at his best, discussing foreign policy in an expert manner in a dialogue with Zhou. The president and the premier clearly dominated these meetings. Kissinger was reduced to the role of the trusted adviser: he made brief interventions, generally to support a point Nixon had already made or to confirm a specific detail if so prompted.

Nixon and Zhou effectively covered the entire globe, from Europe to Japan, from the Soviet Union to Vietnam.

Indeed, one of the first points that Zhou, echoing Mao, made on February 22 was that the meeting was taking place "mainly for the purpose of talks." There was no expectation of agreements or treaties. Nixon was in China to establish a rapport and to set the stage for future normalization. At the outset Nixon also emphasized the high degree of centralization within his own administration on China policy. Only five men—Nixon, Kissinger, Winston Lord, John Holdridge, and Alexander Haig—had seen the full record of Kissinger's previous talks with Zhou. The members of the State Department, Nixon volunteered "in great confidence," had only seen the sanitized versions. Of course he trusted Rogers and Marshall, Nixon added, "but our State Department leaks like a sieve." Zhou laughed. The tone for the relationship, already established during Kissinger's two previous visits, was thus reaffirmed.

Inevitably, the Nixon–Zhou talks focused on three key issues: Taiwan, Vietnam, and the Soviet Union. The script followed, by and large, the one established during Kissinger's earlier visits.

Nixon began his first session with Zhou in the same vein as Kissinger had done during the secret trip, by discussing Taiwan. His policy was based, Nixon explained, on five principles. First, the United States accepted that there was only one China and Taiwan was a part of it. Second, the United States would not support the independence of Taiwan. Third, as the United States removed its presence from Taiwan, it would discourage the Japanese from filling the vacuum. Fourth, Nixon would "support any peaceful resolution" of the Taiwan issue. Lastly, Nixon stressed that the United States wanted "normalization of relations with the People's Republic." Having said that, Nixon emphasized that the "problem is not what we are going to do, the problem is what we are going to say about it." In plain language: this is what I offer to you; but I cannot say it in public.

Two days later, the president returned to this theme when he insisted: "what we say (in the communiqué and to the press) will directly affect whether I can achieve it." He could not allow an impression of secret agreements to permeate the public; he could not "make a secret deal and shake hands and say that within the second term it will be done." But Nixon assured that there would be a gradual withdrawal of U.S. forces from Taiwan, initially in tandem with the ending of the Vietnam War (that would allow Nixon to withdraw two-thirds of U.S. troops in Taiwan and the Taiwan straits). "And," he assured, "I can do this without a question in my mind." But for now, Nixon insisted, he needed "running room."

Zhou did not object to secrecy. Nor did he appear interested in dwelling on Taiwan. It was a subject that "can be discussed easily," he pointed out. "We have already waited over twenty years and can wait a few more years," Zhou added. Taiwan, Zhou implied (echoing Mao), was not such a hot potato to him as it was to Nixon. A few days later, Zhou even said that whatever was written down about Taiwan should be formulated "so that both sides understand some obligation but not to make it so that people know exactly. It should not be so rigid." Nixon, approvingly, answered: "That is what we want." Then Zhou interjected a caveat. Referring to the advanced age of the "present leaders of China," the premier stated, "ten years would be too long" to wait for the solution.[16]

If an agreement to postpone the Taiwan solution was fairly easy to reach, there were plenty of polemics on another key subject. "The crucial question," the Chinese premier surmised, "is Indochina."[17]

* * *

The discussion on Vietnam went nowhere. Showing his keen awareness of Nixon's admiration for the former French president, Zhou argued that the American president should emulate Charles de Gaulle. Just as the French president had shown courage by ending the French involvement in Algeria in the early 1960s, so should Nixon remove American troops from Vietnam. If de Gaulle would not do as a role model, Zhou added, how about General Patton? He knew, Zhou said, that Nixon appreciated Patton "for his daring and for his doing what he thought was right." In the meantime, the premier warned, "As long as you are continuing your Vietnamization, Laoization, and Cambodianzation [sic] policy, and they continue fighting, we can do nothing but to continue to support them."

Nixon repeated the themes from his January speech. The United States was ready to withdraw its troops in six months if the North Vietnamese agreed on a ceasefire and a return of POWs. But Washington would not impose a political settlement on the North Vietnamese. If they did that "the United States would be permanently destroyed insofar as being a country which any nation could depend upon." Moreover, if the North Vietnamese launched further aggression, there would be a "very strong" American response. Nor should anyone think that because of Vietnamization the United States was about to "walk out" of Vietnam; a "residual force" would remain there until an agreement was signed. After delivering the stick, Nixon offered some carrots. He was prepared to offer "very heavy economic assistance to Cambodia, Laos, and North Vietnam." Washington wanted no bases and would be happy to accept a neutralization agreement. Be assured, Nixon maintained, "I am removing this irritant as fast as anyone in my position could."[18]

On one point Zhou and Nixon could agree: the Soviet interest in Indochina. When Kissinger suggested that "the People's Republic wants the war to end and the Soviet Union wants the war to continue," the premier and the president quickly agreed. Nixon, in fact, added, "the only gainer in having the war continue is the Soviet Union." But while the president stressed his inability to abandon Thieu in order to satisfy North Vietnamese demands, the premier stressed that the longer the war, the deeper the Soviet influence, the more painful and complete the American defeat. "The later you withdraw from Indochina, the more you'll be in a passive position," Zhou insisted. With reference to Thieu he added, "you should [choose] your friends more carefully." Ultimately, hanging on in Vietnam did nothing to promote stability, Zhou stressed, but would create "another Middle East."

"How can you talk about a relaxation of tensions?" while the war in Vietnam raged on, the premier wondered on February 22.

Yet, when Nixon tried to enlist Chinese help, Zhou promised little. "The channel of negotiations should not be closed," he said. "We can only go so far," Zhou quickly added. Throughout this exchange Kissinger remained quiet, adopting his role as the adviser, allowing Nixon to revel in the role of the statesman.

It was the Soviet Union that featured most heavily in the Nixon–Zhou conversations. Nixon wanted to convince the Chinese that he had no illusions about the USSR's true intentions. American goals toward the USSR, he repeatedly suggested, coincided with those of China; it was "very important that our policies go together," Nixon maintained. To contain Soviet ambition the United States had taken a hard line against India in 1971, maintained a global (including Asian) military presence, and had not cancelled its missile programs. Zhou agreed that it was necessary to be firm with the Soviets. Yet, he also maintained that the Chinese had nothing at all against a Soviet-American summit and were particularly in favor of the SALT treaty: "If you two big powers can get an agreement limiting armaments, that would be good. We don't have the least opposition to the improvement of relations between the United States and the Soviet Union." Zhou reminded Nixon that the Chinese had even told the Americans to go to Moscow before coming to China. On top of it all, Zhou became a nuclear abolitionist. "Nuclear weapons cannot be eaten, nor worn as clothing, nor can they be used as utensils," the Chinese premier stressed. He added: "They can't raise the standard of living. The only thing they can do is lie there waiting to be used . . . what a great waste they are."

When Nixon wondered why the Soviets were so critical of his trip to Beijing, Kissinger, who had remained fairly quiet throughout most of the meeting, joined in. He echoed the president's bewilderment, adding that Ambassador Dobrynin was "a bit hysterical on this subject. I expect a phone call from the Soviet ambassador at 9:00 A.M. (on the morning of my return to Washington)," Kissinger joked. This prompted Zhou to recount the history of Sino-Soviet hostilities and take a few jabs at the "socio-imperialists" in Moscow. Because of them, Zhou maintained, "the socialist camp no longer exists."[19]

He could not have gone any further to confirm that the Americans had been right in making the trip and in launching triangular diplomacy.

"A PROFOUND NEW RELATIONSHIP"

The trip's public conclusion, the Shanghai Communiqué, reflected the nature of the new Sino-American relationship. It was, by and large, negotiated by Kissinger who, with Nixon's support, kept Secretary of State Rogers in the dark about the progress of the discussions until February 26. At that point, by prior agreement, Nixon discussed the terms of the communiqué with Rogers "so that he won't know that it's an accomplished fact and that it's up to him to go along with it and support it." When Rogers criticized the communiqué in a meeting (one Nixon tried to avoid as much as possible) in Shanghai on the 27th, Nixon, in Bob Haldeman's words, "hit [him] hard, and said he expected him to instruct his bureaucracy to stay behind us 100 percent." Rogers did, Haldeman points out, "get the message."[20]

One of the key points of the Shanghai Communiqué was a message to Moscow: neither the United States nor the PRC would "seek hegemony" in the Asia-Pacific area and would oppose any other power seeking such hegemony. Aside from that, though, the communiqué provided a straightforward list of the two sides' divergent opinions on various issues of the day. For example, while the United States stated its commitment to the peaceful resolution of the conflict in Indochina, the PRC expressed its "firm support to the peoples of Vietnam, Laos and Cambodia."

Most significantly, the Shanghai Communiqué included a formulation on Taiwan that left the island in a juridical limbo for decades. For Nixon, this was mainly a domestic political issue. He feared, rightly so, the angry reaction of his own party's right-wing members—including such members of his own staff as the young speech writer Patrick Buchanan—who vehemently opposed anything that might be interpreted as an abandonment of Taiwan. Indeed, several prominent Republicans—such as California Governor Ronald Reagan, as well as Senators Barry Goldwater from Arizona and James Buckley from New York (duly supported by his brother, the conservative columnist William F. Buckley Jr.)—had expressed severe reservations about the administration's China policy after the expulsion of Taiwan from the UN in October 1971. The last thing Nixon wanted was a revolt from within his own party in an election year.

Thus, the Shanghai Communiqué's Taiwan section was carefully phrased to allow both sides to interpret it according to their political needs. For their part, the Chinese stated that Taiwan was a province of the mainland and its "liberation" was an internal Chinese affair. The American position, though, was the more interesting and complicated one:

> The United States acknowledges that all Chinese on either side of the Taiwan Strait maintain there is but one China and that Taiwan is a part of China. The United States Government does not challenge that position. It reaffirms its interest in a peaceful settlement of the Taiwan question by the Chinese themselves. With this prospect in mind, it affirms the ultimate objective of the withdrawal of all U.S. forces and military installations from Taiwan. In the meantime, it will progressively reduce its forces and military installations on Taiwan as the tension in the area diminishes.[21]

It was a brilliant, if evasive, solution: to accept the differences of view and, effectively, put the entire question on hold. Nixon got what he had wanted: a vaguely phrased formula that allowed him to return home without selling out Taiwan. Even as some hawks were bound to attack him, the damage would not be adequate to spoil his moment of triumph.

The communiqué was, in fact, an accurate reflection of the Nixon visit and the immediate future of Sino-American relations. Throughout the meetings Nixon, Zhou, and Kissinger had been on the same wavelength. The Chinese, without saying so publicly, indicated that Taiwan was not a question of crucial urgency. Nixon and Zhou had agreed that the Soviet Union was a menace to both the United States and the Soviet Union. Ultimately, the visit established the fact that neither China nor the United States was, in 1972, interested in the relationship for its own sake; it was a strategic tool to be used in dealing with the Soviet Union, the reluctant third party in triangular diplomacy. In this sense, Nixon was correct when he told his cabinet: "there's a profound new relationship between the PRC and the United States."[22]

The visit had also confirmed, if it still needed confirming, Kissinger's place as the prime American interlocutor with the Chinese. He would meet with Mao four more times before the Chairman died in 1976. That was, though, a blessing in disguise. For Kissinger's much enhanced role was clearly a concern to Nixon, who soon began complaining to Haldeman that Kissinger was not "getting across on the PR standpoint on the P[resident]'s handling of the situations in China." What Nixon wanted emphasized, undoubtedly given that presidential elections were only eight months away, was his "position as a big-league operator [with the] unusual states-man capability."[23] That was how Kissinger wanted to come across as well. The China trip thus triggered a further intensification of the struggle for the limelight and credit that had begun to infect the Nixon–Kissinger relationship after Kissinger became a media celebrity following his first trip to China. It was, ultimately, a struggle that Nixon would, at least in the short term, lose, in part because he had an immense personal dislike of the press, in part because Kissinger had, from the start of the administration, been one of Nixon's major spin doctors.

What remained to be seen was how the China trip would impact the rest of Nixon and Kissinger's agenda. Would it bring peace in Vietnam any closer? Would it help to make the Soviets any more accommodating and cooperative?

AN EDGY INTERVAL BEFORE THE STORM

On February 28, 1972, when Air Force One was on its way back to the United States, Kissinger got a taste of what some members of the Republican right thought about the opening to China. The thirty-four-year old Pat Buchanan, Nixon's arch-conservative speechwriter, was on the warpath over Taiwan. Kissinger knew of Buchanan's criticism—the previous day Buchanan had pointedly refused to attend Kissinger's press conference in Shanghai—and asked him to explain what was wrong with the communiqué.

Buchanan fumed. Kissinger had conspired to hand over an old ally to the PRC, he argued, and told the national security adviser—in no uncertain words—where to put the communiqué. It represented, Buchanan said, a betrayal of Taiwan.

"Bullshit," Buchanan yelled when Kissinger continued to defend the Shanghai Communiqué.[24]

Whereas Buchanan, disgruntled though he was, decided to stay in the adminis-tration, other conservatives rallied to the cause of Taiwan in public. Conservative columnist William F. Buckley declared that he had "lost interest in Mr. Nixon." Buckley said that he would support the conservative Ohio representative, John Ashbrook, in the 1972 Republican primaries in New Hampshire. Ashbrook voiced many a critic's concern when he said that the Shanghai Communiqué had "set up the framework to abandon 15 million people to the tender mercies of a regime that during its tenure in office has managed to slay 34 million of its own citizens."[25]

Happily for Kissinger and Nixon, most Americans were more impressed by the new relationship with the world's most populous nation than the potential implica-tions of the Shanghai Communiqué to the fate of an island off the coast of Asia. Ash-brook, for one, got only 7 percent of the vote in the New Hampshire Republican primaries; he came in third behind Nixon and California Congressman Pete McCloskey, who got about 20 percent of the vote (his highest in the primaries). The well-managed PR campaign before, during, and immediately after the trip helped the administration sell the visit as a journey for peace. Kissinger himself helped to deflect some of the conservative criticism by contacting two key leaders of the Republican party's right wing—California Governor Ronald Reagan (a strong Taiwan supporter) and Senator Barry Goldwater—immediately upon his return to Washington. Both were satisfied with assurances that Nixon had not abandoned any existing commitments, a fact that Nixon reinforced with his public statements and meetings with congressional leaders. The defense treaty with Taiwan, in other words, remained in force; the United States was not about to hand Taiwan over to the PRC.[26]

Selling the communiqué at home was a priority, but it was not the only challenge. American allies throughout the Asia-Pacific region also deserved a proper briefing on the details of the week that, in Nixon's words, had changed the world. Thus, the president dispatched two senior officials, State Department's Marshall Green and NSC's John Holdridge, for a tour of Tokyo, Seoul, Taipei, Manila, Saigon, Phnom Penh, Vientiane, Bangkok, Kuala Lumpur, Singapore, Jakarta, and Canberra. The trip was a mixed success. In most countries, including Japan, the reaction was surprisingly positive; in some, such as the Philippines and Indonesia, Green and Holdridge managed to head off suspicions over a sellout. But most important, they managed to deflect a strong adverse reaction on the part of Taiwanese leadership. In fact, unlike in South Korea, where the South Korean Foreign Minister Kim Yong Shik treated the Americans to a three-hour cross-examination, Taiwanese Premier Chiang Ching-kuo (Chiang Kai-shek's eldest son) calmly listened to Holdridge and Green's assurances that nothing of substance had changed in American-Taiwanese relations. When they had finished, Chiang pointed at a model U-2 on his fireplace. As long as that stayed, the ROC premier said, there would be no problems. Translation? As long as U.S. military aid continued to flow the Taiwanese would feel secure and would not overtly criticize what, for most Taiwanese, was an American betrayal.[27]

Although they made some feelers toward Chiang Kai-shek, the Soviets, for their part, cared little about Taiwan.[28] Their major concern was the impact of the China trip on Soviet-American relations and the Moscow summit.

*   *   *

During a luncheon meeting in the Map Room on March 1, as Kissinger had predicted, Dobrynin pressed Kissinger on a possible Sino-American "deal against the USSR." The Soviet ambassador was, Kissinger wrote to Nixon, "clearly under instructions not to ask questions or show excessive interest [in the China trip], but violated these instructions consistently, pretending that while his government was not particularly interested, it would be helpful if I volunteered certain information!" A week later Dobrynin was more confrontational. On March 9, he referred to reports in which Kissinger had allegedly offered Beijing "detailed information about Soviet missile deployments and about Soviet forces on the Chinese border." Dobrynin warned: "the gravest view would have to be taken of this if it were true."

Kissinger, disingenuously, denied that he had provided the Chinese with any information of a military nature. But he waffled. "I might have said on one or two occasions that I thought [Chinese] fears of Soviet strength were exaggerated." The following day, Kissinger phoned Dobrynin and explained that the context of such comments to the Chinese had been "one in which the Chinese were afraid of a simultaneous attack by all their neighbors."[29]

Dobrynin was apparently satisfied. During the next two back-channel meetings—on March 17 and 30, respectively—he did not raise China and focused on the preparations for the forthcoming Nixon–Brezhnev summit. Indeed, in January Dobrynin had presented Kissinger with an ambitious agenda that included SALT, the Middle East, the Conference on Security and Cooperation in Europe (CSCE), Germany, and Vietnam. Dobrynin also continued to ask Kissinger to consider the usefulness of an advance trip to Moscow that would prepare the various agreements, as far as possible, prior to Nixon's arrival.

Nixon's China trip had, on balance, been a great success and confirmed Kissinger's role as the architect of the administration's foreign policy. It was a culmination of years of hard work and, potentially, the beginning of a new era in international relations. Triangular diplomacy was a fact and opened seemingly endless opportunities for achieving other goals, most specifically an end to the Vietnam War and an advantageous set of agreements with the Soviet Union. The domestic fascination with China in 1972—that far outweighed the criticism of the slighting of Taiwan—not only improved Nixon's prospects in the November 1972 elections but offered a welcome diversion from the years of domestic disillusionment with the Vietnam War that had dominated American media coverage since the mid-1960s. As Kissinger put it in his memoirs: "the China initiative . . . gave us a chance to shape a new concept of international order even while emerging from a debilitating war and a wrenching decade at home."[30]

The euphoria did not last long. Within a month of their return from Beijing Kissinger and Nixon were confronted with a new series of crises that threatened to unravel the emerging foreign policy architecture.

10

High Stakes

Triangulation, Moscow, and Vietnam

I n March 1972, with China under his belt, Nixon focused on the other major issues on his agenda. In two memos to Kissinger, the president discussed the upcoming Moscow summit and the Vietnam situation. He worried that "the expectations for the Moscow trip are being built up too much" and reminded Kissinger: "it is vitally important that no final agreements be entered into until we arrive in Moscow." Moreover, Nixon ordered "a line of pessimism" that would diminish presummit expectations and, hence, raise the apparent value of the results. This was particularly important on the issue of SALT, Nixon argued, because he worried that "there will be an attempt to make it appear that all this could have been achieved without any Summit whatsoever." On Vietnam, Nixon was no less relaxed. He thought that although domestic critics were, for the moment, relatively silent on the war, this should not give the administration any comfort. Vietnam was not an issue because the Democrats were "not making it an issue and may not even want to do so on massive scale at this point." But Nixon was certain that by the time the Democrats held their convention in July, "with the anti-war crowd constituting a majority of the delegates" the candidate that would oppose Nixon in November was bound to "take us hard on this issue." That is, Nixon added, "unless we have defused it substantially by that time." Barring a peace agreement, the only way to do this was to go ahead with the final troop reductions, leaving only a "residual force" in South Vietnam by the time of the election. An announcement to that effect would need to be made before the Democratic convention. Otherwise, Nixon stressed, "we will be in very serious trouble."[1]

Vietnam did, sooner than Nixon may have anticipated, present serious trouble. To be sure, the North Vietnamese seemed impressed by Nixon's China visit. On February 29, as Nixon and Kissinger were busy selling the Shanghai Communiqué to the press and the American public, word came that the North Vietnamese were ready to return to the negotiating table in three weeks' time. It was the latest in a series of exchanges that commenced after Nixon's January 25 speech. But the hope that Nixon's visit had somehow triggered a chain reaction of Chinese pressures and an appropriate North Vietnamese response was quickly dashed. On March 6 Hanoi reneged on its offer, announcing that Le Duc Tho could not meet with Kissinger until April 15. On March 8, General Abrams provided a gloomy assessment of the situation in Vietnam. Hanoi had amassed large forces just north of the DMZ and an offensive across the seventeenth parallel could be launched at any time. He asked for air strikes to discourage the PAVN. On March 10, Al Haig joined the chorus by warning Kissinger that the North Vietnamese and their allies were ready to attack from Cambodia as well as across the DMZ. Conscious of public opinion Nixon, however, decided not to bomb the North at this point. Instead, Washington refused the April 15 date for a meeting and, instead, suggested the 24th. Kissinger, in the meantime, warned Dobrynin that North Vietnam's continuous postponement of the meetings was bound to cause the United States to cancel the Paris channel completely. Two weeks after this message, on March 27, Hanoi accepted.[2]

The acceptance was bogus. On the morning of March 30, 1972, while Nixon, Kissinger, and Haldeman were discussing the Moscow summit, an aide brought in a note. It had a simple, shocking, yet not entirely unexpected message: the DRV forces had crossed the demilitarized zone into South Vietnam. The Spring Offensive had begun.[3]

Over the next few months Kissinger played with very high stakes indeed. The linkage between triangular diplomacy and Vietnam suddenly became acute. Military action against invading North Vietnamese forces was necessary to prevent the South from collapsing. Yet, such action placed the prospective Moscow summit in jeopardy: how could the Soviets wine and dine Nixon and Kissinger if the two were simultaneously directing a massive bombing campaign of Hanoi? If the summit was cancelled, would the opening to China lose its significance? Would the Chinese perhaps reverse course in order to safeguard their relationship with the North Vietnamese?

In the end, Brezhnev and other Soviet leaders would not cancel the summit and the Chinese would act with restraint. But the North Vietnamese Spring Offensive exposed the inherent limits and weaknesses of triangular diplomacy. Put simply: however carefully Kissinger played his cards with the Soviets and the Chinese, this did not cause the leaders in Moscow or Beijing to restrain their regional allies.

"DO OR DIE"

With the help of Soviet-supplied tanks and rockets the PAVN quickly overran the two northernmost provinces of Vietnam, taking control over the provincial capital of Quang Tri. In a matter of days other offensive forces joined the coordinated attack: one division began to close toward the old imperial capital Hue (the site of some of fiercest battles during the 1968 Tet Offensive); several other divisions attacked the Central Highlands and the Mekong Delta region. By mid-April all of South Vietnam was effectively under fire and the North Vietnamese had managed to take control of the transit routes between Saigon in the South and Hue in the North. The ARVN was in danger of losing the war and the attack presented a serious threat to the longevity of the Thieu government. With approximately 150,000 to 200,000 soldiers, the PAVN and their southern allies had launched the most serious military challenge of the American phase of the Vietnam War.[4]

Militarily, lest it was willing to concede defeat, Washington had few options. By this time the United States did not have the ground troop strength to respond effectively. Of the remaining 95,000 Americans, only 6,000 were combat troops. The ARVN, even with its ample supply of American hardware, was no match for the advancing North Vietnamese. Already on April 2, Ambassador Bunker cabled from Saigon that the ARVN forces "were on the verge of collapse." With re-Americanization out of the question and time seemingly running out, Nixon resorted to heavy bombing. On April 6, 1972, he told General John W. Vogt, the commander of the Seventh Air Force, "to get down there and use whatever you need to turn this thing around." Later the same day Americans started bombing the area immediately north of the DMZ; on April 10 B-52 bombing raids reached the nineteenth parallel for the first time under Nixon's presidency. As Haldeman recorded in his diaries, Nixon considered the situation "a do-or-die proposition." He felt "very strongly that we've got to make an all-out effort."[5]

The bombing of Hanoi started five days later. Although General Abrams had asked Nixon to focus the air operations on those southern areas where the heaviest battles were under way, the president was growing increasingly confident that he needed to hit the source. After making the decision Nixon called Haldeman at about 2:00 P.M. on Saturday, April 15. He was "seriously considering putting on a blockade around North Vietnam later this week," Nixon told his chief of staff. Regardless, the president emphasized "the importance of a good solid PR run" to block an adverse domestic reaction.

The following day, after attending church, Nixon was beaming. The reports from Vietnam indicated that the strikes had been "exceptionally effective, the best ever in the war," he said. The following day, incensed by a critical article in the *New York Times* that suggested Nixon was sacrificing détente, the president defiantly vowed to "do what is necessary." Nixon wanted everyone to know that he would not stop bombing until the North Vietnamese retreated back across the DMZ. They never would.[6]

Kissinger had few qualms about the extensive bombing campaign. It was a military, and to an extent a diplomatic, necessity. If he ever was to achieve that peace with honor, or even a decent interval, allowing South Vietnam to collapse under military pressure was hardly the way to go. His previous support for the bombing and invasions of Cambodia and Laos had been predicated on the belief that the United States could not allow Hanoi to get the upper hand militarily. But, much more than Nixon, Kissinger was keen on taking advantage of the new triangular framework. In practice, however, it meant pressuring Moscow, rather than Beijing.

In fact, from the Chinese perspective the timing of the Spring Offensive was not bad. After all, the Chinese had held their summit and Nixon had, if not publicly, accepted China's insistence that it would not do anything to pressure Hanoi. As a result, the Chinese were not on the spot in the same way as they had been should the Spring Offensive and the American retaliation taken place, say, in early February. Nor could Beijing have missed Nixon's attempt to demonstrate that the China initiative was on track: on April 18 (after the bombing of Hanoi had begun) Nixon met publicly with a Chinese ping-pong team in the White House. And, when they criticized Chinese support for the DRV, Nixon and Kissinger did it only via private channels.[7] It was clear that Nixon would allow nothing to interfere with his emerging relationship with Beijing.

The irony was that the American bombing made it easier for the Chinese to reinstate their support for Hanoi. The Chinese position on Vietnam, which Zhou had repeatedly emphasized during the February meetings in Beijing, thus remained unchanged. On April 12, after Americans had begun their initial response, Zhou Enlai met with the North Vietnamese charge d'affaires, Nguyen Tien and reaffirmed Beijing's support for Hanoi. Nixon's strategy, Zhou assured Nguyen, "will not work."[8] In May, after the Americans started mining Haiphong harbor, Zhou immediately began preparations for sending a team of minesweepers to help out Hanoi. They eventually arrived in July and provided crucial assistance in the reopening of Haiphong for shipping. In the meantime, to help meet North Vietnam's energy demands while its sea access routes were blocked, the PRC also commenced the construction of five pipelines that would help deliver oil from southern China to North Vietnam.[9]

The Chinese, in short, used the Spring Offensive to strengthen their links with Vietnam and to sow discord between Vietnam and the USSR. In this sense, the timing of the offensive was ideal. It put Moscow on the spot.

SECRET TRIP . . . TO MOSCOW

On the afternoon of Sunday, April 9, Kissinger played host at the White House to a small group of guests: in addition to Soviet Ambassador Dobrynin and his wife,

Kissinger's parents, Louis and Paula, had been invited to view some Chinese news-reels about Kissinger's trips to China. After viewing the films in the Situation Room, Kissinger and Dobrynin had a brief conversation in Bob Haldeman's office about the latest developments in Vietnam. Dobrynin expressed concern over U.S. bombings and the impact they would have on Soviet-American relations. Kissinger brushed such complaints aside. "We have been warning you for months that if there were an offensive we would take drastic measures," he told Dobrynin. "That situation has now arisen," Kissinger added. In the next few days, as they met repeatedly, Kissinger kept pressing on the Soviet ambassador the president's wish to get "a word" to Hanoi that he was willing to meet North Vietnamese representatives. On April 10, Nixon took Dobrynin aside after the signing of a Soviet-American treaty against bacteriological weapons.

Two days later, on April 12, Kissinger and Dobrynin met for an hour and forty-five minutes. Kissinger pressed hard: "You are responsible for this conflict, either because you planned it or because you tried to score off the Chinese and as a result have put yourself into the position where a miserable little country can jeopardize everything that has been striven for [for] years." Dobrynin responded by suggest-ing that a pre-summit Kissinger trip to Moscow was now more urgent than ever.

Two hours after the meeting broke up Kissinger and Dobrynin spoke on the tele-phone. Kissinger said that Nixon was "inclined" to approve such a trip. Dobrynin, Kissinger told Nixon, was "slobbering" all over him and had called this the "most cheerful news he had all day." On April 13 Dobrynin agreed to the Moscow visit. After some back and forth over the next few days, the secret trip to Moscow was scheduled to commence on April 20.[10]

At 1:00 A.M. on April 20, Dobrynin met Kissinger at Andrews Air Force Base. They, along with Kissinger's aides Helmut Sonnenfeldt, Winston Lord, John Negroponte, and Peter Rodman boarded a plane and headed off toward Moscow. After a stopover at a NATO base in the United Kingdom (Kissinger counseled Dobrynin not to get out of the plane, lest someone spot him and the secrecy of the trip be blown), the plane arrived in the Soviet capital late the same evening (Moscow time). After a night's rest at a guesthouse in the Lenin Hills overlooking the Moscow River, Kissinger—whose presence in Moscow was kept secret from the American ambassador, Jacob Beam, until the last day of the trip—was ready to get down to business.[11]

*   *   *

Kissinger's secret trip to Moscow—his first direct meeting with key Soviet lead-ers—in April 1972 was remarkably different from the one to China less than a year earlier. To begin with, the objective was quite different: in China Kissinger had opened a contact, in Moscow he was ensuring that progress made would not be jeopardized due to the events in Vietnam. And he was cautiously optimistic. On April 18, two days prior to his departure to Moscow, Kissinger had speculated that it was "doubtful that the Soviets had any control over the scope or timing of the North Vietnamese." Although Moscow must have been "aware of the general nature" of the DRV's intentions, "they took precautionary measures to limit its damage to the summit prospects." Brezhnev had made a reassuring and positive speech on the summit on March 20 and the Soviets had moved ahead "to begin the grain talks, lend-lease talks, and to receive the American delegation for a second round of maritime talks." The Soviets, Kissinger suggested, were playing "an intricate and delicate game." Kissinger summed it all up as follows:

> It seems that the Soviets held their fire until the military situation began to clarify and, once it became apparent that the offensive had not scored a major success, began to ensure that their relations with us would not be damaged, and their association with Hanoi would be limited.[12]

Nevertheless, in the meetings with Brezhnev and Gromyko, Kissinger told Nixon prior to his departure, "Vietnam is agenda item one and nothing will be discussed until it is fully covered and you are satisfied." Although Kissinger was not confident that the trip would bring about a change in North Vietnamese policy, he would make it clear to the Soviets that the North Vietnamese would have to return to pre–Spring Offensive positions. In return, the United States would reduce the aerial attacks and "cease them completely" once Hanoi's withdrawal was complete. Nixon, Kissinger wrote in his memoirs, basically approved of this strategy.[13]

While Kissinger was on board the plane heading toward Moscow, however, somewhat different orders arrived from the president. After a long meeting with John Connally, at the time considered the leading candidate as William Rogers' replacement after the November elections, Nixon had rethought the negotiation strategy. He had his secretary Rose Wood type a long memo to Kissinger in which the president hammered on the necessity of focusing on Vietnam. Forget the "sophisticated approach we used with the Chinese," he added, because Brezhnev's character was very different from that of Zhou and Mao. The Soviet leader, Nixon wrote, was "simple, direct, blunt and brutal." His main interest would be to steer the discussion away from Vietnam; hence it was necessary for Kissinger to keep comments about Nixon's character and discussions on philosophy to a minimum. How a "simple" man like Brezhnev could even dream of discussing philosophical questions with a Harvard professor Nixon did not explain.

In reading the memo it is clear how, even as the summit hung on the balance and fighting in Vietnam intensified, Nixon's mind was preoccupied by public perceptions. He wanted the Soviets to tone down their rhetoric on Vietnam, because if the Kremlin persisted in its propaganda after the trip was made public, "our critics will jump on your trip as being a failure." A key point, Nixon insisted, was "to leave the impression that we have made some progress." Nixon then tried to put words in Kissinger's mouth, suggesting that he should say to Brezhnev: "Mr. Chairman, there are many important matters we will discuss. But the point we have to recognize is that we cannot have useful discussions on the other items on the agenda unless and until we get down to brass tacks on Vietnam and make some progress on that issue."[14]

"Henry isn't going to like it," Haldeman noted in his diaries. He doubted that Kissinger would follow the president's new orders.[15]

* * *

Haldeman, one of the few men who had the privilege to endure the ups and downs of the Nixon–Kissinger relationship, was not referring to the possibility, strong though it was, that Kissinger's ego would not stand being dictated specific instructions on how to talk to his Soviet interlocutors. There was, in fact, a substantial difference between Nixon's and Kissinger's views on how to approach the Soviets after the start of the North Vietnamese Spring Offensive. It boiled down to a simple point: Nixon wanted, first and foremost, a breakthrough on Vietnam while Kissinger considered it more important that the Soviet-American summit not be jeopardized.

Kissinger did not ignore Vietnam during the eighteen hours of meetings he had between April 20 and 24. Soon upon arrival in Moscow, he told Foreign Minister Gromyko: "I am here to see whether there is a possibility of removing the one obstacle we can now see could produce consequences that I don't believe either of our countries want, and which so far as we can tell are not in the interest of either of our countries—namely Southeast Asia." Accordingly, most of Kissinger's first meeting with Brezhnev, on April 21, was spent on the war. "We have two principal objectives," Kissinger said. He then outlined what amounted to a decent interval solution:

one is to bring about an honorable withdrawal of our forces; secondly to put a time frame between our withdrawal and the political process which would then start. We are prepared to let the real balance of forces in Vietnam determine the future of Vietnam. We are not committed to a permanent political involvement there, and we . . . are prepared to withdraw all our forces without any residual forces, and to close all bases within a period of months.

Was the settlement and withdrawal possible in 1972? Ambassador Dobrynin asked. "Yes," Kissinger replied. But the United States must have its POWs returned and "some perspective of what follows afterward." He warned that the North Vietnamese offensive had created a severe problem for Soviet-American relations. "I must in all honesty tell the General Secretary," Kissinger said, "that if developments [in Vietnam] continue unchecked, either we will take actions which will threaten the summit or, if the summit should take place, we will lose the freedom of action to achieve the objectives [of détente]." Brezhnev then read to Kissinger a message from the North Vietnamese that rejected the idea of holding a Tho–Kissinger meeting in

Moscow and went on to demand that before any further secret talks could take place, the United States must accept the resumption of the official peace talks in Paris. Hanoi's note suggested April 27 for the resumption of official talks and May 7 as the date for the secret meeting. Brezhnev insisted that the Soviets had not prompted the Spring Offensive but it was the Chinese and the North Vietnamese, both hoping to prevent the Moscow summit, that were at fault. Brezhnev confided to Kissinger that the North Vietnamese had asked Moscow to cancel Nixon's visit. Although Kissinger had his doubts, understandably, about the sincerity of Brezhnev's comments, he did not doubt the gist of it. "It is hard to overemphasize Soviet eagerness for the Summit," Kissinger cabled Haig.[16]

At 11:00 A.M. the following day, Kissinger responded to Hanoi's proposal. If the North Vietnamese agreed to a Tho–Kissinger meeting no later than May 2, the Americans would be willing to attend a plenary meeting in Paris on April 27, and would restrain the bombing of Hanoi and Haiphong. Brezhnev thought the proposal was "constructive." Kissinger then summarized the offer he was ready to make to Le Duc Tho: Hanoi would need to withdraw the troops that had entered the South since the Spring Offensive began, respect the DMZ, return POWs held over four years, and agree to enter "serious" negotiations. The United States, in return, would stop bombing the North and remove the new personnel that had been brought in since the latest bombing began. "I feel that I have made sufficiently clear that our basic position on Vietnam is an extremely serious one," Kissinger concluded.[17]

That was how he left it. The Soviets dispatched Konstantin Katushev, a member of the Central Committee, to Hanoi to pass on the proposal. On April 24, there was a brief exchange of the possible dates for the next Tho–Kissinger meeting. For the remainder of the trip Kissinger, Brezhnev, and Gromyko focused on other matters: SALT, the Middle East, European security, bilateral trade, and, a new document entitled *Basic Principles of Soviet-American Relations* (that would be approved at the summit in May). Discussions on such issues were generally affable. The Soviets, and Brezhnev in particular, appeared eager to welcome Nixon and hold a successful summit.

Kissinger put the best possible spin on the meetings in his April 24 summary to Nixon. "We did not achieve a breakthrough on Vietnam," he wrote, "we have effectively positioned ourselves for whatever military actions we wish to pursue after first having demonstrated our reasonableness." In large part due to the Sino-American opening, the Soviets had bent over backward on many other issues. Brezhnev, in particular, had staked his reputation and political future on détente. Kissinger thus concluded: "Brezhnev personally, and the Soviets collectively, are in one of their toughest corners in years. They must want the Vietnamese situation to subside and I would judge that there is just a chance that of all distasteful courses open to them they will pick that of pressure on Hanoi."

On April 29, after reading Kissinger's summary of the Moscow trip, Nixon scribbled on the front page: "K—superb job!"[18]

*   *   *

A few days earlier, though, Nixon's assessment of Kissinger's performance had been far different. "We're trapped," Nixon ruminated as Kissinger proved unable, or unwilling, to produce progress on Vietnam. Brezhnev's assurances—as reported by Kissinger—that the Soviets desperately wanted the summit despite events in Vietnam were "bullshit." What mattered was Vietnam. When Kissinger argued that the Moscow trip would send shockwaves to Hanoi, Nixon dismissed this as "typical K[issinger] gobbledygook."[19]

In fact, Kissinger and Nixon, with Alexander Haig usually as the unfortunate middleman, exchanged a series of terse cables throughout the secret trip. On April 22, for example, Kissinger cabled to Washington:

> the situation seems to me as follows: Brezhnev wants a summit almost at any cost. He has told in effect that he would not cancel it under any circumstances. He swears he knew nothing of the offensive . . . Even though untrue, this gives us three opportunities: A) We may get help in deescalating or ending the war. B) If not, we can almost surely get his acquiescence in pushing NVN [North Vietnam] to the limit. C) We can use the summit to control the uproar in the US.

While Kissinger found it hard to estimate how able (or willing) the Soviets were to do anything on Vietnam, he was sure that "they will stand aside and they will have the summit." Thus "we can use this as cover for other actions. Why not play out the string?" Although gaining Soviet cooperation on Vietnam remained an elusive quest, the Soviets were clearly willing to make concessions on SALT. "To kick them in the teeth now would be an absurdity," he concluded.[20]

Nixon disagreed. Feeling "not entirely comfortable" with what he considered Kissinger's eagerness for the summit, he had Haig cable back to Kissinger a simple message: "an honorable conclusion to the Vietnam conflict far exceeds the importance of [the] Soviet summit." Haig, caught in the crossfire between the president and his national security adviser, complained to Kissinger: "despite my efforts [Nixon] tends to equate [Soviet] largess on the Summit with collusion with Hanoi on South Vietnam."[21]

Kissinger, undoubtedly suffering from some stress, finally blew his top. On April 23, he insisted in a cable to Haig that Hanoi and Moscow were not "in direct collusion" and that the leaders in Moscow were "embarrassed and confused" about the Spring Offensive. He asked: "Does the President understand that all concessions have so far been made by Moscow and that we have given nothing including Vietnam?" Indeed, "if this is the President's attitude he had no business approving the Moscow trip."[22]

The following day Kissinger changed tack and promised Nixon that he had made major progress on the SALT agreements by having the Soviets include the SLBMs—a category in which the USSR held a significant advantage—into their latest proposal. "You can claim next week a major accomplishment and at a time when you may have to go very hard on Vietnam," Kissinger cabled.

The ever-modest Kissinger added: "The president can get sole credit for SALT . . . My role can easily be eliminated. I want the result not the credit."[23]

Finally, Kissinger appealed to Nixon's innermost desires by pointing out that the president was at the brink of making history. "Your Moscow summit—if we go through with it and Vietnam is under control—will dwarf all previous postwar summits in terms of concrete accomplishments and have a major international and domestic impact."[24]

In fact, when Kissinger returned from Moscow on April 24, Nixon did not give him the thorough dressing down that Haldeman had expected. When Kissinger arrived at Camp David that evening Nixon had been "all primed to whack Henry, but backed off when he [Kissinger] actually got there," Haldeman noted in his diaries. Instead, Nixon responded to Kissinger's belligerent manner—"he greeted me frostily," Haldeman noted—by agreeing that Kissinger could brief the press on the Moscow meetings as long as he revealed none of their actual substance and focused on atmospherics.

Haldeman also noted that Nixon was at a distinct psychological disadvantage throughout the entire meeting. The president "unfortunately had not zipped up his fly, so during the entire conversation it was noticeably open."

It was, of course, typical of Nixon—whatever the condition of his fly—to avoid open confrontation with anyone. Yet, on this occasion he probably also hoped that Kissinger's Moscow trip and the prospect of the Moscow summit might divert some attention away from Vietnam while Kissinger prepared for the May 2 meeting with Le Duc Tho. Thus, without giving any details of the substance of Kissinger's meetings in Moscow, the White House publicly disclosed the trip on April 25.[25]

On April 26, Nixon gave another TV address on Vietnam. He discussed Vietnamization, the dramatic drop in American casualty rates over the past three years, the administration's intent to stop the draft completely, and the American peace proposal. Nixon insisted that U.S. bombing would continue "until the North Vietnamese stop their offensive," but assured that no American ground troops would be involved. He then made a familiar plea for support:

> let us bring our men home from Vietnam; let us end the war in Vietnam. But let us end it in such a way that the younger brothers and the sons of the brave men who have fought in Vietnam will not have to fight again in some other Vietnam at some time in the future.

The immediate reaction, Haldeman noted, "was excellent." Vietnamization had worked its magic: if assured that no Americans were going to be in harm's way, the public was likely to back Nixon. The president told Kissinger to order more severe strikes against Hanoi over the weekend of April 28–30.[26]

It was a remarkable moment, a moment that illustrated the interconnected nature of the Vietnam War and triangular diplomacy. But it also illustrated the tensions between the president and his national security adviser. While getting ready for his second "journey for peace," Nixon was rushing to order severe air strikes on North Vietnam which, many suspected, could have the eventual result of leading to the cancellation of the Moscow summit. Meanwhile Kissinger was getting ready to step on an airplane headed for Paris and another meeting with the North Vietnamese that had been arranged with Moscow's assistance. It was hardly an ideal working relationship.

"SETTLE OR ELSE": PARIS AND LINEBACKER I

Paris, May 2, 1972. Arriving at the Tuesday meeting Kissinger could hardly be hopeful for a settlement. Nixon, perhaps because he suspected that Kissinger had acted too independently in Moscow, had, once again, given him rigid instructions on April 30. The president had decided that a major bombing and mining effort against Hanoi and Haiphong would commence later that week. "The only factor," he wrote Kissinger, "that would change my decision on this is a definite conclusion at your meeting that the North Vietnamese are ready to make a settlement now, prior to the Soviet Summit." What did he mean by settlement? Not a total capitulation by Le Duc Tho to the Americans' maximum demands "but a very minimum, something like a cease fire, a withdrawal of all their forces to the pre-Easter lines and the return of all POWs." Because of domestic political considerations this was the last chance for Hanoi to avoid being hit hard, Nixon insisted. "Unless we hit the Hanoi–Haiphong complex this weekend, we are probably not going to be able to hit it at all before the election," he added. If they waited, the Moscow summit would be too close; afterward, much like after the Beijing trip, the administration's hands would be tied for a few weeks. Then it would be mid-June, and the last thing Nixon wanted was to give the Democrats a chance to launch fresh criticism of his Vietnam policy at their July convention. He also worried lest the Congress instigate legislation to ban any further bombing and that public support for the bombings, which had so far been surprisingly solid, would erode. Early May was, therefore, the window of opportunity. Thus, when meeting Tho and Thuy Kissinger should demand that they "fish or cut the bait" and show "some very substantial action toward an immediate settlement." And, to make clear that Nixon meant business, he forbid the use of the phrase "reduction of the level of violence" at any time during the talks. "It means absolutely nothing at all and is too imprecise to give us a yard stick for enforcement." Nixon was not concerned that the Soviets would react to new military maneuvers by canceling the summit. During his secret trip Kissinger had "prepared the way (to Moscow) very well," he wrote and "in any event, we cannot let the Soviet Summit be the primary consideration in making the decision" on Hanoi–Haiphong. "We have crossed the Rubicon and now we must win," the president maintained. They both knew that the North Vietnamese "will break every understanding" and "talk in order to gain time." Enough of this, Nixon summed it up,

> In a nutshell you should tell them that they have violated all understandings, they stepped up the war, they have refused to negotiate seriously. As a result, the President had had enough and now you have only one message to give them—Settle or else![27]

To make things worse for Kissinger the city of Quang Tri fell to the North Vietnamese on May 1, 1972. When Kissinger informed Nixon about this, he tried to soften the blow by pointing out that Quang Tri was less significant than the city of Hue, which still remained in South Vietnamese hands. According to Haldeman, Kissinger "hedged around" before getting to a part in General Abrams's report in which he suggested that the South Vietnamese army was losing its will to fight. Kissinger had good reason to be nervous. Not only did Nixon stress that his earlier instructions—that Kissinger should bully the North Vietnamese in Paris— remained unchanged, but he now insisted that the Soviets should be warned that there would be no summit "while we're in trouble in Vietnam." After some brooding the two, mistakenly, seemed to agree that "regardless of what will happen" the war would be over by August.[28]

What happened in Paris was predictable. The first Kissinger–Tho meeting in eight months—since September 1971—was, by all accounts, a disaster. Memories of the meeting made Kissinger rant in his 1979 memoirs that the North Vietnamese "were implacable revolutionaries, the terror of their neighbors." That they may have been, yet the amount of bombing the North Vietnamese had suffered and the violence of decades surely helps explain at least part of their zeal. Le Duc Tho and Xuan Thuy were, given the military situation, understandably confident. Kissinger, given the events in South Vietnam and Nixon's mood, had no real sticks or carrots. Hence, according to Kissinger, Tho immediately went on the attack, accusing the United States of interrupting the secret meetings in late 1971. Kissinger made things worse by losing his temper and putting the blame on the North Vietnamese. Tho then wanted to quote Senator Fulbright's critique of Kissinger and Nixon's policies. Kissinger reluctantly listened. Such exchanges did not exactly break the ice.

Kissinger then followed his script. Among other things he demanded an immediate end to the North Vietnamese military action, return to the pre-Spring Offensive situation, and negotiations based on previous American proposals "leading to a rapid conclusion of the conflict." He indicated that this had been discussed with the Soviets: "I understand that your allies have already told you some of the ideas we have." Kissinger did not, at this point, call for a ceasefire-in-place although he did say that the American "political proposal was not inflexible." Given Nixon's mood that was about the only olive branch he could offer. Tho and Thuy responded by an equally uncompromising stance: the North Vietnamese would not stop their offensive; their earlier offers still stood. Then Tho challenged Kissinger: "show us what flexibility you have and I am prepared to discuss your new flexibility." He then issued an unveiled threat, referring to the lack of U.S. domestic support for the war, the approach of the November elections, and the impossibility of reintroducing American troops: "We know that time is not on your side." After three hours, the two sides decided to end the meeting. Kissinger advised Ambassador Porter to suspend the plenary meetings that were scheduled to reconvene two days later. To Nixon Kissinger wrote that the meeting, while a disappointment, had at least achieved some clarifications. The North Vietnamese intractability was useful "for our own calculations and, when necessary, the public record." It was, Kissinger cabled to Nixon immediately after he had broken off the talks, the "least productive meeting on record."[29]

Nixon, as often was the case, was leaning toward the dramatic and the forceful. But he remained undecided. Much as he had brooded over the decision to order the invasion of Cambodia some two years earlier, the president, notwithstanding his strong instructions to Kissinger and initial determination to begin the B-52 bombings on Friday May 2, still agonized. When Kissinger arrived at Andrews Air Force Base on that evening, he, along with the awaiting Al Haig, were quickly transported by helicopter to the presidential yacht, *Sequoia*, anchored at the Navy Yard. While airborne toward Washington, Kissinger had already received a warning from Haig that Nixon wanted to launch a massive two-day strike the same day and had a "growing conviction that we should move to cancel the Summit now." It would be "ludicrous and unthinkable," Nixon had told Haig, to be "toasting Soviet leaders and arriving at agreements while Soviet tanks and weapons are fueling massive offensive against our allies." While Nixon was not "rigid" in these views, Kissinger needed to give the president's mood some serious thought on his flight from Paris.[30]

Once on board the *Sequoia*, Nixon, Kissinger, and Haig discussed their options. The good thing about the Paris meeting, Kissinger suggested, was that if Tho had offered a ceasefire-in-place, it might have been difficult to refuse. In the existing military situation, such an agreement would have completely demoralized Saigon. Capitulation was, naturally, out of the question and doing more of the same would hardly help shore up the flailing ARVN. Invasion of the North was not a realistic choice. They could bomb the Red River dikes and cause massive flooding throughout North Vietnam. They could use nuclear weapons.[31] It was not a very attractive set of choices.

Nixon, with both Kissinger's and Haig's support, decided in favor of bombing and mining. Kissinger recommended waiting until Monday, May 8. By then, he assured, he would have a plan for a long-term operation, rather than a quick two- or three-day strike against Hanoi that had earlier appealed to Nixon.

Nixon gave him forty-eight hours.[32]

The major issue, though, was no longer whether the United States would commence heavy bombing of the North or mine the Haiphong harbor. That much was
clear. The key question was whether the Soviets would cancel the summit once the
bombing began. If it happened, Nixon's year of triumph might end in catastrophe:
the bombing was, in any event, likely to provoke the antiwar movement and all the
doves to launch a furious anti-Nixon campaign geared at unseating him in November. If the Soviets cancelled the summit, moreover, Nixon's foreign policy record,
so promising only two months earlier, would suddenly be tarnished.

To minimize the possibility of such adverse reactions Kissinger and Nixon
moved to pre-warn the Soviets. In a letter to Brezhnev the president, who had
received several notes from the general secretary calling for restraint in Vietnam,
chastised the Soviets. By providing massive military aid they were, Nixon wrote, in
large part responsible for Hanoi's arrogant behavior. Nixon warned about grave
decisions that were going to be made in the near future. Handing the letter to
Dobrynin, Kissinger commented on his May trip to Paris that Le Duc Tho had
acted "as defiant as if he had won the war." On May 6 Dobrynin brought back
Brezhnev's reply that, yet again, cautioned restraint but offered, perhaps because
the Soviets were not exactly in a position to offer, nothing. Kissinger was clearly
agitated. "Our exchange on Vietnam has not advanced the matter by an inch," he
complained to Dobrynin. Therefore, he added, "we will have to act in Vietnam as
required by the military and political situation."[33]

The final decisions had, in fact, already been made by the time Dobrynin brought
Brezhnev's response. On May 3 Nixon weighed the possibility of canceling the summit. Would it not be better for him to do so, rather than to wait for Brezhnev to
protest and pull the plug? Would canceling the summit do anything to help with the
war, he wondered. Or would it simply allow the Soviets to launch a massive propaganda effort? Would the costs be too high relative to any possible gain? Kissinger, at
that point, appeared certain that canceling the summit was the right thing to do. He
told Haldeman that there was no way to have it both ways; hence it was better to
cancel the summit and then bomb. "The real question," Haldeman paraphrased
Kissinger, "is how can we have a Summit meeting and be drinking toasts to Brezhnev while Soviet tanks are crumbling Hue?" And on it went all day with Kissinger
growing increasingly pessimistic, Nixon trying to rationalize his belief that he could
have it both ways, and Haldeman acting as the middleman between the two. By late
that evening, Kissinger, "deeply disturbed," complained to Haldeman that he had
made mistakes in Moscow and Paris by not leaving "any flexibility." But, in his
defense, Kissinger said that he had simply followed Nixon's orders. Nixon, leaning
toward approving the bombing campaign, decided to wait another day.[34]

May 4 was the day of FBI Director J. Edgar Hoover's funeral.[35] Before heading
for the funeral to give the eulogy, the president met with Al Haig, Kissinger's deputy
and emerging rival. He then called Haldeman, telling him to take Kissinger with

him to see John Connally, who had recently announced his decision to step down as secretary of the treasury.[36] Kissinger's strongest rival in the internal power games of the Nixon administration, Connally—who was about to launch his "Democrats for Nixon" campaign—was poised for a major cabinet post (perhaps secretary of state) after Nixon's reelection. In the spring of 1972 he was one of the few men whom Nixon trusted.

At lunchtime in the Secretary's Office at the Treasury Department Connally listened patiently to what Haldeman and Kissinger had to say. Nixon had decided to commence bombing in the Hanoi–Haiphong area and considered canceling the Moscow summit before the Soviets did so. Haldeman said that he disagreed with the cancellation. Connally agreed. Canceling the summit would gain the president nothing. It would upset domestic opinion (which was likely to be upset by the bombing alone), place the blame for killing détente squarely on the Nixon administration, and, effectively, allow the Soviets to avoid making a difficult decision. This argument, it seems, appealed to Kissinger either on a substantive level or because he could not face being on the losing side of a key decision. Nixon, meanwhile, continued to look for reinforcement from his daughters and from Attorney General John Mitchell. All were, predictably, supportive.[37]

On May 8 Linebacker I commenced. U.S. forces began mining Haiphong harbor. Simultaneously, the bombing of Hanoi was enhanced. Nixon, once again likening the moment to Caesar's crossing of the Rubicon, appears to have been full of adrenalin as he went through the motions. In the morning the NSC met for three hours to discuss the options facing the administration. Nixon presented a seemingly hopeless situation; regardless of what he did in Vietnam, the Moscow meetings would not take place. If he took strong action, the Soviets would cancel the summit or if he took no further measures, the situation in Vietnam would deteriorate, and Nixon could not go to Moscow. If those were the options, clearly action was warranted. Defense Secretary Laird argued otherwise. He did not think that South Vietnam's collapse was imminent or that the bombing and mining would have an immediate impact on the North because it probably had five months' worth of reserves. Rogers called for a delay. Why not wait until after the summit, he asked, ironically echoing what Kissinger had been saying prior to May 4.

As usual, Laird ended up on the losing side. After Nixon questioned Laird's optimism about South Vietnam's ability to withstand the continued attacks, Connally, Vice President Agnew, and Kissinger brought up the various arguments in favor of immediate action. American credibility abroad was at stake, Agnew maintained, whipping up scenarios of further falling dominoes in the Middle East and elsewhere. The American public would not turn a blind eye to the South's collapse, Connally insisted. "If Vietnam is defeated," he said, "Mr. President, you won't have anything." Kissinger then challenged Laird's point about the North Vietnamese reserves, pointing out that Hanoi would never risk the possibility that its reserves would be depleted. With sea routes closed and land routes susceptible to American bombs, Hanoi's capabilities would be seriously hampered. To some extent this was a bogus argument that relied on continued U.S. bombing of all the North's access routes from China, something that was not necessarily going to continue for very long. Still, Kissinger did not fail to warn that there was a strong possibility—"better than even chance"—that the Moscow summit would be cancelled.[38]

Nixon was determined not to have anyone change his mind. When the meeting ended at 12:20 he told the NSC that he would make the decision at 2:00 P.M.; in reality, that was the deadline for allowing the necessary preparations to be completed by 9:00 P.M. the same evening. That was when Nixon had scheduled his announcement to be broadcast on TV. As Haldeman recorded in his diaries, Nixon seems to have drawn some enjoyment from the opportunity to show Kissinger, apparently still not convinced that the timing was right, who the boss really was.

"At 2:00 exactly the P said, 'Well, it's 2:00, the time's up. We go.' Henry was a little dismayed at that point and started arguing some more, but the P said, 'Nope, the decision is made, no further discussion.'"[39]

Linebacker I was officially on.

Later that day, while Nixon met with congressional leaders to inform them of what he had decided, Kissinger briefed Dobrynin. In a "fatalistic mood" about the summit, Kissinger handed the Soviet ambassador Nixon's letter to Brezhnev, in which the president explained what he was about to say in his speech. There had been no progress toward peace on the part of the North Vietnamese. Therefore, the United States was resorting to further military action against Hanoi; until the North Vietnamese ceased their offensive the bombing would continue. But Nixon also offered some modifications to earlier American peace terms. Most significantly, he called for an internationally supervised ceasefire-in-place (rather than the withdrawal of all North Vietnamese troops from the South) and offered the withdrawal of all U.S. troops within four rather than six months after an agreement had been reached. Lastly, Nixon discussed the progress thus far achieved in Soviet-American relations and hinted at even further positive steps that would follow the Moscow summit. In other words, the United States was still ready for the summit; the ball was now in Moscow's court. Dobrynin, as was expected, criticized the American decision and warned that the summit was clearly in jeopardy. If Soviet ships were hit, he said, Moscow would consider it "an act of war." Both men were, understandably, gloomy. They had been less than two weeks away from the culmination of more than three years of back-channel diplomacy.[40]

Meanwhile, Peter Rodman, one of Kissinger's key aides on the NSC staff, had gone to New York to deliver a similar letter to the PRC's UN Ambassador Huang Hua. Much like the letter to Brezhnev, Nixon's letter to Zhou asked for Beijing to put the American action in Vietnam into a broad perspective. "We must consider whether the short-term perspectives of a smaller nation can be allowed to threaten all the progress we have made," Nixon wrote to the Chinese premier. "I would hope," he added, "that after the immediate passions have cooled, we will concentrate on longer-term interests."[41]

Despite gloomy predictions, however, the days that followed Nixon's announcement and the commencement of the mining and bombing campaign proved that the president's instincts had been correct. Of course, there were critics. In public both the Chinese and the Soviets quickly abhorred the "criminal actions" of the Nixon administration. Yet, both governments' formal protests focused on the damage that American bombing had caused to their respective ships. There was no rush to sever relations with the United States over Linebacker I. When Kissinger met with the PRC's UN ambassador Huang Hua in New York on May 16, he tried to stress the confidential nature of his briefing on the upcoming Soviet summit. Among other things he affirmed that the United States would not enter into agreements with the USSR that were directed against China. But Huang simply listened impassively until the discussion turned to Indochina. In light of Chinese protests of U.S. bombing, Kissinger referred to the repeated warnings regarding a U.S. response if the North attacked the South. He assured that a full investigation into the damage suffered by Chinese ships in early May was under way and that the United States was looking into possible compensation. Huang's point was simple: the Chinese would stand behind Hanoi "until the very end," he told Kissinger. While this was hardly an encouraging statement, Kissinger wrote to Nixon that the meeting in New York provided further evidence "of moderate Chinese response to your military actions."[42]

Most important, however, the Soviets did not cancel the Moscow summit. While the Soviets, much like the Chinese, protested against the American bombing and mining, they also chose to focus their strongest criticism on the damage caused to their ships. On May 10 Dobrynin came to Kissinger's office to deliver a note from Brezhnev. To Kissinger's disappointment, the note merely complained about the "criminal activity of the U.S. Air Force" after Soviet ships had been damaged and several sailors been killed. Yet, Dobrynin was "somewhat encouraging" about the prospect that the summit would still take place. In the next few days, it became clear that Moscow had decided to go ahead with the summit and, perhaps more significantly, to try and jump-start the Paris talks. On May 12, Dobrynin and Kissinger met to discuss a proposal for a joint statement renouncing the use of nuclear weapons; on the morning of May 14 they were already discussing gifts to be exchanged at the summit. That same evening Dobrynin brought in a note proposing the resumption of the secret talks in Paris; on May 17, he assured Kissinger that Moscow was "bringing great pressure on the Vietnamese." On May 18, Kissinger and Dobrynin went to Camp David to continue the final pre-summit preparations.[43]

Dobrynin never seriously raised the issue of canceling the summit. For the Soviet leadership there was simply too much at stake. Not only had Brezhnev placed his personal reputation on the line, but there were crucial issues at stake: SALT and other agreements as well as potential breakthroughs on such regional issues as the Middle East. Moreover, the Soviet relationship with North Vietnam was far from a cozy one. Despite massive Soviet aid the Spring Offensive, Dobrynin claims, had come as a surprise to the Soviet leadership and the Politburo's "final verdict was to go ahead with the summit because its members recognized that the alternative would amount to handing Hanoi a veto over our relations with Washington." That, if somewhat overstated, was hardly a welcome prospect for a Kremlin leadership eager to reach superpower status.[44]

In Nixon, the mild Soviet (and Chinese) reaction unleashed demons. If he could get away with it, why not bomb even more? Why not let the North Vietnamese have it while he sat down with their most powerful ally?

On Saturday, May 20, the same day as the presidential party departed from Washington to Salzburg and onward to Moscow, Nixon gave Haig—who was going to remain in Washington while the presidential party traveled to Moscow—detailed instructions about how to fight the war while the commander-in-chief was out of town. "No abatement" of air strikes was to be allowed. More specifically, Nixon insisted that there would be "a minimum of 1200 air sorties a day," about a fifth of which should be directed at the Hanoi–Haiphong area, and that the air attacks should be focused on "those targets which will have major impact on civilian morale"—in other words, on populated areas—"as well as accomplishing our primary objective of reducing the enemy's ability to conduct the war." Nixon was clearly, as Jeffrey Kimball maintains, viewing the Linebacker operations as "a culminating demonstration of his madman theory."[45]

To Kissinger, though, Nixon's determination to bomb the North Vietnamese was an act of courage. Nixon, Kissinger later wrote, acted on his own instincts and "won a brilliant gamble." He could bomb Hanoi and have his summit in Moscow too. He "could leave to Moscow with dignity, for we had not sacrificed those who had put their trust in us," a reference to the South Vietnamese, who actually had not been consulted about Linebacker, although President Thieu naturally welcomed the bombing and mining campaign. Moreover, Kissinger added, Nixon could go to Moscow "with confidence since the interlocking design of our foreign policy had withstood extraordinary stress," meaning that the Soviets had not cancelled the summit and the Chinese had reacted in a muted fashion. Most important, Kissinger concluded, the Americans could fly to Moscow "with hope that we were laying the foundations of a global equilibrium which could bring safety and progress to an anxious thermonuclear world."[46]

Given the unfolding of events, Kissinger's retrospective hyperbole seems far off the mark. The South Vietnamese would, in due course, be "sacrificed" and despite Soviet and Chinese restraint triangular diplomacy would prove to be but a brief interlude in American foreign policy. Ultimately, the Moscow summit hardly produced the basis for a new global equilibrium; indeed, the nuclear arms treaties to be signed in the Soviet capital would do little to curb the arms race (or calm the "anxious thermonuclear world").

MOSCOW SUMMIT

With bombs falling on North Vietnam, the much-awaited Moscow summit between Nixon and Brezhnev commenced on Monday, May 22, 1972. Like Nixon's journey for peace to China, the Soviet summit was a heavily ceremonial affair with the American press corps busy writing stories of the historic 5:00 P.M. signing ceremony in St. Vladimir Hall at the Kremlin. There were, of course, many serious agreements. Most significantly, Nixon signed the SALT I agreements: a five-year agreement on offensive missiles (ICBMs and SLBMs) and another on defensive ones (the ABM Treaty, which was to remain in force for thirty years). Kissinger, in addition to accompanying Nixon to most of his meetings with Brezhnev, spent much time in talks with Foreign Minister Andrei Gromyko about the details of SALT, the potential for a Middle East settlement, and the Vietnam War. There were also discussions about European security and bilateral Soviet-American economic relations. As in Beijing, Secretary of State Rogers and the State Department personnel were kept busy with auxiliary issues (trade, space exploration, cultural and scientific exchanges), while Nixon and Kissinger dealt with the real topics. During his initial one-on-one meeting with Brezhnev on May 22, Nixon made it clear that he did not want to get bogged down in details. "You and I should [not] waste our time on various words and phrases; that is something that Kissinger, Dobrynin and Gromyko can do." Brezhnev agreed. "We shall seek to achieve agreement in principle and then we could entrust the concrete formulations to others." During the first plenary meeting on May 23, they reinforced this division of labor in front of Secretary of State Rogers and others.[47]

The atmospheric differences with the China trip were palpable. Nixon was more firmly in control. Although Kissinger had negotiated a number of the agreements on the back channel and during his secret trip in April, the president had been to Moscow before and had met with Soviet leaders on a number of occasions. Unlike Mao and Zhou, Brezhnev and his fellow leaders did not have the same mystique around them; they were not true revolutionaries but seasoned technocrats. In the end, because even the high-level discussions often focused on more specific issues (such as the number of nuclear missiles each side would be allowed to have) rather than broad outlines about Soviet-American relations, Kissinger's overwhelming feeling was that the summit in Moscow lacked "the uniform texture of the one in Peking; it was more jagged." Unlike in China, Nixon and Kissinger did not spend endless hours in wide-ranging discussions about the state of the world but focused on practical matters. Kissinger, reminiscing about the intellectually more satisfying exchanges in China, remarked that the Soviets always had thick piles of memoranda and drafts with them; Zhou Enlai never used notes. Unlike the urbane and learned Chinese premier, moreover,

> philosophical discussion made [the Soviet leaders] visibly nervous; they considered them either a trick or a smokescreen; they maneuvered them as rapidly as

possible in the direction of some concrete result that could be signed . . . One had the sense that only the literal meaning of documents would be observed (if at all) and that what was not written down had no significance whatever.

The irony of all this was that three years earlier, when Kissinger and Nixon had set up the back channel with Anatoly Dobrynin, concreteness had been a guiding principle of their approach. Whereas Kissinger usually criticized the many "spirits" that had been used to characterize the relaxation in Soviet American tensions (the spirit of Geneva, the spirit of Camp David, etc.), he now derided his Soviet counterparts for the fact that they clearly considered "the 'spirit' of a document a meaningless phrase."[48]

The endless haggling over the SALT agreements is a case in point. During two separate meetings on May 23, Nixon, Kissinger, Brezhnev, and the Soviet leader's national security adviser, Andrei Aleksandrov-Agentov, sparred over the numbers of SLBMs each side could have, over the location of the second Soviet ABM site, and about the question of modernization of existing missiles. By 10:00 P.M. that evening they had reached a tentative agreement. Brezhnev was satisfied. "We have reached an agreement on almost all points," he said.[49]

Yet, it still took Kissinger and Gromyko four and a half hours of debate before the final wording and numbers were settled at noon on Friday, May 26.[50] At that point, the American SALT delegation and its leader, Gerard Smith, were given permission to fly to Moscow from Helsinki to attend the signing ceremony that evening. Not fully appraised of the details of the agreements Smith, not surprisingly, "was thoroughly disgusted" about the way he had been treated. He was no more satisfied when Kissinger decided to hold his own impromptu SALT press conference at the Moscow Intourist Hotel's nightclub after the signing ceremony in St. Vladimir Hall.[51]

Dissatisfaction with the SALT I agreements was not limited to such banter over protocol. To be sure, the ABM treaty of May 1972 that limited the number of ABM sites each side could have to two (one around the capital, the other around a missile site) was generally considered a positive achievement. It certainly allowed each side to cut down spending on an expensive and unproven program. But the five-year interim agreement on offensive weapons was something else. The final terms of the agreement allowed the Soviets higher ceilings on ICBMs (1,618 to 1,054) and SLBMs (740 to 656). To many critics in the United States it was thus easy to charge that Nixon and Kissinger had, in effect, given up U.S. missile superiority. Already on May 24, for example, John M. Ashbrook, a conservative Republican member of the House of Representatives who had unsuccessfully challenged Nixon for the 1972 Republican nomination, attacked the SALT agreement. In a speech on the House floor, Ashbrook denounced the agreement as one that would "lock the Soviet Union into unchallengeable superiority, and plunge the United States and its allies into a decade of danger."[52]

The most outspoken critic was Senator Henry ("Scoop") Jackson (D-WA). The SALT I agreement was "a bad one," the senator charged. Realizing that he would not be able to gather enough votes to defeat the ratification of the treaty, however, Jackson opted for a different course. In mid-August 1972 he introduced the Jackson Amendment to the SALT agreement which stated that in negotiating the next nuclear arms agreement, the president must make sure that the United States would not commit itself "to levels of intercontinental strategic forces inferior to the limits provided for the Soviet Union."

It was a brilliantly worded amendment: could any responsible official or U.S. senator commit to negotiating something that would make the United States "inferior"? The amendment was adopted by the Senate on September 14, 1972, by a sizeable majority (56–35). But, the demand that the United States would either have to have equal (or superior) "levels of intercontinental strategic forces" was also the opening shot in the domestic criticism that would overshadow the next round of SALT negotiations.

The reality was more complex than such critics as Jackson publicly argued. The interim agreement did not cover a number of issues that, in effect, guaranteed the United States an advantage for years to come. For example, the exclusion of MIRVs from the agreement meant that the United States could go ahead with qualitative improvements and use its superior technology to arm missile launchers with multiple warheads; as a result, the United States continued to hold a significant advantage in the overall number of nuclear warheads (in late 1972: 4.146 for the United States vs. 1.971 for the USSR). In addition, the Soviets did not insist on counting either long-range bombers equipped with nuclear weapons (in which Washington had a 450 to 155 advantage) or U.S. forward base systems (medium-range missile launchers based in Europe) as part of the overall American offensive capability.

Pointing out that U.S. overall superiority continued may have satisfied some hawkish critics at home. But another criticism—that received far less attention at the time—was, in fact, more pertinent: the Interim Agreement, particularly due to the exclusion of MIRVs, had done little to curb the arms race. It had merely shifted it to other types of weapons. As one of Kissinger's own advisers, William Hyland, would later point out, the SALT I agreement "actually produced a sizeable buildup in strategic weaponry."[53]

The critics were on the mark: the Moscow summit produced an *imperfect* nuclear arms control agreement. But that misses a major point: to Nixon and Kissinger, the SALT agreements were not about numbers of missiles or about stopping the nuclear arms race dead in its tracks. SALT and the summit produced a politically significant deal, setting Nixon apart as the president who had concluded the first such agreement, while ensuring Kissinger's position as—at least in the public perception—the premier diplomat of his era. And while they were less spectacular in their PR value than the Shanghai Communiqué, the SALT I agreements, both the ABM treaty and the five-year interim agreement on offensive missiles, were at the same time more concrete than anything Nixon and Kissinger had brought home from China. When added to all the other bilateral agreements that were signed in Moscow—on science and technology, medicine and public health, environmental protection, space exploration—and the creation of a joint economic commission, it was hard to escape the conclusion that the Moscow summit had been another "journey for peace." Indeed, it seemed most appropriate that on the last day of the summit, May 29, the United States and the Soviet Union signed what Raymond Garthoff calls the "charter for détente."[54]

This charter was officially called the *Basic Principles of Relations Between the United States and the Union of Soviet Socialist Republics.* Negotiated by Kissinger without the State Department's knowledge prior to the summit, the *Basic Principles* was a wide-ranging and, to many, alarming document. It referred to peaceful coexistence as the key principle of the bilateral relationship and highlighted the role of security interests. The *Basic Principles* downplayed the role of ideological differences and promised that the two countries would not seek "unilateral advantage" at the expense of the other country. The document even promised that the United States and the USSR would work to minimize international tension. Although it was watered down with references to the effect that the document did not affect either country's relations with third countries (and that it was not directed against any third party), the *Basic Principles* was as clear a reflection of the new spirit in Soviet-American relations as one could have conceived. Still, there was little concrete in the *Basic Principles.*

As Kissinger put it at a news conference upon departing Moscow: "I think we are talking here about a general spirit which regulates the overall direction of the policy."[55]

*   *   *

That spirit was lacking in discussions about two pressing regional issues: Vietnam and the Middle East. On the Middle East, Nixon and Kissinger played a waiting game. On the afternoon of May 26, they listened to Brezhnev, Kosygin, and Podgorny's lengthy diatribes about Israel's misbehavior. Nixon handed the Soviets a proposal and suggested that the best way to resolve the Middle East imbroglio was "for the US and Soviet Union privately and with discretion to use their influence to bring the parties together to make a settlement." He proposed that Kissinger and Dobrynin discuss the Middle East on the back channel. In September, Kissinger could come to Moscow and "get to the nutcutting part of the problem." It would be impossible to settle the issue before the U.S. elections in November, Nixon added.[56] In his meetings with Gromyko on May 28, Kissinger continued to press on the need to approach the Middle East problem in steps. "It is better to be as concrete as possible," he insisted, adding,

Total Israeli withdrawal [from the occupied territories] in the sense of an ultimate objective is one thing, but it is not a practical thing without war in the immediate future . . . We are looking for a way for the Arabs to get in the interim period three-quarters of what they want, and leave one-quarter later.

Dobrynin, sensing that Kissinger was trying to avoid any specific commitments, asked for clarification. "Will our agreement be an overall settlement, or an interim settlement that does not include the principle of overall withdrawal? If the latter, it will not be acceptable, you understand. Do you have an idea of the timing? Three to four years? Just give us some idea." Kissinger was not fazed. "Those are very good questions, Anatol. As for the time frame I would like to think about it a little more." Yet, he assured that "what the Arabs would get in the immediate future is a very favorable change in the existing situation." On it went into the evening of May 28 without substantive agreement on anything but the desire to continue "serious" discussions. By the morning of Monday, May 29, all Nixon would promise to Brezhnev was to "do my best to bring about a reasonable solution."[57]

While the Middle East would eventually explode in October 1973, the most immediate regional issue in May 1972 was Vietnam. Given Linebacker I, a showdown could hardly be avoided. It took place on the evening of May 24, at Brezhnev's dacha outside Moscow.

A NIGHT AT THE DACHA

Having learned from Dobrynin that afternoon that the general secretary meant to focus on Vietnam at the scheduled dinner meeting on "outstanding issues," Kissinger had decided to include only two of his aides, Winston Lord and John Negroponte, on the American side. The group was to leave about an hour after the signing of an agreement on cooperation in space that afternoon. But Brezhnev had other ideas. Why don't we ride to the dacha together? Brezhnev asked Nixon and pushed the president into a large Soviet limousine. The astonished Kissinger quickly jumped into the next car that started following Brezhnev's vehicle; a third car, full of panicky secret service agents, joined the race. After a harrowing forty-five-minute ride through Moscow the cars arrived at a heavily guarded mansion in Novo Ogarevo along the Moscow River; Lord and Negroponte, carrying Kissinger's briefing papers, arrived more than an hour later to join a small group that also included Kosygin, Podgorny, and Brezhnev's foreign and security affairs adviser, Andrei Aleksandrov-Agentov. In the meantime, Nixon and Kissinger had been treated to a high-speed hydrofoil ride on the river.[58]

Just before 8:00 P.M. the group went inside the dacha to begin the evening's discussion. After listening to Nixon's statement of the American position—that the United States had not provoked the current crisis and had been forced to react by the North Vietnamese—Brezhnev, Kosygin, and Podgorny each launched into lectures about "shameful" and "cruel" American policy in Vietnam. They demanded that the United States stop bombing, accept Hanoi's proposals, and get rid of Thieu. "It seems to us on the one hand the US wants to improve relations with us and improve the international climate generally, but while continuing the cruel conflict in Vietnam," Brezhnev remarked. "Surely these two things are quite incompatible," he added. Like Zhou Enlai in February, Brezhnev now argued that continuing the war only hurt American prestige. Ending the war was the honorable thing to do, he maintained. As far as Thieu, Kosygin wondered whether it was worth it to sacrifice the lives of "hundreds of thousands of Vietnamese, maybe even a million, and your own soldiers, simply to save the skin of a mercenary President."

Nixon took it all sitting down, waiting until all three had spoken to refute some of the arguments. He then expressed the American willingness to go back to the negotiation table, should the other side be reasonable, adding, "your influence with your allies could be considerable." He promised to "think it over, and maybe Dr. Kissinger out of his brain will come up with a new proposal." Brezhnev then concluded that the United States seemed, after all, eager for a reasonable resolution of the matter.

It was 11:00 P.M. and détente followed confrontation. Dinner, starting off with hors d'oeuvres of caviar and exuberant toasts, was served. Kosygin, Kissinger recalls, was particularly keen "to get his guests to put away as much Soviet cognac as possible. During the meal he drank at least two glasses of cognac for each American guest." Discussion focused on the degree to which Lake Baikal was polluted (Nixon, apparently erroneously, thinking the massive Central Asian Lake was a symbol of the need for Soviet-American environmental cooperation). Brezhnev then joked that perhaps Nixon's inaccurate information came from Kissinger, who should duly be exiled. Nixon suggested Siberia as a suitable site.

After two hours of merriment, drinking, and a four-course dinner, Brezhnev suddenly remembered that there was some serious business waiting for Kissinger in Moscow. Thus, the Americans returned to the Kremlin, where Nixon went to bed. Kissinger, at 1:15 A.M. on May 25, commenced another series of negotiations on SALT with Gromyko.[59]

That, Kissinger writes in his memoirs, was about all there was to it on Vietnam at the Moscow summit. The entire purpose of the Soviets' attacks at the dacha was to create a transcript that could then be sent to Hanoi as evidence that Moscow was not being soft on the capitalists. The entire meeting was a "charade." The only other discussion on Vietnam between the top leaders, he accurately observes, took place on the last day of the summit (May 29) when Brezhnev asked Nixon whether the Americans would accept Thieu's resignation in two months, rather than one month as Nixon had proposed in January 1972, prior to a general election in South Vietnam. The president tentatively agreed. At that time, Brezhnev also offered to send a high-level Soviet emissary to Hanoi.[60]

But was that really it? Or did something more transpire in Moscow? Were the Soviets simply going to pass on a message about the American willingness to have

Thieu resign a bit earlier? In fact, as the Russian historian, Ilya Gaiduk has argued, Kissinger had offered significantly more in trying to entice the Soviets to pressure the North Vietnamese toward serious negotiations. He had, in effect, offered a coalition government and outlined a "decent interval" solution: as long as the Communists did not unite the country immediately after the last Americans left Vietnam, the United States would not intervene.[61]

While inconclusive on the issue of a coalition government, the American record corroborates Gaiduk's argument on the decent interval. "If North Vietnam were wise," Kissinger told the Soviet foreign minister on May 27, "it would make an agreement now and not haggle over every detail, because one year after the agreement there would be a new condition, a new reality." Kissinger further added that

> if the DRV were creative, it would have great possibilities ... All we ask is *a degree of time so as to leave Vietnam for Americans in a better perspective* ... We are prepared to leave so that a communist victory is not excluded, though not guaranteed.

The words amounted to either a clever negotiation strategy or a promise to abandon an ally. Had President Thieu in Saigon been aware of what Kissinger was telling his Soviet interlocutor, he would undoubtedly have exploded in a fit of rage. For what Kissinger was clearly suggesting to Gromyko was that South Vietnam was expendable, that the United States would not be overly concerned about the collapse of the Saigon government or the unification of Vietnam under communist rule. What he asked for, in short, was a reasonable interval between the withdrawal of American troops and the final settlement of the future of Vietnam. It may have been a sheer negotiation strategy, aimed at maximizing the chances that the North Vietnamese would return to negotiations.

Yet, Kissinger's statement also indicated how desperate he was to conclude the frustrating negotiations in Vietnam (at the time almost three years old) and how relatively limited his concern for the future of the South Vietnamese was. They had become, in effect, mere pawns on the grand chessboard of triangular diplomacy. As the triumphs of great power summitry seemed to vindicate the correctness of Kissinger's realpolitik architecture, Vietnam and the Vietnamese had become expendable, while Kissinger suddenly deemed alliance loyalty irrelevant. Any moral concerns over what would happen to those South Vietnamese who had cooperated with the United States over the years if the North did take over all of Vietnam had little room as Kissinger tried to coax Gromyko to do his bidding with Hanoi.

Gromyko was, in fact, easily coaxed. He asked whether this was the "official" U.S. perspective.

"You can communicate this to the North Vietnamese," Kissinger replied.[62]

Soviet President Nikolai Podgorny undoubtedly did so when he traveled to Hanoi four weeks later.

"AN EXTRAORDINARY OPPORTUNITY"

When Nixon and Kissinger left Moscow on Monday, May 29, they did not go straight to Washington. Instead, they flew to Kiev, stayed overnight, and continued on Air Force One to Teheran for another historic meeting, this one with the shah of Iran. On the afternoon of May 31, the presidential party arrived in Warsaw, where Nixon met with Prime Minister Eduard Gierek. On June 1, 1972, they finally headed home. Everyone was tired from jetlag, too much food and drink, and, simply, too many negotiations. Yet, after arriving at Andrews Air Force Base on that Thursday evening, Nixon did not go to the White House for rest. Instead, he took a helicopter to Capitol Hill, and, at 9:40 P.M. gave a televised speech in front of a joint session of Congress. He did not, Nixon spoke, "bring back from Moscow the promise of instant peace but we do bring the beginning of a process that can lead to lasting peace." In short, the president said, "we have before us an extraordinary opportunity." He went on to catalogue the recent agreements with the Soviets and the significance of the opening to China, and added: "The summits of 1972 . . . are part of a great national journey for peace."[63] Nixon did not mention, because he did not have to mention, that the 1972 presidential elections were only five months away.

In mid-summer Nixon was clearly basking in the glory of a series of foreign policy achievements. The trip to China and the summit in Moscow had all but assured Nixon's reelection. And yet, it was exactly at this point in time when the most famous burglary of American history took place: on June 17, 1972, five men were arrested for breaking into the Democratic National Committee's headquarters in the Watergate complex on the Potomac River. In the next two years, spearheaded by *Washington Post* reporters Carl Bernstein and Bob Woodward, a growing investigation gradually linked the White House and Nixon with a disturbing tale of dirty tricks and political racketeering. At the end of that tale, in August 1974, Nixon would leave the White House disgraced; prior to his departure many others, including John Ehrlichman, Bob Haldeman, and John Mitchell were already gone. Ultimately, only one key figure in the first Nixon administration would actually profit from the Watergate crisis: Henry Kissinger.

Watergate would not, though, affect the outcome of the 1972 presidential election. Nixon rode the wave of his Moscow summit and the historic SALT I agreement to begin another term in the White House in January 1973. Kissinger was the great celebrity. An article in *Chicago Sun-Times* declared in June 1972: "Henry Alfred Kissinger . . . has become a legend." Even the most fervent critics of Nixon and Kissinger could find few convincing arguments to use to criticize their impressive summitry with China and the Soviet Union. In 1972, as the historian Robert Schulzinger notes, even the critics, both at home and abroad, "could only mutter and look embarrassed as Nixon and Kissinger rewrote the script of post–World War II foreign policy."[64]

Yet, the script was incomplete. While Kissinger had breached the China wall and engineered détente, he had been singularly unsuccessful in making any significant progress in his negotiations with the North Vietnamese. Even as the drama of great power summitry downplayed the tragedy of Indochina, the Paris talks were a blemish in an otherwise splendid record. It could not stay that way. On July 19, Kissinger returned to Paris with a mandate to negotiate a peace agreement prior to the November presidential election.

He had high hopes. Throughout 1972, particularly after the Spring Offensive commenced, both China and the Soviet Union had indicated that they placed a far higher value on their respective relationships with the United States than on their competition in Indochina. The pieces of the triangular puzzle had fallen in place, the architecture was emerging. Surely, this extraordinary moment in the United States' relations with North Vietnam's two principal supporters, together with the military deadlock that had emerged in Vietnam over the summer of 1972, would finally convince Hanoi's leaders to call it quits. Over the next few months, these assumptions would be severely tested as Kissinger embarked on a negotiation marathon with Le Duc Tho in Paris.

11

Exiting Vietnam

O ctober 12, 1972, was, Nixon's Chief of Staff Bob Haldeman wrote in his
diaries, "a super-historic night."[1]

Earlier that evening Kissinger and Al Haig had returned from a three-day negotiating marathon with the North Vietnamese in Paris. Arriving at the president's
hideaway office in the Executive Office Building adjacent to the White House,
Kissinger was as full of bravado as perhaps at any time during his career (save the
possible exception of his return from China in July 1971). "You've got three for three,
Mr. President," he told Nixon. In the long series of negotiations with Le Duc Tho,
Kissinger maintained, he had ironed out an acceptable agreement. While Haldeman, Haig, and Nixon listened intently, Kissinger argued that the treaty he had
achieved was far better than anyone could have expected. Most important, it guaranteed a ceasefire-in-place by the end of October. The withdrawal of U.S. troops
and the return of American POWs would take place within sixty days after the
ceasefire. In short, America's longest war would be over by the end of the year, a
crowning achievement in the first Nixon administration's foreign policy.

Nixon was elated. He ordered a bottle of his best wine ('57 Lafite-Rotschild) to
be served over dinner. While toasting the triumphs of the past few days, Nixon,
Kissinger, Haig, and Haldeman discussed the next steps. In order to maximize the
political gain Nixon would receive from ending the Vietnam War it was essential,
Kissinger argued, to keep the State Department out of the picture until the very last
moment. Otherwise there might be a leak to the press, causing Nixon to lose the
momentum of surprise that would be so useful in advance of the November elec-

tions. Moreover, there was still a possibility that something might go wrong; the South Vietnamese, for example, could scuttle the deal, believing it too advantageous to the North. If this were to happen amid high expectations for a peace agreement, Nixon would end up suffering in the polls. Thus, the four men cooked up the appropriate scenario on how to mislead the secretary of state. They decided to tell Bill Rogers over breakfast the following morning that Kissinger had achieved a breakthrough on military issues. He would have to go back to Paris for more haggling on political questions (such as the release of political prisoners held in South Vietnamese jails and the role of the International Control Commission). If this all worked out, Kissinger would continue on to Saigon. They would not, however, tell Rogers about Kissinger's additional plan—eventually aborted—to travel to Hanoi after his talks with Thieu. Nor would Rogers be told about the rather specific schedule that was now laid out for the publication of the agreement. If all went according to plan, Nixon would announce it at a press conference on October 26.[2]

All seemed set for a dramatic breakthrough. Another piece was soon to be added to the "structure of peace" and, conveniently enough, just in time for the November 1972 presidential elections. The year that had already featured summit meetings in Beijing and Moscow was to be crowned with the long-awaited peace with honor.

Alas, it was not to be. The October agreements fell victim to the many problems embedded in Kissinger and Nixon's Vietnam policy. In late October, the South Vietnamese president Nguyen Thieu soundly rejected Kissinger's offer. To Thieu, the part of the agreements allowing North Vietnamese troops, more than 100,000 of them, to remain in South Vietnam amounted to suicide. "I want to punch Kissinger in the face," he would later say of the moment when Kissinger tried to convince him that it was a good deal for the South Vietnamese. Meanwhile Nixon, whose wide lead in the polls virtually assured him of victory in the presidential election, became less concerned with concluding a Vietnam agreement. Instead, he worried about being accused of playing domestic politics at the cost of the South Vietnamese. Throughout the fall of 1972, the rift between Kissinger and Nixon—both in a chronically agitated state of mind at the time—grew wider. Indeed, during the weeks after his reelection in November 1972, Nixon contemplated a thorough reorganization of his foreign policy team. He had already decided that Rogers would have to go. But on November 21, 1972, he ruminated with Haldeman that "Henry . . . should leave by midyear (of 1973)."[3]

*   *   *

Kissinger would stay, in part because he would eventually deliver the January 1973 Paris Peace Agreement that would end the war and earn Kissinger the Nobel Peace Prize. All told, however, there would be no peace with honor. The end result was a temporary truce that allowed the United States to withdraw its remaining troops from South Vietnam and retrieve its prisoners of war from Hanoi.

The general outline of the road to the January 1973 Paris Agreements is so well known that it requires no detailed accounting here. It is important, however, to stress that in the months following Kissinger's return from the May summit in Moscow, triangular diplomacy was closely linked to the Vietnam negotiations. Starting in June and July 1972, the Soviets and the Chinese, constantly prompted by Kissinger, advised the North Vietnamese to engage in serious discussions. Whether this was the decisive factor in putting the peace talks back on track is open to some debate. Certainly, the failure of the North Vietnamese Spring Offensive to achieve its maximum results played a role in Hanoi's decision to focus their efforts on what they tended to refer to as the "diplomatic struggle." The near certainty of Nixon's electoral victory may also have been significant in accelerating the talks: Hanoi's worst-case scenario would have been an emboldened Nixon ready to commit extensive American resources to four years of protracted warfare. Within the context of a military stalemate and Nixon's approaching reelection, the Soviet and Chinese calls for serious peace talks thus found a receptive audience among the North Vietnamese leadership. Indeed, it is hard to escape the conclusion that North Vietnam's allies played a more important role in ending America's direct involvement in Vietnam than has previously been recognized.

And yet, this was hardly a vindication of Kissinger's diplomacy. For, as recently released American, Chinese, and Soviet documents reveal, Kissinger offered—and the Chinese and Soviets passed on to Hanoi—the prospect of a decent interval: an American withdrawal in return for a period of North Vietnamese restraint.

"HOW TO LIQUIDATE VIETNAM"

The initiative for renewing the Paris talks had come from the American side. On June 11 Colonel Georges Guay, the American military attaché in Paris, proposed a new secret meeting to the North Vietnamese representative, Vo Van Sung. That much is clear. It is also clear, however, that both the Soviets and the Chinese were in contact with the North Vietnamese in the days that followed. The Soviet president, Nikolaj Podgorny, traveled to Hanoi only two days after Colonel Guay made his proposal in Paris. A few days later, Kissinger's North Vietnamese interlocutor, Le Duc Tho, visited Beijing. Finally, on June 20, Vo, under instructions from Hanoi, responded to Colonel Guay's proposal and proposed that Tho and Kissinger meet in Paris on July 15.[4]

Significantly, Kissinger was in Beijing when the North Vietnamese message was delivered. Between June 19 and 23, Kissinger visited the Chinese capital to brief Zhou Enlai and his aides on the Moscow summit. According to Kissinger's memoirs, there were "no new developments on Vietnam" during these talks. This is partly true: Zhou was happy enough to listen to Kissinger's deprecating comments about Soviet leaders and his assurances that the United States would never collude with Moscow against Beijing. Zhou was ready to engage in a tour d'horizon over the general state of international relations. He asked questions about the SALT agreement and about Soviet policy towards Europe. And Zhou was, as usual, an impeccable host.

But there was so much more to these meetings than that. As the records of the June 1972 Zhou–Kissinger conversations—released only in April 2001—indicate, Vietnam was a key topic in Beijing. To Kissinger's chagrin Zhou returned, again and again, to Vietnam and Indochina. The talks, therefore, deserve special attention as a record of Kissinger's efforts to sell his particular strategy of "liquidating Vietnam" to his Chinese interlocutor.[5]

When Kissinger arrived in Beijing on the evening of June 19, the Chinese premier made the significance of Vietnam clear to his American guest. The previous day, Zhou told Kissinger, he had met Le Duc Tho, Kissinger's North Vietnamese interlocutor, in Beijing. Together Tho and Zhou had "assessed the situation." Accordingly, Zhou politely suggested that Vietnam should be the leadoff topic in the first full session the following day.[6]

In fact, Vietnam was discussed repeatedly over the next three days.

On June 20, Kissinger presented his basic overview of the American approach on "how to liquidate Vietnam." It boiled down to what some scholars have called a decent interval solution; Kissinger himself used the term *respectable interval*. While insisting that the United States could not overthrow the present government in South Vietnam, Kissinger was willing to accept a package deal that included a cease-fire-in-place (which at the time meant that more than 100,000 North Vietnamese troops could stay in South Vietnam), the complete withdrawal of U.S. troops, and the return of American prisoners of war. The real carrot, however, had to do with the political future of Vietnam. Following the American exit, Kissinger maintained, the United States was willing to let the Vietnamese sort out their political future without U.S. involvement, regardless of the fate of the South Vietnamese government. As he put it in a statement implying a willingness to betray the South Vietnamese: "while we cannot bring a communist government to power . . . if, as a result of historical evolution it should happen over a period of time, we ought to be able to accept it."

It was important, though, that fighting cease at least temporarily. But, if the war in Vietnam were to commence again "after a long period [and] we were all disengaged, my personal judgment is that it is much less likely that we will go back again, much less likely."[7]

Kissinger's comments represented, in effect, a plea for helping the United States to exit Vietnam without immediate embarrassment. He was willing to abandon the South, but not to suffer the embarrassment that would follow if the North Vietnamese launched an immediate offensive following the American withdrawal. But the Nixon administration had no interest in prolonging its direct involvement in Vietnam. As Kissinger put it: "In 1954 the reality was that Secretary [of State John

Foster] Dulles was looking for excuses to intervene. We are now looking for the opposite excuses."[8]

Although the message amounted to, in effect, a betrayal of the South, Zhou was not satisfied. On the afternoon of the 21st, the Chinese premier delivered a long critique of U.S. policy in Vietnam. "The present situation is such," Zhou maintained, "that with the turn of one's hand the matter could be settled." He was not happy with Kissinger's insistence that the United States could not simply abandon the Saigon government. "You are pegged down to a point that you say that you cannot give up a certain government . . . set up by yourselves." Zhou complained about the American plan to leave behind a "tail" (a small group of advisers) that could then be used to reintroduce the U.S. presence after a peace agreement was signed. "You know," he further emphasized, "that an end to the Vietnam War is one of the steps that must be taken to normalize relations between the US and China." Zhou ridiculed Kissinger's suggestion that by launching the Spring Offensive in a presidential election year, the Vietnamese were trying to interfere in U.S. domestic politics. "You were saying that Vietnam is interfering in your domestic politics while you are bombing their country. Don't you consider that to be interference in their internal politics?" Kissinger then tried to clarify his earlier points. In particular, he stressed to Zhou that

> it should be self-evident that in a second [Nixon] term we would not be looking for excuses to re-enter Indochina. But still it is important that there is a *reasonable interval* between the agreement on the ceasefire, and a reasonable opportunity for a political negotiation . . . the outcome of my logic is that *we are putting a time interval between the military outcome and the political outcome.*

Indeed, Kissinger assured that "after the agreement is signed there will be an increasing American disinterest in Indochina."

In virtual desperation Kissinger ended his response to Zhou's challenge in a telling manner: "we should not spend most of our time in Beijing talking about Vietnam. It is contrary to what we really want."

Zhou laughed.[9]

*   *   *

It was an exasperating experience. Kissinger had come to Beijing to further the personal bond he believed existed between himself and the Chinese premier. He had hoped that a thorough briefing on the Moscow summit would put to rest any Chinese concerns about collusion between the two superpowers against China. Yet, Zhou only seemed to want to talk about Vietnam.

In the end, Kissinger did make some progress. During the last extensive session in the late evening and early morning of June 22–23, the Chinese premier admitted: "if one were only proceeding from your way of thinking, our thinking would be like yours." But he insisted that China's hands were tied. Zhou would pass on Kissinger's views to Hanoi, yet he could not impose anything on the North Vietnamese; in fact, as long as the fighting continued, Chinese aid to North Vietnam would continue. Still, Zhou would encourage the North Vietnamese to negotiate and he would tell them of the United States' lack of interest in future political developments in Vietnam. He would, in other words, pass on Kissinger's trade-off: the United States would withdraw its remaining troops in exchange for a return of POWs and, most important, an interval before the political and military subjugation of the South Vietnamese government by the North Vietnamese and their southern allies.

On June 24, Kissinger returned to Washington. He paid little attention to a minor news item regarding a break-in at the Democratic National Committee's headquarters in the Watergate building on the Potomac River (the failed break-in and arrests had taken place in the early morning of June 17). Instead, he got Nixon's approval to resume the Paris negotiations with North Vietnam. Within days, the next Kissinger–Tho session was scheduled for July 19. Kissinger also met with Soviet Ambassador Dobrynin, giving him an upbeat account of his recent travels and lambasting the North Vietnamese for their behavior. Dobrynin promised that the Soviets would try to lean harder on Hanoi.[10]

Meanwhile, on June 29, Nixon announced the removal of another 10,000 American troops from Vietnam and proclaimed that in the future only volunteers would be sent to Indochina. Few men would volunteer. The last ground combat troops, the Third Battalion of the 21st Infantry, exited Vietnam on August 23, bringing to a close the Vietnamization process Nixon had initiated three years earlier. For all intents and purposes, even as the peace talks continued, America's war was irresistibly winding down.[11]

* * *

While Kissinger was in Washington, his North Vietnamese counterparts were once again seeking advice from Zhou Enlai. In early July both Xuan Thuy and Le Duc Tho visited Beijing. On July 7, Thuy briefed Zhou on the prospects in Paris. Hanoi was continuing to prepare for two possible outcomes, either a successful agreement "on the basis of reasonable negotiations" or continued fighting. Zhou did not put undue pressure on Thuy. But he did suggest that all depended on whether the Americans showed "a less rigid attitude in the four crucial months from July to October of this year." Five days later he was more forceful with Le Duc Tho, who was stopping at the Chinese capital en route to Paris. Although it was "necessary to prepare for fighting," Zhou said, "you have to negotiate." The discussion then turned to the North Vietnamese demand for a tripartite coalition government for the South and the future role of Thieu. Zhou assured that the PRC would not recognize the legitimacy of Thieu's government, but said, "we can recognize him as a representative of one of the three forces in the coalition government."

Zhou went on to describe his reading of the solution that Kissinger had outlined two weeks earlier. It was necessary to get an agreement now in order to ensure the final exit of American troops; if giving Thieu a role in a coalition government in the South was the prize for that, so be it. After all, once the Americans were gone and should the talks between the three forces in the proposed coalition government (Thieu, PRG, and neutralists) fail, then "we will fight again." Tho was taken aback. "But we still think of a government without Thieu," he told Zhou. This would naturally be the eventual outcome, the Chinese premier maintained. However, in the current situation it was impossible to ignore Thieu, particularly since the Americans were unlikely to go ahead without his ultimate consent. Perhaps, Zhou suggested, "you can talk directly with Thieu and his deputy, thus showing that you are generous." Le Duc Tho persisted. If Thieu does not resign, "we will not talk with the Saigon government." For Tho the key point was to get the American side to accept "the principle of the establishment of a tripartite government." If they did this, then Hanoi would be ready to accept general elections.

Zhou summed up his view with a prophetic remark: "the question is to play for time with a view of letting North Vietnam recover, thus getting stronger while the enemy is getting weaker."[12]

What further advice Le Duc Tho may have received from the Soviets or the Chinese prior to arriving in Paris is unclear. One can, however, reasonably conclude that the Chinese in particular were leaning on the North Vietnamese to conclude an agreement that would allow for the final exit of American forces. To be sure, they did not use exorbitant pressure; the Chinese were also concerned about losing Vietnam to the Soviets. Indeed, while pressing for serious efforts in the Paris negotiations, both Beijing and Moscow continued their economic and military aid (although the Soviet equipment was far more sophisticated) to North Vietnam. Thus, the North Vietnamese could rest assured that concluding an agreement with the United States would not mean abandoning their ultimate goal of unification; they would only be accepting an "interval." That said, the North Vietnamese knew better than to rely on either Beijing or Moscow for guidance. Memories of the 1954 Geneva Agreements—a poor agreement the Vietnamese felt had been forced upon them by their erstwhile Soviet and Chinese allies—still resonated in the collective historical memory of Hanoi's leadership. And promises of an interval suspiciously resembled the agreement of 1954 that had guaranteed nationwide elections in 1956. They had learned the hard way.

Kissinger, for his part, assumed that both Moscow and Beijing were more interested in their new relationship with Washington than in their competition over influence in Southeast Asia. This seems to have been a partially false assumption. To be sure, in 1972 the two major communist powers had separated U.S. military action against their ally in Vietnam from the pursuit of summit diplomacy with Washington. But at the same time China and the USSR were engaged in a continued effort to outmaneuver each other in Vietnam. With the Americans' exit becoming increasingly imminent, regardless of the role that the Soviets or Chinese played, Moscow and Beijing wished to remain on good terms with Hanoi. Zhou, Brezhnev, and other leaders in China and the Soviet Union knew that Kissinger and Nixon were ready to accept a decent interval. The question was how to be in the best position once that interval emerged and once the struggle for Vietnamese unification began. The Chinese were eventually outgunned, but in 1972 the result was still very much up in the air.[13]

PARIS—WASHINGTON—SAIGON

On the appointed day and time—11:00 A.M., July 19—Kissinger arrived at the now familiar apartment at 11 rue Darthé for what turned out to be a six-and-a-half-hour meeting. After initial banter and Kissinger's warning that the North Vietnamese should not try to "manipulate" the American election, Kissinger presented some new points that reflected his discussions with Zhou Enlai the previous month. Instead of demanding, as he had during their previous encounter on May 2, that the North Vietnamese troops had to leave the South as part of an agreement, Kissinger was willing to accept a ceasefire-in-place. Washington was also ready to remove all of its remaining troops within four months after a ceasefire was signed, provided that American POWs were released simultaneously.

Tho did not bite. What about political questions? What about the question of Thieu's resignation?

Tho's minor concession was that Thieu was the only one in the current government that had to go; the others could participate in the type of a three-way coalition Tho and Zhou had spoken about a few days earlier. Given that Kissinger had not mentioned a number of the issues he had discussed with Gromyko in May and with Zhou in June—including Thieu's resignation and a three-party electoral commission—Le Duc Tho was either confused or, more likely, understood that Kissinger was simply starting a negotiation with his maximum position. So the North Vietnamese responded in a similar manner. Indeed, the two sides' assessments of the meeting were strikingly similar. Le Duc Tho thought "in general, the U.S. indicated that it wanted a solution, but it still explored our cards and gave nothing new." Kissinger, meanwhile, wrote to Nixon that while the North Vietnamese "have said nothing which precludes their returning strictly to their old positions, they were about as positive in this first session as we could expect."[14]

After he returned to Washington, Kissinger made sure to brief both Dobrynin and China's UN Ambassador Huang Hua on the Paris talks. As there was little to report, neither the Chinese nor the Soviets—as far as the available documentary evidence indicates—got involved in the negotiation process.[15] Kissinger also cabled Ambassador Bunker in Saigon a vague assessment of the meeting to be passed on to President Thieu. The major implication of the July 19 meeting, Kissinger wrote, was that the North's "non-polemical approach and ambiguous positions are compatible with serious negotiations." While promising little, Kissinger was cautiously optimistic: "The minimum we achieve is building a reasonable negotiating record. The maximum we could gain is either a fair settlement or a temporary ceasefire." The end was not near, he cautioned, but "we are in a good position to explore the chances." According to Bunker, Thieu thought that this was pretty much what could be expected from the North at the time. Disappointed about their military reverses, the North Vietnamese Politburo was, Thieu said, "in the process of considering what course to follow ... it will be another one or two months before we can expect them to come up with concrete proposals."[16]

He was not completely off the mark.

*　*　*

Kissinger and Tho returned to the negotiating table on August 1. According to Kissinger, this meeting gave clear indications that the North Vietnamese were willing to make concessions. Kissinger tabled a twelve-point program that offered, as he put it, "nothing new"; Le Duc Tho, however, considered the American position slightly "more flexible." He was referring to: (1) Kissinger's proposal for a presidential election in the South within six months of a final agreement; (2) the idea of a trilateral electoral commission (PRG, neutralists, and the current South Vietnamese government) that would oversee such an election; and (3) the possibility that Thieu would resign two months (rather than three as in earlier proposals) prior to the election. All this showed some flexibility in the American position.

For his part, Kissinger was apparently elated not only by the sudden hospitality of the North Vietnamese—there was more fruit, cookies, and other snacks available during a break—but their apparent willingness to separate some of the issues, including the particulars of the ceasefire and troop withdrawals. Le Duc Tho dropped a previous demand for an unconditional date for American troop withdrawals (not that there were many troops to withdraw). Nor did he insist that Thieu had to be excluded from a coalition government.

In fact, Kissinger thought that the meeting had been very encouraging. Anticipating even more progress at the next session, Kissinger scheduled a trip to Saigon immediately after his upcoming August 14 meeting in Paris. Still, he guarded his optimism. "Tell Thieu," Kissinger cabled to Ambassador Bunker in Saigon on August 3, "that I cannot visualize a cease-fire situation for at least six weeks and probably well beyond that."[17]

Back in Paris on August 14, the two sides exchanged numerous written proposals. Kissinger gave Tho three documents: a general statement of U.S. principles, a ten-point plan answering all North Vietnamese proposals save the political solution, and a procedural document. Tho rejected Kissinger's suggestion that the secret meetings should focus purely on military questions. Political issues could not be left to the public plenary sessions, he insisted, but only for signing the final agreement. Tho also pressed for Washington's acceptance that the United States had a responsibility "to heal the war wounds in Vietnam"—a controversial point that basically amounted to North Vietnamese demand for reparations payments. The two sides were still far apart. Kissinger and Tho then agreed to meet again on September 15.

Both men headed for Vietnam. Le Duc Tho flew to Hanoi to discuss the latest prospects with his fellow Politburo members, while Kissinger departed for Saigon (with a stopover in Switzerland to celebrate his parents' fiftieth anniversary).[18]

The purpose of Kissinger's August trip to South Vietnam was to assure that America's allies would not create trouble, that they would not interfere in the negotiations that were to decide their fate. On August 17, he tried to convince Thieu that the time to settle had arrived. The military situation was more advantageous for the South than it had been in a long time, Kissinger explained. It had prompted Le Duc Tho to push for a favorable agreement. Thus, the American-South Vietnamese side held good cards and Kissinger would not use them in a way that would undermine the Saigon government. Nevertheless, it was necessary to give something on the political side of the negotiations. Kissinger assured Thieu that he would flatly reject the idea of a coalition government; instead, he would suggest a three-party electoral commission—something he had already proposed to the Soviets and the Chinese. This would be called the Committee of National Reconciliation (CNR). Kissinger further stated that he "would like to accept their proposal that there be no ceasefire until all is done."

Thieu saw an American betrayal in the making. For two days the president and his advisers grilled and criticized Kissinger in meticulous detail. Gradually, Kissinger wrote in his memoirs, it became clear to him that Thieu was simply not ready to accept a deal that would force him to compete politically with his foes in the South; Kissinger failed to mention that this "political" competition was bound to be seriously affected by the presence of North Vietnamese troops. Moreover, Thieu was probably convinced, based on experience from the previous U.S. presidential elections, that postponing an agreement beyond the November polling day would be to his benefit. Should the favorable military trend continue—and Kissinger's promises of enhanced aid did little to suggest otherwise—Thieu's government would have more control over the post-ceasefire political settlement. In fact, Kissinger's own words probably encouraged Thieu to stay the course. Instead of threatening the South Vietnamese president with a possible loss of U.S. assistance, Kissinger assured Thieu that the United States was "prepared to step up the military pressure on the DRV immediately, drastically, and brutally one or two weeks after our election . . . If we can move quickly after the elections, we can destroy so much that they will not be in a position to harm you for a long time to come."[19]

In short: accept a deal before the U.S. presidential election and the Nixon administration will make sure that Saigon will be in a preponderant military position by the end of 1972. Clearly, Kissinger was playing on all sides in a desperate effort to achieve a peace settlement before Americans went to the voting booth. But, as he indicated to Thieu, direct American military pressure would no longer provide a long-term solution for Saigon. An exit was imminent.

After Kissinger left Saigon he heard little from Thieu for almost a month. On August 31, Nixon—or Kissinger in Nixon's name—sent Thieu a message that urged him to stand behind the proposals that Kissinger was about to present in Paris. On September 13, two days prior to the next Kissinger–Tho meetings, the South Vietnamese president responded by soundly rejecting the CNR idea. Although not a coalition government in name, the CNR was, Thieu pointedly noted, tantamount to accepting the principle of power sharing with his southern foes (the PRG). That was unacceptable. Kissinger, who learned the news while in Moscow, argued that it was "imperative to table our plans as they now stand." He did not have the time (or the interest) to go back to Saigon for another session with Thieu. Moreover, he worried that the Chinese and the Soviets would call Kissinger's credibility into question. If, against all odds, the North Vietnamese did accept, "then the fact that GVN was not on board to the last detail will be obscured by the myriad of other complexities in what will essentially be a new ballgame." Nixon accepted the argument. But he insisted that Kissinger establish a hawkish record in his forthcoming meetings with the North Vietnamese in Paris. Not for the first or the last time the South Vietnamese president's views were ignored.[20]

Kissinger was also growing doubtful about Soviet influence on Hanoi. During his brief trip to Moscow and Leningrad in early September, most of the discussion had focused on the further development of Soviet-American détente. Still, it certainly provided an opportunity to describe to Moscow the proposals Kissinger would make in Paris a few days later, a fact that was undoubtedly passed on to Hanoi. But Kissinger's estimation of Soviet influence had sunk fairly low. As he explained to Bunker, the Soviets "clearly want the war to end but do not know what more to do." Sure, Brezhnev and others were "obviously interested in pursuing our bilateral relations without letting Vietnam interfere."[21] However, given all the preparatory work in Moscow and Beijing, Kissinger now faced a new challenge: to assure that the agreement with North Vietnam would be acceptable to the Soviet Union and China. Haig had, under Kissinger's instructions, pressed the point to Nixon that "the important thing is to be able to keep Moscow and Beijing in a position where they cannot claim that we deceived them or are proceeding in our efforts to solve Vietnam in a way which is unacceptably damaging to their interests."[22]

In other words, while the Soviets and the Chinese were not interested in having Vietnam obstruct their respective relationships with the Americans, the United States should not embarrass Beijing or Moscow. A speedy completion of a peace agreement would be the surest way to this end. Thus, the more Thieu resisted, the more he became an obstacle to the conclusion of the peace agreement in Vietnam and the smooth progression of triangular diplomacy. Under the circumstances, Kissinger's efforts helped to enhance Saigon's diplomatic isolation much more so than Hanoi's.

* * *

Soon the situation got even more complicated. On September 15—the same day Kissinger met with Le Duc Tho in Paris—the ARVN scored a significant military victory by recapturing the city of Quang Tri (capital of the northernmost province of South Vietnam). While it did not turn the tide of war, the South Vietnamese victory may, in part, explain why Kissinger found Le Duc Tho's demeanor accommodating when he sat down for another six-hour meeting in Paris. But the fact that Kissinger included a CNR in his new proposal must also have given Hanoi an additional incentive to settle. Tho also made a concession. He presented a modified political plan that allowed for the Saigon government to continue running domestic policy in the areas it controlled. A Government of National Concord (GNC) would be in charge of foreign policy and observe that the various provisions of the agreement were respected. In areas not under Saigon's control (which applied, in Tho's view, to most of South Vietnam), a series of tripartite CNCs would be in charge. Although both sides rejected each other's proposals, Kissinger suggested another meeting in ten days' time. Tho agreed. He then suggested that they set a target date for a final agreement. Kissinger was willing. Shaking hands, the two men agreed on October 15 as their deadline.[23]

Progress with Tho, however, necessitated further pressure on Thieu. Kissinger's subsequent assessment of the situation to Thieu, spread over two long telegrams to Ambassador Bunker, was mixed with optimism and threats. The North Vietnamese, Kissinger cabled Bunker, "displayed extreme eagerness to settle quickly through their most conciliatory tone to date." They had repeatedly requested "a timetable for negotiations and a deadline for overall agreement which they hoped could come within weeks." Yet, "the unacceptable core of their position remains," Kissinger added, and he had "made it very clear that they would have to modify it." He had "tabled only our substantive proposal" which, Kissinger evasively remarked, "was in the framework of our consultations with the GVN." The North was clearly "hurting" and "anxious for a settlement," which would mean that Kissinger needed to make "no new concessions." What it all boiled down to was that Kissinger was making compromises that he knew would be unacceptable to Thieu. Thus, it was necessary for Bunker to "speak quite sternly" to the South Vietnamese president and insist that he "show greater understanding of the tactical situation and confidence in our motives and moves." Thieu, in short, needed to put his trust in Kissinger's negotiation skills and accept the outcome. In fact, Kissinger wrote, "I believe that over the past weeks we have bent over backwards to meet GVN concerns to the point of threatening to undermine our strategy." Lastly, Bunker had to impress on Thieu the need for secrecy. "Tell Thieu in whatever way you believe most appropriate that we will not take kindly to any leaks [about the state of the negotiations] or aspersions on our good faith," Kissinger advised, adding that if such leaks emerged Saigon was "running the greatest of risks."

"This is not 1968," Kissinger concluded.[24]

Significantly, Kissinger gave no details about his discussions with Tho and did not reveal the October 15 deadline. The reference to 1968—similar to one he occasionally used while talking with the North Vietnamese—was to underscore the point that (unlike four years earlier) there was no point in playing games with American electoral politics. Encouraged by the promise of progress in Paris, Kissinger was clearly anxious that the South Vietnamese president might sabotage the agreement.

As Kissinger prepared for his September 26 and 27 meetings in Paris, Thieu's public behavior remained his major concern. On September 20, the South Vietnamese president publicly declared that "no one has the right to negotiate for or accept any solution" on behalf of his government. In two subsequent telegrams Kissinger told Bunker to try and put a lid on Thieu. "Thieu must recognize that his comments get global attention and can seriously complicate our position," Kissinger wrote on September 21. The next day he added: "in the sensitive period facing us it is essential that Thieu stay close to us so that we demonstrate solidarity to Hanoi." That he had to send such warnings to an allied leader was, of course, an indication that little solidarity remained.[25]

Nor was Thieu the only complication in Kissinger's increasingly anxious pursuit of a rapid settlement. In August–September Nixon began to have second thoughts about the negotiations and their impact on the presidential election. On the margins of Kissinger's cautiously optimistic report on the August 14 meeting with Le Duc Tho Nixon scribbled: "It is obvious that no progress was made and that none can be expected. Henry must be discouraged." Nixon was worried that the decision to announce each secret meeting *after* it had taken place (a decision the North Vietnamese grudgingly accepted) was raising hopes that could end up hurting him if no agreement was concluded by mid-October. "The mere *fact* of private talks helps us very little," Nixon noted, while "disillusionment about K[issinger]'s talks *could* be harmful politically."

Over the next two months the tension between the president and his national security adviser became palpable. Essentially, it reflected Kissinger's determination to hammer out a peace deal prior to the November elections and Nixon's concern that the wrong kind of peace agreement might hurt him politically. On the one hand, Nixon could not accept an agreement that would lend itself to charges that the United States had sold out Thieu. Moreover, the president worried that almost any peace deal reached before November would be viewed as a cynical election ploy. He even worried that continuing the talks in Paris beyond mid-September would be presented in this manner. This, Al Haig cabled Kissinger on August 15, was a point that John Connally had successfully impressed on Nixon. On the other hand, the Democratic presidential candidate George McGovern's calls for an immediate peace agreement demanded a serious rebuff. It was particularly important to distinguish Nixon's "peace with honor" from McGovern's "peace by surrender" campaign (as Nixon liked to call it).

In the end, Nixon continued to waver over the pros and cons of the Vietnam negotiations. As one historian puts it, he simply "wanted to keep his options open."[26] To Kissinger, however, the only option was a successful end to the negotiations with Le Duc Tho. Notwithstanding Nixon's skepticism and Thieu's objections, he continued on the set course.

THE OCTOBER AGREEMENT

In Paris, Kissinger found the venue much improved. Instead of a shabby apartment, the two delegations met on September 26 at a villa fifteen miles outside of Paris. The house was former property of the French painter, Fernand Legér, who had donated it to the French Communist Party in his will. Kissinger presented a ten-point plan and Tho responded with his revamped version and a protocol that one of his aides, Luu Van Loi, had recently brought from Hanoi. After taking the customary two hours to agree on the schedule of the talks, Kissinger and Tho got down to business.

Both sides were eager for serious discussions. Over the next two days, they narrowed a number of differences. On the political proposals, for example, Tho was willing to drop the idea that his proposed provisional GNC—a loose coalition government set up of representatives from the PRG, the Thieu government, and other southern representatives—would have responsibility over foreign affairs. Moreover, he was willing to agree that decisions in the tripartite body (that would still have to exclude Thieu himself) were to be on the basis of unanimity. The GNC would have little real power; its function would be to mediate between the CNCs—that would hold local political power in the areas controlled by either the Saigon government or the North's southern allies—and Thieu's government. Although Kissinger was not willing to undercut Thieu by effectively legitimizing the PRG's claim to political power in large areas of South Vietnam, he thought that the proposal was otherwise close to what he wanted. On other issues there were also signs of compromise and give-and-take. Kissinger hinted that the three-month American troop withdrawal period could be shortened if other issues were settled; Tho indicated that his side might not insist on the release of political prisoners held by Saigon if political questions and the issue of U.S. reparations could be agreed upon. At the end of their two-day bargaining session, Kissinger and Tho agreed to reconvene on October 8 for a three-day session.

Le Duc Tho volunteered that the session would be "decisive."[27]

Upon returning to Washington Kissinger lay the ground for his final peace offensive. The first step was to get the president, busy with his reelection campaign, on board. On September 28 Kissinger, Haig, Nixon, and Haldeman had another one of their dinner meetings on the presidential yacht *Sequoia*. Kissinger oozed optimism. He could close the deal with the North Vietnamese during the next series of negotiations. An announcement of the settlement could then be made "sometime between the 20th and 30th of October." A ceasefire-in-place and the start of the POW exchanges would follow in November. Nixon remained skeptical. But the possibility that the North would be less eager to make concessions after the election, and the consensus around the table that present policies could not be continued indefinitely made Nixon relent. Kissinger had a green light to go ahead. Nixon had only one significant proviso: Thieu needed to be on board.[28]

Therein lay the rub. On September 26, while Kissinger and Tho were engaged in their latest tête-à-tête in the outskirts of Paris, Thieu had given Ambassador Bunker a memo that, once again, emphatically stated the South Vietnamese position. Having learned that the Americans had not taken his September 13 objections seriously, Thieu stressed the need to "Vietnamize the peace": to initiate direct negotiations among the Vietnamese themselves. Moreover, Thieu warned that if the Americans were to deviate from the South Vietnamese position he would go public.

This got Kissinger's attention. He tried to buy some time by cabling to Bunker that he saw "practically no possibility of a settlement between now and November unless Hanoi totally reverses its position." The ambassador, who was also obviously kept in the dark, was to tell Thieu: "what we must look to now is how to best insure that we keep the situation under control in this interval and best position ourselves for post-November strategy." To discuss such strategy was, Kissinger added, the purpose of Haig's trip to Saigon in early October. For good measure Kissinger, once again, told Bunker to caution Thieu "against any public characterization of [the Kissinger–Tho] private talks or any other comments that might sabotage the scenario which we have pursued."[29]

*   *   *

When Al Haig arrived in Saigon, he faced a disillusioned President Thieu. After a cordial meeting on October 2, Thieu refused to see Haig the following day. On October 4 he let Haig have it. In front of his entire National Security Council Thieu ranted and raved about American betrayals and Kissinger's arrogance. He had "gained the impression that Dr. Kissinger does not deign to accept GVN [Government of Vietnam] views, but wants to go on his own." Later, Thieu returned to his theme: "if Dr. Kissinger plays the role of middleman, he will be confirming that the GVN is a lackey of the U.S."

Yet, he might as well been talking to a wall. The North's refusal to talk with the South and Kissinger's belief that ultimately he had to play the middle man if any negotiations were to take place made it inevitable that the terms discussed in Paris did not reflect the views of the Saigon government. Indeed, a central structural flaw in the peace talks was simple: the American negotiator (Kissinger) was bargaining on behalf of the South for a goal—American withdrawal—that was ultimately against the South's interests.

At the end of the meeting Thieu gave Haig a memo to Nixon that summarized Saigon's refusal of Hanoi's proposals and insisted that it was up to the South Vietnamese government to negotiate a military solution with Hanoi and a political solution with the Provisional Revolutionary Government.

In principle it was a reasonable argument. In practice it did not stand a chance.[30]

While Haig was in Saigon, Nixon and Kissinger debated the next step. Thieu's attitude, if made public, would easily give the appearance of an American betrayal of their South Vietnamese ally. This would inevitably hurt Nixon's credibility among the voters in the United States by undermining the claim that the administration was working to produce a peace with honor. In the weeks prior to the election, such publicity was the last thing the president wanted. However, refusing to negotiate was certain to result in a North Vietnamese media blitz and provoke further accusations that the administration was unnecessarily prolonging the war. Caught in this dilemma, Nixon gave Kissinger the green light to continue with the Paris talks. But uncertainty prevailed. The October 8–12 meetings, Kissinger estimated, had at best a 50 percent chance of producing an acceptable agreement.[31]

To maximize the chances of success Nixon and Kissinger exerted some extra pressure on the Soviets and the Chinese. The president told Soviet Foreign Minister Andrei Gromyko (who was visiting Washington in early October) that the United States would have to use "other methods" if Hanoi did not accept Kissinger's forthcoming offer. "If the other side said no," Nixon warned, "the negotiation track was closed." Kissinger, meanwhile, passed on the same message to the Chinese. On October 3 he gave Huang Hua the rundown of his last discussions with the North Vietnamese, informed the Chinese that Haig was in Saigon meeting with Thieu, and said that the offer he would make Tho in a few days' time would be the last one. "If rejected," Kissinger added, "we have to conclude that a political solution is impossible." Once again, he stressed that it was not advantageous for the North to postpone because after the November elections the Nixon administration would be in a much stronger position. In this respect, the message to the North, as well as to the South, was strikingly similar: don't play games with American domestic politics.[32]

For good measure, Kissinger also drafted a letter, in Nixon's name, to Thieu. Nixon assured that in the next round of Paris talks Kissinger would "explore what concrete security guarantees the other side is willing to give us as the basis for further discussions on the political point which might be undertaken following consultations with you." He then asked Thieu to sit still and "avoid taking precautionary measures against developments arising from these talks." Nothing would be agreed, the letter stressed, "without full, timely and complete consultation between us."[33]

* * *

His back thus apparently secured, Kissinger—adding Haig, because of his recent encounter with Thieu, to his entourage—arrived in Paris for the October 8 meeting with Le Duc Tho. After initial exchanges, Kissinger tabled an American proposal. It included relatively little new, save some cosmetic changes in the description of the functions of the Committee for National Reconciliation. After Kissinger had finished, Tho called for a lunch break and then asked for some extra time to confer with his colleagues. When they returned to the negotiations at 4:00 P.M. on that Sunday afternoon Kissinger faced, as he later wrote, "the moment that moved me most deeply" in his entire diplomatic career.

What Tho had to propose met, in Kissinger's mind, Nixon's basic demands. The North Vietnamese were ready to separate political and military questions. They did not demand Thieu's removal (in part because they rejected the American offer of presidential elections in the South) and offered a ceasefire-in-place and the return of American POWs within two months after the signing. The remaining U.S. troops were to be withdrawn during the same period. Tho also called for a bombing-mining halt twenty-four hours after the agreement was signed. Most important, Kissinger argued in his memoirs, Le Duc Tho had even further watered down his previous political proposal. He now suggested an "Administration" (rather than a "Government") of National Concord that would be left with little real political power. This tripartite (Saigon government–PRG–neutralists) body would operate on a unanimity principle (thus giving Saigon a veto), supervise the implementation of the agreements, work toward reconciliation, and arrange elections. But the Saigon government and the PRG would, in the meantime, control the areas they occupied.

"The political structure of South Vietnam," Kissinger wrote in his memoirs, "was left to the Vietnamese to settle."[34]

True enough. But while the proposal was very much in line with the discussions Kissinger had held with the Soviets and the Chinese, it was hardly a complete reversal of previous North Vietnamese positions. One could argue that the main new element in Hanoi's political position was completely cosmetic: they had simply changed the term *Government* into *Administration*. While much of this may still have met many of Nixon's conditions, it did not even approximate Thieu's demands. Most significantly, the ceasefire-in-place allowed North Vietnamese troops to stay in the South and effectively legitimized the PRG's political control of large parts of the South. Realizing the grave implications of this for Saigon—and in part to show Thieu his candor—Kissinger, while haggling with Le Duc Tho over the next few days, advised the South Vietnamese president to seize as much territory as possible. In fact, accepting the presence of the PAVN in the South was hardly part of the basic program of May 1971 that Le Duc Tho had, according to Kissinger, now accepted. Nor did the agreement provide more than a vague formulation regarding warfare in neighboring Laos and Cambodia. In those "euphoric" days of October 8–12 Kissinger chose to ignore such loopholes and imperfections. It was time to close shop.[35]

At this stage of the negotiations Kissinger also chose to act as the lone cowboy of American diplomacy; a reference to himself he later slipped to the Italian journalist Oriana Fallaci (thus driving Nixon into an uncontrollable rage). In practice, this meant that Kissinger's and Haig's telegrams to the White House were exceedingly brief and ambiguous, indicating only that progress was being made. The cables sent to Washington during the October 8–12 meetings in Paris described the negotiations alternatively as being "at a crucial point" or as "complex and sensitive." On October 10 Kissinger telephoned Haldeman from Paris stressing the need for "everybody to keep quiet." The Americans in Paris "know what they're doing," he insisted.

Kissinger later gave two less than convincing explanations for this need for added secrecy. First, since there was no Vietnam expert left in Washington to advise Nixon (because Kissinger had taken all of his advisers with him and Nixon could hardly turn to the State Department without jeopardizing the continued obsession with secrecy), sending detailed messages to the White House could only elicit a confused or misguided response. Second, and more astonishingly, Kissinger argued that Nixon himself was prone to leaks! Suspecting that the president might show an interesting cable to anyone who happened to walk into his office Kissinger did not, he wrote in *White House Years,* "think it desirable to put before Nixon's political advisers the temptation to risk four years of negotiations for a fleeting headline." It was an interesting reversal of fortune and logic, although one might suspect that slightly different motives were at work. Kissinger's interest in keeping to maximum secrecy was probably as much linked to his willingness to claim full credit for the agreements as it was to his concern about leaks. There could, after all, be no better way to make him indispensable amid the constant jockeying for influence in the Nixon White House. In addition to the tough negotiations with the North Vietnamese, Kissinger was, in effect, fighting for his own survival. He was determined to survive the inevitable reshuffling at the start of Nixon's second term.[36]

The breakthrough sessions ended on the morning of October 12. Kissinger and Haig flew back to Washington while Winston Lord stayed for another day to complete the collating (and translation) of the documents with the North Vietnamese.

The same evening, Washington time, Haig and Kissinger met Nixon in the president's EOB hideaway office. With Bob Haldeman as the only additional participant, Kissinger argued that the treaty he had achieved was far better than expected: Thieu would stay in office with a ceasefire-in-place by the end of October. Since the agreement stipulated the withdrawal of U.S. troops and return of POWs in sixty days, all would be done by the end of the year.

As Kissinger explained the details of the draft agreement, Nixon's initial skepticism turned into excitement. When Kissinger mentioned that one part of the agreement would be an American economic aid program to North Vietnam, the president concluded that this "admits the failure of their system" and would give Washington "leverage" over Hanoi in the future. This was precisely the reason the PRC had refused any such offers, Nixon added.

As had been the case so often in the past four years, celebration quickly gave way to scheming. Nixon, Kissinger, Haig, and Haldeman discussed ways of maximizing the political effect of the forthcoming announcement. Secrecy, as in the case of

Kissinger's secret trip to China the previous year, was essential; premature leaks should be avoided until Kissinger had completed the next stage of the Vietnam endgame: concluding negotiations in Paris followed by trips to Saigon and, finally, Hanoi. If all went as planned, Nixon would be able to announce the agreement on October 26. In the meantime, information about the talks and the details of the agreement should be shared selectively, if at all. In particular, Kissinger argued that the secretary of state should be cut out of the process until the eve of Nixon's announcement. As Haldeman noted in his diaries: "Kissinger wants to be sure there's no responsibilities assigned to Rogers."

To be sure, even Kissinger understood that the State Department needed to be somewhat involved in the dramatic process that was unfolding. Thus, he proposed taking Deputy Assistant Secretary of State Bill Sullivan with him for the concluding stage of the negotiations. Sullivan was "Henry's man," according to Haldeman, and acted formally as Kissinger's deputy during the tour from Washington to Paris and Saigon that commenced a few days later. Sullivan was also a former ambassador to Laos and hence no lightweight when it came to Indochina. Even as "Kissinger's man," however, Sullivan—in much the same manner as State Department members during and immediately after the February 1972 trip to China—was assigned duties less central to the mission. He would brief the Laotian and Thai leaders on the negotiations and lead the technical discussions on the last phase of the agreements.[37]

Kissinger had only three full days in Washington before departing for Paris. Aside from worrying about keeping the details of the negotiations secret from most of his compatriots, Kissinger used this time to ensure that the Soviets and Chinese remained on board. On October 14 and 15 he pressed Dobrynin about the crucial importance of some of the outstanding issues. In particular, Kissinger wanted a Soviet assurance that they would limit their military aid to Hanoi after an agreement was reached. Dobrynin, while emphasizing that the Soviets were "doing our utmost" to promote a peace settlement, gave no assurance that such linkage was going to materialize. In fact, Dobrynin managed to inject some doubts in Kissinger's mind; the Soviet ambassador showed Kissinger a copy of the North Vietnamese version of the draft agreement that contained some differences in the translation. Considering the Chinese impact at this point only "marginal," and in part because of the time pressure, Kissinger only sent a note to Beijing asking the PRC to reduce its arms shipments to North Vietnam. There was no reply. Indeed, that the United States had suddenly escalated its aid to South Vietnam (in Operation Enhance Plus, which began on October 26), the Soviets and Chinese could hardly have been impressed by Kissinger's pleas.[38]

*   *   *

At 11:00 A.M. on October 16, after a breakfast meeting with Haig, Kissinger took off for another one of his whirlwind tours. He expected it to end with an announcement no less dramatic than the one made in July 1971 after the secret trip to China.

It started off well enough. In Paris on October 17 Kissinger and Xuan Thuy—Le Duc Tho was in Hanoi waiting for Kissinger's potential arrival in a few days' time—put the last touches on an agreement that, Kissinger claimed, "killed" Hanoi's political program. While they could not agree on the question of the replacement of military equipment and a number of technical details, Kissinger flew to Saigon in a fairly optimistic mood. He cabled Nixon that "we have come out of this meeting well," and was certain that the North Vietnamese would not object to a possible delay of a few more days. He could only be further encouraged with news from Washington that Nixon was growing enthusiastic as all of his key cabinet members and military advisers—Laird, Abrams, Rogers—were lining up behind the agreement (while in Paris, Kissinger had consented that Haig show the political draft agreement to Rogers and Undersecretary of State U. Alexis Johnson). Having reviewed the political draft they agreed that it amounted to a "complete surrender" by Hanoi. The only worry was that the supposedly secret agreement was being shared among a growing circle of foreign policy makers. Press leaks, raising public expectations, were becoming endemic. Kissinger did not hesitate to blame the State Department and ordered Haig to "tell Johnson that if he does not keep Rogers under control we will cut him out of everything from now on."[39]

By this time, though, Haig was no longer the loyal deputy he may once have been. In a discussion with Haldeman on October 17, Haig expressed concern over Kissinger's overtly enthusiastic attitude. He agreed with Nixon that Kissinger was driven "by a desire for personally being the one to finally bring about the peace settlement." Haig also told Haldeman that this was probably making Kissinger "push harder for a settlement and to accept a less favorable thing than he might if he didn't have this push." In order to assure that Kissinger did not "feel that he has to prove anything," Haig counseled giving "every possible evidence to him of total support." He also worried, Haig added, that Kissinger might be willing to go to Hanoi even if the agreement were not completely settled. Haig was clearly proving himself a worthy member of the Byzantine structure that was the Nixon White House; a skill that would earn him the questionable honor of serving as Nixon's last White House chief of staff.[40]

Kissinger soon discovered that Haig's skepticism about Thieu's attitude was well founded.

Once in Saigon Kissinger did not immediately rush to meet with Thieu. Instead, he held long consultations with Ellsworth Bunker, Charles Whitehouse (Bunker's deputy), General Creighton Abrams (commander of the U.S. forces in Indochina), and Phil Habib, a veteran diplomat currently serving as the U.S. ambassador to South Korea but with extensive experience in Vietnam.[41] With the exception of Whitehouse, who believed that Thieu would need a considerable period of time to prepare his people for the agreement, all were optimistic that the South Vietnamese president would go along. What they were unaware of at the time was that Thieu had already seen a North Vietnamese version of the draft agreement reached in

Paris earlier in October. The North Vietnamese Politburo had distributed a document called "General Instructions for a Ceasefire" to their cadres in the field. As the South Vietnamese simultaneously stepped up their efforts to grab additional territory, a copy of the document was captured in Quang Tin Province and quickly flown to Saigon. Worst of all, the document went beyond a summary of the provisions regarding U.S. withdrawal, ceasefire-in-place, the North's access to the South for the purposes of resupplying their troops, and the National Council of Reconciliation and Concord; it also laid down a three-phase strategy for the Vietcong that consisted of maximizing its territorial holding prior to the ceasefire and working to undermine Thieu's government immediately afterward. Although the captured document was undoubtedly partly aimed at shoring up Vietcong morale, Thieu was now convinced that he had been sold down the river in Paris. He was determined to resist.[42]

The meetings in Saigon were undoubtedly Kissinger's most humiliating diplomatic experience. In his memoirs, Kissinger wrote that his "strategy was working everywhere with dazzling success—except with our own allies in Saigon." For Thieu did not budge. Between October 19 and 23 he grew gradually more critical, resisting not only Kissinger's arguments but also the letters that arrived from Nixon and were supposed to strengthen Kissinger's hand. No amount of cajoling and threatening helped. Thieu blamed the United States—not entirely incorrectly—for having "connived with the Soviets and China." He asked if Nixon needed the peace agreement to assure his reelection (which Kissinger denied). His people, Thieu added, would assume that accepting the right of the North Vietnamese to remain in the South meant "that we have been sold out by the US and that North Vietnam has won the war." When Kissinger called the course that Thieu was taking "suicidal," the South Vietnamese president responded: "if we accept the document as it stands, we will commit suicide—and I will be committing suicide." As a last resort on the morning of the 23rd (his farewell call to Thieu) Kissinger made a clear-cut threat: "if the war goes on at its present rate in six months US funds will be cut off." Plagued by a chronic fear of assassination (and memories of the fate of Ngo Dinh Diem in 1963), Thieu did not relent. The only thing he would agree upon was to avoid a public quarrel.[43]

Before leaving Saigon—for the last time in his career—Kissinger agreed with Thieu that he would present Le Duc Tho the amendments (sixty-nine of them). The previous day he had already cabled to Hanoi (via Paris) that, unlike previously planned, he was not going to visit the North Vietnamese capital. In a classic understatement Kissinger wrote that he was returning to Washington for further consultations because "the difficulties in Saigon have proved somewhat more complex than anticipated." On the day of his departure he sent yet another cable suggesting that the North Vietnamese set a date for one more meeting in Paris.[44]

The October Agreement was dead.

"WE NEED SOME ASSISTANCE"

Back from Saigon and worried that the North Vietnamese would respond in some other way than compliance, Kissinger met with Huang Hua to request Chinese support. After eliciting a polite laughter from Hua by saying that he had "achieved the unity of the Vietnamese—both of them dislike me, North and South," Kissinger asked for China's help "in the rather complicated state that our negotiations have reached." He summarized his meetings in Paris and his recent trip to Saigon. In a telling remark Kissinger surmised that while the North Vietnamese have "behaved very correctly," it "has not proven possible to obtain agreement in every respect" from Thieu. His suggestion was to hold yet another meeting with Le Duc Tho. Kissinger could not accept the North Vietnamese position that the agreement had to be signed by the end of October because the United States could not have a standoff with Saigon prior to the presidential election on November 7. Again asking for Zhou Enlai's good offices, Kissinger pledged that if the North Vietnamese "agree to this procedure there would certainly be peace during the month of November, and we would make an obligation towards them, but also towards you, whose relations we value so highly. And we would undertake that obligation not only towards them but towards you." However, should the North Vietnamese "insist that we sign on October 30 an agreement whose first article says the U.S. with the concurrence of South Vietnam, whose concurrence we do not have, then we are engaging in an empty exercise which cannot succeed." Kissinger went on:

> The changes we shall propose [to the North Vietnamese] will be mostly on language and one of some symbolic importance. It would enable us to return to Saigon and claim we have taken their views into account. It would certainly be considered a very important gesture by us if the Prime Minister would indicate his experience with our reliability. Because it is obvious that the war is nearly concluded, it would be tragic if negotiations broke down now.

Uncharacteristically, Kissinger even came close to apologizing to the North Vietnamese via the Chinese. "Perhaps I made a promise somewhat too optimistically which we cannot fulfill for reasons which are out of our control," he said. If Hanoi felt that it had been "tricked," Kissinger added that he wanted "to assure you that this was not the case."

In fact, Kissinger was so desperate to salvage the agreement he had spent three years negotiating that he proposed a secret deal on the issue of North Vietnamese forces in South Vietnam. While Thieu wanted the PAVN out, Kissinger thought that all that was needed was a symbolic gesture, say the removal of PAVN forces from the area 20 kilometers south of the border between the two Vietnams. This would not be written into the agreement and the North Vietnamese "wouldn't have to admit their forces are in the South nor change the military situation very much, but it would satisfy the political requirements of the situation." He was not demanding that the agreement reached two weeks earlier be reopened, Kissinger further added. Some cosmetic gestures were necessary, however, in order to "*give Saigon a psychological feeling of having participated.*" Lastly, he warned that, should Hanoi make the agreements public, "a settlement would be delayed indefinitely."[45]

On the same day as Kissinger met Hua in New York, the Soviets urged Kissinger to go to Hanoi and "complete the whole matter." Although trying to assure Moscow, via Dobrynin, that the United States would guarantee that the president "would keep his word and honor the Paris agreements" even after the election, Brezhnev's reply offered no further assistance at this point. Dobrynin summed up the general secretary's attitude: "We cannot have minor considerations of procedure or prestige gaining the upper hand and ruining the whole business."[46]

* * *

At 3:00 A.M. on October 26—two days after his meeting with Huang Hua—a distressed Kissinger called Bob Haldeman. The North Vietnamese had made the peace agreement public and accused the Nixon administration of dragging out the talks in order to uphold Thieu. It demanded that the agreement be signed on October 31.[47]

A coincidence? Or had the substance of Kissinger's meeting with Huang two days earlier been passed on to Hanoi only to convince the North Vietnamese that Kissinger was double-dealing and that their best option was to publicize the talks in the hopes of diplomatically isolating the South even further? After all, the prospect of an agreement before Nixon's reelection had now effectively passed. In any case, one thing was clear: neither the Chinese nor the Soviets were going to (or were able to) deliver at the time.

The North Vietnamese publication of the agreements required an immediate response. Since the news was bad, Nixon was not bound to take the heat; it was Kissinger's time to squirm. In a press conference that same day Kissinger made perhaps the most famous and soon-to-be most controversial of his public comments. It was, in fact, his first news briefing on live national television; the White House public relations people had not considered Kissinger's accent particularly soothing to the average American and he had been confined to giving press briefings with no TV cameras (pictures, obviously, had been allowed).

The news conference on October 26 was special for another reason. If all had gone according to plan, it would have been Nixon standing in front of the TV cameras and announcing that a peace agreement had finally been concluded. Instead, it was Kissinger, visibly nervous, briefing the White House press corps on the state of affairs. His opening remarks included the soon-to-be notorious statement, "we believe that peace is at hand." As far as firsts go he could not have been more dramatic. Unfortunately for Kissinger, as Hanoi refused an early return to the negotiation table the following day, the "at hand" would turn out to

Kissinger at his first National Security Council meeting, January 21, 1969. He would soon overshadow both Secretary of State William Rogers (right of Nixon) and Secretary of Defense Melvin
Laird (left of Nixon). (Photo courtesy of the Nixon Presidential Materials Project)

Kissinger appeared on the cover of *TIME Magazine* eleven times.

Upper Left: "New Approaches to Friends and Foes," *Time,* February 14, 1969. *Time* introduces "Presidential Adviser Kissinger" to the American public as a hardworking and brilliant policy maker ready to move U.S. foreign policy in new directions.

Upper Right: "To Peking for Peace," *Time,* July 26, 1971. *Time* features Kissinger propelling Nixon to China after the announcement of Kissinger's secret trip to Beijing a few days earlier.

Lower Left: "On the Brink of Peace," *Time,* October 30, 1972. Just prior to the 1972 election, *Time* features Kissinger publicly announcing that peace in Vietnam was "at hand."

Lower Right: Men of the Year, *Time,* January 1, 1973. This cover drove Nixon—who was growing increasingly jealous of his assistant's favorable media coverage—mad.

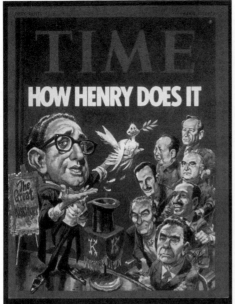

Upper Left: "How Henry Does It," *Time,* April 1, 1974. Following Kissinger's successful mediation of an Israeli-Egyptian disengagement agreement, *Time* portrays him as a magician pulling peace doves out of his hat.

Upper Right: "Mideast Miracle," *Time,* June 10, 1974. After Kissinger produced an Israeli-Syrian agreement, *Time* duly recorded the event on its cover.

Lower Left: "American Jews and Israel," *Time,* March 10, 1975. Kissinger, the most famous Jewish American of his time, is pictured wearing a traditional Arab head garment to illustrate the conflicted attitudes of many American Jews toward Israel.

Lower Right: "Mideast—Is Peace at Hand?" *Time,* August 25, 1975. Kissinger's last *Time* cover seems to imply that Kissinger is tired of trying to bring lasting peace to the Middle East and hints that another war is just around the corner.

Nixon and Kissinger in the Oval Office, February 1971. (Photo courtesy of the Nixon Presidential Materials Project)

Nixon and his entourage meet the aging Charles de Gaulle, February 1969. Kissinger stands behind Nixon, with Secretary of State William Rogers to his left, and Nixon's principal domestic advisers John Ehrlichman and Bob Haldeman to his right. (Photo courtesy of the Nixon Presidential Materials Project)

Nixon and Kissinger with South Vietnamese President Nguyen Thieu during a meeting at Midway Island, June 1969. (Photo courtesy of the Nixon Presidential Materials Project)

Kissinger returning from the secret trip to China. He is seen here arriving at Nixon's Western White House in San Clemente, California on July 13, 1971. (Photo courtesy of the Nixon Presidential Materials Project).

Soviet Ambassador Anatoly Dobrynin is seen here with Kissinger and Nixon in San Clemente soon after the May 1972 Moscow summit. (Photo courtesy of the Nixon Presidential Materials Project)

Kissinger, Alexander Haig, and Nixon at Camp David, November 1972. (Photo courtesy of the Nixon Presidential Materials Project)

Kissinger initialing the Paris Agreements, January 21, 1973. (Photo courtesy of the Nixon Presidential Materials Project)

Kissinger is sworn in as secretary of state, September 1973. His mother Paula stands by her son during the ceremony. (Photo courtesy of the Nixon Presidential Materials Project)

Chairman Mao Zedong, Premier Zhou Enlai, and Kissinger during the latter's visit to the Chinese capital, February 1973. (Photo courtesy of the Nixon Presidential Materials Project)

Nixon, Kissinger, and Israeli Prime Minister Golda Meier during the latter's visit to the United States in 1973. (Photo courtesy of the Nixon Presidential Materials Project)

Kissinger and Haig in the White House following Nixon's resignation announcement, August 1974. (Photo courtesy of the Nixon Presidential Materials Project)

James Schlesinger and Kissinger in a National Security Council meeting, contemplating the proper response to the Cambodian capture of a U.S. ship soon after the collapse of South Vietnam, May 12, 1975. (Courtesy of the Gerald R. Ford Presidential Library)

Donald Rumsfeld and Kissinger, National Security Council meeting, May 1975. (Courtesy of the Gerald R. Ford Presidential Library)

Kissinger, Ford, and General Secretary Leonid Brezhnev at the Conference on Security and Co-operation in Europe, Helsinki, August 1975. (Courtesy of the Gerald R. Ford Presidential Library)

Kissinger pictured in a cartoon spoof of the famous Iwo Jima statue, December 1975. He would suffer another setback in the third world when the Ford administration's covert effort in Angola ultimately failed in early 1976. (Nicholas Garland in the *New Statesman*, 26 December 1975, Copyright (c) *Daily Telegraph*. Reprinted with permission.)

Kissinger with Ford, Brent Scowcroft, and George H. W. Bush, December 1975. Deng Xiaopeng is seated across the table from Kissinger. (Courtesy of the Gerald R. Ford Presidential Library)

Carter and Kissinger on the White House patio, August 15, 1977. During the presidential campaign, Carter attacked what was dubbed the Nixon-Kissinger-Ford Foreign policy. After his victory in November 1976, however, Carter began the long tradition of consulting Kissinger that all subsequent presidents have followed. (Courtesy of the Jimmy Carter Presidential Library)

become a rather lengthy period (eventually almost three months), causing pundits to brand his statement as a preelection gimmick. George McGovern wasted little time jumping on this bandwagon. On November 5 he called the statement "a deliberate deception designed to fool the American people for the sake of Republican votes." What the press conference had also managed to do—perhaps unwittingly because Nixon had ruled out a presidential briefing—was to give the impression that Kissinger was effectively running the show on the American side. As a result, Nixon's growing suspicions about being overshadowed by his national security adviser were fed yet further. Such concerns would be highlighted even more, when the Italian journalist Oriana Fallaci's famous interview in which Kissinger described himself as the "lone ranger" of American foreign policy ran in the *New Republic* in late November 1972. Observers were quick to point out the implications of such a statement: if Kissinger were the Lone Ranger, then Nixon must have been Tonto.[48]

* * *

As press speculation about the possibility of a peace settlement and the nature of the Nixon–Kissinger relationship intensified, Kissinger pressed Hanoi to set a date for another meeting. He turned, yet again, to the Soviets and the Chinese. Kissinger assured the Soviets that an agreement was still within reach and denied accusations that the differences between Washington and Saigon—now so plainly obvious to all sides concerned—were "manufactured."[49] Four days prior to the election Kissinger, who had received several critical notes from Beijing, made yet another plea to the Chinese. Arriving late for a meeting with Huang Hua in New York, he admitted to being too optimistic about the peace talks but insisted that no "foul play" or "crooked dealings" had been involved. The Americans had not tried to "diddle-daddle" the North Vietnamese in order to push the final agreement beyond the U.S. election. Kissinger stressed that after the election "*we will have freedom of action*, not against Hanoi because we have that now, but *against Saigon*." He then betrayed how uncertain the situation was by launching into a long litany of changes that were necessary. Whereas on October 24 he had spoken about a few technical changes and "two substantial ones," there now were four substantive changes and "maybe 8 other technical ones." The four substantive ones turned out to be six (having to do with the ceasefire, administrative clauses, demobilization, future reunification, and the withdrawal of some North Vietnamese troops from the South). Probably aware that such a growing set of demands hardly boosted his reputation as a reliable negotiator Kissinger, unlike in his previous meeting with Huang, even resorted to threats. Should the North Vietnamese continue to attack the United States, they would only make the situation a "matter of prestige." Moreover, "to the extent that the Chinese side repeats these charges this will in time affect our relations which as you know have been one of the central elements of our foreign policy." As a carrot of sorts Kissinger then employed the Soviet threat. In the future Washington was ready to restore its relations with the DRV and offer reconstruction aid "to prevent other big countries further away from having a foothold." To sum it all up, Kissinger said:

> We need some assistance. We are caught in a dilemma between our honor and our intention. There is no sense trying to force us into acting dishonorably. Our interest is to normalize relations in Indochina and to accelerate dramatically the normalization of our relations with the People's Republic, and we know the two are linked. We know they are related ... now that we are heading for a new term we don't want to have to begin with a war in Vietnam and with disagreements between us.[50]

The day after he met with Huang, when Kissinger flew with Nixon to California on the last campaign trip of the election, the North Vietnamese finally responded. After the usual zigzags they eventually settled on November 20 as the date when talks would resume in Paris.

By then Nixon had been reelected with approximately 61 percent of the popular vote (against McGovern's 38 percent) and by winning forty-nine states. Although Nixon was slightly dismayed that his victory fell short of the trouncing that Johnson had given to Goldwater in 1964, the result was, as Bob Haldeman put it, nothing short of "sensational." The turmoil about Kissinger's "peace is at hand" statement had not hurt Nixon (in fact, the announcement that negotiations were to be reopened was made after the election). But by raising expectations, the statement had certainly placed Kissinger and Nixon under pressure finally to deliver an agreement. Moreover, the entire episode had strained the relationship between the two men to such a degree that Kissinger's future in the second Nixon administration looked rather bleak. On November 17, as Kissinger was getting ready to leave for Paris, Nixon told Haldeman to "think in terms of Kissinger's leaving." Having already told—or have Haldeman tell—Rogers that he could not stay on past June 1, 1973, Nixon was probably hoping to commence his second term with a new, fresh, and more unified foreign policy team. Tired of the endless bickering between the secretary of state and the national security adviser, having achieved successes with China and the Soviet Union, and with a clear mandate from the American people, Nixon was looking forward to another four years in the White House assisted by a fresh foreign policy team that would not be divided and would permit Nixon to solidify his public persona without sharing the spotlight with anyone. Kissinger, in part because of his successes, had become expendable. According to Haldeman, Nixon "doesn't think that we should keep him (Kissinger) on very long after Vietnam is settled." He would eventually have to change his mind.[51]

BOMBS FOR PEACE

"The North Vietnamese surprised [Kissinger] by slapping him in the face with a wet fish," Nixon wrote in his diaries on December 9 as the latest round of Tho–

Kissinger negotiations was reaching a dead end.[52] Two weeks after Nixon's land-slide reelection Kissinger, Le Duc Tho, and Xuan Thuy had returned to Paris. Between November 20 and December 12 they met numerous times. But the talks soon became deadlocked as Tho responded to Kissinger's (or Thieu's) proposed changes with some of his own (most significantly, that all political prisoners held by Thieu's government be released within sixty days). For three days they tinkered over details and on November 23 Kissinger delivered Tho another one of Nixon's bombing threats. It did not help. On the 25th Kissinger and Tho took a ten-day break. On December 4 Tho opened the meeting by offering to withdraw all of his new amendments and return to the original October agreement.

It was to no avail. In the absence of any significant concessions from either side Kissinger and Tho continued to haggle about such issues as Cambodia and Laos (the United States wanted a simultaneous ceasefire in these countries and the North Vietnamese maintained that their control over events in the neighboring countries was limited); the specific language used (e.g., "three Indochinese countries" or just "Indochinese countries"); and whether the National Committee of Reconciliation and Compromise should be referred to as "an administrative structure" or not. On December 13 the talks were once again broken off. While Tho flew to Hanoi and Beijing Kissinger returned to Washington in an agitated mood. Le Duc Tho and his companions were, Kissinger confided to Nixon, "just a bunch of shits," who "make the Russians look good, compared to the way the Russians make the Chinese look good when it comes down to negotiating in a responsible and decent way!"[53]

While he negotiated with such characters, Kissinger continued to engage the more "decent" Communists. In between his exhausting sessions with Le Duc Tho, Kissinger met several times with Huang Chen, the Chinese ambassador to Paris. He played, as usual, on Chinese concerns over Soviet influence. Kissinger repeatedly resorted to the same anti-Soviet mantra that the Chinese used when criticizing the possibility of a Soviet-American nuclear no-strike agreement. For example, on November 25, 1972, Kissinger pointed out to Huang Chen that the United States did not "want any for-eign powers that are far away establishing a military position" in Indochina. During a midnight meeting on December 7–8 with Huang, Kissinger stressed that a failure to reach a satisfactory agreement on Vietnam would make it virtually impossible for the United States to act against "the hegemonical desires of others."[54]

On December 13, though, Kissinger outlined two basic options for Nixon. He could either "turn hard on Hanoi and increase pressure enormously through bombing and other means . . . and concurrently try to line up Saigon." Or, the pres-ident could decide to wait until January, resume talks with the North, and, as in the first option, press the South into accepting an agreement. Nixon decided in favor of the first option.[55]

"War by tantrum," as the journalist James Reston called it, followed.

On December 18, 1972, the United States unleashed a massive eleven-day bomb-ing campaign that had no obvious military objective. That is, the 3,420 B-52 sorties that pounded Hanoi and other parts of North Vietnam during Operation Line-backer II (commonly known as the "Christmas bombings") were not responding to a sudden North Vietnamese offensive. Nor were the bombers attempting to cut off the Ho Chi Minh Trail. The key objective of Linebacker II, according to inter-nal instructions, was to make a "psychological impression" on northern morale. Thus, the bombings focused heavily on the key areas near Hanoi and Haiphong, inflicting heavy "collateral" (i.e., civilian) damage. Several residential districts were hit hard, at least one hospital was destroyed (along with a number of foreign embassies), and only an earlier evacuation of the bulk of civilians kept the number of those killed down to a "low" 2,200 (with another 1,500 wounded). For their part, Americans lost over a hundred crewmen and fifteen of the 129 B-52 bombers (12 percent) used in the raids. And even a U.S. Air Force survey later noted that the impact of the Christmas bombings on the morale of the North was minimal.

As in the case of Linebacker I in May, Kissinger had doubts about the Christmas bombings. He initially recommended that any renewed bombing campaign be more limited and not touch the areas north of the twentieth parallel (leaving Hanoi untouched). But once bombing began, he appeared, at least within the confines of the White House, happy with Nixon's policy of "brutal unpredictability."[56]

Reaction elsewhere, though, was furious. In addition to James Reston's quip, complaints of Nixon's ruthlessness and brutality were common themes in Ameri-can editorials. In Europe, all leading politicians and newspapers expressed horror at the sudden U.S. escalation of violence. Some, such as the Swedish Prime Minis-ter Olof Palme, even compared it to the Holocaust.

While hardly hurting morale in North Vietnam and only soliciting outrage at home and abroad, the Christmas bombings were received with some delight in Saigon. As many historians maintain, the goal of Linebacker II was to impress *both* Vietnamese sides. Given that the North had been willing to continue negotiations in any case, the major "target audience" was south of the seventeenth parallel. In a sense, the Christmas bombings were aimed at convincing President Thieu that the agreement that was still in the making, while not perfect, would not diminish American military support for his government. As became evident later Thieu would require more convincing. In particular, he would need further reminding that U.S. support was contingent on his willingness to accept the deal still in the making.[57]

The Christmas bombings made the Soviet and Chinese positions increasingly delicate. Brezhnev, for one, was in a potentially embarrassing position. On Decem-ber 18, the very day that Linebacker II commenced, the general secretary of the Soviet Communist Party was presiding over a large international gathering of socialist leaders who had come to Moscow to celebrate the fiftieth anniversary of the found-ing of the USSR. It was hardly a forum where one could act as Nixon and Kissinger's "messenger"; in fact, the North Vietnamese representatives pressed Brezhnev to use his new influence in Washington and press the Americans; the Soviet leader obliged by publicly stating that future progress in Soviet-American relations was dependent on "the question of ending the Vietnam War." Privately, though, the Soviets stressed the need to compromise. On December 23, 1972, the Soviet ambassador to Hanoi, Ilia S. Scherbakov, met with North Vietnam's Premier Pham Van Dong. Scherbakov patiently listened to Dong's angry complaints about the American bombings and joined in with denouncing the imperialist warmongers. But he then suggested that Hanoi should express to the United States its willingness to resume the talks in Paris. Three days later Hanoi followed Scherbakov's advice.[58]

The Chinese weighed in a few days later by pressing the need for a rapid conclusion to an agreement. On December 29 Mao fumed at the visiting foreign minister of the PRG, Mme Nguyen Thi Binh. Those who still opposed negotiations with the Americans, Mao said, were "so-called 'Communists'" and "bad guys." Two days later Zhou Enlai put the argument in more concrete terms. "It seems that Nixon is truly planning to leave Vietnam," he told Truon Chinh, chairman of the Standing Committee of the DRV's National Assembly. "Therefore," Zhou added, "this time it is necessary to negotiate seriously, and the goal is to reach an agreement." On January 3 he told Le Duc Tho, now on his way to Paris for the final round of negotiations with Kissinger, that

> the U.S. strategy of using bombing to put pressure on you has failed. Nixon has many international and domestic problems to deal with. It seems that the US is still willing to get out from Vietnam and Indochina. You should persist in principles while demonstrating flexibility during the negotiations. The most important thing is to let the Americans leave.

To entice Tho, Zhou then assured that this would only be a temporary solution: "The situation will change in six months or one year."[59]

Set against this context Kissinger's elaborate plea for Chinese help in the last stage of the negotiations was probably unnecessary. On January 3, Kissinger, even more clearly than before, stressed to Ambassador Huang that the United States would press Saigon firmly if Washington's "minimum conditions" were met. He again insisted that the Nixon administration was truly intent on moving toward full normalization of diplomatic relations with China. But it all depended on Vietnam. As Kissinger told Huang:

> What we would like to do—if it were not for the war in Vietnam—is to accelerate the normalization of our relationship with you ... You have been long enough in the US, and you will have some judgment as to which people in the US hold these convictions, and they are not very many. Therefore, the obvious consequences of discrediting the authority of the White House will go far beyond Vietnam, and conversely to get it finished would accelerate and enable us to concentrate on matters we consider to be of real priority ... Our major concern

in Indochina, which is not a central feature of our policy anyway, would be to cooperate with those who want to prevent hegemonies from being established there.

It was a telling remark, indicating how frustrated Kissinger had become over the negotiations that had lasted more than three years and how he liked to stress both the broader implications of the Vietnam War as well as the personal factors operating at the highest levels.

Huang's reply was laconic. Referring to the new talks in Paris he stressed that "if the US side truly wishes a settlement, this opportunity should not be missed."[60]

Kissinger and Tho did not miss it. After some back and forth the two sides agreed to begin low-level "technical talks" on January 3 while Kissinger and Tho would resume their dialogue five days later. By January 9 it was clear that a deal was emerging; on the 13th Kissinger and Tho concluded an agreement that retained the key principles of the October agreement. It still included the ceasefire-in-place and it still effectively recognized the PRG as part of the political settlement that was to be negotiated among the various South Vietnamese parties. Remaining U.S. troops would be withdrawn and American POWs returned by the end of March 1973. Kissinger and Tho initialed the pact on January 23 and Secretary of State Rogers was given the questionable honor of signing the Paris Peace Agreements four days later.[61]

As in October, the final test was to convince President Thieu that his time was up. Even as he prepared for the breakdown of the talks in Paris Kissinger cabled Bunker from Paris on December 13, 1972: "our urgent task remains somehow to bring Thieu to heel."[62] But the Christmas bombings had made the task even more difficult. The South Vietnamese president was no more eager to sign a replica of the earlier agreements; what Thieu expected was some significant modification, such as the withdrawal of North Vietnamese troops from the south. Ironically, Thieu was also in a stronger military position in early 1973 than perhaps at any time since the commencement of the North's Spring Offensive nine months earlier. The Christmas bombings and the enhanced military aid from the United States during the last months of 1972 could only raise his expectations regarding the political future of South Vietnam. Certainly, there seemed little point in voluntarily accepting the permanent presence of enemy troops in his territory. With no American elections around the corner and Nixon feeling pressured to conclude the Paris Agreements before his second term got truly under way, however, the South Vietnamese president had lost the political leverage he had possessed only a few months earlier.

It took a series of letters from Nixon and a visit to Saigon by a stern Al Haig—Kissinger would avoid Saigon for the rest of his career—before Thieu relented. Nixon promised massive aid and offered to send Vice President Agnew to Saigon in the near future. He further invited Thieu to visit the Western White House in San Clemente, California, two months after the signing. But Nixon also insisted that if Thieu rejected the agreement, Congress would probably refuse to grant any future aid to Saigon. Thieu finally bowed to such pressure; on January 21 he offered Ambassador Bunker "no comment except to say that he had done his best and all that he could for his country." He appeared "resigned" to his fate; a fate he had three months earlier described as "suicide."

Kissinger's reaction to the initialing of the Paris Agreements two days later was more upbeat. January 23, 1973, he cabled Bunker, was "a most rewarding day."[63]

A PEACE WITH HORROR

Rewarding though the initialing in Paris may have been, the record of the Nixon administration was hardly anything to be proud of. In the four years after Nixon's inauguration in January 1969, Americans had suffered more than 20,000 casualties (most of them in 1969–71). Their South Vietnamese allies had lost approximately 80,000 soldiers. Estimates (actual figures are impossible to determine) of North Vietnamese and civilian casualties throughout the region run up to half a million for the same period. The United States had dropped more than 4 million tons of bombs in Indochina since January 1969 (the total tonnage in all of World War II has been estimated by the Pentagon at about 2 million tons).

Nixon and Kissinger had not started the war. But the price for an American exit had been high.

Indeed, the six months leading up to the signing of the Paris Agreements were among the most bizarre in the annals of American statecraft and left an enduring mark on Kissinger's reputation. Two aspects in particular stand out. First, there was the scheming and the evident willingness to sacrifice America's South Vietnamese allies. In the end, Thieu had to be effectively blackmailed into accepting the agreement that ill-served his government's interests. Second, the tortuous peace-making in 1972—in particular, Kissinger's willingness to go along with the Christmas bombings—punctured the miracle man's image that had prevailed in the press after his journeys to Beijing and Moscow. Was Kissinger "just a good German lending a cover of respectability to whatever monstrous policy President Nixon is pleased to pursue"? Joseph Kraft asked in a column in the *Washington Post* in early January. The Christmas bombings assured that the question of morality would become a constant scourge in Kissinger's remaining years in office (and beyond).[64]

There had been military overkill and a chorus of domestic and foreign criticism. In Washington, New York, Paris, Moscow, Beijing, and Hanoi there had been triangular efforts and diplomatic intrigue that resulted in the return to the peace table. Finally, there was the bullying of an ally into accepting a treaty that more or less guaranteed its eventual downfall. It had not been pretty. There had been very little honor—and much horror—involved. And, as events would soon show, while U.S. relations with both the Soviet Union and China improved in the first half of 1973, there was not going to be even a temporary peace in Vietnam.

There was, though, at least one positive outcome. With the provision for a return of U.S. troops and POWs the Nixon administration had managed to make the Vietnam War into a relatively insignificant factor in U.S. domestic politics by early 1973. If in 1968 the country had appeared at the brink of a virtual civil war over the conflict in Southeast Asia, it was now eager to forget that such places as Hanoi and Saigon even existed.[65] Indeed, the gradual withdrawal from Vietnam in 1969–73— particularly as it was coupled with the drama of the opening to China and détente with the Soviets—and the subsequent return of American POWs, succeeded in diluting the preponderant impact of Vietnam on American political discourse. Put simply: no war, no antiwar movement.

Underneath it all, though, lay an uneasy sense of betrayal and lost credibility. In 1972–73 Kissinger had gradually given in—pressed by changing circumstances on the ground—to North Vietnamese demands. Through a series of communications with the Chinese and the Soviets he had made it clear that soon after the return of American personnel the United States was ready to abandon Southeast Asia to its own devices. He was not searching for a peace with honor but an exit strategy and a decent interval before South Vietnam's political future was determined. Pressed in part by domestic political considerations, Kissinger's complicated diplomacy thus managed to produce a remarkable role reversal: in 1972 it was South Vietnam's President Thieu, rather than Le Duc Tho or the North Vietnamese, who became the chief villain for refusing to accept an agreement negotiated over his head. Over the next two years the once steadfast allies would bear the burden of the end of America's "Indochinese nightmare." In 1973, the South Vietnamese would suffer more battle deaths than they had in any year since 1968.[66] The decent interval was to be covered in blood.

From the South Vietnamese perspective this amounted to a betrayal. Did Kissinger or Nixon anticipate that the Congress would, in subsequent years, make it impossible for the United States to provide such aid in adequate amounts? Hardly. Were they unaware of the political weakness of the South Vietnamese government if not propped up by massive American aid? Not likely.

Ultimately, the central point about the process that led to the Paris Agreements was unmistakable and reflected what mattered for American policy makers, and particularly for Kissinger, in the early 1970s.

This was the great game; the triangular relationship between the United States, the Soviet Union, and China. Within the context of that game Kissinger and Nixon shared the conviction that Vietnam was an irritant that needed to be removed by any means necessary. Moreover, Kissinger assumed that both Moscow and Beijing were more interested in their new relationship with Washington than in their competition over influence in Southeast Asia. This proved partially correct in the second half of 1972 as the Soviets and Chinese advised Hanoi to conclude an agreement with the United States. But it did not follow from this that either Moscow or Beijing was willing to abandon Southeast Asia to its own devices;

instead, both wished to outmaneuver the other in Vietnam. Zhou, Brezhnev, and others knew that Kissinger and Nixon were ready to accept a decent interval; the question was how to be in the best position once that interval emerged and the struggle for unification began. Even as they held summits with the Americans it was thus perfectly logical for the Soviets and Chinese to stay in as good terms as possible with Hanoi; after the Paris Agreements were signed, Indochina remained an arena of intensified Sino-Soviet competition in which the Vietnamese, Cambodians, and Laotians would continue to bear the heaviest burdens. Triangulation and the Paris Agreements did little to change that fact.[67]

The Americans left behind a situation ripe for further turmoil rather than even a tentative peace. After the American withdrawal, the entire subcontinent gradually descended into yet another vortex of violence that would only temporarily be concluded two years later. With the American presence gone, the competing interests of the various warring parties in Vietnam, Cambodia, and Laos as well as the growing Sino-Soviet interest in safeguarding their respective influence in the region only added fuel to the subcontinent's fire. The war was far from over in Indochina, that is, except for the participation of U.S. ground troops. In fact, Americans would continue to bomb until congressional resolutions banned further American military activity in any part of Indochina in August 1973.

In sum, the negatives of the Paris Agreements—and of Kissinger's overall encounter with Indochina—were numerous. The settlement itself was tenuous and open to immediate violations, particularly in areas of South Vietnam where North and South Vietnamese troops were in close proximity to each other. Kissinger's negotiation performance had not been particularly brilliant; it was his side that had made the most significant concessions. Neither the North nor the South had a particularly strong incentive to observe the agreement religiously. Cambodia and Laos were drawn deeper into the conflict in 1969–71; in 1973 they remained destabilized. Cambodia, which would feel the devastation of American bombs for another seven months, was headed for a human disaster with few parallels in modern history.

It was perhaps befitting that one of the few who expressed strong support for Kissinger's Vietnam policy in early 1973 was Robert S. McNamara, the man who, as Lyndon Johnson's secretary of defense had planned the escalation of U.S. involvement. "You are going to go down in history as the man who finally got us out of there," McNamara told Kissinger in early January 1973. "Henry, you know and I know that there is only one way to resolve this and that's to have conscious ambiguity in the damn thing . . . If it weren't for you I'd be deeply pessimistic about getting out of there."[68]

Kissinger appreciated the support. He did, indeed, get American forces out of Vietnam. But the "conscious ambiguity" that McNamara referred to meant leaving behind a subcontinent poised for further destruction.

12

Highs and Lows

The mood in the White House was somewhat subdued in early February 1973. With all of the accomplishments of the previous years behind them, Kissinger and Nixon could hardly expect that the New Year would bring with it anything equaling the feats just completed.

Yet, there was one obvious change that had taken place. Only three months earlier, in late November 1972, Nixon had contemplated firing Kissinger. In early February 1973, however, Nixon confided to his diaries that, far from having become redundant, Kissinger needed "another goal." Yet, the president was dismayed that his chief diplomat was reluctant to take on the Middle East.

Two things had taken place in the interim. The first was, obviously, Kissinger's role in negotiating the Paris Agreements. He had secured "three for three," as Kissinger had prematurely told Nixon in October 1972. Perhaps more important for Nixon's options, Watergate became, in January–February 1973, a constant scourge. Although the resignations of Haldeman and Ehrlichman, the testimony of John Dean, and the battle over Nixon's ability to prevent access to the White House tapes lay ahead, Nixon's own downfall had, in a manner befitting a life that resembled a Greek tragedy, already begun by the time of his second inaugural on January 20, 1973. Soon Watergate became a daily issue while other matters, including foreign policy, received less of the president's attention. After the conclusion of the Paris Agreements, Nixon became increasingly dependent on Kissinger for setting the overall direction of U.S. foreign policy.

Ironically, Kissinger appeared burned out in early 1973. As Bob Haldeman noted in his diaries on February 6, Kissinger "feels he's running down and getting bored." Most worryingly, Haldeman noted that Kissinger was "obviously not interested in taking the time to work out the details of the [Paris] agreement."[1]

Haldeman was on to something. In the spring of 1973 Kissinger's priorities lay elsewhere. Although he would remain connected to the events in Indochina, Kissinger had bigger fish to fry. In April, he proclaimed—rather disastrously as it turned out—1973 "the Year of Europe," a year when, freed from the distractions of Vietnam, the United States and its NATO allies would reinvigorate the transatlantic relationship. But such an initiative still paled when compared to the unfolding of triangular diplomacy.

"With conscientious attention to both capitals, we should be able to have our mao tai and drink our vodka too," Kissinger wrote to Nixon in early 1973.[2] Throughout the spring of 1973 the careful balancing of U.S. policy vis-à-vis the Soviets and the Chinese remained the major focus of his efforts. Kissinger oversaw the opening of liaison offices (mini-embassies with officially recognized representatives from the two countries that did not carry the formal ambassadorial title) in Beijing and Washington, bringing Sino-American relations as close to normalization as they would be until the formal restoration of diplomatic relations during the Carter administration. After Kissinger's visit to the Soviet Union in May, Nixon welcomed Leonid Brezhnev to the United States in June. While the Washington summit—and Brezhnev's visits to Camp David and the Western White House in San Clemente—did not carry the same PR value as its Moscow predecessor, détente appeared to be taking root firmly. Even as Watergate laid a dark shadow over the Nixon presidency—at the end of April its first major casualties included Bob Haldeman and John Ehrlichman—the broad outlines of Nixon–Kissinger foreign policy appeared, more or less, on track.

But, of course, there was Vietnam.

HANOI AND SAN CLEMENTE

In early February Kissinger left Washington for a tour of Southeast Asia that included stopovers in Thailand, Laos, and Cambodia. He would conclude the eleven-day tour with a series of discussions in the PRC. Significantly, while Kissinger included Hanoi in his itinerary, he would not visit Saigon—a snub that was hardly missed by anyone in Southeast Asia.

What made the snub more extraordinary was Kissinger's "eerie visit to Hanoi." Having experienced four years of endless bargaining mixed with emotional highs and lows as well as recurrent jetlag, Kissinger was not looking forward to a trip to an enemy capital. For the task was, effectively, a hopeless one: to ensure the "strict observance" of the Paris Agreements just concluded. Making stops in Thailand, Laos, and Cambodia, Kissinger tried to reassure the beleaguered American allies that the United States would not tolerate North Vietnamese violations of the peace agreement. In Cambodia, in an attempt to bolster Lon Nol's campaign against the Khmer Rouge and their North Vietnamese allies, American bombing (aimed initially at North Vietnamese supply routes, but gradually escalating to envelop large areas of the Cambodian countryside) resumed on February 9. It would continue unabated until August 1973. The war thus continued when Kissinger landed in Hanoi on February 10, 1973.

To him it was, Kissinger puts it in his memoirs, a moment "equivalent to stepping onto the moon."

This was in part because of the craters left by American bombs in the areas immediately outside of the North Vietnamese capital. In fact, due to the damage caused by American bombing, Kissinger and his entourage—which included Herbert Klein, director of communications for the White House; William H. Sullivan, deputy assistant secretary of state; and NSC staff members Richard T. Kennedy, Winston Lord, Peter Rodman, and David Engel—had to land at Noi Bai military airfield 50 miles north of Hanoi. They then transferred in to a light (Soviet An-24) aircraft, flew to Gia Lam airport closer to the North Vietnamese capital, and crossed the Red River over a pontoon bridge by car.

After settling in the guesthouse, Kissinger and his staff members took a brief walk around the North Vietnamese capital before the first meeting with North Vietnamese officials. Locals stared at Kissinger and his colleagues but expressed little interest—apparently he was not a household name in Hanoi. There was a large billboard showing a map of South Vietnam's "liberated areas" (the areas controlled by the North Vietnamese). Finally, they returned to the guesthouse. There was an aggravating moment: the guards demanded to see everyone's pass and Kissinger discovered that he was the only one in the group not to have one. The North Vietnamese would not let him enter; they had never heard of someone named Kissinger. Only Le Duc Tho's opportune arrival twenty minutes later allowed Kissinger entry to his room.

The trip did not get much better after that.

The February 10–14 negotiations in Hanoi focused on the upholding of the Paris Agreements and the promises—conditional in the American view but apparently unconditional in the view of Kissinger's North Vietnamese interlocutors—of U.S. aid for the reconstruction of Vietnam. On the issues that were linked to the various parts of the Paris Agreements, Kissinger, Le Duc Tho, and Prime Minister Pham Van Dong discussed, among other things, ceasefire prospects for Cambodia and Laos, the release of U.S. POWs, and the continued infiltration of North Vietnamese supplies into the South. Both sides accused each other for creating difficulties and the North Vietnamese explicitly refused to consider the Paris Agreements as anything but a temporary settlement. Needless to say, there was precious little the two sides could agree upon and Kissinger later vented his anger in his memoirs. Le Duc Tho and Pham Van Dong had "lost none of the insolence" that had been evident in Kissinger's haggling sessions in Paris. Clearly, as he listened to the North Vietnamese demands, Hanoi's leaders were unwilling to allow Kissinger's attempt to "encourage any tendencies that existed to favor peaceful reconstruction over continued warfare." In their "monomaniacal" devotion to hegemony in Indochina, the North Vietnamese "were too egotistical to think of foreign policy in terms of an international system; too arrogant to believe in goodwill; too ambitious to restrain their purposes by ideas of concord." As he reported to Nixon afterward, Tho and Pham Van Dong had refused to acknowledge any of the violations of the Paris Agreements; in fact, they pointed out, the ARVN had continued fighting virtually nonstop despite the ceasefire. What the United States needed to do, he wrote to the president, was to force Hanoi to make a choice: either it would need to abide by the agreement (that is, by the American interpretation of the agreement) or forget about U.S. aid. In short, the only, and very slim, hope was to "buy" Hanoi into accepting an agreement while threatening it with renewed bombing; the classic mix of incentives and pressures, carrots and sticks.[3]

The North Vietnamese, though, had reasons to feel confident. They had over 100,000 troops in the South and could expect continued support from the USSR and China. In fact, a day after Kissinger had initialed the Paris Agreements Zhou Enlai had congratulated North Vietnam's ambassador, Ngo Thuyen, and the PRG ambassador, Nguyen Van Quang, on the agreements. Zhou did not ask the two ambassadors to respect the terms of the agreements but instead ruminated: "The victory is easily won. As Prime Minister Pham Van Dong says, it is important to continue the struggle. The important thing is that the Americans have been driven away." It was time, though, to take a breather. A few days later Mao himself advised Le Duc Tho: "you need at least six months to stabilize the situation in South Vietnam [and] to strengthen your forces." Unification, in other words, was merely a question of time.[4]

In fact, already at the time of Kissinger's visit to Hanoi, the North Vietnamese leadership had ambitions extending beyond the unification of Vietnam. While they did not share such goals with the Chinese—who hardly considered it in their interest to have Hanoi establish regional hegemony—the North Vietnamese did apparently confide with the Soviets. In February 1973, the Soviet ambassador to Hanoi, Iliya Sherbakov, cabled Moscow:

> The program of the Vietnamese comrades for Indochina is to replace the reactionary regimes of Saigon, Vientiane, and Phnom Penh with progressive ones, and later when all Vietnam, and also Laos and Cambodia, start on the road to socialism, to move toward the establishment of a Federation of the Indochinese countries.[5]

Given such ambitions, it is not difficult to see why Kissinger's mission to Hanoi was doomed to failure.

*   *   *

Kissinger's principal interlocutor in Hanoi was Prime Minister Pham Van Dong. Born in 1906, Pham, like Le Duc Tho, was a veteran revolutionary, who had joined Ho Chi Minh's movement in the 1920s. In 1954, after the Geneva Agreements, he had become both the prime minister and foreign minister of the DRV (he relinquished the latter post in 1961). After Ho's death in 1969, Pham led the DRV until he resigned from the Politburo in 1986, and was replaced as prime minister in 1987. Kissinger described him as "wiry, short, [and] wary," yet a man he hoped would be more like Zhou Enlai than Le Duc Tho. His hopes were quickly dashed, however, Kissinger later wrote, as Pham Van Dong proved to be "of the stuff of which revolutionary heroes are made . . . while Zhou was of the stuff of which great leaders are made." Whereas he thoroughly enjoyed the sweeping philosophical and geopolitical encounters with Zhou, Kissinger found that "Pham Van Dong's strength was mono-maniacal absorption with the ambitions of one country."[6] It is hard to fathom how the prime minister of North Vietnam, a country that had been at war for the past two decades and was still looking forward to another bout of strife, could have been otherwise. In February 1973, though, it translated into a dialogue of the deaf.

The recently released record of the Hanoi meetings reveals how bizarre (or "eerie," as Kissinger called it in his memoirs) the trip was. After the Americans had settled in the government guesthouse, Kissinger met briefly with Le Duc Tho to discuss the agenda. Both agreed that the meeting was extremely significant. Kissinger suggested that one day they could "look back on this as the beginning of a new relationship." Tho agreed. "Between you and I," he said, "the period of tense sessions is over now."[7]

Such pleasantries quickly disappeared. On the afternoon of February 10, Kissinger opened his first encounter with Pham Van Dong by assuring that the United States was "no long-term threat" to Hanoi. He then went on to list the many violations of the Paris Agreements that had taken place in the three weeks following the signing ceremony in Paris. In an attempt at humor, Kissinger noted: "an analysis leads us to conclude that we have implemented the Agreements somewhat more strictly than has your side." Pham laughed. "I disagree with you on that point," he said. Kissinger went on to list "200 major violations and about 1900 minor violations" of the Paris Agreements, indicating that he had "indisputable evidence that on February 6 . . . 175 trucks crossed the DMZ . . . that over 200 tanks are heading in the direction of South Vietnam through Laos and Cambodia." He demanded a full accounting of the POWs/MIAs.

After a brief break—during which Kissinger and Pham informally stressed the need to make the meetings a success—it was the North Vietnamese turn to list complaints. Pham Van Dong stressed that Hanoi was implementing the Paris Agreements. It was the United States and Saigon, he argued, that were constantly violating it. In particular, Pham said, "we wonder whether the policy of Vietnamization of the war still continues in South Vietnam." The issue he stressed the most—and would come back to repeatedly over the next few days—had to do with U.S. aid to North Vietnam's reconstruction. This was, the North Vietnamese prime minister argued, "an obligation of the US in view of the destruction caused to our country." He added:

> I would like to lay stress on the moral and honor aspect . . . It is known to everyone that heavy damage has been caused by bombs and shells to the system of communication in our country, to seaways, highways, airways, many villages, railways, to the industrial system . . . This is a very significant question between our two countries. We should solve this so as to wipe out the past and open a new period in the relationship between us.

Pham went on to stress the need to move toward normalization of U.S.-DRV relations and the need for the Americans not to intervene in the political future of Indochina. Kissinger seemingly agreed. But he stressed that "we have to act as statesmen, with a long view and have some patience." On the question of U.S. aid, Kissinger stressed the difficulties involved in securing congressional approval and warned: "If you press us too hardly [*sic*] you will jeopardize what we want to do and what we will do."[8]

Subsequent talks produced little indication that the mutual hostility of the previous years was about to be transformed into some form of cooperation. Rather, they read like a catalogue of opposing arguments. On the morning of February 11, Pham Van Dong and Le Duc Tho matched Kissinger's charges of North Vietnamese violations by cataloguing Saigon's breaches of the Paris Agreements. Tho argued that only civilian goods were being sent to the troops in the South. "With tanks?" Kissinger quipped. As Tho and Pham continued to press for the United States to exercise influence on Saigon's behavior, Kissinger responded: "You cannot both want us out of Vietnam and expect us to exercise unlimited influence in [South] Vietnam."

The same afternoon, after visiting Hanoi's History Museum, Kissinger tried to impress the North Vietnamese with his command of French. "Vous avez une histoire très longue, très dure et héroïque," he volunteered. Pham Van Dong thanked him and added: "Et aussi très humaine. Très humaine."

His multilingualism duly proven, Kissinger went on to complain about the activities of the North Vietnamese troops in Laos. Pham denied the accuracy of Kissinger's intelligence; Laos was an internal Laotian matter, he insisted. "Did I get the number of [North Vietnamese divisions in Laos] wrong?" Kissinger sarcastically asked. When the North Vietnamese prime minister wanted to move on to other matters, Kissinger refused. He wanted some commitment from Hanoi to withdraw from Laos. After more fruitless back and forth, he finally exploded (with a hint of black humor):

> I must say this, even at the risk of not being very popular in Hanoi, which would grieve me deeply: Do you gentlemen seriously believe you can keep your forces in South Vietnam and Laos and Cambodia and expect us to implement every provision of the Agreement and start a new era in our relations? Can you really believe this? I assure you that this is not possible.

Pham Van Dong's response was telling: "Putting this question here now is not practical." He would, simply, not enter into a discussion on Laos.[9]

On the morning of February 12, Kissinger and Le Duc Tho had a similarly fruitless exchange on Cambodia. Kissinger again demanded the withdrawal of North Vietnamese troops. Tho declined. The North Vietnamese would not do so, he said, until a political settlement was concluded in Cambodia. Hanoi could not talk to Lon Nol, he added, saying that Prince Sihanouk—who had been living in China since he was ousted in the 1970 coup d'etat—would have to return to Cambodia. "In a word, we can not solve this problem," Tho said. "You should talk to the Chinese," he added.

Kissinger was getting increasingly anxious. "I am very upset at what you say about Cambodia," he insisted. "I can tell you now it is completely unacceptable to us. This is a very serious problem for our relations." But Tho grew even more belligerent. "There are many complexities [in the Cambodian situation]," he insisted. "You talk in a very simple way . . . You don't understand the problem. You are too simple."

Still, thirty years later, one can almost feel Kissinger's anger as he responded to this insult: "Maybe I am too simple, but I know what is possible and what is impossible. And I know that it is impossible to convince Americans that clear obligations in an agreement can be abrogated without any proposed evolution." But Tho only responded in kind: "You should understand me. Only when you understand me, can we find a solution."[10]

*   *   *

Ironically, the only issue that seemed to result in some form of an agreement had to do with U.S. aid to North Vietnam's reconstruction. During the peace talks Kissinger and Tho had agreed to $3.25 billion as a "target figure" for such assistance, and the Paris Agreements (article 21) included a statement to the effect that "the United States will contribute to healing the wounds of war and to postwar reconstruction of the Democratic Republic of Vietnam." Nixon, who clearly believed that North Vietnam's enthusiasm for U.S. aid was a major tool for moderating Hanoi's actions after the Paris Agreements, had later affirmed this commitment in a message to Pham Van Dong that was delivered on January 30, 1973. A general discussion on how the American assistance was to be delivered was then scheduled to take place during Kissinger's trip.[11]

The February 12 meeting on economic reconstruction was surreal. The White House, Kissinger said, was willing to push for the aid but it would require congressional approval. "I think our biggest problem is your lack of understanding of our government process," he added. "It is important for you to understand what is legally possible for us to do and what it is not possible to do." For example, it was not possible for the U.S. government to simply deposit a large amount of money to a North Vietnamese bank account. Kissinger then produced a booklet that discussed a number of issues, including the roles of the White House and Congress in approving and implementing foreign aid programs, the various aid programs in effect at the time, and the possible aid package to the DRV. "It is totally useless for us to discuss theories of why aid should be given," he added, "because until we get the money there is nothing we can do about it." Kissinger volunteered that in order to avoid a major congressional revolt the United States might take the money for DRV reconstruction from the defense budget. But in order to meet the target of $3.25 billion over the next five years, congressional approval would be necessary.

Pham Van Dong was seething. "I would like to express my suspicion," he said. "When the war was going on then the appropriation was so easy . . . when one is unwilling then the legal aspect is a means to this end. And I will not debate that the money will be taken from which budget . . . that is your affair." Kissinger was taken aback. "We have absolutely no interest to trick you," he maintained. But the matter would have to be sold to the Congress and thus required a major legislative effort. The point of all this was that "we cannot do it without your cooperation." The United States could find the technical ways of providing the money; it could be used in a manner the DRV thought most beneficial to its peaceful reconstruction; but "first, you should talk as little as possible about an American obligation, and you should never talk about 'reparation.' Our possibility for getting this money is enhanced if we do it as a voluntary act."

Kissinger and Pham Van Dong agreed to nominate members of a Joint Economic Commission by March 4 to discuss the details of the aid package. But Kissinger also stressed the continued need to keep the issue from becoming public. Those Americans participating in the Economic Commission—if they were not members of Kissinger's NSC staff—would certainly object to the type of deception he had outlined. Thus, if problems should arise, Pham Van Dong or Le Duc Tho should get in touch with Kissinger via the Paris channel.

Once again, Pham Van Dong laughed. But he also said, "We have settled one question this morning." Kissinger, referring to the violations of the Paris Agreements, responded: "We settled only half our question."[12]

The exchange—and seeming agreement—on economic reconstruction was revealing about both sides' motives and goals. Kissinger was, in fact, being sincere, if not even over-optimistic, about the difficulties of getting the U.S. Congress to allocate money for North Vietnamese reconstruction: should Hanoi not cooperate with the release of American POWs or continue military activities throughout Indochina, there was no realistic chance that the Nixon administration could—even if it wanted—assist the North Vietnamese. This fact, then, translated to the only major carrot that Kissinger had at his disposal. The point he made to Hanoi was, essentially, the following: if you live up to the agreements on South Vietnam, limit your engagement in Cambodia and Laos, and tone down your rhetoric, there is a chance that economic reconstruction will follow. Or, as Kissinger put it to Nixon:

> For [the North Vietnamese] the ideal course would be to follow both options at once: violating the Agreement to pursue their objectives and improving relations with us so as to get economic aid. Our essential task is to convince them that they must make a choice between the two.[13]

Over the next few months Hanoi would make a choice, but hardly the one Kissinger and Nixon would have hoped for.

* * *

What about South Vietnam? Kissinger had refused to visit Saigon in early 1973, but, at Nixon's request, Vice President Agnew traveled to the South Vietnamese capital at the end of January. In familiar tones Agnew praised Thieu's performance and promised him continued American support. But Agnew also indicated that U.S. involvement had its limits after the Paris Agreements. While he recognized Thieu's government as the only legitimate one and stressed that the Nixon administration did not approve of the presence of North Vietnamese troops in the South, the vice president was careful not to offer a resumption of American bombing. This reassurance had, however, been the critical point about Nixon's January correspondence with Thieu and, in the South Vietnamese president's view, the one redeeming feature in his relationship with the United States. Moreover, as the realization of another promise—a Thieu visit to Nixon's Western White House in San Clemente— also took longer than initially promised (instead of three to four weeks after the ceasefire, Thieu would go to San Clemente in two months' time, in early April), the South Vietnamese president could not but sense that his country's significance in U.S. policy had dramatically decreased.[14] In short, while trying to use the carrot of economic aid to restrain Hanoi, the Nixon administration was clearly indicating that the future of Vietnam (and Indochina) was not worth risking another major domestic uproar.

Ironically, these bombings—and the massive installments of American military aid in late 1972—had encouraged Thieu to go on the offensive. By the end of March 1973, just prior to Thieu's visit to San Clemente and the return of the last American POWs to the United States, there was not even a semblance of peace in South Vietnam but it was hardly clear who should bear the onus for breaking the Paris Agreements, Saigon or Hanoi. The Nixon administration stopped short of actual military action in Vietnam, but Kissinger and Nixon agreed on the need to continue bombing Cambodia as a way of reducing the continued infiltration of North Vietnamese materiel and men into the South. Washington and Hanoi exchanged protests of violations at regular intervals. As Ambassador Bunker put it on March 30, "the prevailing situation might be characterized as being neither peace nor war."[15]

Thieu's visit to the United States in early April 1973 virtually guaranteed continued warfare. In San Clemente, Nixon promised the South Vietnamese president "vigorous reactions" on the part of the United States should the North or the NLF violate the Paris Agreements. Hoping to capitalize on the Americans' willingness to ignore the ongoing South Vietnamese violations of the agreements and continued U.S. aid, Thieu, in fact, returned to a hero's welcome in Saigon and the ARVN continued to press its land-grabbing operations. Thieu was further encouraged by a U.S. Senate vote on April 5, banning any economic aid to North Vietnam without congressional approval. Pressed by the horror stories of returned American POWs, the Congress was on an anti-Hanoi rampage. Any question about economic aid to those who had jailed and mistreated so many Americans, in some cases for several years, was not going to resonate well—hence the Congress moved to remove the carrot from Nixon and Kissinger's post-Paris Vietnam policy. The American-North Vietnamese Joint Economic Commission that had begun its meetings in Paris in mid-March was called back home on April 17 (the same day that Nixon made his first significant statement on Watergate). Still, this hardly meant that the United States was now ready to turn back the clock and move aggressively. If anything, the American people were fed up with Vietnam and unlikely to accept either limitless American assistance to Saigon or, in the event the administration asked, reconstruction aid to Hanoi. Nixon, with his prestige reduced by Watergate, eventually decided not to resort to bombing against the North Vietnamese. The war was being truly Vietnamized.[16]

For the next two years, Vietnam would remain a constant irritant in Kissinger's otherwise constantly expanding foreign policy responsibilities. Yet, it is worth noting that despite the continuation of the war, Kissinger appeared determined not to allow Indochina to interfere with his pursuit of other objectives. In particular, he used the post–Paris Agreements respite to push ahead with the further development of triangular diplomacy.

FEBRUARY IN BEIJING

When Kissinger departed Hanoi on February 13, 1973, he was happy to leave behind "the most oppressive atmosphere of any foreign capital I have ever visited." His party flew to Hong Kong for a two-day rest. On February 15, Kissinger commenced his fifth visit to Beijing. The contrast to the eerie days in Hanoi could not have been more startling. Not only did Kissinger and Zhou engage in broad discussions about the state of the world but there was an agreement on the creation of special liaison offices in Washington and Beijing. The bilateral relationship, still in its infancy, was moving forward and becoming less of an ad hoc relationship. Yet, while the establishment of the liaison offices in the spring of 1973 made direct communication between Kissinger's office and an official Chinese representative much easier, suspicions of American motives were too deeply entrenched among the Chinese leadership to allow for significant movement in the actual substance of the Sino-American relationship. The Chinese, well aware of the planned Nixon–Brezhnev summit later in the year, remained particularly concerned over possible Soviet-American collusion against China.[17]

During his stay in the Chinese capital on February 15–19 Kissinger met again with Mao who, unlike a year earlier, was in rather good health. While smoking cigars the Chairman summoned Kissinger at short notice just before midnight on February 17 and engaged him in a friendly and wide-ranging two-hour discussion that focused on, in particular, the Soviet threat and the American presence in Europe and elsewhere. He opened, though, by pointing to the Paris Agreements on Vietnam that had, Mao surmised, "basically settled the Vietnamese issue." Kissinger eagerly agreed but also stressed the need for "a transitional period toward tranquility"—a euphemism for a decent interval. Clearly, the January agreements had removed, at least temporarily, a major irritant from Sino-American relations. What the United States and China now needed to do, Mao added, was to "work together to commonly deal with the bastard [i.e., the Soviet Union]." The Chairman added, "sometime we may want to criticize you for a while and you want to criticize us for a while." But that was no problem as long as "fundamental cooperation" existed. Discussion then turned to European affairs and both sides expressed concern about the possibility that Japan and the USSR were to establish closer relations.

In the midst of such banter Mao summarized the Chinese suspicion about the United States and its triangular diplomacy. Should the USSR attack the PRC, the Chairman ruminated,

> then you can let them get bogged down in China, for half a year, or one, or two, or three, or four years. And then you can poke your finger at the Soviet back. And your slogan will be for peace, that is you must bring down Soviet imperialism for the sake of peace. And perhaps you can begin to help them in doing business, saying "whatever you need we will help [you] against China . . ." Your aim in doing that would be to bring the Soviet Union down.

Kissinger strongly denied any such complicity: "We want to discourage a Soviet attack, not defeat it. We want to prevent it."[18]

Toward the end of their conversation Mao injected a reminder of his old age, perhaps in an attempt to push the speed of further reconciliation. "God has sent me an invitation," he told Kissinger.[19]

Given Mao's mixed message Kissinger did his best to convince Zhou that the United States was the strategic partner that China needed in order to deter Soviet ambitions. In what he called "the most candid and comprehensive accounts of our foreign policy that I ever made to any foreign leader"—in itself an admission that the continued improvement in relations with China was absolutely vital—Kissinger did his best to drive home the point that the Americans and the Chinese shared an interest in trying to contain Moscow's expansionism. For the Soviets, he told Zhou, détente with the United States was a mere charade. Moscow's flexibility was aimed "to demoralize Western Europe by creating the illusion of peace; to use American technology to overcome the imbalance between its military and economic capability; to make it more difficult for the US to maintain its military capability by creating an atmosphere of détente and isolate those adversaries ["such as China," Zhou added] who are not fooled by this relaxation policy." But the United States was not fooled by the Soviet "bastard," Kissinger insisted. The Nixon administration was going to build on the successes of the past four years by preventing the Soviet effort to shift the global balance of power in their direction. And therein, naturally, lay the common interest for the United States and China.[20]

It was virtually impossible to try and find the right balance within the triangle without alienating at least one of the two other players. Indeed, Kissinger's own memoirs betray some of the uncertainty of the approach: on the one hand, the United States did not want to become the American card that the Chinese could play against the USSR; on the other hand, Kissinger writes that "we had to resist the temptation of playing the China card in return." He told Zhou in February 1973 that the United States would continue pursuing détente but would always keep the Chinese fully informed on developments in Soviet-American negotiations and the treaties that were to be signed. From the Chinese perspective, however, such complex efforts could easily be interpreted differently. As Mao so forcefully put it, détente—whether the Soviet-American SALT I agreement or such European initiatives as West Germany's *Ostpolitik*—only encouraged the Soviets to push eastward and jeopardize China's interests. Kissinger's obvious reluctance to pursue European détente—including his dismissive stand toward the pan-European Conference on Security and Co-operation in Europe (CSCE) negotiations that had, after much American footdragging, commenced in Helsinki in November 1972—can be seen partly as a way of alleviating such Chinese concerns. Yet, with Vietnam seemingly fading into the background, the future development of triangular diplomacy was increasingly intertwined with a number of other global and regional irritants.

*   *   *

In February 1973, however, Kissinger was not discouraged. To be sure, he correctly noted that the Chinese suspicions may not have been "fully allayed" and the Chinese "will certainly watch our Soviet motives with wariness, and take out insurance with Japan and Europe." (Japan and China had restored full diplomatic relations after Japanese Prime Minister Tanaka's visit to Beijing the previous fall.) Yet, when Kissinger summarized the talks for Nixon in late February and early March, the national security adviser pointed out that the Soviet Union "was the centerpiece and completely permeated our talks." Consequently, Kissinger believed that "*with the exception of the United Kingdom, the PRC might well be closest to us in its global perceptions.* No other world leaders have the sweep and imagination of Mao and Zhou, nor the capacity and will to pursue a long range policy." Of course, Kissinger was wary of the fact that the Chinese leadership was old enough to be removed from the scene at a very short notice. Thus, he pressed the need to speed up the process of normalization, arguing that "before the present dynasty passes from the scene, we must strengthen bilateral ties, get our two peoples used to a closer relationship, and reach out to more layers of Chinese leadership so as to strengthen the advocates of an opening to America."[21]

Kissinger's sense of elation after the February 1973 visit was seemingly well grounded. His trip did, indeed, mark a time when the Chinese viewed cooperation with the United States as a key to countering the Soviet Union in no uncertain terms. Zhou Enlai, once again, summarized the Chinese views at a CCP meeting in March 1973:

> the entire strategic deployment of the Soviet revisionists is global, confronting not only the US but also us. While they simultaneously struggle against and collude with the US, they maintain completely antagonistic relations with us. This is the essence of the problem ... Our basic strategy ... is to oppose the two superpowers, chiefly the most direct, the most perilous and the most real enemy, Soviet revisionist social-imperialism.

What about the United States? Of course, Zhou lamented, "we must still condemn the US for whatever is reprehensible ... [but] of the two world superpowers, one is the most direct enemy. Now the US retires to the second position." Still, Zhou stressed that "we cannot propose 'uniting with the US to oppose the USSR' though we have points in common on certain issues."[22]

Even in the spring of 1973, a number of specific issues continued to plague Kissinger's efforts to bring about a true strategic partnership with China. The Sino-Vietnamese relationship was beginning to show the strain that would eventually lead to a war between the two countries. In this context, Cambodia was a particularly tricky issue. On the one hand, the United States continued to support Lon Nol's government and resumed its air strikes in the aftermath of the Paris peace agreement. On the other hand, the Chinese supported both Sihanouk (who had lived in exile in China since his overthrow in 1970) and the Khmer Rouge. In February Zhou and Kissinger agreed that they should promote a negotiated settlement based on the principles of "independence, peace, neutrality, unity and territorial integrity." At the same time, Zhou made it very clear that "Lon Nol will not do," and the issue became a typical one in the nascent Sino-American relationship: both sides agreed that a solution was needed but also agreed that they respected each other's divergent positions.[23]

They did, though, discuss an alternative scenario for Cambodia that held an eerie similarity to previous Sino-American discussions about a decent (or responsible) interval in Vietnam. Kissinger was ready to abandon Lon Nol provided an agreeable alternative solution could be found: "it might be possible to find an interim solution that is acceptable to both sides and I think, for example, the Lon Nol people would be willing to negotiate with the Chief Minister of Sihanouk here." Kissinger, pressed by Zhou, acknowledged that the "end result could well be without Lon Nol." After long exchanges on February 17 and 18, Kissinger and Zhou agreed to pursue a negotiated settlement that would effectively return Sihanouk as the head of state with an interim coalition government consisting of representatives from Lon Nol's cabinet and its opposition (including the Khmer Rouge). Naturally, Sihanouk's exile in China and the PRC's strong links with the Khmer Rouge more than implied that any such future government would owe a special debt to Beijing.[24]

Adding to the complications over Cambodia, Nixon decided to resume the bombing of the country in February; over the next four months more than 80,000 tons of bombs were dropped in a continued effort to use military force to gain a political solution in this beleaguered country. The Khmer Rouge and Sihanouk's refusal to negotiate with Lon Nol was at least in part a result of this action. Indeed, until the U.S. Congress passed a resolution to stop all bombing in June, the search for a peace in Cambodia resembled in an eerie way the unsuccessful efforts in Vietnam some years earlier.[25]

Another complex issue, more directly linked to the prospect of full normalization, was Taiwan. In the February talks Kissinger repeated the pledges Nixon had made a year earlier about withdrawing American forces from the island and not supporting Taiwanese nationalism. But he also went a step further by offering "to move after the 1974 [U.S. congressional] elections toward something like the Japanese solution with regard to diplomatic relations."[26] The Japanese had closed down their embassy in Taipei as they opened one in Beijing in 1972; his implication was that Washington was considering a similar move. Surely, Zhou could easily interpret it in such a way. Kissinger, unaware of the domestic turmoil in store, was thus raising expectations that would eventually be unmet.

Nevertheless, China and the United States did formalize their diplomatic contacts by establishing liaison offices in each other's capitals in the spring of 1973. With small staffs, the liaison offices acted as each country's official permanent representatives in the other country but lacked the formal stature that comes with an embassy. The new offices minimized the need for back-channel communications links via Paris, Pakistan, or any other far-away venue. Thus, the United States and China moved a step, however small, toward normalization.

Both missions were headed by seasoned diplomats whose experience, by coincidence, came mostly from various posts in Europe. In Beijing, the veteran diplomat David K. Bruce would head the U.S. Liaison Office (USLO). He had previously been ambassador to France and Britain; in July 1970 Nixon had introduced him to the press as his new point man for the Paris peace talks on Vietnam. Bruce was, as his biographer David Lankford puts it, also "an unsentimental realist" and one of those State Department veterans Kissinger got along with. Bruce would stay in Beijing through the remainder of the Nixon administration and, much like his fellow realist Kissinger, could not escape being charmed by Zhou Enlai. According to Bruce's biographer, the discussions with the Chinese premier, whose broad knowledge appealed to the urbane ambassador, were the highlight of Bruce's tenure in the Chinese capital.[27]

To Washington, the Chinese sent their ambassador to France, Huang Chen, whom Kissinger had met several times during his numerous visits to the French capital to broker the Vietnam peace agreement. In fact, after Kissinger's secret trip in July 1971, Huang had been his major contact with the Chinese until the arrival of Huang Hua as China's ambassador to the UN in October 1971.

Despite the new, more formal, arrangements, Kissinger kept the emphasis on back-channel style diplomacy. Bruce was told that he was "the President's man," not a regular diplomat reporting to the secretary of state. Meetings with Huang, while not completely secret, were a privilege in which only Kissinger and his inner circle would indulge. Once he became secretary of state, the special aura of secrecy that surrounded United States–China diplomacy would endure as would the hold that Kissinger had on China policy; after Al Haig became the White House chief of staff in the late spring of 1973, Brent Scowcroft, Winston Lord, and Richard Solomon would be the three key figures involved in U.S. China policy in Washington.[28] And yet, despite the apparent understanding that China had helped to bring about the eventual American extrication from Vietnam, despite Kissinger's numerous efforts to build an atmosphere of trust in his meetings with his Chinese counterparts, Nixon's scandal-filled second term saw disappointingly slow progress.

One of the major reasons was the—for the Chinese alarming—continuance of détente. As Kissinger stressed in his summary of the talks with Zhou Enlai, keeping the Chinese satisfied was a difficult task because the Chinese were most happy when the Americans confronted the Soviets. As he put it to Nixon:

> Mao and Zhou urged a more aggressive American presence—countering Soviet designs in various areas, keeping close ties with our allies, maintaining our defense posture. If the Chinese became convinced that we were heeding the inward impulses of voluble sectors of Congress, the public and the press, we would undoubtedly witness a sharp turn in Peking's attitude.

Thus, Kissinger concluded:

> We are useless for Beijing as a counterweight to Moscow if we withdraw from the world, lower our defenses, or play a passive international game . . . So long as you are president, Peking should certainly be convinced that we will be a crucial factor in the world balance.[29]

Yet, progress on détente was necessary, if only to divert attention away from Nixon's domestic troubles and to focus the American public's attention away from continued difficulties in Indochina. But there were conflicting pressures. On the one hand, it was necessary to build on the concreteness of the previous year's summit agreements and continue negotiations on nuclear arms limitations and other bilateral issues (such as the normalization of trade relations). On the other hand, Kissinger was convinced that any impression of a Soviet-American condominium would alarm the Chinese and cause a breakdown of triangular diplomacy.

Thus, Kissinger was treading a fine line. Ironically, by the spring of 1973—even as he had enjoyed the friendliest reception of any of his visits to China—Kissinger's foreign policy vis-à-vis Beijing and Moscow gradually turned into a holding action in which no dramatic shifts or breakthroughs could be negotiated.

THE "YEAR OF EUROPE"

The "Year of Europe" was an unfortunate sound bite for a commendable initiative. For there was no question that the transatlantic relationship required reassessment. In early 1973 Great Britain, Ireland, and Denmark had become members of the EEC (Norway having declined the honor after a negative referendum). This expansion strengthened the economic power of the EEC and, at least in theory, Western Europe's bargaining power vis-à-vis the United States. At the same time, NATO military strategists argued that Europeans could not rely *only* on the deterrence effect of the American nuclear umbrella as a guarantor of their security. As Kissinger and many others had noted already in the 1960s, the paradox of the strategic nuclear balance was that the growth of nuclear arsenals had made their potential use increasingly less realistic. Hence, a European nightmare scenario: what if the Soviet Union decided to launch a limited conventional attack in some part of Europe because it could rely on the American reluctance not to respond with nuclear weapons?

Theoretical though such thinking was, Soviet conventional superiority on the continent acquired a new, far more menacing, significance that, given its limits, even the political (and to an extent economic) détente of the early 1970s could not remove.[30] In fact, the Soviet Union's current and future policies and possibilities were a key ingredient behind the year of Europe initiative. A National Intelligence Estimate (NIE) of October 1972 had summed it up: "the Soviet leaders hope that while maintaining their position in the East they can wean West Europeans away from their close relations with the US . . . slow further European political and economic integration, and ultimately clear the way for the USSR's emergence as the dominant power on the continent as a whole." It was this sort of thinking, the NIE argued, that would cause the Soviets, in the next few years, "to press vigorously ahead [on détente]."[31]

Kissinger's public entry into the debate over transatlantic relations took place on April 23, 1973. In a speech to the editors of the Associated Press at New York's

Waldorf-Astoria hotel he said seemingly little that was not common knowledge to any observer of international relations at the time. Kissinger touched upon the revival and economic unification of Western Europe, the approximate strategic parity between the United States and the Soviet Union, and the onset of détente. He then stressed that "problems have arisen, unforeseen a generation ago, which require new types of cooperative action." In Nixon's name, he called for the leaders of Europe to join the United States in laying down "the basis for a new era of creativity in the West [and in] reinvigorating shared ideals and common purpose with our friends." He proposed a new Atlantic Charter, a document that would lay out the basic interests and goals of NATO in the new international environment.

Few would have objected to such a high-minded call, or to Kissinger's point about the need to adapt the principle of collective defense with "radically different strategic conditions." But then Kissinger asked for trouble. In an unnecessarily crude way, he stressed the difference between America's global responsibilities and the EEC's regional interests. Specifically, he maintained that the United States, Canada, Western Europe, "and ultimately Japan" had to reconcile the EEC's "regional personality" with the United States' responsibility for "a wider international trade and monetary system."

The ultimate, and oft quoted, faux-pas followed: "Diplomacy is the subject of frequent consultations but is essentially being conducted by traditional nation-states. The United States has global interests and responsibilities. Our European allies have regional interests." In other words, not only did the United States appear to have the monopoly on "responsibilities," it was the only country in the West with legitimate interests outside its own narrow geographic region.[32]

The speech and the diplomacy surrounding it may have been meant as an opening of a new kind of transatlantic relationship. Kissinger may not have said anything that was not true: Europeans were hardly capable of or willing to play a significant role outside of their own continent. In the context of détente there surely was a need to rethink common policies and to find ways of keeping potential trade wars from erupting. And yet, Kissinger managed to provoke a united front in Europe that was potentially detrimental to the goals of his initiative. Moreover, because Kissinger had stressed that the Europeans should have a common proposal for a new Atlantic Charter to be discussed during Nixon's planned tour of Europe later in the year, he had not only insulted America's European partners; he had given them a deadline.

Ironically—and proving that Europe was "irrelevant" to Americans on a number of levels—the Year of Europe was not the most prominent headline news in the United States. There were supportive editorials in the *New York Times* and the *Christian Science Monitor*. But, as the *Washington Post* noted, no far-reaching foreign policy initiatives could be carried through while the Watergate scandal was gripping the nation. Nixon himself was too busy preparing to contain the impact that the sacking of Haldeman and Ehrlichman (announced on April 30, 1973, a week after Kissinger's speech) would have on American public opinion to pay much attention to foreign policy matters. In fact, when Kissinger and Nixon talked in April 1973, they rarely even discussed foreign policy. Instead, on a number of occasions Nixon would protest his innocence to Kissinger and speculate about the need to fire Haldeman and Ehrlichman. The Year of Europe and the protests of the Europeans were understandably irrelevant to a president concerned about his own future.[33]

But if Nixon and the American public were manifestly uninterested in Kissinger's initiative, many European leaders found the Year of Europe idea preposterous. Georges Pompidou, for one, cryptically remarked that for France every year was the "Year of Europe." Willy Brandt thought that the whole notion fit a pattern. Kissinger, Brandt wrote, "wanted to ensure that there was a distinction between Europe's independent regional responsibility and its international co-responsibility." In his memoirs, British Prime Minister Edward Heath wrote, in apparent astonishment, that "for Kissinger to announce a Year of Europe was like for me to stand on Trafalgar Square and announce that we were embarking on a year to save America!"[34]

In subsequent months, Kissinger worked hard to repair the damage. But he had little immediate success. Brandt arrived in Washington on May 1—the day after Nixon had announced the resignations of Haldeman and Ehrlichman—for a series of cordial but inconclusive discussions with a president preoccupied with other issues. On May 10, Kissinger visited London and found the British understanding but clearly more consumed with proving their credentials as "good Europeans" than in acting as a bridge between the United States and the rest of NATO. Finally, in late May, Nixon, Rogers, and Kissinger traveled to Reykjavik, Iceland, for a summit with France's President Georges Pompidou and his foreign minister Michel Jobert. But, as their British and German counterparts, the French proved non-committal to the idea of a new Atlantic Charter. By the summer of 1973 it was clear to Kissinger that "the Year of Europe had lost its meaning."[35]

KISSINGER IN ZAVIDOVO

Two weeks after the "Year of Europe" speech Kissinger traveled to the USSR to prepare the ground for Brezhnev's visit to the United States. Upon arrival on May 4, he, along with Helmut Sonnenfeldt, Philip Odeen, William Hyland, Peter Rodman, and Richard Campbell, were driven to Zavidovo, 90 miles northeast of Moscow. Over the next four days, at the Politburo's hunting preserve, Kissinger, Brezhnev, and Gromyko conducted a series of wide-ranging and erratic discussions that were interrupted by festive meals and an unwelcome (to Kissinger) hunting trip during which Brezhnev managed to bag a wild boar with a single shot. The atmosphere was jovial, with the Soviet leader cracking jokes and drinking with little restraint.[36]

Among the many subjects that Kissinger discussed with Brezhnev were the Soviet proposal for the Prevention of Nuclear War Agreement (PNW), a treaty renouncing the use of nuclear weapons, the principles of a SALT II agreement that would deal with such issues as multiple independently targeted re-entry vehicles (MIRVs), or the ability to equip nuclear launchers with several warheads, bilateral economic relations, the Middle East, and Indochina.

Despite extended discussions there were no major breakthroughs. To Kissinger, the meetings were most significant in establishing the general nature of the Soviet-American relationship—the weaknesses and strengths each side had—on the eve of Brezhnev's visit to the United States. In this regard, Kissinger was confident that the Americans held the upper hand. As he wrote to Nixon after the Zavidovo meetings: "On the basis of Brezhnev's mood and the contents of the talks, you will hold the high cards at the summit." He further added: "Your China policy and Soviet economic difficulties are your strong points."[37]

Indeed, the Soviets had followed the development of Sino-American relations closely. Prior to Kissinger's trip, the opening of liaison offices—and the stationing of one of America's most experienced diplomats in Beijing—had prompted anxious commentary in the Soviet press.[38] At Zavidovo Brezhnev did not hold back on his distaste for China. It was the subject of one of Brezhnev's goriest jokes. At the beginning of a meeting on the evening of May 7, he said: "I always think of the Chinese. They once ate one of their Political Guidance officers in a troop unit. Another man asked, 'How could you do that? He is such a fine man.' The Chinese answered: 'We don't eat bad people.'" After some laughter, Brezhnev's security policy adviser, Aleksandrov-Agentov, quickly confirmed the story by seriously adding: "In regions of China they still do that."[39]

On a more substantive level China was an integral part of the negotiations over the PNW agreement, which, Kissinger thought, was a Soviet attempt to create a public impression of a Soviet-American condominium that would unnerve other countries. This he wished to avoid, in part, because of China but also in order not to create further difficulties for U.S.-European relations. Kissinger considered the talks a success. The major disagreement had to do with the scope of the PNW's nonuse clause: whether Moscow and Washington would commit to the principle of nonuse of nuclear weapons simply against each other or, as the Americans desired, against third parties as well. A bilateral accord on nonuse would, Kissinger maintained, have translated to "a free hand [for the Soviets] to use nuclear weapons against third parties (China or NATO)." Thus, after extensive negotiations on May 5, 6, and 7, Kissinger considered it a major victory that Brezhnev relented and agreed to the inclusion of obligations to third countries. Another negotiation victory was the Soviet agreement to drop a bilateral consultation clause that would have committed the United States to consultations with the USSR should a risk of a nuclear war between, say, China and India appear imminent.

In short, Kissinger's stringent efforts to whittle down the PNW agreement so that it would have the least harmful effect on Sino-American relations were successful. As he concluded in a post-Zavidovo assessment to Nixon: "I believe we have succeeded in creating a web of conditions . . . the Soviets cannot turn on NATO or China without violating this agreement." The PNW agreement, scheduled for Nixon's and Brezhnev's signatures in June, was yet another building block in "the increasingly complex relationship we are developing [with the Soviets]."[40]

*   *   *

As had been the case during the Moscow summit a year earlier, the rest of the discussion—mostly between Kissinger and Gromyko—at Zavidovo focused on two regional issues: the Middle East and Vietnam. On the Middle East—where the outbreak of a major war was only five months away—Kissinger was evasive. "We are not underestimating the danger [of war]," he told Gromyko, "we don't know how to handle it." Gromyko pressed for Kissinger to lean on the Israelis and warned: "if the United States thinks that the Soviet Union will be a partner to agreements promoting the Israeli occupation of Arab lands . . . it is a profound mistake." Kissinger protested. "We are in favor of a major withdrawal [of Israeli forces]," he insisted. But trying to push through a comprehensive peace proposal was a mistake; instead, one should focus on a step-by-step approach. In the end he simply recommended continuing the discussions on the back channel. Kissinger's concluding comment at the May 8 meeting is telling in its vagueness: "I think we have made some progress in understanding how we might proceed."

On Vietnam, Gromyko's and Kissinger's roles were reversed. Kissinger ranted about North Vietnamese violations, continued Soviet aid to Hanoi, and the lackluster performance of the Polish representatives in the International Control Commission that had been charged with overseeing the implementation of the Paris Agreements.

Gromyko was relaxed. He noted that the South Vietnamese were committing "major violations" and that the United States was militarily active. "When will President Thieu be out, by the way?" Gromyko coyly asked, with reference to Kissinger's numerous assurances during the 1972 Vietnam negotiations that the South Vietnamese president was willing to resign and allow free elections to decide the form of the new government in Saigon. Kissinger denied this had ever been a part of any agreement and added: "I think if it is quiet there for a year or two, great power interests would be further dissociated."[41]

Neither the Middle East nor Vietnam would, of course, remain quiet over the next few years. In fact, these were the two regional crises that would soon contribute to the decline of détente. Yet, as Kissinger departed from the hunting lodges of Zavidovo, he was relatively satisfied. While there had been no dramatic breakthroughs, he had negotiated several concessions from Brezhnev, most notably on the PNW agreement. The Soviet leader had indicated that triangular diplomacy was working. In his post-trip assessment, Kissinger even suggested adding to Moscow's China-concerns by inviting Zhou Enlai to visit the UN and Washington in the fall of 1973. Such a visit would never materialize. Nevertheless, in May 1973 Kissinger was optimistic that Soviet-American détente was on a firm foundation. After the June summit Brezhnev, he wrote Nixon, "should be deeply committed to a more positive relationship with the US."[42]

WASHINGTON— CAMP DAVID—SAN CLEMENTE

Given the lack of groundbreaking Soviet-American treaties to be signed, Brezhnev's visit to the United States in June 1973 proved far less dramatic than Nixon's earlier journey to Moscow. Following his arrival in Washington on Saturday, June 16, Brezhnev and his party spent the next day recuperating from their long trip at Camp David (Kissinger and Nixon were at the Southern White House in Key Biscayne, Florida). On June 17, Kissinger flew to Camp David to meet a "buoyant" Brezhnev; for the only time during their acquaintance the Soviet leader kissed the national security adviser. Starting on Monday, June 18, Nixon and Brezhnev held a series of talks in three locations. They began in Washington, then moved on to Camp David on June 20, and closed the summit at the Western White House in San Clemente on June 23. Brezhnev—like Nixon the previous year—gave a nationally televised address. On the morning of June 24 they bid farewell in what Kissinger described as the last time the two "met as equals." At the third Nixon–Brezhnev summit in June—July 1974, Nixon's domestic base had seriously eroded (he would resign a month after that summit) and his ability to act as an effective foreign policy leader was minimized.[43]

The number of issues on the agenda reflected the state of the Soviet-American relationship in the summer of 1973. On the one hand, there was a growing web of linkages. Nixon and Brezhnev discussed arms control and the terms of the SALT II agreement on a broad basis. They signed the PNW Agreement, negotiated by Kissinger in Zavidovo a month earlier. They concluded ten agreements ranging from the peaceful uses of atomic energy to increasing the number of bilateral cultural exchanges. They discussed European security. In addition, the two parties held numerous private talks regarding the Middle East, Indochina, and China. On the other hand, there were few lasting achievements. In particular, Nixon and Brezhnev—or Kissinger and Gromyko in their separate meeting on the Middle East on June 23—could find no solutions to the regional issues that, in the near future, eroded any semblance of mutual trust from the relationship. In short, while the many auxiliary agreements signed at the 1973 summit indicated that the bilateral relationship was deepening, there was little indication that the competitive (and confrontational) nature of Soviet-American relations with regards to regional conflicts had changed.

Again, as in Moscow a year earlier, there were several sets of talks. A new feature was that Brezhnev and Nixon actually met alone with only the Soviet interpreter, Viktor Sukhodrev, present for about an hour on June 18 before Kissinger, Secretary of State Rogers, Foreign Minister Gromyko, Ambassador Dobrynin, and Helmut Sonnenfeldt of the NSC staff were invited into the Oval Office. It is unlikely that the leaders made any secret deals before inviting the rest of the group to join them at 12:35 P.M., to discuss the agenda for the summit meetings and explore, in general terms, the state of U.S.-Soviet relations. From there on, however, the talks followed a usual pattern. After an initial plenary meeting, and a session on economic relations on June 20, Nixon, Kissinger, and Brezhnev held extensive private discussions on the PNW, China, Vietnam, and the Middle East, while Rogers and Gromyko were left to handle such issues as European security and some of the language on the communiqué to be issued at the end of the summit. In between the high-level meetings there was sightseeing and Brezhnev met with members of the Senate Foreign Relations Committee.

The summit did not occur without confrontation on the two regional issues that had marred Kissinger's visit to Zavidovo: the Middle East and Vietnam. Regarding the Middle East, the dialogue of the deaf continued. Although on June 18 Nixon expressed his general hope that "our meetings will help to move the negotiations off dead center," the Soviets did not raise the subject until the last full day of the summit, on June 23. On the morning of that day, at San Clemente, Kissinger and Gromyko first held an extensive discussion over the language of the section of the communiqué that dealt with the Middle East. With the Soviet foreign minister insisting that there should be no mention of the relevant UN Security Council Resolution (No. 242), the two made little progress. In the end, Gromyko suggested that Kissinger would continue discussions on the Middle East with Ambassador Dobrynin after the summit.[44]

It did not end there. At 10:00 P.M. that evening, Kissinger's phone rang. The Secret Service informed him that Brezhnev was noisily demanding an immediate meeting with Nixon on the Middle East. Kissinger called the president and a rendezvous was hastily arranged in Nixon's study for 10:30 P.M.

Brezhnev's behavior reminded Nixon and Kissinger of the previous year's meeting at the Soviet leader's dacha, when Brezhnev, Kosygin, and Podgorny had assailed the Americans about Vietnam. "If we agree on Israeli withdrawals," Brezhnev now suggested, "everything will fall in place." Nixon tried to suggest that the best thing was for Kissinger to send a new American draft of principles to Brezhnev the following day.

But the general secretary was at his most combative. It was necessary to have an agreement on the general principles for a Middle East settlement, he insisted. Otherwise, a war was sure to break out. Brezhnev agreed that there was no point in putting everything into a communiqué, but a general agreement was necessary. "We should know in what direction to act. We could agree on Vietnam. Why can't we do it here?" Brezhnev asked. He promised that everything they could agree upon would remain a secret and suggested a "gentleman's agreement." Brezhnev then issued a not-so-veiled warning: "I am categorically opposed to the resumption of the war. But without agreed principles that will ultimately help situation in area, we cannot do this . . . Do not let me leave without this agreement." Nixon was not fazed. "I will take it into account tomorrow," he said, adding: "We won't say anything in terms of a gentleman's agreement. I hope you won't go back empty handed. But we have to break up now."[45]

The end result of the bizarre exchange was minimal. Three months later a war in the Middle East would catch the Americans unprepared.

Much like on the Middle East, discussions on the situation in Indochina were inconclusive. At their first meeting on June 18 Nixon mentioned the "very vigorous discussion on Vietnam" in May 1972. "The most serious problem now," Nixon added, "is Cambodia."[46]

And indeed it was. While Nixon and Brezhnev were talking, American B-52 bombers continued to bomb Khmer Rouge and North Vietnamese sanctuaries in Cambodia, refugees continued to flood to Phnem Pong (one of the few places that still remained untouched by U.S. bombs), and the Lon Nol government was losing its hold on the countryside. Thus, at San Clemente on June 23, Nixon returned to the topic:

> The subject that concerns me is the continued military action of the DRV in Cambodia . . . If that continues, the reaction of many people in this country will be that Soviet arms made it possible. The U.S. and the Soviet Union must show restraint also towards allies, in relation to our agreement.

"I agree one hundred percent," Brezhnev offered. North Vietnamese Prime Minister Pham Van Dong was coming to Moscow in July, he volunteered. Whatever Pham asks, Brezhnev added, "I see no necessity of sending new equipment. We have no agreement with Cambodia and Laos regarding supplies." Brezhnev went on to blame the Chinese for spreading false stories about Soviet aid. "Do not worry about our supplies."

Brezhnev was hardly being truthful about Soviet intentions. Throughout the spring of 1973 the Soviets had assured the North Vietnamese of their continued military and economic support. A month after the Washington summit, Premier Pham Van Dong visited Moscow and received assurances that the Soviets would continue their aid. In November 1973, North Vietnam and the Soviet Union would sign a new military agreement by which, as the historian Iliya Gaiduk puts it, "Moscow virtually approved Hanoi's plans to overthrow the government of South Vietnam."[47]

Yet, Brezhnev's main goal in this particular meeting was not to discuss Vietnam or Cambodia. Rather, he wanted to warn the Americans that their relationship with the Chinese was bound to hurt Soviet-American détente. The Chinese were, Brezhnev generously volunteered, "treacherous and spiteful, capable of destroying a whole people ... not honorable ... an exceptionally sly and perfidious people." Do not ignore the events of the Cultural Revolution, Brezhnev added. "What sort of people are they who so oppress their people ... gigantic trials were held in public squares and thousands watched public beheadings. What ideas roam in the heads of such leaders?" Nixon and Kissinger should not trust the Chinese, Brezhnev argued. Then he referred to the potential Chinese reaction to the PNW treaty and came to the real point:

> I am sure of one thing; China will never stop the development of its nuclear arsenal no matter what you say. We should continue to exchange [views] on this subject ... We cannot limit our arms while they build up ... we must bring home to them that this cannot go on ... Chinese people are saying they will never use nuclear weapons. I don't believe them ... Of course I do not have the right to interfere in the affairs of your country ... you can make agreements with any state. My idea is that if in the course of this year the US and China will conclude a military arrangement, people's trust will go down ... I would like you to understand me.

When Kissinger responded that the United States had had no military talks with Beijing, Brezhnev issued an ominous warning. "Of course I believe you," he said. "But we are worried about the future, or it will undermine our relationship ... We do not intend to attack China but it will be different if China has a military arrangement with the United States."[48]

When Brezhnev departed from San Clemente on June 24, Soviet-American détente was, in fact, at a crossroads. Despite the broad agenda and the large scale and scope of the issues, very little concrete had come out of the 1973 summit. The PNW agreement was a placid document, the principles for the negotiation of SALT II offered only a hazy road map for the future, and the various agreements that had been signed had to do with peaceful uses of atomic energy, cooperation in agriculture and transportation, and other auxiliary issues. What stood out were the disagreements and anxieties on both sides—on the Soviet side, about China, the Middle East, and lack of progress in normalizing Soviet-American trade relations; on the American side, the future of Indochina and Nixon's own political longevity.

* * *

Kissinger had one additional concern about the Brezhnev visit: the Chinese reaction to the PNW agreement. If he wished to keep drinking mao tai as well as vodka, it was crucial to prevent the impression of undue comity between Nixon and Brezhnev. Thus, Kissinger made a special point of keeping the Chinese informed of Brezhnev's visit even while the general secretary was in the United States. On June 19, three days after Brezhnev's arrival, Kissinger met with Huang Chen at the White House. He began by making deprecating comments about Brezhnev, a man who "doesn't have the same precision of mind as your prime minister." While the

Soviets were trying to create an impression of a partnership between Washington and Moscow, the Chinese should not be fooled by this, Kissinger added. "That is not our policy," he said, adding: "on very practical grounds it makes no sense to support the stronger against the weaker. And we will not do anything practical to support that policy."[49] On July 6 Kissinger pressed this point further. He told Huang Chen about Brezhnev's "violent" attacks on the Chinese leadership, as well as his suggestions—made first during Kissinger's pre-summit trip to the Soviet Union in May 1973—that the United States and the Soviet Union should cooperate to prevent China from reaching "a nuclear capability in 15 years equal to what the Soviets have today." Brezhnev had even warned of "the most serious consequences and drastic [Soviet] measures" should any military arrangements be made between the United States and the PRC. Clearly, the Soviets had been eager to prevent the further improvement of Sino-American relations and Kissinger assured that any Soviet efforts were, as far as he was concerned, going nowhere. He dismissed suggestions—such as the ones Zhou Enlai had made to David Bruce in June 1973 and Mao already in February—that the United States would aid the Soviets against the Chinese in the event of a war as "absurd."[50]

Why was Kissinger being so candid about Brezhnev's remarks and suggestions? He was, clearly, trying to counter a trend against the future improvement of Sino-American relations in the late summer of 1973. It was a losing cause.

ANOTHER INDOCHINA IMBROGLIO

In the aftermath of his successful February meetings in Beijing, Kissinger continued his efforts to enlist Chinese help in Indochina. In mid-April, for example, he complained to UN Ambassador Huang Hua about persistent North Vietnamese violations of the Paris Agreements. "The capacity of lying of your allies is equal to their heroism," Kissinger quipped. He maintained that the United States wanted "nothing more than to end our involvement." He then reemphasized the need for a decent interval: "a reasonable period of time has to elapse after our exit (between the present situation and an evolution)." Thus he urged "the friends of the other side [to] use their influence and not give them the means to start another offensive." He assured that the United States would "not help our friends to start another offensive." With regards to Cambodia he stressed the American willingness to find a "coalition structure along the lines that the Prime Minister and I discussed in Peking." Unlike in the case of South Vietnam in the past, in Cambodia Washington was "not committed to any particular personality"—translation: Lon Nol was expendable. Hua was, as usual, noncommittal, criticizing massive U.S. aid to Saigon and maintaining that the simple removal of Lon Nol was not a basis for a sufficient solution in Cambodia.[51]

By this time the deadlock in Indochina was evident. Negotiations between the PRG and the Saigon government representatives began at La Celle St-Cloud outside of Paris on March 19, 1973. They were, however, hampered by continued fighting in South Vietnam as Thieu's forces attacked NLF strongholds in a concerted land-grabbing operation. At the talks the Saigon delegation, headed by Nguyen Luu Vien, wanted to conclude agreements on holding presidential elections in the South and removing North Vietnamese troops; the PRG/NLF's agenda included upholding the ceasefire, the return of political prisoners, and guaranteeing civil freedoms in South Vietnam. The only common item in the two sides' respective proposals was the makeup of the CNR. No wonder that little progress could be expected at La Celle St-Cloud. On April 20 Nguyen Van Hieu, the NLF's chief diplomat at La Celle St-Cloud, criticized Saigon's agenda at a press conference in Paris while urging Hanoi to plan an all-out military campaign. Five days later both sides presented their formal peace proposals. They were duly rejected.[52]

By this point the likelihood of another military showdown was clearly increasing and the diplomatic struggle relegated, effectively, to a holding pattern. Thieu, who had never considered a negotiated settlement with the NLF/PRG as a serious alternative, had been further emboldened by his visit to San Clemente earlier in the month and continued U.S. bombing of North Vietnamese strongholds in Cambodia. He thus continued to press for more ARVN control in the South. In response, Thieu's South Vietnamese opponents pressed Hanoi to undertake stronger military action. Although the North was still reluctant to commit itself to another war, the Central Committee decided, on April 19 (three days after Kissinger had met with Huang), to begin preparations for an overall offensive because "the likelihood of an American intervention had diminished." In May, as Thieu continued to make gains in the South, Le Duan urged the Vietnamese Communist Party Politburo that there was "no alternative but to use revolutionary violence." On June 1, 1973, he reported strong support in the Politburo for such a course. And still, it would take another several months, until October 1973, before Hanoi would pass Resolution 21 and commence a full-scale counteroffensive in the South. The northerners were, as Robert Brigham has pointed out, reluctant to begin another war in part because of the urgent need to begin reconstruction; in this regard the prospect of American aid was an important consideration for some members of the Politburo. As long as the United States kept bombing Cambodia, moreover, the use of the Ho Chi Minh Trail was hampered. To these considerations one should add the advice from the Chinese that probably influenced Hanoi's decisions in late spring and summer of 1973.[53]

Indeed, Hanoi was in a delicate position—pressed by the NLF/PRG toward an immediate counteroffensive and advised by the Chinese to hold back and retool. The dilemma intensified in early June as Zhou continued to caution the North Vietnamese. The Chinese premier told Le Duan and Pham Van Dong that in "South Vietnam, Laos and Cambodia [one must] play for time and prepare for a protracted struggle." He explained that the Americans were putting pressure on Saigon to "decrease fighting." Obviously aware of the impact of Watergate, Zhou argued, "Nixon was in trouble" and hoped for the South Vietnamese "not to make the situation more complicated." This was, Zhou explained, a major reason why Kissinger had agreed to meet with Le Duc Tho in Paris in late May. It is worth noting that both Le Duan and Pham Van Dong were willing to play the waiting game. Le Duan acknowledged that the Communists were "not in a hurry to turn South Vietnam into a socialist entity." Premier Pham added that the North was "not in a hurry with the goal of national reunification." On June 5, Le Duan clearly accepted Zhou's advice "to solve the problem of US withdrawal first and solve the Saigon problem later." On the next day, Zhou softened the blow by offering to provide aid to North Vietnam at 1973 levels for the next five years.[54]

* * *

While Le Duan, Pham Van Dong, and Zhou Enlai were meeting in Beijing, Kissinger and Le Duc Tho held another series of conversations in Paris. Starting on May 17, Tho and Kissinger engaged in an intermittent tête-à-tête (May 17–23, June 6–9, and June 12–13) that finally resulted in the publication of a joint communiqué. The talks were sandwiched between Kissinger's visit to the Soviet Union and Brezhnev's arrival in Washington (and interrupted by the Nixon–Pompidou summit in Reykjavik). As Kissinger put it to Ambassador Bunker, the purpose of these meetings was to "press North Vietnam and its allies to comply with the Paris Agreements, particularly the provisions concerning (a) the cessation of hostilities, (b) Laos and Cambodia, and (c) the introduction of troops and supplies into South Vietnam."[55] That sounded reasonable.

The results were dismal.

Kissinger later called these talks a "charade with Tho." The problem was that he had few, if any, cards to play. With the absence of U.S. troops and no possibility of reintroducing them, with a Congress challenging the authority of the Watergate-weakened Nixon and about to introduce a resolution banning further U.S. bombing of Cambodia, and with the Saigon government still intent on pursuing the pacification of South Vietnam, Kissinger was effectively reduced to engaging in witty criticism and making empty threats to his North Vietnamese counterpart. On May 19 he complained about the "movement of elephants" to the South and how civilian goods were ingeniously "disguised as tanks." He also stressed that the possibility of U.S. economic aid was linked to "progress on peace throughout Indochina." Although he said two days later that "we do not state a formal linkage [between U.S. aid and North Vietnam's behavior]," the point was clear: if Hanoi wanted money from Washington it had to behave.[56]

Tho, however, was keenly aware of the domestic context in the United States. The argument that Hanoi and the PRG were violating the Paris Agreements, he said, was just another Nixon cover-up. He was clearly skeptical that Kissinger and Nixon would have the power to persuade the Congress to allocate money for North Vietnam's reconstruction. Simply put, the two negotiators lacked, in Kissinger's terminology, the necessary "balance of interests and risks" that make for a true negotiation session. On this instance he was surely correct. The June 13 communiqué, by specifying timetables for the implementation of the Paris Agreements, may have looked fine on paper. But all observers knew that by the summer of 1973 hopes for a true settlement were illusory.[57]

The meager practical results of the Paris talks of May–June were not the only aspect that resembled earlier Kissinger–Tho negotiations. Nixon, gearing up to welcome Brezhnev to Washington and trying to keep domestic critics at bay, was keen on keeping the South Vietnamese on board. Hence, he returned to the time-honored practice of pressuring President Thieu to accept the communiqué, which was being negotiated without Saigon's direct involvement. On May 30, he wrote to Thieu that it was important that the South go ahead with the communiqué lest Nixon "be able to obtain from the Congress the sort of legislative cooperation which will be required to carry out the programs for peace and stability which you and I discussed in San Clemente."[58] In a series of letters in early June, Nixon pressed the need for Saigon to go along or face the loss of U.S. support while Thieu objected to a communiqué he called "very unbalanced and unjust." By June 10 Nixon had reached the same point he had reached back in January when Thieu had objected to the terms of the Paris Agreements. He wrote to Thieu that he had asked Kissinger to return to Washington for "consultations." Kissinger would return to Paris for the signing of the communiqué on June 13. Thieu had a choice, very similar to the one he had had in January. "Either you choose the collapse of all that we have constructed," Nixon wrote, "over a document whose primary significance is the split it threatens between us, or you instruct your representative to join in signature."[59] As in January, Thieu finally relented and agreed to the communiqué.

Kissinger, whose last experience in Saigon in October 1972 had been humiliating, did not get into the middle of all this. Yet, as Charles S. Whitehouse, who was acting as the charge d'affaires in Saigon after Bunker's departure the previous month, explained, Kissinger featured prominently in Thieu's objections. "The impasse," Whitehouse wrote on June 8, "is attributable mostly to the GVN's distrust of both Kissinger's and the North Vietnamese motives for renegotiating the Paris Agreements." Indeed, Saigon's eventual adherence to the June communiqué was "pro forma and will be rationalized here as necessary to help out President Nixon in his current domestic difficulties." Thus, "it should not be assumed that the GVN would pay more than lip service to compliance."[60] Whitehouse was right on the mark.

* * *

As the latest Kissinger–Tho and Nixon–Thieu charades played themselves out in late May and early June, prospects for a peace settlement in Cambodia were going from bad to worse. To be sure, there had been, throughout the spring of 1973, some hope that Kissinger could find a solution for Cambodia with the help of the Chinese. On May 27, Kissinger told Huang Hua: "we are prepared to stop our bombing in Cambodia, and we are prepared to withdraw the very small advisory group we have there." Kissinger also offered "to arrange for Lon Nol to leave for medical treatment in the United States." If he arranged all this, however, Kissinger would require in return "a ceasefire—if necessary, say, for ninety days—a negotiation between the Sihanouk group and the remainder of the Lon Nol group; and while negotiation is going on in Cambodia, we would authorize some discussions between the staff of Ambassador Bruce and Sihanouk in Peking." Huang acknowledged the offer and then read a promising note. "Prince Sihanouk as well as the resistance forces at home [i.e., the Khmer Rouge] are willing to conduct the negotiations with the US side."[61]

A week later the prospects for a negotiated settlement began to dim. On June 4, the Chinese first invited Kissinger for another visit to Beijing; Kissinger agreed that he would come sometime in August and added that Premier Zhou was welcome to visit the United States at any convenient time. But then Huang Chen read an evasive note about Cambodia. It was necessary, the Chinese reiterated, to wait for decisions on Cambodia until Sihanouk returned from his annual travels in Europe and Africa. It was too "inconvenient" to contact the deposed Cambodian leader at the moment. Indications of Beijing's reluctance to push the issue did not stop there. On June 13, after meeting with Le Duc Tho in Paris, Kissinger saw China's Foreign Minister Chi P'eng Fei. Without offering to contact Sihanouk until he returned to Beijing in late June, Chi warned that unless the United States recognized the prince as the sole representative of Cambodia, "it will be very difficult" to reach an agreement. Kissinger was taken aback. "It is important to have a transition period and not push one side against the wall," he said. Five days later, on June 19, he did make another concession by offering to talk with Sihanouk during his projected August 1973 visit to Beijing.[62]

Kissinger would neither talk to Sihanouk nor visit Beijing in August. In fact, his offer to talk directly to the prince was probably prompted in large part because on June 15 the U.S. Congress passed an amendment blocking any further bombing in Indochina. Although not effective until August 15, 1973, the bombing ban removed the last remaining stick in Kissinger's negotiation arsenal. Perhaps more important, however, the Chinese reneged on their earlier offer to mediate a coalition government in Cambodia. On July 6, Huang Chen complained about continued U.S. bombing and about press stories that a Sino-American mediation was under way. In the meeting, which took place at Nixon's Western White House in San Clemente, Huang warned that such leaks would inevitably prolong any agreement. Then, on July 18—the same day as the House of Representatives approved the War Powers Act—the Chinese passed Kissinger a note that called it "inappropriate to communicate to Sihanouk the tentative thinking on the settlement of the Cambodian question as set forth by the US side in late May."[63]

At 11:00 A.M. the next day, July 19, Kissinger gathered his China hands together for a meeting in his West Wing office. Scowcroft, Eagleburger, Lord, Howe,

Solomon, and Rodman listened to Kissinger's pessimistic account about the Chinese note that, he maintained, amounted to "a cancellation or postponement of the Kissinger trip and an opting-out by the Chinese of any involvement in negotiations for a Cambodian settlement." It was "a complete reversal of the Chinese position on both counts." He then, implausibly, explained the reversal as a result of the congressional bombing ban. It had "destroyed the balance in Cambodia" and made it impossible for the Chinese to exercise any pressure on the Khmer Rouge or Sihanouk. "To cancel a Kissinger trip was a major international event," he added with characteristic modesty. Kissinger wanted his staff members to help him figure out whether it was a reflection of a broader change in China's policy toward the United States or limited to the specific changes regarding Cambodia.

A heated exchange followed. No one, of course, knew the real story, yet the consensus seemed to be that the Chinese change was linked purely to the issue of Cambodia. But Kissinger was not convinced. Thus, he decided to advise USLO Chief David Bruce to deliver an "ice cold" note to the Chinese the following week and orally ask Deputy Foreign Minister Qiao Guanhua for a "a general review of our relations." Ironically, five hours after the meeting adjourned, Han Xu, the deputy chief of the CLO, brought in another note from Beijing that suggested Kissinger come to the PRC on August 16. "There was now no need for Bruce to raise 'fundamental questions' with Qiao," the document concluded.[64]

In the end, Kissinger wouldn't go to China until November. This was in part due to continued Chinese delays in responding to U.S. suggestions for alternate dates, Kissinger's nomination as secretary of state on August 22, and, finally, the outbreak of the October War in the Middle East. By then, the North Vietnamese were funneling increasing amounts of aid to their troops and allies in the South. The Khmer Rouge, the one force that had furiously opposed compromise in the summer of 1973, was making headway against the Lon Nol troops in the Cambodian countryside. And the Nixon administration, further weakened by the continued unfolding of Watergate, had effectively lost its ability to influence events through military means in Indochina.

In fact, a realignment of forces was taking place in Indochina. North Vietnam was looking ultimately toward establishing a united, perhaps federated, communist subcontinent in which Vietnam would play the role of big brother to Laos and Cambodia. However, the Cambodians were less than eager to play second fiddle and anxious to preserve their independence from Hanoi. As this contest intensified in subsequent years, the Chinese grew concerned about the emergence of an independent communist power, supported by their archrivals in Moscow, on their doorstep. To minimize that power they began to gravitate toward the weaker link, the Khmer Rouge in Cambodia, while the Soviets—eager to support a challenger to China—continued supporting Vietnam. Even as American involvement was decreasing, triangles and power games would continue to tear Indochina apart.

"SUPERCILIOUS ATTITUDE"

During their meeting on July 10, 1973, Anatoly Dobrynin was being particularly candid with Kissinger about the state of Soviet-American relations. While the Brezhnev visit had gone well, Moscow was disappointed about the obvious lack of enthusiasm for détente in the American press and the administration's unwillingness to seriously discuss the Middle East. Dobrynin "volunteered the opinion that the Democrats were certain to win in 1976 and this was bound to affect Soviet calculations" about the future of their relations with the United States. And he flatly told Kissinger that the Soviets "knew we [the Americans] were playing them [China and the Soviet Union] off against each other."

Kissinger's responses were predictable. He said that a Democrat victory in 1976 was "not a foreordained conclusion" and denied that the United States was playing triangular games. He assured Dobrynin "that we were as circumspect with the Chinese in talking about the Russians as we were with the Russians in talking about the Chinese." This, given Kissinger's candid account of the Brezhnev visit to the Chinese was patently untrue. But it fit well with his general notion that tilting toward China was essential for maintaining the ability to—as he had told Nixon at the beginning of 1973—"drink our mao tai and vodka too."

Notwithstanding the difficulties with the post-Paris endgame in Indochina and the lack of success with his Year of Europe initiative, Kissinger's architecture appeared well in place in 1973. There had been no similar breakthroughs as in 1972, but the establishment of liaison offices in Washington and Beijing, together with the series of agreements signed in the United States during Brezhnev's visit, indicated that all was on track in U.S. relations with China and the Soviet Union. His various meetings with the Soviets and the Chinese gave no reason to doubt that triangular diplomacy was a reality. Kissinger's only obvious concern about his meeting with Dobrynin in July 1973 had to do with a "perceptible note of superciliousness in the Ambassador's attitude." Not only had Dobrynin made an accurate prediction about the 1976 elections, but he had noted that the congressional opposition to further bombing in Cambodia left the Nixon administration with "little bargaining leverage" in Indochina.[65]

Ironically, it was the general lack of leverage in his dealings with the Congress—caused in large part by Watergate—that would cause Nixon to make an agonizing decision a few weeks after Kissinger and Dobrynin surveyed the state of the world. In August 1973 the president would nominate Kissinger secretary of state.

13

Secretary of State

At 11:06 A.M., September 22, 1973, Henry Kissinger was sworn in as the fifty-sixth secretary of state of the United States by Chief Justice Warren Burger in the East Room of the White House. Kissinger's parents (Paula and Louis) and children (David and Elizabeth) were there to witness the occasion and visibly brimmed with pride. Paula Kissinger held the bible while her son took the oath. History had been made: America had its first Jewish, non-native-born secretary of state.

Nixon, however, was less than exuberant. Although he duly noted in his brief remarks that Kissinger was the first naturalized U.S. citizen to assume the leadership of the State Department and ventured a joke about the varying hairstyles of Kissinger's predecessors, Nixon's last comments were perhaps the most poignant. "Dr. Kissinger knows, as I know, and as everybody in this audience knows," Nixon stressed, "that success in any area, and particularly in foreign policy, *do[es] not come simply from the activities of one person.*"

It was a telling statement, indicative of the fact that Nixon had—in part as a result of Watergate, in part as Kissinger's breakthroughs on the various back-channel negotiations—lost the struggle for the limelight to Kissinger. By September 1973, as Nixon was fighting to prevent the release of the White House tapes that would ultimately tie him directly to the Watergate cover-up, Kissinger continued to relish the aura of the president's secret agent, the man who had opened China, engineered détente, and negotiated the end of American involvement in Vietnam.

Nixon's statement was also an attempt—in his case prophetic—to remind those in the audience, including Kissinger, that no one was, ultimately, indispensable.

Kissinger chose not to mention this part of Nixon's comments in his memoirs. Instead, the new secretary of state remembered only Nixon's futile attempts at humor; his comment that Kissinger was the first secretary of state since 1945 not to part his hair. "I replied, evading this fascinating subject but saying what was in my heart," Kissinger later wrote. "In his heart" was, understandably, pride for the achievements of the past years and for being at the center stage of a historic occasion. "There is no country in the world where it is conceivable that a man of my origin could be standing here next to the President of the United States," Kissinger said. He pledged to continue the pursuit of past policies and inserted a note of idealism: "We will strive not just for a pragmatic solution to this or that difficulty, but to recognize that America has never been true to itself unless it meant something beyond itself."

One can interpret such an idealistic pronouncement in any number of ways. Perhaps Kissinger's comments were, indeed, genuinely conceived, illustrating that the ultimate realist actually justified his policies in idealistic terms or that he pursued what appeared immoral policies for deeply moral ends. Or perhaps Kissinger was simply recognizing the demands of his new post: as the public spokesman for U.S. foreign policy he needed to take into account the traditional sensibilities of the American people. A note of idealism was required in order to sell realpolitik.

After Nixon and Kissinger had spoken, there was a brief reception. Showing their ambivalence for the appointment, the president and the First Lady, Pat Nixon, did not linger. In fact, Nixon was by this point consumed with his effort to keep the White House tapes—that would eventually reveal a smoking gun tying him to the Watergate cover-up—from being released to special prosecutor Archibald Cox's office. The president's ratings in the polls had plummeted in the ten months since his landslide reelection: a Gallup poll released on September 23, 1973 (the day after Kissinger was sworn in), showed that only 35 percent of Americans approved of Nixon's performance, while 55 percent expressed disapproval. Two weeks later the figures would be 32 and 59 percent, respectively. Although Nixon would fight on for another year, his effectiveness in and the sheer amount of time he could spend on foreign policy declined in tandem with his overall popularity.[1]

This meant that Kissinger, for better or worse, was at the helm. By September 1973, his leadership of U.S. foreign policy was unquestioned. He was not merely the chief adviser. Kissinger was the leading policy maker.

WHITE HOUSE MANEUVERS

Nixon had not envisioned Kissinger in this role. In early 1973 the two front-runners to succeed Bill Rogers were Kenneth Rush and John Connally, while Kissinger had repeatedly appeared on Nixon's hit list. By the summer of 1973, however, the unfolding of Watergate and the resignations of a number of Nixon's key aides made it imperative for the president to nominate a strong and widely respected figure to head the State Department. Kissinger, due to his immense success as national security adviser during Nixon's first term, was the obvious choice. Not only had Kissinger—to Nixon's fury—shared the *Time* magazine's "Men of the Year" honor with the president, he was widely credited as the architect of the administration's successes. Nor could it have been otherwise. Kissinger had, after all, gone to China in July 1971, negotiated the January 1973 Paris Agreements with the North Vietnamese that provided for the final withdrawal of U.S. troops, and engineered the SALT I agreement through his back-channel talks with Soviet Ambassador Anatoly Dobrynin. In the eyes of the general public, Kissinger had emerged as the globe-trotting super-diplomat, who had tirelessly crisscrossed the globe and pulled one rabbit after another out of his hat. In contrast, Nixon was trying desperately to hold on to the presidency. In April 1973 he had lost a number of his key aides, including Bob Haldeman and John Ehrlichman. In July 1973, Alexander Butterfield, Haldeman's key aide who had taken up a new post as the head of the Federal Aviation Authority, revealed the existence of the White House taping system during the Ervin Committee hearings into the Watergate affair. Nixon was searching, desperately, for ways of shoring up his support base.[2]

One way of doing so was by highlighting the successes of the administration's foreign policy. In short, Kissinger's nomination as secretary of state was largely a result of Nixon's own political weakness and the strength of the American public's image of Kissinger. "With the Watergate problem," Nixon later recalled, "I didn't have any choices." What made Nixon's lack of choices even more evident was that he did not ask Kissinger to step down as the NSC adviser, making him the only man ever to hold the two preeminent foreign policy posts simultaneously. It was the ultimate confirmation of Kissinger's position as the Nixon administration's foreign policy czar. Yet, without Watergate, Kissinger might have been a "one-term wonder."[3]

The most influential man pushing for Kissinger's appointment in the summer of 1973 was the new White House chief of staff, General Alexander Haig. In early 1973 Haig had left the position of Kissinger's deputy at the NSC to become army vice chief of staff. Prior to that post he had impressed Nixon and acted, at times, as the president's informant on Kissinger's various maneuvers. Indeed, by early 1973 Kissinger had seen Haig—who acted as Nixon's special envoy to South Vietnamese President Thieu during the last stages of the Vietnam negotiations and, particularly during those many occasions that Kissinger was out of the country, had ingratiated himself with Nixon—as a potential threat of sorts. In May 1973, when Nixon wanted to appoint Haig as Haldeman's replacement, Kissinger initially objected. And yet, Haig, soon after returning to the White House, started pushing for Kissinger's appointment as a way of boosting the administration's fledgling domestic base. He also kept Kissinger appraised of these lobbying efforts.

Nixon eventually saw no way around the choice. Kissinger would not "tolerate competition," he later ruefully explained. Appointing someone else would undoubtedly result in Kissinger's resignation and another media circus. So eventually Nixon told Haig that Kissinger was the man for the job. But then he asked Haig to do what Haldeman had done so many times during Nixon's first term: go deliver the news to Rogers. Ask him to resign.

Haig tried. But the usually mild-mannered Rogers, fully aware that his time at the State Department was over, got incensed by this latest slight from his old law partner. "Tell the president to go fuck himself," he promptly responded. If Nixon wanted Rogers to resign, the president had better ask in person.

In mid-August Nixon did gather up the courage and Rogers, gracefully, came to Camp David with a resignation letter. At poolside in San Clemente a few days later, on August 21, 1973, Nixon informed Kissinger of his promotion.[4]

Against such a background it is hardly surprising that when Nixon announced Kissinger's nomination at a news conference in San Clemente, California, on August 22, the president was neither exuberant nor enthusiastic. He shared few accolades with the White House press corps and simply stated that "Dr. Kissinger's qualifications for this post . . . are well known by all of you as well as those looking to us and listening to us on television and radio."

It seems that the press agreed. There were no follow-up questions on the nomination. Instead, the reporters used the opportunity to grill Nixon on Watergate and his alleged abuses of power. In subsequent weeks the press fawned over Kissinger in the wake of his appointment. "A Super Secretary to Shake Up State," reported *Time* magazine. *Newsweek* hailed Kissinger as "the White House genius in residence."[5]

None of this, in the end, helped Nixon. To him, appointing Kissinger was in part an acknowledgment that the president had failed to absorb the credit for the administration's foreign policy achievements. The irony was complete: the ultimate American politician had lost the battle for the limelight to an immigrant with a heavy accent. But, as an omen of things to come, in 1973, the limelight was not always full of accolades, even for Kissinger.

THE WIRETAPS AND THE HEARINGS

In the atmosphere of Watergate, it was hardly an accident that the press homed in on the 1969 wiretapping of Kissinger's staff members. In May 1969, when reports of the secret bombing of Cambodia had suddenly appeared in the *New York Times*, Kissinger had agreed that the FBI could wiretap several of his staff members. In the spring of 1973 news of the wiretaps themselves began to leak to the press. In February a report in *Time* magazine confirmed their existence. On May 14, 1973, Acting FBI Director William Ruckelshaus confirmed that the records of the wiretaps had been found in John Ehrlichman's safe in the White House after Ehrlichman had resigned at the end of April.

At this point Kissinger made one of his few serious gaffes with reporters, comparable only to his "lone cowboy" interview with Italian journalist Oriana Fallacci in the fall of 1972. This time his interviewer was none other than Bob Woodward of the *Washington Post* (who, together with Carl Bernstein, had played a major role in publicizing the Watergate scandal as early as 1972). Understandably intrigued by the question of wiretaps, Woodward called his (unnamed) source at the FBI, who confirmed that many of the orders for the 1969 wiretaps had come from Kissinger. So Woodward called the White House and left a message. Given Woodward's background, Kissinger should probably have refused to even talk to the reporter. But, perhaps hoping to diffuse the issue, he returned Woodward's call. After telling Woodward that he simply did not remember, Kissinger admitted that he may have given a few staff members' names to the FBI. "It is quite possible that they (the FBI) construed this as authorization," Kissinger added. When Woodward said that he was going to quote him, Kissinger erupted. He had only been talking "on background," Kissinger insisted, adding: "I've tried to be honest and you're going to penalize me. In five years in Washington I have never been trapped into talking like this."

After a series of frantic phone calls Kissinger managed to get Ben Bradlee, the executive director of the *Post*, and Howard Simons, the managing editor, to agree not to rush Woodward's story into print.

The problem was that the *New York Times* journalist Seymour Hersh had the same information as Woodward from an independent source: William Sullivan, a high-ranking FBI official. Despite Alexander Haig's attempts to dissuade Hersh from publishing the wiretap story, the *New York Times* headline on May 17, 1973 (ironically the same day as the Senate commenced its televised hearings on Watergate) read: "Kissinger Said to Have Asked for Taps." Although the *Washington Post* columnists Rowland Evans and Robert Novak argued that the story was but a smear campaign against Kissinger and Nixon issued a statement taking full responsibility for the wiretaps, Kissinger's reputation had suffered a blow. While the taps could, with a stretch of the imagination, be claimed to have been ordered in the name of national security, Kissinger would, rightly so, remain associated with the abuses of power that were collectively known as Watergate.[6]

If anything, the publication of the wiretaps certainly showed that despite his close links to such newspapers as the *Washington Post* and his ability to spin stories to his advantage, Kissinger had not been inoculated against the scrutiny of investigative journalists.

Still, when he came to Capitol Hill to commence two weeks of testimony, Kissinger need not have worried about the end result. As Kissinger himself put it in his memoirs, almost all the seventeen members of the Senate Foreign Relations Committee were "well disposed toward me and eager to confirm me . . . My confirmation was a certainty."[7] This surely was the case. During the two-week hearings (September 7–21, 1973) no one seriously questioned the appointee's foreign policy credentials. To most, Kissinger was the architect of triangular diplomacy and the negotiator who had finally secured a peace agreement in Vietnam. Attacking him on such substantive issues would have hurt the attacker more than the one being attacked. Only George McGovern, the Democrats' 1972 presidential candidate, openly opposed the confirmation.

Of course, the hearings did not pass without serious questions. A number of senators questioned Kissinger's role in the secret bombing of Cambodia and the role of the United States in the coup that toppled Chile's socialist President Salvador Allende while the hearings were in progress (on September 11, 1973). But, reflecting the mood of the Watergate era, the tightest scrutiny focused on the wiretaps. In a series of closed sessions Kissinger denied (in a manner that resembled Bill Clinton's admission during the 1992 presidential campaign that he had smoked but "not inhaled" marijuana as a student) having ever *recommended* the actual practice of wiretapping but admitted having *provided* the names of several staff members to the FBI. In short: it was not his idea but he decided to go along.

In the end the senators accepted Kissinger's explanation, perhaps because it effectively shifted the blame to Nixon (who had, as already noted, taken full responsibility for the wiretaps). As Senator Frank Church (D-Idaho) put it: "Responsibility should be placed where the power resides; in this case the President." Kissinger was eventually confirmed by an overwhelming 16–1 vote by the Senate Foreign Relations Committee (George S. McGovern was the lone dissenter) on September 19 and an equally impressive 78–7 (in addition to McGovern and four other Democrats, the opponents included Republicans Jesse Helms and Lowell Weicker) vote in the Senate on September 21.[8]

*　　*　　*

But the issue of wiretaps would not go away. In early June 1974 the charges reappeared. Instead of asking him questions about his latest feat—the Israeli-Syrian disengagement agreement concluded in late May—journalists focused on selected statements from the Nixon White House tapes that appeared to suggest that Kissinger had, in fact, "initiated" the wiretaps. And there were more embarrassing questions. Had Kissinger ordered wiretaps on his former aide, Anthony Lake, after the latter had joined Senator Edmund Muskie's staff in 1970? Had Kissinger been involved in the creation of the Plumbers unit (a Nixon White House task force set up in 1969 to plug undesirable leaks of information)? While no clear evidence was available, the American press was suddenly full of speculation about such matters (most of which turned out to be true). Was there "An Ugly Blot on Mr. Clean?" *Newsweek* wondered, while a series of articles and editorials in the *New York Times* (by Hersh) and the *Washington Post* (Woodward and Bernstein) suggested that by denying knowledge of the Plumbers' operations during his confirmation hearings, Kissinger had committed perjury. Kissinger was furious. During one particularly difficult press briefing he stomped his feet and walked out of the room. Finally, against White House advice, he decided to take on the press.

On June 11, 1974, Kissinger held a press conference in Salzburg, Austria, where he and Nixon had stopped for two days en route to Egypt. His deep raspy voice was, if possible, graver than before. If the questions about his character were not cleared, Kissinger said, he would have to resign. "I do not believe that it is possible to conduct the foreign policy of the United States when the character and credibility of the Secretary of State is at issue," Kissinger fumed.

The reaction to that press conference, which was held less than two months before Nixon's resignation, amply testified to Kissinger's aura. A large number of senators and congressmen from both parties—including Senators Muskie, Mansfield, Fulbright, Humphrey, Cranston, Javits, and Percy—quickly issued statements supporting Kissinger. On June 13, a resolution in support of Kissinger's "integrity and veracity" was introduced and received broad bipartisan support. Although no one called him Mr. Clean, Kissinger was exonerated, for the time being, for Watergate-related crimes and misdemeanors. Yet, he had also managed to create another—equally pervasive and undoubtedly quite accurate—impression about himself. Kissinger was, many observers noted, perhaps too prone to temper tantrums, too sensitive to press criticism. "Just cool it," Hubert Humphrey advised Kissinger.

Kissinger did not cool it. On July 12, 1974, he told Ambassador Dobrynin: "I think I need to show some of my opponents in this town that I did not survive for five and a half years by being a pushover. . . . I want to stay here for about four weeks and restore a little discipline." He did. On August 6, the Senate published a report affirming that his role in the wiretappings during the first Nixon administration had not been adequate "to bar his confirmation as Secretary of State." Three days later Nixon left office in disgrace. The contrast between the two men's reputations could hardly have been greater.[9]

Clearly, as long as Nixon was in office, Kissinger appeared to many in the U.S. Congress as well as to most of the press, the irreplaceable man.

THE NEW EMPIRE: KISSINGER'S STATE DEPARTMENT

Moving into the massive office of the secretary of state at the top floor of the State Department's Foggy Bottom building "took some getting used to," Kissinger wrote in his memoirs. Not that the new secretary of state was loath to accept the special privileges, the spacious quarters, the panoramic views on offer. That hardly presented a problem. It was a huge step up from the West Wing of the White House basement.

It was the nature of the job that took more getting used to.

As NSC adviser, Kissinger had presided over a staff that was small by comparison to the State Department. He had been able to focus on a relatively few key areas of foreign policy, and had been able to operate—at least until the 1971 trip to China—in secrecy when he needed to by using a series of back channels. Perhaps most important, there had been the sheer proximity to Nixon, a fact that—if not

always easy on a personal level—had been immensely helpful in Kissinger's accu-
mulation of influence. Kissinger's description of the NSC adviser's role in the first
volume of his memoirs, although written in the third person, captures in essence
his own modus operandi during the first Nixon administration:

> The security adviser . . . is human; he seeks status; he is only too well aware that
> his own power depends on his ability to demonstrate a unique kind of useful-
> ness . . . If he is skillful, he can position himself in bureaucratic debates close to
> the President's predilections, which he usually has the possibility to learn more
> intimately than his competitor in Foggy Bottom.[10]

Of course, as of September 22, 1973, and until November 1975, Kissinger was his own
competitor.

Becoming secretary of state—even as he did not have to worry about a serious
bureaucratic rival—meant a dramatic, and often frustrating, series of transforma-
tions. The number of personnel under his guidance dramatically increased. When
he came to office in 1969, Kissinger had raised some eyebrows by tripling the number of NSC staff to 34. By 1971 he had enlarged his empire to include 46 assistants
and 105 administrative personnel; most of who worked in the Executive Office
Building adjacent to the White House. But the State Department was in a different
league. Throughout the 1970s its personnel hovered around 13,000. Half of them
were stationed abroad in the American embassies and consulates that spanned the
150 or so countries with which the United States enjoyed diplomatic relations.

On the face of it, Kissinger faced substantial challenges. For all his considerable
abilities at the negotiation table, Kissinger had, after all, alienated many within the
State Department's bureaucracy. While Soviet-American summitry and the opening to China were major achievements, they were, decisively, White House triumphs.
Moreover, in cases such as the Indo-Pakistani War of 1971, Kissinger had pushed for
policies that contradicted the advice of those who were actually aware of the regional
context of such crises. There was also the sheer size of the State Department that
reflected the major difference between the NSC and State: the former focused on a
limited number of issues and, usually, on grand strategy; the latter was in charge of
a far wider range of issues ranging from the familiar ones of arms control and political relations to foreign assistance and visa and immigration policy. For a new secretary of state it was easy to get lost in the sheer volume of paperwork and the weight
of the ceremonial aspects of the job. This, in fact, had been one of the major disad-
vantages that William Rogers had experienced in his rivalry with Kissinger.

In short, the immediate challenge in September 1973 was to organize the State
Department in a way that allowed Kissinger to focus on key foreign policy issues
without jeopardizing the smooth functioning of the day-to-day diplomacy of the
United States. In addition, he needed, somehow, to balance the dual roles of secretary of state and NSC adviser.

The latter problem was relatively easy to solve. Kissinger's deputy, Brent Scowcroft, simply assumed a more prominent, if still subservient, position. Other top aides moved with Kissinger to prominent positions in the seventh floor of the State Department. Winston Lord became the chief of the Policy Planning Staff. Helmut Sonnenfeldt was given the post of counselor, a purposely nondescript title that, in this case, meant that Sonnenfeldt remained as Kissinger's closest adviser on Soviet policy and East-West relations. William G. Hyland, another trusted associate, became the head of the Bureau of Intelligence and Research. Kissinger also convinced Lawrence Eagleburger, who would later become the only career Foreign Service officer ever to serve as secretary of state, to become his executive assistant and, later, deputy undersecretary of management. One of the few men to have the guts to tell the temperamental secretary of state when he was "full of shit," Eagleburger's role was more significant than his position in the hierarchy may have suggested. He became, in effect, the man who ran the State Department during the frequent absences of the secretary himself.[11]

* * *

Still, Kissinger's adjustment to the new post was difficult. There was little time left in his schedule for the kind of strategic conceptual thinking to which he had become accustomed at the NSC. His temperament was not necessarily best suited for running such a vast organization. Kissinger would frequently rant about the lack of conceptual thinking in the State Department, about being a "clearing house" for cables. During a meeting of American ambassadors to the Far East in mid-November 1973, for example, he stressed the need for the State Department "to be more conceptual, less geared to just reporting facts, and more geared to determining where we are going rather than where we are." Kissinger found the "mass of facts to be stifling."[12] In February 1974, when State Department press secretary Robert McCloskey pointed out that Kissinger had a reputation for not letting anyone else make decisions, Kissinger responded testily: "Well I will let them [make decisions] if I have the confidence that the decisions will be what I want." The State Department people would have to "be philosophically on my wave length first," he added. He continued: "What I can do is to try to set the overall strategy and to infuse the Department with a certain spirit, so that people know where they are going. With a little bit of lift we can get things done. Cable clearing is incidental to my work."[13]

The real challenge, though, did not come from getting accustomed to the size of the foreign service, reframing the organizational structure of the State Department, or trying to reduce the flow of cable traffic across his desk. The true test of Kissinger's abilities was to be his guardianship of American foreign policy. Most particularly, the new secretary of state needed to build on the successes of the first Nixon administration in triangular diplomacy and détente, to respond effectively to the sudden explosion of such regional crises as the October 1973 War in the Middle East, all the while maintaining America's traditional alliance systems intact.

Given Watergate, an emasculated chief executive, and the run-up to the 1976 presidential elections, this was a tall order. As secretary of state, Kissinger was now subjected to continuous congressional oversight. The confirmation hearings of September 1973 were but the first in a series of appearances in front of the Senate Foreign Relations Committee, where Kissinger would be called upon to justify the administration's foreign policy. His calls for a bipartisan approach were frequently ignored in the atmosphere of the mid-1970s, as politicians seized the opportunity to attack the secretive methods and the un-American realpolitik of what, in due course, became known derisively as the Nixon–Ford–Kissinger foreign policy. Although he would later attempt to educate the American public about the benefits of détente, Kissinger would eventually find himself the subject of a bipartisan critique rather than a beneficiary of a consensus.

DOMESTIC CONUNDRUMS AND FOREIGN POLICY

One of those who wished Kissinger well upon his confirmation was George F. Kennan. The Truman administration's Policy Planning Staff chief, the ambassador to Moscow and Yugoslavia, the Princeton University professor, and sometime foreign policy contrarian dispensed detailed advice in a long letter to Kissinger on September 19. Kennan focused his comments on détente and the emerging domestic challenge to Kissinger's conduct of Soviet-American relations. Kennan was highly critical of Senator Henry Jackson's efforts to link the question of Jewish emigration from the Soviet Union to the granting of Most Favorite Nation (MFN) status to the USSR via the so-called Jackson–Vanik Amendment that had been formally introduced in March 1973 (see chapter 15). "It is improper, confusing to everyone, and usually ineffective when a government tries to shape its policy in such a way as to work domestic-political changes in another country," Kennan wrote. He went on to emphasize the basic affinity that he and Kissinger shared regarding the conduct of U.S. foreign policy:

> The proper concern of this government, and the only one that can, in the long run, be made intelligible to our people and the world, are the interests of this country, generously and enlightenedly [sic] conceived, not the interests of any faction, however put upon, of the citizens of any other country.

Kissinger had little time to study Kennan's letter and only sent a pro forma response to the veteran foreign policy analyst. Yet, the newly minted secretary of state undoubtedly took heart in the fact that Kennan's thoughts seemed to parallel his own. Foreign and domestic policies should be kept separate as far as possible; at the minimum the latter should not be allowed to influence the former so as to jeopardize the so-called national interest.[14]

Such separation of powers, or immunization of foreign policy from the influence of domestic politicking, did not, because it simply could not, occur. After all, it had been exactly this particular linkage—the close interconnection between domestic and foreign affairs—that had forced Nixon's hand in the summer of 1973 and elevated Kissinger to the position of secretary of state. Between 1973 and 1976, the impact of Watergate would be compounded by persistent attacks on both the substance and style of Kissinger's foreign policy. Indeed, by the time he moved into Foggy Bottom, executive authority had already been challenged by the passing of the war powers resolution, which limited the president's ability to authorize the long-term use of American troops abroad without express congressional support. At the same time as Nixon nominated Kissinger, the Congress passed a resolution banning further bombing in Cambodia. Over the next few years, during the remainder of Nixon's presidency and throughout Ford's, a battle between the legislative and the executive branches would continue to complicate Kissinger's conduct of American foreign policy.

In effect, it was a supreme irony—which to some may carry a sense of historical justice—that Kissinger reached the pinnacle of his powers and influence at a time when America was rocked by the worst domestic crisis since the Civil War. While Kissinger seemed all-powerful in September 1973, while he had taken over the reins of foreign policy from a beleaguered president, he was ironically in the process of losing control over the course of events. Although Gallup polls showed that 80 percent of Americans had a favorable impression of Kissinger at the time of his confirmation, the wiretap controversy had already exposed the dark side of Kissinger's character. Moreover, his policies were now under much tighter congressional scrutiny and the conduct of secret diplomacy had become all but impossible.[15]

Growing domestic criticism in the United States was, though, only part of the explanation for the demise of Kissinger's architecture in the years after he became secretary of state. However powerful the American foreign policy establishment, and Kissinger at its helm, were, its control over events around the globe was limited. In particular, no American statesman could control, let alone predict, the actions of various individuals, groups, and countries in all regions of the world. And yet, given its preponderant position around the world, the United States had to respond to most, if not all, regional crises that erupted unexpectedly. In some cases the response could have wide-ranging implications for the overall conducting of American foreign policy.

The war that erupted in the Middle East less than a month into Kissinger's tenure as secretary of state would be such a defining moment.

14

Unilateral Advantage

The October War and Shuttle Diplomacy

Soon after 6:00 A.M. on October 6, 1973, Assistant Secretary of State Joseph Sisco rushed into Kissinger's suite at the Waldorf Towers in New York. A war in the Middle East, pitting Israel against Egypt and Syria, Sisco announced, was about to begin. He had just received a cable to this effect from the U.S. ambassador to Israel, Kenneth Keating, who had received a stern warning to this effect from the Israeli prime minister, Golda Meir. Only rapid and decisive action from the newly appointed secretary of state, who was in New York to participate in the annual UN General Assembly meetings, could avert the outbreak of war.

Over the next few hours Kissinger made frantic phone calls to Soviet Ambassador Dobrynin and the Israeli charge d'affaires, Mordechai Shalev (both in Washington). He also spoke with the Egyptian and Israeli foreign ministers Mohamed el-Zayyat and Abba Eban (who were in New York for the same purpose as Kissinger); he tried, unsuccessfully, to reach the Syrian vice foreign minister Mohammed Zakariya Ismail (the Syrian UN embassy in New York was not answering their phone); and he sent telegrams to Jordan and Saudi Arabia. By 8:30 it appeared clear that a war was about to start. Kissinger spoke with Al Haig in Key Biscayne, who passed on the message to Nixon. An hour later Kissinger spoke again with Dobrynin, telling the Soviet ambassador his, correct, interpretation of events: the Egyptians and Syrians had launched a surprise attack on Israel. Dobrynin responded that the Egyptians were arguing that it was Israel that began the attack.

"You and I know that is baloney," Kissinger replied and stressed that the war in the Middle East should not be allowed to harm détente. The improvements in

Soviet-American relations during the past few years were too important to be "destroyed by maniacs" in the Middle East.

The Yom Kippur, or October, War had begun.[1]

A MODEL OF CRISIS MANAGEMENT?

The October War and its resolution, particularly the shuttle diplomacy that followed, were to cement Kissinger's reputation as a skillful negotiator. Later on, he would take great pride in his performance of 1973–74, devoting eleven out of twenty-five chapters of the second volume of his memoirs either entirely or predominantly to the October War and shuttle diplomacy. In August 2003 Kissinger published *Crisis*, a book devoted, for the most part, to the Middle East crisis during which, Kissinger wrote, his "policy was designed to shape events in conformity with America's values and national interests."[2]

Perhaps this is understandable. For in retrospect, the period from October 1973 until Nixon's resignation in August 1974 saw few other triumphs: in Indochina fighting continued, with the Chinese progress stalled over Taiwan, and Nixon's last summit with the Soviets in the summer of 1974 did not produce substantive results. Meanwhile, Watergate continued to erode the Nixon administration's morale and effectiveness. Any foreign policy move requiring congressional support faced an uphill struggle. In fact, from the domestic perspective, solving a crisis in the Middle East—especially if it could be done while simultaneously reducing the USSR's role in the area—might even help restore some of the beleaguered president's credibility. Perhaps most significantly from Kissinger's perspective, however, the Middle East was, unquestionably, his show. In October 1973, Nixon was in no condition to execute U.S. policy in the Middle East. Depressed, the president reverted to drinking. On October 11, for example, Kissinger told Brent Scowcroft to refuse a call from the British Prime Minister Edward Heath to Nixon because the president was "loaded."

Because he was in charge, the October War and the diplomacy that followed thus offers an excellent opportunity for evaluating Kissinger's performance as a diplomat, strategist, and crisis manager. It is thus an ideal case study for answering two broad questions: Was the outcome of the October War a great achievement? Did Kissinger's behavior and American policy truly reflect American "values" as well as the country's "interests"?

A close look at the evidence now available shows, in fact, a mixed record with some disturbing side effects and outcomes.

One key aspect deserves special attention: the Soviet-American jockeying that made the crisis into one with potentially global ramifications. For Kissinger's unilateral approach elicited Soviet protests that, though unheeded, were portents of the impending decline of détente and probably had an impact on Soviet behavior in other regional crises. While Kissinger talked of a multilateral approach, he worked hard to sideline the Soviets and searched for unilateral advantage.

In particular, given that the end result of the October War and the diplomacy that followed was an enhanced U.S. prestige and a coinciding decline in Soviet influence in the Middle East, Moscow's restraints on supporting North Vietnam were diminished: unilateralism would breed unilateralism. This, in turn, made it important for Beijing to step up its efforts in Southeast Asia, which eventually amounted to increased support for the Khmer Rouge in Cambodia. By 1975, the Middle East and Indochina would see a remarkable reversal of fortunes: as U.S. influence in the Middle East increased due to the success of Kissinger's unilateralism, American ability to influence the course of events in Southeast Asia evaporated. In a very concrete sense, Kissinger made the United States into the preeminent Middle East power in 1973–74. But while doing so he also treated Indochina increasingly as a mere sideshow: in meetings with the Soviets and the Chinese in 1973–74 he hardly brought up the area that, in previous years, had repeatedly been a centerpiece of these talks. And he effectively abandoned direct diplomatic efforts with North Vietnam in December 1973.

By the summer of 1974 the press would once again idolize Kissinger for his Middle East successes. Most of the Congress, even as they prepared for the impeachment of Richard Nixon, agreed that the secretary of state had put in another virtuoso performance. But one of the untold side effects of his unilateralism in the Middle East was that Kissinger, in effect, conceded that the United States could do little to change the course of events in Indochina, where the Soviets were stepping up their aid to North Vietnam and the Chinese (and North Vietnamese) continued to bolster the Khmer Rouge. It was almost the reverse of Nixon and Kissinger's earlier postulations about linkage: by 1974 unilateral advantage in one place would translate into unilateral disadvantage in another.

THE ROAD TO WAR

By the time Sisco woke him up on that October morning Kissinger had already spent several years in shaping U.S. Middle East policy. This was the case despite Nixon's initial concern that Kissinger's Jewish background made him susceptible to the pressures of various Jewish-American interest groups. Although the majority of Americans tended to sympathize with Israel, Nixon wanted to keep an open mind in the Middle East, where the conflicting interests of Arab nationalism and Israel's survival had for decades been further complicated by the importance of the region's oil resources and Soviet efforts to gain a foothold by supporting various Arab nations.

In fact, the Nixon administration inherited a Middle East poised for further bloodshed. In the 1967 Six Day War the Israeli army had thoroughly humiliated, with the help of American arms, its Arab neighbors. By capturing Sinai, the Golan Heights, and the West Bank, Israel had perhaps improved its national security from a narrow military perspective, but such an enhanced position came at a very high price. Neither Egypt nor Syria was willing to accept the status quo and plotted ways of retrieving the lost territories. In addition, the 1967 war had made Israel responsible, in the eyes of most of the world, for a refugee crisis, the ramifications of which are still one of the major obstacles in trying to obtain a durable solution to the Middle East labyrinth. Because of the large oil depositories, the Arab-Israeli conflict had, moreover, global consequences, as any serious disturbance to the flow of oil from the area to, in particular, Western Europe and Japan, threatened to cause economic carnage to America's foremost allies. It was no wonder that Richard Nixon called the Middle East a "very explosive powder keg" in a press conference in late January 1969.[3]

To Kissinger it was always clear that the Middle East was a testing ground of Soviet-American relations; the Soviets' interest in discussing the region throughout the early détente process had only confirmed this assumption. Accordingly, as Secretary of State Rogers' efforts to come up with a comprehensive solution to the Middle East situation showed little hope of success in 1969–70, Kissinger had gradually maneuvered himself into a key position on U.S. Middle East policy. This position was confirmed during the September 1970 Jordanian crisis, when an Israeli mobilization and U.S. naval movements apparently worked to stabilize a potentially explosive situation (see chapter 6). For the next three years American policy relied heavily on supporting Israel's military force as a stabilizing factor in the region, helping to achieve the twin objectives of preventing a future Arab (Syrian and/or Egyptian) attack on Israel while undermining Soviet influence in the region.[4]

Kissinger and Nixon's faith in this approach did not waver even when the new Egyptian leader Anwar Sadat, who had replaced Nasser after his death in September 1970, signaled his readiness to cooperate with the United States. Unfortunately, in 1972—the year that saw the drama of Nixon's trip to China, the North Vietnamese Spring Offensive, and the Moscow summit—U.S. Middle East policy was devoid of much experimentation. Indeed, while on his secret trip to Moscow in April 1972 Kissinger told Gromyko that everything, including any progress on a Middle East peace settlement, was "conditional on the end of Vietnam." At the Moscow summit the following month the two sides agreed on a broad statement of principles that did not even mention Israeli withdrawal from occupied territories. This, it seems, prompted Sadat to expel the roughly 15,000 Soviet advisers from Egypt in July 1972 and search for a negotiated settlement with Israel via the United States. Unfortunately, the timing could not have been worse. The Egyptian efforts to launch into secret negotiations with the Americans had to wait for several months while Kissinger focused on the Vietnam peace talks. In the meantime, Kissinger and Nixon had roped in Iran as another strong regional ally when they stopped in Teheran after the Moscow summit. The application of the Nixon Doctrine for the Middle East, the idea that American national security interests were best served by relying on militarily strong allies (such as Israel and Iran) to maintain regional stability, effectively closed out a search for a comprehensive peace settlement.[5]

By the spring of 1973 the countdown to war was on. On the one hand, the United States did little to entice Israeli interest in a peace process. To be sure, when Prime Minister Golda Meir visited Washington in late February and early March 1973 Kissinger suggested that Nixon should stress the Israeli need to move toward peace while "Israel is still in control of the situation and while the US is in a position to keep the USSR in a secondary role." Yet, he did not suggest putting pressure on the Israeli prime minister but recommended that Nixon promise to keep U.S. economic aid at the same level and continue aircraft deliveries "at a level close to what Israel has requested." The memoranda of Meir's meetings concluded that there had "not [been] a great deal of discussion about the question of peacemaking."[6]

On the other hand, Sadat became increasingly frustrated with American policy. Freed from the political handicaps of the presence of an unpopular Soviet contingency, Sadat embarked on a buildup of the Egyptian military. He relied in large part on massive material aid from the USSR and on special equipment from West Germany. Sadat also formed a secret agreement with the Syrians (who were also receiving massive Soviet aid). Perhaps most important, the Egyptian president sought to enlist the support of those states in the region that could be expected to have influence on American policy. In practice, this meant strengthening ties with the major oil-producing nations, such as Saudi Arabia, who could use the specter of increased oil prices or the threat of cutting down production as a tool of economic diplomacy.

By the early fall of 1973 Sadat's efforts to enlist the oil weapon on his side bore fruit. Saudi Arabia, the major oil-producing nation and traditionally an American ally, indicated to the United States that it would initiate grave measures lest Washington took action "to change the direction of events in the Middle East." In late August King Faisal secretly pledged to support Sadat with $500 million and to use oil to sway world opinion. Undoubtedly, the Saudis were not simply concerned about correcting the losses that Egypt had incurred in the 1967 war. In fact, the leaders in Riyadh, as well as those in other oil-producing capitals, were presented with a tempting opportunity to transform the economic benefits of oil into a political tool.[7]

In 1973, such developments within the Arab world went unnoticed on Kissinger's radar screen. He paid seemingly little attention to numerous Egyptian and Soviet warnings. Intelligence in Israel and the United States stressed that any Arab attack would be virtual suicide and thus foreclosed the possibility of a military offensive. The analysis was simple and apparently convincing: "The Arab armies must lose; hence they would not attack."[8] What such analyses did not take into account was the immense domestic pressure on Sadat, who had replaced Nasser three years earlier after the longtime Egyptian leader's death, to break the unfavorable deadlock that had existed in the Middle East since the 1967 war.

* * *

Between the Brezhnev–Nixon meeting at San Clemente in June 1973 and the out-break of the war in October the Soviets issued one more warning. On September 28, Foreign Minister Gromyko met with Nixon and Kissinger in the Oval Office. Although the discussion covered a large number of issues, from SALT to trade, Gromyko kept coming back to one specific point. It was necessary for the Ameri-cans and Soviets to move to defuse the situation in the Middle East, he insisted. But Nixon, his mind preoccupied by a tug-of-war over the release of the White House tapes, had little to offer. The president frequently deferred to Kissinger—something he had rarely done in such high-level meetings during his first term. He promised that he would have something concrete to offer in a few months' time.[9]

By then it would be too late to deter a war.

WAR, THE SOVIETS, AND THE AIRLIFT

A clear indication that the combating of Soviet influence was constantly at the top of Kissinger's list was the simple fact that Ambassador Dobrynin received the first phone call from Kissinger after Sisco had so rudely woken him up. "You and we have a spe-cial responsibility to restrain our respective friends," Kissinger told the Soviet ambas-sador. Later the same day, Kissinger argued that it was necessary for the Americans and the Soviets to act rapidly. This was in the interest of the Arabs, he argued, because Israeli military strength meant that by Monday, October 8, Egyptian and Syrian armies would be thrown back. "If you and we could find a way of settling this now," he told Dobrynin, "then it would be an overwhelming argument (in favor of détente)."[10]

From the outset, Kissinger considered the joint Egyptian-Syrian attack a Soviet-supported (if not necessarily Soviet-inspired) move; the fact that the Soviets had removed their civilian advisers from Egypt a few days prior to the attack was ade-quate evidence of Moscow's knowledge of the forthcoming aggression. Still, Kissinger did not believe that the Soviets were keen on becoming overtly engaged and thought that they were ready to find a quick negotiated resolution to the cri-sis. Yet, while Dobrynin may have shared Kissinger's belief that Israel would quickly rebound from the initial shock and drive the attackers back, the Egyptians and Syr-ians were unlikely to yield as long as their offensive was successful. Nor did the Soviets see much point in pressing them.

"The Arabs will say to us, 'You are in collusion with the U.S. and Israel,'" Dobrynin responded to Kissinger's suggestion that Moscow apply pressure on Cairo and Damascus. "For us to tell [the Arabs] you cannot free your land, it is ridiculous," he added.[11]

After several days of frantic diplomacy and emergency meetings, it became increasingly clear that an early solution to the crisis was not possible. On Tuesday,

October 9, the Israelis made an emergency appeal to Washington for help. The next day, the first Soviet military supplies were airlifted to Damascus while El Al planes were picking up the first set of American resupplies from Norfolk, Virginia. Yet, Kissinger and Nixon—the latter preoccupied with the resignation of Vice President Spiro Agnew on October 10—held back from a full military commitment to Israel. As the Soviets continued their airlift and Israelis made increasingly urgent pleas the possibility of an early resolution quickly faded.

Finally, on October 13, after initial UN diplomacy failed to produce a ceasefire (the Egyptians rejected it before it was even introduced), Nixon ordered a full airlift of materials to Israel. The Americans commenced the transport of 1,000 tons of goods per day. Already on October 14, the Israelis scored a massive victory over the Egyptians in a tank battle on the Sinai Peninsula. By the 18th Israelis were on the offensive, notwithstanding the oil embargo imposed on countries supporting Israel (a total embargo was placed only on the United States and the Netherlands), causing many of America's allies to distance themselves from the conflict. The oil embargo, however, did press Kissinger to accelerate his diplomatic efforts. On October 19, he agreed to Anatoly Dobrynin's suggestion of an emergency visit to Moscow. The next morning, Kissinger, his staff, and Dobrynin took off from Andrews Air Force Base.[12]

As the crisis evolved from the initial Egyptian-Syrian attacks to Kissinger's trip to Moscow, it would be logical to assume that Kissinger had little time for meeting with representatives from countries that were not directly involved. Yet, the secretary of state made a point of seeing China's UN Ambassador Huang Chen on two occasions. Clearly, triangular diplomacy remained at the forefront of his thinking and influenced, to a degree, Kissinger's policy toward the October War.

In particular, Kissinger considered it important to emphasize to Beijing that his policy was driven, first and foremost, by a resolve to stand firm vis-à-vis the USSR. Kissinger's point was similar to the one he had repeatedly used in trying to enlist Chinese support for his earlier efforts in Vietnam: the United States was trying to prevent the Soviets from achieving a dominant position in the region. "Israel," he told Ambassador Huang Chen, "is a secondary, emotional problem having to do with domestic politics here. Our objective is always, when the Soviet Union appears, to demonstrate that whoever gets help from the Soviet Union cannot achieve his objective, whatever it is." Clearly, when discussing his goals in the Middle East with the Chinese ambassador, the realist had abandoned the idealism he had publicly flirted with when Kissinger had been sworn in as secretary of state a month earlier. What mattered was countering the USSR, not that America "should mean something beyond itself." A week later, a few days prior to flying off to Moscow for a meeting with Soviet leaders, Kissinger returned to the theme, expressing confidence in the success of the American airlift and his forthcoming negotiations.

"This is a competition we can win," he told Huang.[13]

He would take the most important steps toward that victory in Moscow.

MOSCOW, TEL-AVIV, AND UN RESOLUTION 338

Before Kissinger's arrival in Moscow the Soviets had engaged in a long internal debate about how to respond to the developments on the ground. But by October 15, the Politburo was seeking to bring about a ceasefire and Premier Kosygin had flown to Cairo for this purpose the following day. On the 18th—with the fortunes of war turning against the Arabs—the Soviets had decided to work with the Americans. Dobrynin invited Kissinger to come to Moscow. He accepted.

By the time Kissinger was ready to depart for Moscow in the early hours of Saturday, October 20, the strategy that he would follow had effectively been laid out. At a meeting with Scowcroft, Schlesinger, Colby, and Moorer the previous evening, Kissinger stressed that the airlift needed to continue at full speed during the negotiations in Moscow. The trip, he maintained, would give the Israelis a few extra days to push the Egyptians and Syrians back before a joint Soviet-American UN resolution. It would also "give [the Soviets] a face-saver," Kissinger said, adding that, for the sake of détente, "we can't humiliate the Soviet Union too much." He had no intention of cooperating with the Soviets because "everyone knows in the Middle East that if they want a peace they have to go through us."[14] In short, the point was to give the Soviets the impression that they were involved while keeping true bargaining power in Washington's hands. But in Moscow, Kissinger had insisted, the only item on the agenda should be a ceasefire. He was not going to discuss a comprehensive Soviet-American sponsored settlement.

Kissinger—along with Ambassador Dobrynin, Assistant Secretary of State Joseph Sisco, Ambassador Robert McCloskey, Deputy Assistant Secretary of State Roy Atherton, Eagleburger, Sonnenfeldt, Lord, Rodman, and Hyland—arrived in Moscow on Saturday evening, October 20. Brezhnev, eager to get down to business as soon as possible, invited Kissinger and his group for a private dinner in the general secretary's quarters. Despite his initial wish to wait until the following morning, Kissinger could not refuse.[15]

Brezhnev, as he usually did on such occasions, opened the first informal meeting with a long speech on the grave situation in the Middle East. Although suffering from an infection of his vocal cords, the general secretary made a forceful presentation. The situation was, he maintained, a severe test case for Soviet-American détente. "Realistically, if our two countries could come to conclusion, then we would be believed by all parties," he concluded. Kissinger and Brezhnev then agreed to use a Soviet proposal for a ceasefire resolution as a base for discussions. The first meeting ended at 10:30 P.M. Moscow time.[16]

Soon after the meeting broke out, Kissinger—operating on too little sleep and too much heavy food—blew his top. During the meeting, Nixon had sent a set of instructions including an oral message to Brezhnev that stressed the need for Moscow and Washington to "bring the necessary pressure on our respective friends for a settlement which will at last bring peace to this troubled area [the Middle

East]." In effect, Kissinger deduced, Nixon wanted him to commit to a joint comprehensive Soviet-American peace plan, rather than a mere formula for a ceasefire. He quickly cabled back to Scowcroft: "If I carry out the letter of the President's instructions, it will totally wreck what little bargaining leverage I still have. Our first objective must be cease-fire. That will be tough enough to get the Israelis to accept; it will be impossible as part of a global deal."

He also telephoned Alexander Haig.

"Will you get off my back? I have troubles of my own," the White House chief of staff replied.

Kissinger could not imagine how anything inside the beltway could compare to the gravity of the situation he was dealing with in Moscow. Haig explained. As a conclusion of a long effort to avoid handing over his White House tapes Nixon had just fired Special Prosecutor Archibald Cox, Attorney General Elliott Richardson, and Deputy Attorney General William Ruckelshaus.[17]

It was surreal. What had transpired in Washington while Kissinger and his companions were en route to Moscow was the climax of a lengthy domestic upheaval that all but sealed Nixon's fate. In May, under considerable pressure after the resignations of Haldeman and Ehrlichman, Nixon had appointed Archibald Cox, a professor at Harvard Law School, as a special prosecutor in charge of the Watergate investigations. Meanwhile, the Erwin Committee (named after its chairman, Senator Sam Erwin of North Carolina) had started holding televised hearings. In mid-July Alexander Butterfield, a member of Nixon's White House staff, testified that Nixon had, in 1971, installed a taping system in his offices. The inevitable follow-up was that Cox, after being rebuffed by the White House, asked Federal District Court Judge John Sirica to compel the White House to disclose all relevant tapes. Sirica complied, but the White House then appealed to the Washington, D.C. court of appeals. While the Senate was confirming Kissinger and Syria and Egypt launched their attacks on Israel, the decision regarding the tapes preoccupied Nixon. While the Saturday Night Massacre, as it came to be known, was troubling as an indication of Nixon's faltering domestic base, it was not entirely a disaster— at least from a tactical point of view—for Kissinger's Moscow negotiations. Nixon's preoccupation with Watergate made it undoubtedly easier (and even more justifiable) for Kissinger to ignore the president's instructions. Unlike his marathon talks with the North Vietnamese during the first Nixon administration, the Middle East peace process became, clearly and irrevocably, a one-man show.

Israeli military advances further strengthened Kissinger's hand in Moscow. At 4:00 A.M. on October 21, the Soviet ambassador to Egypt, Vladimir Vinogradov, called Brezhnev to inform him that he had just met with Anwar Sadat. The Egyptian president, Vinogradov told Brezhnev, had made a desperate plea for an immediate ceasefire. Sadat's national security adviser, Hafiz Ismail, had even acknowledged that the Israeli army would soon pose a threat to Cairo. Pressed by such an appeal, Brezhnev took the case to the Politburo the following morning. He recommended dropping demands for a comprehensive solution and focusing on an immediate ceasefire in his discussions with Kissinger. After vigorous debate the Politburo approved Brezhnev's suggestion. Although Kissinger did not know it at the time, he had little concrete to negotiate; Israeli military pressure had already guaranteed the desired result.[18]

Thus, when Kissinger and Brezhnev reconvened at noon on October 21, it took only four hours to reach an agreement on the text of what would become UN Security Council Resolution 338. The text read as follows:

The Security Council

1. *Calls upon* all parties to the present fighting to cease all firing and terminate all military activity immediately, no later than 12 hours after the moment of the adoption of this decision, in the positions they now occupy;
2. *Calls upon* the parties concerned to start immediately after the cease-fire the implementation of Security Council resolution 242 (2967) in all of its parts;
3. *Decides* that, immediately and concurrently with the cease-fire, negotiations start between the parties concerned under appropriate auspices aimed at establishing a just and durable peace in the Middle East.

There was a brief tragicomic exchange as Kissinger read out a translation of the initial Russian version's point 3 as "a just and honorable peace."

Brezhnev: Durable peace.

Kissinger: I was wondering, I have never seen the word 'honorable' before . . .

Brezhnev: It is durable . . .

Most of the discussion on that afternoon, however, focused on two other parts of the resolution: first, on what the term *under appropriate auspices* (point 3) would mean and, second, when the resolution should go into effect.

Kissinger got his wish on both counts. The resolution would go into effect only twelve hours after the UN Security Council approved it. This effectively meant that the Israelis, who had gained the upper hand on the battlefield, were given extra time to improve their position on the ground. In short, the Israelis would be in a better bargaining position, the Arabs would be weakened and more prone to make concessions, and the Soviets would have lost some more face with their allies. As to "appropriate auspices," Kissinger did agree to initial an "understanding" with Gromyko to the effect

that the phrase . . . shall mean that the negotiations between the parties concerned will take place with the active participation of the United States and the Soviet Union at the beginning and thereafter in the course of negotiations when key issues of a settlement are dealt with . . .

Yet, Kissinger was already finding excuses for ignoring Moscow's role. He could not envision cooperation "in every detail," Kissinger told Brezhnev.[19]

With the agreement on the resolution reached, Kissinger and his group set out to transfer messages to Washington and New York. Kissinger also met with the British, French, and Australian ambassadors to Moscow to brief them on the resolution and urge them to pass it on to their respective governments. There were technical difficulties and mix-ups. In the end the Security Council met in the late evening of October 21. Resolution 338 passed at 12:52 A.M. EST on October 22, or just before 8:00 A.M. Moscow time.[20]

Less than an hour later Kissinger had breakfast with Gromyko. They initialed the understanding on "appropriate auspices." Kissinger showed Gromyko another text that called for the United States and the USSR to "use their maximum influence" to ensure that all POWs would be released within three days of the ceasefire. After a brief discussion Kissinger and Gromyko agreed that they did not need to initial it. Gromyko assured that Brezhnev was committed to the release of POWs. "I'll take the word of the General Secretary," Kissinger said. The Soviets and the Americans exchanged a series of congratulatory toasts: to the American delegation, to Gromyko, Dobrynin, Nixon, and Brezhnev.

Perhaps most revealing of the uneasiness underneath the celebratory façade on that morning was the following brief exchange:

> *Kissinger:* One other question: Can I tell newsmen at the airport that I'm going [to Israel]? Would it be embarrassing?
>
> *Gromyko:* Psychologically . . . It would be preferable if you not tell your destination from Moscow.[21]

Although he was laughing at the time, Gromyko realized that Kissinger left Moscow with a strong hand: a representative of the only country that could influence Israeli decisions and with an improved position vis-à-vis those Arab countries that had relied on Soviet military aid.

"IF YOU NEEDED A FEW HOURS AT THE OTHER END . . ."

The Israeli prime minister, Golda Meir, was not ready to follow Kissinger's advice blindly. "She was an original," Kissinger would later describe one of the foremost leaders of Israel. Leonard Garment, the occasional Kissinger–Nixon envoy to Israel, put it in somewhat more familiar terms. Meir, Garment writes, "radiated a warm intelligence that reminded American Jews of their nurturing, nagging mothers. (Just ask Henry Kissinger.)"

No doubt, the genuine respect and even affection that Kissinger felt for Meir was partly a result of certain similarities in their respective personal histories. Born in

Kiev in 1898, the seventy-five-year-old Meir was a veteran Zionist devoted, above all, to the survival of Israel. Originally named Golda Mabovitch, Meir had immigrated to the United States in 1906. Unlike the Kissingers in the 1930s, the Mabovitches had settled in Milwaukee. In 1921, after a brief career as a schoolteacher, Meir emigrated with her husband, Morris Meyerson (the name was hebraized to Meir in 1956), to Palestine. She joined the Palestine labor movement and in 1936 became head of the political department of the Histadrut (General Federation of Jewish Labor). After World War II, Meir served briefly as Israel's envoy to Moscow. She was minister of labor in 1949–56 and foreign minister in 1956–66. In 1966 she became secretary-general of the Mapai Party (later the Labor Party) and became prime minister after the death of Levi Eshkol in 1969. A brilliant politician and consummate negotiator, she earned a special distinction from Kissinger: she became the only major international leader that Kissinger would refer to by using only her first name.[22]

But "Golda" was as tough a negotiator as Kissinger had ever faced. After the Americans landed at Lod (later renamed Ben-Gurion) Airport between Jerusalem and Tel-Aviv, Kissinger had a brief, fifteen-minute, one-on-one with the prime minister at the Israeli government's guesthouse in nearby Herzliyya. They were then joined by Peter Rodman and Meir's assistant, Mordechai Gazit, for another forty-minute private discussion.

Kissinger started on the defensive. There were no secret Soviet-American understandings, he assured. The term *appropriate auspices* in the Resolution 338 meant "nothing . . . until there are negotiations." He said that Brezhnev had given his "word of honor" that the Soviets would press Egypt and Syria for the return of Israeli POWs and recommended that negotiations should only begin after that had occurred. Perhaps most revealingly, however, Kissinger and Meir had a fateful exchange on the observance of the ceasefire:

> *Kissinger:* Did you get our message that if you needed a few hours at the other end . . .
>
> *Meir:* What does standstill ceasefire mean?
>
> *Kissinger:* Frankly we haven't thought it through . . . [but] You won't get violent protests from Washington if something happens during the night [of October 22–23], while I'm flying [to Washington].
>
> *Meir:* If they don't stop, we won't.
>
> *Kissinger:* Even if they do . . .

Kissinger's message was simple: if you wish to continue your military advances for a few hours after the ceasefire was formally in effect, the Americans would not protest. It was a troubling comment, showing not only Kissinger's obvious wish to see the Israelis in as strong a position as possible when the fighting ended, but indicating that he had little respect for formal agreements. Luckily, the comments did not become known in Egypt or Syria at the time. Yet, Kissinger's almost off-handed comments to Golda Meir most likely incited the Israelis to do exactly what Kissinger had told them they could: continue advancing after the initial ceasefire was supposed to take hold.

Kissinger would later write that he simply stopped in Israel "to establish the cease-fire." That was certainly the major purpose of the quick stopover. But Kissinger's casual attitude toward the strict observance of the time when the cease-fire was to go into effect managed to contribute to the prolongation of the war. Indeed, Kissinger explained a central element of his overall approach to the war and its aftermath to Meir in straightforward terms: "It is important that I not *appear* as your spokesman."[23] Over subsequent months Kissinger would work hard and successfully to avoid such an appearance, to the extent that Meir would later criticize Kissinger for being too willing to haggle with Arab leaders.

* * *

At 2:30 P.M. Kissinger's entire group joined Meir, Deputy Prime Minister Yigal Allon, Foreign Minister Abba Eban, Defense Minister Moshe Dayan, Ambassador Yitzhak Rabin, and others for a luncheon meeting. Of all the Israeli cabinet members Dayan was the most belligerent. "I do not like to stop," he said when discussing a message from Sadat indicating that the Egyptian army was ready to stop firing at 6:00 P.M. "That is your domestic jurisdiction," Kissinger replied. "I'll be on an airplane," he added. Clearly, Kissinger had no problem with and even encouraged further Israeli advances.

The luncheon finished at 4:00 P.M. General David Elazar, the chief of staff of the Israeli Defense Force (IDF) then gave a military briefing and Kissinger's group went back to the airport. Before heading back to Washington, Kissinger flew to London's Heathrow Airport and gave a quick briefing to British Foreign Secretary Sir Alec Douglas-Home.[24]

At 4:00 A.M. on Tuesday, October 23, Kissinger and his weary group finally landed at Andrews Air Force Base, only to discover that impeachment proceedings against Nixon—whose interest in the Middle East War was severely curtailed by his mounting domestic troubles—were a certainty. But they also discovered that the ceasefire agreement negotiated in Moscow was failing to take hold, perhaps partly due to Kissinger's flippant comments to the Israelis.

THE THIRD ARMY, "THE ALERT," AND THE CEASEFIRE

It did not take long for the Soviet-American sponsored ceasefire to break down. Neither the Egyptians nor, in particular, the Israelis (encouraged by Kissinger's comments), were ready to stop firing at each other at 6:52 P.M. local time on October 22 as called for in the UN resolution. The key issue was the Egyptian Third

Army of 25,000 men, which, at the time the ceasefire went into effect was on the southern sector of the eastern bank of the Suez Canal. The Third Army had a narrow overland link to the west (Egypt) and the Israeli military was eager to encircle it completely. They undoubtedly assumed that Kissinger's comments at Herzliyya had, in effect, given them a green light to do exactly that (in his memoirs Kissinger admits that this was possible). He did not accept Golda Meir's explanation that the Israeli cabinet had decided on the renewed offensive because of continued Egyptian attacks. Nor did the Soviets.[25]

Another crisis ensued.

On the morning of October 23, Kissinger met with his staff and with Soviet charge d'affaires Vorontsov (Dobrynin was still in Moscow). He sent and received several cables to and from Moscow, Tel Aviv, and Cairo. Before noon it was clear— on the basis of a phone call from the Israeli ambassador Simcha Dinitz—that the Israelis had cut off the Egyptian Third Army's supply routes. At 12:36 P.M. Kissinger received a message from Brezhnev addressed to Nixon, proposing (significantly not 'demanding') an immediate implementation of the ceasefire and suggesting "that the [UN] Security Council be convened most urgently." By the afternoon of October 23, a new ceasefire resolution was finally assured as the UN Security Council passed Resolution 339. It instructed Israel and Egypt to uphold a ceasefire as of 7:00 A.M. local time the following morning (1:00 A.M. EST). Even Syria, which had not concurred with the earlier ceasefire resolution, indicated its approval.[26]

*   *   *

But the crisis was hardly over. In the morning of October 24 EST (afternoon in the Middle East), Israelis and Egyptians were still fighting. At 9.45 am Kissinger placed a call to Dobrynin. "Anatol, the madmen in the Middle East are at it again," he offered, adding that "this time the Egyptians may have started it." He was putting pressure on both sides and wanted Dobrynin to "understand that we are not playing any games here." Then, Anwar Sadat called for a joint U.S.-Soviet peacekeeping force.

Such cooperation was never seriously contemplated on the U.S. side. But the Soviets seized the opportunity. On the evening of October 24, Dobrynin called Kissinger saying that the Soviets were ready to support a joint, UN-approved, military mission to enforce the cease-fire agreement. A few hours later a letter from Brezhnev reaffirming Dobrynin's oral message arrived. Kissinger quickly rejected any such notion (whose implications would have been huge not only in the Middle East but also in terms of China). Under no pretext, he later wrote, was the United States going to allow Soviet troops in the area. Perhaps most important, however, he interpreted Brezhnev's comment on possible unilateral Soviet action as an ultimatum.

As historian Raymond Garthoff and others have argued, this was an alarmist interpretation that represented a worst-case interpretation of the facts. Brezhnev had, in fact, ordered an end to the Soviet airlift on October 24 as a showcase of Moscow's willingness to cooperate with the United States. But Kissinger and others interpreted the move as a decision to focus on the possible deployment of Soviet troops.

Thus, on the night of October 24–25, Kissinger convened a meeting of the key officials in Washington (including CIA Director William Colby, Secretary of Defense James Schlesinger, White House Chief of Staff Alexander Haig, Kissinger's deputy Brent Scowcroft, and Joint Chief of Staff Chairman Thomas Moorer). Nixon did not attend in person, although Haig would leave the meeting several times to inform the president.[27]

What instructions the president gave are still somewhat uncertain. Nixon was clearly depressed from the after-effects of the Saturday Night Massacre a few days earlier and had been drinking; he was in no condition to make informed decisions. According to Haig, the president likened the situation to the 1962 Cuban Missile Crisis and simply told him: "We've got to act."

Kissinger and others did act. They issued DEFCON III, a directive that put U.S. strategic nuclear forces on high alert. Whether this was what Nixon had in mind is not entirely clear. Yet, given his penchant for toughness—similar incidents of brinkmanship over, for example, 1970 reports that the Soviets were building a naval base in Cuba—does not foreclose the possibility that a sober Nixon would have done more or less the same thing as Kissinger, Haig, Scowcroft, Colby, Moorer, and Schlesinger did.[28]

Whoever ordered it, the alert was, as Raymond Garthoff puts it, basically "an excessively dramatic maneuver by Kissinger for diplomatic leverage."[29] A few days later, on October 30, Ambassador Dobrynin actually asked Kissinger: "What kind of a relationship is this if one letter produces a [nuclear] alert."[30] In fact, Brezhnev, who had apparently inserted the reference to possible unilateral Soviet action into his letter merely as a way of putting more pressure on the Americans to agree on joint action, simply replied to the alert by agreeing to send a joint group of observers to the Middle East. Meanwhile the UN passed yet another ceasefire resolution (No. 340).

The ceasefire took hold. Yet, it was probably not the result of the issuing of DEFCON III but the subsequent pressure that Kissinger put on the Israelis to stop their continued attacks against the Egyptian Third Army. On the evening of the 26th he made it clear to the Israelis that the United States would not allow the destruction of the Third Army, demanded that the Israelis allow nonmilitary supplies to reach the Egyptians, and insisted that subsequent negotiations between Egypt and Israel were necessary. Otherwise, the United States would have to reconsider its relationship with Israel, Kissinger threatened. The Israelis eventually gave in. The third ceasefire resolution took hold and the imminent crisis passed.

Perhaps most important, it was the United States, and ultimately Kissinger, that had been placed at the center of the storm. The manner in which the final ceasefire resolution was achieved, moreover, gave the impression—most likely faulty—that the U.S. decision to issue DEFCON III had saved the Middle East from a potential Soviet intervention. As much as Kissinger's brinkmanship had apparently impressed the Egyptians, however, it had angered the Israelis, who thought they had been robbed of an even more decisive victory. The Soviet leadership undoubtedly felt double-crossed by Kissinger's assurances in Moscow that the United States would press the Israelis toward accepting a ceasefire.

*   *   *

The story of the alert would not be complete without noting the reaction in Beijing. Although the Chinese were not deeply involved in the Middle East crisis, Mao and Zhou were keenly observing the Soviet-American tug-of-war over influence in the region. Not unexpectedly, they agreed with Kissinger's goal of marginalizing the Soviets. On November 12 in Beijing, Mao and Kissinger brought up the alert and its consequences. "Every once in a while we have to take some strong measures as we did two weeks ago," Kissinger told the Chairman. "Those were not bad, those measures," Mao responded. He then added: "[The Soviets] can't possibly dominate the Middle East, because, although their ambition is great, their capacities are meager."[31]

With the ceasefire finally in place, diplomacy and Kissinger were placed at the epicenter of the Middle East settlement. In the months that followed his strategy would reflect three specific elements: the need to win Anwar Sadat's trust, the necessity to impress the Israeli government that they would actually have to compromise with their neighbors, and the conviction that the Soviets should and could be marginalized. While he would not succeed in solving all of the Middle East's problems, Kissinger would manage, by May 1974, to place the United States in a position of a unilateral advantage.

A "PARTNERSHIP FOR PEACE"? KISSINGER AND SADAT

Two weeks after the nuclear alert and ceasefire, large, enthusiastic Egyptian crowds in Cairo greeted the Jewish-American secretary of state. He arrived in the Egyptian capital, after stopovers in Morocco and Tunisia, late on Tuesday evening, November 6, 1973. It was, in a number of ways, a historic visit and the first of Kissinger's numerous forays to the land of the pharaohs. To be sure, Kissinger's predecessor, William Rogers, had been to Cairo only two years earlier to discuss the moribund Jarring initiative, one of the many plans that aimed for a comprehensive solution to the Arab-Israeli conflict. But prior to that unsuccessful visit, American secretaries of state had boycotted Egypt throughout most of the Cold War (only John Foster Dulles had been to the country in 1953). Most important, though, what made Kissinger's November visit a proverbial turning point was the simple fact that as a result of the previous weeks' developments, he had an extraordinary opportunity for launching a significant peace process in the Middle East. Much depended, though, on the attitude of Anwar Sadat.

In his fourth year as Egypt's president, the fifty-five-year-old Sadat ruled in the formidable shadow of the charismatic Gamal Abdal Nasser, whom he had replaced after Nasser's death and sixteen-year reign in September 1970. Less charismatic than his former mentor, Sadat had been a loyal supporter of the nationalist leader ever since entering the Abbasia Military Academy in the 1930s. To the Israelis—and undoubtedly to Kissinger—Sadat's brief tenure as a German agent during World War II was hardly comforting. He had been in British jails twice: first in 1942 as a spy and in 1946–49 for participating in terrorist acts against pro-British Egyptian officials. In 1952 Sadat took part in the bloodless coup that deposed King Farouk. Throughout the 1950s and 1960s he held a variety of government positions, including director of army public relations; secretary-general of the National Union, Egypt's only political party; and president of the national assembly. In 1969 he became Nasser's vice president, and then succeeded to the presidency a year later. Sadat was ultimately a pragmatist eager to consider all options to ensure his country's security. Kissinger would later call him "a world leader . . . a great man."[32]

In 1973 the question was whether Sadat would be willing to compromise and, if necessary, lose face at home and abroad for the cause of peace.

The odds were hardly in Kissinger's favor. To begin with, there was a legacy of distrust, fed by generous American support to Israel and the slipping of the recent ceasefire initiatives. There was the oil weapon: with every passing day the price hikes and the embargo increased international pressure on the need for Israel to make concessions; on November 6, for example, the European Community (EC), whose member countries were more heavily dependent on Middle East oil than the United States, had approved a declaration urging Israel to withdraw back to the original October 22 ceasefire line. Sadat's willingness to accommodate Israeli demands was hardly increased by this apparent international show of support (and, as Kissinger points out, the EC declaration was bound to make it difficult for the Egyptian president to accept anything less than what the Europeans called for). On top of all this, Kissinger was, once again, under pressure from Nixon. The day prior to Kissinger's arrival in Cairo, Senator Edward Brooke of Massachusetts had become the first Republican to join the growing ranks of Democrats calling for Nixon's resignation. Eager for an international breakthrough to divert attention away from his Watergate troubles, the president thus told his cabinet that he might have to tighten the screws on Israel in order to solve a potentially severe energy crisis. In short, Kissinger may have arrived in Cairo with a clear-cut strategy of placing the United States in the middle of the postwar peace process, but he had few cards to play. At best, he would have to produce a quick breakthrough with Sadat.

To Kissinger's relief, the Egyptian president did not believe that the oil embargo would have a decisive impact on the outcome of the October War. He had also concluded—already during the war—that the only way of breaking the deadlock of the Egyptian-Israeli confrontation was by employing the services of the United States and, in effect, turning his back on other external players (including the Soviet

Union). It was the United States, he well knew, that had pressured the Israelis against the complete destruction of the Egyptian Third Army which, as of the commencement of Kissinger's visit, was still under Israeli encirclement. Sadat's alternatives were, in fact, severely limited and hardly enviable. He could hang tough and wait for the Israelis to blink. That they would was unlikely in the current situation, however, and would require American pressure on Jerusalem. Alternatively, Sadat could offer concessions and reopen the peace process. Whatever road he chose, though, he needed Kissinger's help.

During their November 7 meeting, Sadat made it clear to Kissinger that Egypt was ready to deal. As any negotiator would, he started off by demanding more than was reasonably possible; Sadat suggested a "Kissinger plan" that would call for the Israeli forces to withdraw from two-thirds of the Sinai. After flattering Sadat with questions about his remarkable surprise attack on October 6, Kissinger made it clear that such a "Kissinger plan" was impossible. Should Sadat even insist on an Israeli withdrawal to the October 22 ceasefire line, he would have to rely on Soviet (and EC) support. Instead, Kissinger suggested that Sadat accept the status quo in the near term, while the United States—or, more accurately, Kissinger himself—would arrange a disengagement agreement as a first step; this would then induce further steps on the way toward a more acceptable long-term solution than could ever be possible in a climate poisoned by continuous military pressures. In short, Kissinger asked Sadat to accept two things: (1) the continued isolation of the Egyptian Third Army over the next several weeks (possibly months); (2) that the United States alone could be trusted to produce an Egyptian-Israeli agreement beneficial to Cairo's long-term interests.

Sadat bit the bullet. Without a fight, he accepted Kissinger's proposal. The two discussed a six-point Israeli-Egyptian plan detailing specific steps toward reducing the tension on the front lines (such as establishment of UN checkpoints, exchange of POWs) and a commitment to discuss the return to the October 22 line. Sadat's only condition was that he would not be able to reestablish formal U.S.-Egyptian diplomatic relations until there was "some tangible diplomatic success." (After the first Israeli-Egyptian disengagement was signed a few months later, formal relations were restored on February 28, 1974.) On that morning of November 7, 1973, in Cairo, Anwar Sadat effectively made a decision that started the U.S.-dominated Middle East peace process that has continued, with its ups and downs, for over three decades.

Why did Sadat so quickly accept what Kissinger had to offer, hence bestowing on the U.S. secretary of state the mantle of peacemaker? Was his move a huge risk that eventually cost Sadat his own life?

The Egyptian president's decision was both a courageous reversal of policy and a calculated move to pass the onus of responsibility for the potential failure of peacemaking to Kissinger's shoulders. On the one hand, Sadat had to go against most of his advisers and face a potential popular revolt. His decision effectively removed Sadat's ability to claim that Egypt and its president were the leaders of the pan-Arab movement that drew much of its strength from the rejection of Israel's right to exist. Instead of banking on the support of the oil-rich Arab nations, the Soviet Union, or the radical pan-Arab movement, Sadat threw his lot in with the United States. On the other hand, Sadat also put Kissinger on the spot. "I am making this agreement with the United States, not with Israel," the Egyptian president pointed out. The next step would, clearly, have to be a concession from the other side, Sadat stressed.

MULTILATERAL NECESSITY: THE GENEVA CONFERENCE

Even if Sadat was on board with the peace process, much more remained to be done. Most urgently, Kissinger needed to assure that the Soviets—and others—would not intervene in his forthcoming negotiations with the Israelis and Egyptians. To this effect—and to highlight the role of the United States—the next step in Kissinger's post–October War strategy was to appear supportive of the Geneva Conference while simultaneously assuring that it could not result in substantive progress. In short, the conference in Geneva that opened in mid-December amounted to a diversion, a multilateral façade to obfuscate the reality of Kissinger's unilateral diplomacy. The Soviets were, though, getting anxious. After the ceasefire and the alert, the Soviets made repeated complaints that the United States was acting "against the spirit and letter" of détente and the October Moscow meetings. [33]

Just prior to the opening of the Geneva Conference Kissinger went on a whirlwind tour of the Middle East that made it clear that the only step that might produce results was through an opening of an Egyptian-Israeli dialogue. As in November, Sadat was the most forthcoming of Kissinger's negotiating partners: on December 14 the Egyptian president agreed to devote the opening session in Geneva to "ceremonial and procedural matters," on a broad agenda for the disengagement negotiations, and not to raise the question of Palestinian representation during the disengagement phase. Later the same day Kissinger met King Faisal in Riyadh and pressed the Saudi leader for his cooperation on the oil embargo. On December 15–17, Kissinger stopped in Damascus, Amman, Beirut, and Jerusalem. He managed to secure Israeli attendance at the Geneva Conference but eventually failed to induce the Syrians to come. After a six-and-a-half-hour meeting with Asad, Kissinger concluded that although the Syrians were keen on maintaining close contact with the United States, they would "be hard to deal with." In particular, they would not send a delegation to the Geneva Conference. Kissinger then flew to Europe, visiting Lisbon, Madrid, and Paris (where Kissinger held his last face-to-face talks with Le Duc Tho). Finally, on December 20, Kissinger attended the opening of the Geneva Conference.[34]

By the time he arrived in Geneva, Kissinger was increasingly optimistic that his strategy was working successfully. On December 19, he cabled to Nixon:

The strategy we developed in the wake of the Arab-Israeli war is unfolding largely as planned. We have built on the ceasefire and negotiating formula worked out during my October 20–22 trip to Moscow to stabilize the ceasefire on the Israeli-Egyptian front and to launch the negotiating process that will begin in Geneva. This is a historic development, the first time Arabs and the Israelis will negotiate face to face in a quarter of a century. We have done this while enhancing our influence in the Arab world and reducing that of the USSR.

What about the absence of the Syrians? "A blessing in disguise," Kissinger maintained. It had made it easier for the Israelis, facing a domestic election the following month, to attend the Geneva Conference. "We should let Asad stew in his own juice for a while and let moderate Arab pressures and possibly some Soviet pressure build on him as he watchfully awaits developments at Geneva," he added. Two days later, amid the conference, Kissinger cabled Nixon, "your strategy is working well. We are the only participant who is in close touch with all the parties, the only power that can produce progress, and the only one that each is coming to in order to make that progress."[35]

Kissinger's prognosis and predictions were all positive:

> There is a real chance of an Egyptian-Israeli agreement on disengagement. Sadat has bought our concept of a step-by-step phased approach . . . The prospects between Jordan and Israel are also hopeful since they share a mutual interest in keeping out the Palestinian radicals from the West Bank . . . As to Syria, its participation later may prove possible if progress can be made behind the scenes.[36]

The Middle East was working out much in the way Kissinger had planned: the Egyptians and Israelis had turned to him as the peace broker and the most disruptive elements in the region—the Palestinians and the Syrians—had been marginalized. Even the Soviets appeared willing to play the game by U.S. rules. On December 22, Kissinger and Peter Rodman met Gromyko at the USSR's Geneva mission. They drank toasts to U.S.-Soviet cooperation and hardly touched upon the Middle East aside from a few jokes about the trustworthiness of the Arabs. Instead, their three-hour meeting focused on bilateral Soviet-American matters and preparations for the 1974 summit.[37]

Shortly after Kissinger returned to Washington, Anatoly Dobrynin came to the Oval Office to meet with Nixon and Kissinger. The Soviet ambassador seemed to agree that Moscow and Washington were, in fact, cooperating closely on the Middle East. He even complimented Kissinger on his recent efforts. Nixon, whose role in the Middle East process had been severely circumscribed by constant Watergate problems, was equally effusive. He emphasized "that we must not be in conflict and we must not have one side try to drive the other out." Then he made a promise: "I will deliver the Israelis. It will be done."[38]

It is hard to tell whether Nixon was being genuine in his promise of cooperation and offer to deliver the Israelis. If he was, it reflected another difference in his and Kissinger's approach to the Middle East conflict. For Kissinger, as later events would show, had little interest in engaging the Soviets outside the Geneva multilateral process.

DUCKY'S CHALLENGE AND HENRY'S MISSIVE

On December 20, 1973, as Kissinger prepared for the opening of the Geneva Conference, Vietnam suddenly resurfaced. He met in Paris, for the last time, with Le Duc Tho to discuss the many violations of the Paris Peace Agreements. It was a meeting that Kissinger dismisses with one simple sentence in his memoirs. "Tho," Kissinger writes, "was growing more unbearably insolent as America's domestic divisions gradually opened up new and decisive strategic opportunities for Hanoi."[39]

While Kissinger's statement is part of his overall effort to place the blame for the collapse of South Vietnam on the shoulders of American domestic opposition, it is a fairly accurate characterization as far as the atmosphere of the meeting is concerned. For on December 20 Tho was anything but jovial. He blamed the United States and South Vietnam for all the problems in Vietnam and admonished: "I should frankly say that the signature you affixed on the [January 1973 Paris] Agreement and the [July 1973] Joint Communiqué have no longer any value. You never know to respect your honor and your signature. Your pledges are nothing but empty promises." Tho then went on to say that "if you continue to practice the Nixon Doctrine and to Vietnamize the war in South Vietnam, if you and the Saigon administration, which you encourage and assist, do not correctly implement the provisions of the Agreement, then the South Vietnamese people have no other way than using every means to counter with the greatest determination."[40]

And so it went on. The transcript of the meeting runs to forty-four pages of charges and countercharges, with Le Duc Tho demanding an immediate ceasefire followed by talks and Kissinger insisting that it was necessary to agree on zones of control and stop the influx of weapons and ammunition from the North to the South before a full ceasefire could be agreed upon.

Yet, Kissinger's report of the meeting to Nixon was optimistic. There was little in it about the dangerous impact of "American domestic divisions." There was little about the North Vietnamese having new "strategic opportunities." Quite the contrary. Given that Tho had not pressed on political demands, it appeared to Kissinger that the North Vietnamese "have unmistakably abandoned any expectation of gaining politically in South Vietnam." Indeed, Kissinger agreed with Ambassador Martin's optimistic report about South Vietnamese military performance in late 1973: "The NVA got nowhere and it is the GVN that has been gaining territorially in the prolonged fighting."[41]

This was true, but it was also wholly misleading. Although the North Vietnamese had not yet moved to the next stage of their unification campaign, Hanoi had not abandoned its ultimate goal. In October 1973, a few days after the outbreak of the Middle East war, the North Vietnamese Politburo had passed Resolution 21, confirming that "the path of the revolution in the South is the path of revolutionary violence." Responding to growing pressure from their southern comrades, Hanoi's central organ had, in effect, decided to approve the planning for the final military showdown with the Thieu government. While Resolution 21 did not call for an immediate all-out offensive, on October 15, the NLF/PRG publicized its "legitimate right to take all measures possible to counteract the Thieu administration's sabotage of the [Paris] Accords." Within weeks, fighting between the PRG and ARVN forces in the south escalated. By early 1974 President Thieu, apparently still confident of U.S. support and buoyed by some military successes in late 1973, declared that the Third Indochina War had begun. To Kissinger, Tho's accusations in their Paris meeting about the aggressive actions of the South Vietnamese may well have appeared to be a sign of desperation.[42]

In the long run, Thieu's optimism, as reflected in his open denunciation of the January 1973 Paris Peace Accords, would do little to help South Vietnam's fortunes. Perhaps, as many have suggested, Thieu was calculating that the United States would continue to support him and, if need be, eventually bail him out. Paradoxically, his and Ambassador Martin's optimism may even have strengthened the hand of those in the United States who argued for reducing American aid to Saigon. If Thieu was doing as well as he said he was with the aid he had received, what was the rationale behind the Defense Department's February 1974 request for additional funding? In fact, as late as October 1974, Deputy Secretary of Defense Walter Clements, visiting Saigon, told South Vietnamese Prime Minister Tran Thien Khiem that one reason for the Congress's cuts was "growing confidence in the strength of the Government of Vietnam."[43]

In retrospect, the facts of the case are, of course, quite clear: with American aid on the decline, Chinese aid continuing at roughly the previous levels—although gravitating toward the Khmer Rouge—and Soviet aid on the increase, the odds were increasingly against the South. Mounting oil prices after the October 1973 War in the Middle East meant that the Saigon government had to devote a larger portion of its budget to purchasing fuel, leaving less money for other expenses. If anything, one could surmise that the North Vietnamese were acting cautiously; that in late 1973 and throughout most of 1974, Hanoi was still respecting the appearance of the decent interval while allowing the Saigon government to exhaust itself in a continued, costly, and eventually self-defeating effort to regain control of the areas south of the seventeenth parallel. In the meantime, Hanoi continued to expend its resources into expanding and perfecting a supply network—the Ho Chi Minh Trail—through Cambodia and Laos.[44]

The North Vietnamese also continued to argue, with regular intensity and with evident justification, that the South Vietnamese were violating the Paris

Agreements. Thieu's January 1974 declaration of war made that argument, not withstanding Hanoi's own obvious disregard of the agreements, ring true. Hanoi also complained repeatedly that the Thieu government was not living up to the agreement to release civilian (political) prisoners and that the United States was in violation of the January 1973 agreements by continuing to send military supplies (this was true) and introducing "military personnel disguised as civilians" (certainly, if CIA officers fell under this category, this charge was equally true).

Although they never met again, Tho and Kissinger continued to exchange acerbic letters after their December 1973 meeting. On February 19, 1974, Le Duc Tho warned Kissinger of "unforeseeable consequences." In May, Le Duc Tho expressed dismay over continued American support for the "fascist regime" of Nguyen Thieu. Moreover, the North Vietnamese could no longer respect the work, much less contribute to the funding of, the International Control Commission that was charged with overseeing the implementation of the Paris Agreements, because the United States was clearly "seeking by every means to delay and to refuse carrying out its obligations to contribute to the healing of the wounds of war and to the postwar reconstruction of the DRV." Kissinger, in his sporadic replies to Tho's complaints, responded with countercharges and demanded that Hanoi and its allies observe a "genuine ceasefire."[45]

There never would be a genuine ceasefire in Indochina. But that much had been accepted already in January 1973. The trouble was that in late 1973 and early 1974, Kissinger paid but scant attention to the developments in Indochina. The meeting with his old negotiation partner and Thieu's aggressiveness went almost unnoticed in Washington as Kissinger's Middle East strategy continued to unfold. Vietnam had become a sideshow.

UNILATERALISM: ISRAELI-EGYPTIAN SHUTTLE

After the Geneva Conference Kissinger stayed in the United States for several weeks in stark contrast to the previous months' hectic traveling (in addition to his Middle East travels and attendance at the Geneva Conference, Kissinger had been to China, Japan, South Korea, and numerous European capitals during the last three months of 1973).[46] Amid preparations for the next round of Israeli-Egyptian talks, Golda Meir's ruling Labor Party lost 5 percent of its parliamentary seats. While she was still able to muster a coalition cabinet after the December 31 elections, Meir's authority—and the credibility of her defense minister, Moshe Dayan—had been badly damaged by furious attacks from Ariel Sharon's newly formed right-wing Likud Party. With Israel's domestic fragility clearly in evidence, Dayan arrived in Washington on January 3.

Dayan came with a plan. He offered to withdraw Israeli troops to a line 20 kilometers east of the Suez Canal. Dayan also proposed the establishment of a UN zone and a limit on the number of Egyptian and Israeli forces allowed in the areas immediately adjacent to the UN-controlled area. The Israeli minister's political demands included an Egyptian pledge to reopen the Suez Canal and end the state of belligerency between the two countries. In addition, Dayan demanded assurances of long-term U.S. military aid.

Although presented as a series of virtual ultimatums, Kissinger accepted Dayan's plan as the basis for negotiations. He and Dayan then agreed that the best way of pushing disengagement toward a conclusion as rapidly as possible was for Kissinger to act as the mediator. They quickly decided—and from his earlier discussions in Egypt Kissinger knew that Sadat would agree with this approach—not to take the Israeli proposal to Geneva. Instead, Kissinger quickly cabled the proposal to Sadat, who in turn invited the secretary of state to come to Aswan. Shortly after midnight on January 11, 1974, Kissinger left Andrews Air Force Base for his first tour of shuttle diplomacy. [47]

Over the next week, Kissinger shuttled back and forth between Aswan, Jerusalem, and Tel-Aviv on a U.S. Air Force Boeing 707 (named SAM 86970). He negotiated with both sides over the exact placement of the Egyptian and Israeli forward lines, over the size and location of the UN zone, and over assurances of access to the Suez Canal. There were a number of tense and awkward moments. Throughout the period Golda Meir was struck with a severe case of shingles. But in the end, an agreement between Israel and Egypt was signed on Friday, January 18, 1974. The Kilometer 101 agreement (named after the Kilometer 101 marker along the Cairo–Suez road) provided the first step toward the ultimate restoration of Israeli-Egyptian diplomatic relations and confirmed that American power in the Middle East was on the rise. It would be followed by further Israeli disengagement in March 1974 and September 1975. Moreover, it provided Nixon an opportunity to announce a foreign policy triumph in the midst of his Watergate troubles.

Kissinger was not quite finished with his foray to the Middle East. Hoping to build on the momentum of the Egyptian-Israeli agreement, he visited Jordan and Syria on January 19 and 20. Upon leaving Damascus, he made one last stop in Israel to hint that he was ready to participate in another similar mediation effort. Israelis were, Kissinger later wrote, "opaque."[48] But the germ had been planted. Shuttle diplomacy was not about to remain a one-off affair.

This, in particular, caused anxiety in Moscow. To Brezhnev, Gromyko, and others, it was becoming increasingly evident that Kissinger's shuttle diplomacy was aimed at reducing the Soviets' role in the peace process and, hence, cutting down Moscow's influence in the region. Already on January 17, 1974—while Kissinger was still flying back and forth between Israel and Egypt—Brezhnev had written to Nixon about his concerns. The general secretary called the Geneva Conference a "good beginning which opened the way to a settlement of one of the most complex and acute problems of the present international life." But Brezhnev then pointed out that "the important agreement between ourselves on active participation of Soviet and American representatives . . . together with Arab and Israeli delegates of the key issues of the Middle East settlement is actually not being carried out." He proposed that Kissinger and Gromyko meet in the next few weeks to "outline and carry out next joint or parallel steps by the Soviet Union and the United States."[49] In other words, Brezhnev was calling for Nixon to include the Soviets in the peace process. On February 1, after Kissinger had returned to Washington, Ambassador Dobrynin complained further. He explained that "a bitter debate" had taken place within the Soviet Union" over American unilateralism in the Middle East. Dobrynin warned that "an interval of bad feelings" was descending over the Soviet-American relationship. Kissinger agreed that such an "interval" should be avoided and promised that the United States would cooperate with the USSR and not "interfere" with Gromyko's forthcoming trip to the Middle East in March.[50]

Gromyko arrived in the United States a few days later. On February 4 the Soviet foreign minister met with Nixon and Kissinger at the Oval Office. Gromyko was tangibly anxious. "What happened to our agreement that the [Geneva] conference would be under the auspices of the US and the Soviet Union?" he inquired. Despite repeated assurances to the contrary, the Americans had acted without consulting the Soviets. Clearly, the United States had "decided to take matters into its own hands and to act in circumvention of the agreement." Nixon was defensive. The United States was not trying to push the Soviets out of the Middle East but simply working toward peace, he insisted. The impression of a "one-man show" was incorrect. It was just a matter of tactics, the best way toward a disengagement of forces.

"We have no interest in proceeding unilaterally," Kissinger added.

When Gromyko reemphasized the need for "joint action," Kissinger assured that he would "follow up on this."[51]

He would do no such thing. Kissinger was determined to marginalize the Soviets' role in the Middle East. But while doing so, while focusing so intently on the situation in the Middle East, Kissinger was undermining, in the eyes of Soviet leaders, the ground rules of détente. He would pay the price later, as the Soviets would pay scant attention to Kissinger's protest of Soviet action in other regional conflicts.

MOSCOW AND THE SYRIAN SHUTTLE

Having completed the Israeli-Egyptian disengagement agreement, Kissinger moved quickly to work on the next steps of his Middle East diplomacy. Over the next four months he achieved two important feats. On March 1, 1974, OPEC countries lifted the oil embargo in place since October 1973. In May, after an intense and lengthy shuttle between Israel and Syria, another disengagement agreement was announced. Kissinger was quickly on his way to becoming the most successful Middle East peace broker in the modern era.

Kissinger began his second round of shuttle diplomacy in late February. Between February 26 and March 2 he visited Syria (twice), Egypt (announcing the reestablishment of formal diplomatic relations), Israel, Jordan, and Saudi Arabia. In Cairo, Anwar Sadat promised to press Syrian President Asad to follow the Egyptian example in negotiations with the Israelis. Both Syria and Israel agreed to send representatives to Washington for further talks on various disengagement proposals. The Saudis were positive about the peace process and optimistic that OPEC would soon lift the oil embargo—on March 18, the Arab oil ministers finally announced that the embargo was being lifted unconditionally and production would be increased in order to stabilize world prices. The only dark spot on the horizon was Jordan. On March 2, King Hussein was less than optimistic about the future settlement of the West Bank. Concerned over the large Palestinian minority in Jordan—many of whom had rebelled against his rule in September 1970 and demanded that Israel relinquish the occupied territories of the West Bank—Hussein's domestic maneuvering room was, in fact, far more limited than that of either Sadat or Asad. Making a deal with Israel could easily have resulted in another bout of major unrest.

Yet, progress had, once again, been evident. Kissinger's flying State Department, complete with sympathetic journalists and loyal staff members, was beginning to acquire an almost legendary status. "The Return of the Magician," *Time* magazine announced upon Kissinger's return to the United States after the Syrian shuttle. "The master of the diplomatic coup has done it again," reported the *Christian Science Monitor.* "It's a Bird, It's a Plane, It's Super K," blurted *Newsweek.*[52]

Even Nixon, despite his mounting problems at home and jealousy over the public accolades awarded to Kissinger, could do nothing but signal his approval. "K[issinger]: good job in an almost impossible situation," he scribbled on one of Kissinger's situation reports in early March.[53]

Upon Kissinger's return to Washington, he and Nixon explained the Middle East strategy to key cabinet and congressional leaders. "What we have been able to do is gain the trust of the Arabs," Nixon told his cabinet on March 8. Kissinger elaborated on the new strategy and its success as follows:

Our idea in October [1973] was that we would move Israel and the Soviet Union would move the Arabs. We are now in a position where we can best move both. We not only don't need the Soviet Union, but their style is bad for the Middle East.

But Kissinger also cautioned that future success was not going to be easy because

the Soviet Union is extremely frustrated. We succeeded with the Egyptian disengagement because they [the Soviets] didn't know what was going on. Now, in a clumsy way, the Soviet Union is trying to push its way in [to the negotiations].

The major problem in the months to come would, indeed, be the role of the USSR. Somehow, Kissinger would have to keep the Soviets from exploding. Or, as Nixon put it, "the Middle East is important. Vietnam was important. But relations

between the two superpowers is [*sic*] most important. We can't brag about pushing the Soviet Union out of the Middle East. Let them preserve their pride." "It is
not in our interest to drive them [the Soviets] to an explosion," Kissinger added.
Although Moscow was unable to produce a settlement in the Middle East, he
stressed, "[it] certainly can prevent one." Thus, Kissinger summed up the rationale
behind his strategy: "It is a vital US interest to keep [the Soviet Union] sufficiently
involved to keep them in line."[54]

Kissinger's unilateralism in the Middle East was, in fact, contributing to the
decline of Soviet-American détente already in evidence in the spring of 1974. To
be sure, Nixon's domestic travails and the Congress's reluctance to award the
USSR MFN status were clearly hurting the momentum of détente in 1973–74. But
Kissinger's monopoly over the Middle East negotiations was, from the Soviet perspective, clear evidence that the United States was unwilling to abandon the zero-
sum games of the Cold War. During Kissinger's trip to Moscow in late March 1974,
the Soviets made their disappointment with U.S. Middle East policy crystal clear.
Whenever the Middle East was discussed "Brezhnev bristled," Kissinger later wrote.[55]

During his March 24–28 visit to Moscow, the Soviets vented their anger over the
Middle East. In what Kissinger described as the "most acid [negotiations] I have
had with Brezhnev," the Soviet leader (correctly) complained about being purposely shut off from the Middle East peace process. On March 27 Brezhnev
demanded "that we will cooperate with one another completely as was initially
agreed upon by our two sides." To drive the point home Brezhnev then added: "I
stress the word 'cooperate,' and by that I mean not simply inform each other. That
should characterize our relationship in the Middle East." Disingenuously, Kissinger
assured that the United States was "prepared to cooperate and not seek unilateral
advantage." As further assurance, Kissinger added: "I agree that we should coordinate our moves." Kissinger had no intention of following up on such assurances.
He had already managed to place himself and the United States at the center of the
process that had produced the January 1974 disengagement agreement between
Israel and Egypt and would produce another one, between Israel and Syria, in late
May (not to mention the lifting of the oil embargo just over a week before the
Brezhnev–Kissinger talks). Clearly, he was seeking unilateral advantage. And yet,
he would complain to the new British foreign secretary, James Callaghan, a few days
later that the "capacity of the Soviet leaders to lie is stupendous."[56]

Like Gromyko had done in February, Brezhnev accused Kissinger of two things:
not trying to prevent the outbreak of the Yom Kippur War despite repeated Soviet
warnings and breaking the October agreement on cooperation in the Middle East.
The spirit of the October agreements had worked fairly well through the December 1973 Geneva Conference, Brezhnev maintained, but the United States had
clearly violated them through Kissinger's unilateral diplomacy in subsequent
months. "If the United States continues to act separately," Brezhnev warned, "nothing good will be produced and there will be no final settlement." In February

Kissinger had promised to cooperate with Gromyko, the general secretary added, but had then continued with his personal unilateral diplomacy.

"We have no intention of achieving unilateral advantage," Kissinger again disingenuously responded. His tactics in the Middle East were necessary due to the "extremely complicated domestic situation [in the United States]," the secretary of state explained. He cited a February 19 letter to Gromyko that had informed the Soviets of Kissinger's forthcoming shuttle diplomacy as evidence of American forthrightness and offered to hold regular meetings in Geneva, Washington, or elsewhere.

"You favor that role for the Soviet Union—just to be informed?" Gromyko interjected. "I have not heard any clearer case of direct ignoring of the Soviet Union's role than the one you just described . . . You have gone back on the understanding reached between us on Egypt; now you want to do it on Syria," added Brezhnev. "What other violations will there be?" he wondered.

The Soviets clearly understood Kissinger's strategy. Gromyko and Brezhnev warned Kissinger that, much as the Americans had insisted on Vietnam, one could not isolate certain aspects of the Soviet-American relationship from others. "All these questions—strategic arms, Middle East, Europe—are linked," Brezhnev said. They brought up the question of cooperation repeatedly during Kissinger's stay in Moscow. But they could not bring about a change of heart. While agreeing to meet with Gromyko on a regular basis, Kissinger was simply following the strategy he had outlined at the cabinet meeting in early March: of pacifying the Soviets while keeping them at arm's length from the actual peace process.[57]

In the end, Kissinger's strategy was successful for several reasons. First, neither the Egyptians nor the Syrians wanted the Soviets deeply involved in the disengagement negotiations. For the Egyptians, Soviet aid had outgrown its usefulness; for the Syrians, the success between Egypt and Israel had apparently been possible only because Moscow's role had been extinguished. Second, because of this, the Soviets had no way, especially after the January 1974 Kilometer 101 agreement, of pushing themselves into the Middle East without being endorsed by the United States. Third, the end of the oil embargo in March 1974 removed the major point of contention between the United States and its European allies. Hence, the transatlantic divide that had been one of Moscow's assets vis-à-vis Washington over the past year, had begun to heal.[58]

The end result was clear. As Brezhnev and Gromyko correctly pointed out, Kissinger had, in effect, managed to hijack the Middle East peace process. Nixon was not moved when Gromyko assailed U.S. Middle East policy during a brief meeting in the Oval Office on April 15. The Soviet foreign minister called U.S. actions "separatist." In fact, on the same day, Kissinger told UN Secretary General Kurt Waldheim that Gromyko "had bowed to the inevitable." By the end of the month, after a series of meetings with Gromyko in Geneva, Kissinger reported to Nixon in a similar fashion. "My impression is," he cabled the president, "that if one gives the Soviets some face-saving formula, they will not obstruct the current effort and may even be moderately helpful."[59]

This was, indeed, the case. The Soviets did not—because they could not—intervene in the month-long Israeli-Syrian shuttle that followed. When Kissinger met, as previously agreed, with Gromyko on Cyprus for three hours on May 7, the Soviet foreign minister simply confirmed what Kissinger already knew from his earlier meetings with Egyptian President Sadat: that the Syrians considered the small town on Quneitra on the Golan Heights a necessary precondition for the settlement. Most important, Gromyko—on his way to Damascus—did not demand an explicit role in the negotiations. In fact, he moved the discussion to European security.[60]

Kissinger had sidelined the Soviets.

"SUPER-K"

Throughout the month of May, Kissinger shuttled back and forth between Damascus and Jerusalem (with a few stopovers in Cairo, Amman, and Riyadh). He traveled a total of 24,230 miles in thirty-four days, staying out of the United States for a longer period of time than any secretary of state since Robert Lansing in 1919.

Quneitra, a deserted town at the foothills of the Golan Heights that had served as the provincial capital of the area before the Israelis occupied it in the 1967 war, dominated much of the Jerusalem–Damascus shuttle until May 18, when the two sides agreed to a compromise of sorts: Syria gained control of the town, while the Israelis maintained military presence on three surrounding hills. But there had been many tense moments, particularly in Kissinger's encounters with the Israelis. At one point (on May 14) during his intensive shuttling when Kissinger got tired of haggling over the streets of Quneitra, he lashed out at Golda Meir: "I am wandering here like a rug merchant in order to bargain over one hundred to two hundred meters! Like a peddler in the market!"[61]

The "peddler" eventually secured his deal. Through painstaking negotiations, Kissinger eventually managed to settle a number of other issues: buffer zones, UN forces, limited-weapons areas, and Syrian enforcement of the ceasefire on Palestinian guerrillas living in the Golan area. Finally, the Israeli-Syrian disengagement agreement was announced on May 29. There were accolades all over. Most famously, *Newsweek* depicted Kissinger on its cover as "Super-K" (superman with a Kissinger face) and *Time*'s headline read: "The Miracle Worker does it Again." His former student, the incoming Israeli foreign minister Yigal Allon, toasted Kissinger as "the foreign minister of the century." The outgoing prime minister Golda Meir (soon to be replaced by Yitzhak Rabin), though, was a bit more subdued. After Kissinger kissed her on the cheek during the celebratory banquet in Jerusalem, she looked at him and, with a reference to Kissinger's ability to embrace those Arab leaders who had launched a war on Israel, said: "I have been afraid you only kissed men."[62]

Meir's jibe may have hurt. Ultimately, the most disappointing fact of the Israeli-Syrian disengagement agreement was that it would remain the highlight of Kissinger's shuttle diplomacy. After May 1974, he would be unable to pull any more rabbits from his magician's hat. By October 1974 it was clear that there would be no Jordanian shuttle as an Arab summit in Morocco designated the PLO and Yasir Arafat, rather than Jordan and King Hussein, to be the negotiators on behalf of the West Bank. In March 1975, the Israelis refused to negotiate further withdrawals on the Sinai. Ultimately, only a massive military aid package of $2.6 billion would make the Israelis change their minds in August 1975. By then, however, the special position Kissinger had acquired through the 1974 Egyptian and Syrian shuttles was gone.[63]

It had been an impressive performance. The Jewish-American secretary of state had managed to gain the trust of an Egyptian president and the respect of the Syrian government. He had successfully pressed for an end to the oil embargo. Kissinger had been able to nudge the Soviets out of the Middle East. While the changes on the map of the Middle East were minimal, Kissinger had, in effect, introduced a new atmosphere to the region, an atmosphere that all but precluded another major Arab-Israeli war. Not that the region had suddenly become immune to violent conflict: the unresolved issue of the Palestinians and the West Bank would continue to mar any efforts at a comprehensive solution to one of the world's most volatile areas. Indeed, Kissinger's remarkable successes would always have to be counterbalanced with his unwillingness to take on this particular issue.

Shuttle diplomacy was also bound to have a negative effect on Soviet-American relations. Kissinger's disingenuous assurances that he wanted the Soviets engaged in the Middle East peace process rubbed the Kremlin leadership the wrong way. Despite arguing otherwise, he had searched for and secured a unilateral advantage for the United States. For Gromyko and Brezhnev, however, it was a humiliation they would find difficult to forget. Kissinger's unilateralism in the Middle East would certainly not give any inducement to the Soviets for acting with restraint in other areas of the globe. Vietnam, for one, appeared almost forgotten amid the frenzy of Kissinger's shuttle diplomacy. By 1975, as Vietnam, Cambodia, and Laos would fall under communist rule, the price for the relegation of Indochina—an area that had formerly been so central for Kissinger's diplomacy—to the position of a sideshow would become painfully clear. Indeed, as Dobrynin had suggested to Nixon and Kissinger during the first back-channel meeting in 1969, there was a linkage between Washington and Moscow's policies in the Middle East and Vietnam. They both, in their own ways, eroded the basis for Soviet-American détente and, hence, exposed the shaky structure of Kissinger's foreign policy architecture.

Still, in the aftermath of the 1973 October War, few would have seriously expected the extent of progress that Kissinger had made within the subsequent eight months. And no one was more anxious to share the credit than the beleaguered occupant of the White House.

15

Nixon's Farewell

Watergate, Kissinger, and Foreign Policy

Richard Nixon almost died in Cairo in June 1974. The president, Kissinger, and their entourage had arrived in the Egyptian capital, after brief stops in Austria and Germany, on June 12. Throughout the two-day visit to Egypt, as well as subsequent travels to Saudi Arabia, Syria, and Israel, Nixon suffered from phlebitis in his leg. If the blood clots broke loose—a strong possibility—and traveled toward his heart, the president would be in mortal danger. Yet, perhaps buoyed by the cheering crowds in Cairo, perhaps in a suicidal mood due to the impending end of his presidency, Nixon soldiered on. On June 14, he beamed as Anwar Sadat called him "a great statesman."[1]

Less than two months later, on August 9, 1974, Nixon boarded a helicopter on the White House lawn, flashed his trademark "V-for-victory"-sign, and flew off. Watergate had done him in.

The departure of his boss had a multifaceted impact on Kissinger. As recounted earlier, he would probably never have become secretary of state if it had not been for the havoc that Watergate wrecked within the confines of the Nixon White House and on the president's credibility. Because Nixon became so obsessed with Watergate, Kissinger was able to conduct American foreign policy without much interference from his mentor: by July 1973 the extensive one-on-one strategy sessions of the early years were gone as Nixon spent increasing amounts of time brooding and planning, usually with Alexander Haig, his next attempt to avoid handing over the White House tapes to the Watergate special prosecutor. Moreover, as Kissinger shuttled in the Middle East and recorded a series of triumphs, his reputation soared while the president's plummeted. In June 1974, 44 percent of Americans believed that Nixon should resign. In contrast, 75 percent of the people thought that Kissinger should remain as secretary of state regardless of who was in the White House.[2]

But did Watergate have an impact on foreign policy aside from the rise of Kissinger's influence and popularity?

It surely did. "I would not link foreign policy with Watergate. You will regret it for the rest of your life," Kissinger had told Haig in October 1973.[3] Over subsequent months it became clear that such linkage could not be avoided. Nixon's obvious political weakness emboldened congressional opponents to challenge the administration more openly. Opposition to the granting of MFN status to the Soviet Union, for example, became increasingly vocal and produced roadblocks to Soviet-American détente. Full normalization with China was rendered impossible, as Nixon could not fathom alienating his conservative supporters by breaking off diplomatic relations with Taiwan. Nixon was unable to prevent cutbacks in military and economic aid to South Vietnam. In short, Watergate made the task of running American foreign policy increasingly complicated.

"It is extremely in our interest to keep the present world going as long as possible," Kissinger had told a gathering of American ambassadors on November 15, 1973.[4] By August 1974, however, it was clear that while the world may not have changed dramatically, the domestic context of foreign policy making had gone through a remarkable transformation. On August 8, 1974, as Nixon made the most agonizing announcement of his political career, the structure he and Kissinger had endeavored to build in years past was being seriously undermined at home.

WATERGATE AND VIETNAM

According to Kissinger, Watergate clinched South Vietnam's fate. As he later wrote,

> The debacle of Watergate finally sealed the fate of South Vietnam by the erosion
> of Executive authority, strangulation of South Vietnam by wholesale reductions
> of aid, and legislated prohibitions against enforcing the peace agreement in the
> face of unprovoked North Vietnamese violations.[5]

One may disagree with the argument that Watergate, which in Kissinger's mind translated to a Congress eager to use the excuse of a third-rate burglary to launch an overall assault on executive privilege, was the *primary* factor that doomed South Vietnam. Yet, it is hard to escape the conclusion that American domestic politics played an important role in determining the *timing* of the North Vietnamese offensive or that the U.S. aid cuts had a severe impact on the morale in Saigon.

In 1973–74 the Nixon administration's ability to live up to the president's private promises to Saigon was severely affected by Watergate and the growing congressional resistance to the administration's Vietnam policy. In July 1973 the House had already cut down Nixon's original $1.6 billion aid package for fiscal year 1974 (July 1973 to June 1974) to $1.3 billion; in October 1973 the Senate cut the funds further to about $1 billion. In the meantime, General John Murray, who was in charge of administering the U.S. aid package, had acted as though the amount Nixon had originally requested would be forthcoming; as a result there was only about $200 million left in the U.S. aid budget for the first six months of 1974. Exactly at the moment when the North gradually accelerated its military campaign and President Thieu in the South confidently declared the opening of the Third Indochina War, the administration found itself undercut at home, with a resulting lack of funds for Saigon. This, one might add, came on the heels of rising oil prices that swallowed a larger chunk of the remaining aid budget than previously anticipated. When the Defense Department in February 1974 requested that the budget for Vietnam be reset at $1.6 billion, moreover, the Senate Armed Services Committee moved in the opposite direction. In the context of Watergate, the Middle East War, and the oil crisis, continued massive aid to South Vietnam was simply not politically feasible. Add to this the fact that on November 7, 1973, the Congress overrode Nixon's veto of the War Powers Act. The inevitable conclusion was that by late 1973 and early 1974, the possibility of the United States reentering the war had virtually disappeared and Kissinger's ability to influence events in Indochina was severely limited.[6]

From the North Vietnamese perspective these developments were naturally encouraging. As Zhou Enlai had predicted to Le Duc Tho in 1972, Hanoi had become stronger while the enemy got weaker. Yet, an overall offensive was still on hold in early 1974. This was in part due to Chinese and Soviet policies. Military aid from Beijing peaked in 1973; by 1974 Beijing started cutting its aid to Hanoi while also gravitating toward the Khmer Rouge as China's major, if still emerging, regional ally. The Soviets, meanwhile, remained reluctant to risk détente while Nixon was in office. The South Vietnamese, moreover, still maintained a significant military force. There was also probably some concern in Hanoi about a possible renewed U.S. bombing campaign, although congressional pressure and Watergate made this exceedingly unlikely. As long as Nixon remained president, the North Vietnamese remained cautious. But there was no doubt which way the conflict was heading. As Kissinger himself retrospectively admitted, already "after the summer of 1973, Cambodia was doomed, and only a miracle could save South Vietnam."[7]

That was in retrospect. At the time, however, Kissinger seems to have been under the illusion that North Vietnam had effectively given up the hope of conquering the South. In congressional hearings between May and July 1974 to determine the following year's aid budget for South Vietnam, the final decision was to cut the aid further, from the proposed $1 billion to $700 million for the next fiscal year. Undoubtedly, reports that confirmed a significant decline in ARVN casualty figures (one-third of the figures before the January 1973 agreements, Kissinger wrote to Senator Ted Kennedy in March 1974) helped the Congress to conclude that it was "unlikely that the North Vietnamese can win a military or political victory in the South in the foreseeable future."

Notwithstanding his future criticism of the Congress, Kissinger made relatively little noise about the cuts at the time. It is very possible that he still believed—as he had implied in November 1973—that the combination of Sino-Soviet restraint, North Vietnamese concern about Nixon's willingness to reintroduce American bombing, and ARVN's successes would keep the Vietnam irritant contained for some time to come. Given his preoccupation with the Middle East throughout much of 1974 he, as well as Nixon, may also have been eager to accept Ambassador Graham Martin's confidence in Thieu's ability to preserve his independence. Martin wrote as late as June 22, 1974, ten months prior to the collapse of Saigon, that the South Vietnamese government was "more stable than at any time just before 1939." He added that the ARVN, particularly its air force, "was getting stronger every day." Indeed, Martin even advised Kissinger and Nixon to let the Soviets know

that the insatiable appetite of fanatic true believers in Hanoi is no longer allowed to provide destabilizing influence in an area where it is obviously in the interests of both the Soviets and the United States that this not [be] allowed to happen, and that we are aware that it is within Soviet capability to influence Hanoi.[8]

Martin clearly made a serious misjudgment by equating the 1973–74 apparent ARVN successes with Hanoi's weakness. Equally important, Soviet support for U.S. efforts to restrain North Vietnam was becoming increasingly unlikely, because of the emergence of a tense rivalry within Indochina in 1974 that eventually pitted the USSR and Vietnam against China and Cambodia. Indeed, while triangular diplomacy had been important in bringing about the North Vietnamese acceptance of the Paris Agreements of January 1973, the Chinese and Soviet restraint that had followed was beginning to evaporate as both engaged in the struggle over influence in postwar Indochina.

One of the most significant turning points in the struggle over influence in post-American Indochina occurred in April 1974, when Mao met with Khieu Samphan, the deputy prime minister of the anti-Lon Nol Royal Government of National Union of Kampuchea (GRUNK), a coalition of the Khmer Rouge and Sihanouk supporters. Samphan was the first Khmer Rouge leader to be accorded such an honor. In late May, China and the GRUNK signed an agreement that guaranteed the Khmer Rouge Chinese military aid. Prompted by the prospect of Vietnamese-Soviet domination of Indochina, the Chinese had made a conscious decision to support Pol Pot and his comrades—still allied with the Beijing-based Prince Sihanouk—as a regional counterweight to Hanoi. Indeed, even before South Vietnam collapsed the continued Sino-Soviet competition prompted a reshuffling of external aid: while growing Chinese military support for the Khmer Rouge coincided with Beijing's decreasing aid to North Vietnam, the Soviets increased their assistance to Hanoi.[9]

Unlike Kissinger implies in his memoirs, therefore, Watergate and American funding cuts were not the *only* reasons why South Vietnam's survival as an independent entity was looking exceedingly bleak by the time Nixon left office in August 1974. To be sure, one could speculate that the Nixon administration's inability to continue massive funding of either the Saigon government or Lon Nol's regime in Cambodia may have encouraged the North Vietnamese and the Khmer Rouge to act more aggressively; when Nixon resigned any remaining restraint seems to have evaporated.

"What could we do?" Kissinger asked the author when queried about the demise of South Vietnam.[10] With no domestic support and a beleaguered president, there was indeed little room to maneuver. And yet, to blame Watergate and later the "McGovernite Congress" for all the failures in Vietnam after 1973 seems to overstate the case. After all, through his own actions Kissinger had indicated that Vietnam had become a low-priority item after 1973. After his trip to Hanoi in February 1973, he never again set foot on Vietnamese soil, an indication of the relative significance of the region to his policies. He protested, but only mildly, against congressional aid cuts. Most significantly, he did not put significant diplomatic pressure on the USSR or China to restrain their allies in Indochina. Whether such pressure would have yielded significant results is open to question; the point is Kissinger hardly tried.

While Watergate undermined the administration's plans in Vietnam, within the context of triangular diplomacy Vietnam almost ceased to exist in the last year of the Nixon presidency.

"THIS NONSENSICAL WATERGATE ISSUE"

In November 1973 Kissinger went to China for meetings with Zhou and Mao. In part because of Watergate and the uncertainty of Nixon's political future, he was in an awkward situation. There was nothing new he could offer on Taiwan; hence Nixon's promise to move toward full U.S.-PRC normalization during his second term was becoming increasingly unlikely. A Watergate-weakened Nixon could not even dream of abandoning Taiwan—an act that, surely, would have hurt his support among the conservatives. Of course, there were other issues separating China and the United States in 1973–74. Despite Kissinger's protests to the contrary, Beijing criticized the June 1973 Soviet-American PNW agreement as Soviet-American collusion against China. In Indochina the Chinese were providing increasing amounts of support for the Khmer Rouge's war against the American-backed Lon Nol. After the U.S. ban on bombings went into effect in mid-August the Khmer Rouge assaults against the Lon Nol government only increased. In Vietnam, the war for reunification also gained additional impetus in the fall of 1973.[11]

Still, the top Chinese leadership remained generally supportive of Sino-American rapprochement in late 1973. One of the major themes at the conference was the open criticism of Lin Biao that, among other things, focused on his alleged interest in a rapprochement with Moscow. The mood of this party congress was apparently captured in Zhou's strong statement that stressed the need for realpolitik and the use of the United States (and Japan) as counterweights to the USSR. As Zhou put it:

> The US made much noise but did not attack us. The so-called Asian alliance headed by Japan is in fact designed to defend them from our attack. But the so-called brothers, namely the Soviet revisionists, are attacking us, threatening us . . . Therefore, *we have to base our policy on our national interests*. Otherwise our policy will be incorrect and wrong . . . We have to be flexible, taking into account different opportunities.[12]

In essence, as Kissinger prepared for his Middle East diplomacy and Nixon fought his Watergate ghosts, the Sino-American relationship—and triangular diplomacy—was at a crossroads. On the one hand, Zhou was still a prime player and felt secure enough (and was undoubtedly prompted by Mao) to issue statements downplaying ideology and emphasizing realpolitik. This indicated that the relationship with the United States was an important part of China's security policy. On the other hand, as David Bruce reported, the Chinese were manifestly unwilling to compromise on the question of Taiwan in order to move toward full normalization.[13]

When Kissinger arrived in China he chose to play it safe and preempt some of the Chinese criticism. From experience the Soviet card was the one that tended to elicit the most favorable Chinese responses; accordingly, Kissinger emphasized the tough stance of the United States toward the USSR, citing his actions in the Middle East crisis as evidence. Kissinger even promised American help for China to strengthen its defenses and prepare appropriately for a potential clash with the USSR. In their opening meeting, Kissinger, in a manner that was by now part of the two men's repartee, assured Zhou Enlai that he believed that "the destruction of China by the Soviet Union, or even a massive attack on China by the Soviet Union, would have unforeseeable consequences for the entire international situation." He then went on to hint at having "some ideas on how to lessen the vulnerability of your forces and how to increase the warning time," insisting that if the United States was to provide any assistance in this field, "it has to be done in such a way that it is very secret."[14]

Two days later, when Kissinger had his audience with Chairman Mao, he pressed the idea of evil Soviet intentions and the need for Sino-American cooperation to combat Moscow's expansionist designs even further. "Our strategy is the same," he told Mao, assuring the Chairman that while "the Soviet Union likes to create the impression that they and we have a master plan to run the world, that is to trap other countries. It is not true. We are not that foolish." But Kissinger also warned that he used to consider the possibility of a Soviet attack on China merely "a theoretical possibility. Now I think it is a more realistic possibility . . . I think they above all want to destroy your nuclear capability." Mao, whose sense of humor seems to have improved with age, pointed at a small place between his thumb and forefinger and retorted that China's "nuclear capability is no bigger than a fly of this size."

Kissinger and Mao then launched into a wide-ranging discussion of world politics, touching on almost every corner of the globe from Finland to Japan and the Middle East. Interestingly, Vietnam—or Cambodia for that matter—hardly surfaced in this discussion. But, as the following extract shows, Mao did show his grasp of the situation in the United States:

> *Mao:* "Why is it in your country, you are always obsessed with that nonsensical Watergate issue? The incident itself is very meager; yet now such chaos is being kicked up because of it. Anyway, we are not happy about it."
>
> *Kissinger:* "But not in the conduct of foreign policy, Mr. Chairman, which will continue on its present course, or in our capacity to take actions in crises we've shown."
>
> *Mao:* "Yes. And even in the domestic aspects, I don't think there's such an overwhelming issue for you and the President."
>
> *Kissinger:* "No. For me there is no issue at all because I am not connected with it at all. The President too, will master it."

Mao, later on in the conversation, expressed his attitude toward Watergate. It was just a "fart in the wind."[15]

In the end, the November 1973 visit to China was significant mainly for two reasons. One was the list of concessions that Kissinger offered at the outset of the talks and the attempt to play up the Soviet threat. In addition to sharing military intelligence, Kissinger told Zhou that the Americans would remove all their U-2 spy planes, F-4 Phantom jets, and nuclear weapons from Taiwan by the end of 1974. Those were the carrots. But the real point of his visit was that Kissinger wanted to somehow convince Mao and Zhou to accept the full normalization of Sino-American relations while the United States still maintained a diplomatic and military relationship with Taiwan. Nixon had, after all, promised during his February 1972 visit to China that normalization would take place during his second term. Moreover, ultimately normalization was the only clear way of demonstrating to the Soviets and to American domestic audiences that the early progress in Sino-American relations had not halted, that American foreign policy had not been paralyzed due to Watergate.

The end result was a deadlock. Kissinger could not offer a complete break with Taiwan. There was the potential of a strong domestic reaction, something Nixon was unwilling to brave in his severely weakened state. In 1973–74 Nixon's chances for weathering the storm of Watergate relied heavily on the support of the same conservative wing of the Republican Party that had criticized him in 1972 for the ambiguity of the Shanghai Communiqué's references to Taiwan (see chapter 9).

Equally important, Nixon and Kissinger realized that Mao and Zhou were on their last legs. What would happen after they were no longer in power? Would China descend into chaos? Would power, especially the control of China's military forces, be transferred to a radical faction? In that case, if the United States had abandoned Taiwan would the PRC simply annex the island by force? And what, then, would be the U.S. policy? In other words, the fudging on Taiwan can also be viewed as a way of simply buying time until China's imminent internal power struggle would be over.

Of course, none of this could be discussed with Zhou. Thus, Kissinger responded to the Chinese premier's persistent pressure on Taiwan with an evasive statement: "I have in mind something like the Shanghai Communiqué, which would make clear that the establishment of diplomatic relations [between the United States and the PRC] does not mean giving up the principle of one China [even as the United States did not break its defense treaty with Taiwan]."[16]

Even when cloaked in such verbiage Kissinger's message was simple: whatever they may have implied earlier, the Nixon administration was not about to abandon Taiwan any time soon; normalization and a one-China policy could only be bootlegged to the United States in two-China bottles.

Although no significant agreements had been reached, the November 1973 meetings in Beijing represented the culmination of the Nixon administration's China policy. Kissinger's report to Nixon after his return from Beijing said as much. The fourteen hours with Zhou and almost three hours with Mao amounted to a "confirmation and deepening of the close identity between you and the Chinese leaders' strategic perspectives on the international situation." In short, Kissinger summarized the situation: "we have become tacit allies." The Chinese "crucial calculation is the steadiness and strength of America as a counterweight" to Moscow —a point that Nixon emphasized by writing "K—the key" on the side of Kissinger's report.

Yet, Kissinger had to admit that there were a number of caveats. One was Taiwan, although Kissinger considered it a minor nuisance. The Chinese had made a major concession, he argued, by requiring only the recognition of the "principle of one China" as a precondition to full normalization of Sino-American relations. In Kissinger's view the more substantial difficulty was continued Chinese anxiety about détente. "We are walking a tightrope of public détente with Moscow and tacit alliance with Peking," Kissinger maintained, adding: "This will continue to require the most careful handling. The meticulous care and feeding of the Chinese on our

Soviet policy has paid off, but Peking sees our détente pursuit as at least objectively threatening its security, whatever our motives."[17]

The relationship was, in fact, approaching a dead end. Despite positive atmospherics, Kissinger had nothing concrete to take home to the beleaguered president. The Chinese had clearly indicated that they were not going to compromise on Taiwan. They were skeptical about Soviet-American relations. Although Kissinger—or a "senior administration official"—told the press that there was "a definite movement to normalization," the reality was very different. Movement toward normalization had stopped. Constrained by the domestic situation in the United States, Kissinger was unable to deliver what the Chinese really wanted: Taiwan.

In the immediate aftermath of his latest trip to Beijing, however, Kissinger's optimism about his China policy was unwavering. On November 15, as he presided in Tokyo over a large gathering of American ambassadors to Asia, Kissinger summed up his thinking:

> I think the Chinese are impressive because they are tough, unsentimental, calculating. They understand the world situation better than I would say anyone I have dealt with—not because they love us sentimentally, but precisely because they can overcome their sentiment in order to deal with us and to understand the necessities.[18]

As before, Kissinger considered the Chinese as his partners in the practice of realpolitik. The trouble was that the comfort that Kissinger clearly drew from his ability to discuss the state of the world with Mao and Zhou did not carry obvious implications for practical policy questions. As already noted, the Chinese had little interest in cooperation with the Americans on Indochina. They may have understood the world but they still had some specific interests of their own (such as Taiwan). Perhaps most important, within the domestic American context the realism that Kissinger celebrated in November 1973 was no badge of honor.

DÉTENTE AND THE HOMEFRONT: JACKSON–VANIK

The key figure among the domestic critics of détente was Senator Henry ('Scoop') Jackson. A Democrat from Washington state, Jackson had first been elected to the Senate in 1952 at the age of forty. A Cold War liberal and a mentor to such modern neoconservatives as Richard Perle, Jackson focused his criticism of détente on two issues: Kissinger and Nixon's alleged willingness to bargain away American nuclear superiority and the linkage between Soviet-American trade and emigration from the USSR. Jackson had taken up the banner already in the aftermath of the 1972 Moscow summit. First, Jackson had introduced an amendment to the SALT treaty that specified that any future arms control agreements would not leave the USSR in a position of superiority. This Jackson Amendment had been passed in September 1972 and would, after Nixon's resignation, complicate the SALT II negotiations.

It was the second of Jackson's causes—his effort to link the question of Jewish emigration to improvements in Soviet-American trade—that aroused more controversy in 1973–74. It started haunting the administration as the new Congress convened in January 1973. The original cause had been a heavy education tax levied by the Kremlin in August 1972 on all Soviet citizens who wished to leave the USSR; since Jewish citizens were the only ones allowed to emigrate to Israel they were, clearly, the target of such an exit tax. Although rarely applied, the tax gave the initial impetus for the introduction of two draft bills in Congress in October 1972, one by Jackson in the Senate and the other by Representative Charles Vanik.[19]

After a congressional recess, the issue picked up again in January 1973. Jackson, who would enter the 1976 Democratic presidential race the following year, clearly recognized a winning political issue and rounded up support from Jewish groups and from labor organizations, who saw increased trade with the USSR as a threat to American jobs. Jackson managed to enlist endorsements for the Jackson–Vanik Amendment from many Israeli politicians with close connections to the United States (although Prime Minister Golda Meir would not make public statements to this effect) and the American-Israel Political Action Committee. On March 15 the Jackson–Vanik Amendment was formally introduced as an attachment to the Nixon administration's 1973 Trade Reform Act (TRA). The controversy that would continue into the Ford presidency had truly begun.

The primary purpose of the 1973 TRA was broad: to authorize the administration to undertake multilateral negotiations for the reduction of tariffs and the removal of other trading blocs. But the administration had included the granting of Most-Favored Nation status, which simply indicated that the United States would treat trade with the Soviet Union in a similar manner as that with any other country, to the USSR as part of the TRA. As a result, when the Jackson–Vanik Amendment was introduced granting of the MFN status was tied to the Soviets lifting restrictions on emigration.

A long period of triangular diplomacy between the White House, congressional leaders, and the Soviet Union followed. Already in late March 1973, the Soviets agreed to stop implementing the exit and pass on the Nixon administration data on Jewish emigration from the USSR. On April 18, when Nixon met with Jackson and other Senate leaders he undoubtedly hoped that the problem was solved. But the senators were not moved. "You're being hoodwinked," said Jackson to Nixon. Jackson insisted that the Soviets had not gone far enough—that they needed to specify a minimum number of exit visas and extend their pledge to non-Jewish would-be-immigrants. His colleagues silently assented. Undoubtedly, their faith in Nixon's authority had been shaken with the latest turn of events in the Watergate scandal the previous day. On April 17, Nixon had issued a press release saying that all his previous statements on Watergate were "inoperative" and guaranteed that all the members of his staff would appear voluntarily in front of the investigative committee then being headed by North Carolina Senator Sam Irvin. Moreover, Nixon had already told Haldeman and Ehrlichman that they would have to resign (these resignations were formally announced on April 30).[20]

The Jackson–Vanik Amendment would remain a scourge on détente throughout the remainder of Nixon's presidency. Over time, the issue became another example of Nixon's inability to keep promises to foreign leaders—such as aid to South Vietnam or the full normalization of Sino-American relations—that were dependent on domestic approval.[21] This was the case despite the fact that Kissinger could show impressive growth in the number of Soviet Jews that were allowed to emigrate to Israel. In 1973, for example, the number was up to 35,000 from 400 in 1968.[22] The Soviets, who tried to comply with Kissinger and Nixon's requests, were understandably angered and confused about the issue that, despite their cooperative attitude, was holding back the much-desired MFN legislation. While Kissinger was visiting Zavidovo in May 1973, for example, Brezhnev at one point brought up the issue of Jewish emigration. "All those who want to can go," he said. "It's peripheral," Kissinger, who was incapable of foreseeing the power that the Congress could yield in order to block his foreign policy initiatives, misleadingly assured.[23]

During Brezhnev's trip to the United States the following month, the issue came up again. While Brezhnev (or Nixon) never brought up the word *Watergate*, it was clear to the Soviet delegation that the president's power was being undermined. Moreover, while he may not yet have been able to fathom the possibility that Nixon would be forced out of office, Brezhnev was keenly aware of the linkage in U.S. domestic discourse between Jewish emigration from and MFN status for the Soviet Union. His favorite bete noire was, naturally, Senator Jackson. "Don't even remind me of that man," he said on June 18. The following day, after meeting with Senator Fulbright and the rest of the Senate Foreign Relations Committee, Brezhnev volunteered that one of the senators had asked him about the Jackson Amendment. "I told them any amendment can have a counter amendment," Brezhnev said.[24]

Watergate had not created the Jackson–Vanik Amendment but it clearly provided a favorable overall context—already in 1973—for a rising congressional challenge to the administration's détente policy. When Kissinger became secretary of state in September 1973 the Soviet MFN status remained unresolved. When the October War in the Middle East broke out, the 1973 Trade Reform Act itself was shelved. But the amendment was included in the next year's TRA. While Nixon's power grew weaker and Kissinger shuttled in the Middle East, the issue stayed alive.

"THESE BASTARDS ON THE HILL"

On March 18, 1974, Kissinger vented his anger during a staff meeting. He was concerned that "the Soviets are getting nothing out of détente. We are pushing them everywhere and what can I deliver in Moscow?" When Helmut Sonnenfeldt mentioned the trade bill, Kissinger raged:

> God damn it, we are going to have a public brawl with them. The same sons of bitches who drove us out of Vietnam and said it would be immoral for us to tamper with the North Vietnamese internal system now try to destroy détente and assert that its our moral obligation to change internal Soviet policies.

He went on to quip that "[Senator Henry] Jackson has obviously been convinced that I am a hostile country" and referred to him as the leader of "these bastards on the hill [who] ignore the fact that 400 Jews were leaving the Soviet Union in 1969 and now say that 30,000 a year is inconsequential." In summing up trade and SALT problems Kissinger said: "What I want to give the Russians is something to start the SALT process working smoothly. I do not want to give them a final position and tell them to take it or leave it ... [because] trade is no good, SALT can't go down the drain." While resigned to the fact that no major Soviet-American agreements would be concluded in 1974, Kissinger needed something. He had to have "an analysis which convinces him [Brezhnev] there is something to be gained from the small ones," Kissinger concluded.[25]

The issues in Soviet-American relations that Kissinger was referring to were obviously not new. But in the spring of 1974, his difficulties were compounded by the president's now almost total inability to use the bully pulpit to forge decisions that would have kept détente on course. A January 1974 Harris survey poll found that only 26 percent of Americans thought their president was telling the truth. On February 6, 1974, as Kissinger was en route to Panama City to sign a statement of principles for the negotiation of a new Panama Canal Treaty, the House of Representatives formally authorized the Judiciary Committee to start considering possible articles of impeachment against the president.[26]

It was in such a context of declining presidential authority and looming impeachment hearings that Kissinger traveled to Moscow. Once he arrived in the Soviet capital on March 24, Kissinger, not unexpectedly, made little progress on a future SALT II agreement. For all his dislike of Senator Jackson, Kissinger was under sufficient domestic pressure not to give anything to the Soviets; thus he rejected Brezhnev's proposals for cuts in forward based systems (FBS) deployed in NATO territory and put forth proposals that would have allowed the United States to retain its numerical advantage on MIRVs by equalizing the number of nuclear delivery systems. While the Soviets would never accept that proposal, Kissinger tried out the idea of "offsetting asymmetries"—allowing the Soviets a slight lead on ICBMs but still protecting the American advantage on MIRVs. After much bargaining over numbers, the possibility that a SALT II agreement might be concluded during Nixon's visit to Moscow three months later remained as murky as ever, in fact, just as murky as the possibility of Sino-American normalization. "We remain far apart on SALT," Kissinger cabled Nixon. Brezhnev also registered his unhappiness over the Jackson–Vanik Amendment. Trying to insist that a certain level of exit visas was a precondition to granting the USSR MFN status was "tantamount to interference in our internal affairs," he noted on March 26.[27]

* * *

Much as his talks with Mao and Zhou in November 1973 had signaled a deadlock in Sino-American relations, Kissinger's meetings with Brezhnev, as well as the Nixon trip that followed a few months later, were indicative of the limits of détente in the context of the second Nixon administration. The summitry that had shook the world in the early 1970s, the back-channel agreements that seem to have indicated that linkage worked, all of that was gradually in the process of being unraveled.

The ironies of the situation were evident. On the one hand, Kissinger was pursuing policies that specifically aimed at marginalizing the USSR in the Middle East. On the other hand, he was determined to keep détente alive, to build on the structure that had been developed in the past five years. Only in this way, he reasoned, could the mounting frustration in Moscow over U.S. Middle East policy be countered. But he was no longer getting any lucky breaks. While searching for ways to reassure the Soviets, Senator Jackson and others cut him no slack. Emboldened by Nixon's weakness, they pressed ahead with their own agenda, ignoring Kissinger's foreign policy prerogatives.

"THE EASY STEPS ARE OVER"

In 1974 the United States was not the only country engulfed in internal turmoil. Soon after Kissinger's November 1973 visit, internal developments in China took an ominous turn. Perhaps most important, Mao appeared to be losing some of his faith in the cooperative line Zhou had so openly advertised at the August 1973 CCP Party Congress. In late November, only a few weeks after Kissinger departed Beijing, Mao openly criticized Zhou for a "rightist error" (i.e., tilting too much toward the United States) in his diplomacy. Diagnosed with cancer in 1973, Zhou was physically ailing and gradually fell victim to the constant jockeying between radicals and moderates in Mao's court.[28]

"Our bilateral relations with Beijing are immobilized," Richard Solomon argued in early 1974. He blamed this state of affairs on the continued back and forth between Zhou's moderates (who were committed to Sino-American rapprochement and a program of economic modernization) and Mme Mao's radicals (who criticized the opening to America and promoted the ideological program of the Cultural Revolution). While Solomon still thought that Zhou was in control, the fact that he had to defend his policies constantly—and that the military was raising questions about the wisdom of the rapprochement with the United States—indicated that China's policy toward the United States had little room for maneuver. By March 1974 Solomon was fairly certain that the two factions were heading for an imminent show-down. "The delicate stand-off between the Premier and his supporters on the one hand, and a combination of Mme Mao's 'leftists' and military politicians on the other," he wrote Kissinger, "[is] unlikely to endure for any length of time." Solomon declined to speculate which way the pendulum would ultimately swing.[29]

The man who ultimately emerged from this internal Chinese power struggle as the next supreme leader of China was Deng Xiaopeng.

By 1974, Deng's political career had been one of high drama. Born in the Szechuan province in 1904, Deng had joined the Chinese Communist Party while studying in France (1920–25). A veteran of Mao's Long March, he had risen quickly in the CCP hierarchy. In 1945 he became a member of the Party Central Committe, in 1952 the deputy premier, and in 1956 a member of the Politburo Standing Committee. Although committed to the revolution, Deng was also a pragmatist and worked with Liu Shaoqi to restore China's economy after Mao's disastrous Great Leap Forward (1957–60). That association had almost cost Deng his life. When Mao launched the Cultural Revolution in 1966, Deng was attacked as the "Number Two Capitalist Roader" (Liu held the top spot). Purged and stripped of his power, Deng was sent to work in a tractor factory. After his reinstatement in 1973 and due to Zhou's illness, however, Deng was suddenly more powerful than before. But, knowing that he essentially served at the pleasure of the Chairman, he treaded carefully. Memories of the purge and inside knowledge of the fickleness of the Great Helmsman certainly made Deng eager to follow the political currents of the times with care. In the context of 1973–74, this meant that he needed to avoid any notion of pandering to the American imperialists.[30]

In addition to the impact of the precariousness of Deng's internal position on the substance of his diplomacy, Deng's negotiation style was markedly different from that of the Chinese leaders Kissinger had grown accustomed to. Instead of Mao's "cryptic philosophical allusions" and Zhou's "smooth professionalism," Kissinger later described Deng as a man with an "acerbic, no-nonsense style" whose dialogue was filled with "sarcastic interjections" and who had a "disdain of the philosophical in favor of the eminently practical." Unlike his previous contacts on the Chinese side, "Deng rarely wasted time for pleasantries. He did not envelop one with solicitude as Zhou was wont to do, nor did he treat me, as Mao had, as a fellow philosopher worthy of his personal attention."[31] Indeed, from Kissinger's description—taken from his 1999 memoirs *Years of Renewal*—Deng comes across as a poor follow-up to Zhou. His habit of occasionally interrupting his dialogues with Kissinger by disposing some phlegm into an adjacent spittoon hardly helped. If anything, the vice premier emerges, perhaps quite accurately, as the ultimate pragmatist in contrast to the more philosophical and always urbane and charming Zhou.

In early April 1974, as Kissinger was honeymooning with his new wife, Nancy Maginnes-Kissinger, in Acapulco, Mexico, Deng arrived in New York as part of the PRC's delegation to the Sixth Special Session of the UN General Assembly on economic development. Considering the vice premier as a man "primarily interested in economics," Kissinger had little interest in Deng's—retrospectively historical—visit to the United States. Only about a week into his stay in New York did Deng get an invitation for dinner with the secretary of state. On the evening of April 14, with a number of colleagues in tow, the man who would lead China's massive economic transformation in subsequent years arrived at Kissinger's suite at the Waldorf Towers. As the discussions unfolded, Kissinger later recalled, "it immediately became evident . . . that, far from having been restored to ease Zhou's burden, Deng's assignment was, in fact, to replace him."[32]

Nor was the replacement simply a shift in personnel. To be sure, Deng assured (and Kissinger repeated) that "our relationship has not changed." But Deng also minimized the significance of the heavy Soviet deployment of troops on China's border and, in effect, implied that it was useless for Kissinger to try and play upon the Sino-Soviet conflict. "There are one million Soviet troops deployed on our very, very long border, and they are scattered all over the place," Deng said. But this meant nothing, he said. "[The Soviets] use this simply to scare people with weak nerves!" Using selected statements from the Mao–Kissinger conversations of November 1973, Deng added: "I believe that, when you discussed this with Chairman Mao, he said even one million was not enough for defensive purposes and for an offensive purpose they must increase them by another million." Kissinger replied with a weak attempt to stress that the Soviets were hoping to destroy China's nuclear power. Deng was not impressed.

During their three-hour working dinner that evening, Deng and Kissinger discussed a number of other issues. Kissinger gave his appraisal of the forthcoming Israeli-Syrian negotiations and framed his overall Middle East policy—accurately enough—as a strategy of reducing Soviet influence in the region. They touched briefly upon Pakistan, Europe, and on the Soviet-American SALT negotiations. Kissinger reviewed, briefly, his late March visit to Moscow and Nixon's forthcoming summit with Brezhnev.

Toward the end of the dinner, the talk shifted to domestic politics. First, Deng initiated a brief exchange on Watergate:

Deng: "Why is there such a big noise being made about Watergate?"

Kissinger: "That is a series of almost incomprehensible events, and the clamor about it is composed of many people who for various reasons oppose the President."

Deng: "Chairman Mao told you that we are not happy about this. Such an event in no way affects any part of our relations . . . We do not care much about such an issue."

Kissinger: "When I first met the Prime Minister [Zhou Enlai in 1971] I spoke of China as the land of mystery. Now the U.S. must seem a very mysterious country."

Deng: "Such an issue is really incomprehensible to us."

Deng was apparently satisfied with Kissinger's assurances of continuity in foreign policy for he rose to give a toast to U.S.-Chinese friendship. Not that he went overboard with praise. "Relations between our two countries can be said to be fine," he temporized.

Perhaps to shift the topic away from Watergate, to prod for further information, or to stress the insignificance of domestic events to the bilateral relationship, Kissinger then, somewhat implausibly, said, "I have been observing your foreign policy for a long time, and I conclude that it has always been consistent." (In fact, he had been observing it for only a few years, during which the PRC had gone through a major shift in its external policies.) Then Kissinger made his central point: "We, of course, do not comment on your internal policies and your internal situation."

The implication of Kissinger's comment was straightforward: we are both realists, he was stressing, let's not worry about either side's domestic developments.

Deng may or may not have required such reassurances. For, in the end, the relationship, with or without Watergate, with or without Zhou, was already at a standstill. This became clear at the end of the Deng–Kissinger meeting, as discussion turned to normalization. Taiwan was the key both Deng and Vice Foreign Minister Qiao Guanhua insisted. The United States should follow the Japanese model and break off all diplomatic relations with Taipei. Without doing so, there was no possibility for establishing full relations between the United States and China.

And then Deng made a typically elliptical comment: "there are two points. The first point is that we hope we can solve this question relatively quickly. But, the second point is that we are not in a hurry on this question."[33]

Deng's two points on Taiwan effectively summed up the state of Sino-American relations in 1974. For a number of reasons—domestic politics in the two countries, differences over the nature of the Soviet threat, and the question of Taiwan—normalization was on hold. The Kissinger–Deng meeting in New York had merely confirmed that fact. As Solomon, Lord, and Arthur Hummel Jr. wrote to Kissinger on May 24: "Our China policy is drifting without a clear sense of how we will move toward normalization, or indeed what the shape of a future normalized relationship with the PRC will look like." Emphasizing the significance of solving the riddle of Taiwan in order to restore the momentum in Sino-American relations, the three aides argued that since "the relatively easy first steps of the opening to Peking are over . . . we must have an overall strategy tailored to the goals of the Administration's China policy."[34]

Such overall strategy was not forthcoming anytime soon. At the time that Solomon, Lord, and Hummel submitted the report (or "Action Memorandum"), Kissinger was deeply engaged in the Israeli-Syrian shuttle that, a week later, would produce a disengagement agreement on the Golan Heights. When he returned to Washington at the end of May, the severely jetlagged secretary of state had ten days to take in the situation at home, including a bout of media scrutiny over the wiretaps (see chapter 13), before another series of trips to Europe, the Middle East, Canada, and the Soviet Union. During the month of July, most of his time would be spent on the, by then inevitable, presidential transition. An in-depth overview of U.S. China policy was simply not possible until after Nixon's resignation.

In fact, aside from shuttle diplomacy and Nixon's self-serving 'victory lap' in the Middle East, Kissinger's focus was on two issues: the preparations for the third Soviet summit, scheduled to commence in late June, and the repairing of transatlantic relations.

THE ATLANTIC DECLARATION

As we have seen, 1973 had been a bad year for the transatlantic relationship. Kissinger's "Year of Europe" speech in April had touched off a round of fruitless negotiations about a prospective Atlantic Charter, a European-American statement about common interests and shared goals. The October War and the oil crisis that followed had further inflamed the relationship by causing the Europeans to distance themselves from the United States. As OPEC states threatened countries that helped Israel with embargoes and price increases, the United States discovered that there were very few countries left to line up behind Washington's policies. Most Europeans (and the Japanese) complied with the OPEC price hikes (from $2.90 a barrel in September to $11.65 a barrel in December) to secure a sufficient supply of energy as the winter approached. Given their heavy dependency on Middle Eastern oil imports this was, of course, quite understandable. But this also meant that only Portugal—but only after Kissinger threatened that the United States would "leave Portugal to its fate in a hostile world" if it declined to do so—was willing to allow the United States to use airbases in its territory (in the Portuguese case, the Azore Islands base of Lajes) during the arms airlift to Israel that had been instrumental in turning the tide of war against the Arabs. Two allies, Turkey and Greece, even refused to allow American use of their airspace for overflights to Israel. As a result, by 1974 the transatlantic relationship was, at best, a troubled one.[35]

At a November 15, 1973 chief of missions meeting in Tokyo, Kissinger vented his frustration with the Europeans' attitudes:

> A different perception has grown up between Europe and the United States about the nature of their interests, and the European opinion is now being organized— since it is too risky to organize it on an anti-Soviet basis, and since an anti-Soviet basis would force it toward us—those who want to organize European unity are doing it deliberately on an anti-American basis.

To prevent suggestions that he might be too thin-skinned for the job of dealing with European leaders, Kissinger added:

Now I don't say this emotionally. I am saying it analytically. We have to understand what we are up against . . . we act sharply . . . not because we are angry; (but) to tell the Europeans the party is over, they cannot have all the benefits of special relationships, unlimited military protection, the pretense of eternal American friendship, and take all the cheap shots they do, vis-à-vis our domestic public opinion by beating us around the head in every crisis.

What about the proposed Atlantic Charter? someone asked. Kissinger explained that he was not after a far-reaching or path-breaking document. Rather,

what we want is really something like the Shanghai Communiqué. Has anybody read the Shanghai Communiqué? It is not one of the great documents of history. . . . all we have asked the Europeans is, twenty years after the end of the war, when conditions have changed, when every country in the western world is trying to gain domestic support in relations with its adversaries, it is time to give some emotional content to relations with friends. All we have wanted from them is some declaration done in some decent way that could create some American and European emotional commitments, to the proposition that the non-Communist countries have some common tasks they can perform together. A month after the document would have been signed no one would have known what was in it. And that would have made no difference whatsoever.

Kissinger assured the U.S. ambassadors that there would be an Atlantic Charter. The problem, however, was that it "will be achieved in the most ungracious manner possible"—that it would require Kissinger to play diplomatic hardball (perhaps by threatening with American troop reductions or economic sanctions). He then reminded the ambassadors about most European countries' unwillingness to support the American airlift to Israel in October 1973 that he clearly viewed as an unfriendly act (justified though it had been by the need to avoid an Arab oil embargo). Kissinger ominously added: "The Europeans will have to learn that in foreign policy there is a price to pay and that if they want to pursue anti-American policies, they will have to pay the price for it."[36]

Kissinger was either blowing off steam or trying to impress his cohorts with his toughness. Most Europeans had no interest in picking a fight with Washington.

Indeed, by the time he attended a NATO foreign ministers meeting in Brussels the following month, Kissinger was, as his reports to Nixon indicate, rather confident that the Europeans were coming back to the fold. Although he criticized the Europeans for their difficult attitude toward the oil crisis and his Year of Europe initiative, most foreign ministers responded with a series of cordial speeches. To be sure, there was one exception. French Foreign Minister Francois Jobert attacked numerous recent American policies. Jobert argued—and Kissinger vehemently denied—that the 1973 Soviet-American PNW agreement "has called the US nuclear commitment to Western Europe into question." Because of this Jobert, at least rhetorically, recalled the Gaullist idea of an independent European defense and nuclear force, pointing to the existence of French and British nuclear capabilities. The French foreign minister also attacked the United States for its failure to consult NATO allies on the Middle East, particularly with reference to the nuclear alert (see the previous chapter).[37]

Such criticism notwithstanding, Kissinger concluded that even the French might be willing to work with the United States. The two-day meeting was, Kissinger concluded in his assessment to Nixon, an indication that "we can expect the Europeans to curb their impulse to show their 'identity' by kicking us." In fact, Kissinger added, "We may be on a threshold of an event of historic significance that would justify a presidential visit." The trip had gone well and "should put US-EC relations on a better footing."[38]

A number of things contributed to the subsequent "restoration of western unity" (as Kissinger calls it in his memoirs). The lifting of the OPEC oil embargo in March 1974 removed an important factor that had contributed to the increase in transatlantic friction. West Europeans had, in fact, contributed to the change in OPEC policy through participation in the February 1974 Washington Energy Conference. By creating at least an impression of Western (and oil consumer) solidarity, the Energy Conference put pressure on OPEC to lift its price controls and production quotas. Moreover, the conference served as an indication that, despite European (and Soviet) complaints of American unilateralism in the Middle East, a united Western front did exist.[39]

Equally important, however, were the sweeping changes in the leadership of the key NATO countries. For Nixon was not the only one destined for the political wilderness in 1974.

*   *   *

On the last day of February 1974, Harold Wilson's Labour Party won an unexpected plurality in the British Parliament. With 301 seats and 47.4 percent of the popular vote, Labour narrowly defeated the Conservatives (46.8 percent and 297 seats) and formed a minority cabinet. In October, after another general election, Wilson would confirm his party's hold on power by winning over 50 percent of the vote (319 out of the 635 seats in the Parliament). Ted Heath, the Conservative leader who had led Great Britain into the EEC after his 1970 triumph over Wilson, had probably been the most pro-European prime minister to date. Whereas Heath had moved away from the special relationship between the United States and Britain, Kissinger felt reassured by the attitude of the new Labour government in Britain. More skeptical of the continentals than their Conservative predecessors, Wilson and his foreign minister (and successor), James Callaghan, clearly wanted "to emphasize the US relationship." While Kissinger was hardly a big believer in the so-called special relationship, he recognized that in the aftermath of the Year of Europe fiasco and the oil crisis, the shift at 10 Downing Street played into Washington's hands. As he summed up his March 28 meetings with Wilson and Callaghan: "the attitude here has greatly improved with the new government."[40]

Less than two months later, on May 7, 1974, Willy Brandt announced that he was stepping down as the chancellor of the Federal Republic of Germany. Brandt's exit had nothing to do with elections. Instead, a week earlier, Günther Guillaume, a member of Brandt's personal staff, had admitted to being a communist spy; Brandt had no choice but to resign amid such a scandal. His post fell to Helmut Schmidt, who was ready—if only to distinguish himself from Brandt's *Ostpolitik* and the political baggage it now carried—to emphasize European unity and transatlantic relations rather than East-West détente. As Kissinger puts it, Schmidt "was a mainstay of close Atlantic ties" during his first few years in office. Schmidt also managed a feat that would elude Gerald Ford: although Schmidt had "inherited" his post due to a predecessor's scandal-ridden resignation, he would go on to win a nationwide election in 1976.[41]

Twelve days after Brandt announced his resignation, Valery Giscard d'Estaing was elected the president of France. His predecessor, Georges Pompidou, had suddenly died on April 2. In a brief presidential campaign that boasted twelve candidates, Giscard received the second highest number of votes in the first round of voting on May 5; two weeks later he defeated the frontrunner, the Socialist Party's Francois Mitterand. Throughout his seven-year term Giscard turned out to be a new kind of French president. For one, he was not a Gaullist like Pompidou but a leader of the center-right Independent Republicans. More important from Kissinger's perspective, the new French leader was willing to take modest steps toward improving his country's inflamed relationship with the United States, while simultaneously maintaining his country's central role in European integration. In fact, Kissinger's assessment of the new president was as generous as any American assessment of a French politician could ever be: "Giscard's presidency transformed [the Franco-American relationship] to a close approximation of genuine partnership."[42]

Such changes in the leadership of the three most important West European countries undoubtedly contributed to Kissinger's success in finally hammering through the Atlantic Declaration of June 1974. The text was approved in Ottawa, during a ministerial meeting immediately after Nixon's Middle East tour. Nixon signed it at the end of a NATO heads of state meeting in Brussels on June 26. The document was not, as Kissinger put it, "the far reaching embodiment of shared purpose we had in mind in initiating Year of Europe." At the same time, it did signal an end to a long period of uncertainty in transatlantic relations. The United States and its allies reaffirmed their commitment to close consultations, burden sharing, and the need to improve American-European economic and political relations. The Atlantic Declaration repeated the mantra of the 1967 Harmel Doctrine that acknowledged a two-track—détente and defense—NATO policy. While it did not transform the alliance's focus dramatically, the June 1974 Atlantic Declaration, together with the more Atlantic-oriented efforts of the new European leaders, definitely buried the acrimony that the Year of Europe had created. In terms of transatlantic relations, the remainder of Kissinger's time in office would, indeed, be "one of the best periods of Atlantic cooperation in decades."[43]

The signing of the Atlantic Declaration was also a potential asset during the Nixon–Brezhnev summit that immediately followed.

NIXON'S LAST RITES: MOSCOW AND OREANDA

A number of developments overshadowed Richard Nixon's final visit to Moscow in late June and early July 1974. There was the forthcoming culmination of the Watergate scandal. The link between Soviet domestic politics and Soviet-American economic relations continued to imperil détente. The expelling of the author Alexander Solzhenitsyn from the USSR (he would later settle in Vermont) in February had brought the issue of Soviet dissidents into the headlines. On top of this, two days prior to the opening of the summit, Senator Jackson tapped into the general mood by announcing his intention to lay down yet another new set of conditions for the granting of MFN status to the USSR. He did not specify what such conditions would be. But Jackson clearly wanted to keep the issue alive and to deprive Nixon and Kissinger of the ability to secure far-reaching deals while in the USSR. Four days later, while Nixon and Kissinger were in the Soviet Union, the public image of the Moscow summit was complicated further when Andrei Sakharov went on a hunger strike.[44]

Still, the administration hoped to make the summit a high-profile event. In a joint NSC–State Department paper prepared for Nixon and signed off on by Kissinger, the authors—Hyland, Sonnenfeldt, Lord, and Smyser—evaluated the strengths and weaknesses of the president's position. They listed the new Atlantic Declaration and Nixon's Middle East trip as the immediate factors that had strengthened the president's hand. Although admitting that American unilateralism in the Middle East had "probably raised some question in Moscow about the validity of pursuing détente," the June 19 study also argued that a number of the "objective factors" that made détente attractive to the USSR remained unchanged. The Soviets still needed Western credits and technology, they were still under pressure from China, and Brezhnev had staked his personal reputation on having the USSR recognized as an equal superpower. "This combination of factors," the study concluded, "makes your [Nixon's] bargaining position in Moscow a strong one."

Kissinger and his staff offered five general objectives for Nixon. On a general level, Nixon had the opportunity "to demonstrate that each year we are making steady gains toward a relationship that is more stable, and less subject to sudden reversals." If he were able to make progress toward a SALT II agreement, moreover, the summit "could constitute a major political breakthrough." Thus, Nixon's "second aim is to close [the] gap, if possible, on SALT issues." The key issue in this regard was "how to limit MIRVs." Third, Nixon should try "to make some progress in the mutual reduction of forces in Europe." In practice, this meant that given the superior strength of Warsaw Pact troops, Nixon should press Brezhnev to accept that troop cuts should be based on percentages rather than numbers (i.e., that NATO and the Warsaw Pact countries should reduce their strength by, say, 5 percent rather than 50,000, respectively). The fourth of Nixon's objectives was more defensive: "to reassure Brezhnev on economic relations." Lastly, Kissinger and his staff expected that Nixon would need to hold a full overview of the state of international relations. In this context, his guidance was to "impress on Brezhnev that mutual restraint, as laid down in the Basic Principles of 1972, must still be the code of conduct."

It was a tall order. Nixon was, in effect, asked to do almost the impossible: he would have to dismiss charges of American unilateralism in the Middle East and convince the Soviets to accept the American arguments on a number of other issues.[45]

In the first plenary meeting of the summit, on the morning of June 28, Nixon followed the script. After Brezhnev's general overview of the positive developments in Soviet-American relations over the past three years, Nixon responded in the same vein. He then went on to catalogue his personal dissatisfaction with Congress's rejection of MFN status. Nixon admitted to having problems at home and with his allies. The Middle East was also a difficult area, Nixon said, but stressed that while "the US will play whatever role it is useful to play to bring about a more peaceful atmosphere in the Middle East . . . there has not been, and will not be any effort to push the Soviet Union out of its traditional role." What that "traditional role" was, Nixon did not explain. The president then stressed that to him SALT presented the "most difficult" problem and the one issue that the summit should make progress on (which effectively meant that it was one problem on which there *could* be progress).

As an incentive for the Soviets, Nixon said: "I want to add that on MFN we will get it."

"That is a good sign," Brezhnev replied.[46]

At this meeting, Watergate was never mentioned. Like most external observers of Watergate, Brezhnev was puzzled and concerned over Nixon's internal difficulties. Indeed, to a leader of a communist dictatorship, the possibility that the U.S. president could be removed by an act of Congress for breaking American laws was utterly incomprehensible and suggested that sinister forces were at work in the United States. As Anatoly Dobrynin wrote in his memoirs: "the Kremlin believed that the real source [of Watergate] was some conspiracy by anti-Soviet and pro-Zionist groups trying to scuttle Nixon's policy of good relations with Moscow." In late May, Brezhnev had sent Nixon a message, delivered orally by Dobrynin, expressing "satisfaction" with his determination to resist the "shortsightedness" of those trying to oust him. Nixon was apparently moved and said that historians would one day be talking about a "Nixon–Brezhnev doctrine" as a major shift in Soviet-American relations. In the end, Dobrynin maintains, "neither Watergate nor the prospect of impeachment had any appreciable effect on the conduct of [Soviet] leaders" at the 1974 summit".[47]

This may well have been the case. The Soviets certainly did not feel pressured to offer Nixon any special concessions as a way of boosting the president's domestic clout. But Watergate was, clearly, in Brezhnev's thoughts at the beginning of the summit. On June 27, after escorting Nixon from Vnukovo II airport outside Moscow to the Kremlin, the two leaders spent half an hour alone with only Viktor Sukhodrev, Brezhnev's interpreter, present. Although Nixon did not share the contents of the meeting with Kissinger, Brezhnev had apparently indicated that he hoped and expected the president to stay in office until the end of his second term.

While Kissinger was not too concerned about this brief encounter at the start of the summit, he became more worried about another private Nixon–Brezhnev discussion a few days later. After spending the first two days in Moscow, the Soviets and Americans flew to Oreanda, a resort town in the Crimea. From the perspective of American domestic politics, it was an unfortunate choice for a location: Oreanda was located close to Yalta, where the ailing Franklin Roosevelt had conferred with Stalin and Churchill almost thirty years earlier. The atmosphere at Yalta in 1945 had been congenial, with Roosevelt appearing more inclined to side with the Soviet leader than the British prime minister. As the Cold War unfolded, however, Yalta became a symbol of appeasement and Roosevelt's last summit was interpreted as having amounted to a sellout of Eastern Europe to the Soviets. For those in the United States who considered détente a similar showcase of American weakness vis-à-vis the USSR, the Nixon–Brezhnev meetings in Oreanda thus held a special symbolism.

At noon on Sunday, June 30, Brezhnev took Nixon to a beach house in Oreanda for a private meeting, while Kissinger, Gromyko, and their aides took in the sun at a nearby swimming pool. The meeting lasted three hours. After that, Kissinger and others joined the two leaders for an inconclusive meeting on SALT II and MIRVs.

What did Brezhnev and Nixon discuss at their private meeting? "The subject clearly had not been SALT," Kissinger would later write. Nor had it resulted in any significant agreements. In fact, when Kissinger next visited Moscow in October 1974, he discovered that Brezhnev had proposed to Nixon a significant modification to the 1973 PNW agreement. As Brezhnev put it on October 26, he had proposed to Nixon a treaty agreeing that if a third party ("we could even name it," he added) attacked the United Sates, the USSR, or their allies, the other country would help in subsequent retaliation. Brezhnev, clearly keen on this revolutionary concept, would discuss this idea further with Ford during their Vladivostok summit in late November 1974.

Nixon could only have turned down such a clumsy attempt at a Soviet-American alliance. He may have felt that a major breakthrough at the summit, such as ironing out a framework for SALT II, was important in order to divert attention away from Watergate. But there was a limit to how far even a president undergoing impeachment proceedings would go.[48]

In the end, Summit III yielded an adequate number of minor agreements to allow the appearance of continued détente to be sustained. Instead of a breakthrough on SALT II, Nixon and Brezhnev agreed to an amendment to the 1972 ABM treaty: the number of ABM sites would be limited to one, instead of two as in the original agreement. Nixon also signed a threshold test ban treaty (which would not, however, be ratified by the Congress), and a number of agreements on economic, technical, energy, housing, and medical research cooperation. And, as had become customary, Nixon invited Brezhnev for a return visit to the United States the following year.[49]

That visit never took place. Détente had reached a plateau. The United States and the Soviet Union had reached a point in which substantial breakthroughs and far-reaching agreements were hard to come by. Kissinger's claim that the summit "by all normal criteria . . . had been a success" was in some ways disingenuous, for the Moscow–Oreanda meetings hardly met the standards of concreteness that had been laid out at the outset of the Nixon administration. The agreements reached were not mere window dressing, but they added little to the overall structure of the Soviet-American relationship. In fact, Kissinger had been extremely concerned that something concrete would have been agreed behind his back during the Nixon–Brezhnev tête-à-tête at Oreanda.[50]

Even as détente stalled, Kissinger put on a brave face in public. After departing Moscow, he toured Europe for a few days: between July 3 and 9 he stopped in Brussels, Paris, Rome, Dusseldorf, Munich (he managed to see the final of the World Cup), London, and Madrid. Briefing the NATO Council on July 4, 1974, Kissinger outlined the results of the summit. Nixon had had, he explained, three basic objectives: first, to "review with the Soviets the world situation so that tensions do not arise as a result of miscalculation or misunderstanding"; second, to review and make further steps toward reducing the nuclear arms race; and third, "to find areas of bilateral cooperation so as to strengthen the network of U.S.-Soviet relationships which gives to both countries an incentive for moderation and restraint in times of crises."

Kissinger argued that there had been progress. Yet, he took a somewhat defensive posture. "As these US-USSR summits continue," Kissinger maintained, "they cannot make the same fundamental achievements that they made in the beginning which was marked by a complete turn in orientation." Indeed, he argued, "the worst mistake we could make would be to let ourselves be trapped by publicity into creating the impression that every time [the] President and Brezhnev meet there will be world-shaking occurrences."

The most illuminating comment Kissinger made at the NATO Council meeting was, though, the following: "the mere fact that we had a summit in this atmosphere and in the face of the domestic pressures to which we are exposed and the temptations that the assault on central authority must entail, is in itself an extraordinary event."[51] Perhaps. But was having a summit without substance truly significant? For no clever rhetoric could hide the fact that despite Kissinger's often impressive performance during his various meetings with the Soviets, the Chinese, and the Europeans, he was running a holding action. Largely due to Nixon's domestic weakness, Kissinger could offer little to his interlocutors—no MFN status for the Soviets, no severing of relations with Taiwan to the Chinese—and could therefore expect little in return. By 1974 triangular diplomacy was running on empty. Given this Kissinger's performance as a negotiator appears, though, even more impressive. While there was no obvious breakthrough on the big ticket items of China and the USSR, there was no evident deterioration either. The diplomatic holding action during the unfolding of Watergate was, ultimately, successful.

As a result, to most Americans Kissinger remained "Super-K." On June 1, 1974, the *New York Times* reported that a Harris Poll had found that an astonishing 85 percent agreed that Kissinger was doing a "splendid" job and 88 percent considered him a "highly skilled negotiator." He was "the most popular member ever of Federal Government's Executive branch."[52]

Such reports were undoubtedly satisfying. But it was also a fleeting moment, soon eclipsed by unprecedented events in Washington.

NIXON'S TWILIGHT

"Well, Al, there goes the presidency," Nixon told his chief of staff Alexander Haig on July 23, 1974. The two men were sitting at Nixon's Western White House office in San Clemente. The president had just gotten off the phone with Governor George Wallace of Alabama, who had refused to help Nixon in his latest effort to line up enough congressional support to avoid impeachment. By this point, Nixon later wrote, he had lost all hope of hanging on to the presidency.[53]

In fact, by the time Nixon returned from his summit with Soviet leaders, the juggernaut culminating in his resignation had become unstoppable. His last feeble hopes were dashed on July 24, when the Supreme Court unanimously ordered Nixon to release more of his tapes. At the end of the month, the Judiciary Committee of the House of Representatives voted to recommend that Nixon be impeached on three charges, including obstruction of justice.

On August 5, 1974, Nixon finally released three tapes that proved he had ordered a cover-up of the Watergate burglary only six days after the June 1972 break-in. The tapes indicated that he knew of the involvement of White House officials and the Campaign for the Re-election of the President (CREEP) in the burglary. Known as the "smoking gun," the tapes prompted the eleven Republicans on the Judiciary Committee who had voted against impeachment to say that they were ready to change their votes. It was clear that Nixon was headed for impeachment and even faced a criminal conviction. Instead, at 9:00 P.M. on August 8, 1974, the president addressed the nation in a live television and radio broadcast. "I have never been a quitter," Nixon said. "But America needs a full time President and a full-time Congress," he added, before announcing that he would resign the presidency at noon the following day. He offered no full confession and went on to catalogue the Nixon administration's successes in foreign policy.[54]

The next day, August 9, after yet another farewell speech, Richard and Pat Nixon flew to San Clemente. After five and a half years, the Nixon presidency was over.

To Kissinger and many others who had observed the unfolding of Watergate at close hand, the resignation was both a relief and a shock. In the last days of the presidency, Kissinger had been asked to exert pressure on Nixon. Although he hardly threatened the president, Kissinger, at least according to his own account of Nixon's last days in the White House, repeatedly pointed out the difficulties that prolonging the Watergate crisis created to the conducting of U.S. foreign policy.

Finally, Nixon bowed to the inevitable. On the evening of August 7, after telling Kissinger of his decision to resign, the president spent several hours with the secretary of state ruminating about past achievements.

Nixon appeared particularly concerned over how his achievements would be treated by historians.

"History will treat you more kindly than your contemporaries have," offered Kissinger.

"It depends who writes history," Nixon growled back.[55]

Although he felt "honored" to have spent the last night prior to the announcement of the resignation with Richard Nixon, Kissinger could hardly have looked toward the future without serious foreboding. True, foreign policy had become his special preserve in 1973–74. The latitude Kissinger had enjoyed in making decisions without the endless—and sometimes fruitless—daily dialogues with Nixon that had characterized foreign policy making in 1969–72 may have been somewhat gratifying. Similarly, the accolades from the press, the enhanced reputation he had gained as a miracle man due to the Middle East negotiations, must have boosted Kissinger's already bloated ego. Were he to stay on, and it was fairly certain he would, Gerald Ford was unlikely to challenge Kissinger's foreign policy leadership anytime soon. Not only was Kissinger, in August 1974, still, more or less, "Mr. Clean," he also remained the undisputed czar of American foreign policy. And much of it had to do with Nixon's illegal activities.

But Watergate had left an imprint on foreign policy. As Nixon's reputation fell, Congress's ability to attack the executive branch's prerogatives increased. To Kissinger's chagrin, by August 1974 this "challenge to central authority" had already translated into the passage of the War Powers Resolution, the ban on the further bombing of Cambodia, deep cuts in U.S. aid to South Vietnam, and a severe threat to such impending legislation as MFN status for the Soviet Union. Indeed, in mid-July Ambassador Dobrynin and Kissinger had berated the domestic "crusade against détente" in the United States. As Dobrynin recounts: "we agreed that the country was entangled in contradictions, while the administration's authority had been collapsing disastrously."[56]

If Kissinger agreed to acknowledge this sad state of affairs, he was being uncharacteristically candid with his major Soviet interlocutor. It could not but confirm— if such confirmation was needed—that in the late summer of 1974 U.S. foreign policy was, in part as a result of the Watergate scandal, in a flux. There were impending regional crises everywhere: in Indochina, in Africa, in the Mediterranean. U.S. China policy was deadlocked. Although Kissinger had taken the first steps to ensure that another full-blown war in the Middle East would not break out, he had also managed to create tension in Soviet-American relations. Moreover, the Congress was itching to launch new investigations into alleged abuses of power that would, within a few months, lead to investigations of the CIA's covert activities.

Upon his departure for San Clemente on August 9, 1974, Nixon had left behind a nation in the grips of a major institutional and domestic crisis that had partly paralyzed American foreign policy. The final culmination of the Watergate scandal and the arrival of a new president in the White House called for a reassessment. It was a reassessment in which Kissinger, still at the peak of his powers, was destined to play the decisive role.

16

Renewal? Ford, Vladivostok, and Kissinger

Leonid Brezhnev was in a playful mood.

On the afternoon of October 26, 1974, the general secretary was meeting in his Kremlin office with Kissinger, Gromyko, Sonnenfeldt, and the Soviet interpreter, Viktor Sukhodrev. Brezhnev opened with a joke: "There is always good and evil in the world. I am the epitome of good. Gromyko and Sonnenfeldt are the epitome of evil." Then, the Soviet leader started playing with a miniature mortar. He aimed it, in turns, at Kissinger and Sonnenfeldt, while simultaneously discussing the subject of his mysterious July private meeting with Nixon at Oreanda. "The gist of the conversation," Brezhnev started, "was this."

At that point Brezhnev had managed to insert a shell into his toy mortar and pulled the lanyard, but nothing happened. "I must ask Sadat for spares," Brezhnev joked. "He probably has them in the wrong guns," Kissinger, relieved that nothing had happened, retorted.

Brezhnev began his account of the Oreanda meeting:

Could we not give thought to the possibility of our two powers who possess for the foreseeable future immense strength, especially in the military realm, achieving a treaty or an agreement in some form . . . to the effect that, in the event of an attack on either of us by any third power—we could even name it—each side, in the interest of keeping the peace, would use military power in support of the other.

Such a treaty could also apply to our allies, Brezhnev said, adding that the matter—and the memorandum of his conversation with Nixon—had not been discussed with other members of the Soviet Politburo.

"Let me understand," Kissinger responded. "If either of us or one of our allies is attacked with nuclear weapons the other one would come to his assistance."

A loud bang, as if a firecracker had exploded under their noses, went off as Brezhnev finally succeeded in his efforts to fire the miniature mortar. A brief silence followed as Kissinger and Sonnenfeldt glanced at each other. But Brezhnev, who had anticipated the bang, moved to the punch line of his joke.

"Now they will say you are under duress," the general secretary quipped, looking extremely amused.

Brezhnev then began the conversation on what, in effect, amounted to a proposal for a joint statement warning other nuclear-armed countries against using their weapons against any other country. But, as the exchange made clear, the mysterious "third country" was the PRC. Kissinger promised to discuss the proposal with President Ford before the November 1974 Vladivostok summit.[1]

Brezhnev's proposal was a nonstarter. Given the extensive Chinese (and U.S. allies') criticism of the 1973 PNW agreement as a measure indicating an emerging Soviet-American condominium, Kissinger had little interest in a bilateral superpower arrangement that went beyond that earlier, watered-down pronouncement. Yet, he was in a tough spot. On the one hand, Soviet criticism of Kissinger's unilateralism in the Middle East had not waned since Kissinger last saw Brezhnev three months earlier. On the other hand, Nixon's resignation in August 1974 had done little to discourage the Congress from criticizing détente. Prior to Kissinger's arrival in Moscow, Senator Jackson had, in fact, managed to embarrass Kissinger, Ford, and the Soviets by publicly announcing that Moscow had agreed to raise emigration quotas to levels Jackson and his supporters had demanded. Such apparent American meddling with Soviet internal matters, albeit condemned by Kissinger, only added to Brezhnev's suspicions that the era of détente was drawing to a close. Fully aware of Soviet suspicions, embarrassed by Jackson's antics, and eager to demonstrate the continuance of détente, Kissinger needed a breakthrough.

In the fall of 1974, the best means of renewing détente was the conclusion of the SALT II agreement. It was to this end that Kissinger had traveled to Moscow on the eve of the U.S. congressional elections. A month later, Ford would join his secretary of state at a working summit in Vladivostok, a Pacific city near the Chinese and North Korean borders. At both meetings there was progress. By late November 1974, a breakthrough appeared imminent, renewal of détente achieved, and the foreign policy transition from Nixon to Ford successfully managed. On December 10, 1974, Kissinger and Dobrynin exchanged confidential memoranda confirming the SALT II agreements. Ten days later, however, the U.S. Congress passed the Trade Act of 1974, which tied MFN status for the Soviet Union with the liberalization of the USSR's emigration policies. In a letter to Ford on December

25, 1974, Brezhnev called the bill "fundamentally unacceptable." Détente had suffered yet another blow.[2]

The first few months of Gerald Ford's presidency did, indeed, set back the course of détente. To be sure, Kissinger retained his high approval ratings. In December a Gallup Poll revealed that Americans, for a second year in a row, found him the most admired man in America. But the search for renewal in U.S. foreign policy was not cut down due to Kissinger's unwillingness to pursue an active agenda. Rather, détente was severely hampered by the inability of the new president to dominate— or even lead—an unruly post-Watergate legislature. Not only did Ford face large Democratic majorities in both houses, but he made a number of moves guaranteed to alienate his former colleagues. The worst of these was, undoubtedly, Ford's decision to pardon Nixon in early September. As a result, Ford had but the shortest of honeymoons with the American public; if Kennedy and Nixon had had their 100 days, Ford had, at best, a month. And he did not use it well.

FORD TEAM

When Gerald Ford assumed the presidency in August 1974, he brought with him, in stages, a new team that would feature such future luminaries of the Republican Party as Richard ("Dick") Cheney and Donald Rumsfeld. Ford and his aides were keen on getting rid of Nixon's last chief of staff and Kissinger's former deputy, Alexander Haig. But the new president had no intention of messing around with the remaining original of his predecessor: Henry Kissinger.

The two men's paths had crossed several times prior to Ford's nomination as vice president in 1973. In the early 1960s, the Michigan congressman had been to Harvard as guest lecturer in one of Kissinger's seminars. Ford had also participated in Nelson Rockefeller's Critical Choices program, a series of seminars on foreign policy matters for senior Republican legislators that Kissinger organized during the 1960s, and had attended numerous Republican leadership briefings during Nixon's first term. As early as March 1974, Ford, by then vice president, had indicated to John Osborne, a reporter at *The New Republic*, that should he ever become president, Kissinger would stay on as secretary of state. Later the same month, Ford personally boarded Kissinger's plane as the secretary of state was preparing for his trip to Moscow. Kissinger, perhaps already anticipating that the vice president was bound to move up on the ladder in the not-too-distant future, clearly saw the potential importance of cultivating Ford. Thus, on his return trip from Moscow, Kissinger advised his deputy, Brent Scowcroft, to thank Ford for such "a warm personal gesture [that] had profound symbolic political importance." Kissinger also promised that he would keep Ford fully informed of all the talks with Soviet leaders.[3]

That may seem a rather prudent message; surely, a secretary of state should keep the vice president informed of major diplomatic maneuvers. There was, however, probably more to it than sheer common sense. After all, Kissinger had always been extremely careful about sharing his diplomatic record with anyone; certainly former Vice President Spiro Agnew was not a man in whom he had ever confided. In the atmosphere of Watergate and with the possibility of Ford becoming the new commander-in-chief, however, it was important that Kissinger break in and win the confidence of his future boss. In the months to come his contacts with Ford would, therefore, continue to increase. By July 1974, Kissinger personally took over from Scowcroft the job of briefing Ford on foreign policy.[4]

* * *

Like Nixon before him, the new president came from a very different background than Kissinger. Born in Omaha, Nebraska, in 1913 as Leslie Lynch King, Ford grew up mostly in Grand Rapids, Michigan, with his mother and stepfather (his parents divorced when Ford was two years old), Gerald R. Ford Sr. (like Kissinger, Ford thus changed his name, albeit for very different reasons). A University of Michigan football star and Navy lieutenant during World War II, Ford was elected to Congress in 1948. During his thirteen terms, he rose steadily in the Republican hierarchy and served on the Warren Commission that investigated the assassination of John F. Kennedy. In 1965 he had become the House Minority leader. Ford had some, but not excessive, experience or interest in foreign affairs.[5]

Ford had none of the political baggage (or enemies) and few of the negative personality traits of his predecessor. Whereas Nixon had become increasingly jealous over the accolades that Kissinger received from his various feats, Ford allowed Kissinger to revel in the public eye. If Nixon had been awkward and, particularly in the earlier years, interested in endless discussions about foreign policy matters at all hours of the day, Ford was usually content with early morning sessions in which Kissinger and Scowcroft briefed the president on foreign policy. If Nixon had been secretive and manipulative, Ford appeared open and honest. Perhaps most important, though, Ford was convinced that Kissinger was a genius. As a result, the running of foreign policy tilted even further into Kissinger's hands after August 9, 1974.

This hardly meant that turf battles, backbiting, and personal jealousies suddenly disappeared. But the cast of characters changed and, reflecting Ford's limited foreign policy experience, did not present a clear and present danger to Kissinger's position as the foreign policy czar in the early Ford administration. In fact, some of the changes initially benefited Kissinger. In the last year of the Nixon presidency, for example, Alexander Haig had emerged as a rival of sorts. Although Ford and his staff needed the retired general to smooth the transition, they were equally keen on getting rid of the future secretary of state. In the fall of 1974 Haig was sent off to Europe as the new supreme commander of NATO, while Donald Rumsfeld, a forty-two-year-old former Republican congressman from Illinois and the U.S. ambassador to NATO during Nixon's last year in office, took over as White House chief of staff. As his assistant, Rumsfeld chose the thirty-three-year-old Dick Cheney, who had served in various lower-level positions in the Nixon administration. In time, Rumsfeld would clash with Kissinger, but in the fall of 1974 he represented no serious threat to the secretary of state's position.[6]

Many other key members of the Ford team were trusted assistants from his years in Congress with little experience in working at the epicenter of federal politics. Such key aides as Robert T. Hartmann, Philip Buchen, and L. William Seidman may have shared a long relationship with America's accidental president. They were, however, ill prepared for the running of the White House and would never develop the brusque, but brutally efficient, managerial style of, say, Bob Haldeman or Haig. In Kissinger's memoirs "the Grand Rapids group" emerges as basically "decent" and "honest" but lacking the necessary "energy and malice" of their more successful predecessors in the Nixon White House. But the "Grand Rapids group" presented, clearly, no immediate threat to Kissinger's position until electoral considerations began to dominate all aspects of policy planning in the Ford White House in late 1975.[7]

The major competitor for influence in the early Ford administration was another Nixon administration holdover, Secretary of Defense and former CIA Director James R. Schlesinger. Prior to replacing Elliott Richardson in July 1973, Schlesinger had enjoyed a wide-ranging career. A Harvard Ph.D. like Kissinger, Schlesinger had been a professor of economics at the University of Virginia and published a well-received book, *The Political Economy of National Security,* in 1960.[8] In 1963–69 he had worked at the RAND Corporation. At the start of his administration, Nixon appointed Schlesinger the assistant director of the Bureau of the Budget with primary responsibility for defense matters. In 1971 Nixon made him the chairman of the Atomic Energy Commission and, in February 1973, chose Schlesinger as the new CIA director after firing Richard Helms (at least in part due to Helms's efforts to protect the agency against Watergate-related investigations). Three months later, however, Nixon nominated Schlesinger for the top Pentagon job and, after confirmation hearings, he was sworn in, at the age of forty-four, on July 2, 1973 (William Colby assumed the leadership at Langley). Aside from Kissinger, Schlesinger was the most experienced of Ford's cabinet members. He even received the most flattering of Kissinger's compliments when the secretary of state noted: "Intellectually [Schlesinger] is my equal."[9]

Such equality guaranteed a tense relationship.

By the fall of 1974 the relationship between Kissinger and Schlesinger had already been through some stormy moments. In October 1973 they had argued over the timing and method of the U.S. airlift of arms to Israel (with Schlesinger insisting on the use of American military aircraft and Kissinger worrying about the impact of such a course on the Soviets and the Arabs). Schlesinger had eventually carried the day and neither the Soviets nor the Arabs had protested voluminously about the method the Americans used to deliver arms and ammunition to Israel (after all, the Soviets were airlifting goods to Egypt and Syria). Most of all, though, the two clashed over their different conceptions of U.S. strategy vis-à-vis the Soviet

Union. In 1974–75, Schlesinger was the foremost critic of the SALT process within the administration and a strong advocate of increased defense spending. At times, to Kissinger and Ford's consternation, Schlesinger would emerge as a valuable ally to Senator Jackson in the fight against détente. In the fall of 1974, though, he represented the most influential counterweight to Kissinger's dominance of U.S. national security policy.[10]

Kissinger's own "empire," with its two arms at the NSC and State, remained by and large intact throughout the presidential transition. The now trusted aides—Scowcroft, Lord, Sonnenfeldt, Eagleburger, Solomon, Smyser, Rodman, and others—stayed in place. Such continuity in a time of transition was remarkable, an indication that despite his often abrasive management style, Kissinger clearly inspired loyalty among those who worked for him. Having an experienced team also, at least in the short term, strengthened Kissinger's influence within an administration that was quickly being assembled to step in. But, in addition to holding on to his loyal subordinates, Kissinger's position in the new administration was significantly improved when Ford made a decision on his vice president.

"ROCKY" AND "TRICKY DICK"

Ford's choice ultimately boiled down to two names: George H. W. Bush and Nelson Rockefeller. Both belonged to the moderate wing of the Republican Party, both were men of great, if not equal, inherited wealth. The fifty-year-old Bush, who had served in the House of Representatives, as the U.S. ambassador to the UN, and as the Republican National Committee chairman, appeared the more appealing candidate to the GOP's rank and file than the sixty-six-year-old mercurial former New York governor (Rockefeller had resigned in 1973 amid accusations that his lengthy governorship had, in effect, bankrupted the Empire State). Although Bush received 255 to 181 votes in a private White House poll of leading Republicans, his chances were suddenly destroyed when *Newsweek* published a story about a secret Nixon slush fund that had donated $100,000 to Bush's 1970 senatorial campaign against Lloyd Bentsen. Although Bush had lost the election, such a link to Nixon-era abuses of power undoubtedly weighed heavily on Ford's decision. On August 17, 1974, he called "Rocky" and offered him the job. Rockefeller accepted the next day. As a consolation prize, Ford nominated Bush as the new U.S. liaison chief in Beijing, to replace the veteran diplomat—and Kissinger trustee—David Bruce.[11]

From Kissinger's perspective there had never been much of a contest between the two men considered for the vice presidency. Although Bush had worked with Kissinger on China issues, the two had never developed more than a respectfully distant relationship. In fact, in 1971, as Kissinger and Nixon had discussed the names of possible secret envoys to China, Nixon had suggested both Bush and Rockefeller. Kissinger, of course, had secured the job for himself. But he had also made it clear that Bush was "too soft and not sophisticated enough," while a Rockefeller mission had "possibilities."[12]

Nelson Rockefeller was indeed, as Kissinger would later note, one of the "seminal influences on [his] life." Since their working relationship had come to an amicable end in 1968 (Rockefeller gave Kissinger a check for $50,000 as a departing gift), the two men had remained distant but friendly. Having Rockefeller join the new administration was, therefore, a momentous personal victory for Kissinger (Kissinger's second wife, Nancy Maginnes-Kissinger, had also worked on Rockefeller's staff in the 1960s). Yet, as Kissinger points out, for Rockefeller the vice presidency turned out to be an experience that "would have demoralized a lesser man."[13] His nomination was also one of the early political miscalculations of the Ford presidency.

For one, Rockefeller's vice presidency began with a tortuous confirmation process: after his nomination in August 1974, he was held up in congressional hearings until December, in large part because the Democrats did not want Rockefeller to participate actively in the November 1974 congressional elections. Between September 23 and December 5, Rocky testified on seventeen different occasions. Once confirmed he would find that Ford's promise that he could act as a domestic policy czar was not honored. Worst of all, in early November 1975, less than a year in office, Rockefeller was pressured off the 1976 presidential ticket as part of what became known as the Halloween Massacre. It was, Kissinger would later note, "the single worst decision of Ford's presidency."[14]

Whether one agrees with Kissinger's judgment or not, Rocky's lengthy confirmation hearings in the fall of 1974 were a clear reflection of Ford's excessively short honeymoon with the U.S. Congress and the American people. The real reasons for this brevity, however, lay elsewhere. The approaching congressional elections in November naturally played an important role in accelerating Democratic criticism of Ford. In the final analysis, though, Ford did it to himself. As his biographer John Robert Greene writes, on September 8, 1974: "With the stroke of his pen, Ford destroyed his month-long honeymoon." What Ford did at 11:00 A.M. on that Monday was straightforward: he pardoned Richard Nixon for any federal crimes he may have committed while in office. It was supposed to lift the shadow of Watergate and allow Ford to move on and commence his own presidency by preventing a high-profile, endless, and, in all likelihood, inconclusive trial of the former president.

Much has been written about the pardon's disastrous reception. The problem was not necessarily the act itself but the way Ford had gone about it. He had, in effect, negotiated or been pressured into a deal by those who had worked for Nixon. Indeed, a week prior to Nixon's resignation Alexander Haig had discussed the pardon with Ford. Although he made no deal at that time, the pressure on Ford continued to build after August 9. The most active proponents of such action were the two principal holdovers from the Nixon administration, Haig and Kissinger. By late August Ford had made his decision. In early September, he sent John Miller and

Benton Becker to San Clemente for negotiations. By then, Nixon and his aides knew that they had the upper hand. They played hardball and offered no statement of contrition. Ford accepted. No wonder most Americans reacted with shock as "Tricky Dick" got off without publicly acknowledging any wrongdoing.

Within a month of taking office Ford, who had successfully cultivated an image of honesty and decency, appeared as just another corrupt politician.[15]

Congressional leaders, particularly Democrats trying to cash in on the Republican Party's eminent weaknesses in the wake of Nixon's resignation and pardon, were quick to attack the new administration. On September 16, fourteen members of the House of Representatives led by New York Democrat Bella Abzug submitted a resolution asking the president for more information on the details leading to his decision to pardon Nixon. Ford responded with apparent shrewdness: he testified, on October 17, in front of the House Subcommittee on Criminal Justice and denied that any deal had been negotiated. Yet, whether people believed the new president's firm affirmation or not—Ford, red-faced, announced that "there was no deal, period, under no circumstances"—was almost inconsequential.

By becoming the first president since Abraham Lincoln to appear in person before a congressional committee, Ford had confirmed an essential fact of American political life in the immediate post-Watergate era: the executive branch, through the actions of Ford's predecessor, had lost much of its authority and power to the legislative branch.[16] This fact, coupled with the congressional election campaign and resultant Democratic victories in early November, had immediate consequences for the efforts toward renewing American foreign policy in the fall of 1974. Kissinger got a taste of it when he went to Capitol Hill to testify on September 19, 1974. The subject was détente.

"SCOOP" JACKSON AND DÉTENTE

In the weeks after Nixon's resignation the question of Jewish emigration (see chapter 15) returned with a vengeance. The issue was the same: the Jackson–Vanik Amendment that tied increased emigration of Soviet Jews to the granting of MFN status to the USSR. The amendment itself was part of a larger Trade Reform Act that the new administration needed to get approved in order to have the power to negotiate a multilateral agreement for the reduction of tariffs and other disincentives to free trade.

In 1974 the issue had been reduced to a numbers game: Jackson and his supporters offered 100,000 per year as a figure that would allow them to support MFN. Soviet Foreign Minister Andrei Gromyko had grudgingly agreed to a figure of 45,000 in April 1974 "as approximately the trend" (this was roughly 25 percent higher than the previous level). In Moscow in July, Ambassador Dobrynin made another—what Kissinger later called "more realistic"—proposal: the Soviets could,

although not in writing, guarantee that they would not reject more than 1.6 per-
cent of the exit visa applications. In other words, if there were, hypothetically,
100,000 applicants, 98,400 would be approved. Yet, Gromyko, Brezhnev, and
Dobrynin repeatedly made it clear that any open demands of such nature—which
Kissinger called "highly irresponsible"—amounted to interference in the Soviet
Union's internal affairs. And they refused to commit to anything in writing.

After Nixon's resignation, Kissinger and Ford were determined to resolve the
imbroglio as soon as possible. On August 14, Ford and Kissinger met with Soviet
Ambassador Dobrynin and explained yet again that the question of Soviet MFN
status could only be solved if the Soviets *formally* agreed to specified number of
exit visas. Dobrynin offered to give oral assurances that 55,000 annual exit visas
were possible (subject to an adequate number of applications). The next day,
Ford and Kissinger met with Jackson and his colleagues, Senators Abe Ribicoff
(D-Connecticut) and Jacob Javits (D-New York). Kissinger had prepared the
ground with his friend Javits, who was apparently ready for a deal.

Jackson was not. He started to haggle for more: 75,000 was the minimum he
would accept. "Boy, was Scoop ever adamant," Ford later recalled. Kissinger then
assigned Helmut Sonnenfeldt to work out a letter with Jackson's staff outlining the
deal. Kissinger informed Dobrynin, who warned against any public reference to
specific Soviet guarantees of emigration numbers.[17]

Over the next two months the issue continued to simmer. Kissinger negotiated
with the senators and a number of 60,000 per year was eventually agreed upon as
a benchmark for Jewish emigration. On September 19 Kissinger took his case to the
Senate Foreign Relations Committee. He attacked efforts to tie Soviet "domestic
political practices" with American-Soviet economic relations. Whatever the moral
justifications of Senator Jackson, such efforts had no place in state-to-state relations. The senators should, Kissinger said, maintain "a sense of proportion about
the leverage our economic relations give us with the USSR." Lastly, the Jewish-
American secretary of state noted the achievements that had been possible without congressional resolutions, including the Soviets' dropping of the exit tax and
the rapid increase in the number of Jews who had been able to emigrate from the
Soviet Union.[18]

Kissinger's efforts to pacify the senators did not work. On October 18, 1974—the
day after Ford testified in front of the House Sub-Committee on Criminal Justice
regarding Nixon's pardon—Ford and Kissinger met with Jackson, Javits, and Representative Vanik at the White House. At the meeting, Jackson and Kissinger—who
had recently returned from a weeklong trip to the Middle East—exchanged letters
that were supposed to resolve the trade-emigration issue once and for all. The first
letter summarized the Soviet guarantees—based on Ford and Kissinger's talks with
Gromyko and Dobrynin—and the second gave Jackson's interpretation of them.
Unfortunately for the administration's credibility with the Soviets, Ford ("in an
excess of generosity," as Kissinger puts it[19]) allowed Jackson to brief the press on

the letter exchange in the White House Briefing Room. Naturally, Scoop took advantage of the situation, presented a figure of 60,000 as a "benchmark" for future emigration from the Soviet Union, and generally displayed the letter exchange as a moral victory over Soviet repression.

The Ford administration's inability to effectively counter Jackson's challenge proved a major blow to détente. In retrospect, though, the timing of the Washington senator's somewhat mischievous behavior seems perfectly logical. He was, after all, playing for domestic audiences as much as he was trying to ease the USSR's emigration rules. In fact, Jackson could hardly have expected that Brezhnev and his fellow leaders could be bullied into submission by American public opinion. He may have, as Jackson's biographer Robert Kaufman puts it, "infuse[d] American foreign policy with greater moral clarity and confidence about U.S. virtues and our adversaries' vices" (a very Reaganesque approach, Kaufman further stresses). But Jackson undoubtedly did this as much for the headlines and for his own political advantage as because of any deep-seated moral conviction. And what better time to make such headlines than mid-October 1974, a few weeks prior to the congressional elections in which Democrats triumphed (the election increased the Democrats' majority in the Senate and House to 23 and 143 seats, respectively)? By 1974 Jackson, in short, had emerged as a front-runner for the 1976 Democratic nomination.[20]

However noble or opportunistic Jackson's motives may have been was irrelevant to Kissinger. Referring to the apparent congressional victory that the October 1974 letter exchange indicated, Kissinger later wrote: "All this was no doubt very impressive in senatorial back rooms where no one was obliged to negotiate any of it with Soviet leaders."[21] For the secretary of state, the main point was that Jackson's victory not be allowed to hurt Kissinger's efforts to convince the USSR that Washington was still interested in continuing détente. This was particularly the case because Kissinger and Ford (as Nixon had earlier) had given repeated assurances that they were not going to allow Jackson to bring the emigration issue to the forefront of Soviet-American relations. Together with the backlash the new president had incurred after his pardon of Nixon, the emigration debacle hardly reassured the Soviets of the reliability and stability of the new administration.

Kissinger, in particular, felt hoodwinked. As he traveled to Moscow a few days after the exchange of letters and Jackson's press briefing, Kissinger had a lot of explaining to do.

"I AM AS ANGRY AS YOU"

Soon after he sat down with Brezhnev on October 24, it became clear to Kissinger that the Soviet leader was in no mood for small talk. Brezhnev complained about the United States' failure "to live up to its obligations and agreed positions." In particular, he berated the Americans for their failure to live up to the agreement, reached in October 1972, under which the United States would grant the Soviets MFN status and the Soviets would, in return, pay back their World War II lend-lease obligations. But now, under pressure from Jackson, the United States appeared to be reneging on this agreement, Brezhnev complained. "We don't see any of that agreement fulfilled," he added. The Soviet leader, pounding on a table for emphasis, wondered about Jackson's claims that the Soviets had agreed to allow 60,000 Jews to emigrate annually. "Dr. Kissinger, you must know me well now after eight meetings," Brezhnev said, adding that "what I have said makes me think that the United States is not doing all it can to improve relations [with the USSR]."[22]

Kissinger naturally protested Brezhnev's interpretation of Jackson's influence. He denied that the White House had ever agreed to any figures, and had recently released a statement to the effect that "all the Soviet Union had done was to give us the principle for applications and visas." Kissinger stressed that neither he nor the president had anticipated Jackson's remarks after the White House meeting regarding a Soviet agreement to hike up the emigration numbers. "What happened last Friday was a trick of Jackson's. We didn't know what he would do when he stepped on the White House podium," Kissinger said.

Nevertheless, Kissinger had to admit that although "we said we are not bound by the Jackson figure, we would take it under consideration." Foreign Minister Gromyko, quite justifiably, complained that such a statement "gives grounds for one-sided interpretation." Kissinger was defensive and evasive. "I have believed and have said publicly that it was a mistake for the United States to involve itself in an internal Soviet issue." But all the blame, he argued, belonged to Jackson, whose "manner is as humiliating for me as it is for you."

To punctuate the point Kissinger hit the table with his hand. "I am as angry as you are," he insisted. He then, theatrically, left the meeting room for a few minutes to cool off.[23]

Whether Kissinger's table-pounding over Jackson's behavior was mere theatrics or not, the meetings that followed during the next two days indicated some progress toward a SALT II agreement. On the evening of October 26, Brezhnev, Kissinger, and Gromyko discussed a Soviet proposal that would allow the USSR a maximum of 2,400 strategic missiles and bombers in contrast to 2,200 for the United States for 1977–185 (the period the SALT II agreement was to be in force). Each side, Brezhnev proposed, could build up to 1,320 MIRVs in the same period.

What justified a higher overall aggregate for the Soviets? Kissinger wondered. Because, Brezhnev explained, the British and French missiles were to be counted on the American side of this bargain. Of course, he joked, if the British prime minister were to come to Moscow and announce his country's decision to join the Warsaw Pact, "then we will add his missiles [to our total]." In effect, Brezhnev maintained, the United States and its allies would have roughly 2,400 missiles by 1985; "unfortunately, we don't have an ally we can either add or subtract."

Kissinger conceded that the Soviet proposal had "positive elements." It might, he added, provide the basis for an agreement between Brezhnev and Ford the following month. But he emphasized that, for the time being, it was necessary to keep the details of the proposal secret. Before the Vladivostok meetings, Kissinger suggested, he should discuss the details with Dobrynin, which could then be ironed out at the Ford–Brezhnev working summit. "I do this in order to prevent those people who are looking for difficulties to cause trouble," Kissinger said. In particular, it was important to prevent Senator Jackson from holding hearings. Still, Kissinger assured that the Americans "will try to work by all available means to come to an agreement by the time you [Brezhnev] visit the United States in 1975."[24]

Kissinger also stressed the need for secrecy in his reports to Ford. Having clashed over the acceptable terms for a SALT II agreement with Secretary of Defense Schlesinger at an NSC meeting shortly prior to his departure for Moscow, Kissinger was keen on avoiding a costly internal battle and maintaining all the cards in his hands. On October 27, Kissinger thus told Ford that the Soviet proposal brought the positions of the two countries much closer to each other. Yet, he pressed that it was "essential that elements of the Soviet position be kept totally outside [the] interagency process until I have had [an] opportunity to analyze it further and discuss next steps with you." Even with the easy-going Jerry Ford at the helm and many old rivals gone, Kissinger felt threatened by internal enemies and competitors.[25]

* * *

The discussions in Moscow and Kissinger's report to Ford exemplified his concern about growing domestic opposition to détente. As the administration braced for heavy Republican defeats in the mid-term congressional elections in November 1974, the secretary of state clearly felt that he was walking a delicate tightrope between the need to hammer out a SALT II agreement and the prospect of being undercut by the criticism of Schlesinger from within and Jackson from without the administration. The problem was that by 1974 secrecy, even if justified as a means of inoculating Soviet-American negotiations against the virus of domestic criticism, was bound to be counterproductive. In the United States that was still riddled with the after-effects of Watergate-era abuse of power, back channels reeked of the age of Nixon, the era that Americans in general and Ford in particular wanted to put behind them. In short, in late 1974 secret diplomacy was, in more modern idiom, politically incorrect. It would only lead to a mounting backlash, no matter what the substance of the policies advanced might have been.

VLADIVOSTOK

In November 1974, the tentative SALT II agreements were further solidified when Kissinger accompanied Gerald Ford to Vladivostok. Sandwiched between Ford's visits to Japan and South Korea, and Kissinger's trip to Beijing, the choice of the meeting place reflected a Soviet effort to complicate the delicate nature of Sino-American relations (the Chinese would in fact comment on the fact that the meeting took place close to the Chinese border).

One of the most telling exchanges took place, at President Ford's initiative, on November 23 during a fifty-mile train ride from the Vozdvizhenka airport to Okeanskaya Sanatorium, near Vladivostok. Ford was direct:

> I should tell you Mr. General Secretary . . . that I intend to be a candidate in 1976. I believe it most important, therefore, to have coordination of our foreign policies, coordination which I am convinced benefits not only the United States and the USSR but also the entire world. I am apprehensive that if others were elected the policy of 72–76 could be undercut.

"I'm for Jackson," joked Brezhnev.

Kissinger, accustomed to the Soviet leader's rough sense of humor, retorted: "Our intelligence reports say so."

Ford refused to join the banter (causing Ambassador Dobrynin to complain later to Kissinger about the president's poor sense of humor). He stressed the need to show progress on détente, and to prevent "people such as Senator Jackson" from continuing to undermine the favorable course of Soviet-American relations. Pressing the point further, Ford added: "I want to point out that 1975 is a crucial year, because an election year is not the best time for the US President to engage in serious negotiations." Ford did not bother explaining why his predecessor had chosen 1972—the previous presidential election year—as the time for signing the SALT I agreement.[26]

*   *   *

It was an extraordinary moment: an American president using his domestic political calendar as a negotiation tool with the Soviet Union. In retrospect, it was also a huge mistake. Ford effectively promised that should the Soviets agree to a SALT II agreement it would be signed within a year, boost his reelection campaign, and, in effect, produce an unstoppable forward movement of détente for the remainder of the 1970s. In the near term, it seemingly worked: the Soviets did make important concessions to their earlier stand on the terms of the SALT II agreement. But such Soviet action produced none of the long-term benefits Ford suggested. The new president had oversold his hand in a way that would only produce further Soviet resentment.

During the Vladivostok summit, Kissinger clearly—and in a way that would never have been possible during Nixon's presidency—dominated the American side of the discussions. As Dobrynin recounts:

> Ford did not yet know all the details [and] preferred not to get involved in long arguments with Brezhnev or Gromyko; he had Kissinger for that. Ford was a solid

and decent American who meant business when he understood it. Otherwise he listened to the disputes and quietly smoked his pipe.[27]

In his memoirs Kissinger disagrees with Dobrynin's assessment. "Ford conducted much of the technical discussion himself," he wrote in *Years of Renewal*. In fact, it was Brezhnev who "simply did not know what he was talking about."[28]

While he was being exceedingly complimentary to Ford (Kissinger was clearly the dominant American throughout the negotiations), Kissinger's low opinion of Brezhnev's performance at Vladivostok was accurate. Brezhnev was ill at ease and left the meeting room repeatedly. He was surprisingly willing to yield to Gromyko on a number of occasions and did not press the extension of the PNW agreement he had originally discussed with Nixon in July and then with Kissinger in October.[29]

The explanation for Brezhnev's aloof manner, however, had little to do with his inability to understand the details of the SALT II agreement. At the time of the Vladivostok meetings, the general secretary—a chain smoker and a heavy drinker—suffered several seizures that could not but affect his performance. Despite advice from his doctors, Brezhnev refused to miss any of the meetings that had been scheduled with Ford. Yet, his long illness, concealed from the public though it was, was gradually affecting the ebullient general secretary's grasp of detail and mastery of negotiation.[30] In the spring of 1975 Brezhnev's declining health would become increasingly evident to such frequent interlocutors as Kissinger. By then, the general secretary would often be described as the "old man in a hurry."[31]

Although Ford, Brezhnev, Kissinger, and Gromyko discussed a wide range of issues, from the Middle East to MFN and from the CSCE to Jewish emigration from the USSR, their main goal was to conclude a SALT II agreement. Ford, in his few substantive contributions to the talks, stressed that the United States needed a "politically acceptable" agreement that would emphasize the "equivalence" of the two countries' nuclear forces. Kissinger explained further that any agreement with differentials "would not be possible" from a domestic viewpoint. By the evening of November 23—the first day of the meetings—an outline for the SALT II treaty was reached. It had two main stipulations. First, each side would be allowed 2,200 nuclear delivery vehicles (ICBMs, SLBMs, and long-range bombers). Second, out of this total a maximum of 1,320 on each side could have MIRVs.

The following morning, November 24, the two sides further clarified a number of rules regarding throw weights and missile-equipped bombers. Ford also promised that after 1983 the United States would stop using the Rota naval base on the Spanish coast for stationing nuclear submarines.[32]

As it happened, this was the high point of Soviet-American relations during the Ford administration. As a number of the American delegation to Vladivostok suspected, even an agreement that acknowledged the United States' nuclear parity with the USSR was bound to provoke intense domestic criticism in the United

States. During 1975 the two countries' SALT delegations met constantly in Geneva and, as they appeared deadlocked over such issues as verification, the back channel was reactivated in May 1975. Neither this nor the high-level attempts to break the deadlock over mostly technical issues, however, brought SALT II any closer to actual treaty status in 1975. By the end of the year, as the 1976 elections beckoned, Ford began to sidestep the whole issue. Indeed, as Dobrynin writes in his memoirs, the Vladivostok meeting was the moment when "détente reached its height and began its decline." Kissinger, in his own way, concurs. In *Years of Renewal,* he wrote that the ensuing domestic debate in the United States eventually "transformed Vladivostok from a spur to improving Soviet-American relations into a further obstacle to them."[33]

Before facing the barrage of domestic criticism Kissinger flew to Beijing. On November 25 he commenced five days of discussions with Deng Xiaoping.

"TWO COULD PLAY TRIANGLES"

By 1974 Kissinger's visits to China had almost become an annual ritual. Since the secret trip in July 1971, he had been to Beijing five times. He had met with Chairman Mao and had spent hours in sweeping conversations with Zhou Enlai. After Nixon's trip to China in February 1972, Kissinger had, in fact, made U.S. policy toward China as virtually his personal reserve. Watergate and Kissinger's nomination as secretary of state had only further confirmed that fact. Yet, as he commenced his first encounter with the Chinese of the Ford presidency, change was clearly in the air. Most significantly, Zhou was gone and Kissinger faced a new, more intransigent, interlocutor, Deng Xiaoping.

Kissinger's position was hardly made easier by evident Chinese respect for Kissinger's domestic tormentor, Senator Jackson. For a number of years, Senator Jackson had been nurturing a special relationship with the PRC. As early as February 1969, he had delivered a major speech calling for normalization of Sino-American relations. Since early 1973 Jackson had argued that the United States should sever its diplomatic ties with Taiwan (eventually done in 1979). He had met with representatives of the Chinese liaison office in Washington on a regular basis since it was opened in the spring of 1973. The following spring the Chinese, appreciative of the combination of Jackson's critique of détente and his attitude toward China, invited the senator to Beijing. Consequently, one of the foremost U.S. critics of détente visited the Middle Kingdom only a month prior to Nixon's resignation. The Chinese were hardly inept at playing triangular games.

While in China, Jackson met several times with Deng. According to Jackson's biographer, the two men got along particularly well. They agreed on the dangers of détente and compared it with the British and French appeasement policies prior to World War II. Jackson and his wife, Helen, also briefly saw the ailing Zhou Enlai.

Although terminally ill with cancer and hospitalized, the premier echoed Deng's sentiments regarding détente and emphasized the need for the United States to keep up its troop levels in Europe (something Jackson had supported through his resistance to the Mansfield Amendment). Yet, the Chinese appeared far less concerned about the "Soviet menace" than Jackson had expected. The Soviets "were not as fierce as Jackson thought," Deng had told the senator. In fact, the vice premier was more keen on pressing the United States to "treat its allies better" than complaining about the Soviets. Lastly, the Chinese quietly stressed that further progress on trade and cultural exchanges depended on Washington's attitude on Taiwan.[34]

Another American whom Kissinger worried about was none other than George Bush. As noted earlier, Ford had appointed Bush as David Bruce's successor at the U.S. Liaison Office in Beijing. Unlike Bruce—a career diplomat willing to keep secrets—Kissinger did not trust the former UN ambassador and future president. Nor had Bush much reason to be admiring of Kissinger. He could not but assume that in the debacle over the vice presidency, Kissinger had played some role in tilting the balance toward Rockefeller. In 1971, Bush had been furious over what he considered Nixon and Kissinger's duplicity regarding Taiwan's UN seat. In the fall of 1974, as Bush prepared for his new post, Kissinger only grudgingly made available the transcripts of his July and October 1971 discussions with Zhou Enlai.

In mid-October, Bush was granted only a ten-minute audience with President Ford. Kissinger's talking points for the president were indicative of the secretary of state's intention of keeping China policy in his own hands. Ford was advised to tell Bush: "I am confident that you will take in stride some of the frustrations of working and living in Peking, including the low-key nature of our public posture there." You will "be bored out of [your] mind from the inactivity," Kissinger himself told Bush. But the inactivity that Bush was to encounter was part of the secretary of state's design: he did not wish to have anyone, even the chief U.S. diplomat in Beijing, engage with the Chinese without Kissinger's permission. Indeed, as Kissinger prepared for his visit to China, he continued the pattern of undermining Bush. In a November 11, meeting with the PRC's liaison office chief, Huang Chen, Kissinger apologized for Bush's "lack of subtlety" and stressed that the future president was not "always up on all the nuances of our previous conversations." He then added: "I want your leaders to understand that what I have discussed with Premier Zhou regarding our basic strategy is unchanged." Real policy, in short, was up to him.[35]

Notwithstanding his concerns about Jackson and Bush, Kissinger's real troubles awaited in Beijing. To be sure, an outside observer would have found it hard to believe that Sino-American relations were not on course for further improvement. Kissinger's entourage was the largest of his visits to date. His new wife Nancy, as well as his children David and Elizabeth, joined the secretary of state. White House Chief of Staff and future Secretary of Defense Donald Rumsfeld was also part of the group. For all appearances, it was the first true state visit since Nixon's journey in February 1972.[36]

Despite the pomp that surrounded Kissinger's November 1974 visit to China, however, the negotiations themselves lent little cause for optimism. There was, to begin with, a lack of rapport between Kissinger and his new major Chinese sparring partner, Deng. As reports from Jackson's trip had suggested, Zhou Enlai's health had severely deteriorated and the premier remained hospitalized for cancerous malignancies in his bladder, lung, and colon. Like Jackson in July, Kissinger was allowed to see the ailing Zhou briefly; like Jackson, Kissinger was invited to bring his wife (and two children) with him. Unlike Jackson, who had to wait until the second to last day of his trip, Kissinger and his family were taken to Zhou's hospital near the Imperial City immediately upon arrival.

It was Kissinger's last meeting with his principal Chinese interlocutor. And, for the first time, the purpose was purely ceremonial. There was no discussion of "serious" subjects; his doctors had, Zhou explained, advised him not to engage in anything but small talk. The meeting simply confirmed—if such confirmation was still necessary—that the torch had been passed. Kissinger would have to deal with Deng Xiaoping, someone he would in private call "that nasty little man."[37]

The November 1974 visit to China was also notable because Kissinger did not have an audience with Mao. While Kissinger considered this a diplomatic snub and a reflection of the Chinese displeasure that the secretary of state had only a few days earlier been meeting with Soviet leaders, there was, in fact, a good excuse. The Great Helmsman was suffering from Lou Gehrig's disease and going blind. In July—at the time of Henry Jackson's visit to China—Mao's doctors had determined that he had, at best, two years left to live (Mao eventually died in September 1976). To further complicate matters, the combination of Mao's and, in particular, Zhou's ill health did not mean that Deng, now the vice premier and Zhou's effective successor, was in full control of the situation. Indeed, the "nasty little man" was under a close watch from a group of even nastier individuals: the party radicals that included Mao's wife, Jiang Qing. The recently rehabilitated Deng could under no circumstances risk being seen as soft on the Americans.

This meant, among other things, that there was no chance of Deng giving any ground on the issue of Taiwan. The Chinese attitude was as unmovable as before: if the United States did not break its diplomatic relations with Taiwan, a full normalization of Sino-American relations was impossible. Deng, with an eye on the Japanese government's decision to follow such a course in 1972, called this procedure "the Japan way." Nevertheless, he again elliptically emphasized that while "you owe us a debt" on this issue, the Chinese side was "not so much in a hurry." On Taiwan, the vice premier reverted to the line that Mao had repeatedly taken and Deng himself had expounded during his visit to New York in April 1974.[38]

Throughout his meetings with Deng, it was clear that the only way Kissinger could gain the vice premier's attention was by berating the Soviets. It was an old strategy, but doubly necessary now that Nixon was gone. Given that he arrived in China after the Vladivostok summit, Kissinger probably felt compelled to assure

Deng that the United States still considered Moscow its primary adversary. Jokingly referring to the PRC's "ally and northern neighbor" (the USSR), Kissinger on November 26 assured Deng that "we believe Soviet purposes are still essentially hegemonic." Therefore, he added, "we will not permit a strategic gain for Soviet power [and] we do not intend to create a condominium with the Soviet Union, because such a policy—by removing all obstacles to Soviet expansion—would eventually, with certainty, turn against us." While the Soviets clearly hoped for such a condominium and were eager to give an impression that Washington and Moscow were cooperating rather than merely negotiating, Kissinger maintained that the Vladivostok agreement on nuclear weapons was "very favorable in the overall strategic balance." Further, he explained that Brezhnev had proposed—in Vladivostok as well as a month earlier in Moscow—a Soviet-American defensive alliance. Although Brezhnev's proposal had been limited to a possible nuclear attack on either superpower or their respective allies, Kissinger argued that because the proposal had clear anti-Chinese undertones, "we did not accept a serious discussion . . . Nor will we."

Deng and Foreign Minister Qiao Guanhua said they appreciated Kissinger's explanation and the general American refusal to enter any treaties that were directed, even by implication, against China. Still, Deng was not impressed. Even if there were such a treaty as "the Doctor" had described, "what role would those treaties play?" he rhetorically asked. "They would not be able to play much of a role." In short: thank you for the information, but it makes no real difference.[39]

In attempting to strike an anti-Soviet tone, Kissinger made much of his shuttle diplomacy in the Middle East, U.S. attempts to improve relations with India to balance the growth of Soviet influence since the Indo-Pakistani War of 1971 (see chapter 8), and Washington's growing ties with Iran. His goal was, Kissinger stressed, "the erosion of Soviet influence" throughout the Middle East and South Asia. Deng was somewhat responsive, but clearly skeptical. He "approved" of the United States' efforts to improve relations with India. Deng called the Middle East "the most sensitive area," and warned that the Soviets "were making a comeback against our [U.S.] earlier inroads." It was important that the Americans continue helping both the Arabs and the Israelis, the vice premier added. As for the PRC, "it must support the Arab/Palestinian cause." It was hardly a whole-hearted endorsement.

When discussion turned to Indochina all pretenses of common interests and objectives disappeared from Deng's discourse. On Cambodia, Deng suggested that the United States leave the country alone. He had no interest in acting as a mediator or working toward any kind of coalition government with or without Prince Sihanouk (who was still staying in a nearby guesthouse). On Vietnam, Deng "stonewalled." When Kissinger brought up North Vietnamese violations of the Paris Agreements, the vice premier responded by listing American and South Vietnamese infringements.[40]

In the end, the most significant outcome of Kissinger's visit was an agreement that President Ford would travel to China in 1975. It was preceded, however, by a very different invitation. On the afternoon of November 26, Deng invited, on Mao's behalf, Secretary of Defense James Schlesinger for a visit to China. This would be a good way to "show progress in US-Sino relations," Deng said. It was a shrewd move. By now the differences between Schlesinger and Kissinger were well known: the secretary of defense had distinguished himself as the administration's chief critic of détente and an ally of Senator Jackson in a drive to increase U.S. defense spending and maintain American nuclear superiority. Moreover, Deng suggested that Schlesinger might well include some of the military regions on the Sino-Soviet border in his itinerary. Schlesinger's visit could, therefore, be easily viewed as a confirmation of an anti-Soviet "strategic alliance." This was something that Kissinger had carefully avoided doing over the past three years. In a cable summing up the meeting, Kissinger assured Ford that he would "turn" the Schlesinger invitation "into an invitation to you [Ford]."

On the morning of November 27, this was exactly what happened. Kissinger explained that a visit to the PRC by the secretary of defense was "premature" and could only lead to similar visits to "places that I don't believe are desirable." In the past year, Washington had, he said, repeatedly turned down similar invitations from the USSR. Kissinger then offered a visit by any other cabinet member or the president. Deng immediately accepted and suggested that the final communiqué issued at the end of Kissinger's trip should include a statement to this effect. In a cable to Ford later that same day, Kissinger suggested that the Schlesinger invitation had, in fact, been "designed precisely to bring about your visit."

It was a revealing exchange. The Chinese were clearly well informed of the internal battles over foreign policy within the United States. Earlier in the year, Beijing had hinted at this by inviting Senator Jackson. Now, with the secretary of state sitting across the table, Deng had gone even further.

As Kissinger put it in a memo to Ford, Deng had effectively demonstrated "that two could play triangles."[41]

Kissinger left China on November 29, 1974. He was, undoubtedly, disappointed. Deng, "the nasty little man," had been quite a different negotiator than the now terminally ill Zhou. The Chinese, despite receiving fuller briefings of Kissinger's negotiations with the Soviets than American allies—sometimes fuller than many cabinet members—were drifting away and playing their own triangular game.

Kissinger's assessment of the trip was, as usual, a bit more upbeat. He stressed that the basic rationale that had made the Sino-American opening possible remained in place. This was "the Chinese preoccupation with Soviet hegemony." Kissinger added that while he and Deng had not moved closer to full normalization, at least there was "a mutual agreement to leave the normalization issue where it is now with our studying possible formulas."[42] Compared to the significant breakthrough in Vladivostok the visit to Beijing had clearly been a disappointment.

"IF THIS BECOMES LIKE THE TRADE ISSUE"

On December 2, 1974, upon Kissinger's return to Washington, Ford convened a session of the NSC. The president was upbeat on the Vladivostok agreement. He had developed a good relationship with Brezhnev. "We put a cap on the arms race," Ford claimed. It was now important to rally public opinion behind the Vladivostok agreement.

Kissinger was equally optimistic. He told "war stories" about the negotiations and explained that Brezhnev had probably been willing to make concessions because he wished to establish a good rapport with Ford, wanted to strengthen détente against those opposing it, and was afraid of a renewed arms race with the United States. Kissinger thought that U.S. allies would see the agreements "as an unbelievable achievement." But he then stressed that if SALT II "becomes like the trade issue, I think we will see a massive reversal of the Soviet position on détente."

Kissinger was also positive on his experience in China. It had been a good move to go there directly after making the Vladivostok deal. "Nothing helped us as much," he said. Deng had been keen on inviting Ford and restoring the momentum of Sino-American relations, Kissinger argued. He then outlined the complicated and delicate rationale of the renewed triangular diplomacy: "We have this triangular game going on again as a result of Vladivostok. The more we talk Soviet strategic superiority, the more it hurts us with China. It is imperative that they don't believe we are inferior militarily to the Soviets." The renewal of triangular diplomacy hinged on the conclusion of a SALT II agreement that could receive both domestic support and Chinese approval.

The mood at the NSC meeting was optimistic. Surprisingly, after Kissinger and Ford were finished with their briefings, Secretary of Defense Schlesinger gave his seal of approval to the Vladivostok agreement. It should be acceptable to domestic audiences, he observed. "Mr. President, you can win this one. You have the high ground," Schlesinger concluded. There would be attacks from within the Congress but the agreement was solid. It represented a potential turning point for the Ford administration's foreign policy. And, Kissinger insisted, it was the best possible deal at the moment. When Fred Ikle, the director of the Arms Control and Disarmament Agency, raised the question of additional reductions in both sides' nuclear arsenals, Kissinger quickly cut him off. "We should not get too cute about further reductions and restraints until we get this one signed."[43]

The optimism that was evident during the December 2, 1974 NSC meeting appeared well founded. Kissinger met Dobrynin on the same afternoon to discuss the details of the agreement and, on December 10, 1974, exchanged confidential memoranda confirming it. The U.S. Congress passed resolutions supporting the Vladivostok agreement in January and February 1975, while Soviet and American delegations began meeting in Geneva to hammer out the details of the SALT II treaty (there was no formal treaty as of yet).[44]

Amid such support, however, a revolt, again spearheaded by Jackson, was brewing. Already on December 4, questions about the details of the agreement had appeared in the press and during Kissinger's briefing of a select group of senators. A week later Jackson argued that the Vladivostok agreement legitimized "the massive continuation of Soviet arms expenditures." While Jackson did not object to equal ceilings to the USSR and the United States, he called for a drastic reduction in the numbers agreed to in Vladivostok. Otherwise, the end result would be "an arms buildup agreement," he maintained. Jackson vowed to conduct intensive hearings in Congress in order to convince the general public that it was necessary "to insist on strategic force reductions in a SALT II agreement." In short, Jackson's argument effectively linked the concerns of the left and the right that had been expressed in the aftermath of the 1972 SALT I agreements: the deal Kissinger and Ford had negotiated in late November allowed a Soviet buildup and potential nuclear superiority to continue, while doing nothing to cut down the size of the two countries' nuclear arsenals. Whatever the merits of his case, Jackson's opposition ultimately resulted in shelving the Vladivostok agreement for the remainder of Ford's term.[45]

By early 1975 the debate on SALT II was further complicated by the effective collapse of economic détente. Through a series of amendments, the Trade Reform Act of 1974, passed by both houses of Congress on December 20, managed to single out the Soviet Union as a country subject to such specific conditions regarding its domestic conduct. Export-Import Bank credits to the USSR were limited to an annual $75 million; further allocations would require congressional approval. The much-sought-after MFN status was similarly constricted and tied to Soviet compliance on observing the freedom of emigration rules embedded in the Jackson–Vanik Amendment. In fact, MFN status was subject to an annual review—the first one of which was slated, as Kissinger acidly noted, for April 1976, in the midst of the presidential primaries. And yet, because such restrictions were but a part of the comprehensive Trade Act that was necessary for the overall functioning of the United States' international trade, Ford had little choice. On January 3, 1975, he signed it into law while warning that the language of the ACT "can only be seen as objectionable and discriminating by other sovereign states." Kissinger had issued similar warnings repeatedly throughout December and early January.[46]

The Soviets responded on January 10, 1975: they refused to accept the 1974 Trade Act and abrogated the 1972 Soviet-American trade agreement. It was hardly a surprise. On December 18, the day a House-Senate conference committee had begun its discussions of the Trade Act, the Soviets had released a letter that Gromyko had handed to Kissinger during the secretary of state's visit to Moscow. In it—which

Kissinger had chosen to keep secret—the Soviet foreign minister stated his objection that the USSR was under any obligations regarding specific emigration quotas. The Soviet press release, which Kissinger learned about while having breakfast with Dobrynin, also stated that Moscow "flatly reject[s] any attempts to interfere in internal affairs that are entirely the concern of the Soviet state and no one else." On December 25, Brezhnev had sent another letter to Ford declaring the new trade legislation "fundamentally unacceptable." Although Brezhnev still suggested that détente should continue, it was clear that the final episode in the saga of the Jackson—Vanik Amendment amounted to a severe blow to Soviet-American relations.[47]

"OUR HOLD ON THEM IS GONE"

The collapse of economic détente and the emerging debacle over the Vladivostok Agreements left Kissinger in a somber mood in early 1975. His policy vis-à-vis the Soviet Union was in danger of coming apart at the seams. With the Soviet rejection of the Trade Act and the cancellation of the 1972 Trade Agreement, the United States had, Kissinger believed, lost one of its most important tools of linkage. As he put it to Ford at a meeting in the Oval Office on January 6, 1975, the inevitable result would probably be that the Soviets would feel less restrained in their overall policies. "Our hold on them is gone," Kissinger remarked the following day. "The question in [the] Soviets' minds is, 'how dependent can the USSR become on United States domestic decision[s]?'" Kissinger told the cabinet on January 8.[48]

The high hopes of the immediate post–Vladivostok period were proving groundless. 1975 might well not be a breakthrough year. And according to Kissinger, it was all due to domestic forces beyond his control.[49]

But why had it happened? Were the declining prospects due simply to the ambitions and political opportunism of Senator Jackson? Or was there something more fundamental at play?

There is little question that Jackson, even if he truly believed in the cause itself, had used the issue of Jewish emigration as a platform for his own political ambition. He was ready to enter the 1976 presidential contest and had emerged, largely as a result of his success in the fall of 1974 as the Democratic Party's front-runner.

Similarly, it appears clear that Kissinger had misjudged his ability to, yet again, negotiate his way out of a difficult position. It was one thing to shuttle between the capitals of the Middle East where he could pose as a mediator, or sit down and discuss world events with Mao. It was something completely different to try and mollify an American senator whose major goal was to complicate—or even destroy—the basic tenets of Kissinger's policy toward the Soviet Union. It was a costly mistake on his part to assume that there was room for compromise with Jackson or that Kissinger—or Ford—could sway the Congress to back their policies. All told, by the end of 1974 Kissinger and the new president were in danger of losing control of the foreign policy agenda for the remainder of his term. As the historian John Robert Greene puts it: "By the end of 1974 it was clear that Congress, not the Ford administration, controlled the nation's agenda."[50]

It was, in the end, much more than the Vladivostok Accord or the issue of Jewish emigration from the USSR that was undermining U.S. domestic support for détente. Ultimately, the policy was almost impossible to market at home. It was doubly difficult to do so in the atmosphere of the Vietnam trauma and Watergate, both of which had increased cynicism about the role of the chief executive. Détente was not the answer to the deep need among the American body politic to see their country's external affairs as an extension of the American dream or as an expression of democratic values. When adopting détente, the Nixon administration had bargained away, consciously, the ability to explain U.S. foreign policy in the context of a struggle between good and evil. Kissinger had been a key figure in advocating the new realpolitik. Despite his best efforts, however, Kissinger ultimately failed to minimize the role of ideology within the context of Soviet-American relations. It was this failure that would greatly contribute to the collapse of his architecture in 1975–76.

But there was even more. On Wednesday, January 8, 1975, Kissinger, Scowcroft, and Ford met again in the Oval Office. The president asked about Vietnam. Kissinger was gloomy. The Congress, while not objecting to large military aid budgets for Israel, was sabotaging any effort to provide direct or indirect assistance to South Vietnam. Defense Secretary Schlesinger, Kissinger argued, was also obstructing his plans. If the United States did not act fast, the South Vietnamese would lack "the mobility and firepower to survive," he insisted. It was imperative to ask for supplemental aid from the Congress or the South Vietnamese resistance was likely "to unravel."

Ford promised to put the request into his forthcoming State of the Union address. He would. But it would be to no avail.[51]

17

Not Our Loss

Exit from Vietnam

The morning of April 30, 1975.

Saigon was in chaos. Over the previous days, as North Vietnamese troops approached the South Vietnamese capital, the remaining American marines had overseen a frantic evacuation effort. Thousands of South Vietnamese, fearing retribution from the conquerors, had already been helicoptered out of the beleaguered city. Many more were waiting outside the American embassy compound, hoping that their allies would fly them to safety. But timTe had run out. At about 6:00 A.M., the remaining marines moved from the gates of the compound to the embassy building and locked the door to the stairwell leading to the helicopter pad. Realizing they were about to be left behind, South Vietnamese climbed over the compound's walls and tried to break through the locked doors. Marines panicked. They fired teargas canisters and Mace into the stairwell. Finally, the helicopters arrived. At 7:53 A.M. the last helicopter lifted off the embassy roof. A few hours later tanks flying the flag of the NLF entered the center of Saigon and accepted the surrender of the South Vietnamese government.

To countless South Vietnamese (and most Cambodians), the events of spring 1975 would be a tragedy of immense proportions. Yet, from Washington's—and Kissinger's—perspective Vietnam had, after the conclusion of the January Paris Agreements, become a sideshow. Already by the fall of 1973, public attention focused on the October War in the Middle East and the impact of the oil crisis; Kissinger's shuttle diplomacy would help maintain the world's focus on the region in 1974. The unfolding of the Watergate crisis grabbed far more headlines than the gradual collapse of America's once erstwhile allies. In fact, in his memoirs Kissinger would explain: "After the events of the summer of 1973, Vietnam disappeared as a policy issue. There was nothing the administration could do to alter the course of events." Citing the demands of the Middle East War and the severe cuts that the Congress enacted on U.S. aid to Vietnam, Kissinger added: "I observed [Indochina] with the melancholy shown toward a terminally ill relative, hoping for a long respite and a miracle cure I was unable to describe."[1]

In short, Kissinger transferred responsibility for the collapse of Vietnam and Cambodia elsewhere. Neither the Nixon nor the Ford administration could provide the necessary aid to Saigon to prevent the collapse of South Vietnam. And it was Congress, rather than decision makers in the White House, the State Department, or elsewhere in the executive branch, that should be held responsible.

Shameful and self-serving though Kissinger's assertions clearly are they were not entirely without foundation. As relayed earlier, in 1973 and 1974 American assistance to Vietnam and Cambodia did decrease as a result of congressional decisions. The victory of the North Vietnamese and the Khmer Rouge was made possible in part by the inability of their opponents—the South Vietnamese and the Lon Nol government in Phnom Penh—to field adequate military defenses, while those victorious in 1975 could count on Soviet and Chinese support.

There were plenty of excuses.

But ultimately, the collapse of South Vietnam was not simply a result of a combination of American domestic callousness and North Vietnamese trickery. The events of April 1975 also signaled a major fault in Kissinger's overall architecture: triangular diplomacy was not an effective means of restricting Soviet (or Chinese) involvement in regional conflicts. Indeed, if Kissinger's diplomacy in 1972–73 had encouraged the conclusion among Chinese and Soviet leaders that the United States was willing to accept Vietnam's unification after a time interval (see chapter 11), his 1973–75 negotiation record leads to a similarly disappointing assessment. To put it bluntly: after the summer of 1973, Kissinger did not treat Vietnam and Cambodia as anything but of marginal significance. He occasionally protested to the Soviets—but, according to the available record, hardly ever to the Chinese—about North Vietnamese violations of the Paris Agreements. But the nature of such protests was so mild as to suggest that Vietnam was, in fact, expendable. While Congress's cutbacks may have sealed South Vietnam's fate, Kissinger's diplomacy hardly improved Saigon's chances. The secretary of state's own policies contributed heavily to the disaster in Indochina in 1975. His attempt to blame others should not be allowed to obfuscate the simple fact that Vietnam constituted, ultimately, perhaps the darkest chapter in his career.

STAY THE COURSE?

On August 8, 1974, shortly before Nixon announced his resignation, Brent Scowcroft met with Soviet charge d'affaires Yuli Vorontsov. Kissinger's deputy handed over a communiqué that expressed concern over increased military activity in South Vietnam. Continued attacks by the North Vietnamese "could pose obstacles to further progress in our bilateral relations in the coming months," the communiqué read.[2]

It was, by this point, a rather empty threat. As relayed in the previous chapter, there were numerous other obstacles—most impressively the Jackson–Vanik Amendment—to the smooth progression of Soviet-American relations in the first months of the Ford administration. And yet, in the frantic months of trying to renew the course of American foreign policy that had suffered from Nixon's ill-advised effort to hold on to the presidency at all costs, the new president seemingly thought that he could halt the imminent collapse of South Vietnam. On August 9, 1974, his first day in office, Ford, Kissinger, and Scowcroft met with South Vietnamese Ambassador Tran Kim Phuong in the Oval Office. Ford, whose experience in Congress may have given him the illusion that he would be able to influence his former colleagues in a way that Nixon had not, assured Phuong that he would continue Nixon's policies in Vietnam. He expressed disappointment that U.S. aid had been subjected to congressional cuts earlier in the year. Ford also passed on a letter to President Thieu, assuring that "the existing commitments this nation has made in the past are still valid." Kissinger, referring to the latest congressional cutbacks on aid to Vietnam, blurted that it would be "disgraceful to let Vietnam go down the drain, after 50,000 Americans died there."[3]

Ford, who soon became aware of Nixon's private assurances to Thieu, could never live up to his promises. He tried to convince the Congress that South Vietnam was worthy of continued U.S. aid. But his former colleagues were less than enthusiastic: in early September 1974, the Congress approved $722 million of a requested $1 billion package; Ford's supplemental $500 million aid request was immediately criticized by congressmen gearing up for the November elections. No politician running for reelection wished to be associated with a losing and certainly unpopular cause. By this point Kissinger was growing increasingly frustrated. Lack of money would mean cuts in the number of sorties the ARVN could fly, cuts in ammunition, cuts, in short, in the military effectiveness of the South Vietnamese, he told Ford. "First we make an undesirable settlement, but with the promise of unlimited aid—and then aid is cut off within two years," he complained in an Oval Office meeting with the president and Scowcroft on September 10. "The impact over two to five years is bad," Kissinger added.[4]

Of course, Kissinger did not bother mentioning that he was, to a large extent, responsible for that "undesirable settlement."

Against this background, it is almost inexplicable that the new president continued to imply to President Thieu that he would be successful in the quest for further aid. Visiting Saigon in early October, Deputy Secretary of Defense Walter Clements told Thieu that a supplemental aid package for South Vietnam was likely to be approved in January.[5] "American policy remains unchanged," Ford wrote

Thieu as late as October 24, 1974. His administration "will continue to make every effort to provide you the assistance you need." And yet, Ford was sufficiently canny a politician to refuse to meet personally with Thieu. The tragedy was that Thieu, much as during the closing stages of the Kissinger–Tho negotiations in Paris, was being deceived about real American intentions and capabilities.[6]

Of course, Ford and Kissinger wished to increase aid to South Vietnam. In the aftermath of Nixon's exit they may even have thought that the Congress would be more sympathetic to their quest. But realistically, after Ford's month-long honeymoon was destroyed in September when he announced Nixon's pardon, as he and Kissinger felt the power of congressional resistance with the passing of the Jackson–Vanik Amendment to the Trade Bill, there was no real chance for a change of course.

The North Vietnamese were well aware of the new administration's difficulties. Thus, when Kissinger tried to impress Le Duc Tho about continued U.S. support for the Thieu government and Ford's complete agreement with Nixon's policies in Indochina, the response was dismissive. On August 25, 1974, Tho wrote to Kissinger:

> In case the United States continues the implementation of the Nixon Doctrine without Nixon and the use of the fascist and dictatorial Nguyen Van Thieu group to pursue the war and to undermine the Paris agreement on Viet Nam, then the Vietnamese people will resolutely carry on their struggle to defend peace and the Paris agreement until complete victory.

Kissinger, growing increasingly weary of the fruitless correspondence with his North Vietnamese counterpart, simply expressed concern over the direction that Tho was implying.[7]

Tho's "insolence" was no longer mere bravado. In October 1974, Hanoi's leadership concluded that South Vietnam could no longer count on American support and that the potential for a renewed U.S. intervention was extremely remote. In subsequent weeks attacks throughout South Vietnam intensified greatly, contributing to an escalation of desertion rates from within the ARVN (up to 20 percent of the total strength of one million may have deserted in 1974). In December 1974, Hanoi's leadership was engaged in detailed planning for the final offensive.

* * *

As was the case during Nixon's last months in office, congressional cutbacks were reinforced by Kissinger and Ford's reluctance to convince the Soviets and the Chinese of the need for further restraint. During his late October trip to Moscow, Kissinger focused, inevitably, on diffusing Soviet criticism about the Jackson–Vanik Amendment and on laying out the framework for the SALT II agreement (see chapter 15). Brezhnev brought up Vietnam, but merely as a model of Soviet-American cooperation to be used in the Middle East. "The situation [in Vietnam] is still complicated," Brezhnev said, "but there is no war." Kissinger made no response.[8] A month later, at Vladivostok, despite Ambassador Martin's strong lobbying that Ford and Kissinger bring up Vietnam, Indochina was never mentioned.

Soon after Vladivostok, Kissinger spent several days in China. This time he did discuss Indochina and suggested to Deng Xiaoping that the Chinese participate in a new peace plan for Cambodia: a coalition government consisting of Sihanouk and some of Lon Nol's supporters (but not Lon Nol himself). Deng rejected the offer out of hand: by this point the Chinese were heavily supporting the Khmer Rouge who, within six weeks, would commence their all-out offensive. Kissinger also discussed Vietnam. On November 28, he asked for help in recovering American soldiers still missing in action and warned that a North Vietnamese offensive against the South would lead to "serious consequences." Deng, Kissinger reported Ford, "stonewalled us on this issue, saying that both the South Vietnamese and we [the United States] were bogged down in Vietnam with our military assistance." Despite Deng's cool manner, however, Kissinger came out of the meeting with a sense that the Chinese did not "want Hanoi to heat things up."[9]

The Chinese, whose relationship with Hanoi was growing increasingly tense, may not have wanted to see a rapid North Vietnamese takeover of the South. But the prospect that a Chinese-supported Khmer Rouge would rule over Phnom Penh sometime in the spring of 1975 was a disheartening prospect for the USSR as well as North Vietnam. In December 1974, Marshall Viktor Kulikov visited Hanoi and, in all likelihood, affirmed substantial material support for the final offensive against Saigon that would commence that year. By the end of 1974, a forceful constellation of forces was coming together: in Cambodia, the Khmer Rouge readied to launch a major attack at Phnom Penh supported by Chinese materiel aid and the aura of Prince Sihanouk, the country's deposed ruler. In Vietnam, the rapidly disintegrating and under-funded southerners faced an offensive from the Soviet-supported North Vietnamese and their southern allies. The Ford administration, weakened at home and unable to forge a renewal of foreign policy, was faced with the hitherto unimaginable: an impending collapse of an American ally under a communist offensive.

"BLEEDING HEART"

By early 1975 the outlook in Indochina was even more bleak. In Cambodia, the Khmer Rouge commenced its final offensive campaign on New Year's Day. Over subsequent weeks and months two million refugees flooded Phnom Penh. By March Lon Nol started making plans for his departure to Hawaii. The North Vietnamese, meanwhile, captured an important provincial capital, Phuoc Binh, on January 6, prompting the Politburo in Hanoi to consider the "liberating" of South Vietnam in 1975 a serious possibility. As America did not restart bombing or reintroduce troops, and as the South Vietnamese retreated from the central highlands after the next major North Vietnamese offensive in March, Hanoi's leadership became determined to complete the unification campaign.

Kissinger's mood grew increasingly pessimistic by the day. On January 7, the day after the collapse of Phuoc Binh, Kissinger asked the Joint Chiefs of Staff to provide, within two days, an assessment of the amount needed to rescue South Vietnam and Cambodia. But the prospects were hardly good. While convinced that only an urgent installment of aid could turn the tide in Southeast Asia, Kissinger and his aides discussed in great detail the "best timing" of such a request to the Congress. Kissinger also recommended that the United States should move a carrier task force to the Gulf of Tonkin and B-52s to either Guam or Thailand. But the prescient point was that none of these moves was expected to do much more than, in CIA Director William Colby's words, send "a message to the North Vietnamese."[10]

On January 8, 1975, Kissinger made the urgency of the situation clear to Ford: unless the Congress granted further allocations for aid to Saigon, the South Vietnamese resistance "will unravel."[11]

He was right. But the president, fully aware of the strength of the administration's opponents in Congress, acted slowly. While moving American aircraft carriers closer to Vietnam and alerting U.S. marines on Okinawa did little to deter the North Vietnamese, Ford took three weeks before making his pitch for supplemental U.S. aid to Saigon. Finally, on the morning of January 28, Ford, Kissinger, Rockefeller, Scowcroft, Schlesinger, and the JCS chairman, General George Brown, met with congressional leaders. Ford gave a gloomy assessment of the situation in Indochina and said that he was going to submit a request to the Congress for additional funds. It would include $300 million for Vietnam and $222 million for Cambodia, the president added. Brown gave a briefing on the military situation and Kissinger pitched in with a plea about honoring old commitments. The administration's line was apparently straightforward: only by acting forcefully, by being tough, could the South Vietnamese be saved and the North Vietnamese convinced about the wisdom of renewed negotiations.

The congressmen and senators present at the Oval Office meeting that Tuesday morning, however, were mostly unmoved. To be sure, Senator Strom Thurmond (R-South Carolina), freshly returned from a trip to South Vietnam, was ready to back the president's request. "I am convinced they can make it if we help them," Thurmond said.

He was an exception in a meeting in which partisanship was obvious: the only other senator to voice his support for Ford's aid request was Hugh Scott, the Republican minority leader. Senator John Stennis (D-Mississippi) and Representative Al Ullmann (D-Oregon) summed up the majority opinion among the congressional leadership (and probably around the country). Stennis demanded that the Congress needed "proof" that the proposed aid package would actually succeed in achieving its goals. Ullman put it as follows: "What concerns us is their ineptitude and their lack of will to carry on. We see the divisiveness on the streets of Saigon. We are putting money in a place that is doomed to fall." House Speaker Carl Albert (D-Oklahoma), Representative Tip O'Neill (D-Massachusetts), and Senator Mike Mansfield (D-Montana) agreed. Only Senator Scott joined Thurmond in support. When Ford submitted his supplemental aid request later that day, he could hardly have hoped for a positive outcome.[12]

The skeptical mood was not limited to Democratic members of Congress. At a cabinet meeting the following day, January 29, Ford stressed that the administration had to back up his request for funds unanimously. He suggested, with reference to a *Christian Science Monitor* article that had appeared that morning, that the loss of Vietnam would result in a profound "guilt complex" in the United States and had to be avoided. Many cabinet members, however, were not certain what they should say in public if asked about the supplemental request. Secretary of Interior Rogers C. B. Morton blurted out the question in many cabinet members' minds: "What can that kind of money do in Vietnam?" Schlesinger and Kissinger responded, in uncommon unison, that the purpose of the $522 million was simply to keep the South Vietnamese and Cambodians from collapsing. Kissinger put it in these terms:

> We are asking for only enough to make it. We must have enough! We are out of Vietnam, we brought 550,000 troops home with honor; but now the dissenters who wanted those troops out are asking for even more. The dissenters want to retroactively destroy everything that we have achieved. We maintain that this will hurt our credibility worldwide. Our allies must know that we will stand by them and by any agreements we have with them. It will hurt our international negotiating power, if we do not stand in South Vietnam. We will need this support for two, perhaps for three years before the Vietnamese will be able to handle themselves adequately.

Ford and Vice President Rockefeller echoed Kissinger's sentiments. Aid to South Vietnam, Rockefeller put it, "is a necessity for our global relationships." It will eventually be impossible to do business effectively with China, the Soviet Union or any other country, Ford added, "if it always hinges on the domestic question of whether or not Congress will approve."[13]

In retrospect, the exchange was as bizarre as it was in character. It was a reminder of the significance that Kissinger continued to place on credibility as the cornerstone of American foreign policy and his ability to play the triangular game with the Soviets and the Chinese. As Nixon before him, Ford—and Rockefeller—shared this conviction. Moreover, similar arguments had been made in previous years to support American bombing campaigns.

The bizarre part was that no one questioned the assumptions about the impact that the collapse of the Thieu government would have on America's global role or that somehow, if only given more time, the South Vietnamese would be able to create a sustainable independent nation. In retrospect, the first of these assumptions proved incorrect: American allies did not consider South Vietnam's collapse a test case of American reliability. There was no appreciable impact on NATO allies and no noticeable change in attitudes of the countries most immediately affected by changes in Indochina (such as Thailand). If anything, some of the countries in the region, most notably Indonesia, would take advantage of the situation by convincing the Americans of a renewed necessity to provide them with additional aid and support in some questionable foreign policy adventures (such as the invasion of East Timor that is discussed in the following chapter).

If one could see some merit to the argument that credibility was important, the assumption, introduced by Kissinger and supported by Ford and Rockefeller, that South Vietnam only needed a bit more time was downright bizarre. How could one possibly make the case in early 1975 that if the United States only gave aid for another two-year period, South Vietnam would finally be viable on its own? That there was light at the end of the tunnel?

The answer probably is that Kissinger did not believe that South Vietnam would ever be a viable nation. But in his worldview that did not matter. What he believed in was that any sign of American weakness would hurt his already fragile foreign policy architecture by prompting the Soviets to engage more actively in other faraway places. Sadly, he, as well as many of his colleagues, still viewed the world through Cold War spectacles and reduced the significance of the events in Vietnam to a zero-sum Soviet-American game of power, influence, and credibility.

Meanwhile, a true human tragedy was unfolding.

"NOTHING CAN BE DONE"

By this point South Vietnamese President Thieu had come to realize that his constant letters to Ford and pleas to Ambassador Martin were of little consequence. Thus, Thieu had attempted to influence the Congress by throwing lavish banquets and showing extreme hospitality to a congressional delegation visiting South Vietnam in February 1975. When some of the delegates asked Thieu to release political prisoners held in South Vietnamese prisons, the president acceded. But none of it worked. There simply was no support for additional aid.

Meanwhile, a gloomy pessimism began to set in among the principal American policy makers. Ambassador Martin, back home for a brief visit in mid-February, not only argued that a minimum sum of $722 million was necessary, but that Hanoi was watching the Washington scene closely. If the Congress refused further aid requests, the North Vietnamese would unleash a forceful offensive. Martin had, moreover, already come to the conclusion that any hope of rescuing Cambodia from Khmer Rouge domination had vanished. Ten days later, on February 25,

Kissinger effectively presented Ford and Scowcroft with a similar assessment: Cambodia was sure to collapse, he argued, but a slim chance remained in Vietnam.[14]

That slim chance—real or imagined—quickly vanished. On March 10, 1975, the North Vietnamese began attacking Ban Me Thuot, a major city in the Central Highlands of South Vietnam. In two days, the ARVN was in full retreat and Thieu ordered his troops to abandon northern and central provinces in order to focus on the defense of Saigon. Within ten days, Hue, the old imperial capital, and Danang, a major provincial capital, were under North Vietnamese control. On March 12, the day that Ban Me Thuot fell, the U.S. Congress turned down Ford's request for additional funds.

Thieu was starting to panic. On March 25, he wrote Ford, asking him to "order brief but intensive B-52 air strike against the enemy's concentration of forces and logistic base within South Vietnam, and to urgently provide us with necessary means to contain and repel the offensive." In a meeting that same day, Ford, fresh from a golfing holiday in Palm Springs, ordered the army chief of staff, General Fred C. Weyand, to go to Vietnam and return with a full assessment of the situation. Kissinger punctuated the need for rapid action. "If we don't move fast we will be in big trouble," he stressed. Ironically, Ford had another Vietnam-related meeting that same evening. The president and Scowcroft met with a South Vietnamese delegation of parliamentarians and labor leaders. The impending collapse was clearly on the minds of the South Vietnamese, yet Ford had little else than empty words to offer: "Be tough and keep up the good fight."[15]

Even as they waited for Weyand's return from South Vietnam in early April, Kissinger had evidently come to the conclusion that the situation had gone from bad to hopeless. On the morning of Thursday, March 27, he put his feelings of hopelessness in plain terms to Ford and Scowcroft:

> We are on the wrong wicket. It seems that they [South Vietnamese] have lost virtually everything and North Vietnam has suffered very little. I say this with a bleeding heart—but maybe you must put Vietnam behind you and not tear the country apart again.[16]

The next day's NSC meeting—on March 28, 1975—was the first time during the Ford administration that Vietnam made it on the agenda. Interestingly, perhaps because the president was still waiting for Weyand's return from Saigon, it was not the lead-off topic. In fact, Kissinger's most recent (March 8–23) Middle East voyage dominated the discussion. The secretary described an emerging deadlock in his negotiations and warned that a renewed war in the region was now a possibility. A "complete reassessment" of U.S. policy in the Middle East was necessary, Kissinger argued.

After about an hour and a half, the discussion finally shifted to Vietnam. CIA Director Bill Colby provided a pessimistic estimate: at best, Thieu's troops could hold on in the immediate area around Saigon until 1976. There were roughly a million refugees in Saigon and "some grumbling about Thieu in the army as well as the political circles." Danang, a coastal city that had been a major U.S. military base, was on the verge of collapse and witnessing chaotic evacuation scenes; "law and order has broken down completely." After Colby gave an equally cheery report on Cambodia, Secretary of Defense Schlesinger predicted—quite accurately—that the remaining opposition to the Khmer Rouge's victory would collapse within two weeks (it took just under three).

"We have to make an evacuation decision," Kissinger blurted. "If we wait," he added, "it could collapse all at once before we can get our people out."[17]

The fight was over. The broad plans for the evacuation were drawn up during a WSAG meeting on April 2, 1975. The basic conclusion of the meeting was that "the evacuation of US personnel in South Vietnam and those US citizens who left the cities in the north will begin immediately." The airlift in Cambodia would continue, if possible, for another two weeks. Noticeable at the meeting was how shocked Kissinger was about the speed of South Vietnam's collapse. He had suggested three months; Schlesinger retorted: "I would say we should be prepared for the collapse within three weeks . . . I wouldn't count on any more than 45 days." Others agreed.

"Basically, then, nothing can be done," said Kissinger.

"I can't think of anything," agreed Schlesinger.

Discussion turned on the categories of people the United States should try to get out from South Vietnam before the North Vietnamese overran Saigon. Philip Habib suggested that it might be worth approaching Hanoi in order to negotiate a deal, a respite, on fighting. There could be no negotiated withdrawals, Kissinger argued. When Habib suggested that the North Vietnamese had done so with the French two decades earlier, Kissinger retorted:

> They did it with the French in 1954 because they were opposed by force. We have no cards to play. We have no leverage. We have nothing left. I guarantee you that we will get no cooperation whatsoever from Le Duc Tho . . . *The US will not negotiate a surrender of South Vietnam.*[18]

We will never know whether another negotiation attempt with the North Vietnamese would have relieved some of the pain and suffering inflicted upon the South Vietnamese in 1975. But Kissinger's decision not to even try and cite a lack of "leverage" as a reason is telling. What still mattered was American (and Kissinger's) credibility, not the human dimension. Observing the collapse of South Vietnam was bad enough; sitting down and discussing the terms of surrender with Ducky would have been thoroughly humiliating. Impressions still mattered most and Kissinger could not accept legitimizing North Vietnam's impending victory at the negotiation table.

The next morning, April 3, Kissinger told Ford and Scowcroft that he was going to write the Norwegian Nobel Committee and offer to return the Peace Prize. When he actually did so, however, the response from Oslo was negative: once awarded and accepted, the prize could not be returned. Rules were rules.[19]

EAGLE PULL AND YEAR ZERO

Cambodia collapsed first. On April 1, a weeping Lon Nol fled with his family from Cambodia to Hawaii. Nine days later, President Ford made yet another passionate plea for aid to Cambodia. "It may be too late," the president remarked. That same day, George Bush saw Prince Sihanouk in Beijing. The future president suggested, yet again, that Sihanouk return home to form a coalition government now that Lon Nol had left the country and had been replaced by Prince Sirik Matak, a former contender to the throne. Sihanouk refused. He was well aware that the Khmer Rouge was not interested in anything but a complete and unconditional victory. The next day, April 11, 1975, Ford decided to execute Operation Eagle Pull, the final U.S. evacuation from Phnom Penh. "All Americans must be on board the last chopper," Ford insisted.[20]

Heart-wrenching scenes, indicative of what was to be in store for Cambodia under the Khmer Rouge's subsequent rule, followed. There were displays of uncommon, if hopeless and futile, courage on the part of some Cambodian officials. Sirik Matak, for example, refused to accept an offer that he should escape Phnom Penh on an American helicopter. "I cannot leave in such a cowardly fashion," Matak wrote. "I have only committed this mistake in believing you, the Americans," he added in a note—much publicized later on—to the U.S. ambassador, John Guenther Dean. Lon Nol's brother Lon Non and acting Prime Minister Long Boret also refused the evacuation offer. On April 12, Dean and other remaining Americans boarded helicopters headed for a U.S. navy ship in the Gulf of Thailand. As they lifted off from the embassy compound, Dean and others watched in horror while Khmer Rouge mortars shelled the Cambodian crowd that had gathered to watch their liftoff.

A few days later, on April 17, the Khmer Rouge took over all of Phnom Penh. Long Boret was shot on the spot. Lon Non suffered a similar fate. They were the lucky ones. Sirik Matak had to suffer for three days without medical help until a bullet wound in his stomach killed him.

As Kissinger pointedly remarked, the *New York Times'* headline a few days earlier, on April 13, had read: "Indochina Without Americans: For Most, a Better Life."[21] For Cambodians, it would be anything but. Over subsequent months and years, the Khmer Rouge would make its mark in history as one of the most homicidal regimes of the twentieth century.

While Kissinger (or Nixon, or any other American policy maker) can hardly be held responsible for the bloodthirsty fantasies of Pol Pot and his comrades, U.S. policy had, since the late 1960s, helped create the conditions in which the Khmer

Rouge's ascendancy became possible. Kissinger had not single-handedly destroyed Cambodia, as some authors would later have it, but his support for the many policy decisions, from the secret bombings in 1969 to treating Cambodia as one of the minor sideshows of triangular diplomacy, did ultimately nothing to improve the chances of that nation's survival. They surely showed an abhorring disregard for Cambodian lives (however touching Kissinger's later recollection of the Khmer Rouge's atrocities may appear). Kissinger's policies may have saved some American and South Vietnamese lives in 1969–72; the bombings and the 1970 invasion were, in that narrow sense, a legitimate military strategy. But the destruction wrought on Cambodia, whether as a result of American policy or as an indirect and unintended consequence thereof, was a microcosm of the worst facets of his realpolitik.

CRUEL APRIL

The collapse in Vietnam occurred two weeks later. On April 4, General Weyand returned from his mission to Vietnam and reported to Ford. The brief was, as expected, depressing reading. "The probability of the survival of South Vietnam as a truncated nation in the southern provinces is marginal at best," Weyand wrote. He then went on to plead for an additional $722 million in American aid and U.S. air strikes. Recognizing the "significant legal and political implications" of such aid, however, Weyand also urged the development of plans for mass evacuations of U.S. citizens, South Vietnamese, and third-country nationals. The army chief of staff closed his assessment with a familiar argument: "United States credibility as an ally is at stake in Vietnam. To sustain that credibility we must make a maximum effort to support the South Vietnamese now."[22]

There was little in Weyand's report that could have surprised Ford or made him change his mind about the course in Vietnam. Like Kissinger, the president was determined to get out and place the blame for South Vietnam's collapse on the Congress. Thus, fully aware that it had no chance of being approved, Ford decided to pass the request for $722 million to the Congress. Air strikes in April 1975, as they had been since 1973, were out of the question: even if they had produced a temporary respite in North Vietnam's attacks, ordering such strikes amounted to political suicide in the United States.

Indeed, plans for the airlift of Americans and others were already under way when Ford asked the Congress, in a nationwide address delivered to a joint session of the House and the Senate on the evening of April 10, for an emergency package of $722 million. The response on Capitol Hill was an awkward silence, followed by immediate denunciations of the request. Two Democratic House members, Toby Moffett (Connecticut) and George Miller (California) walked out of the chambers while Ford was talking. The next morning, Kissinger and Ford were already making contingency plans in case the request, as expected, would be refused. "If you lose the Vietnam aid," Kissinger said, "you should speak for 10 minutes and say you are pulling the Americans out." Already thinking ahead to November 1976, Kissinger then added:

> What are the Democrats going to run on next year? They got us into it, and we got out of it, and they won't even fund poor GVN that they got into the whole thing. They will have no issue on Vietnam—but you will. I think you should go out and sell this.[23]

On April 14, members of the Senate Foreign Relations Committee made it clear that any additional funds would be strictly limited to finishing the evacuation. Meeting with Ford, Kissinger, Scowcroft, and Schlesinger, the senators only wanted to discuss evacuation plans. Jacob Javits (D-New York) put it succinctly: "I will give you large sums for evacuation, but not one nickel for military aid for Thieu." There was much discussion about how many South Vietnamese should be pulled out. Frank Church worried that the administration was trying to use a large-scale evacuation as a pretext for putting American troops in indefinitely. Ford denied any such plan, but argued that it was essential to give the impression that American troops were going in "for some period" to avoid panic among the South Vietnamese.[24]

Whereas Kissinger had not confronted the members of the Foreign Relations with anything but a plea for help in evacuating Americans and South Vietnamese, he vented his frustration at a cabinet meeting two days later. After a gloomy briefing on the forthcoming collapse of Saigon, Kissinger placed the blame squarely on Capitol Hill. "This is the first time that American domestic reactions, principally in the Congress, have impacted seriously on the action of a foreign government," he argued, adding: "It is the age old problem of internal domestic argument and competition affecting the conduct of foreign policy." He continued:

> The United States had encouraged the South Vietnamese to resist and fight for its right of self-determination. By not giving aid to South Vietnam and with the Russians and Chinese giving consistent aid to North Vietnam, there developed an imbalance whereby the North Vietnamese Army had much greater force.

Given his almost desperate effort in 1971–72 to sell the notion of what he had called "a responsible interval" between the American exit and the determination of Vietnam's political future, there was more than a small amount of hypocrisy in Kissinger's argument. (Of course, few in the cabinet room were at the time privy to the secret record of Kissinger's negotiations with the Chinese and the Soviets.) Now that the interval was coming to an end, he was finding fault everywhere, except in his own actions.

As far as South Vietnam was concerned all was, in effect, lost. What remained to be done in Vietnam was to evacuate Americans and as many friendly South Vietnamese as possible. And

> the great challenge to the United States is how does the country manage its exit from this tragic situation. The answer to that will be the world's perception of the United States foreign policy. These events have a profound impact on world leaders. They are very interested in the United States position, not only in South Vietnam, but how it relates to their specific countries all across the globe.[25]

In fact, "managing the exit" in the second half of April neither created problems at home nor had an appreciable impact on the attitudes of U.S. allies abroad. Gerald Ford decided that it was politically more expedient to ignore Vietnam rather than start playing the blame game with the Congress. On April 23, 1975—a week before North Vietnamese troops entered Saigon—Ford delivered the convocation address at Tulane University in New Orleans. He declared that the war was over. After evoking images of Andrew Jackson's 1815 victory in the Battle of New Orleans, Ford noted that the former president's epic triumph, although it occurred after the war with Britain had formally ended, had "restored America's pride." He went on to say: "Today, America can regain a sense of pride that existed before Vietnam. But it cannot be achieved by refighting war that is finished as far as America is concerned . . . I ask that we stop re-fighting the battles and the recriminations of the past." After Ford uttered the word *finished,* his audience burst out in thunderous applause, perhaps the loudest Gerald R. Ford ever received.

There was no doubt that Ford had judged the national mood on Vietnam correctly; there was no point in campaigning against the Congress in a way that Kissinger had suggested he do. Indeed, as John Robert Greene notes, Ford's convocation address at Tulane "represents a significant break between Ford and Kissinger over foreign policy." One should add, though, that the break was not so much over foreign policy as such, but the uses of foreign policy in U.S. domestic politics: while Kissinger had pushed for a campaign of vitriolic attacks against the "spineless" Congress, Ford had opted for reconciliation.

Ford was undoubtedly correct. But the incident was an indication of one of the major reasons why Kissinger was, ultimately, unable to build a consensus behind his overall foreign policy architecture: his inability to read and relate to the overall mood of the American public.

With his Tulane speech Ford effectively removed Vietnam as an issue in U.S. domestic politics (at least for the forthcoming electoral season). While they hardly took pride in the Vietnam experience, most Americans were willing to observe a brief moratorium on the debate over the causes of the country's longest war. In 1976, as the election season was fully under way, Vietnam—perhaps because it was, after all, a bipartisan failure of momentous proportions—would hardly figure in as an issue in the campaign.[26]

The relative ease, even relief, with which Ford, the Congress, and the American public at large accepted South Vietnam's collapse in April 1975, however, should not lead one to ignore the very real tragedy that was unfolding in Saigon. Two days prior to Ford's speech, on April 21, Thieu, pressured by U.S. Ambassador Martin, had finally announced his resignation. His successor, for a few days, was Tran Van Huong. On April 27, General Duong Van Minh ("Big Minh") was installed as the last president of South Vietnam. Minh immediately asked Hanoi for a ceasefire and negotiations but was rebuffed. Hanoi promptly rejected these requests and Minh, on April 29, issued an order for all remaining Americans to leave Vietnam within twenty-four hours. The next day, April 30, 1975, North Vietnamese forces took over Saigon.

By the time Minh made his demand for the immediate departure of all Americans, an airlift of U.S. personnel and friendly South Vietnamese had been under way for over a week. Yet, the last two days of evacuation were dramatic. On April 28, the North Vietnamese began pounding Saigon's Tan Son Nhu airport with artillery fire, making the use of planes for evacuation purposes impossible. At 11:00 P.M. that evening—coinciding almost to the hour with Minh's ultimatum—Kissinger phoned Ambassador Martin to "pull the plug" and use helicopters to evacuate all Americans and as many South Vietnamese as possible. At the end of it, harrowing scenes of desperate people in overfilled helicopters being flown to U.S. ships were flashed around the world. Ambassador Martin left at 4:58 A.M. (Saigon time) on April 30 on what was thought to have been the last helicopter. A few hours later, it turned out that 129 marines were still on the U.S. embassy compound. They had to be rescued in broad daylight. Two hours after the last marine had been airlifted, North Vietnamese troops entered Saigon and smashed through the gates of the presidential palace.

During those last days before the fall of Saigon, Kissinger grew increasingly irate and short-tempered. He was clearly upset with President Ford for not consulting him about the Tulane University speech. At a WSAG meeting on April 28, he sniped at everyone in the room. He interrupted CIA Director William Colby's briefing on the airlift by asking—without evidently getting the irony—why there was so much contradictory information. "Can't we keep each other informed around here?" Kissinger blurted. At the same meeting there was much discussion of the many small groups that were on the airlift list because they might suffer retribution from the conquering North Vietnamese. Someone mentioned the Mormons. "Well, I feel sure that as long as Brent Scowcroft is Deputy Assistant to the President [for National Security Affairs], the Mormons will get out of there," Kissinger quipped. "How about the Jews?" he asked. "Does anyone care about the Jews?" No one answered.[27]

At the WSAG meeting on April 29, Kissinger again blew his top. Ford had earlier decided that only Americans were to be airlifted, but this was not the reality in Saigon, where masses of South Vietnamese were bursting through U.S. embassy gates in the hopes of being airlifted. To avoid complete panic, U.S. helicopters were taking on some. Kissinger demanded: "Can somebody explain what the hell is going on? The orders are that only Americans are to be evacuated. Now what the hell is going on?"[28]

The answer was simple: a war was ending. But the battle over blame had only just begun.

"AN AURA OF [IN]COMPETENCE"

Despite his attempt to blame others—the Congress, North Vietnamese trickery, the Soviets—for the collapse of South Vietnam, Kissinger's own policies had contributed to the final outcome in Indochina in 1975. Ever since the signing of the Paris Agreements in January 1973, he had viewed the war as a sideshow, as indicated in the limited space that was allotted to discussions on Indochina in Kissinger's meetings with the Soviets and the Chinese. Although he would later argue that the collapse of Saigon was inevitable within the context of a weakened executive and a rebellious Congress, Kissinger failed to use his remaining asset—diplomacy—as a tool in counteracting (or at least prolonging) that inevitability.

Inevitable or not, the effects of the collapse of Saigon worried Kissinger. Not because he had a soft spot in his heart for the South Vietnamese or worried deeply about the moral implications of the sudden end to American involvement in Indochina. Instead, he remained concerned over the same issue that had, from the beginning of the Nixon administration (and before), been a central consideration in determining the nature of U.S. involvement in Vietnam: American credibility. The events of April 1975 were sure to damage the image that U.S. allies had of the country's trustworthiness. Robert Tucker in *Commentary* put it as follows in May 1975: "To be militarily frustrated, and eventually defeated, by so small a state is humiliating, and nothing we say can deny this." *Time* magazine, which two years earlier had chosen Nixon and Kissinger as its men of the year, summed up the dreaded credibility crisis somewhat differently. "What was imperiled by America's performance in South Vietnam," an article declared on April 14, 1975, "was not so much the nation's credibility as its aura of competence."[29]

Kissinger, undoubtedly, took the insult personally.

The ignoble end of the Vietnam War also prompted Kissinger to call for another decent interval: the United States should, he argued, refrain from recognizing Hanoi's legitimacy for the foreseeable future. In his remaining time in office, Kissinger was relatively successful in his efforts at isolating the unified Vietnam internationally. He blocked efforts at restoring even a semblance of a bilateral relationship and personally pushed for the use of an American veto against Vietnam's UN membership in December 1976 (the vote at the UN Security Council was 14–1). The Vietnamese, of course, greatly helped the cause of their own isolation: albeit not similarly homicidal as the Khmer Rouge in Cambodia, the establishment of reeducation centers and the introduction of one-party socialism in the country was exactly what Kissinger (and his predecessors) had predicted. In June 1976, any pretense that the PRG was an independent entity was demolished when the country was officially united as the Socialist Republic of Vietnam. The refusal to deal with Vietnam was, of course, also domestically expedient. In the context of the approaching 1976 elections, with Ford trying to protect his conservative flank against criticisms from Ronald Reagan, there was much to lose and little to gain from opening the wound within American society. It seemed better to ignore Indochina.[30]

The unification of Vietnam further eroded the framework of triangular diplomacy. After the spring of 1975, the Ford administration would find it virtually impossible to make concessions to either the Soviet Union or China, the two other external powers that had played a major role in Indochina's transformation. If American leaders in the 1960s had viewed the need to uphold South Vietnam as crucial in the containing of Chinese expansionism, Kissinger and Ford now thought that the fall of South Vietnam and Cambodia—the final disaster in America's long crucible in Southeast Asia—made it essential to put plans for normalization on ice. Meanwhile, the victory of Soviet arms in North Vietnamese hands (and Chinese arms in Cambodian hands) showed that, at least in this case, Moscow (and Beijing) was clearly unwilling to practice self-restraint in the third world. Indeed, both the United States (in the Middle East) and the Soviet Union (in Vietnam) had now clearly violated the "Basic Principles of Soviet-American Relations" that condemned the search for unilateral advantage.

Such structural problems aside, the key issue remained, in Kissinger's mind, the problem of lost credibility. In the aftermath of cruel April, it appeared necessary that the impression of an American retreat be counterbalanced. For Kissinger, in particular, the question was largely one of prestige and credibility, the two things that he valued as keys to an effective foreign policy. With three dominoes gone in a short span of time it was imperative not only to show some guts through the rescue of the crew of *Mayaguez*—an American cargo boat that was captured by the Cambodians in May 1975—but also to restore, as far as was possible, the image of the United States as a tough power and a reliable ally.

In short, one of Kissinger's goals in the aftermath of Saigon's fall was to show the world that the Americans were not, as the *Chinese People's Daily* argued, in a period of "strategic passivity."[31]

18

The Worst Hour

Angola and East Timor

Huang Chen could not resist twisting the knife.

"It was a gross mistake for the U.S. to have its feet mired in the quagmire of Indochina," the PRC's liaison office chief told Kissinger. "We have urged you to disengage yourself and not dilly-dally," Huang added.

The two men were meeting on May 9, 1975, a little over a week after Saigon's collapse. It was an effort at damage limitation. Kissinger explained that the collapse of Saigon was of limited consequence to overall U.S. policy. Americans were, Kissinger maintained, merely in a brief regrouping period. He even tried to turn the unification of Vietnam into a net gain for the United States: "we are in a psychologically stronger period as we don't have to debate Vietnam every week," Kissinger temporized.

Huang Chen was not convinced. The Americans had clearly taken a very passive approach toward the USSR, he said. More important, he added, "the U.S. has engaged, and shaken off this burden. It should learn lessons from this experience."

"Everyone should learn lessons from this," Kissinger interjected.

"You should learn correct lessons from this," Huang replied.[1]

The next time Kissinger met with Huang Chen, on May 29, 1975, they didn't discuss Vietnam. Instead, Kissinger promised that the United States would "organize . . . barriers to Soviet expansionism."[2]

If this was the lesson Kissinger had learned, the question was how to apply it; how to organize those "barriers."

Two Portuguese colonies, in different parts of the world, merit special attention in this context: Angola and East Timor. In Angola, the Soviet and Cuban military role in the struggle for the political control of the nation that became formally independent in November 1975 virtually assured an American engagement. In the case of East Timor—an archipelago in Southeast Asia that had no obvious direct interest to the United States—Kissinger and Ford cast their policies more clearly with reference to the regional context of post-Vietnam War Southeast Asia and a search for an improved relationship with Indonesia. In neither of the two countries did the Ford administration choose a course that could, by any stretch of imagination, be viewed as either carefully construed or successful. They became prime examples of how Kissinger's overall foreign policy outlook, when applied to complex regional crises, not only contributed to the havoc in those regions but, particularly in the case of Angola, contributed to the demise of his entire foreign policy architecture.

For in Angola, he proved manifestly incapable of organizing the "barrier" he was looking for.

PORTUGUESE REVOLUTION

While Richard Nixon was still fighting for his political life in Washington, the series of crises that would eventually bring Cuban troops to Angola erupted. On April 25, 1974, the Movimento das Forcas Armadas (the Armed Forces Movement, MFA) overthrew Marcello Caetano's dictatorship in Portugal and established a military council, with General Antonio de Spinola becoming the interim president. Three months later, a leftist group of young officers, headed by Colonel Vasco dos Santos Goncalves, overthrew Spinola and included Communists in the new government.[3]

In Washington, the significance of the Portuguese revolution was largely related to its impact on NATO's future. The April coup itself was of little concern to the Nixon administration. It was only after mid-July, during Nixon's final weeks in office, when the left-leaning Goncalves replaced Spinola and included Communists in his cabinet, that they became concerned. Kissinger later described Goncalves as one who "if not an outright communist, only refrained from membership in order to save paying his party dues."[4] In subsequent months, as the Ford administration was establishing itself in Washington, seemingly related developments in Greece (where a right-wing junta collapsed after a Turkish invasion of Cyprus) raised the specter of instability in NATO's southern flank. The following year, a strong communist showing in Italy's parliamentary elections in June 1975 and the death of General Franco in Spain five months later, added to such fears.[5]

The fear of Portugal going communist, with the potential loss of America's base in the Azores islands and weakening of NATO's southern flank, proved overstated. As the situation in Portugal vacillated throughout the first half of 1975, moreover, Kissinger's focus gradually moved toward the fate of the country's colonies. For the continuous shifts in political power in Lisbon more or less assured that an earlier American expectation—that Portugal's participation would ensure a smooth transformation to postcolonial rule—was clearly unrealistic. While Angola became a focal point of his interest, East Timor was equally indicative of the flawed and morally questionable approach that guided Kissinger's policies at the time.[6]

EAST TIMOR

The collapse of South Vietnam presented opportunities to countries in Southeast Asia that understood the basic realpolitik outlook of Kissinger's policies. It boiled down to a simple point: the United States had lost allies in the region; it needed new ones. One leader who was poised to take advantage of the new situation was Indonesia's President Mohamed Suharto. In the second half of 1975, Suharto managed to gain Washington's backing for his government's decision to annex the former Portuguese colony of East Timor. The end result was a decades-long bloodbath. Interestingly, the events in which Kissinger participated are completely left out from his memoirs.

Visiting Camp David in early July 1975, Suharto described Indonesia's "long-standing struggle" against communism and made a strong case, to a receptive President Ford, for U.S. economic aid. Suharto then described how the collapse of the Portuguese empire was creating an unstable situation in its soon-to-be former colony of East Timor which, Suharto patiently explained, shared the island of Timor with one of Indonesia's provinces. Most disturbingly, Suharto continued, a communist-inspired minority dominated the independence movement in East Timor. "The majority" of the East Timorese, Suharto added, favored integration to Indonesia.[7]

The reality in East Timor was far more complex than Suharto indicated. There was indeed a division within East Timor over the half-island's future. The Timorese Democratic Union (UTD), was supported by Timorese elites and senior Portuguese colonial administrators, while the Revolutionary Front for an Independent East Timor (Fretilin) had the support of younger Timorese and lower-level colonial officials. In January 1975, following the Portuguese revolution of 1974 and Lisbon's move to abandon its imperial holdings in the Far East and Africa, the two East Timorese groups had formed an uneasy coalition. In July 1975, Fretilin, openly calling for a quick move toward independence, won 55 percent of the vote in local elections, while the UTD strengthened its ties with Indonesia. Fretilin was, essentially, a left-leaning nationalist movement. But it was hardly communist-inspired.[8]

But such complexities of the local East Timorese situation were easily overlooked within the Ford administration that was, in the summer and fall of 1975 still reeling from the collapse of South Vietnam, Cambodia, and Laos. If anything, Kissinger and Ford were looking for new strong allies in the Far East.

On December 8, 1975, Indonesian forces invaded East Timor, touching off a long and bloody conflict that would only end when an international peacekeeping force entered the country in 1999. They did so with at least a yellow light from Ford and Kissinger, who met with Suharto in Jakarta only days prior to the invasion; an event completely left out from Kissinger's otherwise detailed memoirs. "We want your understanding if we deem it necessary to take rapid or drastic action," Suharto told Ford and Kissinger on December 6. He claimed that the four other main political parties in East Timor resisted the Fretilin and had asked for integration into Indonesia.

"We will understand," Ford responded. Kissinger then expressed concern over the possible use of American arms. But neither objected to the forthcoming invasion. In fact, Kissinger even volunteered a wry, shockingly cynical, qualification: "We would be able to influence the reaction in America if whatever happens, happens after we return [to Washington]. If you have made plans, we will do our best to keep everyone quiet until the President returns home."[9]

The people of East Timor, an estimated 60,000 of whom were killed during the first year of the long Indonesian occupation (and approximately 200,000 over the next two decades), were one of the first to pay the indirect price for the collapse of American policies in Vietnam because of the renewed search for regional strongmen that Suharto skillfully exploited. As Kissinger had put it in a memo to Ford prior to their visit to Jakarta, Indonesia was "the largest and most important non-Communist Southeast Asian state." The major goal of the visit to Jakarta, Kissinger maintained, was "to encourage Indonesia's sense of self-reliance commensurate with its importance to the region, and to focus our dialogue increasingly on broader issues." The most important of such issues was, Kissinger elucidated, the changing American role in East Asia "in the post-Vietnam environment." Within that context, Kissinger advised Ford to assure Suharto that the United States was "determined to maintain close ties with friends such as Indonesia." The visit was to be "a dramatic reaffirmation of the significance we attach to our relations with Indonesia."

What about East Timor? Its relative significance to Kissinger was reflected in the fact that it was the last of twelve items in his briefing paper. He did not seem to anticipate an invasion but advised Ford to tell Suharto that a merger of East Timor into Indonesia "with the assent of the inhabitants would appear to be a reasonable solution."[10]

It was a classic case of a grand strategy creating misery at the grassroots level. The most important point about the meeting with Suharto was the big picture: to keep his "non-communist state" on America's side. The people of East Timor, although their "assent" was desired, were but minor pawns in such a game.

In the end, Kissinger and Ford's cynical attitude and quiet assent regarding Suharto's plans for an invasion of East Timor did little to rescue American credibility or remove the stain of incompetence that the collapse of Saigon had placed over the Ford administration. If anything, the ease with which Ford and Kissinger accepted Suharto's arguments showed a monumental lack of foresight and a moral insensitivity that helped produce a massive human catastrophe. While Suharto remains the man most responsible for the fate of East Timor, American policy did nothing to discourage him from moving ahead with the December 1975 invasion. Whether Kissinger and Ford could have persuaded Suharto not to invade East Timor—his troops were already poised to make their move—is questionable; the simple fact is that they did not even try.[11]

For all the human tragedy involved in the Indonesian invasion of East Timor, there was only limited interest among the American public in the events in Southeast Asia in late 1975 and early 1976. Later, of course, critics would harp on Kissinger's conduct with vehemence (see chapter 20). At the time, however, the public's focus was on Angola.

ANGOLA'S INDEPENDENCE

Like the tragedy of East Timor, the conflict in Angola that preoccupied the Ford administration in 1975 was an outgrowth of the Portuguese revolution. Unlike the French (in Algeria), the British (throughout their Commonwealth), and the Belgians (in the Congo), the Portuguese had managed to hold on to their colonies in Africa—Angola, Mozambique, Guinea-Bissau, and Cape Verde—through the 1960s. Under the dictatorships of Salazar and Caetano, Lisbon had expended considerable resources into suppressing resistance movements by force. After the April 1974 revolution, however, Portugal ceased all military offensives in Angola and commenced a process of decolonization that was accelerated after the second coup in July. Whereas Mozambique, Guinea-Bissau, and Cape Verde gained independence relatively peacefully and with limited external involvement, and the conflict in East Timor remained, for a long time, a regional issue, the situation in Angola produced a major international crisis.

In 1974–75, the Portuguese withdrawal exacerbated a civil war between the three main liberation movements in Angola. The Soviet Union, Cuba, the United States, the PRC, East Germany, Great Britain, France, Romania, India, Israel, Algeria, Zaire (former Congo), South Africa, Uganda, North Vietnam, and North Korea all took part in the struggle for Portugal's colonial legacy. Not since the Belgians had abruptly departed Congo some fifteen years earlier had a former European colony become a subject of this sort of magnified international interest.

To the external eye, the Angolan factions themselves were less than clearly defined. The MPLA—Movimento Popular de Libertacao de Angola, or the Popular Movement for the Liberation of Angola—was based around the capital of Luanda, where its main tribal support base, the Mbundus, was dominant. Its leader, Agostinho Neto, was a gynecologist and a poet. Born in 1922, Neto had married a white Portuguese woman, become a Marxist, and spent six years (1956–62) in Portuguese prisons for his open criticism of colonial rule. Neto's personal history, as well as the MPLA's effort to avoid racial rhetoric, made the MPLA more appealing to various ethnic groups than its two major contenders. In the mid-1960s, Neto had established himself as the most important leader of the MPLA and would eventually become the first president of the People's Republic of Angola (1976–79). His main supporters were the Soviet Union, Cuba, East Germany, and Yugoslavia.

Founded in 1962, the FNLA—Frente Nacional de Libertacao de Angola, or the National Front for the Liberation of Angola—had its strongest local support among the Bakongo tribe in the northwestern part of Angola, along the Zairian border. The leader of the FNLA was Holden Roberto, who was married to the sister in-law of Zaire's President Mobutu Sese Seko. Roberto had been on a modest CIA retainer since the Kennedy administration. Although hardly a pro-Western capitalist, Roberto became Kissinger's choice ally in early 1975 when he approved a $300,000 aid package to the FNLA leader. It was, though, a mistake to bet on the FNLA: the Bakongos were French-speaking and more interested in an independent Congolese state than a united Angola, the FNLA was heavily dependent on Zaire, and the FNLA had, at best, a regional support base. That Roberto himself spent most of the 1960s and early 1970s in Zaire did little to prop up his popular appeal in Angola. Yet, in addition to the United States, Roberto managed to receive various forms of aid from such countries as China, Romania, India, and Algeria.

The third Angolan grouping was UNITA, Uniao Nacional para a Independencia Total de Angola, or the National Union for the Total Independence of Angola. Its leader, Jonas Savimbi, had originally allied himself with the FNLA and been courted by the MPLA but decided, in 1966, to form his own movement. Flamboyant and charismatic, Savimbi would continue his struggle through the 1980s and 1990s; in fact, the civil war in Angola would continue until Savimbi was killed in 2002. Based in the south among the Ovimbundu tribe, the UNITA had the largest ethnic base (about 31 percent of the population). The strength of ethnic influence and reliance on that bond—at least at this stage of Savimbi's career—was, however, one of UNITA's problems: it lacked appeal among other ethnic groups. Its other serious problem was that it had accepted assistance from apartheid South Africa. Yet, Savimbi's charisma and political skills managed to land him support from a number of the same countries, including, China, Romania, the United States, and North Korea, as the FNLA.[12]

*   *   *

In early 1975, despite the evident tensions between the three major Angolan movements, the Kenyan president, Jomo Kenyatta, managed to assemble Neto, Roberto, and Savimbi around the same table in Mombasa. The three leaders agreed to cooperate in negotiations with the Portuguese authorities, leading to the conclusion of the Alvor Accord on January 15, 1975. The accord called for the establishment of a transitional government on January 31, and set November 11, 1975, as the date for Angola's independence.

It looked neat on paper. But the Alvor Accord was dead on arrival.

While the three movements welcomed Angola's forthcoming independence, the hopes that a peaceful transfer of power would occur were quickly dashed. By March 1975, small-scale fighting between the FNLA and MPLA had already become endemic. The Portuguese, caught in their own internal crisis, could do little to enforce the Alvor Accord. Despite having 20,000 troops in Angola, Ambassador Carlucci cabled from Lisbon in March 1975, "Portugal has neither the will nor the capability of major military intervention to save the precarious peace in Angola." He was correct. In the months leading up to November 11, Angola became mired in a civil war that would continue, with fits and starts, to the next millennium.[13]

The impending Portuguese detachment prompted the Soviets to take another look at Angola. Although Moscow had supported the MPLA since the early 1970s, the divisions within the movement (it had three major factions in the spring of 1974) had been disappointing to the Kremlin. The Soviets had been further discouraged by Neto's unwillingness to consider forming a united national liberation front with the FNLA as a first step toward a future consolidation of power. Indeed, only a month before the coup in Lisbon, Soviet observers in southern Africa had been thoroughly pessimistic about the prospects of the Angolan revolution. Yet, by May 1974, the Kremlin had moved to strengthen the MPLA and boost Neto's claim to leadership. The task was made more urgent as both the FNLA and UNITA strengthened their respective positions in the summer of 1974.[14]

The arrival of Chinese advisers to help train Roberto's troops in Zaire in June 1974 was an added reason for the Soviet interest in Angola. Since the Sino-Soviet split and the emergence of détente, the Kremlin had been concerned that Beijing would be able to use the Soviet-American relationship to advance China's prestige in the developing world. In February 1971, for example, a Soviet Communist Party Central Committee Report summarized how

> Beijing is trying to take the non-aligned movement and the developing countries under its own influence. For this purpose, and in order to alienate the states of the "third world" from their dependable support in the struggle with imperialism—the Soviet Union and other fellow socialist countries—the Chinese leadership is tactically using the PRC's opposition to both "superpowers," which allegedly "came to terms" to "divide the world amongst them."[15]

Happily—from the Soviet perspective—the Chinese had made their claim to such opposition to both superpowers questionable by inviting Nixon to Beijing in 1972. Nevertheless, in 1974 Mao's China continued to make a claim to leadership of the third world. As the Chairman put it to Zambia's President Kenneth Kaunda in February 1974: "We are the Third World."[16]

In January 1975, only a week after the Alvor Accord was signed, the Forty Committee (which Kissinger chaired) approved an additional $300,000 in aid to

Roberto. Although not massive, the aid indicated a continued American interest in the future of Angola. The CIA's involvement further undermined the shaky legitimacy of the transitional government and was likely to prompt the FNLA—already supported by Zaire—to escalate its attacks on the MPLA in the spring of 1975.[17]

* * *

Ironically, the most significant non-African contribution to the Angolan War did not come from the United States, the Soviet Union, or China, but from Cuba. Cubans had, in fact, played a significant role in Africa ever since the early 1960s. Fidelistas had appeared in Algeria before 1964; Cuban advisers had fought in Zaire and Congo Brazzaville in the mid-1960s, and engaged successfully in the long campaign for Guinea-Bissau's (another Portuguese colony) struggle for independence in 1966–74. In 1964–65 Che Guevara, the legendary Argentinian-born guerrilla warfare expert, had toured the continent for three months. During this tour Che met, among others, Agostinho Neto. Although Cuba's relations with the MPLA and Neto remained intact in subsequent years, Havana's interest in Angola rapidly increased only after the Portuguese revolution in 1974. In late December of 1974 and January 1975, two Cuban emissaries visited Angola to explore the MPLA's prospects for success. Their report was glowing. But Castro still hesitated to grant the MPLA significant aid.

In April 1975, after suffering several defeats at the hands of the FNLA, Neto dispatched another emissary to Havana. Talks between the MPLA and Cuba were complicated by Soviet reluctance, as late as August 1975, to give its blessing to a large-scale Cuban military mission. While a few hundred Cubans did trickle into Angola in the late summer and early fall of 1975, the significant escalation of Havana's involvement not occur until November. By the end of the year, however, about 7,000 Cuban "advisers" (a number that would ultimately climb to 12,000) would be fighting alongside the MPLA. At that stage, their role would be decisive.[18]

In the spring of 1975, when the Ford administration was focused on the events in South Vietnam and Cambodia, Angola remained a sideshow. The collapse of Saigon at the end of April increased the significance of the Angolan conflict in the minds of Kissinger and his advisers. Moreover, given the involvement of the PRC in Angola, the conflict was bound to have its triangular implications by bidding the United States and the PRC on one side of the proxy conflict against the Soviet Union on the other. The problem was that in this case, the MPLA, the Soviet "horse," would end up on the winning side.

SEARCHING FOR A ROLE

Given the unfolding of events in Indochina, continued Middle East shuttle diplomacy, and the deadlock in SALT negotiations, it was not easy to get Kissinger's attention in the spring of 1975. Still, several of his key aides tried. In early April, the new assistant secretary of state for African affairs, Nathaniel Davis, co-authored a memo to Kissinger with Winston Lord and William Hyland. The three men accurately predicted a rapid internationalization of the Angolan conflict. Davis, Hyland, and Lord argued that the MPLA would be seeking increasing amounts of Soviet aid in the near future. This fact alone, they maintained, necessitated a decision regarding potential American involvement. As the April 2, 1975 memo put it: "We must decide on a U.S. position . . . Specifically, at what level, if any, should we covertly support FNLA's Holden Roberto or other Angolan leaders?" The last point was an oblique reference to potential U.S. support for UNITA's Jonas Savimbi.[19]

Another source of pressure on Kissinger and Ford came from a visiting African leader. In a meeting with Ford and Kissinger on April 19, Zambian President Kenneth Kaunda, whose relationship with Mao was particularly strong among African leaders, stressed the chaotic nature of the situation in Angola and the dangers inherent in a potential MPLA victory. Kaunda's advice was far from reassuring. He doubted that Roberto, allied with Zambia's northern neighbor Zaire as he was, represented a credible Angolan faction. In effect, Kaunda lobbied for the United States to support a third force, Savimbi's UNITA (its base of operations was along the Zambian-Angolan border). Savimbi, Kaunda said, was "the compromise leader" who could unite the country. But he would need significant external assistance. Kaunda also somewhat implausibly claimed that he represented the views of a number of other African countries.[20]

In addition to African pressure, the specifics of Sino-Soviet engagement in Angola preyed on Kissinger's mind. After all, both China and the Soviet Union were already active participants in the Angolan war. Although debate still continues regarding the actual relationship between Soviet and Cuban assistance to the MPLA, there is little doubt that the Soviets provided some military assistance throughout the spring of 1975 (although the most significant amounts during the first months of 1975 apparently came from non-aligned Yugoslavia). Similarly, the PRC had, as already noted, supported the FNLA via Zaire and, albeit to a lesser extent, given aid to UNITA.[21]

To Kissinger, the situation was hopelessly complex. At one level, it seemed that Angola provided a pretext for Sino-American collaboration in preventing the emergence of a Soviet-supported government. Such action would even carry the blessing of several regional leaders, including, but not limited to, Kaunda's Zambia. But it was hardly that simple.

To begin with, neither Beijing nor Washington wished to be seen as collaborating openly with the other. Moreover, the Chinese had limited resources and were not keen on active engagement in the conflict, particularly if it would damage Beijing's claim to leadership of the third world by linking Chinese policy in Africa with that of the United States and, worse yet, South Africa. While Kissinger wished to maintain an active Chinese role in Angola, the PRC—chronically concerned over Soviet-American détente—hoped that the United States would take a more assertive stand against the USSR. Kissinger, in turn, considered toughness vis-à-vis the Soviets the surest way to the Chinese hearts, but he was equally aware of the damage that a concerted military effort in Angola would do to his hopes of keeping détente alive. Moreover, there was the domestic political impossibility of direct American involvement in a far-away land immediately after the collapse of Saigon. In the end, covert action, combined with material and diplomatic encouragement to regional opponents of the MPLA, became the only logical—if ultimately disastrous—course to follow.

The State Department's African Bureau did not agree with Kissinger's prescriptions. Both Nathaniel Davis, as of April 1975 the new head of the bureau, and his deputy, Edward Mulcahy, saw few benefits in any kind of American entanglement in Angola. On May 13, the bureau produced an options paper that laid out three potential courses of action for the Ford administration. The United States could: (1) embark on a strong diplomatic effort to restrain external aid to the MPLA; (2) remain neutral in the conflict; or (3) step up its support for the anti-MPLA factions, FNLA and UNITA. To make clear where the bureau's preferences lay, Mulcahy flashed out the dangers embedded in "actively support[ing] one or more of the liberation groups." He argued that increasing assistance to FNLA would "constitute a clear political commitment with an increasing risk of exposure which would have a negative impact on our relations with other Angolan factions." Mulcahy further opposed broadening covert assistance to UNITA, adding that such a course would have the additional disadvantage of provoking Zaire and its leader, Mobutu. Overall, Mulcahy simply stressed the importance of "avoiding direct, overt involvement" in the Angolan conflict. Nathaniel Davis, whose confirmation hearings had been complicated by his alleged role in the 1973 overthrow of Salvador Allende's government in Chile (where Davis had served as the U.S. ambassador), also made his opposition to covert involvement clear.[22]

The African Bureau's advice notwithstanding, Kissinger continued to search for alternatives that better fit his penchant for action. He ordered a newly created NSC task force on Angola, headed by Davis, to prepare a study on U.S. policy toward Angola (National Security Council Memoranda, NSSM 224). In the meantime, Kissinger also asked the CIA to propose a potential program of assistance to UNITA.[23]

*   *   *

Kissinger also consulted the Chinese on Angola. On May 29, 1975, while waiting for the Davis Task Force's report, Kissinger met with Huang Chen, the PRC's liaison chief in Washington. The discussion veered rapidly toward Chinese concerns over Soviet expansionism. Kissinger, still recovering his composure after Saigon's fall and eager to placate the Chinese in advance of President Ford's planned state visit to Beijing later in the year, vowed to "organize barriers" against Moscow's hegemonic designs. In Africa, the United States was, Kissinger confided, ready to increase military aid to Zaire, where Chinese "advisers" were training FNLA troops.

While Huang had no problem with such assistance—which Ford would finally approve in July—he stressed a broader point. The MPLA's success "is inseparable from US policy towards the Soviets." Indeed, Huang argued that American policies thus far had "abetted the Soviet efforts." Soviet-American détente, in short, had given Moscow a chance to pursue expansionistic policies in Africa. The "barriers" Kissinger talked about were made of paper. According to Huang, détente was rendering the United States ineffectual as a serious counterweight to the USSR.[24]

The Chinese criticism could only have increased Kissinger's belief in the necessity of countering the MPLA.

The Davis Task Force delivered its report on June 13 (two weeks before its deadline). Unsurprisingly, it recommended against "any direct over-involvement" and called for the United States to search for a "peaceful solution through diplomatic political measures." Significantly, the task force also recommended against covert involvement, arguing that any leak would be highly damaging to U.S. interests in Angola and Portugal, as well as throughout Africa and the third world in general. Davis also warned about the damage that covert activities would do to the administration's position at home. The CIA, in turn, proposed an initial $6 million aid package to FNLA and UNITA in early June.[25]

Kissinger was clearly unhappy with what he later described as Davis's undue eagerness to follow "conventional wisdom" and lack of "stomach for covert operations." He worried about the possibility of falling dominoes and asked the State Department's African Bureau to reconsider the situation in Angola in broad regional terms: "Forget for a moment how important Angola itself may be. I am concerned about the impact on Nyerere and Kaunda and Mobutu when they see we have done nothing."

When he reviewed the Davis report at the NSC Senior Review Group on June 19, Kissinger conceded that there was little support for clandestine activities and a generally shared preference for accelerated diplomatic efforts. His skepticism, however, was clear. Kissinger considered the report weak and made no commitment to push the Africa Group's line at a decisive NSC meeting on Angola the following week. Later, in July 1975, Kissinger put his thinking in even more straightforward terms: "If Angola goes communist, it will have an effect in Angola, in Zaire, and in Zambia etc. These countries can only conclude that the U.S. is no longer a factor in Southern Africa. We will pay for it for decades."[26] It was all there. What Kissinger had in mind in Angola was a triad of ideas that had dominated much of American foreign policy throughout the Cold War: credibility, containment of communism, and fear of the domino theory. In fact, he had all but decided that activism was necessary and that covert action, combined with support for the regional players that opposed the MPLA was the only plausible way to success.

A central figure among those leaders was Zaire's President Mobutu, whose opposition to the MPLA was unwavering. To Mobutu, decolonization of Angola offered an opportunity to increase his role in the region and, possibly, even grab control of Angola's oil-rich Cabinda province. Roberto, who had resided in Zaire for a number of years, was Mobutu's favored candidate. In the months following the Alvor Accord, Mobutu had become increasingly critical of U.S. inactivity in Angola. Frustrated and searching for ways of forcing Washington's hand, Mobutu even accused the CIA of collaborating with assassination plots against him and eventually expelled the U.S. ambassador, Deane Hinton, from Kinshasa in early June, just as Kissinger was bombarded by advice urging him not to get involved in Angola.

As a sign of his interest in collaborating with Zaire, Kissinger sent Sheldon Vance, who had gotten along well with Mobutu while serving as the U.S. ambassador in Kinshasa, to meet with the Zairian president. On June 23, 1975, Vance had a friendly discussion with Mobutu, who described a Soviet-MPLA drive for power in Angola, complained about his own lack of funds and arms, and suggested that the United States start actively supporting Roberto and Savimbi. Zaire, Mobutu added, would be happy to coordinate such efforts.[27]

The Zairian president had, more or less, described what U.S. policy would look like for the next several months.

"DOING NOTHING IS UNACCEPTABLE"

The National Security Council met on the afternoon of Friday, June 27, 1975, to discuss Angola. The principals at the meeting were Ford, Kissinger, Colby, Schlesinger, Rumsfeld, and the acting chairman of the Joint Chiefs of Staff, General David C. Jones. In addition, Kissinger's deputy at the NSC, Brent Scowcroft, Deputy Secretary of State Robert S. Ingersoll, Deputy Secretary of Defense William Clements, and NSC staff member Harold E. Horan attended the meeting. Expertise on Angola—and Africa in general—was sorely lacking in the cabinet room, making it undoubtedly easier for Kissinger to paint the objectives of American policy in broad terms. This was not about Angola. It was about the global credibility of American foreign policy in the wake of the collapse of Vietnam.

In his briefing, CIA Director William Colby described the situation in Angola as "highly unstable." The MPLA, FNLA, and UNITA were all "trying to stake out territory and gain military superiority before independence on November 11." The transitional government installed in January 1975 was "unworkable" and Portugal had basically adopted a position of neutrality (the remaining 24,000 Portuguese troops were stationed around Luanda) although Colby argued that Lisbon was likely "to expend considerable diplomatic effort to reduce tension in Angola." Colby then went on to describe the involvement of various outside powers, particularly the Soviet Union's aid to the MPLA, and the PRC and Zaire's assistance to the FNLA. In the end, Colby was pessimistic:

The prospects for Angola between now and November are poor. Further violence could take place and edge the territory closer to civil war. At best, Angola will lurch along and become independent without a strong leader ... After independence, it now appears that no single liberation group in Angola will have the power to impose its own ideology as national policy.[28]

After asking a few basic questions about literacy rates and the size of the white population in Angola, Ford—whose lack of knowledge of Africa was palpably in evidence during the meeting—passed the floor to Kissinger.

"Henry, can you give us the options?" Ford asked.

Kissinger had, in fact, prepared the ground by providing Ford with a six-page memo on Angola in advance of the NSC meeting. In most respects, Kissinger echoed Colby. Yet, the secretary of state had added his own spin on events. Kissinger described, for example, the MPLA as a group with "a strong Marxist strain." Jonas Savimbi, although he headed the least influential, most obviously tribal group (UNITA) and had shown strong Maoist tendencies in his rhetoric, was, according to Kissinger, "the most active and politically skilful of Angola's nationalist leaders." He was also, much as Kaunda had argued during his visit to Washington two months earlier, the "compromise candidate."[29]

At the June 27 meeting, Kissinger acknowledged that "this is an area where no one can be sure of judgments," but argued that the key to power in Angola lay in the capital, Luanda. "Whoever has the capital has a claim on international support," Kissinger maintained. The immediate danger was that large Soviet arms shipments—reported by the CIA at the time but later contested by several historians[30]—had turned the situation in the MPLA's favor. As a result, the Portuguese government was "tilting towards Neto (the leader of the MPLA) and the Soviets are putting important equipment into Neto's hands." To counter the trend, Mobutu was urging the establishment of a coalition between UNITA and FNLA. Kissinger downplayed Mobutu's support for a separatist movement in the oil-rich Cabinda province (FLEC, Front for the Liberation of the Enclave of Cabinda).

There were three possible courses of action, Kissinger continued, adding that he was not "in wild agreement with" any of them. First, the United States could opt to stay neutral "and let nature take its course." Choosing this option had a certain appeal. It "would enable us to avoid a costly involvement in a situation that may be beyond our control; protect us from some international criticism; avoid tying us to any group; and avoid further antagonizing the MPLA." But the end result, Kissinger predicted, of choosing neutrality would be problematic. The MPLA would probably emerge as the dominant force and "Angola would go in a leftward direction; and Zaire would conclude we have disinterested ourselves in that part of the world and move towards anti-Americanism."

Judging from Kissinger's briefing, Mobutu's recent complaints about the CIA had achieved their objective.

The second option was no more promising. The idea was to launch a diplomatic offensive "to get the Soviets, the Yugoslavs and others to lessen arms shipments to the MPLA, get Portugal to assert its authority, and encourage cooperation among the groups." But such diplomacy was unlikely to lead anywhere because it depended on getting third parties do Washington's bidding. Most significantly, any discussion about Angola with the Soviets would expose the weak American position to the USSR: "If we appeal to the Soviets not to be active, it will be a sign of weakness; for us to police [Angola] is next to impossible and we would be bound to do nothing."

The third alternative course of action, clearly preferred by Kissinger and Ford, was to "actively support the FNLA and/or UNITA." In practice, this option translated to added U.S. support for Zaire and South Africa, the two regional powers most actively engaged in supporting FNLA and UNITA. Specifically, the active engagement option consisted of various forms of covert action, such as financial support to Roberto and pressure on Zaire, Zambia, and Tanzania to influence Savimbi and Roberto to conclude an alliance. Most fatefully, Kissinger's plan—developed in the Forty Committee—called for the buildup of Savimbi's UNITA "up to comparable strength with FNLA and MPLA." To avoid public exposure and "widespread negative domestic and international repercussions," Kissinger recommended that such efforts should be channeled via Zaire, by using Mobutu "as an offset" (although Kissinger envisioned also establishing direct contact with Savimbi). In short, the third option boiled down to supporting all the Angolan and regional forces that were—for whatever reason—fighting against the Soviet-supported MPLA.

Not everyone at the NSC meeting was eager to go ahead with the idea of throwing more money at the civil war in Angola and building up UNITA. As in a number of previous cases, the most penetrating questions came from Secretary of Defense Schlesinger. "We might wish to encourage the disintegration of Angola," Schlesinger, almost casually, noted. Would the oil resources of the Cabinda province not be more secure if they were controlled by Mobutu's Zaire (in other words, why not support the separatist movement in that province)? Most important, however, Schlesinger pointed out, "if we do something, we must have some confidence that we can win, or we should stay neutral."

"Doing nothing is unacceptable," Ford interjected. "As for diplomatic efforts," he added, parroting Kissinger, "it is naïve to think that's going to happen."

In the end, there was no real debate. Kissinger had clearly convinced Ford that, in the aftermath of the collapse of Vietnam, Angola was a test case of the credibility of the Ford administration's foreign policy. Schlesinger's objections—his pessimism about the FNLA and UNITA—were brushed aside. While direct U.S. troop involvement was out of the question, Colby and the NSC were charged with developing a plan that would bring a number of the elements from the first two plans together: work to produce an alliance between Savimbi and Roberto, push Mobutu into supporting such an alliance, and provide military assistance to the FNLA.[31]

* * *

In the weeks following the NSC meeting, changes in the situation on the ground provided the final push for stepping up American activities. On July 9, heavy fighting broke out throughout Angola. Within a week, the MPLA, boosted by the prospect of increased Soviet and Cuban material support, took control over Luanda. A pro-Soviet Angola appeared to be in the making with only four months before formal independence and the MPLA controlling the capital city.

Kissinger and Ford responded rapidly. Davies's NSC task force was shelved and the Forty Committee directed the CIA to draft a full proposal for covert action. At a meeting on July 17, 1975, Kissinger endorsed a detailed covert action plan, code-named Operation IAFEATURE. Ford approved IAFEATURE the following day, authorizing an initial expenditure of $14 million. In August, he would sign off on $11 million; an additional $7 million would be approved for IAFEATURE on November 11, the day of Angolan independence. By the end of July arms were being transferred to the FNLA via Zaire. Nathaniel Davis, for his part, resigned in protest, only four months after he had taken the oath as the new assistant secretary of state for African affairs. He was named U.S. ambassador to Switzerland and would present his credentials in Bern at the beginning of 1976.[32]

From almost any perspective—regional, global, domestic, moral, strategic—the course of action that Ford and Kissinger approved was the worst possible one. With each passing day, bloodshed in Angola increased and foreign involvement escalated. Even before its formal independence, the former Portuguese colony had become chronically plagued by warfare that would last, in fits and starts, for the remainder of the twentieth century (indeed, until Jonas Savimbi's death in 2002). An estimated 750,000 Angolans would perish over the next twenty-five years, while another four million would become refugees.

From Kissinger's perspective, informed as it was by his concerns over the impact to U.S. credibility of another Soviet-backed communist victory in the third world and Chinese concerns over American weakness, there had been few credible alternatives. The collapse of Saigon had magnified concerns over credibility. The tide in Angola threatened to bring into power a liberation movement with strong ties to Moscow; while the Soviet-MPLA bond was probably exaggerated at the time, it seemed, to decision makers in Washington, an objective reality. Pressure from Zaire and other African countries, as well as Chinese taunts about American ineffectiveness, further increased the perceived necessity to intervene and prove the administration's credibility in countering Soviet expansionism in the third world.

Thus, in late July 1975, the CIA began channeling aid to its chosen warriors in Angola, while encouraging Zairian and eventually South African support for Holden Roberto and Jonas Savimbi's anti-MPLA campaigns. Over the next three months the decision appeared to have been the correct one.

IAFEATURE AND ZULU

The CIA aid for FNLA and UNITA clearly had an impact. In late July 1975 Neto's troops controlled twelve of the sixteen provinces in Angola. The initial delivery of American military aid to the FNLA and UNITA via Zaire halted the MPLA's advance. Holden Roberto arrived in Angola, for the first time in years, in late July. In August and September as additional U.S. assistance arrived, the situation grew increasingly unfavorable to the MPLA. In addition to IAFEATURE, aid to the FNLA continued to arrive from China and North Korea, while Mobutu, encouraged by American aid deliveries, sent Zairian paracommandos into northern Angola. In October, 1,500 FNLA and Zairian troops presented a clear and present danger to MPLA's control of Luanda. And Kissinger grew increasingly confident. Meeting with Ford and Scowcroft on the morning of October 16, Kissinger briefly remarked that "We [*sic!*] apparently won a victory in Angola between Caxito and Luanda."[33]

South Africa, secretly encouraged by Washington, took the lead in supporting UNITA. An infusion of South African arms commenced in August–September, allowing Savimbi to commence offensive operations. Then, on October 14, the South Africans launched Operation ZULU. Over subsequent weeks, up to 3,000 regular troops of the South African Defense Force (SADF) cooperated with a simultaneous UNITA drive to the capital from the south. A few weeks later the SADF, having scored a number of victories, was closing in on the Angolan capital from the south. By early November, the MPLA had been reduced to controlling Luanda and only three provinces (including Cabinda). Agostinho Neto's troops were under siege; Jonas Savimbi and Holden Roberto were issuing triumphant statements. Apparently, everything was going according to plan.[34]

*   *   *

Just as victory beckoned, however, the tide in Angola turned yet again. On Independence Day, November 11, 1975, the MPLA—supported by Cuban artillerymen and Soviet rocket launchers—defeated the combined FNLA-Zairian-mercenary force north of Luanda. Neto, in control of Luanda, declared independence from the new nation's capital. The following day, MPLA forces scored another victory in the battle of Cabinda in the far northern part of the country. Suddenly, the FNLA, UNITA, and their supporters were on the run.

The shift was, in effect, the result of Fidel Castro's decision to pull out all stops from Cuban aid to the MPLA. Although the MPLA had lobbied Havana aggressively throughout the year, only the entry of South African troops into Angola in mid-October finally convinced Castro to engage deeply in the conflict. While Cuba had sent a trickle of military aid and advisers earlier, the major decision was made in Havana on November 4, without prior consultation with Moscow. Concerned over the rapid South African advance and worried that Brezhnev might veto or obstruct the delivery of Cuban troops and aid (as he had done in August), Castro thus acted independently. Yet, faced with the fait accompli, the Soviets were enthusiastic and supported the effort by providing transport planes and additional military aid. As a result, beginning on November 7, 1975, when the first major contingent of Cuban forces arrived in Angola, the MPLA was being rapidly fortified by a massive infusion of external assistance. The arrival of 12,000 Cuban troops in Angola (Operation Carlota) over the next few months dramatically improved the MPLA's military capabilities and transformed the situation on the battlefield. By the end of the year, Operation ZULU had been halted. The FNLA and UNITA were under siege.[35]

"The intervention of Cuban combat forces came as a total surprise," Kissinger wrote in his memoirs.[36] Not only that, but it basically destroyed his strategy in Angola. In November, Kissinger was unable to launch—covertly, overtly, or with the help of allies—a meaningful military response to the massive infusion of Cuban and Soviet aid and men (the first Soviet military advisers started arriving in Luanda on November 12, the day after independence). Suddenly, the money that had been allocated to hire mercenaries and to provide arms was insufficient to deal with the arrival of a strong Cuban contingency.

The stakes had clearly been raised. Something more than a group of mercenaries was needed. And it was not just the Cubans giving trouble.

"OUR VIEWPOINT PERHAPS IS NOT ALIKE"

A deescalation of the limited Chinese role in the Angolan conflict coincided with the gradual increase of Soviet and Cuban assistance to the MPLA. While the Chinese removed their advisers before independence in November 1975, the Soviets started providing growing amounts of military aid to the MPLA at that time. Although it was the largely independent Cuban role that clinched the military conflict to the MPLA's favor, by 1976 Moscow emerged as the PRA's major external benefactor, supporting the MPLA throughout the remainder of the Cold War.

In retrospect, the Angolan conflict provided a significant challenge for Kissinger vis-à-vis China. At one level, Angola seemed to provide a pretext for Sino-American collaboration: while neither had a clear national security interest at stake in Angola, both Beijing and Washington wanted to avoid the emergence of a Soviet-supported Angola. At the same time, neither country wished to be seen as collaborating openly with the other. Moreover, the Chinese were far less keen on active engagement in the conflict, particularly if it would hurt their image as a nonwhite anticolonial power. While Kissinger wished to maintain an active Chinese engagement in Angola, the Chinese—chronically concerned over Soviet-American détente—wished that the United States would take a more assertive stand against the USSR. Kissinger, in turn, considered toughness vis-à-vis the Soviets the surest way to the

Chinese hearts. And yet, Kissinger was also acutely aware of the need to stroke the flames of détente.

The extent of Chinese concern over Angola is debatable. It is fairly clear, though, that in the mid-1970s the PRC was reconsidering the value of its overall involvement in Africa. Not that Mao wished to cut off Beijing's links to the newly independent states on the continent. "We are the Third World," the Chairman had, after all, told Kenneth Kaunda, during the Zambian president's state visit to Beijing in February 1974. As to Angola, however, the Chinese, given their long-standing relationship with several countries in the region, were more attuned to the ethnic sensitivities of the local populations. Since the mid-1950s Beijing had actually granted more aid to southern and south-central regions of the continent than the Soviet Union (with such countries as Tanzania, Zambia, the Congo, and Zaire topping the list of aid recipients). In 1975, this experience meant that the Chinese were quick to cut their losses and disengage from the war. In October, soon after the South Africans launched Operation ZULU, the PRC started withdrawing military advisers from Zaire (where they had been based) and ceased supporting any faction in Angola before November 11. Whatever the Chinese hoped to achieve in Africa, an association with the apartheid regime in Pretoria was hardly a way of winning the hearts and minds of black Africa, while the growing role of other outside powers and lack of Chinese resources made Angola a losing cause for Beijing. In fact, as Raymond Garthoff puts it, "the United States would have been better advised to have emulated the Chinese in disengaging from a lost cause."[37]

* * *

Sino-American differences on Angola first became evident when Kissinger met Chinese Foreign Minister Ch'iao Kuan-hua (who headed a Chinese delegation to the annual UN General Assembly meeting) in New York on September 28. Kissinger tried to enlist Chinese cooperation by describing how "the Soviet Union [has] greatly increased its arms deliveries in Angola" and had managed to prop up the MPLA. He expressed "surprise" that the Chinese had indicated that they would be neutral in the conflict. Kissinger went on to ask: "If we are concerned with hegemony, why let the Soviet Union stretch its hands into an area as far as this from the Soviet Union?"

"Our viewpoint perhaps is not alike," Ch'iao responded. While he agreed that the Soviets were deeply involved and had "provoked" the civil war, Ch'iao reverted to his public statement of neutrality and argued that Moscow "will eventually fail even though it may gain some military advantages for a time."

"Forget about the speech," Kissinger snapped. "What do we do now?"

Ch'iao replied: "Some of our friends want to enlist the help of South Africa. This is short-sighted."

Kissinger agreed. "This has to be done by the blacks there," he added, mentioning his co-operation with Tanzania and Zambia. "We have studied the situation," he further added. "Do you want to exchange ideas on it?"

Ch'iao acknowledged that in some cases, like the Middle East, it was "necessary to use dual tactics." But he insisted that "Angola is different. So far we haven't given up hope that this problem can be solved between the African countries and the three liberation movements."

Kissinger, growing exasperated with Ch'iao's refusal to discuss the specifics and eager to reach some sort of cooperative agreement, had had enough of the diplomatic game and gave a succinct summary of his position:

> I will be precise. Roberto and Savimbi have to be stronger. I get daily reports of Soviet military shipments to Luanda. It is mathematically certain that Neto will prevail unless Roberto and Savimbi are strengthened—or else when the Portuguese leave Neto will take over. So unless Roberto and Savimbi are strengthened, then there will be no agreement between the three liberation movements and the African governments . . . I understand that Chinese arms are held up somewhere. It is important that Roberto and Savimbi control the large part of Angola before independence. Otherwise Neto will declare independence and go to the UN. Our people think this is a soluble problem if we act quickly. I repeat, we favor an outcome negotiated between the three liberation movements. But in a few weeks the outcome will be decided . . . We are prepared to help Roberto and Savimbi with weapons. Indeed, we are helping already to some extent.

Balance the forces to create a stalemate and conditions for negotiation was Kissinger's basic message.

"Good. I have taken note of your views," was Ch'iao's noncommittal conclusion.[38]

Three weeks later Kissinger visited Beijing to prepare for President Ford's forthcoming arrival. The situation had, by this time, changed dramatically: the PRC had commenced its withdrawal, the South Africans had launched ZULU, and the MPLA was losing ground. Cubans had yet to arrive and the prospects of FNLA-UNITA victory appeared bright. Thus, in his talks with Deng Xiaoping, Kissinger boasted that the Ford administration was resisting Soviet expansionism in Africa. It made little impact.[39]

Three weeks after Kissinger departed Beijing came the FNLA's defeat near Luanda and the arrival of the first Cuban troops in Angola.

CONFRONTATIONS AND OPEN SECRETS

Given the covert nature of both countries' involvement in Angola, as well as a shared interest in maintaining the pretenses of détente, Kissinger and his Soviet interlocutors did not approach the subject until fairly late in the game. Kissinger's meetings with Foreign Minister Gromyko in Geneva in July 1975, a week prior to the authorization of Operation IAFEATURE, explored almost all other issues: the

Middle East, China, Japan, SALT II, and the Conference on Security and Co-operation (CSCE). The same was the case with meetings during CSCE in Helsinki in late July and early August (see chapter 19). In September, Kissinger and Gromyko continued their discussions over a possible SALT II in New York, but did not exchange views on Angola.

In the end, it was only in November—after events on the ground suddenly shifted to the MPLA's advantage and the Chinese had withdrawn their advisers from Zaire—that Kissinger started peppering the Soviets on Angola. On November 20, Kissinger handed Ambassador Dobrynin a warning that Soviet actions were "passing all 'reasonable bounds'" in Angola.[40]

By then it was too late. The Soviets, whose aid to the MPLA had been limited up to this point, felt compelled to support the Cubans and the MPLA in Angola. If they did not, the Cubans were likely to continue their campaign and any loss of the MPLA could easily be blamed on the USSR. Thus, the Soviet reply, on November 22, denied American accusations as "groundless" and simply called for an end to all foreign interference.

Two days later, on November 24, Kissinger went public. In a speech in Detroit, he tied the "continuation of an interventionist policy" to the continuance of détente. Meanwhile, Ford approved an additional $7 million for IAFEATURE on November 27, bringing the total funding for the Angolan operation to $31.7 million, a sum that depleted the funds available from the CIA reserves. The president then submitted to Congress a request for an additional $28 million. It was the lowest of three figures discussed (the highest had been $100 million; Kissinger had recommended submitting a request for $60 million) and the first time that the Congress could openly discuss U.S. funding with reference to the administration's policy in Angola.[41]

*　*　*

When Gerald Ford landed in China a few days later, he and Kissinger had no illusions that the visit would do much more than "maintain common perceptions." This was, in fact, the crux of President Ford's two-hour meeting with Chairman Mao on December 2, 1975. While, once again, treating his American visitors to wide-ranging discussion of world events and criticizing the United States for its weak approach to the Soviet Union, Mao emphasized that until a full normalization took place, "there will not be anything great happening between our two countries."

When discussing Angola, Mao and Deng pointed out that South Africa was "a complicating factor" because it did not "have a very good reputation," but Ford defended Pretoria's anti-Soviet stand. Kissinger asked the Chinese to help by pressing Mozambique to cease its support for the MPLA. "It would probably be difficult," Mao responded. "Impossible," Deng concurred. When Kissinger persisted, Mao finally offered to "make a try." Ford closed the discussion by stressing, for the third time, that "time is of the essence."[42]

The following day, in a conversation with Deng, Kissinger continued lobbying for Chinese military assistance to the FNLA and UNITA, asking that the PRC resume its training operations in Zaire. "We have no way of transferring weapons into their hands," Deng stressed, once again returning to the problem of South Africa.

Ford upped the ante: "Will you move in the north if we move in the south?" Deng made no promises. As before, there was no agreement on joint or simultaneous action. And time was, as Ford had indicated, running out on the FNLA and UNITA.[43]

Although the discussion on Angola had been, at best, elliptic and inconclusive, there were some concessions and olive branches. Kissinger offered to help the Chinese circumvent export regulations on computers.[44] There was also Ford's assurance that he would "oppose any governmental action as far as Tibet is concerned," adding that in his opinion the Dalai Lama "should stay in India." But if anything, the final meeting between Ford, Kissinger, Deng, Huang Chen, and others on December 4 was unique in that the two sides completed the agenda with excess time on their hands. In order to put the right spin on the meeting, Ford asked if they could stay in the room the allotted time in order to avoid "giving ideas" to the press.

Kissinger joked: "See, if the meeting runs longer than planned, it proves we quarreled. If it runs shorter than planned, it also proves we quarreled."[45]

They had not exactly quarreled. But there had been no forward movement, no significant agreements. On Angola, the hot international topic of the moment, Ford and Kissinger had only elicited the vaguest of commitments while the Chinese had made it clear that they were extremely reluctant to get involved unless South African troops were withdrawn.[46]

Yet, Kissinger, Ford, and Scowcroft tried to put the best possible spin on the presidential visit to China. Meeting with a congressional delegation on December 10, Ford told his former colleagues how he had been surprised about "the vigor of [Chinese] anti-Sovietism." Kissinger described the PRC leadership as "cold-blooded pragmatists." The issue of Taiwan, certainly a major obstacle to full normalization, was not, Kissinger argued, "the major issue in our relations . . . the major issue is the international situation." He then went on to offer the following insight:

> They are one of our best NATO allies. In fact, our relations with them are better than with some of our allies . . . All we have to fear is if they decide our internal weakness prevents our acting with strength; then they will turn on us.[47]

It was vintage Kissinger. On the eve of the 1976 electoral season, he was tying together domestic U.S. politics with the maintenance of the strategic partnership with the PRC as well as the strength of the United States to act in such places as Angola.

Such elaborate linkage had little impact. As Cuban troops and Soviet aid continued to boost the MPLA's fortunes on the battlefield, the Congress turned down the administration's request for further aid to Angola.

CONGRESSIONAL REVOLT

In early December, while Ford and Kissinger were in China, Indonesia (where they flashed a green light to President Suharto's forthcoming invasion of East Timor), and the Philippines, the Congress considered the administration's request for an additional $28 million aid package to Angola. Domestic politicking was evident. Although the CIA had held several briefings on IAFEATURE in previous months, most senators and congressmen had exhibited limited interest in the details of the operation. Prior to November, only two senators, Joseph Biden (D-Delaware) and Dick Clark (D-Iowa) had voiced their concerns over the CIA's involvement in Angola. This lack of interest was particularly noticeable since details of IAFEATURE had appeared in the *New York Times* in late September (Clark actually went to Africa to see whether the story was true; he returned convinced that it was) and various congressional committees, including the Church Committee in the Senate and the Pike Committee in the House, had spent most of 1975 examining the CIA's clandestine activities.[48] Such silence, the Congress's notorious lack of interest in Africa ("I knew nothing of Africa. I had not been there had not studied it and wasn't particularly interested in it," Clark, the chair of the Senate Subcommittee on Africa, later reminisced), and the relatively small amount of aid being requested had, probably, given Ford and Kissinger some hope that the money would be appropriated. The administration could also take heart in the fact that it had a strong spokesman in UN Ambassador and future Democratic Senator Daniel Patrick Moynihan, who publicly ranted about "Soviet neocolonialism in Africa."

But then "the shit hit the fan," as the Senate Foreign Relations Committee's chief of staff, Pat Holt, later described it. In late November and the first half of December, stories of the true nature of South African involvement appeared in the press, linking U.S. activities with the apartheid regime. On December 13, journalist Seymour Hersh reported on Operation IAFEATURE and the brawl between Kissinger and Davis on the front page of the *New York Times*. The possibility, far-fetched though it was, that the Ford administration was about to lead the United States into another Vietnam-like quagmire quickly permeated the press. Senator Clark introduced an amendment that called for cutting off all covert aid to any Angolan faction.

Finally, on December 19, 1975, the day after Kissinger returned from yet another trip to Europe, the Senate turned down Ford's request and passed the Tunney Amendment to the Defense Appropriations Bill by 54 votes to 22. It banned any use of funds for Angola unless it was specifically appropriated in the budget. A month later the House passed a similar amendment (323–99). Unwilling to fight a losing cause amid the presidential election campaign, Ford eventually signed the legislation into law on February 9, 1976.[49]

*   *   *

While the Congress deliberated, Kissinger and Ford decided "to bring matters to a head with the Soviets." On December 8, Kissinger met with Dobrynin and asked the Soviets to halt their arms shipments to the MPLA. The following day, Ford told the Soviet ambassador that while he was committed to the continuance of détente, the situation in Angola was helping his domestic critics to mount an anti-Soviet offensive. Kissinger suggested that the withdrawal of all foreign forces, an end to external military assistance, and the creation of a coalition government under the auspices of the Organization of African Unity (OAU) would provide a solution. A seemingly sympathetic Dobrynin passed the message to Moscow.

In the next few weeks the Soviets responded with a series of mixed signals. On December 10, the CIA reported that the Soviets had ceased their airlift to Angola. On December 16, Soviet President Nikolai Podgorny apparently indicated to a British diplomat Moscow's willingness to consider the formation of a coalition government as long as the MPLA had a strong presence. But then, on December 18, the day before the Congress banned all further aid to Angola, Brezhnev's formal reply arrived. The general secretary only reiterated earlier arguments. The situation in Angola was not a civil war but a case of outlandish foreign intervention on the part of South Africa. Until the SADF withdrew its troops, there would be no discussion. Yet, like Ford on December 9, Brezhnev stressed that Angola should not become a test case of détente.[50]

The next day came the Senate vote. Despite Kissinger's public warnings that Soviet actions in Angola were "incompatible with a relaxation of tensions," the Soviets resumed their airlift on December 25. Cuban troops continued to assert themselves, and in early 1976 the MPLA quickly established its dominant position in Angola. On January 14, 1976, South African troops were ordered to withdraw from Angola (the last troops departed in early February).[51]

*   *   *

In his memoirs Kissinger argues that the decisive step in determining the outcome in Angola was the U.S. Congress's decision to ban any further aid to the FNLA and UNITA. He blames the "McGovernite Congress" for the MPLA's victory. There is something to the argument. After all, the congressional vote on December 19, 1975, occurred at a crucial point in the conflict: the Soviets appeared to be vacillating and had, in fact, suspended their military aid. Diplomatic efforts to forge a compromise were under way and might have produced a coalition government following the withdrawal of external forces. Less than a week after the Congress voted, however, the Soviet airlift resumed and American "allies"—including South Africa and Zaire—were undoubtedly disillusioned by the sudden pause in American aid and diplomatic support. As Kissinger puts it: "the Congress exploded our design."[52]

But what, exactly, was that design? A negotiated settlement orchestrated by the OAU was an unlikely solution to a civil conflict that had already claimed thousands of lives. If anything, the immediate period after the signing of the Alvor Accord in January 1975 had shown how limited the possibility of cooperation between the three Angolan movements was. It is also worth asking—as the historian Piero

Gleijeses does—whether another $28 million would have made a significant difference. While the Soviets paused their airlift, the Cubans continued to arrive in Angola throughout December. As a result, the FNLA, in particular, was on the run. Backing up South African involvement in the conflict would certainly have been politically unsustainable in the United States and have further eroded the American position amongst nonwhite African countries. As it stood, even the hidden cooperation between Washington and Pretoria was a public relations disaster that, more than anything else, hurt American prestige.[53]

* * *

By January 1976, the only chance for a negotiated settlement in Angola was to get the Soviets on board. But, as Brezhnev's responses had already indicated, this was a forlorn hope.

"PROSPECT FOR CHAIN REACTION"

In early 1976, Kissinger had the opportunity to make his case on Angola directly to Brezhnev, Gromyko, and other Soviet leaders. On January 21 he arrived in Moscow for two days of talks with the Soviet leadership. Although SALT dominated these discussions and Brezhnev publicly announced at the beginning of the talks that he had "no questions about Angola," Kissinger gave the Soviets a long exposition of the American position during his opening statement and argued:

> We have made it a cardinal principle of our relations that one great power must exercise restraint and not strive for unilateral advantage. If that principle is now abandoned, the prospect is for a chain of action and reaction with the potential for disastrous results.

Brezhnev was blunt. The talks in Moscow should focus on SALT, he maintained. "If we raise all sorts of extraneous matters, we will accomplish nothing." Moreover, Brezhnev disingenuously argued, "there is no Soviet military presence in Angola." And if Kissinger wished to raise the prospect of "disastrous results" arising from unilateral action, then the Soviets might as well "talk of disastrous consequences for the United States in the Middle East." When Kissinger persisted, Brezhnev grew more aggressive. "Are we here to discuss SALT? Or Angola?" he asked. "We [the USSR] need nothing in Angola. But the whole world can read in the press that the West, and America, is sending arms and mercenaries in Angola. And you turn everything on its head."[54]

Kissinger would not let the item drop. The following day, he raised Angola again. Brezhnev was no more accommodating: "Don't mention that word [Angola] to me. We have nothing to do with that country. I cannot talk about that country."

Kissinger turned to Gromyko, asking whether the Cuban troops would be withdrawn if the South Africans pulled out of Angola. Gromyko, however, denied that the Soviets had provided the Cubans transportation. "We have given some equipment—that's all," the Soviet foreign minister maintained. Yet, if South Africa would withdraw, Gromyko offered, the Soviet Union "will react to it." He did not specify the nature of that reaction.

"I must tell you in all seriousness that we can never accept 8,000 Cuban troops in Angola," Kissinger threatened. "[You are] continuing to depict our position in a distorted light," Brezhnev retaliated.[55]

When Kissinger met with Gromyko on the morning of the last day of his last trip to Moscow, he made yet another pitch on Angola:

> We cannot accept that 10,000 troops be sent as an expeditionary force carried in Soviet aircraft, with Soviet equipment. We must take public notice. The tragedy is that those of us who have supported the policy of détente with the Soviet Union will increasingly be put into the position of attacking this policy.

Gromyko was no more forthcoming than he had been in previous days. On Angola, Brezhnev had said what there was to be said, Gromyko retorted. If the Americans wanted to throw away détente because of Angola, so be it. But from Moscow's perspective, "all Soviet-American relations, and all that has been achieved, will override momentary considerations or momentary events in Angola. So, objectively speaking, there is no reason for events in Angola to have an adverse effect on Soviet-American relations." They sparred for a while on the ins and outs of the South African and Cuban involvement. But there was no meeting of minds, no effort at finding a joint solution.

"It is a pity that this has come to pass," Kissinger finally concluded.

"I have nothing to add," Gromyko retorted.

They moved on to discuss Japan.[56]

*   *   *

The recalcitrance of Soviet leaders on Angola should have come as no surprise. Although Soviet materiel was important for the success of the MPLA, Cuban engagement in Angola was not dependent on Soviet approval, or, by late January 1976, subject to Moscow's veto. In fact, there was general delight among many circles within the Soviet elite at the success of the MPLA and even a sense, as one foreign ministry official later put it, that history was moving in the direction of socialism. The unification of Vietnam and now, the success of the MPLA in Angola, seemingly vindicated those ideologues who had long spoken about the inevitable rise of socialism.[57]

In addition to such ideological considerations, there was the opportunity to teach a lesson to the Americans about the rules of détente. If Kissinger had felt free to exclude the Soviets from the Middle East, then Angola was payback time. Brezhnev, for his part, hardly minced words about this particular connection.

Lastly, there was little the Soviets could do, lest they were willing to alienate not only Cubans and the MPLA—both often acting independently of Moscow—but also other potential allies and sympathizers in the third world. If Kissinger worried about prestige and credibility, so did Brezhnev and Gromyko.

All in all, by the time Kissinger arrived in Moscow, the Soviets had little incentive to cooperate.

THE WORST HOUR

The South African decision to withdraw in mid-January had not been publicly announced, yet it was clear after Kissinger returned to Washington from Moscow that Pretoria's involvement was coming to an end. That, ultimately, determined the outcome of the war. By the end of February 1976, the MPLA reigned in Angola. The People's Republic of Angola (PRA) was formally recognized by the OAU on February 11; the Portuguese government followed suit eleven days later. The Soviets promised and delivered economic and military aid to the new government.

Unable to block the OAU's recognition of the PRA, Mobutu followed Pretoria's lead and ordered his troops out of Angola by the end of February. Meanwhile, the embedded tensions between FNLA and UNITA increased, evaporating any hopes of a united anti-MPLA front (although Savimbi would continue to fight in the bushes for decades). The CIA's scramble for mercenaries in early 1976 did little to change the course of events. In the end, Zairians, South Africans, mercenaries, and, most significantly, the Ford administration's attempts to harness together all anti-MPLA factions had been frustrated. The Ford administration was further embarrassed as mercenaries were exposed and prominently displayed in the international press.[58]

Ultimately, Operation IAFEATURE was a disaster. It provided ammunition to the critics of détente in the United States: while some berated the ineffectiveness of the Ford administration to counter a Soviet challenge in the third world, others raised questions about the morality of covert action and the confluence of U.S. and South African policies. Angola, Walter Isaacson pertinently writes, "was a paradigm of an unnecessary, self-inflicted defeat."[59]

To his credit, Kissinger seems to have learned lessons from the crisis. After April 1976 he would help transform the administration's policy toward Africa by publicly taking up the banner of majority rule and using, in effect, his Middle East-tested shuttle diplomacy to bring about the gradual transformation of Ian Smith's apartheid Rhodesia into Zimbabwe (that was finally completed in 1979).[60]

Such belated changes in Kissinger's approach to Africa, however, did little to hide the failure of his policies toward Angola. Nor was he a true convert to the cause of majority rule. Kissinger's logic was straightforward: no more Angolas. As he explained during an NSC meeting after his first trip to Africa in April 1976, the Ford administration's new Africa strategy had a straightforward goal:

> Find a platform on which we could rely that would arrest the armed struggle in southern Africa, preclude foreign intervention, and give the moderate regimes something to hold on to and the radicals something to think about. The strategy was to slow down the struggle and get control of the process as we did in the Middle East.

Given the failure of covert action and the boost that Angola had provided for radical forces, diplomacy and dangling the carrot of economic aid were now the keys to Kissinger's African policy. And, as he indicated, the model was to be found in the one aspect of his foreign policy that still commanded much respect: Middle East peacemaking.

In contrast to hiring mercenaries and supporting unpopular regimes, Kissinger's new approach was laudable. He also had relatively modest expectations. "I think we can defuse the southern African situation so there will be no outside intervention," Kissinger added. But the positive outcome of the new strategy would be no panacea: "We will confine the situation to a black/white African war, and we can get black/white African negotiations."[61]

In addition to bringing about a shift in U.S. policy toward Africa in 1976, the Angolan conflict had the curious effect of producing a Soviet-American confrontation while simultaneously exacerbating the difficulties in Sino-American relations. Already by late 1975, as was evident during Kissinger's and Ford's trips to Beijing, the Chinese considered the United States a fairly ineffective counterweight to the Soviet Union. Having promised to raise barriers to Soviet expansionism in the aftermath of the collapse of Saigon, Kissinger had not delivered. In fact, when he visited Moscow in January 1976, Brezhnev and Gromyko had been downright rude in their denials—partly accurate though they may have been—about Soviet involvement in Angola. One senior official later summed up the overall sentiments within the Soviet leadership in straightforward terms: "The world was turning in our direction."[62]

In a number of speeches and internal meetings Kissinger expressed his frustration and concerns about the broader impact of the MPLA's victory. During Senate hearings in late January 1976, as the MPLA was routing its enemies, Kissinger argued that the United States "must make it clear that Angola sets no precedent." A few weeks later, he stressed that Angola was "the first time that the United States has failed to respond to Soviet military moves outside the immediate Soviet orbit." The crux of the problem was, Kissinger argued that "the failure of the United States to respond effectively will be regarded in many parts of the world as an indication of our future [lack of] determination to counter similar Communist interventions."[63] Four months earlier, during a meeting of the NSC, Kissinger had warned in similarly apocalyptic terms:

> There is one reason why Angola is so important; we don't want to whet the Soviet
> appetite . . . They have a game going in Angola. But it is not the ultimate test yet.
> They might want it if they can pick it up at a low price. Even if they don't pick it
> up, they will want to run around Africa and Europe and say: "The Americans
> can't cut the mustard."[64]

To Kissinger Angola was, therefore, a serious blemish. But ultimately it also reflected the prominent flaw in his overall architecture. By viewing the crisis in Angola essentially as an issue in Soviet-American relations, he had basically paid no heed to the complexities of the regional situation in southern Africa or the possibility that the Cubans had, as they evidently had, acted largely independently. He had judged the crisis not on its own merits but within the context of his overall analysis of what he considered to be a crisis of American credibility in the post-Vietnam situation. The end result was, ironically, almost preordained: because he had made Angola, unnecessarily, into a test case, it was inevitably perceived as such.

The end result amounted to one of the worst hours of Kissinger's career in office. By early 1976, the Angolan war resulted, as Walter Isaacson puts it, in "a total Soviet-Cuban victory, an unnecessary loss of American credibility, a political debacle at home, and a costly program that pointlessly fueled a distant war."[65] Angola also exacerbated Chinese criticism of American ineffectiveness vis-à-vis Soviet imperialism. Ironically, a distant war in a far-away land with minimal significance to U.S. national security managed to further erode the already shaky foundation of triangular diplomacy.

19

"Worse Than in the Days of McCarthy"

Kissinger and the Marathon of 1976

I t became known as the Halloween Massacre.

On November 3, 1975, Nelson Rockefeller announced that he was withdrawing from the 1976 presidential ticket. The same day, President Ford revealed a number of other changes within his cabinet. Ford's White House chief-of-staff, Donald Rumsfeld, was to replace James Schlesinger as secretary of defense, while Dick Cheney would step into Rumsfeld's shoes. George Bush was returning from China to take over from William Colby as the director of the CIA (or DCI, director of Central Intelligence; the director of the CIA was responsible for coordinating the activities of the various U.S. intelligence agencies, and thus held the title of DCI). Elliott Richardson was named the new commerce secretary to replace Rogers Morton. Last but not least, Henry Kissinger, while retaining his job as secretary of state, would no longer be the national security adviser. Brent Scowcroft, Kissinger's deputy at the NSC, was promoted to that post.[1]

The Halloween Massacre was also a clear indication that Kissinger had, at least in the minds of Howard Callaway and some other members of the President Ford Committee (PFC), become a political liability. This was a remarkable change. When Ford had been sworn in on August 9, 1974, it had seemed clear that one of the keys to victory in 1976 was to build on the success of the Nixon-era foreign policy. To assure this, Ford needed Kissinger and had asked him to maintain his two portfolios as the secretary of state and national security adviser. "I need you. The country needs you," Ford had told Kissinger.[2]

How different the situation was fourteen months later! Détente was in difficulty, Vietnam had collapsed, the Middle East peace process had come to a halt, and relations with China were at a standstill. Moreover, Kissinger was widely, and largely correctly, assumed to have virtually complete control over the administration's foreign policy making. This, in turn, made Ford appear less 'presidential.' Thus, it was politically imperative to scale down Kissinger's role, to minimize his visibility, and postpone such important issues as the prospective SALT II agreement beyond the elections. In November 1975 his campaign staff had advised Ford: "Détente is a particularly unpopular idea with most Republican primary voters and the word is worse. We ought to stop using the word whenever possible."[3]

In February 1976, facing an increasingly populist challenge from Reagan, Ford followed the advice and told his staff to stop using *détente* in his campaign. The next month he did so in public. Kissinger refrained from criticizing the move publicly, yet he was obviously dismayed. "Except for Angola, I think the Soviets are getting a bum rap," he argued during a meeting with Ford on March 18, 1976. "The problem with the Soviet Union is that détente is really right," Kissinger maintained a month later.[4]

By 1976, the merits of détente hardly mattered. Far from being an asset, foreign policy—and its chief practitioner—had become a hindrance to Ford's pursuit of the presidency. Finally, on November 2, 1976, almost exactly a year to date after the Halloween massacre (the press also called it the Sunday Morning Massacre), Ford lost in one of the closest presidential elections of the twentieth century.

The demotion of Kissinger in November 1975 and Ford's loss in 1976 would be intimately linked to a broad criticism of U.S. foreign policy. In this regard Vietnam and Angola were important but hardly the linchpin of domestic discontent. After all, Vietnam was a heavily bipartisan mistake and Angola inhabited but a minor space in the collective mental map of the American electorate. In the end, the "Nixon–Ford–Kissinger" foreign policy was one that emphasized the perceived immorality of détente and the secrecy that surrounded Kissinger's operational methods. Overall, the 1976 presidential campaign became, in part, a referendum on détente and Kissingerian realism that Kissinger, never one to underestimate his own importance, took personally.

KISSINGER AND THE YEAR OF INTELLIGENCE

What Kissinger would describe in his memoirs as a sustained long-term attack on executive authority by the "McGovernite Congress"—codename for the heavily Democratic Congress elected in November 1974—began with a series of unprecedented investigations into the activities of the CIA. The most damaging and public of them was the Senate Select Committee to Study Governmental Operations with Respect to Intelligence Activities, known as the "Church Committee" after its chairman Frank Church (D-Idaho), which conducted a wide-ranging investigation of the intelligence agencies in 1975. The Church Committee took public and private testimony from hundreds of people, collected huge volumes of files from the FBI, CIA, NSA, IRS, and many other federal agencies, and issued fourteen reports in 1975 and 1976.[5]

The Church Committee's investigations provided a rare glimpse at the U.S. intelligence services' activities. Among the revelations were the following:

- The CIA had developed a program to open the mail of selected American citizens that had generated a database of 1.5 million names.
- The FBI had carried out 500,000 investigations of suspected subversives between 1960 and 1974; no court convictions had resulted from the effort.
- The NSA had monitored all cables sent overseas from the United States or received by Americans between 1947 and 1975.
- The CIA had conducted drug experiments that had resulted in two deaths.
- The CIA had targeted a number of foreign leaders by assassination plots (none successfully).
- The CIA had manipulated foreign elections (Chile being the most prominent case).

Thirty years later, Kissinger would write that the "CIA did not deserve the opprobrium various investigations heaped on it." At the time, though, he was more critical. As the NSC adviser and the secretary of state, Kissinger had often worked closely with the CIA. To be sure, his relationship with former DCI Richard Helms had been far better than the ones with either Schlesinger or Colby. But the point was that he had more than a passing knowledge of some of the recent cases that the Church Committee exposed. As the chairman of the Forty Committee, Kissinger had certainly been involved in planning U.S. efforts to overthrow the Allende government in Chile. Thus, aside from Kissinger's tendency to view any investigations by the Congress into the activities of the executive branch as part of an overall attack of executive authority, Kissinger took the revelations and the outcry they created personally.

"What is happening is worse than in the days of McCarthy," Kissinger told Ford and Scowcroft on the morning of January 4, 1975. His judgment of the intelligence crisis never changed, at least in his speaking and writing about it.[6]

The background to the intelligence crisis of 1975—the Year of Intelligence, as the press would call—went back to May 1973, when James Schlesinger, two days before the end of his brief tenure as the DCI, had ordered a study on the potentially controversial activities of the CIA. Schlesinger, who had replaced Richard Helms earlier in the year, was concerned over revelations that CIA equipment had been used in domestic operations related to Watergate. Thus, Schlesinger had ordered his deputy, William Colby, to conduct a full internal investigation into all clandestine domestic operations so that the agency could prepare contingency plans in the case of further inflammatory reports. As Schlesinger's immediate successor, Colby, a veteran of the wartime predecessor of the CIA, the Office of Strategic Services (OSS) and a career intelligence officer, oversaw the study after Schlesinger moved to the Pentagon.[7]

The end result, instantly dubbed "the family jewels," was a 700-page report. Some of the jewels, including evidence that the CIA had spied on antiwar activists, leaked to the press. On December 18, 1974, the Pulitzer Prize winning journalist Seymour Hersh—who had earlier exposed Kissinger's role in the wiretap controversy—informed Colby that he was about to publish an article in the New York Times that would expose the Nixon administration's use of the CIA against the antiwar movement (it was illegal for the CIA to spy on American citizens at home). Colby alerted Scowcroft, who in turn warned Ford. Yet, on December 22, 1974, when Hersh's story appeared on the front page of the Times, the Ford administration was apparently caught unawares.

Although much of the article focused on the Johnson years and none of it extended to the Ford presidency (nor did Hersh implicate Kissinger), Hersh revealed the so-called Huston plan: a CIA operation directed by Nixon's former aide Tom Huston to combat civil disturbances fomented by what was euphemistically referred to as "black extremists." A week later Hersh published another piece, in which he revealed that the CIA did, in fact, have a division devoted to domestic operations. Senators and congressmen from both parties were soon echoing the growing public outrage. In January Ford, who had spent the Christmas holidays in Vail, Colorado, established a Blue Ribbon Committee to investigate the allegations and encourage the Congress to look into the allegations.[8]

* * *

The Blue Ribbon Committee was Ford's attempt to preempt the congressional investigation. In the political climate of the day, it had little chance of being taken seriously. Chaired by Vice President Rockefeller, the committee's eight members included former cabinet members, military leaders, and prominent politicians, such as C. Douglas Dillon (secretary of the treasury, 1960–65), Ronald Reagan (who had completed two terms as the governor of California), and Lyman Lemnitzer (former chairman of the Joint Chiefs of Staff). The committee's 299-page Final Report was submitted to the president in early June. After a brief controversy, the White House made the Rockefeller Commission's findings public on June 10.

Ford had hoped to preempt a major crisis of confidence by establishing the Rockefeller Commission. In the end, the report—and the possibility that it might have been kept secret—merely stirred more doubts about CIA activities. Moreover, under pressure from Kissinger and Ford, neither of whom had been mentioned in Hersh's articles, the commission had steered away from one of the most controversial topics: CIA involvement in the assassination plots against foreign leaders.

But such pressure leaked. On February 28, 1975, Daniel Schorr of CBS Evening News announced to an astonished prime time audience: "President Ford has reportedly warned associates that if current investigations go too far they could uncover several assassinations of foreign officials in which the CIA was involved." The report itself did little to erase doubts about the CIA as a means of executive abuse of power while Rockefeller's own performance on NBC's "Meet the Press"— program on June 15, 1975, merely raised further concerns about a cover-up. Thus, the Rockefeller Report created an opening for the Church Committee's damning accounts of CIA activities.[9]

"WE HAVE TO ESTABLISH SOME FENCES"

The Church Committee did a thorough job. It took public and private testimony from hundreds of people, and collected huge volumes of files from the FBI, CIA, NSA, the IRS, and many other federal agencies, before issuing fourteen different reports in 1975 and 1976. One of the first was an Interim Report on American involvement in plots to assassinate five foreign leaders: Patrice Lumumba (Congo), Fidel Castro (Cuba), Rafael Trujillo (Dominican Republic), Ngo Dinh Diem (South Vietnam), and Rene Schneider (Chile). The committee found that the United States initiated plots to assassinate Fidel Castro and Patrice Lumumba. In the other cases, either U.S. involvement was indirect or evidence was too inconclusive to issue a definitive finding. In Lumumba's case, the committee asserted that the United States was not involved in his death, despite earlier plotting.

Although he would never be publicly charged with involvement in the one plot that had occurred during his time in office (Schneider), Kissinger was anxious about the Church Committee's work for personal and substantive reasons. On the one hand, he clearly believed that the CIA was, at times, a necessary tool of U.S. foreign policy that required, indeed relied upon, tight secrecy in order to undertake its operations successfully. Kissinger had cooperated with the CIA director Richard Helms in the Nixon years on such issues as Chile and was, in 1975, using the CIA as a means of implementing American policy in Angola (see chapter 18). Given the strict limits to the use of force that the 1973 War Powers Act and various congressional rulings on Cambodia and Vietnam had erected, the CIA's ability to conduct covert operations had been magnified as a foreign policy tool. Kissinger believed that if one could not intervene overtly, then one needed to preserve the ability to intervene covertly. If the Congress is allowed to tamper with the U.S. intelligence community, "you will end up with a CIA that does only reporting, and not operations," he warned Ford in early 1975.

Personal concerns, though, were also apparent in Kissinger's comments about the intelligence investigations and the possibility that the "family jewels" would become public. In particular, he worried about revelations of his role in the Nixon administration's plans to prevent the 1970 election of Salvador Allende as Chilean president, including the foiled coup attempt that resulted in the assassination of General Schneider. "This could end up worse for the country than Watergate," Kissinger told Ford and Scowcroft in January 1975.[10]

As suggestions for a law banning such assassination plots were heard during the Church Committee hearings, Kissinger grew anxious. During an NSC meeting on May 15 he was particularly upset. The word was that the Church Committee would propose a law explicitly prohibiting the CIA or any other government agency from contributing to the assassination of foreign leaders. This was utter nonsense, Kissinger insisted. The United States should not back away from clandestine and morally questionable methods if the national interest was at stake. Or as he put it: "It is an act of insanity and national humiliation to have a law prohibiting the President from ordering assassination."[11]

Five months later, as the Church Committee completed its Interim Report on assassinations, Kissinger worried about the impact of revealing such gory aspects of U.S. policy on American diplomacy. "If those things get put out, senior officials will stop speaking frankly and foreign governments will wonder about their ability to work with us confidentially." Kissinger then returned to his historical analogy. "The new element in these investigations is the turning over of documents. During the McCarthy era there was testimony, but it did not involve all the documents involved, we have to establish some fences around the Executive."[12]

There was something to these concerns. Once details of American clandestine activity filtered out into the open, American credibility was hurt and the United States' covert activities could easily be compared to the less than sanguine policies conducted by the USSR. Similarly, if Kissinger was personally branded with involvement in such clandestine activities, his ability to negotiate in good faith might be jeopardized.

Of course, Kissinger's antagonism toward the congressional hearings reflected more than just these philosophical concerns. Once he was identified as someone who had been engaged in planning clandestine operations, Kissinger's reputation suffered a blow from which it would never entirely recover. The making of "Kissinger-the-criminal" school that would be popularized initially by Hersh in the early 1980s and reinvoked by Christopher Hitchens two decades later, began with the Church Committee and the simultaneous Pike Committee in the House of Representatives reports in 1975–76.[13]

*   *   *

The results of the Year of Intelligence were mixed. For one, the Rockefeller, Church, and Pike reports (February 17, 1976) prompted Ford to issue Executive Order 11905, which established new ground rules for intelligence collection and reorganized the American intelligence community. Assassination plots, for example, were made illegal and domestic intelligence activities drastically curtailed. As a result, the CIA and the U.S. intelligence community in general became less inclined to operate outside the law and, in effect, more suitable for the world's leading democracy. Yet, the damage done to the CIA's effectiveness, internal morale, and the overall respect it had commanded was undoubtedly severe, not unlike the damage inflicted on the State Department during the worst days of McCarthyism in the early 1950s. Only in the aftermath of the September 11, 2001 terrorist strikes on New York and Washington would the CIA and intelligence services in general begin to claim back its lost stature and significance.

Perhaps most important in the near term, however, the Year of Intelligence helped to foment the political atmosphere in which the 1976 presidential elections were held. While Ford was not personally identified with any of the revelations, the Blue Ribbon Committee and the president's attempt to suppress the reports on assassination plots served to project an image of a secretive administration. In part because he was the main survivor of the Nixon years and in part due to his own penchant for suppressing information, Kissinger would become a natural target of such attacks. Yet, excessive secrecy was only one of the many charges leveled against his policies.

SOLZHENITSYN, THE HEARTLAND, AND THE HELSINKI ACCORDS

When the Rockefeller Committee delivered its final report, the CSCE was moving toward its long-awaited conclusion: a thirty-five-nation summit to be held in Helsinki in late July and early August. Few in the United States had paid attention to the painstaking negotiations in Geneva and Helsinki over the past two years. But in the summer of 1975 the CSCE became a lynchpin of domestic criticism of détente.

On the face of it, this seems to make little sense. The CSCE was as carefully drafted a document as one could imagine. For more than two years representatives of all European countries (including the Soviet Union but excluding Albania) as well as the United States and Canada had been negotiating on various aspects of European security. Although the Soviets had spearheaded the conference for decades simply as a way of ratifying the postwar borders of Europe, they had secured Western participation in the early 1970s only by agreeing to expand the agenda of the meetings and by including the United States in the talks. In 1973, the CSCE had been divided into three so-called baskets that eventually formed the final text, the Helsinki Final Act (or the Helsinki Accords). The first one dealt with such traditional security issues as borders while the second focused on trade and scientific cooperation. The third basket was titled "Humanitarian and Other Fields" and included such soft issues as the free movement of people and respect for individual rights. Although he had paid little attention to the CSCE earlier, in the spring and summer of 1975 Kissinger himself had, to his credit, pressed Soviet Foreign

Minister Gromyko to accept the last basket despite its potential for being used as an argument for relaxing the Soviet bloc's states' control of their citizens.[14]

The problem was with basket 1. Not only did it recognize the inviolability of borders. It also included a phrase about the noninterference in other states' internal affairs. It was something that the Soviets cherished as a guarantee that Westerners would not try and spread propaganda within their sphere. But it was also an issue that the most famous Soviet dissident in America used to launch a broad attack on détente.

The Russian writer Alexander Solzhenitsyn was expelled from the Soviet Union in February 1974 and arrived in the United States a few months later. He quickly became a potent symbol of Soviet oppression and was courted, among others, by Senator Henry Jackson. Two conservative Republicans, Strom Thurmond and Jesse Helms, spearheaded a campaign in the U.S. Senate to declared Solzhenitsyn an honorary American citizen.

On June 30, 1975, a month prior to the Helsinki Conference, Solzhenitsyn was invited to address a dinner hosted by the AFL-CIO, then headed by the staunch anticommunist, George Meany. Ford was invited but, at Kissinger and Scowcroft's advice, refused to accept an invitation to the dinner because the Russian writer was likely to criticize the administration's policy in his speech. Ford also turned down a public offer to meet with Solzhenitsyn in the White House on July 4. Ford did have a good excuse for the latter refusal: Independence Day was a busy time for the American president. He also tried to counter the mounting criticism by issuing an open invitation to Solzhenitsyn to come and meet him in the future.

It was to no avail. Solzhenitsyn suddenly lost interest in a meeting with the president. On July 15, after turning down Ford's open invitation—"nobody needs symbolic meetings," Solzhenitsyn said—the Russian delivered a stinging denouncement of détente, singling out the forthcoming Helsinki conference as a "betrayal of Eastern Europe."

Ford and Kissinger were seething. Although on holiday in the Virgin Islands in early July, Kissinger—the architect of détente—was generally viewed as the villain of the Solzhenitsyn debacle. Largely correctly, the press considered Ford's initial refusal to meet a Russian dissident as a way of avoiding a stormy reaction from the Soviets. In broader terms, the press and the growing number of détente's critics saw Ford's behavior as an example of the "immoral" attitude toward foreign policy.[15]

*   *   *

Kissinger, unwittingly, had played a role in provoking this crisis. To make matters worse, beginning in 1975 he made a series of major speeches throughout the country outlining the administration's foreign policy. Kissinger made an unprecedented effort in these so-called heartland speeches to reach out and "educate," as Winston Lord, the Policy Planning Staff chief who was in charge of the program, put it, the American public on the rationale behind his nonideological approach to foreign policy. And, for the most part, he was relatively successful, retaining a high favorability rating. Yet, while the heartland speeches certainly increased his celebrity status and provided a forum where Kissinger could showcase his self-deprecating wit, the message appeared blurred behind the messenger.[16]

Kissinger's central point—whether the specific speech was titled "Constancy and Change in American Foreign Policy" (June 23, 1975, in Atlanta) or "American Unity and National Interest" (August 14, 1975, in Birmingham, Alabama)—reflected his unapologetic realpolitik. While paying lip service to American ideals, Kissinger argued that the nuclear age demanded a more cooperative relationship with such foes as the Soviet Union. His other point, made repeatedly and increasingly forcefully as the 1976 elections approached, was that foreign policy was a nonpartisan activity. And, as he did in Detroit on November 24, 1975, Kissinger would usually wrap the two themes together:

> In a world of thermonuclear weapons, shrunken distances, and widely dispersed power, we cannot afford disunity, disarray, or disruption in the conduct of our foreign affairs. Foreign policy requires authority . . . this country cannot have a moratorium on a responsible foreign policy . . . A great responsibility rests upon both the Congress and the Executive. Our foreign policy has been most effective when it reflected broad bipartisan support . . . Our free debate once again must find its ultimate restraint in the recognition that we are engaged in a common enterprise.[17]

Kissinger gave one of the most publicized of these heartland speeches in the midst of the Solzhenitsyn controversy and only two weeks prior to the signing of the Helsinki Accords. On July 15, after stopping in Milwaukee to throw out the first ball of baseball's All-Star Game, Kissinger addressed an audience in Minneapolis. The speech, titled "Moral Foundations of Foreign Policy," began with the trademark nod to American values. He cited Woodrow Wilson and John F. Kennedy. But the bulk of the address focused on "the age-old quandary of the relationship between principle and power" and its relevance to U.S.-Soviet relations. Kissinger, with an implied reference to his own efforts at raising the levels of emigration from the USSR, stressed that the United States'

> immediate focus is on the international actions of the Soviet Union not because it is our only moral concern, but because it is the sphere of action that we can most directly and confidently affect. As a consequence of improved foreign policy relationships, we have successfully used our influence to promote human rights. But we have done so quietly, keeping in mind the delicacy of the problem and stressing results rather than public confrontation.

Kissinger then issued a challenge:

The critics of détente must answer: What is the alternative that they propose? What precise policies do they want us to change? Are they prepared for a prolonged situation of dramatically increased international danger? Do they wish to return to the constant crises and high arms budgets of the cold war? Does détente encourage repression—or is it détente that has generated the ferment and the demands for openness that we are now witnessing?[18]

It was a fine speech, containing few surprises to those familiar with Kissinger's thinking. His critics, however, chose not to take the bait and answer Kissinger's challenge.

*   *   *

Instead, on July 16, back in Milwaukee, Kissinger was peppered with questions about the Solzhenitsyn case. Kissinger tried to deflect: he had the utmost respect for Solzhenitsyn, a great writer, but maintained that a meeting with a senior official always had a "symbolic effect" and in this case such an effect could well have been "disadvantageous." Kissinger also suggested that Solzhenitsyn had effectively advocated that the United States should seek the overthrow of the Soviet system. Such views, Kissinger reasonably argued, "cannot guide our actions, much as we admire [Solzhenitsyn's] writings."[19]

It all seemed so reasonable. Be moderate and consider the period of extreme tensions that had preceded the Nixon–Kissinger–Ford years, the secretary of state was effectively saying. What was wrong with the tranquility that détente and triangular diplomacy had brought?

But the critics of détente had no intention of letting Kissinger off the hook. In fact, the Solzhenitsyn case had the impact of bringing together the odd coalition that would ultimately help unseat President Ford: the Republican right was joined by such Democrats as Senator Henry Jackson in denouncing the immorality of the administration's policy. "If Kissinger and Ford had met with Solzhenitsyn rather than cowering with fear of the Soviet reaction to such a meeting," Jackson complained, "they would have learned that all Solzhenitsyn is asking for is détente without illusions, for an American-Soviet relationship that promoted the cause of human rights and genuine peace." When Ford and Kissinger returned from the CSCE summit in Helsinki a few weeks later, they discovered that Jackson, who had announced his bid for the presidency already in February 1975 and looked very much the likely Democratic candidate for 1976, was even more ferocious—and certainly more articulate—in his critique of the CSCE than Reagan. Eastern Europe had been bargained away and the human rights provisions of the Helsinki Accords were, in Jackson's opinion, "so imprecise and so hedged as to raise considerable doubt about whether they can and will be seriously implemented."[20]

The irony of Jackson's critique is that over the next fifteen years, the CSCE and its human rights provisions became, as no less an observer than Anatoly Dobrynin put it in his memoirs, "the manifesto of the dissident and liberal movement" inside the Soviet bloc. The CSCE provided the basic reference point for, for example, Vaclav Havel's and Lech Walesa's challenge of the authoritarian rule in Czechoslovakia and Poland. Of course, as Kissinger himself admits in his memoirs, this was not something that he, nor anyone else, had anticipated at the time.[21]

Kissinger and Ford knew at the time that, given Solzhenitsyn's high visibility and support base among Democrats and Republicans alike, trying to sell the Helsinki Accords to American domestic audiences as a major achievement would be extremely difficult. Yet, they tried. In his speech in Helsinki on August 1, 1975, for example, President Ford stressed that the principles of human rights included in the CSCE "are not clichés or empty phrases." While the Ford administration would "spare no effort to ease tensions and to solve problems" with the USSR, the president added, "it is important that you realize the deep devotion of the American people and their government to human rights and fundamental freedoms and thus to the pledges that this conference has made regarding the freer movement of people, ideas, and information." While speaking these words, Ford later said, he "looked directly at Brezhnev."[22]

Judging from continued Soviet suppression of dissidents, the general secretary had either fallen asleep or paid little heed to Ford's words. To him, the text on human rights amounted to empty phrases.

Kissinger, for his part, rejected any criticism of the CSCE. During a cabinet meeting on August 8, he bemoaned the negative view of the CSCE. The acknowledgment of the inviolability of borders in the Final Act was meaningless, Kissinger argued, because "the [European] borders were legally established long ago." Instead, Kissinger maintained,

> all the new things in the document are in our favor—peaceful change, human contacts ... At the conference ... it was the West which was on the offensive ... [no one] observing from another planet would have thought Communism was the wave of the future.[23]

This was, though, exactly what the critics of détente in the United States, which assuredly was on this planet, charged at the time. The Helsinki Accords aroused immense controversy in the United States. While few people bothered to read through the accords, many were quick to equate one part of the vast document—the statement recognizing the "inviolability of borders"—as a de facto recognition of the legitimacy of the Soviet hold over Eastern Europe. The United States had, such presidential hopefuls as Ronald Reagan argued, been weakened by the Ford administration's immoral appeasement of the USSR. Reagan, about to challenge Ford in the 1976 Republican primaries, famously announced that "all Americans should be against" the Helsinki Accords. He was prudent enough not to explain why.

By 1976, the CSCE, which remained popular in Europe and clearly helped the case of various dissident groups in Eastern Europe, was rarely mentioned in the

United States except by those who criticized the Nixon–Ford era foreign policy as immoral. Although the justification of such attacks appears, in retrospect, questionable, the Helsinki Accords exposed one of the Ford administration's key problems both with regards to the Soviets and in terms of domestic opinion. The president and Kissinger lacked consistency and credibility when it came down to promoting human rights. Their failure to prevent the passing of the Jackson–Vanik Amendment had already exposed this in late 1974. In 1975, the CSCE helped confirm this fact and set the stage for a vociferous bipartisan critique of détente during the election year.[24]

And the issue would live on because for those gearing up to challenge Ford in 1976, the attacks on détente worked well. In a Gallup poll released on November 24, Ford and Jackson were in a dead heat, each receiving 44 percent.[25] The Solzhenitsyn debacle and the negative reaction to the Helsinki Accords helped make Kissinger the lynchpin of domestic attacks on détente and contributed to Ford's decision to remove Kissinger's NSC hat in November 1975. By early 1976, the bipartisan attacks and Ford's growing concerns over his election campaign had virtually frozen the administration's ability to conduct meaningful foreign policy. Perhaps the most important casualty was SALT II.

DEADLOCK ON SALT

In addition to the CSCE, the Solzhenitsyn debacle, and a general critique of immoral foreign policy, attempts to finalize a SALT II agreement were faced with a mounting domestic onslaught. To be sure, in early 1975 the Congress had passed resolutions in support of the Vladivostok Accord. By that time, however, critics were hard at work. Senator Jackson, for example, had already in December 1974 argued that the agreements, which provided a ceiling of 2,400 intercontinental delivery vehicles (ICBMs and SLBMs) and limited both sides to 1,320 MIRVed missiles, needed serious revision. Jackson criticized MIRV levels as too high and argued for reductions in the overall numbers. Vladivostok had produced an "arms buildup agreement," he maintained. Jackson also argued that the exclusion of the Soviet Backfire bomber from the Vladivostok agreements did not make sense because Backfire, if refueled mid-air, could reach American territory and be used to deliver missiles on the United States. Jackson also called into question the reliability of the Soviet Union by charging that Moscow had violated both the 1972 ABM and SALT agreements. In short, Jackson argued throughout 1975, the SALT II agreement "must be precise."[26]

Jackson's criticism of the Vladivostok agreements was undoubtedly politically motivated. But he did raise substantive concerns that were, to an extent, shared by a number of Ford's cabinet members, including Secretary of Defense Schlesinger. Most important Jackson had homed in on the one general problem that would prevent the treaty from being adopted during Kissinger's time in office: the vagueness of some of the details. In addition to the Backfire bomber—which Raymond Garthoff calls "the albatross of SALT II"—there was the question of cruise missiles (missiles that are jet-propelled to the targets rather than blasted through space like ballistic missiles).[27]

The complicated details of SALT II almost guaranteed its downfall in 1975. To be sure, at an NSC meeting in late January, a few days prior to the opening of the Soviet-American SALT II negotiations in Geneva, the mood was still fairly optimistic. CIA Director William Colby stressed that the "Vladivostok agreement, if implemented, will remove one worry: that the Soviets might achieve a numerical edge." The CIA, Colby added, did not "foresee technological advances which would sharply alter the strategic balance in the USSR's favor in the next ten years." Kissinger added that the Soviets, despite setbacks on trade legislation, still wanted an agreement "before Brezhnev's visit here in June" and that the Soviets "will put their cards on the table by mid-March at the latest."[28]

* * *

In the end, there was neither a SALT II agreement nor a Brezhnev visit. Starting in early February 1975, the American delegation, headed by U. Alexis Johnson, met with its Soviet counterparts in Geneva. Kissinger, who spent much of the month in unsuccessful shuttles in the Middle East, stopped in Geneva in mid-February for a meeting with Andrei Gromyko. They discussed rules for verifying and counting MIRVs and the issue of whether cruise missiles should be included in the treaty or not. "The differences are manageable if the Soviets really want an agreement," Kissinger reported to the NSC. The real concern to him remained Senator Jackson's Senate hearings. But there was general agreement around the table with Secretary of Defense Schlesinger's view that the opposition to SALT II was "a political loser to Jackson." Hopes for an agreement and a Ford–Brezhnev summit were still relatively high.[29]

The next full NSC discussion on SALT II took place on July 25, at the same time as the CIA was beginning Operation IAFEATURE in Angola. The mood had completely changed. In part, this had to do with the gradual defection of Schlesinger to the hardliners' camp. He exchanged acerbic comments with Kissinger about a number of details of the Geneva negotiations. "Our positions have been bilaterally preposterous," Schlesinger argued when the discussion turned to the yield limits for SLBMs. He also complained that the United States was considering "bigger concession[s] than any [the Soviets] have made." After Kissinger completed his briefing on the state of negotiations, Schlesinger criticized any concessions:

> It is clear Brezhnev is anxious for this agreement. We would be inclined to give only little ground, showing a considerable degree of firmness, responding to their tactics in kind. Brezhnev reiterated their Geneva position. The package Henry outlined is as forthcoming as they have been.[30]

In fact, this was not a hearty recommendation. Schlesinger effectively argued that the United States should drive a hard bargain. The problem was that from the Soviet perspective, the deal had been sealed in November 1974 in Vladivostok and it was the Americans who, for whatever reason, had started demanding more and more concessions. Yet, Schlesinger's more hard-line views, because they did reflect the position of a large segment of the hawkish opinion in both parties, did push the president to press the Soviets for concessions.

*   *   *

The Soviets' confusion over this turn of events—stemming in part from Brezhnev's health problems—became evident when Ford, Kissinger, Brezhnev, and Gromyko met on August 2, 1975 (during the CSCE Helsinki summit in late July and early August). They made no substantive progress and engaged in a bizarre exchange over the yields and counting rules of cruise missiles. The Americans claimed that the Soviets had to "compensate" for "geographical disparities": because major U.S. cities were based mostly on the coasts, it was arguably possible for Soviet submarine-based cruise missiles with a yield of 300 to 500 km to hit major population centers in the United States. The following exchange, only partly in jest, ensued:

> *Kissinger:* "So we have a choice: either you give us a longer range or move your cities closer to the coast."
>
> *Gromyko:* "A very revolutionary proposal! What kind of binoculars do you use?"
>
> *Kissinger:* "Our Secretary of Defense proposed moving your cities to the sea coast."
>
> *Brezhnev:* "Put them on barges."
>
> *Ford:* "I thought you would suggest moving our cities farther from the sea!"

After some more intelligent back-and-forth, Brezhnev, growing exasperated, looked at Gromyko and sighed: "I can't invent anything new here."

Kissinger turned to Backfire. Brezhnev, again, argued that Backfire should not be counted as a long-range (intercontinental) bomber and therefore not included among the total aggregate of 2,400 intercontinental ballistic missiles that had been agreed on at Vladivostok in November 1974. Ford insisted that American intelligence sources indicated otherwise. "It is most difficult," Brezhnev started. "Your intelligence reports to you certain things that are news to me, so what does it mean when you don't believe what I tell you?"

There were long pauses and some more small talk. Kissinger suggested that perhaps he should go to Moscow to discuss these matters further. But Brezhnev was less than enthusiastic.

"It is apparently difficult to solve the problem before us," he said.[31]

It proved impossible to solve the riddle of SALT II during the Ford administration. To be sure, this was not for the lack of meetings and negotiations. Ford and

Kissinger met with Gromyko on September 18 and Kissinger then flew to New York for another set of negotiations a few days later. He passed on a proposal that set a new subceiling for the Backfire and submarine-launched cruise missiles (SLCMs). In early October both Kissinger and Ford made direct appeals to Brezhnev via Ambassador Dobrynin. "Let Brezhnev give me anything, at least something of a positive nature," Ford reportedly told Dobrynin. But the Soviets, who were well aware of the fact that the United States had no SLCMs at the time, soundly rejected the proposal in late October.[32]

A week later came the Halloween Massacre. The Soviets were alarmed. To them, understandably enough, Kissinger was the key American orchestrator and practitioner of détente. Since the opening of the back channel in 1969, Kissinger had personified to the Soviets the new relationship with the United States. Indeed, as Ambassador Dobrynin puts it: "From the point of view of Soviet-American relations and especially SALT, this shake up did not look promising."[33]

"DON'T THINK UP ANY MORE PROBLEMS"

Thus, on January 21, 1976, when Kissinger landed in Moscow for his last official visit to the Soviet Union, the prospects of a SALT II agreement were extremely limited. To make matters worse, Kissinger found himself undercut during the first day of the meetings when he learned that the NSC had held a meeting in the White House in his absence. Although Ford had blown his top when Admiral James Holloway, chief of naval operations, outlined the Defense Department's new plan for cruise missile deployment on submarines (rather than surface ships as had been the position during the NSC meeting only two days earlier), Scowcroft cabled to Kissinger: "I really don't know where we stand now." Kissinger, having just completed a warm-up session with Brezhnev, was incensed about what he clearly considered a bureaucratic ploy to undermine his negotiation position, because it contradicted the negotiation positions that had been carefully ironed out in previous NSC meetings. In a separate response, Kissinger's aide, Helmut Sonnenfeldt, and Scowcroft's deputy, William Hyland, both in Moscow, wrote a telegram summing up the situation:

> We do not see how we can proceed in these weird circumstances. It is all the more devastating when you consider that the Soviets are showing a serious interest and obviously trying to find some middle ground without capitulating . . . We could make progress here today, but not without absolute, unqualified support from Washington.[34]

Brezhnev did, in fact, offer a compromise on January 22. He offered "assurances" that the USSR would develop the Backfire bomber into a strategic weapon (i.e., a long-range bomber) but still rejected a linkage between cruise missiles and the

Backfire. After agreeing to a proposal that the two countries start cutting their strategic arsenals by 1980, the general secretary clearly thought that an agreement was possible and even expressed a desire to meet Ford at Camp David in 1976. But he made
a plea: "Don't think up any more problems. Or else you leave and suddenly I get a
telegram from Washington with some entirely new problems invented."[35]

That was more or less what happened. Kissinger, unsure of Ford's position in
light of the previous day's NSC meeting, could only offer that he would take the
Soviet proposals back and respond to them as soon as possible. In the end Ford had
decided on a course: SALT needed to be shelved until the presidential election was
over. In February he wrote Brezhnev, suggesting that the issue of cruise missiles—
the one major concern for the Soviets—be deferred until 1979 and that the agreement be based on the overall Vladivostok numbers plus temporary restrictions on
the Backfire. Brezhnev rejected the offer as a new "setback." For the rest of the Ford
presidency, SALT II remained on hold.[36]

The internal squabbles within the Ford administration aside, it was clear that
SALT II had become equally political as its predecessor. If SALT I had been an
imperfect nuclear arms treaty, it had also been a milestone in Soviet-American relations and, for the most part, a domestic political success for Nixon in the run-up
to 1972 elections. Thus, the push for SALT II had, from the beginning, been tied to
both the advancement of détente and the political fortunes of the Ford administration. However, as much as SALT II was more complex (and comprehensive) in
detail, the political situation in 1975–76 was dramatically different from the one in
1971–72. While Nixon had operated in an overall mood that looked upon détente
as a new, generally favorable, approach to international relations, Ford had to face
politicians from the left and right that were busily attacking the legacy of his predecessor and tapping into popular moods that shifted from disgust regarding the
apparent lack of morality in U.S. foreign policy to accusations of self-inflicted
weakness vis-à-vis the USSR.

A future president and a former actor issued the first formidable challenge.

THE REAGAN CHALLENGE

On November 19, 1975, Ronald Reagan had called the White House to inform the
president that he would announce his candidacy the following day. A few weeks later
Gallup polls showed that Reagan was 12 percentage points ahead of the president.
In other polls, both Ford and Reagan were ahead of the most likely Democratic candidate (at the time considered to be Hubert Humphrey or Edmund Muskie).[37]

Over subsequent months, the Ford campaign began responding to the Reagan
challenge. Dick Cheney, Stuart Spencer, a convert from the Reagan team, pollster
Robert Teeter, who had worked for the Nixon campaign in 1972, and advertising
professional Peter Dailey, another Nixon campaign alumnus, took charge. In par-

ticular, the Ford team started working on polishing an image of a "decisive" president, fully in charge. As Teeter explained in a memo to Cheney:

> our most important job is to repair the President's perception so that he is seen as a decisive, forceful leader with a plan for the country. In doing this, it is critical that the President not only have a simple, understandable plan of his own but that he avoid any more situations where he is perceived to be indecisive.

Ford never fully accomplished either of these goals. His public image remained, if anything, indecisive and impressionable, albeit generally likeable. Ford was unable to articulate a simple plan with a simple name. He was, of course, at a natural disadvantage: having inherited Nixon's legacy Ford may not have been obliged to defend it but could hardly shake away the five and a half years that had preceded August 1974. And the one area that he had, from the beginning, consciously refused to break away from was Nixon's foreign policy.

It was in that field that pressure came to bear. As Teeter explained in December 1975:

> In the foreign affairs area, the country has become more hard-lined toward our adversaries and, more significantly, they see the President to the left of themselves on détente. Any actions or statements that would put the President in the position of taking tough stands with our adversaries would be helpful.[38]

In short, as 1976 commenced and Kissinger tried to continue the SALT II negotiations, Ford was under growing pressure from the right. Yet, although he did, for example, criticize Soviet-Cuban actions in Angola, Ford's initial response was to try and minimize the role of foreign policy in the primary season.

*   *   *

In the first months of 1976, the Ford campaign seemed to turn the corner. The president eked out a narrow victory in the New Hampshire primaries of February 24. In Florida two weeks later Ford got 53 percent of the primary vote, buoyed by his catering to the large cohort of senior citizens residing in the state. But a month later came an unexpected shock: Reagan won the March 23 North Carolina Republican primary. The sudden rejuvenation of Reagan's campaign was in part based on a series of attacks that focused on Ford's foreign policy record. Although the charge that the administration was about to relinquish the U.S. rights to operate the Panama Canal was the most specific issue that scored Reagan points in North Carolina, détente and Kissinger bore the brunt of the critique throughout the remainder of the Republican primary season.[39]

"Henry Kissinger's recent stewardship has coincided precisely with the loss of U.S. military supremacy," was one of Reagan's favorite lines in the spring of 1976.

Détente, he argued, was a "one-way street." Rejuvenated by his success in North Carolina, Reagan—not unlike Ross Perot in 1992—purchased time to deliver a nationwide television address on March 31. His sharpest attacks focused on détente. "'Wandering without aim,'" Reagan argued, "describes U.S. foreign policy." He complained about American weakness in Angola. He then wondered aloud why Ford had refused to invite Solzhenitsyn to the White House and why he had traveled to Helsinki to sign the CSCE, "putting our stamp of approval on Russia's enslavement of the captive nations [of Eastern Europe]."

Reagan's anti-détente campaign was further assisted by the revelation of the so-called Sonnenfeldt Doctrine. On March 22, Rowland Evans and Robert Novak of the *Washington Post* reported on a memo written by Helmut Sonnenfeldt on his December 1975 briefing to U.S. ambassadors in Europe. The State Department counselor and long-time Kissinger aide had allegedly called for U.S. support for "an organic union" between the Soviet Union and Eastern Europe. His real point was that the United States should strive to promote conditions that would create a less volatile situation within the Soviet bloc, one that was not based on the overwhelming presence of the Soviet military. But Sonnenfeldt had done so in an easily misinterpreted prose. "It sent shivers up the spine" to read that American officials were so cynical, C. L. Sulzberger of the *New York Times* wrote. In late March and early April a series of articles blasted the obvious moral callousness of such policies. The Romanian government issued a note of protest. And Reagan, naturally, upped the ante. The Sonnenfeldt Doctrine was further proof, if such was needed, that détente amounted not only to appeasement, but also to a de facto call for the Soviet Union to formally incorporate Eastern Europe.

There was no such thing as the Sonnenfeldt Doctrine. But in the charged atmosphere of the day, the leaked memo gained notoriety far out of proportion to its true significance. Kissinger, initially bemused, grew restive and outraged as the notion lingered on even beyond the Republican primaries, despite his denials at congressional hearings that the United States "emphatically" rejected the legitimacy of a Soviet empire in Eastern Europe. In a meeting with Ford, Rumsfeld, and Scowcroft he exploded: "Reagan doesn't know what he's talking about and he's irresponsible."[40]

"IF WE PISS ON EVERYTHING"

The attacks on détente might have offered Ford a chance to appear presidential. He could have stood firmly by his (and Kissinger's) foreign policy record. Instead, as Walter Isaacson puts it, the president "scurried away from defending détente like a startled rabbit." On March 5, in a speech in Peoria, Illinois, the president publicly banished détente from his vocabulary; a move that his campaign staff had urged for months. But "peace through strength"—Ford's replacement—did little to improve his defensive position vis-à-vis Reagan's straightforward rhetoric.

Ford's campaign staff was, in fact, fully aware of the problems of their candidate. And they, by and large, agreed with Kissinger's assessment of Reagan. But in the world of American politics in 1976, there were no simple answers. As one campaign memo put it on April 7: "[Reagan's] messages capitalize on an existing perception of indecisive leadership with President Ford, and the lack of clear voter comprehension of current defense/foreign policy." While that might have sounded clear enough, the prescription was far from straightforward:

> As such, a dramatic response and argument on the limited focus of national defense is insufficient ... a continuing argument may even provide credibility to the charge while quietly recalling the existing impressions of indecisive leadership. Rather, we must assert a *strong leadership* stance by the President.

In his forthcoming speeches Ford should simply emphasize

> That the public is being misled by ambitious, irresponsible campaign rhetoric. The President must deliver a personal message to the American public ... and communicate his saddened, somewhat righteous indignation with his challenger. Importantly, Ronald Reagan must not be mentioned or singled-out of the group of Presidential aspirants, but it must be *implied that:*
> He is an irresponsible and ambitious man. He has sacrificed his principles for ambition. He must be depicted as naive. He would commit our young men to another "Vietnam war" in Africa or elsewhere. His "eyeball-to-eyeball" diplomacy really means nuclear confrontation with the Soviet Union.

"We must go for the jugular and eliminate, the credibility of the Reagan candidacy," the memo concluded.[41]

Ford thought it over and apparently decided it was time to take off the gloves and go after Reagan. But, having already abandoned détente, he could not suddenly go back and start emphasizing its virtues. Thus, while meeting with Kissinger and Rumsfeld on April 15, Ford told them that he was going to make a "tough" speech against Reagan and against the Soviet Union. Kissinger was skeptical. "The problem with the Soviet Union is that détente really is right," he mused. There was little point in going overboard with criticism of the Soviet Union, because it would never satisfy the conservative critics and would, in all likelihood, lead to charges of inconsistency. Moreover, criticizing the USSR would unnecessarily inflame Soviet-American relations and, possibly, wreck détente beyond repair.[42]

"If we piss on everything, we will lose the whole policy," Kissinger warned.[43]

Such arguments fell on deaf ears. Instead, Kissinger was advised to scale back his extensive heartland speech tours. Détente remained a four-letter word for the remainder of the election season (if not the remainder of the Cold War). And Kissinger spent an astonishingly large part of the 1976 primary season cicumnavigating the globe, avoiding, perhaps, the increasingly aggressive press corps in Washington. In late April he went for an extensive two-week tour of seven African countries; on May 20—after less than two weeks in the United States—he departed for a week in Europe, followed by a week-long tour of Central and South America, and another week in Europe in late June. In August he would again leave the country just prior to the start of the Republican convention, an event he had not missed since 1960. While such trips surely had their diplomatic significance, they also indicated that in 1976 no serious foreign policy achievements were in the cards.

Indeed, even Kissinger's most commendable efforts in 1976 became campaign fodder. Touring Africa in April Kissinger delivered a speech in Lusaka in which he openly pronounced U.S. support for racial justice and attacked Ian Smith's apartheid regime in Rhodesia. The Lusaka Declaration received an enthusiastic response from black African leaders and Kissinger followed up by putting pressure on Smith to agree to a negotiation process that eventually—during the Carter administration—led to the independence of and majority rule in Rhodesia (to be renamed Zimbabwe). Kissinger deserves a great deal of credit for unleashing this anti-apartheid process. A few days after the Lusaka Declaration, however, Reagan crushed Ford in the May 1 Republican primaries in Texas. Pointedly, in a speech at the Alamo in late April, Reagan had criticized Kissinger's efforts in Africa as a recipe for immense bloodshed (presumably against the white minority).[44]

The May 1 loss in Texas was not unexpected, but Ford's campaign would hit even harder times. On May 4, Reagan won in Alabama, Georgia, and Indiana and a week later in Nebraska. Despite Ford's victories in West Virginia, Maryland, and his home state of Michigan, Reagan remained ahead in delegates as the primary season was headed for its final showdowns on June 8. On that day, Reagan won in his home state, California, while Ford triumphed in Ohio and New Jersey. In states that did not hold primaries, conventions chose the remaining delegates. Ford managed to close the gap and inch ahead, by 40 delegates out of a total of approximately 2,200. But 94 delegates to the Republican convention remained undecided, at the beginning of August, leaving Ford 28 votes short of his party's nomination. Astonishingly, Ford's candidacy was only determined when Reagan announced that he would chose a liberal Republican senator from Pennsylvania, Richard Schweicker, as his running mate. This move, combined with the Ford campaign's aggressive lobbying, cost Reagan some of his conservative base and did not assure him what he had hoped for: the votes of the undecided delegates from Pennsylvania. Thus, on August 18, 1976, Ford was nominated after the first ballot at the convention in Kansas City with 1,187 votes to Reagan's 1,070.[45]

But there had been a price. The 1976 Republican platform, adopted at the Kansas City convention, bore the hallmarks of the Reagan challenge. This was particularly the case with foreign policy. For example, the platform included the following:

We recognize and commend that great beacon of human courage and morality, Alexander Solzhenitsyn, for his compelling message that we must face the world with no illusions about the nature of tyranny. Ours will be a foreign policy that keeps this ever in mind. Ours will be a foreign policy which recognizes that in international negotiations we must make no undue concessions; that in pursuing *detente* we must not grant unilateral favors with only the hope of getting future favors in return. Agreements that are negotiated, such as the one signed in Helsinki, must not take from those who do not have freedom the hope of one day gaining it. Finally, we are firmly committed to a foreign policy in which secret agreements, hidden from our people, will have no part.

It was all too evident that the target of much of this thinly veiled criticism was Kissinger. The president's own party, in effect, condemned Kissinger and Ford as guilty of a weak and immoral foreign policy. It was almost as though the Democrats and Jimmy Carter, if they needed one, were being handed a straightforward blueprint for criticizing détente.

In addition to losing the détente card, moreover, Ford had little to brag about his record on China.

TURMOIL IN CHINA

Unlike in 1972, when Nixon's trip to China had boosted his election campaign and strengthened the statesman's image he coveted, Sino-American relations were a handicap to Ford in 1976. Ford's visit to Beijing in December 1975 had been generally considered a flop. Then, on January 8, 1976, Zhou Enlai died. To the confusion of outside observers, Beijing announced a month later that Hua Guofeng, an unknown provincial chief, was to take over as the acting premier. Kissinger's latest sparring partner, Deng Xiaopeng, was purged for the second time in his career.

On February 5, the Chinese government threw another curveball. Beijing announced that it had invited Richard Nixon for a visit, causing Kissinger (who had seen Nixon only three days earlier), Ford, and others to go ballistic. "Nixon's a shit," commented the usually subdued Brent Scowcroft, while a number of commentators condemned the former president's private diplomacy in the press. Joseph Kraft, for example, called the trip a "sleazy act" in a *Washington Post* column. Yet, Nixon instantly became, upon his visit to Beijing on February 21–29 (almost exactly four years after his previous trip to China) the first Westerner to have talked with the new premier, forcing Kissinger to ask the former president for a full report.[46]

Nixon's brief return to China coincided with George Bush's departure from Beijing. The future president had returned to Washington to head the CIA and, during the first months of 1976, the Chinese held their liaison office chief in Beijing waiting for Bush's replacement to arrive. Eventually Thomas S. Gates, a Philadelphia banker, was selected for the delicate task. Kissinger, probably still seething over Nixon's personal diplomacy and the Chinese ability to play games with the Americans in the early part of an election year, warned Gates just before his departure in late March that the Chinese "are cold, pragmatic bastards." Showing just how "cold" they were, Premier Hua Guofeng did not receive Gates until June, months after he had arrived in China.[47]

* * *

In 1976 the Chinese also played hardball on Taiwan, exactly at the same time as the domestic pressure from both the Republicans and Democrats to hold firm on issues related to the island's security increased. Alarmed by rumors that the administration was considering full recognition of the PRC, the 1964 Republican presidential candidate, Barry Goldwater, threatened to join the Reagan camp if there was any change in U.S. policy toward Taiwan. "I don't mind telling you," Goldwater warned in a letter to Kissinger, "if we are going to sell Taiwan down the river, it's going to have a decided effect on what I do for the rest of the campaign." To appease Goldwater, Reagan, and other Taiwan supporters, Ford eventually accepted the following de facto two-Chinas policy in the July 1976 Republican Party platform:

> The United States government, while engaged in a normalization of relations with the People's Republic of China, will continue to support the freedom and independence of our friend and ally, the Republic of China [Taiwan], and its 16 million people. The United States will fulfill and keep its commitments, such as the mutual defense treaty, with the Republic of China.[48]

The Chinese reaction to the Republican platform was immediate. In mid-August Kissinger and Huang Chen engaged in their hottest exchange on Taiwan. Chen warned that recent "comments about Sino-U.S. relations" constituted a flagrant threat against China." Kissinger, in a desperate attempt to maintain the illusion— for it surely was an illusion by this point—that U.S. domestic politics would have little bearing on the issue of normalization, responded by saying that the U.S. government would not act "on the basis of what is written on this or that platform."[49]

* * *

While the unresolved question of Taiwan and the impact of the American presidential election surely put a further damper on the question of normalization, they were mere window dressing when compared to the events that unfolded in early fall of 1976.

Although much anticipated, Mao Zedong's death on September 8, 1976, raised the already existing level of uncertainty in Sino-American relations to new heights. The Great Helmsman had been, after all, the central figure in the history of the People's Republic for almost three decades. While living in virtual isolation—much like the Chinese emperors before him—during the last years of his life, Mao had pulled the strings and set the course of China's internal and external policies. Without Mao's approval there would hardly have been an opening to China; with Mao gone the future of the Sino-American relationship was extremely uncertain.

The power struggle within China between Deng Xiaopeng and the Gang of Four—which included Jiang Qing (Mao's wife), Zhang Chunqiao, Yao Wenyuan, and Wang Hongwen—had, in fact, clearly swung in favor of the radical Gang in early 1976. While Hua Guofeng had been brought in, Deng had been dismissed from his duties as the vice premier in early April, thus suffering a second purge as a capitalist roader.

It seems, though, that the Gang of Four could remain in power only as long as Mao acted as their unwitting or witting front. Merely a month after Mao's death, the Gang was overthrown. In early 1977 Deng Xiaopeng returned. He was to rule China for the next two decades and effectively transform a backward nation into an emerging economic giant while keeping the CCP firmly in charge of politics. The Ford administration and Kissinger, however, had seen the last of their serious dialogues with the Chinese.

JIMMY CARTER AND MORALITY IN FOREIGN POLICY

After the Reagan challenge had finally been defeated in July 1976, Ford was hopeful that he would have a fairly straightforward run to the November election. Sure, he had made some concessions, including the Party platform's criticism of détente. He chose the Kansas senator Bob Dole as his running mate largely in part because of pressure from Reagan and his supporters. Still, in his acceptance speech, Ford exuded confidence:

> I am proud to stand before this great convention as the first incumbent President since Dwight D. Eisenhower who can tell the American people America is at peace. Tonight I can tell you straightaway this Nation is sound, this Nation is secure, this Nation is on the march to full economic recovery and a better quality of life for all Americans. And I will tell you one more thing: This year the issues are on our side. I am ready, I am eager to go before the American people and debate the real issues face to face with Jimmy Carter.[50]

In private, Ford was equally optimistic. "Now that we've gotten rid of that son-of-a-bitch Reagan, we can just do what is right," he told Kissinger and Scowcroft.

"I think Carter is vulnerable on a number of areas," offered Kissinger.[51]

On the face of it, Ford and Kissinger's optimism was well founded. Although Carter, who had become the official Democratic candidate in July, had been far ahead in the Gallup polls at the time of the Republican convention, his lead had slipped from 25 percent (57 to 32) in early August to 13 percent by August 26. Two months prior to Election Day Ford clearly had the momentum vis-à-vis his challenger.[52] But, in November, Carter emerged triumphant, not least because of his ability to tap into the reserves of resentment over the state of U.S. foreign policy.

* * *

Little in his past suggested that the former one-term Georgia governor would clinch his party's nomination, let alone be sworn in as the thirty-ninth president of the United States in early 1977. His electoral record was mixed. Carter had been elected to the Georgia Senate in 1962. In 1966 he had lost the race for governor, but was elected in 1970. In 1972 the peanut farmer-politician set his sights on the presidency and in 1974 built a base for himself as chairman of the Democratic Campaign Committee. Throughout 1975, however, Carter's campaign was short of money and his name recognition remained limited. In a poll of possible Democratic candidates conducted in January 1976, Carter received only 4 percent of the prospective vote, behind Hubert Humphrey, George Wallace, George McGovern, Henry Jackson, Edmund Muskie, and several others. But by March he was in the lead and ended up winning nineteen out of the thirty-one primaries. In July, Carter officially became the Democratic Party's nominee at Madison Square Garden in New York.[53]

Carter's sudden surge is explained by a combination of factors. First, like Ronald Reagan, Carter ran a campaign as an outsider; even more than Reagan, he was a fresh face. He repeated, sometimes to the point of exasperation, a few simple messages, such as: "I'm Jimmy Carter and I'm running for president. I will never lie to you." In contrast, his Democratic opponents, such as Jackson, were beltway insiders. But, most of all, Carter ran as an unabashed Wilsonian moralist. As the historian Robert Greene puts it: "Carter planned to corner the market on morality and beat the Republicans senseless with it." In the post-Watergate era of intelligence investigations and concerns over the morality of American foreign policy, this was a fruitful political strategy.[54]

The main target was, often, Kissinger. While faulting Ford for allowing Kissinger to run foreign policy, Carter, who had earlier declared Kissinger "a remarkable man and a very good friend of mine," now argued that the secretary of state was "obsessed with power blocs, with spheres of influence." This sort of obsession had resulted in "a policy without focus [that] is not understood by the people or the Congress." In numerous speeches authored partly by Zbigniew Brzezinski, Kissinger's old academic competitor from Harvard and Carter's future NSC adviser, the Democratic candidate attacked "a kind of secretive, 'Lone Ranger' foreign policy, a one man policy of international adventure." In fact, Carter charged, "the president is not really in charge. Our policies are Kissinger's ideas and his goals, which are often derived in secret." In early October Carter told the Foreign Policy

Association that the heart of the problem was that "a foreign policy based on secrecy inherently has had to be closely guarded and amoral."[55]

* * *

How did Ford respond? His campaign staff thought that the president had essentially two choices: either hit the campaign trail actively, displaying his image as a "nice guy," or rely on what one White House staffer, Michael Raoul-Duval, referred to as "the no-campaign campaign." By early September, the approach boiled down to three points: an active advertising campaign emphasizing the nice guy image; the vice presidential candidate, Bob Dole, would lead the negative attacks against Carter; and Ford himself would try to maintain his presidential image by remaining in Washington as an active chief executive. "Mister President, as a campaigner you are no fucking good," Stuart Spencer told Ford when outlining the necessity of keeping the president's stump speeches and campaign trips to a minimum.

In the first month after the Republican convention some of this seemed to work. Carter's earlier lead in the polls shrunk to 12 points and was further cut to 8 after the first presidential debate on September 26. As in the famous Nixon–Kennedy debate of 1960, Carter, having spent days preparing for the debate by poring over detailed briefing books, looked tired and acted a bit deferential. Ford, however, had prepped in a TV studio and focused on style rather than substance. The topic of the debate, the state of the economy, also gave Ford the chance to offer a $10 billion tax cut, while Carter floundered when asked whether he would raise taxes. It was one of the high points for the Ford campaign.

The low point came during the second nationally televised presidential debate.

"KISSINGER WILL BE A PRINCIPAL TOPIC"

Ford's preparation for the October 6 presidential debate, focusing on foreign policy, appeared immaculate. He was briefed on all key issues. NSC deputy adviser, William Hyland, had prepped Ford for almost any eventuality, including a potential challenge from Carter regarding the alleged American acceptance of Soviet domination in Eastern Europe and the administration's lackluster performance on human rights. Ford had also been advised that Kissinger was likely to "be a principal topic." In particular, Carter was likely to argue that the secretary of state had been running American foreign policy as a secret, private reserve, with Ford playing Tonto to Kissinger's Lone Ranger.[56]

Carter, reeling from his lackluster performance in the first debate and eager to stop Ford's momentum, did as expected: he went on the attack. "This Republican administration has been almost all style and spectacular, and not substance," he began. He then moved on to the central criticism:

Mr. Ford, Mr. Kissinger have continued on with the policies and failures of Richard Nixon. Even the Republican platform has criticized the lack of leadership in Mr. Ford, and they've criticized the foreign policy of this administration. This is one instance where I agree with the Republican platform . . . as far as foreign policy goes, Mr. Kissinger has been the President of this country. Mr. Ford has shown an absence of leadership and an absence of a grasp of what this country is and what it ought to be.

Ford, rather effectively, deflected Carter's criticism. The candidates went back and forth, trading charges and countercharges over proposed cuts in defense budgets and potential plans for a Middle East settlement. Then Max Frankel of the *New York Times*, one of the reporters posing questions to the two candidates, raised the Helsinki Accords and Eastern Europe.

"We've virtually signed, in Helsinki, an agreement that the Russians have dominance in Eastern Europe . . . Is that what you call a two-way street of traffic in Europe?" Frankel asked the president.

Ford's response was one of the most memorable and significant moments in the history of televised presidential debates. He had been prepped, extensively, to deny any existence of a Sonnenfeldt Doctrine or American acceptance of a Soviet sphere. Most of his answer followed the prepared response in his briefing book. But it was the last line that stuck: "There is no Soviet domination of Eastern Europe and there never will be under a Ford administration."

Frankel appeared baffled. "Did I understand you to say that the Russians are not using Eastern Europe as their own sphere of influence and making sure with their troops that it's a Communist zone?"

Ford, unfortunately for him, did not grab the opportunity to clarify his remarks and minimize the damage. Instead, he continued to hand Carter ammunition:

I don't believe, Mr. Frankel, that the Yugoslavians consider themselves dominated by the Soviet Union. I don't believe the Rumanians consider themselves dominated by the Soviet Union. I don't believe the Poles consider themselves dominated by the Soviet Union.

It was an unexpected gift to Carter, who immediately responded:

We've seen a very serious problem with the so-called Sonnenfeldt document which, apparently, Mr. Ford has just endorsed, which said that there's an organic linkage between the Eastern European countries and the Soviet Union. And I would like to see Mr. Ford convince the Polish-Americans and the Czech-Americans and the Hungarian-Americans in this country that those countries don't live under the domination and supervision of the Soviet Union behind the Iron Curtain.

Almost as overkill, Carter went on to talk about Solzhenitsyn.

Ford's gaffe on Poland was a major blunder and the reaction among the administration's foreign policy staff was immediate. "You've got a problem," Brent Scowcroft, watching the debate in a room near the podium, told Stuart Spencer. When Spencer appeared miffed, Scowcroft explained the reality of Soviet dominance of Poland. In the White House William Hyland let out a moan when he heard Carter's response to Ford's gaffe.

During a press conference an hour after the debate had ended, Scowcroft and Cheney tried to explain that Ford had really meant that the administration understood the reality of Soviet domination but did not accept or approve of it. It was to no avail. The press replayed the comment over and over. Ford only managed to quiet down the uproar a week after the debate when he admitted that he had perhaps been less than clear when addressing the particular question. But he had clearly lost the second debate: polls showed that the margin was a staggering 45 percent in Carter's behalf. "The engines of the President's comeback drive had stalled," one analyst later commented.

The interesting point was that neither the president nor Kissinger seemed to immediately understand the significance of the blunder. "I was stepping through a minefield, but I failed to recognize it," Ford wrote about his answer to Frankel's question. Kissinger, who called Ford from Washington an hour after the debate, only congratulated Ford for a superb job and never mentioned Eastern Europe. In fact, most Americans might not have noticed the "no Soviet domination"-gaffe had there not been the relentless press queries and analysis: initial polls, taken by Ford's campaign staff, showed that he had won the debate by 11 points. It was only in the days following the debate and in the ensuing furor that the perception of Ford's performance, influenced by media criticism, dipped lower in the polls.[57]

*   *   *

Did the "no Soviet domination" blunder cost Ford the presidency? It is impossible to measure the exact impact of the gaffe, let alone count the number of votes it may have cost. Yet, it surely did confirm one popular image of Ford that had been popularized by such scenes as the thirty-eighth president stumbling down the ramp of Air Force One, shown on popular TV shows such as "Saturday Night Live."

That image was one of a likeable, somewhat simple, and clumsy guy from the Midwest, who lacked strong leadership skills and displayed little moral conviction. When he put his foot down—as he apparently did during that second debate—Ford lost his way and fed the image of an aloof, weak, and out-of-touch president. It was this image, undoubtedly, that hurt him more than anything else and undermined his appeal to the voters.

As election day approached, Kissinger could not avoid being asked about Carter's continued attacks regarding the lack of a moral dimension in American foreign policy. His responses followed two general outlines. For one, Kissinger would intimate that Carter was simply playing an irresponsible political game.

"I really don't think that foreign policy lends itself to a detailed partisan debate," he responded to one reporter's query in late October.

If pushed a bit harder, however, Kissinger would defend his record on human rights. As an example, he would point to his role in the negotiations that had pushed Rhodesia toward accepting a transition from apartheid to majority rule.

But why was he not openly pushing a human rights agenda with the Soviets if he was doing so with the Rhodesians? Was there a double standard: one rule for countries like Rhodesia, another for the USSR? Kissinger was asked.

"No," was the quick response. Kissinger would stress that his nonconfrontational policies toward the Soviet Union had been instrumental in raising emigration numbers. Finally, he would point to the Helsinki Accords of 1975 as "the first time there has been an international acceptance by the Communist countries that participated that certain essential human rights were part of an international agreement." In short, Kissinger did have a human rights agenda, "but the method of application will have to differ with circumstances."[58]

That, of course, meant that the real answer to the question of double standards was, in fact, "yes." There was one rule for the Soviets and one for the Rhodesians. Morality had a contingent quality in his foreign policy and Kissinger could not explain it away. And it was that simple fact that allowed Carter to keep the issue at the forefront of his presidential campaign.

In the end, the election was extremely close. Although he narrowed Carter's lead in the last weeks of the campaign, the Ford campaign—even as the president hammered on a pledge to cut taxes—never fully recovered from the second debate's embarrassment. When Election Day finally arrived on November 2, 1976, Carter clinched the popular vote by two percentage points (49.9 percent to 47.9 percent). Ford had lost the presidency. Kissinger had two months to prepare for a life after government.

"I PASS ON A WORLD THAT IS AT PEACE"

On his last day in office, January 19, 1977, Kissinger gave an interview to three *New York Times* reporters, James Reston, Hedrick Smith, and Bernard Gwertzman. He ruminated about his legacy and about the eight years that had passed. The feeling was mixed, the departing secretary offered. On the one hand, he was proud of many achievements, arguing that the world in 1977 was "more peaceful, more hopeful, and with more chance for progress" than the world of 1969. On the other hand, Kissinger added, he was sad about "the anguish that the country suffered during this period, the bitterness of the debate on Vietnam, in the disintegration of authority on the Watergate, the destruction of some people I knew [notice past tense], and in the sense of things that one didn't quite finish." He mentioned SALT II as an example of those in the last category.

During the interview Kissinger flashed out some of his achievements, made predictions about the course of future relations with the Soviet Union and China, and argued that his overall approach to the Middle East and Africa was based on a carefully developed strategy, rather than a knee-jerk reaction to specific events. Overall, Kissinger did not succumb to any temptations for modesty. He summed it all up as follows:

> I have to say that I [*sic*] pass on a world that is at peace, more at peace than in any previous transition, in which, in addition, in every problem area solutions can be foreseen even if they have not been fully achieved and the framework for solutions exist, in which the agenda of most international negotiations was put forward by the United States. Therefore it cannot be entirely by an accident and it cannot be a series of tactical improvisations.[59]

The departing secretary of state thus summed up his view regarding the major debate that, in subsequent decades, would influence his place in history. The question was, in essence: Was Kissinger a stuntman or a statesman, a diplomatic svengali or a geopolitical genius? The secretary of state left no doubt about how "Kissinger's Kissinger" would appear in the forthcoming memoirs. On January 19, 1977, he displayed not a trace of the famous self-deprecating humor.

Despite the self-congratulatory assessment, it was clear that Kissinger's public image was partly to blame for the downfall of the 1976 Ford bid for the presidency. The secretary of state was, simply, too visible a target for those wishing to move into the White House in early 1977. Kissinger's penchant for secrecy, his unapologetic realpolitik, his celebrity status had all become election issues. Gerald Ford, for all his apparent decency and likeability, could never escape the stain of the intelligence investigations, convincingly argue that his administration championed human rights, or persuade his audiences that the Ford administration had moral clarity. Perhaps most important of all, despite the Halloween Massacre of November 1975 and the efforts to minimize Kissinger's visibility, the president appeared to lack the authority and decisive leadership skills that most Americans expected from their commander-in-chief.

One of the paradoxes of the 1976 election was that even with the compounded indignities and attacks on Kissinger that undermined the appeal of détente and other substantive parts of the Ford administration's foreign policy, the secretary of state remained highly popular among and generally trusted by the American people. In contrast, the president himself could never project an image as a decisive or inspiring leader: in an October 1976 poll only one in three thought that Ford had "strong leadership qualities" (as opposed to one in two for Carter).[60] The perception of Kissinger as the commander-in-chief of foreign policy, a message that both Reagan and Carter stressed, surely played a role in fomenting this, not entirely faulty, impression of Ford. While Ford lost the presidency for a number of reasons—such as poor campaign strategies, the relentless populism of his opponents, the economic problems in the United States, and the difficult legacy of Nixon—his inability to visibly take charge of foreign policy ranked high among Ford's handicaps. This fact, along with Richard Nixon's earlier undignified exit from the White House, helps to explain why Kissinger, after eight years in office, was bound to remain a higher-profile figure than the president who had brought him to Washington and far more prominent than the president who had kept him on.

But there were other reasons why Kissinger would remain a household name throughout the world a quarter of a century after he left office in January 1977. Like many other former secretaries of state, he was ready to write his memoirs. Unlike most of his predecessors, however, Henry Kissinger was not prepared for a life in relative obscurity.

20

The Chairman "On Trial"

T he announcement, on December 13, 2002, was puzzling.
The seventy-nine-year-old Henry Kissinger, former secretary of state and national security adviser, media celebrity, and globetrotting businessman, had changed his mind and not agreed to chair the commission on the terrorist attacks of September 11, 2001. It was "a moment of disappointment for me," Kissinger wrote in a letter to President George W. Bush. "For over a half a century, I have never refused to respond to the call from a president," he added, citing demands that he disclose a full list of the business clients of his consulting firm, the Kissinger Associates.

It was an end to the latest of many Kissinger controversies. Only two weeks earlier, on November 27, President Bush had appointed Kissinger to head the high-profile commission. "We must uncover every detail and learn every lesson of September the 11th," Bush had said in his remarks at the White House. Kissinger and the vice chairman of the committee, former Senate majority leader George Mitchell (D-Maine), vowed to do a thorough job. "We are under no restrictions and we will accept no restrictions," Kissinger had told reporters at the news conference following the announcement. "We will get all the facts," he had added. In the end, neither he nor Mitchell stayed on the commission, both citing what they considered unreasonable demands that they sever ties to their private clients. But it was Kissinger, not Mitchell, who became the true subject of press scrutiny, the one whose past resurfaced with a vengeance.[1]

The sudden uproar in late 2002 spoke volumes of the unprecedented name recognition and controversy that Kissinger still commands a quarter century after departing government service. Indeed, when he left office in January 1977, Kissinger had hardly turned his back on a potential return to the seventh floor of the State Department. Not yet fifty-four, with a worldwide reputation and a powerful circle of friends, the possibility that he might have a second act with another Republican administration under the right circumstances was hardly out of the realm of possibility.

The call from the White House or from a president-elect never came. Although all future chief executives consulted Kissinger in one way or another, he would never again hold an official government post. Instead, Ronald Reagan and George H. W. Bush—the two Republican presidents who served when Kissinger was still young enough to be considered for the grueling position—chose as secretaries of state men who were well known and had worked for or alongside Kissinger in the Nixon and Ford administrations: Alexander Haig (1981–82), George Schultz (1982–89), James Baker (1989–92), and Lawrence Eagleburger (1992–93). Other aides and foes— Winston Lord, John Negroponte, Paul Bremer, Peter Rodman, Richard Solomon, Robert McFarlane, Anthony Lake, and Morton Halperin, among others—could be found in high positions in all subsequent administrations. Although he was a god-father to a generation of American foreign policy makers, Kissinger was destined to remain in the political wilderness for the remainder of his active career.

One obvious explanation for Kissinger's inability to resuscitate a career in government was, ironically, his high profile. Kissinger's intensely scrutinized record made Super-K a political liability to any administration. To most, his legacy consisted of mostly negative elements: an unapologetic realpolitik, a disregard for human rights, an eagerness to work with American adversaries in Moscow and, in particular, Beijing, questionable conduct and judgment regarding the use of covert operations (such as in Chile and Angola), and a seeming willingness to bypass the Constitution in organizing secret military campaigns (such as the Cambodian bombings of 1969). Unlike Haldeman, Ehrlichman, Mitchell, and others, Kissinger may have escaped legal proceedings and jail terms. But the stain was there, and it would not wash away.

Equally, if not more, damning for Kissinger's future role in a Republican (let alone Democratic) administration was his domineering personality. As Nixon had found out to his fury and Ford accepted with some reservations, Kissinger was not one to share the limelight. He was a junkie for public praise and almost maniacal about guarding his reputation. Despite the light self-deprecating touch that Kissinger often inserted into his dealings with the press, there was no greater ego in Washington or New York. Few politicians were either secure enough to share the spotlight with Kissinger, or insecure enough to crave for someone of his stature to take charge of the country's foreign policy. Ronald Reagan and George H. W. Bush fit neither of these categories. A related problem was Kissinger's ability to make acerbic comments about those he considered his intellectual inferiors. In the world of American politics and statecraft, this applied to almost everyone.

Kissinger's famously thin skin also made the possibility that he would run for elected office improbable. To be sure, in the late 1970s and 1980s Kissinger twice considered a life in politics (how serious these flirtations were is another matter). As early as October 1978 there were rumors that Super-K might run for the New York Senate seat that Jacob Javits had occupied since 1957. By the time of the 1980 elections Javits, who suffered from Lou Gehrig's disease, was going to be seventy-six. Yet, the delicious prospect of having New York's Senate seats occupied by two brilliant egos—Daniel Patrick Moynihan and Henry Kissinger—never materialized. Pundits and potential supporters judged Kissinger's temper ill-suited for the hard-hitting life of American politics, and Alfonse d'Amato ultimately became the Republican senator from New York. In early 1986, Kissinger was again rumored to be considering a run for office. This time, his potential target was Mario Cuomo, the New York governor. In the end, Kissinger did not warm to the idea of moving to Albany. As Walter Isaacson puts it: "the notion of [Kissinger] as governor, milking cows at state fairs and wrestling with legislators over highway funds, was on the face of it ridiculous."[2]

By the time the brief flirtation with the New York governorship passed, Kissinger had apparently become resigned to the fact that his career as a high-ranking government official had ended in January 1977. It was equally clear, though, that he would never retire. Over the years he wrote three massive volumes of his memoirs and several other books, contributed editorials and articles to prominent newspapers and magazines, appeared regularly as a commentator on world events on major TV networks, served as an informal foreign policy adviser to presidents, joined high-level nonpartisan commissions, traveled the world giving speeches for high fees and, perhaps most important for his bank account, led a successful international consulting company that capitalized on Kissinger's worldwide reputation, geopolitical acumen, and unparalleled contacts.

While such activities allowed Kissinger to continue a jet-set lifestyle even while living in the political wilderness, they had a dual impact for his reputation. On the one hand, Kissinger remained a household name throughout the globe, a world figure like few others. On the other hand, he would also remain a subject of controversy. At regular intervals, Kissinger would be questioned about his past role in the Nixon and Ford administrations, as well as for the alleged conflicts of interest that arose from his chairmanship of Kissinger Associates. As the twenty-first century dawned, Kissinger had become a chairman permanently on trial for activities past and present.

SENIOR STATESMAN IN WAITING

During the first five years after leaving office, Kissinger was occupied with a number of different pursuits. While maintaining a base in Washington as a part-time professor at Georgetown University and a senior fellow with the Aspen Institute, Kissinger established his permanent home in New York. In addition, he and Nancy purchased a country residence in Kent, Connecticut. Perhaps to fund his expensive lifestyle, which included a privately paid squad of bodyguards, Kissinger became a paid consultant to the Chase Manhattan Bank's international advisory committee, and gave several speeches to corporate audiences for fees ranging from $10,000 to $15,000. He also signed a five-year contract with NBC worth $200,000 a year to act as a consultant for special reports and to be on stand-by for commentary for news shows when necessary. It was the first of a series of media deals that further cemented the retired secretary of state's celebrity. His relationship with NBC did not go entirely smoothly. His first special report, on Eurocommunism, had extremely low ratings. Then, in an hour-long interview, talk show host David Frost peppered Kissinger with questions on Cambodia, prompted by accusations in a book by William Shawcross called *Sideshow*, which had been published in the spring of 1979. Shawcross, who helped Frost prepare for the interview, argued, in effect, that the decisions to bomb and invade Cambodia had plunged the country into chaos and allowed the Khmer Rouge to gain power. Kissinger, along with Nixon, was therefore indirectly responsible for the genocide of up to two million Cambodians that followed as Pol Pot and his comrades perfected their warped vision of a communist utopia. Kissinger naturally denied the charges, arguing that the bombings (and the invasion) had been necessary for military reasons and that the targets had been carefully selected to avoid civilian casualties. After the interview was taped, Kissinger was so incensed that he tried to have the Cambodia portions of the interview excised before it was aired. Frost, in retaliation, released the transcript and NBC broadcast the interview in full. And the first volume of Kissinger's memoirs, *White House Years*, that was published at the time of the October 1979 interview, received much additional publicity and controversy, boosting its sales (at least three bookstores in New York capitalized on the controversy by offering buyers of *White House Years* a free copy of *Sideshow*).[3]

After his five-year contract with NBC was complete, Kissinger joined ABC, becoming a regular on Ted Koppel's "Nightline." Throughout the 1990s and into the new millennium, he remained a regular guest on news shows, in sharp contrast to his forgotten successors.

In addition to his role as one of the prime media analysts of the 1980s and 1990s (albeit somewhat less so as his age and heavy accent began to fit less well into the fast-pace world of such popular debate formats as the "McLaughlin Group"), Kissinger's influence on public opinion and continued name-recognition was guaranteed through the proliferation of articles and books. Starting in the early 1980s Kissinger would write some dozen major newspaper columns a year for the *Los Angeles Times* syndicate that were usually reprinted in the *Washington Post*. Although his prose remained heavy and the length of his op-eds far exceeded that of the usual commentary on editorial pages, the papers continued to print the former secretary of state's postulations on major events at regular intervals. Kissinger also contracted several pieces a year for *Newsweek.*

While appearing on TV, writing columns, and giving speeches took up some of his time, Kissinger's major project in 1977–82 was to write his memoirs. Published in 1979 and 1982 respectively, *White House Years* and *Years of Upheaval* were unprecedented in length and detail. Instant best-sellers, the books were products of intensive teamwork with former aides Peter Rodman, William Hyland, and Rosemary Niehuss. Yet, the prose was unmistakably Kissinger's and the spin expectedly in his favor. Nevertheless, critics often praised them—if not for anything else then surely for the often revealing descriptions of such foreign leaders as Mao, Brezhnev, Zhou, Golda Meir, and others. In the *New York Times,* for example, James Reston called the *White House Years* "the most remarkable insider's political memoir of our time," while William Safire argued that it was "a credit to Kissinger's mind and energy." Perhaps the most astonishing fact of the first two volumes was that in close to 2,500 pages they had only covered the Nixon administration's five-and-a-half years in office. The Ford administration's turn would have to wait for the late 1990s, when Kissinger would publish *Years of Renewal* (1999).[4]

* * *

While working on the first two volumes of his memoirs, Kissinger unsuccessfully flirted with a potential return to office. The closest he came was in July 1980, at a time when, in an effort to reach out to the more moderate Republicans, Ronald Reagan was considering asking Gerald Ford to be his running mate. On July 15, during the Republican convention, Ford agreed to consider the possibility. The same evening Kissinger met with Reagan's campaign manager and future CIA Director William Casey as well as two other top aides, Edwin Meese and Michael Deaver. Meese, who would go on to serve as Reagan's White House political counselor and attorney general, asked Kissinger to help them persuade Ford to join the Reagan ticket. Ford, in turn, wanted Kissinger to become secretary of state. When he told this to Reagan on July 16, the future president was taken aback. "I've been all over this country the last several years," Reagan told Ford, "and Kissinger carries a lot of baggage." By the end of the day Ford had declined and Reagan picked up the phone to call George Bush. The former UN ambassador, envoy to China, and CIA director, who had lost the vice presidency to Nelson Rockefeller in 1974 in part due to Kissinger's influence, immediately accepted.

After his victory over Carter, Reagan appointed Alexander Haig as his secretary of state. Kissinger remained on the sidelines, making, on occasion, snide comments about Haig's less than distinguished stewardship of the State Department.[5] In 1988, the Republican nominee George Bush had little need for Kissinger's foreign policy experience and even less interest in sharing the limelight with the man who had cut him out of policy making on several occasions in the early 1970s. Like Reagan, Bush did, however, bring Kissinger's former aides to the administration. Two of them emerged as particularly influential. Brent Scowcroft began his second term as NSC adviser in January 1989 and Lawrence Eagleburger became the deputy secretary of state at the same time. Eagleburger would later be elevated to the top post in the State Department when James Baker took over as Bush's campaign manager during the 1992 presidential elections.

SHADOW SECRETARY

Although he was never called back to active duty, Kissinger maintained his influence on policy in two important ways: as an informal adviser to presidents and as a member or head of numerous committees related to the conduct of foreign policy. Every president after Ford would call upon him for advice on major foreign policy questions of the day. He clearly carried clout and was not viewed as overtly partisan. Although his advice was not always welcome, Kissinger's insights into the various leaders around the world he had met during his years in office, made him a valuable bipartisan source. At times, though, when he did meddle in actual policy matters, Kissinger could arouse both publicity and controversy.

An early example of Kissinger's ability to attract controversy had to do with his attitude toward the Iranian revolution. In 1979, the shah, whom Kissinger and Nixon had met only days after the historic Moscow summit of May 1972, was overthrown. While the Carter administration was reluctant to grant the exiled shah asylum in the United States, Kissinger, along with David Rockefeller and John J. McCloy, championed the cause. They arranged for the shah and his family to find temporary homes in the Bahamas and Mexico City. In October 1979, the shah was finally allowed to enter the United States to receive medical treatment. Soon thereafter, buoyed by the news that the Americans had let in the major target of the Iranian revolution, the hostage crisis erupted.

The Iranian revolution was a classic example of what would later be dubbed "blowback": the United States, in implementing the Nixon Doctrine, had been the shah's best friend and anti-Americanism had, as a result, been closely linked in the minds of students, radical Islamists, and others who acted as the driving force of the Iranian revolution. Kissinger (and Nixon) had made their mistakes much earlier by treating Iran as a pawn in the strategic game of the early 1970s without paying attention to the specific regional circumstances and potential internal consequences to Iran such policies might produce. They had, in essence, been guilty of some of the same shortsightedness that had resulted in unintended negative consequences as earlier U.S. policies in Southeast Asia or later efforts in Afghanistan.[6]

*   *   *

During the Reagan administration, Kissinger's most high-profile role had to do with another region that had not been at the top of his agenda while in office. In

July 1983, Reagan appointed the former secretary of state to head a bipartisan commission on Central America. The Kissinger Commission consisted of twelve voting members and eleven senior counselors, a mixture of foreign policy, congressional, and business leaders. In addition to Kissinger, some of the primary members included William P. Clements, former Republican governor of Texas; Nicholas Brady, former Republican senator (and future namesake of the Brady Bill); Henry G. Cisneros, mayor of San Antonio and future secretary of interior under Bill Clinton; and John R. Silber, president of Boston University. The senior counselors were a collection of prominent members of the House and Senate, including Senators Lloyd Bentsen (D-Texas) and Pete Domenici (R-New Mexico); and Representatives Jim Wright (D-Texas) and Jack Kemp (R-New York). In addition, UN Ambassador Jeanne J. Kirkpatrick served as President Reagan's representative, while two former Kissinger aides—William D. Rogers (the former assistant secretary of state for inter-American affairs who had rejoined his law firm in Washington) and Winston Lord (who was at the time serving as the president of the Council on Foreign Relations)—filled the remaining two counselor seats.

Between August and December 1983, the Kissinger Commission held thirty full days of open hearings in addition to a score of other meetings and heard from more than 400 witnesses regarding the social, humanitarian, religious, economic, security, and political considerations affecting U.S. policy toward Central America. Commission members traveled twice to Central America for fact-finding missions (in October and December). Finally, in January 1984 the Kissinger Commission delivered its final report.

Given the bipartisan composition of the commission, its final report was, inevitably, a consensus study that, by and large, endorsed the Reagan administration's policies. The commission agreed that the roots of the crisis in Central America, where left-wing revolutionaries were fighting right-wing groups in Guatemala, Honduras, El Salvador, and Nicaragua, "are both indigenous and external," thus giving a tacit endorsement to Reagan's charge that Central America had become a target of Soviet-Cuban aggression. "The United States Must Act Urgently" was another part of the report that, in effect, endorsed the Reagan Doctrine, the anticommunist blueprint of the Reagan administration that vowed to take on any Soviet-inspired liberation movement anywhere in the world, at the opening of the 1984 election year. Kissinger, viewing Central America as a potential replay of his 1975–76 debacle with the Soviets and Cubans in Angola, even went a bit further in the dissent notes of the report. While supporting the conditioning of U.S. aid to El Salvador on human rights improvements (government-supported death squads were reportedly patrolling the Salvadoran countryside in search of left-wing rebels), Kissinger, along with Nicholas Brady and John Silber noted that they "do not want conditionality interpreted in a manner that leads to a Marxist-Leninist victory." Before President Reagan sent a bill to the Congress asking for the recommended military aid, he made it clear that the White House would remain the final arbiter on conditionality.

The end result was that the Kissinger Commission's report became politicized almost at the moment it was released. While Reagan made it clear that he had no interest in accepting restrictions to his ability to boost Central American anticommunists regardless of the methods they employed, the Democrats, including commission members Lane Kirkland and Robert Strauss, soon denounced the commission's report. Although it had hardly been his intention, Kissinger had once again managed to step into a domestic political minefield.[7]

By this point, Kissinger had most likely abandoned any serious thoughts about returning to government. Yet, he continued to engage—but with no noticeable success—policy making at the highest levels. Perhaps the worst indignity came in 1989, when Kissinger was among the many who seriously misread the developments in the Soviet Union and tried to revitalize back-channel diplomacy.

In January 1989, as the Bush administration took office, Kissinger, with Bush's blessing, met with Gorbachev. The former secretary of state proposed a tacit Soviet-American understanding: the USSR would allow liberalization to go ahead in Eastern Europe and the United States would not attempt to exploit this to its advantage by luring countries away from the Warsaw Pact. Once the news of the plan leaked, it was instantly dubbed "Yalta II" or "new Yalta" by such commentators as Zbigniew Brzezinski, drawing the contrast to the 1945 American-British-Soviet summit, where President Franklin Roosevelt had, arguably, accepted Stalin's demands for Soviet control over East-Central Europe. In the end, Secretary of State James Baker publicly disassociated the administration from any such plans and Kissinger, probably feeling as though he was being accused of something akin to the nonexistent Sonnenfeldt Doctrine of 1976, criticized the administration for both distorting his views and for not engaging the USSR adequately. "Once there is anarchy and the tanks roll it is too late for diplomacy," he wrote in a column in the *Washington Post* on April 16, 1989. As the events in Eastern Europe unraveled rapidly during the remaining months of 1989, however, Baker's dismissal of Kissinger's role and proposal appeared justified.[8]

*   *   *

The other issue in 1989 that brought Kissinger unwelcome publicity—although in this case his views were almost identical to those of the Bush administration—revolved around his perception regarding the proper U.S. response to the Chinese regime's crackdown on student demonstrators on Tiananmen Square.

Throughout the 1980s Deng Xiaopeng had eased the state's control over the economy and prompted a remarkable boost in the PRC's economy. Yet, there had been no relaxation of the Communist Party's hold on political power. Throughout the spring of 1989 thousands of students demonstrated throughout China's major cities, prompting the government to declare martial law on May 19. Finally, on June 3, 1989, tanks "rolled" on to Beijing's Tiananmen Square and soldiers opened fire on demonstrators.

While the world watched in shock the footage featuring, most memorably, a solitary demonstrator attempting to block the forward movement of a Chinese tank, many called for the imposition of economic sanctions on the PRC as a minimum response to such flagrant violation of human rights. For commentary, American networks turned, naturally, to the man who had been instrumental, eighteen years earlier, in opening the Sino-American relationship. Kissinger counseled restraint. "China remains too important for America's national security to risk the relationship on the emotions of the moment," he wrote.[9]

The Bush administration, and the president himself as its foremost China expert, generally agreed with Kissinger. Yet, it could not simply go on as if nothing had happened. Ultimately, the administration chose a two-track policy. On June 5, President Bush announced the first series of economic sanctions and invited all Chinese students in the United States to extend their stay if they wished. Most Americans left China in subsequent months and all official high-level contacts were suspended.

Yet, hoping to keep the relationship alive even as its forward movement was impossible, the Bush administration also reverted to the practice of secret diplomacy. Late on June 30, 1989, National Security Adviser Brent Scowcroft and Deputy Secretary of State Larry Eagleburger—the most prominent former "Kissinger hands" in the Bush administration—left Andrews Air Force Base for a clandestine visit to Beijing. After spending twenty-four hours and meeting with Deng, they returned without being discovered (news of the trip only leaked in December). The trip was followed by subsequent meetings in Paris and New York (at the UN), as well as another Eagleburger–Scowcroft visit to China in December (this time in public view). On December 19, Bush announced the first relaxation of economic sanctions and the Chinese followed up by lifting martial law a few weeks later. The relationship began to return to normalcy. "Our approach to this crisis had avoided setting the relationship back for decades," Secretary of State Baker wrote in his memoirs.[10]

*   *   *

The two contrasting experiences that occurred during the first year of the Bush administration—Yalta II and Tiananmen Square—were clear indications that Kissinger still yielded some influence, directly and indirectly, in the White House. Although his proposals on the reconfiguration of Soviet-American relations had been rejected (even ridiculed), Kissinger's advice on China had clearly been a different matter. Not only was there a close match between Kissinger's thinking and the Bush administration's policies, but there was a resemblance of method: secret trips and clandestine meetings, aimed, undoubtedly, to disabuse the Chinese of the idea that the United States was keen on challenging the PRC's internal political structure. This was reminiscent of many of Kissinger's meetings with Chinese leaders in the 1970s, when he had repeatedly told Mao, Zhou, and Deng to ignore domestic American bickering about China's internal political structure. The Scowcroft—Eagleburger mission was but a latest example of the longevity of Kissinger's legacy in U.S.-China relations. As James Mann puts it, with tongue only partly in cheek, "American officials who followed Kissinger to Beijing sang many of the same tunes, in the same rhythm and style, as the Meistersinger."[11]

There was another eerie coincidence. Less than a year earlier, the two men who had gone secretly to China in late June 1989 had been closely associated with Kissinger Associates.

KISSINGER ASSOCIATES

In early 1982, as *Years of Upheaval* was going into print, two events in Kissinger's personal life foreshadowed a profound change in his career choices. First, he had to undergo open-heart surgery. A few weeks after that Kissinger's father, Louis, died at the age of ninety-five. "These two things together concentrated my mind," he later told a reporter. Although Kissinger joked in public about his heart problems— "at least it proves that I do have a heart"—and had never been emotional with his father, the fifty-nine-year-old did undertake important lifestyle changes. He began to be careful about what he ate. At the same time, Kissinger kept busy; he and a group of former associates, friends, and aides launched a successful international consulting firm.[12]

In July 1982, Kissinger Associates Inc. (KAI) became an active business. Over the next twenty years, it became an immensely successful and constantly evolving consulting operation, offering confidential advice to dozens of multinational companies around the world. In addition to Kissinger, the other early principals of KAI were Scowcroft and, as of 1984, Eagleburger. Scowcroft had stayed in Washington after the end of the Ford administration to act as a paid consultant and continued such work on the side, while running KAI's Washington office in the 1980s. In the early 1990s, after serving as national security adviser to George Bush, he would go on to found his own consulting firm, the Scowcroft Group. Unlike Scowcroft, Eagleburger, a career foreign service officer, had remained in the Carter administration. In June 1977, he had been appointed ambassador to Yugoslavia, where he served for three years. In the first Reagan administration Eagleburger served as assistant secretary of state for European affairs (1981–82) and undersecretary of state for political affairs (1982–84). Like Scowcroft, Eagleburger would leave KAI to join the top echelons of the Bush administration in 1989, initially as deputy secretary of state and briefly as secretary of state (1992–93). In the 1990s Eagleburger became the chairman of the International Commission on Holocaust Era Insurance Claims, and a senior foreign policy adviser for the Washington, DC firm Baker, Donelson, Bearman and Caldwell.[13]

In 1989, as Scowcroft and Eagleburger joined the Bush administration, Kissinger hired another former aide, Paul ("Jerry") Bremer III, as the managing director of KAI. Like Eagleburger, Bremer had been Kissinger's executive assistant at the State

Department and had served as ambassador to the Netherlands and as ambassador-at-large for counter-terrorism. This is the same Paul Bremer who in the spring of 2003, at the age of sixty-one, returned to government as the second Bush administration's top civilian official in post-Saddam Iraq.

* * *

KAI was not a massive enterprise. In addition to the high-profile consultants, there was a small secretarial staff in the two, outwardly unassuming, offices in New York (Fifth Avenue) and Washington (K Street). The total staff size hovered around twenty-five in the 1990s. But the client list and the profits—although no exact accounting is possible—were substantial. KAI was, in large part due to the magnetic effect of its chairman, an extremely successful business, boosting Kissinger's personal earnings—that also included his substantial royalties and media and speaking tour fees—to somewhere around $8 million a year by the conclusion of the firm's first decade.

In 1985, *Business Week* reported that "some 28 U.S. and foreign multinational corporations and banks pony up $150,000 to $250,000 of their stockholders' money to put Kissinger himself on retainer." KAI's revenues in 1985 totaled $4 million. In an April 1986 article in the *New York Times Magazine*, Leslie Gelb revealed that, in that year, "25 to 30 corporations paid KAI between $150,000 and $420,000 each per annum for political influence and access." The key to success was simple. As Gelb put it: "The superstar international consultants [at KAI] were certainly people who would get their telephone calls returned from high American government officials and who would also be able to get executives in to see foreign leaders." By the early 1990s, KAI's earnings were hovering at the $10 million mark. Its client list was impressive, ranging from American Express and Chase Manhattan Bank to ITT, Heintz, and Coca-Cola. Eagleburger, courtesy of his service as ambassador to Yugoslavia, brought such clients as Yugo, a phenomenally unsuccessful car in North American markets. In part through the links of Per Gyllenhammer, president of Volvo, there was a long list of Swedish multinationals—in addition to the automobile maker, KAI's client list included Ericsson (telecommunications) and Skandinaviska Enskilda Banken, one of the largest Scandinavian financial institutions.[14]

But while KAI was financially successful and engaged an impressive array of clients, it also managed to perpetuate—as it built its success upon—one of the most negative images of its namesake: secretiveness. As Kissinger himself put it in an interview: "I don't advertise. There's no booklet about me. They [the clients] have to come to me."[15] Given Kissinger's controversial reputation, the business relied on absolute confidentiality, making it extremely difficult for reporters to uncover, for example, the company's client list (let alone provide a full accounting of its revenues). In a sense, Kissinger Associates was conducting a series of back-channel operations, albeit this time for financial profit rather than in the service of U.S. foreign policy interests. There was nothing illegal in all of this. Yet, the noteworthy point was that

Chairman Kissinger himself was simultaneously engaged in a number of highly public pursuits. The cohabitation of secrecy and extreme publicity, a trademark of Kissinger's period in office, thus continued into his career in the private sector.

In the United States, however, secrecy tends to provoke exaggerated interest, no less so when the guardians of such secrecy are high-profile public figures earning sizeable sums of money. Such interest, translated into journalistic scrutiny has, in general, only one outcome: public controversy. Kissinger Associates proved no exception, particularly when two of its senior partners returned to government service in 1989.

CONFLICTS OF INTEREST?

Roughly at the same time as Kissinger was engaged in his foiled attempt at reinvigorating his role as a back-channel communicator as a special envoy to Mikhail Gorbachev, Larry Eagleburger and Brent Scowcroft were involved in controversy of their own. After his victory over Massachusetts Governor Michael Dukakis in November 1988 elections, president-elect George H. W. Bush had invited both Eagleburger and Scowcroft to join the new administration. Both accepted: Eagleburger a position as Secretary of State Jim Baker's second in command and Scowcroft as Bush's national security adviser (making him the only man to have served in that post under two different presidents). Both resigned from KAI. Both faced questions about the so-called revolving door, that is, the cycling back and forth between government and private industry, and the attendant conflict of interest. Had the two men used their extensive governmental contacts for private gain and could they compartmentalize the public and the private spheres?

While both Scowcroft and Eagleburger served full terms in the Bush administration, the controversies over their business dealings were only part of a long list of conflicts of interest charges that Kissinger and his company faced. To his credit, though, the chairman at times acted quickly if a potential conflict appeared on the horizon. But given his high profile and controversial reputation, Kissinger was often assumed to be guilty before (and sometimes even after) proven innocent.

Instructive, for example, is the relationship between the Bank of Credit and Commerce International (BCCI) and KAI. Dubbed as the "Bank of Crooks and Criminals" by CIA Director Robert Gates, BCCI was indicted on October 11, 1988, for money laundering charges, pleaded guilty in 1990, and was fined $15 million for offering such services to the likes of Panama's Manuel Noriega. Proving that the Republicans weren't the only former government officials hiring out their services, the legal representative of BCCI during the proceedings was former Johnson administration Secretary of Defense Clark Clifford.

Kissinger had never been in business with BCCI; the damning fact was that BCCI had *tried* to hire KAI and that it took Kissinger a long time to turn down the invitation. In fact, the indirect relationship between BCCI and KAI dated back to the fall of 1986, when a retired Brazilian ambassador, Sergio da Costa, signed up as a consultant for both companies. In subsequent months and years, Da Costa had worked on creating a connection between Kissinger's partner Alan Stoga and BCCI representatives. Although the episode ended soon after BCCI's indictment in 1988—da Costa's consultancy with KAI was terminated at the time and Kissinger personally put a stop to any further discussions with BCCI in early 1989—the issue was revisited in 1991–92, when a subcommittee of the Senate Committee on Foreign Relations subpoenaed a number of KAI and BCCI documents relating to the contacts. While the documents showed a strong interest on the part of the BCCI in developing a relationship with Kissinger, there was little evidence of reciprocity, aside from a few meetings between Stoga and Abol Helmy of BCCI. In December 1992, the final report to the Senate Foreign Relations Committee concluded that "Kissinger was never himself especially interested in this potential client . . . recognized the risk to the reputation of his firm and instructed Stoga to advise BCCI that no relationship was possible."[16]

Kissinger and his firm had done nothing illegal. But the BCCI case is instructive about the way many would easily assume the worst when the former secretary of state's name was even mentioned.

The other major scandal that touched Kissinger Associates in the early 1990s was tied to the unauthorized loans to Iraq that came to be known as Iraqgate. In 1985 Kissinger had become a member of the international advisory board of the Banca Nazionale del Lavoro (BNL), an Italian bank with offices around the world. During the 1980s, the BNL's Atlanta branch made $4 billion in unauthorized loans to Iraq. In 1991–92 the House of Representatives held hearings into the BNL scandal. Although much of the attention focused on National Security Adviser Brent Scowcroft, Kissinger was once again considered to be implicated by association; Iraq's invasion of Kuwait in August 1990 guaranteed that the BNL scandal made it to the headlines. Nor did the drama stop there. In a lengthy statement to the House, Texas Democratic Representative Henry Gonzalez, the chairman of the House banking committee, even described how Kissinger's partner at KAI Alan Stoga had met with Saddam Hussein during a trip to Baghdad in June 1989.

In February 1991 Kissinger severed his ties with BNL. As with BCCI, there was no evidence that he had been engaged in illegal activities. And yet, the sheer mention of Kissinger's name often invited public scrutiny and journalistic attention. Even if he did nothing illegal, controversy was bound to follow him.[17]

After the hearings on BNL and BCCI were completed in 1992, KAI did not make much news until, in the late 1990s, another potential conflict of interest association arose. In the fall of 1999 Kissinger joined forces with President Bill Clinton's former White House chief of staff, Thomas F. ("Mack") McLarty III. A new affiliate was born, known as Kissinger McLarty Associates, with its two namesakes serving as chairman and vice chairman. McLarty's particular external strength was links to Latin America, a relatively weak (albeit no less controversial) spot in Kissinger's own resume but a growing market for the services of KAI in the first decade of the

North American Free Trade Agreement (NAFTA, which had been signed in late 1992). Among the new clients of Kissinger-McLarty was GlobalNet, a telecommunications firm planning for substantial expansion to Latin America.[18]

*   *   *

In the end, Kissinger (-McLarty) Associates has never been involved in anything strictly illegal—at least nothing that would have led to criminal prosecution. That Kissinger waited five years after leaving office to commence his business was, in fact, an extraordinary delay (although explained in part by his evident interest in returning to government and the sheer length of the memoirs he compiled at the time). Nevertheless, given the nature of his business, the high profile of its associates, and the continued links between Kissinger and high government officials at home and abroad, Kissinger Associates inevitably became and remained a subject of controversies. *New York Times'* Jeff Garth and Sarah Bartlett put the basic point as follows:

> In a field as subtle as foreign policy, can people like Mr. Kissinger and his associates wall off what they know of confidential Government discussions from what they can legitimately advise their corporate clients? And when people of their stature help shape Government decisions, can they ignore what they know of their corporate clients interests?[19]

Perhaps they could. But such an argument, in all honesty, could never truly wash and did not have a fighting chance of being accepted by the scandal-hungry American media of the late twentieth century. And yet, being chased after by journalists may have been a blessing in disguise; it certainly kept Kissinger in the public eye and increased—particularly as the confidentiality of his consulting firm and its operations remained untouched—the KAI's market value. The lesson, after all, from the BCCI and BNL investigations was twofold: Kissinger could keep secrets and he did nothing illegal.

In fact, already by 1993, when he turned seventy and Bill Clinton was serving his first year in the White House, Kissinger, once again, appears to have changed the focus of his pursuits. His financial situation secured, his reputation still remained under the eye of skeptical researchers. The "glittering twilight"—as Walter Isaacson summed up Kissinger's lifestyle in the early 1990s—was simply inadequate to make up for his apparent need to guard his plummeting historical reputation. Thus, the former professor-statesman and successful businessman returned to active writing.

SEARCHING FOR REPUDIATION

Richard Nixon died in April 1994. Kissinger had maintained a respectful relationship with his former mentor for the two decades between Nixon's resignation and the former president's death. It had never, of course, been more than a working relationship. While the two men may have spent much time together strategizing and impressing each other; they had never become friends. "We never went to a baseball game together," Kissinger later ruminated, with some regret in his voice in an interview with the author. Yet, Kissinger owed his success in large part to Nixon, who had chosen the Harvard professor as his national security adviser and eventually elevated him, even if unwillingly, to secretary of state.

In a moving eulogy delivered at Yorba Linda, California, on April 27, 1994—with all the living presidents (Ford, Carter, Reagan, Bush, and Clinton) in attendance—Kissinger spoke of Nixon's (and hence his) foreign policy successes. In this field, Kissinger maintained, Nixon had been a "seminal president." He contrasted the situation in 1969 and 1974:

> When Richard Nixon took his oath of office, 550,000 Americans were engaged [in Vietnam], America had no contacts with China . . . no negotiations with the Soviet Union . . . and Middle East diplomacy was stalemated . . . When Richard Nixon left office, an agreement to end the war in Vietnam had been concluded, and the main lines of all subsequent policy were established: permanent dialogue with China, readiness without illusions to ease tensions with the Soviet Union, a peace process in the Middle East, the beginning via the European Security Conference of establishing human rights as an international issue, weakening the Soviet hold on Eastern Europe.

Of course, Kissinger stretched the point of Nixon's foreign policy achievements. A balanced assessment would have been somewhat less rosy: Vietnam had hardly ended with the prospects of peace high; the dialogue with China was, at best sporadic; détente had already begun to evaporate; the Middle East process was haphazard and less than straightforward; and Nixon had expressed no interest in the European Security Conference negotiations that continued for almost a year after his resignation. But such subtleties were hardly appropriate in the context of a former president's funeral. Nor was Watergate, understandably enough, a word to be uttered out loud, except in code. As Kissinger put it, Nixon "stood on the pinnacles that dissolved in the precipice. He achieved greatly and he suffered deeply." That the achievements were partly Kissinger's doing and the suffering mostly self-inflicted by Nixon was implied.[20]

In the spring of 1994, almost coinciding with Nixon's death, Kissinger published *Diplomacy*, a massive book that became yet another best-seller. Part history, part memoir, part policy analysis and advocacy, *Diplomacy* took Kissinger back to his roots as a diplomatic historian: he commenced by examining European diplomacy in the age of Richelieu.

The main thrust of *Diplomacy* juxtaposed two early twentieth-century U.S. presidents, Theodore Roosevelt and Woodrow Wilson. While acknowledging the necessity of an idealistic element in American foreign policy, Kissinger left no doubt where his sympathies lay. Teddy's more realist approach was clearly more in tune with the former secretary of state's thinking. Not unexpectedly, when Kissinger the memoirist took over, the Nixon and Ford years emerged as the golden age of American Cold War diplomacy. Prior to the Nixon presidency, Teddy Roosevelt had been, according to Kissinger, the last chief executive to have conducted U.S. foreign policy "in the national interest." In the Nixon–Ford years—Kissinger refrained from using the first-person pronoun when discussing the 1970s—the United States moved, finally, toward a realistic appraisal of its interests and capabilities.[21]

A few years after the publication of *Diplomacy*, Kissinger finally completed the trilogy of memoirs of his time in office. Published by Simon & Schuster in 1999, *Years of Renewal* celebrated the Ford presidency as a period during which President Ford (or, more accurately, Secretary of State Kissinger) "navigated his country through a series of extraordinary events" ranging from "the conflicts in Cyprus and Lebanon to transition to majority rule in Southern Africa." Kissinger basically argued that the Ford administration had laid the groundwork for what ultimately transpired during the 1980s: a tough-nosed, but realistic approach to the Soviet Union that, eventually, paid dividends with the collapse of the USSR.[22]

An equally lengthy tome as its predecessors, *Years of Renewal* received mixed reviews. Given the passage of time, Kissinger had had the opportunity to reexamine events with greater hindsight than in *White House Years* or *Years of Upheaval*. Yet, this also made the memoir a more blatantly revisionist account. *Years of Renewal* was undoubtedly aimed as a preemptive strike against historians about to take advantage of the massive opening of new archival materials on the Nixon and Ford years (on which the present book is heavily based). It also provided another target for one of the favorite "blood sports" among scholars of American foreign policy. As the historian John Lewis Gaddis put it in his review of *Years of Renewal*, "historians are likely to regard this book as an elaborate smokescreen designed to conceal what really happened."[23]

*   *   *

While *Diplomacy* and, in particular, *Years of Renewal* were aimed at rehabilitating Kissinger's reputation, he also produced a series of contemplations about the state of American foreign policy that appeared during the 1990s. In the pages of *Newsweek* and *Foreign Affairs*, as well as in regular columns in major newspapers like the *Washington Post*, Kissinger continued to consider the major issues of the day. U.S.-China policy, the Middle East peace process during the Clinton administration, relations with the new Russia, and the state of the transatlantic alliance were all subjected to his reflections and criticism. Particularly during the Clinton years, Kissinger was often sharply critical of what he saw as an American foreign policy sorely lacking in direction and tempted by the influence of moral prerogatives. "Outrage is not a policy," Kissinger ruminated in 1997 when critics charged that the United States should be more critical of China's human rights record. A few years later, when the United States used its air power to help liberate Kosovo from the oppressive hold of Slobodan Milosevic's Yugoslavia, Kissinger worried about a "New World Disorder." In particular, he argued: "The ill-considered war in Kosovo had undermined relations with China and Russia and put NATO at risk." In January 2000, Kissinger summed up the Clinton administration's foreign policy in a simple phrase: "Our Nearsighted World Vision."[24]

Finally, in 2001, a few months prior to the September 11 terrorist attacks, Kissinger published *Does America Need a Foreign Policy?* In 300 pages, he provided a geopolitical analysis of the post–Cold War world and a critique of the Clinton administration's custodianship of U.S. foreign policy. Although clearly written as a guidebook of sorts to foreign policy makers in the post–Clinton era, Kissinger— revisiting familiar themes from his earlier writings—called for a balanced approach. Both the hyper-idealists and hyper-nationalists that Kissinger saw as dominating the debate over American policy at the dawn of the new millennium had it wrong. While the idealists tended to "treat foreign policy as social work," assuming that the United States had a democratic solution for every ill in the world, the nationalists were equally mistaken in basing their thinking on the belief that American hege-mony could be imposed to solve the world's trouble spots. Kissinger, as he had done in many of his other works, called for a balance, arguing:

> The ultimate dilemma of the statesman is to strike a balance between values and interests and, occasionally, between peace and justice. The dichotomy postulated by many between morality and interest, between idealism and realism, is one of the standard clichés of the ongoing debate over international affairs. No such stark choice is, in fact, available. Excessive "realism" produces stagnation; exces-sive "idealism" leads to crusades and eventual disillusionment.[25]

As this quote indicates, *Does America Need a Foreign Policy?* had few surprises for those familiar with Kissinger's thinking. Its impact on actual policy making was probably limited; after September 11, 2001, there was little room for balance as the United States engaged in a global struggle against terrorism, sent troops to Afghanistan, and, in 2003, attacked Iraq. Hyper-nationalism—in the way Kissinger described it—clearly ruled the day in Washington. His advice may have been sound, but unforeseen circumstances made postulations over the need to find balance between extremes less relevant to the policy makers in the Bush administration.[26]

*   *   *

Indeed, Kissinger's latest memoir did little to preempt the merciless attacks of scholars and journalists. His somewhat somber defense of the Ford administra-tion's record was not enough to counter the critics who, in the late 1990s, were finally gaining access to the original documents of the Kissinger years. Nor did

Kissinger's 2003 book, *Ending the Vietnam War,* make the many journalists who considered him a war criminal change their minds.[27]

"ON TRIAL"

The two men who have been the most prominent in arguing, consistently, that Kissinger was neither a master of geopolitics nor a decent human being are Seymour Hersh and Christopher Hitchens. Both are prolific authors whose reputations have been based, in large part, on critical assessments of high-profile public figures. Their respective works on Kissinger fit into a broader framework of exposing abuses of power, hypocrisy, and other failings of leadership.

Of the two, Hersh had been a constant scourge already throughout Kissinger's years in office; he was also the more widely respected of the two as a journalist and analyst of foreign policy. In 1970, Hersh had received the Pulitzer Prize for international reporting, for his work in exposing the My Lai massacre in Vietnam. He had received his second (out of four) George Polk Awards in 1974 for reporting on the secret bombing of Cambodia. In late 1974, Hersh's reports about the CIA's domestic activities prompted, in part, the Church Committee's subsequent investigations into intelligence activities. Then, in 1983, only a year after Kissinger published the *Years of Upheaval,* Hersh's critical assessment of Kissinger's role in the Nixon White House hit the bookshelves, earning him the National Book Critics Circle Award.

Hersh's book *The Price of Power: Kissinger in the Nixon White House* was instantly dubbed the "Kissinger anti-memoirs" by Stanley Hoffmann in a July 1983 review. Although Hoffman did not give *The Price of Power* a ringing endorsement, Kissinger became furious at his former colleague (and rival) for not trashing the book. For months he raged about Hersh's "slimy lies" and even hired researchers to check Hersh's footnotes. Clearly a nerve had been touched.

Based on hundreds of interviews, *The Price of Power* laid out the basic points of criticism that, over the next two decades, clouded Kissinger's reputation. In essence, the former secretary of state was revealed in all his most negative characteristics: secretive, manipulative, "realist" to a fault, and deceitful. Hersh burrowed into the controversies over Vietnam and Cambodia, provided a detailed account of Kissinger's consolidation of power, criticized his secretive China policy, and went into great length about the Nixon administration's efforts to get rid of Salvador Allende in Chile, concluding that Kissinger was motivated in his anti-Allende actions by "his need to please the President and dominate the bureaucracy and his belief that no action to stop the spread of communism was immoral."[28] Although he ended the 600+ page book with the 1972 Christmas bombings, Hersh's portrayal would stand as the counterweight to Kissinger's memoirs—at least to the first volume of them— for decades. He ended with the following, largely accurate assessment:

Nixon and Kissinger remained blind to the human costs of their actions—a further price of power. The dead and maimed in Vietnam and Cambodia—as in Chile, Bangladesh, Biafra, and the Middle East—seemed not to count as the President and his national security adviser battled the Soviet Union, their misconceptions, their political enemies, and each other.[29]

Whatever Kissinger thought of it, *The Price of Power* was as solid an antidote to the view of Kissinger as the realpolitik genius as the secretary state's own memoirs had portrayed him. In particular, Hersh, in the best tradition of investigative reporters, had effectively exposed the human costs of Kissinger and Nixon's policies. No wonder he won the National Book Critics Circle Award in General Non-Fiction and the book was named the Best Book of the Year by *The New York Times Book Review*, *Newsweek* and the *San Francisco Chronicle*. It was, in short, a major success.

*   *   *

For the next two decades Hersh's book did, as Hoffman had indicated in his review, provide the basic counterweight to Kissinger's memoirs. It may have been one of the factors that caused Kissinger not to publish his third tome until fifteen years after *The Price of Power*. Rather than rousing up controversy and exposing himself to further charges, perhaps it was better to keep a low profile.

But the trick of time meant that a trickle of documentary evidence, enabling historians and journalists to assess the Nixon–Kissinger record in detail, started turning into a flood in the second half of the 1990s. Helped by numerous Freedom of Information Act requests spearheaded by the Washington-based National Security Archives (NSA) and the Clinton administration's decision to relax classification rules, old charges began to reappear. Several critical books on the Vietnam War, reassessments of the secretive China diplomacy of the Nixon–Kissinger–Ford years, and a collection of transcripts edited by NSA's William Burr foreshadowed a reinvigoration of Kissinger scholarship in the new millennium.[30]

Then, in 2001, Christopher Hitchens published *The Trial of Henry Kissinger*.

Hitchens's 150-page book was as inflammatory as its title suggested. Kissinger, Hitchens argued, had seemingly single-handedly—with some necessary support from Nixon and Ford—engineered a series of proxy massacres and underhanded political deals. With his considerable talent for engaging prose, Hitchens charged the former secretary of state for, among other crimes, engineering Nixon's electoral victory in 1968 by promoting the continuation of the Vietnam War; ordering and directing the secret bombing of Cambodia and creating a situation in that country that allowed the murderous regime of Pol Pot to seize control; assuring the downfall of Salvador Allende in Chile and the installing of the military dictatorship that followed; and giving a green light to the Indonesian invasion of East Timor in late 1975. Kissinger was the prince of darkness, a war criminal on the loose. In 2002, when the BBC released a documentary based on Hitchens's book, the charges reached even wider audiences.

The arguments and conclusions in *The Trial of Henry Kissinger* were clearly pre-conceived and very much in line with the tenor of Hersh's 1983 book. But although Hitchens's specific target was, like Hersh's, Kissinger, he also went after what he, rightly so, considers the uneven and hypocritical application of universal jurisdiction. In a broad sense, Hitchens called for Americans to acknowledge that many of their leaders had committed immoral acts that resulted in the deaths of thousands and not allow them to argue that any act committed while in high office was, in effect, immune to prosecution. Kissinger was a case study. The book—and the film—was not a trial but, in effect, the case for the prosecution. As Hitchens put it:

> Many if not most of Kissinger's partners in crime are now in jail, or are awaiting trial, or have been otherwise punished or discredited. His own lonely impunity is rank; it smells to heaven. If it is allowed to persist then we shall shamefully vindicate the ancient philosopher Anacharsis, who maintained that laws were like cobwebs: strong enough to detain only the weak, and too weak to hold the strong. In the name of innumerable victims known and unknown, it is time for justice to take a hand.[31]

According to Hitchens, the victims of Kissinger's statecraft included those who perished in Indochina as a result of the Nixon administration decision to prolong the war when it first came to office (this included 20,000 American GIs), to bomb and invade Cambodia in 1969–70 (and continue bombing the country until 1973), to arm the South Vietnamese and bomb the North. There were the millions of Bengalis who died as a result of mistaken action during the Indo-Pakistani conflict of 1971. There was the CIA-abetted killing of General Schneider of Chile in 1970 and the policies that followed that would lead to the deaths of thousands in the aftermath of the 1973 coup against Salvador Allende. And there was the green light given to the Indonesian invasion of East Timor in late 1975 that ultimately resulted in the deaths of at least 100,000 East Timorese. All told, Kissinger's policies resulted, as Hitchens argues, in the deaths of hundreds of thousands, perhaps millions, of innocent civilians.

After exploring the documentary record in the previous chapters of this book on these issues, it seems difficult to deny the charges. Kissinger did support the secret bombing and invasion of Cambodia, he did pursue a pro-Pakistani policy during the Indo-Pakistani crisis, he did politely nod when Suharto told Kissinger and Ford that an invasion of East Timor was about to be unleashed. Yet, one is left wondering whether it is Kissinger or American Cold War policy at large that should be on trial? Were Kissinger's actions, perhaps, mere symptoms of a warped mentality that devalued human life and allowed policy makers to make numerous costly decisions in the name of national security and a global struggle against communism? Were the decisions taken with full knowledge of their impact?

Take, for example, the secret bombing of Cambodia and its broader context, the Vietnam War. What was at stake in 1969? As incredible as it may seem from today's perspective, most in the Nixon administration—and surely the president him-self—believed in the notion of peace through strength. A permanent division of Vietnam remained a goal, one that had been inherited from the Johnson adminis-tration. Another goal of the Nixon administration was to withdraw American troops from South Vietnam without handing Saigon over to Hanoi. The Ho Chi Minh Trail that ran through the eastern part of Cambodia was a major threat to both of these goals: it was the main infiltration route for men and materials from the North to the South and was used as a base for attacks on both American and South Vietnamese troops. To attack it made military sense and the United States was, after all, still in a war. Moreover, it is hard to see what was the desire for "domes-tic and personal profit" that Hitchens argues lay behind Kissinger's support for the expansion of the war to Cambodia (and Laos). If anything, the secret bombings and the invasions of Cambodia and Laos in 1970 and 1971 resulted in a severe domestic backlash (as described earlier in this book).[32]

None of this excuses the carnage and the deaths of civilians. Yet, if put into per-spective, the real problem—the true crime—was that neither Kissinger nor Nixon truly changed American strategies in Indochina to reflect the situation in the area itself. Afraid of losing the war, they continued to bomb (secretly and openly), they continued to employ clandestine counter-guerrilla terror operations—the so-called Phoenix program—aimed at pacifying South Vietnamese countryside. The death toll on their watch was close to 30,000 Americans, more than 80,000 South Vietnamese soldiers, and perhaps as many as half a million others (North Viet-namese soldiers and civilians, NLF guerrillas, Cambodian and Laotian civilians). Could these have been avoided? Perhaps, although the nature of the future rulers of, say, Cambodia, hardly offers an image of a peaceful transition in Indochina after the American exit. We will, of course, never know for sure. In the end, though, one conclusion is fairly certain: if Cold War idealism had led America to its disillu-sioning engagement in Vietnam in the 1960s, Cold War realism—as practiced by Kissinger—offered ultimately no better alternative. In both cases, American lead-ers appear to have been anesthetized to the human suffering they caused. And that, surely, calls for even a broader indictment than the one Hitchens is arguing for.

The case of East Timor is equally disturbing if vastly different in its circum-stances. To begin with, the events in question are completely omitted from Kissinger's memoirs; they have been "airbrushed," as Hitchens puts it. As has been discussed earlier in this book, Kissinger and Ford did nod politely when Indone-sian President Suharto told them in December 1975 that his troops were ready for an invasion of East Timor. The invasion in fact started while Kissinger and Ford flew from Jakarta to Hawaii on December 7, 1975. The United States was Indone-sia's major arms supplier but the Congress had stipulated that American arms could be used only for self-defense. And, as Kissinger's meeting with his staff on December 18, 1975, indicates, he was seriously concerned that something illegal had taken place and that it would leak and cause him problems. Most important, the

Indonesian invasion resulted in a death toll of at least 50,000 civilians by mid-1977 and perhaps more than 200,000 by the late 1990s when the conflict was finally approaching its conclusion.[33]

Yet again, one can argue that American support for Suharto followed a certain— immoral and misconceived—logic. In late 1975 the domino theory appeared more real than perhaps at any time during the Cold War. South Vietnam, Laos, and Cambodia had all fallen under communist control in the spring of 1975. The Ford administration was clearly concerned about Soviet activities in Africa, particularly in Angola. However, Kissinger still clung to the Nixon Doctrine, the idea that strong regional allies would maintain stability in various parts of the world. In Southeast Asia, South Vietnam had been such an ally; its collapse had created a vacuum that Indonesia, the most populated country in the region, might well fill. Moreover, Suharto himself was capable at playing this particular game: he had told Ford already in July 1975 that his main goal was to combat communism; later he consistently (if mistakenly) described the independence movement in East Timor (FRETILIN) as communist-dominated.

In short, there is no excuse for Kissinger's conduct vis-à-vis East Timor. But again, perhaps the indictment should be broader and Kissinger's flippant attitude toward the fate of the East Timorese civilians be viewed as resulting from two interrelated factors. First, there was a mistaken and simplistic foreign policy architecture (the Nixon Doctrine and the domino theory) that, in true realist fashion, did not necessitate deep thinking about the nature of the regime that the United States was supporting (i.e. Suharto's Indonesia). Second, there was an unwillingness to question Suharto's arguments about the communist nature of the East Timorese independence movement because, in the context of 1975, such claims appeared to ring true given the recent events in Indochina. Indeed, as Kissinger himself has admitted, to him and Ford, East Timor was just "a little speck of an island in a huge archipelago."

The last point is grounds for, of course, repeating one of the central points of the present book. Simply put: there were real people, hundreds of thousands of them, living on that "little speck of an island." But Kissinger had little interest in them, because they were ultimately mere pawns within the framework of his overall foreign policy architecture. Morality may be an impossible compass for statesmanship. But realism clearly offered its own type of disillusionment and disappointment. That, ultimately, is the fundamental point of the criticism that Hersh and Hitchens so abundantly have weighed upon Kissinger.

The publication of *The Trial of Henry Kissinger* clearly rekindled the ongoing debate about the former secretary of state's reputation. Many applauded Hitchens. One reviewer called it a welcome "beginning of a new and honest assessment of Kissinger's uncomfortable place in American life." *The Village Voice*, with reference to former Yugoslav president on trial at the International Court at The Hague, even dubbed Kissinger "Manhattan's Milosevic." But others went on the defensive. Conrad Black, for example, called Hitchens a "Stalinist."[34]

What about Kissinger himself? Publicly, he has essentially refused to comment on Hitchens and his book, perhaps on the theory that acknowledging that the charges had been made would give them some legitimacy. Yet, Kissinger hardly overlooked the charges and the eagerness with which so many were ready to put him on trial. A disturbing reminder of this occurred in the spring of 2001, when a judge in Paris sent officials to the Ritz hotel, to serve a summons for the former secretary of state to appear in his chambers to answer questions about American involvement in Chile in the 1970s. Judges in Argentina, Spain, and elsewhere—all countries whose nationals had disappeared during the early stages of the Pinochet regime when Kissinger oversaw the normalization of American-Chilean relations after the overthrow of Salvador Allende—announced they were about to make similar demands. Kissinger declined to oblige and there was little any foreign court could do to force him do otherwise.[35]

But Kissinger, never able to take criticism lightly, was clearly in need of some form of repudiation.

"HE'S BA-A-ACK!"

Traveling in Germany at the time of the September 11 terrorist attacks, Kissinger briefly offered his comments, by phone, on CNN, stressing that the Bush administration needed to take rapid retaliatory action. By September 17, 2001, he was on CNN with journalist Paula Zahn, contemplating the next moves of the Bush administration in a brusque manner. Going after the Taliban in Afghanistan and the al-Qaeda camps there was a necessary first step in the Bush administration's response Kissinger maintained. As to further moves that the administration might take, he contemplated: "I don't think we have to attack Syria because Syria will close down these [terrorist] camps if they are brought under enough pressure." Kissinger then added: "Iraq, I would be open-minded on. If they have ties to any of these terrorist networks, they should be attacked."[36]

Given subsequent developments, Kissinger was clearly on the same wavelength with the Bush administration. Thus, it was hardly anomalous that, on November 27, 2002, the president announced that Kissinger would be the chairman of the bipartisan 9–11 Commission.

Although the nomination eventually led to controversy, many of the initial comments were cautiously positive. "Our position: Having Henry Kissinger Lead the 9–11 Panel will give it the Credibility it Deserves," headlined the *Orlando Sentinel* on December 1. "A very good choice," offered Sandy Berger, President Bill Clinton's national security adviser, in an interview with the *New York Times*. "A really smart choice," agreed Walter Isaacson, whose 1992 critical biography of Kissinger had led to a lengthy break in their relationship. The chairman and chief executive officer of CNN at the time, Isaacson added that the former secretary of state had "both an appreciation and a healthy skepticism of American intelligence." Later, as criticism of Kissinger started to mount, Isaacson acknowledged that Kissinger's "greatest weakness" was a penchant for secrecy, but stressed that Kissinger's own worldview was far more "nuanced than the for-us-or-against-us approach that the Bush administration, in rhetoric if not always in practice, has promoted." Most important, Isaacson argued that Kissinger "is capable of being analytically brilliant and intellectually honest, even brutally so" and was optimistic that Kissinger understood "that it is now in the nation's interest, and his own, to apply that analytic rigor with an unflinching candor." The 9–11 Commission was, after all, Kissinger's chance to "burnish his reputation for history."[37]

William Safire, a former colleague from the Nixon administration, agreed. He thought that Kissinger's long experience in government would be a useful asset in circumventing any bureaucratic attempts at concealing intelligence failures leading up to 9–11. Safire derided the "hate-Henry industry" for bringing up age-old complaints about the Vietnam War and argued that Kissinger was well equipped to discover the problems and recommend changes in U.S. intelligence community. Safire did not accept the argument that Kissinger was either willing to cover up mistakes or would allow himself to be misled by alleged conflicts of interest arising from his business contacts. "He is working for his historic reputation now, not his clients," Safire wrote. Abroad, Fraser Nelson of *The Scotsman* explained the opposition to Kissinger's appointment in somewhat similar terms: "The desire to do something about Henry Kissinger is a popular pursuit for many; for some, an obsession. He is the enemy, for reasons many of them obvious: he is a Harvard intellectual who served Richard Nixon intimately, and survived with honor."[38]

The *Seattle Post-Intelligencer* thought that "Kissinger probably regards leadership of the commission as one of his final opportunities to be of service to the country," a sentiment shared by Lee Hamilton, the former Democratic congressman from Indiana who, after the original choice, former Democratic Senator George Mitchell resigned (two days before Kissinger), eventually ended up as the 9-11 Commission's vice chairman.[39]

*   *   *

Ultimately, the criticism outweighed the defenses. The first act took place on the December 1 Sunday morning news shows. On NBC's "Meet the Press," Senator John Kerry (D-Massachusetts)—a soon-to-be Democratic presidential candidate, raised the issue that ultimately brought about Kissinger's detraction. "I think it is going to be extraordinarily important for Dr. Kissinger to prove to the nation that he comes to this without any linkages that could remain suspect," Kerry stressed, referring to the business contacts of Kissinger Associates. Kissinger defended himself on CNN's "Late Edition," telling Wolf Blitzer that he would sever relations to any clients that might be perceived as creating a conflict of interest and assuring that he would never "permit a foreign government to affect my judgment." When Blitzer referred to a sharply critical editorial in the *New York Times*, Kissinger snapped. The *Times* "will apologize for this editorial when our report is submitted," he assured.[40]

In the editorial—titled "He's Ba-a-ck!"—Maureen Dowd had been acid. "If you want to get to the bottom of something you don't appoint Henry Kissinger. If you want to keep others from getting to the bottom of something, you appoint Henry Kissinger," she had written. Neither Dowd, nor the *New York Times*, would apologize.

In the end, it was not Kissinger's client list that got the 'hate-Henry' industry going; it was his record in the Nixon and Ford administrations that did the job. "Kissinger's shady record is a bad omen for his new record," Clarence Page of the *Chicago Tribune* noted on December 1, the same day as Kissinger defended his record with Blitzer. "From Cambodia to Chile," Page added, Kissinger's career has been "widely reviled." Others joined in. "A September 11 Investigator Brings a Lot of Baggage," one headline pronounced on December 3. "An appalling choice," a columnist wrote in the *Los Angeles Times* the same day. Throughout the two weeks between his nomination and resignation, newspapers and Internet sites filled up with accusations and outrages. "Grand Canyon-size discrepancy between man and job," Mary McGrory opined in the *Washington Post* on December 5.[41]

Even as negative criticism mounted, Tim Rutton of the *Los Angeles Times* complained that the media had been too nice to Kissinger. "Kissinger kiss-up," Rutton's editorial pronounced on December 5. Investigative reports on Kissinger's past and present abuses of power, secret dealings, and other infractions are "conspicuously missing" he argued. Syndicated columnist Helen Thomas, who had been part of Kissinger's traveling press corps during the years of shuttle diplomacy in the Middle East, was quick to pick up the charge. "President Bush must have been kidding when he named Kissinger," Thomas wrote. "It is difficult to imagine anyone in the country fonder of operating in secrecy, more protective of the government establishment and less forthright in many of his past activities," she added. Should Kissinger produce a reliable and forthright report, Thomas added, it would constitute "one of the greatest role reversals ever."

Columnist Molly Ivins summed up the negative perception in similar terms: "Good grief. I turn my back for 10 minutes and they bring back the old War Criminal."[42]

Given the criticism it was no wonder that Kissinger finally turned down the chairmanship of the 9–11 Commission. Thomas Kean, former New Jersey governor and president of Drew University, became the chairman; Lee Hamilton, director of the Woodrow Wilson International Center for Scholars and a former Democratic congressman from Indiana had already been named the new vice chairman after Mitchell's exit. The 9–11 Commission controversy was over and quickly became a footnote in history as the Bush administration geared up for its war against Iraq.

In retrospect, the episode was hardly surprising. For while Kissinger remained, a quarter century after he had left office, the most high-profile of the many former secretaries of state, he was also the most controversial. Indeed, the two-week saga that ended with Kissinger's letter to President George W. Bush explaining the reasons for the decision was an example of Kissinger's unique and multifaceted status among retired American statesmen. While in office, he had been the most publicized American diplomat during the Cold War, perhaps even during the history of the United States. Out of office, Kissinger maintained an unprecedented level of name recognition and influence. Yet, both while in office and during his postgovernment career, Kissinger was and remained a subject of heightened scrutiny.

KISSINGER AT EIGHTY

Despite being out of office for a quarter century and notwithstanding the repeated controversies over his alleged conflicts of interest and past policies, Kissinger, celebrating his eightieth birthday on May 27, 2003, remained a player in more ways than one. He continued to write columns and appear on the news, his consulting business showed no sign of slowing down, and his links to the business and political elites in the United States and abroad remained intact.

It was a feat like no other. Yet, Kissinger's reputation remained tarnished by a past record that was becoming intensely scrutinized as previously classified records were opened, while questions about conflicts of interest related to his dual role as the head of a consulting firm and an integral member of the United States' foreign policy elite continued to be raised. In particular, there was the unlikeliest of accusations: that the man whose family had escaped genocide in 1938 was responsible, because of his policies while in office, for the acts of U.S. and foreign governments that had resulted in the deaths of innocent men and women. Even as the likelihood was limited that Kissinger would actually have to appear in a courtroom somewhere in the world to testify of his activities during the 1970s, Kissinger remained, more or less permanently, on trial. In 2003 he published two books—*Ending the Vietnam War* and *Crisis* (which focused mostly on the October 1973 Middle East War)—that were aimed at refurbishing his battered reputation and preempting some of the inevitable swipes that the historians of the twenty-first century, with their enhanced access to new sources, were likely to take.[43]

In short, the dichotomy that had appeared in the early 1970s when Kissinger first became a household name persisted. To many, he was the respected, if somewhat out-of-date, super-diplomat: the man who had opened China and navigated American foreign policy through a tumultuous period in its history and had then turned into a thoughtful commentator on international relations. To others, Kissinger remained the prince of darkness: the villain who got away when other top Nixon administration officials were purged and who had, since the early 1980s, amassed a sizeable fortune by capitalizing on his unparalleled access to American and foreign leaders.

Both critics and defenders would probably agree on one fact: whether he was guilty of war crimes or simply a statesman who had pursued his country's national interest with secretive methods, Kissinger had escaped the fate of most of his predecessors. He had never become even close to irrelevant. And that, ultimately, was why he was such an attractive target of critics and why he was so vehemently defended by his supporters.

His place in history, though, remains to be determined.

Conclusion

The Flawed Architect

"History," Henry Kissinger told Richard Nixon on the eve of the president's resignation in August 1974, "will treat you more kindly than your contemporaries have." He was correct in this assessment. Over the years the fiction that the Watergate scandal had been but a third-rate burglary gradually took hold. By the time of his death in 1994, Nixon's achievements, particularly in the field of foreign policy, dominated the historical assessments of the only president in the nation's history to have resigned. In an amazing recovery, showing his curious political acumen, Nixon had spent twenty years in running for ex-president. And he had, apparently, succeeded. Even Oliver Stone's (1995) movie *Nixon* portrayed the ex-president as a tragic, rather than a criminal, figure.

Ironically, the opposite seems to have been the case with Kissinger. While journalists had tended to fawn on Kissinger during his time in office, Super-K has become a favorite target for historians and journalists. Over time, his reputation suffered, and his conduct in office was questioned for substantive as well as coincidental reasons. The image of a war criminal came to replace, at least for some, that of a globetrotting super diplomat, the notion that Kissinger's main concern was his own glorification rather than the pursuit of a vision of American national interest permeated the writings of many. If Nixon's reputation was resuscitated, Kissinger's aura gradually evaporated.

Historical reputations have, of course, a contingent quality. Men and policies that may seem reasonable and carefully thought out one day are often judged as mistaken or shortsighted the next (or vice versa). "Each generation"—the facile but nevertheless largely accurate law of historiography goes—"will write its own history." Our interpretations of the past are irrevocably linked to our understanding of the present.

That obvious fact notwithstanding, it seems appropriate to consider, by way of conclusion, Kissinger's place in the history of American foreign policy from the vantage point of early 2004, when many of the issues he dealt while in office—most obviously the Cold War—are no longer with us.

What were his major achievements and shortcomings? How should one ultimately judge the actions of a realist in an age that seems so different from ours, an age that was besieged by Cold War rivalries and an overriding fear of a nuclear holocaust?

*   *   *

It is, in fact, the absence of the Cold War that makes many of Kissinger's policies appear somewhat mystifying today. Given the collapse of the Soviet Union less than fifteen years after Kissinger left office, it seems that his relentless pursuit of détente with the USSR, a nation we now know was already moving toward its demise, was based on a mistaken assumption that the Cold War would provide the basic structure of international relations for decades to come. He may have been correct about the need to constrain the Soviet Union's appetite for third world adventurism (as was evident in his reaction to the Angolan crisis), but Kissinger clearly overestimated Moscow's ability to withstand such costs in the long term.

And yet, Kissinger was hardly an exception to the rule. One searches in vain for the statesman or scholar who, in the 1970s, would have predicted the events of 1989–91. If anything, at the time Henry Kissinger took office in early 1969, U.S. foreign policy—with the Vietnam War as the major symptom—was in a deeply troubled state. Kissinger effectively argued that America had overstretched and needed to cut back its commitments without jeopardizing its central goal of containing Soviet power. Under Richard Nixon he then proceeded to change the methods of fighting the Cold War. Instead of military interventions and nation-building—the staples of American Cold War policy in the 1950s and 1960s—there was creative diplomacy vis-à-vis the Soviet Union and China, and search for strong regional allies.

This was all reasonable. Kissinger was responding to the challenges of his time and did so in a manner that, at least in principle, was logical. He took advantage of many opportunities, most obviously the Sino-Soviet split, to try and restore the United States' position as the central player in international relations that it had, arguably, lost in the late 1960s. Triangular diplomacy and détente were the central elements of this new approach to fighting the Cold War.

But what, exactly, was Kissinger's role in implementing the new strategy? Was he simply a messenger boy, implementing the decisions of the true mastermind, Richard Nixon? Was this a co-presidency as far as foreign policy was concerned? Or did Kissinger, in fact, run the show by carefully manipulating the president?

From his first day as president, Nixon depended on Kissinger. Already during the transition period and the early months of the Nixon administration, it was the newly appointed national security adviser who helped the president to clarify a clear foreign policy agenda. In subsequent years, Kissinger's role in the breakthroughs with the People's Republic of China and with the USSR was central, not incidental. Over time, as Nixon became mired in Watergate, Kissinger took charge and managed, among other issues, to place the United States into a central position in the resolution of the 1973 Middle East War. Many of these successes ultimately depended heavily on Kissinger's negotiation skills.

Such success, however, was built by methods of operation that appear—as much in 2004 as they did in 1974—highly questionable and ultimately counterproductive. While Kissinger's acknowledgment that there were limits to American power, so evident in light of the Vietnam War, and a need to embark on creative approaches to the United States main adversary, the Soviet Union, one is left baffled by the proliferation of back channels, stunned by the obsession over leaks of information, and incensed by the bureaucratic maneuvering that accomplished the centralization of foreign policy making in Kissinger's hands. To be sure, Nixon was ultimately responsible for minimizing the role of such men as William Rogers. But Kissinger was more than eager to cooperate. Justifying the secrecy by the argument that large bureaucracies such as the State Department were prone to inertia may have made some sense. But to launch U.S. foreign policy on a new course with secret methods created a long-term problem. While the breakthroughs made good headlines, they provided a poor base for building broad domestic support for such policies as détente.

The secrecy so deeply embedded within the Byzantine Nixon White House—an atmosphere Kissinger did not create but certainly manipulated and profited from—ultimately exploded in the worst domestic crisis since the Civil War. And Watergate did change everything. It eroded Nixon's power base and his interest in foreign policy. It created an atmosphere in which it was increasingly difficult to conduct foreign policy via back channels, the trademark of Kissinger's operational methods during the first Nixon administration. Watergate, in short, proved the close linkage between foreign and domestic politics that, starting in 1973, complicated Kissinger's policy making. His major achievement as secretary of state came early on, during his 1973–74 forays to the Middle East.

In fact, one of the ironies of Kissinger's career was that he achieved the pinnacle of his influence at the same time as the scrutiny of the executive branch became the most popular pastime of American politicians and journalists. By September 1973 the clout of the presidency vis-à-vis the Congress was already greatly diminished, a fact of life that did not change after Nixon resigned and Gerald Ford took over. Kissinger's complaints about the difficulties of running foreign policy in such a charged political climate were not entirely off the mark.

But blaming "the McGovernite Congress" for the shortcomings of the Ford administration's foreign policy record is neither a satisfactory explanation nor the entire story. For Kissinger's critics—then and now—had a point. The most admired man in America had his flaws. Some very serious ones.

There was the domineering, scheming, at times almost paranoid personality. Kissinger was a volcano that threatened to erupt; when State Department officials complained that he did not give them enough leeway to make decisions, Kissinger's reply was telling. He would allow such leeway only once he was sure that the officials fully understood his thinking; that they were on his wavelength. Many, it is clear, never reached that frequency. Indeed, as a boss, Kissinger was demanding but also too often demeaning. He could elicit the best from many, but drive others to resign (and turn into critics). As a co-worker he was competitive. He could be charming at one point and stab you in the back the next. He would be respectful toward his superiors and funny with the journalists. But he could also make snide and deprecating comments about the presidents he served and rant and rave about the idiocy of the American media.

For a man with a reputation for realism, he was incredibly human.

Perhaps most of all, there was the famously thin skin that would—although Kissinger would probably be the last one to accept it—only encourage critics. While Kissinger became accustomed to using self-deprecating humor, one searches in vain for admissions of much more than "tactical mistakes." Blame for obvious failures lay elsewhere, with the Congress, the power-hungry bureaucracy, the untrustworthy foreign leader.

Kissinger's sensitivity to criticism translated, in the years after 1977, to a sustained effort at spinning future history books to reflect his version of events. A good example of Kissinger's selective reading of history was an interview on August 10, 2003, with Wolf Blitzer of CNN's "Late Edition." Kissinger was plugging his latest book, *Crisis,* which provided detailed analyses of his response to the October 1973 War and the April 1975 collapse of South Vietnam. The book was based on Kissinger's previously classified telephone conversations and portrayed, in minute-by-minute detail, a secretary of state under siege from various quarters but maintaining his cool. The most revealing comment Kissinger made in his interview with Blitzer was his explanation for choosing these two particular crises. The October War, Kissinger said, was an example of a crisis that was, or that he, handled successfully. The collapse of Saigon, however, constituted a "tragedy." Not a failure, a tragedy.

Of course, the collapse of Saigon and the coinciding events in Cambodia were an immense tragedy. But Vietnam also represented a failure that revealed a basic conceptual flaw in Kissinger's approach to foreign policy. In essence, Vietnam showed that it was impossible to find solutions to complex regional problems without active involvement with the local players. Improved Sino-American or Soviet-American relations and the application of triangular diplomacy were essentially irrelevant in determining the ultimate fate of Vietnam.

But Kissinger's comment also reflected his hierarchical worldview. To him, the countries that truly mattered were the Soviet Union and China. Of course, he differentiated between them: while the Soviets were adversaries to be outmaneuvered, the Chinese were potential allies to be wooed. But other players—the Vietnamese, the Europeans, the Angolans, the Chileans, the Indonesians, the East Timorese, the Indians, the Pakistanis, the Bengalis, the Arabs, and the Israelis—were ultimately pawns in a bigger game that revolved around an ultimately futile search for international stability through the application of détente and triangular diplomacy.

The flaws thus extended far beyond the quirky personality of the man or his inability to connect with domestic audiences. While Kissinger's recognition of the limits of American power was a healthy departure from the previous administrations' overextension, his overall emphasis on the "great powers" blinded him to the specific local circumstances that determined the course of the numerous regional conflicts the Nixon and Ford administrations encountered. More specifically, Kissinger's efforts in China, Vietnam, Angola, the Middle East, South Asia, and Europe were all calculated within the context of the U.S. relationship and rivalry with the Soviet Union. His approach, ultimately and inexorably, thus reflected the Cold War logic so prevalent in Washington at the time. While the means for pursuing the long twilight struggle were less militaristic and more diplomatic, they were also less open and more covert. But the basic thinking behind Kissinger's policies were neither revolutionary nor particularly far-sighted.

*   *   *

Ultimately, an assessment of Henry Kissinger would be incomplete without considering the relationship between morality and foreign policy.

The general consensus has always been that Kissinger had a conception of American national interest that left no room for idealism and was rabidly devoid of moral content. It seems that Kissinger's record proves the point. How else could he have justified his policies toward the Soviet Union and China or conspired in the secret bombing of Cambodia? What else but a callous attitude could account for his ability to countenance the human costs of some of his policies in the various regional crises, such as the Indo-Pakistani conflict of 1971 or the Angolan civil war? What else could have been behind his seemingly inexplicable ability to negotiate with both the Israelis and the many Arab leaders than a cool, calculating mind that did not let his personal background interfere?

In fact, Kissinger's thinking was not as rigid as a superficial analysis might suggest. He was critical of moral crusaders (whether on the left or the right of the political spectrum) not because they were wrong, but because moral absolutes, when used as guidelines for foreign policy, had a poor track record. Yet, he would not argue that realism offered any panacea either. As Kissinger pondered in 2001:

> The ultimate dilemma of the statesman is to strike a balance between values and interests and, occasionally, between peace and justice. The dichotomy postulated by many between morality and interest, between idealism and realism, is one of

the standard clichés of the ongoing debate over international affairs. No such stark choice is, in fact, available. Excessive 'realism' produces stagnation; excessive 'idealism' leads to crusades and eventual disillusionment.[1]

Such statements had permeated Kissinger's public addresses—the so-called heartland speeches—in 1975–76. America should not choose between realism and idealism but fuse the two.

Few today would argue against such postulations. As Les Gelb and Justine Rosenthal wrote in a 2003 article in *Foreign Affairs*:

> We have passed from an era in which ideals were always flatly opposed to self-interests to an era in which tension remains between the two, but the stark juxtaposition of the past has largely subsided. Now, ideals and self-interests are both generally considered necessary ingredients of the national interest.[2]

So was Kissinger ahead of his times? Not exactly. The trouble is that while Kissinger's public speeches often recognized the need for idealistic content in the running of U.S. foreign policy, much of his record while in office suggests that he was very much the hard-nosed realist. There are the bombings that resulted in the deaths of civilian populations in Indochina. There is no question that the Nixon administration meddled in the internal affairs of Chile and that Kissinger and Ford politely nodded when Indonesian President Suharto told them that he was about to send his army into the former Portuguese colony of East Timor. Humanitarian considerations had little impact on such decisions.

But even if the cases of Cambodia, Chile, East Timor, and others are indications of an immoral realpolitik at play, do they confirm the charge that Kissinger is, in effect, a war criminal on the loose?

As abhorrent as they appear today, before passing such firm judgment, one needs to, yet again, consider the contexts in which the decisions were taken.

The bombing of enemy targets that were the source of numerous attacks against American forces—even if the bombings resulted, as they did, in the deaths of civilians (collateral damage in today's horrendous parlance)—can also be considered a legitimate military strategy. Such bombing further destabilized Cambodia and may have improved the Khmer Rouge's ascendancy. But it did not, alone, cause the rise of Pol Pot's murderous regime; many other factors, including the role of the North Vietnamese, the Chinese, and the Soviets in Cambodia need to be considered to fully fathom the killing fields. Moreover, such bombings would never have occurred without the authority of the commander-in-chief, President Nixon. While Kissinger had emerged as immensely influential in the spring of 1969, he was not, at the time, Super-K. Nixon remained firmly in charge. It is also important to note that covert operations to prevent an undesirable political change within the

Western Hemisphere were hardly an invention of the Nixon administration; economic pressure aimed at reversing such a political change even less so. On East Timor, when President Suharto briefed Ford and Kissinger on the invasion, he had already amassed his troops; the strike did not depend on the Americans' approval. Suharto was not asking for permission, he was giving advanced warning.

Thus, as unfashionable as it may be, this author does not consider Henry Kissinger a war criminal. In fact, most of Kissinger's time in office was not spent in waging war but pursuing peace and forging settlements, whether it was nuclear arms agreements with the USSR, opening a relationship with the Chinese, mediating an end to the October War in the Middle East, or even trying to negotiate a settlement in Vietnam. His field was diplomacy and negotiation.

Indeed, if Henry Kissinger can be categorized as a war criminal then most American foreign policy makers during the Cold War would fit that category. Think of, for example, the Truman administration using the CIA to influence elections in Italy in the 1940s; the Eisenhower administration orchestrating coup d'etats in Iran and Guatemala in the 1950s; the Kennedy administration's policies vis-à-vis Cuba, the Congo, or Vietnam in the early 1960s; Lyndon Johnson and the Gulf of Tonkin or the invasion of the Dominican Republic in the mid-1960s; Reagan's shenanigans with Iran and Central America in the early 1980s. One could compile a far longer list of unsavory conduct for any U.S. administration before or after Kissinger was in office.

Does this fact justify all of his actions? Absolutely not. If anything, a study of Kissinger's custodianship of American foreign policy is ultimately one of disappointment.

It is disappointing to find that Kissinger found it so difficult to break with the same mistaken traditions of other American Cold Warriors whose policies he often criticized. Moreover, it is sad—if hardly surprising—to find that Kissinger, who repeatedly talked about the inevitable dispersion of power, seems to have spent very little time considering the negative long-term consequences of his policies in the areas of the world where that power was being dispersed to. Nor did he ultimately have a much better understanding of the underlying forces that were shaping the direction of international relations in the 1970s. He held fast with the assumption that the Soviet Union was and would remain America's primary foreign policy nemesis. Everything was predicated to meet that challenge and the consequences were predictable: dictators were supported in the third world and grassroots movements for human rights and independence were by and large ignored as inconsequential.

Ultimately, what Kissinger is guilty of—a "crime" that would again place him alongside many of his predecessors and successors—is shortsighted policies that were particularly evident in his inability to grasp the intrinsic significance of local and regional circumstances to the unfolding of the Cold War. Instead, his policies relied on preconceived notions, not particularly innovative for their time, about the overarching significance of American credibility and the Soviet-American relationship.

Perhaps this was understandable, Kissinger was, after all, of a generation that grew up with the Cold War and by and large came to assume that the division of the world was, if not normal, at least unavoidable. Sadly, he was unable to seriously challenge that basic paradigm—indeed, a conventional wisdom—of his day.

It does not make him a war criminal. It makes Henry Kissinger a flawed architect of foreign policy.

Notes

Introduction

1   Doris H. Linder, *Aase Lionës: En politisk biografi* (Oslo: Det norske arbeiderparti, 1997), 199–207; Aase Lionës, *Tredveårskrigen for freden: Høydepunkter i Nobelkomitens historie* (Oslo: Ashehoug, 1987), 77–105. Reischauer cited in Schulzinger, *Henry Kissinger*, 140. For a somewhat more elaborate description, see Jussi Hanhimäki, *A Prize-Winning Performance? Henry Kissinger, Triangular Diplomacy, and the End of the Vietnam War, 1969–1973* (Oslo: Norwegian Nobel Institute, 2001). This work was written during a fellowship at the Norwegian Nobel Institute which, as all my much-cherished friendships with several Norwegians, left me with two enduring impressions. First, the Kissinger prize was consistently considered to have been the most controversial selection in the century of peace prizes. Second, perhaps most important, the Norwegians *do* have an excellent sense of humor.

2   *Les Prix Nobel En 1973*, (Stockholm: Almqvist & Wiksell, 1974), 47–53.
3   Cited in Schulzinger, *Henry Kissinger*, 238. For an example of the continued comparisons between Kissinger and his successors, see Nicholas Lemann, "Without a Doubt: Has Condoleezza Rice Changed George W. Bush, or Has He Changed Her?" *The New Yorker*, October 14 and 21, 2002, 164–179.
4   Kissinger, *Years of Renewal*; idem, *Does America Need a Foreign Policy?*; idem., *Ending the Vietnam War*; idem, *Crisis*.
5   For a recent realist appraisal, see Robert Kaplan, *The Coming Anarchy: Shattering the Dreams of the Post Cold War* (New York: Vintage, 2000), 127–155; Hitchens, *The Trial of Henry Kissinger*.

Chapter 1

1   "Presidential Adviser Kissinger: New Approaches to Friend and Foe," *Time*, February 14, 1969.
2   This is a reference to the title of Mazlish's book *Kissinger: The European Mind in American Policy*.
3   Isaacson, *Kissinger*, 43–47; Kalb and Kalb, *Kissinger*, 38–42; Kissinger interview with the author.
4   Cited in Isaacson, *Kissinger*, 56.
5   Graubard, *Kissinger*, 8.
6   Kissinger, *World Restored*, 325.
7   Gaddis, "Rescuing Choice from Circumstance: The Statecraft of Henry Kissinger," in *The Diplomats, 1939–1979* (Princeton, 1994), 564–592.
8   Isaacson, *Kissinger*, 82–83.
9   Kissinger, "Military Policy and the Defense of the Grey Areas," *Foreign Affairs* (April 1955).
10   Kissinger, *Nuclear Weapons and Foreign Policy*, 4.
11   Ibid., 14, 15.
12   Ibid., 166.
13   Ibid., 167–168. See also Richard Weitz, "Henry Kissinger's Philosophy of International Relations," *Diplomacy and Statecraft* 2, no. 1 (1991): 111–113.
14   "Kissinger: The Uses and Limits of Power," *Time*, February 14, 1969.
15   Kissinger, *World Restored*, 326.
16   Ibid., 328.
17   Kissinger, *Nuclear Weapons and Foreign Policy*, 247.
18   Ibid.
19   Isaacson, *Kissinger*, 72.
20   For example: "Arms Control, Inspection and Surprise Attack," *Foreign Affairs* (July 1960); "Limited War: Nuclear or Conventional? A Reappraisal," *Daedalus* (Fall 1960); "The New Cult of Neutralism," *The Reporter* (November 24, 1960).
21   Isaacson, *Kissinger*, 105.
22   Kissinger, *White House Years*, 9.
23   Cited from *Troubled Partnership* in Andrianopoulos, *Kissinger and Brzezinski*, 96.
24   Isaacson, *Kissinger*, 118.
25   Kissinger, *White House Years*, 5.
26   Isaacson, *Kissinger*, 128.
27   Kissinger, *Necessity for Choice*, 1.

Chapter 2

1   Isaacson, *Kissinger*, 157–158; Reeves, *President Nixon*, 26–28.
2   Ambrose, *Nixon: The Triumph of a Politician*, 10. For an overview of Nixon's career prior to the 1968 election victory, see ibid., and idem, *Nixon: The Education of a Politician, 1913–1962* (New York: Simon & Schuster, 1987).
3   Kimball, *Nixon's Vietnam War*, 57–58.
4   Bundy, *Tangled Web*, 35–48, citation from 40. The latest rendition is in Hitchens, *The Trial of Henry Kissinger*.

5　In mid-September Humphrey was trailing Nixon by about 15 percentage points in the polls. Bundy, *Tangled Web*, 29.

6　See Isaacson, *Kissinger*, 133.

7　Hoff, *Nixon Reconsidered*, 150.

8　Peter Rodman interview, May 22, 1994, Association for Diplomatic Studies Oral History Collection, Georgetown University.

9　Cited in Kalb and Kalb, *Kissinger*, 27.

10　*Haldeman Diaries*, 23 (January 18, 1969).

11　"Kissinger: The Uses and Limits of Power," *Time*, February 1969, 20.

12　For these maneuverings, see, for example, Isaacson, *Kissinger*, 151–156; Schulzinger, *Henry Kissinger*, 23–25.

13　See Isaacson, *Kissinger*, 204.

14　Rodman interview; Kissinger interview with the author.

15　Isaacson, *Kissinger*, 151. For a book that captures the atmosphere in the Nixon White House—even if it makes some errors in fact—see Reeves, *President Nixon*.

16　Nixon–Kissinger Telcons, April 7, 1971, at 9:31, 10:21, 10:35, and 11:13 P.M. RC 393–10, 3945, 394–10, and 394–21, WHT, NPMP. In between these calls, Nixon spoke to a number of others as well, including his secretary Rose Mary Woods and Chief of Staff Bob Haldeman, several times. For the text of Nixon's speech see *PPP: Richard M. Nixon, 1971* (Washington, DC: GPO, 1972), 522–527.

17　Morris, *Uncertain Greatness*, 195–196.

18　Nixon to Kissinger, Haldeman, and Ehrlichman, August 7, 1969, "HAK/President Memos 1969–70," box 341, NSC Subject Files, NPMP.

19　Kissinger interview with the author, June 24, 2003.

20　Reeves, *President Nixon*, 178.

21　Kissinger, *White House Years*, 69–70.

Chapter 3

1　Mann, *About Face*, 19–20. See also Tucker, *China Confidential*, 226.

2　On the Europe trip, see Bundy, *Tangled Web*, 59–61; Kissinger, *White House Years*, 73–111.

3　Cited in Bundy, *Tangled Web*, 76.

4　See Dobrynin, *In Confidence*, 52–54.

5　Robert Ellsworth to Kissinger, January 29, 1969, USSR I, box 709, NSC Country Files, NPMP; Kissinger, *White House Years*, 135–136.

6　Dobrynin, *In Confidence*, 201.

7　*Haldeman Diaries*, 38 (February 15, 1969).

8　Memcons: Kissinger and Sedov, December 18, 1968, and January 2, 1969, USSR, Memcons, box 725, NSC Country files, NPMP. Kissinger recounts these meetings briefly in his memoirs: Kissinger, *White House Years*, 127–128.

9　Rogers to Nixon, February 13, 1969, USSR Memcons, Dobrynin/President, box 340, NSC Subject Files, NPMP. It is not clear if Nixon saw this memo until the 15th, when it was attached to Kissinger's Talking Points.

10　Kissinger to Nixon, February 15, 1969, USSR Memcons, Dobrynin/President, box 340, NSC Subject Files, NPMP.

11　Memcon: Nixon, Kissinger, Toon, Dobrynin, February 17, 1969, USSR Memcons, Dobrynin/President, box 340, NSC Subject Files, NPMP.

12　Kissinger to Nixon, Talking Points, February 15, 1969, USSR Memcons, Dobrynin/President, box 340, NSC Subject Files, NPMP. Malcolm Toon to Kissinger, February 17, 1969, NSC Subject Files, USSR Memcons, Dobrynin/President, box 340, NSC Subject Files, NPMP. At least before he sent it to Kissinger, Toon did not discuss the message with Rogers.

13　Kissinger, *White House Years*, 143–144.

14　Memo for records, February 22, 1969, USSR Memcons, Dobrynin/President, box 340, NSC Subject Files, NPMP.

15 This account of the Sino-Soviet border clash is based mainly on Yang Kuison, "The Sino-Soviet Border Clash of 1969: From Zhenbao Island Incident to Sino-American Rapprochement," *Cold War History* 1, no. 1 (August 2000). See also Christian Ostermann, "New Evidence on the Sino-Soviet Border Dispute," *CWIHP Bulletin* 6–7 (Winter 1995–96): 186–189; Tyler, *Great Wall*, 48–50.

16 Ostermann, "New Evidence," 188; Tyler, *Great Wall*, 60.

17 "Soviet Report to GDR Leadership on 2 March 1969 Sino-Soviet Border Clashes," *CWIHPB* 6–7 (Winter 1995–96): 189.

18 Yang, "Sino-Soviet Border Clash."

19 *Haldeman Diaries*, 48 (March 10, 1969).

20 Memcon: Kissinger–Dobrynin, March 11, 1969; Telcon: Nixon–Kissinger, March 11, 1969, Dobrynin/Kissinger, 1969, part 2, box 489, PTF, NSC, NPMP.

21 On their respective views of Vietnam, see Kimball, *Nixon's Vietnam War*, 63–86. See also Kimball, ed., *Vietnam War Files*, 48–52.

22 See Bundy, *Tangled Web*, 64–65.

23 Kimball, *Nixon's Vietnam War*, 137–139; idem., *Vietnam War Files*, 76–79, 82–86; Berman, *No Peace, No Honor*, 50–51. For the texts of these announcements, see *PPP: Richard Nixon, 1969*, (Washington, DC: GPO, 1970), 443–445 (Midway Island) and 544–556 (Guam press conference).

24 The number of American troops in Vietnam declined from a high of 540,000 in early 1969 to almost half of that by the end of 1970 (280,000), to 140,000 by 1971, and to a mere 24,000 by late 1972.

25 Kissinger, *White House Years*, 265.

26 Kissinger, *American Foreign Policy*, 130.

27 The COSVN was, according to U.S. intelligence information, located in the Fish Hook area of Cambodia, a mere seventy-five miles northwest of Saigon. If the United States managed to destroy these headquarters then, surely, the enemy's war-making capacity would be reduced, U.S. negotiating position would be improved, and the war would be brought closer to a conclusion.

28 For an extensive discussion of MENU, see Kimball, *Nixon's Vietnam War*, 124–145.

29 "K[issinger] very disappointed," Bob Haldeman pointed out in his March 1, 1969 diary entry. *Haldeman Diaries*, 42, 45 (February 24 and March 1, 1969). For Kissinger's account of the decisions, see Kissinger, *White House Years*, 240–244.

30 *Haldeman Diaries*, 47, 48, 51 (March 9, 10, and 17, 1969). Kissinger vehemently criticized Rogers in a memo to Nixon. Kissinger to Nixon, March 8, 1969, Dobrynin/Kissinger, 1969, part 2, box 489, PTF, NSC, NPMP. Nixon cited in Kimball, *Nixon's Vietnam War*, 134.

31 Andrew, *For the President's Eyes Only*, 361–362. On the wiretappings, see Isaacson, *Kissinger*, 212–233.

32 Zhou Enlai's discussions with COSVN delegation, April 20, 1969, *77 Conversations*, 158, 159. See also Qiang Zhai, *China and the Vietnam War*, 179.

33 Li Xiannian and Le Duc Tho in Beijing, April 29, 1969, *77 Conversations*, 160.

34 Memcons: Dobrynin and Kissinger, April 3 and 14, 1969, Dobrynin/Kissinger, 1969, part 2, box 489, PTF, NSC, NPMP.

35 See, for example, Berman, *No Honor, No Peace*, 49–52. For the May 14 speech, see *PPP, Nixon, 1969*, 369–374.

36 Beam to State, April 23, 1969, NSC Country Files, USSR II, box 709: NSC, NPMP.

37 See on these issues: Qiang Zhai, *China and the Vietnam War*; Barnouin and Changgen, *Ten Years of Turbulence*; Kuo-kang Shao, *Zhou Enlai and the Foundations of Chinese Foreign Policy*, 179–200.

38 Much has been written on the differences between American and Soviet conceptions of détente. For a thorough assessment, see, for example, Garthoff, *Détente and Confrontation*, 27–76.

39 Dobrynin, *In Confidence*, 200; Kissinger, *White House Years*, 147–149. For a good general overview of the early SALT developments, see John Newhouse, *War and Peace in the Nuclear Age* (New York: Knopf, 1988), 209–223. See also Smith, *Doubletalk*, 15–27.

40 Cited in Kissinger, *White House Years*, 136.

41   See Garthoff, *Détente and Confrontation*, 146–152; idem, *Journey through the Cold War*, 243–246; Bundy, *Tangled Web*, 83–91; Smith, *Doubletalk*, 21–36.

42   Kissinger, *White House Years*, 204–209.

43   Isaacson, *Kissinger*, 316–318; Kissinger, *White House Years*, 210–212.

44   Kissinger, *White House Years*, 212. On the MIRV decision, see, for example, Bundy, *Tangled Web*, 96–100; Smith, *Doubletalk*, 33–35.

45   On the debate, see Michael Mastanduno, *Economic Containment: CoCom and the Politics of East-West Trade* (Ithaca, NY: Cornell University Press, 1992), 136–142.

46   Kissinger, *White House Years*, 152–155.

47   Mastanduno, *Economic Containment*, 142.

48   See Gaiduk, *The Soviet Union and the Vietnam War*, 214–215; Qiang Zhai, *China and the Vietnam War*, 136.

49   William Burr, "Sino-American Relations, 1969: The Sino-Soviet Border War and Steps towards Rapprochement," *Cold War History* 1:3 (April 2001), 15.

50   Gaiduk, *The Soviet Union and the Vietnam War*, 227; Garthoff, *Détente and Confrontation*, 243–245, Kissinger, *White House Years*, 179–180. Halperin to Kissinger, June 27, 1969, USSR III, box 710, NSC, NPMP.

51   Isaacson, *Kissinger*, 239–242; Kissinger, *White House Years*, 222–224.

Chapter 4

1   Ambrose, *Nixon: The Triumph*, 287.

2   Kissinger, *White House Years*, 691. The term *compensating gains* was used by Assistant Secretary of State Marshall Green in his letter of opposition to an early opening to China. For some interesting reminiscences into the early Nixon administration's thinking about China by Winston Lord and John Holdridge, see Tucker, *China Confidential*, 226–228.

3   See Yang Kuison, "Sino-Soviet Border Clash," 66–68; Shu Guang Zhang, "In the Shadow of Mao: Zhou Enlai," in *The Diplomats, 1939–1979*, 362–364; Keith, *The Diplomacy of Zhou Enlai*, 160–185; Kuo-kang Shao, *Zhou Enlai and the Foundations of Chinese Foreign Policy*, 147–150.

4   Yang, "Sino-Soviet Border Clash," 71.

5   Kuo-kang Shao, *Zhou Enlai and the Foundations of Chinese Foreign Policy*, 171–172. On American perspectives on these proposals, see memcons June 17 and 24, 1969, Rogers, Tcherniakov, Richardson, USSR II, box 709, NSC, NPMP.

6   Report by Four Chinese Marshals to the Central Committee, "A Preliminary Evaluation of the War Situation," July 11, 1969. Excerpts printed in *CWIHP Bulletin* 11 (Winter 1998): 166–167.

7   Yang, "Sino-Soviet Border Clash," 39; the mobilization order in *CWIHP Bulletin* 11 (Winter 1998).

8   Burr, "Sino-American," 28–29.

9   Ibid., 16–18; Holdridge, *Crossing the Divide*, esp. 31–43. Kissinger, *White House Years*, 180–183.

10   Kissinger, *White House Years*, 182.

11   Burr, "Sino-American," 34–37; Tyler, *Great Wall*, 67.

12   E.g., Tyler, *Great Wall*, 67–68.

13   Hyland to Kissinger, August 28, 1969, USSR IV, box 710, NSC, NPMP; State Department Intelligence Note # 640, September 8, 1969; unsigned memo, September 10, 1969, USSR V, box 710, NSC, NPMP.

14   Burr, "Sino-American," 26. On the meeting with Stoessel, see also Kissinger, *White House Years*, 188; Mann, *About Face*, 22. Tyler mistakenly asserts that the meeting with Stoessel took place in October. Tyler, *Great Wall*, 74.

15   Kissinger to Nixon, September 20, 1969; Kissinger to undersecretary of state, September 24, 1969, USSR V, box 710, NSC, NPMP.

16   Yang Kuisong, "Sino-Soviet Border Clash," 56

17   "Our Views about the Current Situation," Report by Four Marshals, September 17, 1969, printed in *CWIHP Bulletin* 11 (Winter 1998): 170. Marshal Chen Yi's "Further Thoughts," ibid., 171.

18   See Tyler, *Great Wall*, 73; and John Wilson Lewis and Xue Litai, *China Builds the Bomb* (Stanford: Stanford University Press, 1988), 243–244.

19   Yang Kuisong, "Sino-Soviet," 58–60.

20   Nixon received the reply on August 30, 1969, only three days prior to Ho's death. See Kimball, *Nixon's Vietnam War*, 153, 158 and Kimball, *Vietnam War Files*, 87–93.

21   The group of ten, or the "September Group," included Anthony Lake, Winston Lord, Laurence Lynn, Roger Morris, Peter Rodman, Helmut Sonnenfeldt, William Watts, Alexander Haig, William Lemnitzer, and Rembrandt C. Robinson. Kimball, *Nixon's Vietnam War*, 162–163. For Lake's September 17, 1969, memorandum to Kissinger, see Kimball, *Vietnam War Files*, 102–104.

22   Ibid., 164; Berman, *No Peace, No Honor*, 54–56; Small, *Johnson, Nixon and the Doves*, 182–187. See also Kissinger, *White House Years*, 284–285.

23   Kimball, *Nixon's Vietnam War*, 173–175. As Kimball notes, the impact of the "Silent Majority" speech was perhaps less dramatic than initially seemed. Even while critical of the antiwar movement's tactics, 81 percent of Americans believed they were raising important questions.

      Nixon's decision not to go ahead with Duck Hook may also have been prompted by the administration's efforts to reach out to China. After all, a major U.S. military move in Vietnam could easily preempt any chance of an opening. Worse yet, it might provide a pretext for at least a temporary Sino-Soviet rapprochement during the two countries' border talks that had been scheduled to commence on October 20. See also Small, *Johnson, Nixon and the Doves*, 187–192.

24   Kissinger to Nixon, October 13, 1969, box 3, Presidential Handwriting File, POF, NPMP.

25   Memcon (with aide memoire as an attachment): Kissinger, Nixon, and Dobrynin, October 20, 1969, Dobrynin/Kissinger, 1969, part 2, box 489, PTF, NSC, NPMP.

26   Burr, "Sino-American," 32; Aijazuddin, *From a Head*, 27–30.

27   Mann, *About Face*, 22–23.

28   In Burr, "Sino-American," 34.

29   Mann, *About Face*, 23–24.

30   Nixon memo, December 12, 1969; Kissinger to Nixon (with Nixon's comment in the margin), December 27, 1969, USSR VI, box 711, NSC, NPMP. Memcons: Kissinger and Dobrynin, December 22, 1969, and January 20, 1970, Dobrynin/Kissinger, 1969, part 2, and Dobrynin/Kissinger, 1970, vol. 1, part 2, box 489, PTF, NSC, NPMP. Kissinger, *White House Years*, 192–193, 523–524.

31   On the Helsinki talks, see Smith, *Doubletalk*, 75–107; Kissinger, *White House Years*, 149–150.

32   Cited in Kissinger, *Diplomacy*, 712. For the entire text of the report, see *PPP: Richard Nixon, 1970* (Washington, DC: GPO, 1971), 116–189.

33   For more on these meetings, see the following chapter.

Chapter 5

1   Loi and Vu, *Le Duc Tho-Kissinger Negotiations in Paris*, 111.

2   On Tho and the 1968 talks, see Berman, *No Honor, No Peace*, 25–30.

3   On the first series of Tho–Kissinger talks, see ibid., 63–72 (citations, 66, 69); Loi and Vu, *Le Duc Tho–Kissinger Negotiations in Paris*, 111–137; Kimball, *Nixon's Vietnam War*, 187–192 (Nixon citation, 188); Kimball, *Vietnam War Files*, 127–129 (February 21, 1970 discussion).

4   *Haldeman Diaries*, 179 (April 13, 1970). Nixon's comments on a report of Kissinger's secret meetings with Le Duc Tho in Paris.

5   Shawcross and Kimball, among others, would strongly dispute that Sihanouk ever "acquiesced" to the bombings; yet, the fact remains that the prince failed to launch a major criticism once the bombings got under way. See Kimball, *Nixon's Vietnam War*, 132; Shawcross, *Sideshow*, 28, 33.

6   Bundy, *Tangled Web*, 148; Shawcross, *Sideshow*, 64. On Chinese relations with Cambodia prior to the overthrow of Sihanouk, see Qiang Zhai, *China and the Vietnam War*, 55–57, 68, 99, 157–162, 182–186. Sihanouk's talks with Mao, see *77 Conversations*.

7   Ibid. See also Ralph Smith, "The International Setting of the Cambodian Crisis," *The International History Review* 18, no. 2 (May 1996): 303–335.

8   Bundy, *Tangled Web*, 129–150; Shawcross, *Sideshow*, 114–122.

9   Kimball, *Nixon's Vietnam War*, 199; Kissinger, *White House Years*, 465; *Haldeman Diaries*, 172 (March 30, 1970).

10 Full text of the speech is in *PPP: Richard Nixon, 1970* (Washington, DC: GPO, 1971), 373–377.

11 Kissinger to Nixon, April 17, 1970, box 334, Lord Files, PPS, RG 59, NA.

12 *PPP: Richard Nixon, 1970*, 405–410. Kissinger cited in Kimball, *Nixon's Vietnam War*, 211. At the time Kissinger had simply indicated that he thought the speech "will work."

13 *Haldeman Diaries*, 184 (April 24, 1970).

14 Lord to Kissinger, April 2, 1970, box 338, Lord Files, PPP, RG 59, NA. The discussion below is based heavily on Kimball, *Nixon's Vietnam War*, 197–210; Isaacson, *Kissinger*, 256–267.

15 Lord, Morris, and Lake to Kissinger, April 22, 1970, box 338, Lord Files, PPP, RG 59, NA. Lord sent another memo on April 24, stressing the open-ended commitment that the invasion would entail.

16 Isaacson, *Kissinger*, 262–265. Kissinger had Bill Watts listen on the phone call from Camp David, where Nixon and Rebozo had been drinking martinis and watching the movie *Cincinnati Kid*.

17 *Haldeman Diaries*, 182–188 (April 19–29, 1970). "The Decision," ibid. (May 4, 1970).

18 The discussion of the incursion is based on Kimball, *Nixon's Vietnam War*, 210–225; Isaacson, *Kissinger*, 268–275; Shawcross, *Sideshow*, chapter 15.

19 Shawcross, *Sideshow*.

20 Small, *Johnson, Nixon and the Doves*, 201. For more on the public reaction, see ibid., 201–208; Kimball, *Nixon's Vietnam War*, 213 223.

21 Isaacson, *Kissinger*, 263–265, 275–278; Kimball, *Nixon's Vietnam War*, 208.

22 Holdridge and Sonnenfeldt to Kissinger (to RN), April 15, 1970, USSR VII, box 711, NSC, NPMP.

23 Winston Lord to Kissinger, May 3, 1970, box 333, Lord Files, PPP, RG 59, NA.

24 Kosygin as told by Sihanouk in his memoirs. Cited in Qiang Zhai, *China and the Vietnam War*, 187. "Blundering fool" in Shawcross, *Sideshow*, 123.

25 On Soviet zigzagging: Kissinger to Nixon, April 17, 1970, and Holdridge to Kissinger, April 18, 1970, USSR VII, box 711, NSC, NPMP. Nixon himself seems to have been too elated on April 17 about the safe return of the *Apollo XIII* crew to pay too much attention to these particular Soviet uncertainties. See *Haldeman Diaries*, 330–332 (April 17 and 19, 1971).

26 Qiang Zhai, *China and the Vietnam War*, 187–191; Gilks, *Breakdown of the Sino-Vietnamese Alliance*, 56–58.

27 Qiang Zhai, *China and the Vietnam War*, 189–192; Gilks, *Breakdown of the Sino-Vietnamese Alliance*, 57–62; Tyler, *Great Wall*, 80. For a table of China's military aid to North Vietnam, see Qiang Zhai, *China and the Vietnam War*, 136.

28 Shu Guang Zhang, "In the Shadow of Mao: Zhou Enlai and New China's Diplomacy," in *The Diplomats, 1939–1979*, 362–63; Keith, *Diplomacy of Zhou Enlai*, 181–209.

29 Kissinger to Nixon, April 29, 1970; Sonnenfeldt for the record, April 29, 1970, USSR VII, box 711, NSC, NPMP.

30 Kissinger to Nixon, May 6, 1970, USSR VIII, box 712, NSC, NPMP.

31 Sonnenfeldt for the record, April 29, 1970, USSR VII, box 711, NSC, NPMP.

32 For an account of the Vienna phase in April-August 1970, see Smith, *Doubletalk*, 121–153.

33 Garthoff, *Détente and Confrontation*, 159. For a discussion of the preparations for this proposal, see ibid., 155–159. See also Paul H. Nitze, *From Hiroshima to Glasnost: At the Center of Decision* (London: Weidenfeld and Nicolson, 1989), 308–309; and Garthoff, *Journey through the Cold War*, 243–276.

34 Garthoff, *Détente and Confrontation*, 161; Bundy, *Tangled Web*, 170–172.

35 Garthoff, *Détente and Confrontation*, 162; Nitze, *Hiroshima to Glasnost*, 311–313. The Americans also suggested another ABM possibility: zero-deployment, as part of the new comprehensive package. The Soviets rejected this alternative in favor of the already accepted NCA swap. Garthoff, *Détente and Confrontation*, 165; Bundy, *Tangled Web*, 172–173.

36   Memcons: Kissinger and Dobrynin, February 18, March 10 and 20, April 7 and 9, June 23, July 7 and 20, 1970, Dobrynin/Kissinger, 1970, vols. 1–2, box 489, PTF, NSC, NPMP.

37   Memcons: Kissinger and Dobrynin, April 7, July 7 and 9, 1970, Dobrynin/Kissinger, 1970, vols. 1–2, box 489, NSC, PTF; Kissinger to Nixon, July 13, 1970, USSR VIII, box 712, NSC, NPMP.

38   Kissinger to Nixon, August 22, 1970, USSR IX, box 713, NSC, NPMP; *Haldeman Diaries*, 226 (August 15, 1970); Kissinger, *White House Years*, 552–556.

39   On Brandt's early career, see Barbara Marshall, *Willy Brandt: A Political Biography* (London: Macmillan, 1997), 5–65. On his Scandinavian connections, see Jussi Hanhimäki, *Scandinavia and the United States since 1945: An Insecure Friendship* (New York: Twayne's, 1997), 129–130.

40   For an outline of *Ostpolitik*, see Michael J. Sodaro, *Moscow, Germany, and the West.* 108–202. On Bahr's concept see 167.

41   Andrianopoulos, *Kissinger and Brzezinski*, 232.

42   Kissinger to Nixon, February 16, 1970, Germany, IV, box 683, NSC, NPMP.

43   Kissinger, *White House Years*, 410.

44   Memcon: Nixon, Rogers, Kissinger, Brandt, Kiesinger, et al., February 26, 1969, Conference Files, 1966–72, CF 340-CF 342, lot 70d 387, box 484, RG 59, NA.

45   Brandt, *My Life in Politics*, 167.

46   Richard J. Barnet, *The Alliance: America-Europe-Japan: Makers of the Postwar World* (New York, 1983), 287. Bahr, like Kissinger, was a German Jew, but had stayed behind and had even tried to become an officer in Hitler's army.

47   Kissinger to Nixon (drafted by Sonnenfeldt), October 14, 1969, box 917, VIP Visits, NSC, NPMP; and Kissinger to Nixon, October 20, 1969, Germany III, box 682, NSC, NPMP. Bahr's memcon in *Akten zur Auswartigen Politik der Bundesrepublik Deutschland* (AAP) 1969, Band II, 1114–1118. Kissinger and Bahr's versions are also in their memoirs: Kissinger, *White House Years*, 410–412; Bahr, *Zu Meiner Zeit*, 271–273.

48   Brandt, *My Life in Politics*, 176; Kissinger, *White House Years*, 416. Rush to Rogers, April 2, 1970; Kissinger to Nixon (drafted by Sonnenfeldt), April 3, 1970, box 917, VIP Visits, NSC, NPMP.

49   Kissinger, *White House Years*, 424. Memcon: Brandt, Schmidt, Nixon, Rogers, Laird, Kissinger, box 917, VIP Visits, NSC, NPMP.

50   Sodaro, *Moscow, Germany, and the West*, 174–179, 183–185; Bundy, *Tangled Web*, 173–179.

51   Sodaro, *Moscow, Germany, and the West*, 201.

52   Telcon: Kissinger–Dobrynin, July 28, 1970, Dobrynin/Kissinger, 1970, vol. 1, box 489, PTF, NPMP.

53   Kissinger to Nixon, September 1, 1970, Germany VII, box 684, NSC, NPMP.

54   Kissinger to Nixon, October 23, 1970, France VII, box 677, NSC, NPMP.

55   Kissinger to Nixon, December 1, 1970, USSR XI, box 714, NSC, NPMP.

56   *Haldeman Diaries*, 226–227 (August 15–17, 1970).

Chapter 6

1   The most comprehensive account of the crisis can be found in Quandt, *Peace Process*, 94–115. Much of the discussion below is based on this and on Bundy, *Tangled Web*, 123–133, 179–182. For an informative biography of Arafat, see Rubin and Rubin, *Arafat*.

2   Memcons: Kissinger and Dobrynin, June 11 and September 27, 1969; telcon: Nixon–Kissinger, September 27, 1969, Dobrynin/Kissinger, 1969, box 489, NSC, PTF, NPMP.

3   Memcons: Kissinger and Dobrynin, February 10 and March 10, 1971, Dobrynin/Kissinger, 1970, box 489, NSC, PTF, NPMP. In practice this meant that Dobrynin had two sets of Middle East discussions under way: with Kissinger he discussed "general principles" and with the Assistant Secretary of State Joseph Sisco, the State Department's top Middle East official, "the details." Sisco had, in fact, been the man charged with the implementation of the Rogers Plan. But in the course of 1970 and the Jordanian crisis, Sisco, who clearly sensed where power on U.S. Middle East policy rested, gradually developed a strong, if at times volatile, relationship with Kissinger. In 1973, Sisco would be one of the few members of Rogers' inner

circle who would stay on when Kissinger was made secretary of state. On the Kissinger–Sisco relationship, see Isaacson, *Kissinger*, 304, 507.

4   Memcons: Kissinger and Dobrynin, February 10, March 10, March 20, April 7, April 9, June 23, July 7, July 16, July 20, 1970; telcon: Dobrynin and Kissinger, July 27, 1970, Dobrynin/ Kissinger, 1970, box 489, NSC, PTF, NPMP.

5   There were unconfirmed U.S. intelligence reports to this effect.

6   Bundy, *Tangled Web*, 183–188; Isaacson, *Kissinger*, 289–308; Rubin and Rubin, *Arafat*, 50–53.

7   Kissinger, *White House Years*, 631.

8   On these, Bundy, *Tangled Web*, 187; Quandt, *Peace Process*, 101–105.

9   Kissinger to Nixon, September 17, 1970, box 922, VIP Visits, NSC, NPMP.

10 Kissinger to Nixon, October 14, 1970, box 334, Lord Files, PPS, RG 59, NA2.

11 Kissinger to Nixon, June 1, 1970, USSR VII, box 712, NSC, NPMP.

12 Memcons: Kissinger and Vorontsov, August 4 and 7, 1970, Dobrynin/Kissinger, 1970, box 489, NSC, PTF, NPMP.

13 Cited in Isaacson, *Kissinger*, 293. See Bundy, *Tangled Web*, 193–194.

14 Memcon: Kissinger and Dobrynin, September 25, 1970, Dobrynin/Kissinger, 1970, box 489, PTF, NSC, NPMP. Isaacson, *Kissinger*, 308; Bundy, *Tangled Web*, 191–194; Kissinger, *White House Years*, 638; Hersh, *Price of Power*, 250.

15 Memcon: Kissinger and Dobrynin, October 6 and 9, 1970, Dobrynin/Kissinger, 1970, box 489, PTF, NSC, NPMP.

16 Dobrynin, *In Confidence*, 208.

17 Telcon: Kissinger–Nixon, September 24, 1970, NSecA webpage; Kissinger, *White House Years*, 652.

18 Hersh, *Price of Power*, 257.

19 Hitchens, *Trial of Henry Kissinger* and Kornbluh, *Pinochet File*.

20 Bundy, *Tangled Web*, 199–201.

21 Hersh, *Price of Power*, 263.

22 This remark apparently made a strong impression on Nixon, who cites it in his memoirs. The businessman reportedly said: "If Allende should win, and with Castro in Cuba, you will have in Latin America a red sandwich. And, eventually, it will all be red." Nixon, *RN*, 490.

23 Cited in Isaacson, *Kissinger*, 290.

24 Isaacson, *Kissinger*, 288–289; Bundy, *Tangled Web*, 203.

25 Korry to State Department, September 9 and 11, 1970, in www.gwu.edu/~nsarchiv/NSAEBB/ (hereafter NSArc Chile documents).

26 Korry to State, September 22, 1970, NSArc Chile documents.

27 Helms's notes can be found in NSArc Chile documents. Also see Helms, *Look Over My Shoulder*, chapter 8.

28 Memcon: Kissinger, Karamessinis, Haig, October 15, 1970, NSArc Chile documents; Isaacson, *Kissinger*, 291–297, 303–308; Bundy, *Tangled Web*, 201–202; Kornbluh, *Pinochet File*, 1–22.

29 Isaacson, *Kissinger*, 310–312; Kornbluh, *Pinochet File*, 22–35; Bundy, *Tangled Web*, 202–203; author's interview with William Rogers.

30 Kornbluh, *Pinochet File*, 25–26; 79–115; NSSM 97: "Options Paper on Chile," November 3, 1970; NSDM 93: "Policy Towards Chile," November 9, 1970, NSArc Chile Documents.

31 Since the September 11, 2001 terrorist attacks on New York and Washington, the date has assumed a certain ironic implication in U.S.-Chilean relations.

32 Telcon: Nixon–Kissinger, September 16, 1973, NSecA webpage.

33 Dwight Chapin to Haldeman, November 4, 1970, "NSC 9-1-70 to 11-4-70," box 28, Subject Files: Conference Files, 1969–74, WHCF, NPMP.

34 Isaacson, *Kissinger*, 314.

35 Tyler, *Great Wall*, 81.

36 Kissinger, *White House Years*, 696, 698. Kissinger to Nixon, September 12, 1970, "Cookies II" and memcon: Kissinger and Sainteny, September 27, 1970, box 1032; "Exchanges Leading up to HAK Trip to China—December 1969—July 19171 (1)," box 1031, NSC, NPMP.

37 Kissinger, *White House Years*, 697–699; Tyler, *Great Wall*, 81. *Time*, October 5, 1970. Most of the interview focused on the Jordanian crisis discussed above.

38   Kuo-kang Shao, *Zhou Enlai and the Foundations of Chinese Foreign Policy*, 200–201.

39   On the Lushan Plenum and debates within, see Roderick MaqFarquhar, "The Succession to
        Mao and the End of Maoism," in *The Politics of China: The Eras of Mao and Deng* (Cam-
        bridge: Cambridge University Press, 1993), 262–264; and idem, ed., *The Cambridge History
        of China*, vol. 15: *The People's Republic, Part 2: Revolutions within the Chinese Revolution,
        1966–1982* (Cambridge: Cambridge University Press, 1991), esp. chapters 3–5.

40   These documents are in *77 Conversations*, 174–178.

41   Bundy, *Tangled Web*, 165. Kissinger writes: "Unfortunately, they overestimated our subtlety,
        for what they conveyed was so oblique that our occidental minds completely missed the
        point." Kissinger, *White House Years*, 698; Tyler, *Great Wall*, 82.

42   Tyler, *Great Wall*, 83. Kissinger, *White House Years*, 736; Winston Lord interview. On Trudeau,
        see Andrew Cohen and J. L. Granatstein, eds., *Trudeau's Shadow: The Life and Legacy of Pierre
        Elliott Trudeau* (Toronto: Vintage, 1998).

43   Memorandum of conversation: Nixon, Kissinger, Khan, October 25, 1970, box 334, Lord Files,
        PPS, RG 59, NA.

44   Memcon: Kissinger and Ceausescu, October 27, 1970, "Cookies II," box 1032, NSC, NPMP.

45   Kissinger to Nixon, December 10, 1970 (est.), "Exchanges Leading up to HAK Trip to
        China—December 1969—July 1971 (1)," box 1031, NSC, NPMP; Aijazuddin, *From a Head*,
        39–45. See also Bundy, *Tangled Web*, 165–166; Kissinger, *White House Years*, 701.

46   Memcon: Kissinger and Bogdan, January 11, 1971, "Exchanges Leading up to HAK Trip to
        China—December 1969—July 1971 (1)," box 1031, NSC, NPMP.

47   Ibid.

48   Kissinger, *White House Years*, 980–981; Lankford, *The Last American Aristocrat*, 360–361;
        Kissinger to Nixon, October 26, 1970 (Bruce quoted from an enclosed telegram), Lord Files,
        box 334. For the September meetings, see Loi and Vu, *Le Duc Tho–Kissinger Negotiations in
        Paris*, 142–148, 151–152; Kimball, *Nixon's Vietnam War*, 230–234.

49   *Haldeman Diaries*, 202 (October 7, 1970); Kimball, *Nixon's Vietnam War*, 235.

50   Telcons: Kissinger and Nixon, Kissinger and Haig, December 9, 1970, NSecArc website;
        Smith, "The International Setting of the Cambodian Crisis"; Kimball, *Nixon's Vietnam War*,
        241–48; and Kimball, *Vietnam War Files*, 139–42.

51   Lord to Kissinger, November 25, 1970, box 334, Lord Files, PPS, RG 59, NA.

52   *Haldeman Diaries*, 282 (January 18, 1971).

53   Ibid., 285–286 (January 21, 1971).

54   Ibid., 287–288 (January 26, 1971).

55   Kimball, *Nixon's Vietnam War*, 248; Castle, *At War in the Shadow of Vietnam*, 108–109. See
        also Roger Warner, *Back Fire: The CIA's Secret War in Laos and Its Link to the War in Vietnam*
        (New York: Simon & Schuster, 1995), 300–303.

56   Kissinger, *White House Years*, 1009–1010.

57   Nixon televised address can be found in *American Foreign Relations, 1971: A Documentary
        Record*, 279–284.

58   Small, *Johnson, Nixon and the Doves*, 213–219; *Haldeman Diaries*, 284 (May 4, 1971). See also,
        Reeves, *President Nixon*, 301–307.

59   Rusk to Acheson, March 3, 1971; Acheson to Rusk, March 10, 1971, Acheson Papers, Yale Uni-
        versity. I am grateful to Andrew Preston for sharing these documents with me.

Chapter 7

1   Zhou Enlai to Nixon, April 21, 1971 (handed to Kissinger on April 27); Haig to Vernon Wal-
        ters (with attachments), April 27, 1971, both in "Exchanges Leading Up to HAK Trip to
        China—December 1969—July 1971 (1)," box 1031, NSC, NPMP.

2   Kissinger, *White House Years*, 736–737; Lord interview with the author.

3   Cited in Isaacson, *Kissinger*, 357.

4   Telcon: Nixon and Kissinger, 8:16 P.M., April 27, 1971, WHT: 2–52, NPMP.

5   Tyler, *Great Wall*, 93–94; Kissinger, *White House Years*, 713–724; *Haldeman Diaries*, 282 (April
        28, 1971).

6   Message from Nixon to Zhou ("Handed to Ambassador Hilaly by Kissinger 12.00 5/10/71"), "Exchanges Leading up to HAK Trip. to China—December 1969—July 1971 (1)," box 1031, NSC, NPMP.

7   Zhou to Nixon, May 29, 1971, "Exchanges Leading up to HAK Trip to China—December 1969—July 1971 (1)," box 1031, NSC, NPMP; *Haldeman Diaries*, 357, 358 (June 2 and 3, 1971); Kissinger, *White House Years*, 726–727.

8   *Haldeman Diaries*, 358 (June 3, 1971).

9   Qiang Zhai, *China and the Vietnam War*, 194. Ålågrd had played a key role in a Norwegian channel that aimed at bringing the United States and North Vietnam together in the late 1960s. Svein Gjerdåker, "Norsk menneskerettspolitikk," in *Norges Utenrikspolitikk*, ed. Torbjørn L. Knutsen et al. (Oslo: Cappelen, 1995), 217.

10   Stephen J. Morris, *The Soviet-Chinese-Vietnamese Triangle in the 1970s: The View from Moscow*, CWIHP Working Paper no. 25 (Washington, DC, 1999). Citation on page 14. See also Gilks, *Breakdown of the Sino-Vietnamese Alliance*, 66–67.

11   Conversation between Zhou Enlai, Le Duan, and Pham Van Dong, Hanoi, March 7, 1971, in *77 Conversations*, 179–180. See also Quang Zhai, *China and the Vietnam War*, 194.

12   Gilks, *Breakdown of the Sino-Vietnamese Alliance*, 70.

13   The Foreign Policy Report is in *PPP: Richard Nixon, 1971* (Washington, DC: GPO, 1972), 219–345.

14   Tyler, *Great Wall*, 89–90; Nixon and Bray in *American Foreign Relations, 1971: A Documentary Record*, 340–342. See also Kissinger, *White House Years*, 706–708.

15   Telcon: Nixon and Kissinger, April 15, 1971, 7:31 P.M., WHT: 1–101.

16   Telcons: Nixon and Kissinger, April 16, 1971, 10:45, 11:05, and 11:22 P.M., WHT: 1–108, 1–114, 1–119, NPMP. Nixon's comments at the press meeting in. *PPP: Richard Nixon, 1971*, 534–550.

17   Telcons: Nixon and Kissinger, April 18, 1971, 10:23 A.M. and 10:41 A.M., WHT: 1–124, 1–146, NDMP.

18   Tyler, *Great Wall*, 90–91; Kissinger, *White House Years*, 709–711; Kuo-kang Shao, *Zhou Enlai*, 201; NSSM 124: "Next Steps Toward the People's Republic of China," April 19, 1971, NPMP.

19   Telcon: Nixon and Kissinger, 8:16 P.M., April 27, 1971, WHT: 2–52, NPMP.

20   *Haldeman Diaries*, 271 (April 12, 1971); Telcons: Kissinger and Nixon, April 13, 1971, 7:46 P.M.; April 14, 1971, 8:05 P.M., WHT: 1–79 and 1–91, NPMP. Less than two weeks earlier Kissinger had pointed out, in his report of Leonid Brezhnev's foreign policy speech at the Soviet Communist Party Congress, that Soviet interest in developing détente was forthcoming. Brezhnev's speech, he wrote Nixon, "all but commits the Soviet Union to a major effort at détente." Kissinger to Nixon, March 31, 1971, USSR XII, Box 714, NSC, NPMP.

21   Radio–Television Statement by Richard Nixon, May 20, 1971, *American Foreign Relations, 1971: A Documentary History*, 104.

22   Dobrynin, *In Confidence*, 209.

23   Memcon: Dobrynin and Kissinger, January 23, 1971, Dobrynin/Kissinger, 1971, vol. 4, part 2, box 490, NSC, NPMP. See also Kissinger, *White House Years*, 804–805; Dobrynin, *In Confidence*, 210–211; Garthoff, *Détente and Confrontation*, 107–108. Kissinger's title for the subsection that follows is, indeed, "The Channel Becomes Operational."

24   Memcon: Dobrynin and Kissinger, April 26, 1971, Dobrynin/Kissinger, 1971, vol. 5, part 1, box 490, NSC, NPMP; Kissinger, *White House Years*, 823–833; Bahr, *Zu Meiner Zeit*, 358–371; Garthoff, *Détente and Confrontation*, 136–139. Kissinger did not consider Ulbricht's resignation particularly significant at the time. Kissinger to Nixon, May 4, 1971, Germany 685, NSC, NPMP.

25   Memcon: Dobrynin and Kissinger, January 9, 1971, Dobrynin/Kissinger, 1971, vol. 4, part 2, box 490, NSC, NPMP. See also Kissinger, *White House Years*, 802–803; Dobrynin, *In Confidence*, 210.

26   On the domestic debate, see Garthoff, *Détente and Confrontation*, ch. 5; Bundy, *A Tangled Web*, 250–253.

27   Memcons: Dobrynin and Kissinger, February 4, 22, 26, March 5 and 12, 1971. Dobrynin/Kissinger, 1971, vol. 4, part 2, box 490, NSC, NPMP; Kissinger, *White House Years*, 813–816.

Dobrynin has little to add on this phase of the back-channel negotiations. Dobrynin, *In Confidence*, 213–214.

28 Kissinger made such comments during meetings with Dobrynin on February 26 and March 2, 1971. Dobrynin/Kissinger, 1971, vol. 4, part 2, box 490, NSC, NPMP. For the negotiators' perspective, see Smith, *Doubletalk*, 201–221; Garthoff, *Journey Through the Cold War*, 260–261.

29 Andropov to Ustinov, April 19, 1971, in *CWIHP Bulletin* 4 (Fall 1994) 69–70; Garthoff, *Détente and Confrontation*, 170–171.

30 *PPP: Richard Nixon, 1971*, 648; *Haldeman Diaries*, 351 (May 21, 1971); Kissinger, *White House Years*, 822.

31 "As a member of the SALT I delegation," Garthoff maintains, "I am virtually certain that a better agreement could have been reached by negotiations between the delegations." Garthoff, *Détente and Confrontation*, 167 n. 57; see also Smith, *Doubletalk*, 233–235. Stephen Ambrose disagrees. "For once," he writes, "[Nixon] was not indulging in hyperbole." Ambrose, *Nixon: Ruin and Recovery*, 442.

32 Garthoff, *Détente and Confrontation*, 167.

33 Ibid., 166–167; Kissinger, *White House Years*, 814–819; Smith, *Doubletalk*, 225–235; Bundy, *Tangled Web*, 252–253; *Haldeman Diaries*, 350 (May 19, 1971). See also Arkady N. Schevchenko, *Breaking with Moscow* (London: Jonathan Cape, 1985), 205.

34 Ambrose, *Nixon: The Triumph of a Politician*, 442–443.

35 Reeves, *President Nixon*, 326.

36 Kissinger, *White House Years*, 727–728; Kuo-kang Shao, *Zhou Enlai and the Foundation of Chinese Foreign Policy*, 201.

37 Kissinger, *White House Years*, 1017–1020; Kimball, *Nixon's Vietnam War*, 265–266; Kimball, *Vietnam War Files*, 166–173; and Luu and Loi, *Le Duc Tho–Kissinger Negotiations in Paris*, 164–168.

38 Kimball, *Nixon's Vietnam War*, 266.

39 Instead of a number of easy chairs as in previous meetings, the room now featured a conference table. Kissinger, *White House Years*, 1021; Kimball, *Nixon's Vietnam War*, 267.

40 Luu and Loi, *Le Duc Tho–Kissinger Negotiations in Paris*, 170–175; Kissinger, *White House Years*, 1021–1024; Kimball, *Nixon's Vietnam War*, 267–271.

41 Memcons: Kissinger–Dobrynin, June 8, 14, 21, 1971, Dobrynin/Kissinger, 1971, vol. 6, part 2, box 491, NSC, NPMP.

42 Haig to Nixon and Haig to Kissinger, July 5 and 6, 1971, Dobrynin/Kissinger, 1971, vol. 7, part 2, box 492, NSC, NPMP.

43 *Haldeman Diaries*, 358 (June 4, 1971); Kissinger, *White House Years*, 729; Isaacson, *Kissinger*, 342; interview with Winston Lord. Isaacson calls Laird's request "a puckish trick," while Kissinger writes that by agreeing to rearrange his schedule "Laird was a good soldier."

44 Isaacson, *Kissinger*, 327–331, 342; Kissinger, *White House Years*, 729–730. Haig in *Haldeman Diaries*, 363 (June 13, 1971). As an example of his moral standards Nixon claimed in his memoirs that the break-in to Ellsberg's psychiatrist's office (on Labor Day 1971), while excessive, "was not as excessive as what Daniel Ellsberg did" by leaking the Pentagon Papers to the *New York Times*. Nixon, *RN*, 514. For Ellsberg's viewpoint, see Ellsberg, *Secrets*.

45 *Haldeman Diaries*, 383 (July 8, 1971); Mann, *About Face*, 30–31.

46 Once the plane crossed into Chinese air space, the Pakistani crew handed the controls over to the Chinese.

47 The discussion of the secret trip that follows is based on the following books: Isaacson, *Kissinger*, 343–347; Bundy, *Tangled Web*, 234–238; Mann, *About Face*, 31–36; Tyler, *Great Wall*, 95–103; Kissinger, *White House Years*, 733–755; Nixon, *RN*, 553–554; Holdridge, *Crossing the Divide*, 53–63.

48 It was, Winston Lord later recalled, typical of Kissinger to rant and rave about such minor details as missing shirts but be cool about the big issues. At another instance Kissinger, upset about a busy appointment schedule, erupted at his secretary: "Who do you think I am! A dentist?!" Winston Lord interview. The shirt incident can be found in Kissinger, *White House Years*, 753; Holdridge, *Crossing the Divide*, 55.

49 Kissinger, *White House Years*, 743–745; Chen Jian, *Mao's China*, 266; Han Suyin, *Eldest Son: Zhou Enlai and the Making of Modern China, 1898–1976* (New York: Hill & Wang, 1994), 376–377.

50 Memcon: Kissinger, Zhou, et al., July 9, 1971, China HAK Memcons, July 1971, box 1033, NSC, NPMP.

51 See, in particular, Mann, *About Face*, 33–34; Tyler, *Great Wall*, 98–100.

52 Kissinger, Zhou, et al., July 9 and 10, 1971, "China visit: Record of previous meetings," box 90, HAKOF, NPMP. Although he has little to say about the secret trip, see also Berman, *No Peace, No Honor*, 104–105.

53 Memcon: Kissinger and Zhou, July 10, 1971, "China visit: Record of previous meetings," box 90, HAKOF, NPMP. Mao cited in Zhai, *China and the Vietnam War*, 196. See also Tyler, *Great Wall*, 101; and Mann, *About Face*, 34.

54 Memcons: Kissinger and Zhou, July 10, 1971 (afternoon and evening), China HAK Memcons, July 1971, box 1033, NSC, NPMP. "I did not have the impression that Zhou was unhappy about this," Kissinger later wrote, implying that the Chinese premier had actually agreed to the sequence of summits. Kissinger, *White House Years*, 751.

55 Chen Jian, *Mao's China and the Cold War*, 268.

56 Memcons: Kissinger, Huang Hua, et al. July 11, 1971 (12:00 A.M. to 1:40 A.M. and 9:50 A.M. to 10:35 A.M.), "China HAK Memcons, July 1971," box 1033, NSC, NPMP. Lord interview. Citation in Kissinger, *White House Years*, 760.

57 Memcon: Kissinger and Zhou, July 11, 1971, "China HAK Memcons, July 1971," box 1033, NSC, NPMP.

58 Kissinger, *Years of Renewal*, 155, 157. Similar views were expressed in his first volume, published in 1979. See Kissinger, *White House Years*, 742ff. Kissinger's positive views of Zhou raised much criticism. Some of the most biting was offered by then undersecretary of state (and previously ambassador to Japan) Alexis Johnson, who wrote in his memoirs: "I am afraid that the scintillating Kissinger mind let itself get mesmerized by the charm and urbane intelligence of the cosmopolitan Zhou En-lai." U. Alexis Johnson, *The Right Hand of Power*, (New York: Prentice Hall, 1984), 555.

59 In the July 11 message Kissinger simply stated that the talks had been a success and insisted that secrecy be maintained until he arrived in California two days later. Kissinger to Haig, July 11, 1971, "China HAK Memcons, July 1971," box 1031, NSC, NPMP.

60 Kissinger, *White House Years*, 756.

61 Lankford, *Last American Aristocrat*, 367–368.

62 He was not the only journalist to have missed this particular scoop by a whisker. The more famous case is that of James ("Scotty") Reston, whose arrival in Beijing was delayed by the Chinese to allow Kissinger to make his way back to Pakistan. James Reston, *Deadline: A Memoir* (New York: Random House, 1991), 210–212.

63 For a full text, see *American Foreign Relations 1971: A Documentary Record*, 348–349.

64 Schulzinger, *Henry Kissinger*, 89.

65 "Rogers ably took charge," Kissinger somewhat condescendingly writes in his memoirs. Kissinger, *White House Years*, 758. Haldeman thought that "Rogers really reacted extremely well and was most gracious in congratulating Henry." *Haldeman Diaries*, 319 (July 13, 1971).

66 Schulzinger, *Henry Kissinger*, 90.

67 Tyler, *Great Wall*, 112–113.

68 Michael Schaller, *Altered States: The United States and Japan Since the Occupation*, (New York: Oxford University Press, 1997), 228.

69 Ibid., 225–229; Johnson, *The Right Hand of Power*, 553–555; Kissinger, *White House Years*, 758, 761–762. On the Sato cabinet's internal divisions over China, see Sadako Ogata, *Normalization with China: A Comparative Study of U.S. and Japanese Processes* (Berkeley, CA: Institute of East Asian Studies, 1988), 38–43.

70 Ogata, *Normalization with China*, 47–55; Schaller, *Altered States*, 246.

71 Dobrynin, *In Confidence*, 225.

72 Ibid., 226–227.

73   Memcon: Kissinger and Dobrynin, July 19, 1971, Dobrynin/Kissinger, 1971, vol. 7, part 2, box 492, NSC, NPMP.

74   Memcons: Kissinger and Dobrynin, July 29, August 5 and 17, 1971, Dobrynin/Kissinger, 1971, vol. 7, parts 1–2, box 492, NSC, NPMP. Burr, *Kissinger Transcripts*, 44–45. Kissinger, *White House Years*, 837–838; Dobrynin, *In Confidence*, 231–233.

75   Memcon: Kissinger, Huang Chen, Lord, et al., July 26, 1971, box 330, Lord Files, PPS, RG 59, NA.

76   Kissinger to Nixon, August 16, 1971, ibid.

77   Kissinger, *White House Years*, 1024.

78   Kimball, *Nixon's Vietnam War*, 272.

79   Kissinger, *White House Years*, 1024–1031; Kimball, *Nixon's War*, 276; Loi and Vu, *Le Duc Tho–Kissinger Negotiations in Paris*, 191–192.

80   Kimball, *Nixon's Vietnam War*, 276–277.

81   Kissinger, *White House Years*, 1035–1037; Kimball, *Nixon's Vietnam War*, 277.

82   There were, in fact, four options in Kissinger's memorandum. One of them is still classified while the other—essentially an exchange between a fixed withdrawal date and POW releases—was dismissed by both Nixon and Kissinger as leading inevitably to the collapse of South Vietnam. Kimball, *Nixon's Vietnam War*, 279–280; Kissinger, *White House Years*, 1038–1039.

83   Kimball, *Nixon's Vietnam War*, 281.

84   Kissinger, *White House Years*, 1038–1040; Kimball, *Nixon's Vietnam War*, 281–282.

85   Quang Zhai, *China and the Vietnam War*, 196–197. Le Duan cited in *77 Conversations*, 180.

86   Le Duc Tho and Ieng Sary, September 7, 1971, CWIHP website (*77 Conversations*).

87   According to the Australian Labor Party leader, Gough Whitlam, Zhou had mentioned this during their talk on July 5, 1971; Whitlam announced this upon his return to Australia on July 14. Quang Zhai, *China and the Vietnam War*, 198–199.

88   Zhou Enlai and Le Duan, (undated, presumably October) 1971, *77 Conversations*.

89   Memcon: Kissinger and Dobrynin, September 20, 1971, Dobrynin/Kissinger, 1971, vol. 7, part 1, box 492, NSC, NPMP. Schulzinger, *Henry Kissinger*, 101.

90   See Ramesh Takur and Carlyle Thayer, *Soviet Relations with India and Vietnam* (London, 1992), 117; Gaiduk, *Soviet Union and the Vietnam War*, 239–241.

91   See Gaiduk, *Soviet Union and the Vietnam War*, 231–232; and Quang Zhai, *China and the Vietnam War*, 198–200.

92   Kissinger, *White House Years*, 442.

Chapter 8

1   Memcon: Kissinger, Zhou, et al., July 11, 1971.

2   Kissinger, *White House Years*, 913–914.

3   Christopher Van Hollen, "The Tilt Policy Revisited: Nixon–Kissinger Geopolitics and South Asia," *Asian Survey* 20, no. 4 (1980): 340. "That idiot Van Hollen drives me crazy," Kissinger once remarked. Memcon: Kissinger, Harold Saunders, James Farland, July 31, 1971, in *The White House and Pakistan: Secret Declassified Documents, 1969–1974*, ed. F. S. Aijazuddin (Karachi, 2002), 220. It is likely that their obvious anti-Kissinger and/or anti-Nixon stands have influenced Van Hollen, Garthoff, and Bundy. After all, Van Hollen and Garthoff were among the large group of State Department officials who felt marginalized, even betrayed, in the Nixon–Kissinger years; as a member of the previous presidential administration, Bundy, who appears convinced that Nixon stole the 1968 election, carries a rather obvious grudge. Yet, it is remarkable that virtually all historians who have written about the issue agree, by and large, with Van Hollen's statement about White House policy. Garthoff, *Détente and Confrontation*, 295; Bundy, *Tangled Web*, 269–292. Christopher Hitchens considers the policy toward the Indo-Pakistani conflict as one of Kissinger's crimes against humanity in Hitchens, *Trial of Henry Kissinger*, 44–54. For further critiques, see William Brands, *India and the United States: The Cold Peace* (New York, 1990), 122–139; Isaacson, *Kissinger*, 371–379; Van Hollen, "Tilt Policy"; Morris, *Uncertain Greatness*, 213–228; Hersh, *Price of Power*,

444–464. Kissinger's and Nixon's views are summarized in their memoirs: Kissinger, *White House Years*, 842–918; Nixon, *RN*, 525–531.

4   On the general history and background of the 1971 war, see McMahon, *Cold War on the Periphery*; Kux, *United States and Pakistan*; idem, *India and the United States*; Sumit Ganguly, *Conflict Unending: India-Pakistan Tensions since 1947* (New York, 2001).

5   Rena Fonseca, "Nehru and Nonalignment," in *The Diplomats, 1939–1979*, 394.

6   There is not, as of yet, a satisfying biography of Indira Gandhi. For a recent treatment see Katherine Frank, *Indira: The Life of Indira Nehru Gandhi* (New York: Houghton Mifflin, 2002).

7   For example, Thomas P. Thornton, "U.S.-Indian Relations During the Nixon and Ford Years," in *The Hope and the Reality: U.S.-Indian Relations from Roosevelt to Reagan*, ed. Harold A. Gould and Sumit Ganguly (Boulder, CO, 1992), 93–94. On the 1965 war, see Robert J. McMahon, *The United States, India, and Pakistan* (New York, 1994), 305–336; and Ganguly, *Conflict Unending*, 31–50.

8   Brands, *India and the United States*, 121.

9   For a summary of the Johnson administration's policy toward India, see Sumit Ganguly, "U.S.-Indian Relations During the Lyndon Johnson Era," in *Hope and Reality*, 81–90.

10   Nixon cited in Thornton, "Nixon and Ford Years," 93.

11   Kissinger, *White House Years*, 849.

12   Indeed, while visiting India in 1962 Kissinger had responded to a question about the importance of Kashmir—the most volatile region in the area—that he simply "did not know enough about it to form a judgment." Kissinger, *White House Years*, 847. Ironically, Kissinger managed to provoke a minor diplomatic incident when he said at the same conference that he did not expect the Pakistanis to be so foolish as to open a mutual relationship with the PRC because of the obviously aggressive nature of Beijing's policies. Accordingly, he was at the time accused of having a pro-Indian bias.

13   See Kux, *United States and Pakistan*, 181–183.

14   These developments are summed up well in, among others, Bundy, *Tangled Web*, 269–271; Ganguly, *Conflict Unending*, 57–61; Kux, *United States and Pakistan*, 184–187. For a more detailed assessment, see Sisson and Rose, *War and Secession*, esp. 54–133.

15   Ibid., 153.

16   Bundy, *Tangled Web*, 271–272; Garthoff, *Détente and Confrontation*, 296–297. See Van Hollen, "Tilt Policy," 340–341.

17   Kenneth Keating to Secretary of State, July 8, 1971, POL 7: US/Kissinger, box 2693, Subject Numeric Files, 1970–1973, RG 59, NA.

18   Cited in Brands, *India and the United States*, 133.

19   Summary cables of Kissinger's talks can be found in *White House and Pakistan*, 152–158. See also Hersh, *Price of Power*, 451; and Holdridge, *Crossing the Divide*, 52–53.

20   Nixon's handwritten comments on Haig to Nixon, July 9, 1971, USSR XIV, box 715, NSC, NPMP.

21   Kux, *United States and Pakistan*, 190, 194.

22   The State Department, for example, imposed a hold on the shipping of military equipment to Pakistan in March. See Van Hollen, "Tilt Policy," 344. Nixon discussed South Asia in only two full NSC meetings and only once after July 16; this was during a meeting on December 6 (after the war had broken out). Ibid., 345 n. 14. This does not mean that Nixon had no interest in the manner, but indicates how the NSC as such had lost much of its significance.

23   Kissinger, *White House Years*, 863; Isaacson, *Kissinger*, 373; Bundy, *Tangled Web*, 272; Kux, *United States and Pakistan*, 193–195.

24   Memcon: Kissinger, Farland, and Saunders, July 30, 1971, *White House and Pakistan*, 217–220. There is no record of the discussions between Kissinger and Farland after Saunders's departure from the meeting.

25   Kissinger *White House Years*, 865; Hersh, *Price of Power*, 454. See Bundy, *Tangled Web*, 272–273; Van Hollen, "Tilt Policy," 346–347. For the text of Nixon's August 4, 1971 press conference, see *PPP: Richard Nixon, 1971*, 849–861.

26 Kissinger, *White House Years*, 863–865.

27 For the text of the treaty, see Ganguly, *Conflict Unending*, 164–167.

28 Cited in Gaan, *Indira Gandhi and Foreign Policy Making*, 179. The discussion below is based partly on 175–199.

29 Kux, *United States and Pakistan*, 195; Ganguly, *Conflict Unending*, 65–66.

30 Kissinger, *White House Years*, 767.

31 Memcon: Nixon and Senior Review Group, August 11, 1971, in *White House and Pakistan*, 258–263; Kux, *United States and Pakistan*, 196.

32 Memcon: Kissinger and Dobrynin, August 17, 1971, Dobrynin/Kissinger, 1971, vol. 7, part 2, box 492, PTF, NSC, NPMP. See also *Kissinger Transcripts*, 45–46.

33 Kissinger, *White House Years*, 768.

34 Walters to Kissinger, July 19, 1971 and Kissinger to Walters (via Haig), July 20, 1971, "China exchanges—July—October 20, 1971," box 849, NSC, NPMP.

35 Memorandum of Conversation: Kissinger, Walters, Lord, Huang Chen, Tsao Kuei Sheng, and Wei Tung, July 26, 1971, box 330, Lord Files, PPS, RG 59, NA.

36 Memcon: Kissinger, Chen, et al., August 16, 1971; Kissinger to Nixon, August 16, 1971, box 330, Lord Files, PPS, RG 59, NA.

37 Kissinger, *White House Years*, 769.

38 For an extensive account of the Lin Biao affair, see, for example, Barnouin and Changgen, *Ten Years of Turbulence*, 199–246; and Teiwes and Sun, *Tragedy of Lin Biao*.

39 Teiwes and Sun, *Tragedy of Lin Biao*, 166–167.

40 Indeed, the two versions of why Lin Biao boarded the plane on September 13 illustrate the debate: the official version that Lin left because his plot had been uncovered; his daughter, Lin Doudou has indicated that Lin was virtually kidnapped by two of his close supporters who had panicked because of indications that Mao was about to launch a purge against Lin Biao and his associates. See Teiwes and Sun, *Tragedy of Lin Biao*, esp. 156. For a fairly up to date historiographical essay on the issue, see ibid., 1–6.

41 Chen Jian, *Mao's China and the Cold War*, 269–271.

42 Kissinger to Nixon, September 13, 1971, box 330, Lord Files, PPS, RG 59, NA.

43 Holdridge, *Crossing the Divide*, 68; Tucker, *China Confidential*, 241, 258–259.

44 Holdridge, *Crossing the Divide*, 70–71; Kissinger, *White House Years*, 776–777.

45 Kissinger to Nixon, November 11, 1971, "Book III China Trip—Record of Previous Visits," box 847, NSC, NPMP.

46 Tyler, *Great Wall*, 115–116; Kissinger, *White House Years*, 781–784. For a Chinese version, including an account of Mao's role during the talks, see "Kissinger's Second Visit to China in October 1971," Diplomatic History Institute of the Chinese Ministry of Foreign Affairs, *Xin zhongguo wenjiao fengyun* [New China's Diplomatic Experience] (Beijing, 1991), 3:59–70 (translated by Gao Bei, History Department, University of Virginia), NSArc website. While bidding farewell to Kissinger, Zhou spoke, for the first time, in English: "Come back soon for the joy of talking," he told the exhausted national security adviser.

47 Kissinger and Zhou, October 21, 1971, "Polo II—HAK China Trip October 1971 Transcript of Meetings," box 1034, NSC, NPMP.

48 Kissinger to Nixon, November 11, 1971, "Book III China Trip—Record of Previous Visits," box 847, NSC, NPMP. Both Zhou and Kissinger made a number of oblique references to the USSR throughout the talks, but their discussions never extended to specifics.

49 Memcon: Kissinger, Zhou, et al., October 22, 1971, "Polo II—HAK China Trip October 1971 Transcript of Meetings," box 1034, NSC, NPMP. "Five powers," reference on October 20.

50 Ibid.; and Kissinger to Nixon, November 11, 1971, "Book III China Trip—Record of Previous Visits," box 847, NSC, NPMP.

51 For Bush's version of events: George Bush with Victor Gould, *Looking Forward* (New York: Doubleday, 1987), 114–116.

52 Nixon and Kissinger, September 30, 1971, WHT 582–3, NPMP.

53 *Haldeman Diaries*, 368 (October 26, 1971); Tyler, *Great Wall*, 116–117; Kissinger, *White House Years*, 784–787; Mann, *About Face*, 38.

54   See Kissinger, *White House Years*, 785–787; Tyler, *Great Wall*, 117.

55   Haig to Kissinger, November 22, 1971, box 330, Lord Files, PPS, RG 59, NA (about the safehouse); Kissinger, *White House Years*, 786.

56   Kissinger, *White House Years*, 880–881; Reeves, *President Nixon*, 391; Isaacson, *Kissinger*, 374; Bundy, *Tangled Web*, 275–276; Van Hollen, "Tilt Policy," 348–350.

57   Keating to State, October 9, 1971, in *White House and Pakistan*, 303–304. Also, Rose and Sisson, *War and Secession*, 242–245; Kux, *United States and Pakistan*, 194; Ganguly, *Conflict Unending*, 66.

58   Memcon: Nixon, Gromyko, et al., September 29, 1971; memcon: Kissinger and Dobrynin, October 8, 1971, Dobrynin/Kissinger, 1971, vol. 7, part 1, box 492, PTF, NSC, NPMP.

59   Memcon: Nixon, Gandhi, Kissinger, Haksar, November 4, 1971, "Memcons May 1971–Sept 1973 [2 of 2]," box 1030, HAK + Presidential Memcons, NSC, NPMP.

60   Hersh, *Price of Power*, 456; Brands, *India and the United States*, 134.

61   Saunders to Kissinger, November 11, 1971 and memcon: Kissinger and Sultan Khan, November 15, 1971, in *White House and Pakistan*, 345–346, 353–361; memcon: Kissinger and Dobrynin, November 18, 1971, Dobrynin/Kissinger, 1971, vol. 7, part 1, box 492, PTF, NSC, NPMP.

62   *Haldeman Diaries*, 377 (November 22, 1971); Tyler, *Great Wall*, 118.

63   Memcon: Kissinger, Huang Hua, November 23, 1971, box 330, Lord Files, PPS, RG 59, NA. Emphasis added.

64   Tyler, *Great Wall*, 120.

65   Rose and Sisson, *War and Secession*, 227–230; Kux, *United States and Pakistan*, 199; Van Hollen, "Tilt Policy," 350. The Pakistani attacks in the West were quickly followed by Indian retaliation.

66   For a Pakistani criticism of the Khan government's naiveté—its belief that the Pakistani role in helping to bring about the opening to China would help it through the East Pakistani crisis—see the book by Ali Bhutto's son: Raza, *Zufikar Ali Bhutto and Pakistan*, esp. 91–141.

67   For details of the UN debate, see Gaan, *Indira Gandhi and Foreign Policy Making*, 232–237; Sisson and Rose, *War and Secession*, 218–220; Raza, *Zufikar Ali Bhutto and Pakistan*, 120–129; Kux, *United States and Pakistan*, 200–204.

68   Memcons: Nixon and Matskevich, Kissinger and Vorontsov, December 9, 1971, Dobrynin/Kissinger, 1971, vol. 8, box 492, PTF, NSC, NPMP; Sisson and Rose, *War and Secession*, 262–263; Dobrynin, *In Confidence*, 236–237.

69   Memorandum of Conversation: Kissinger, Huang Hua, George Bush, et al., December 10, 1971, in *Kissinger Transcripts*, 48–57.

70   For an extensive account of the war, see Sisson and Rose, *War and Secession*, 206–236.

71   Ibid., 236ff.; and Ganguly, *Conflict Unending*, 69–72.

72   Kissinger, *White House Years*, 918.

73   Kux, *United States and Pakistan*, 206.

74   Dobrynin, *In Confidence*, 237. According to Dobrynin, Kissinger later acknowledged, albeit never in public, having acted in a somewhat unreasonable manner during the crisis. Ibid., 238.

75   Ibid.

76   Memcon: Kissinger and Dobrynin, January 28, 1972, Dobrynin/Kissinger, 1972, vol. 9, part 2, box 493, PTF, NSC, NPMP.

77   Zhou Enlai's report to the CCP, December 1971, excerpts printed in Barnouin and Yu, *Chinese Foreign Policy During the Cultural Revolution*, 188–196.

Chapter 9

1   Nixon's remarks at Andrews Air Force Base are in *PPP: Richard Nixon, 1972* (Washington, DC: GPO, 1973), 381–383.

2   The best succinct account of the Watergate scandal is Olson, *Watergate*.

3   Isaacson, *Kissinger*, 380–397; *Haldeman Diaries*, 481–482 (January 13–15, 1972); Reeves, *President Nixon*, 409–427.

4   Nixon's complete speech is in *PPP: Richard Nixon, 1972,* 100–106.

5   Reeves, *President Nixon,* 427–429.

6   Memcon: Kissinger and Dobrynin, January 28, 1972, Dobrynin/Kissinger, 1972, vol. 9, part 2, box 493, PTF, NSC, NPMP.

7   Kimball, *Nixon's Vietnam War,* 290–292.

8   *Haldeman Diaries,* 498 (February 14, 1972).

9   Ibid., 498–499 (February 14, 1972); Kimball, *Nixon's Vietnam War,* 296–299. Berman mistakenly writes that the invitation came while Kissinger was in China. Berman, *No Peace, No Honor,* 122.

10   Burr, *Kissinger Transcripts,* 58; Tyler, *Great Wall,* 129. See also Li Zhisui, *The Private Life of Chairman Mao,* 553–564.

11   Kissinger, *White House Years,* 1058–1060.

12   Memorandum of Conversation: Nixon, Mao, Kissinger, Lord, Zhou, et al., February 21, 1972, *Kissinger Transcripts,* 59–65. See also Mann, *About Face,* 44–46; Tyler, *Great Wall,* 134–135; Nixon, *RN,* 567–568: Kissinger, *White House Years,* 1070–1073.

13   Memcon: Nixon, Zhou, et al., February 21, 1972, Memoranda for the President, "Beginning February 20, 1972," box 87, POF, NPMP. Kissinger hardly said a word during the meeting.

14   With obvious disdain Kissinger calls these issues "the obsessions of the East Asian Bureau" of the State Department. Kissinger, *White House Years,* 1070. For an embittered view of a State Department representative, see Green, Holdridge, and Stokes, *War and Peace with China,* 159–161 (a chapter by Green).

15   *Haldeman Diaries,* 422 (February 27, 1972); Hersh, *Price of Power,* 494.

16   Memcon: Nixon, Zhou, et al., February 21 and 24, 1972, Memoranda for the President, "Beginning February 20, 1972," box 87, POF, NPMP.

17   Memcon: Nixon, Zhou, et al., February 22, 1972, Memoranda for the President, "Beginning February 20, 1972," box 87, POF, NPMP. See also Tyler, *Great Wall,* 134–135, which in turn is based on Nixon, *RN,* 567–568.

18   Memcon: Nixon, Zhou, et al., February 22, 1972, Memoranda for the President, "Beginning February 20, 1972," box 87, POF, NPMP.

19   Ibid.; Memcon: Nixon, Zhou, et al., February 23 and 24, 1972, Memoranda for the President, "Beginning February 20, 1972," box 87, POF, NPMP.

20   *Haldeman Diaries,* 421–422 (February 26 and 27, 1972).

21   The Shanghai Communiqué can be found in Mayall and Navari, *The End of the Post-War Era,* 114–117.

22   *Haldeman Diaries,* 423–424 (February 29, 1972).

23   *Haldeman Diaries,* 424 (March 2, 1972).

24   Tyler, *Great Wall,* 143. See also Kissinger, *White House Years,* 1093; *Haldeman Diaries,* 423 (February 28, 1972).

25   Tyler, *Great Wall,* 144. Ashbrook cited in Schulzinger, *Henry Kissinger,* 100.

26   Kissinger, *White House Years,* 1093. On the primaries, see Small, *Presidency of Richard Nixon,* 262–263.

27   Holdridge, *Crossing the Divide,* 97–102; Green, Holdridge, and Stokes, *War and Peace with China,* 167–173.

28   On Soviet policy toward Taiwan, see Michael Share, "From Ideological Foe to Uncertain Friend: Soviet Relations with Taiwan, 1943–1982," *Cold War History* 3, no. 2 (January 2003): 1–34.

29   Memcons: Dobrynin and Kissinger, March 1, 9 and 10, 1972, Dobrynin/Kissinger, 1972, vol. 9, part 1, box 493, PTF, NSC, NPMP.

30   Kissinger, *White House Years,* 1091.

Chapter 10

1   Nixon to Kissinger (two memos), March 11, 1972, "HAK/President Memos 1971–," box 341, NSC, NPMP. See also Schulzinger, *Time for War,* 294.

2   Kimball, *Nixon's Vietnam War,* 299–300; Memcon: Dobrynin and Kissinger, March 10, 1972, Dobrynin/Kissinger, 1972, vol. 9, part 1, box 493, PTF, NSC, NPMP.

3 *Haldeman Diaries*, 434 (March 30, 1972).

4 For more detailed discussions of the Spring Offensive, see Kimball, *Nixon's Vietnam War*, 302–308; Schulzinger, *Time for War*, 295–297; James S. Olson and Randy Roberts, *Where the Domino Fell: America and Vietnam, 1945–1990* (New York: St. Martin's, 1991), 246–249.

5 Bunker cited in Olson and Roberts, *Where the Domino Fell*, 248; Nixon in *Haldeman Diaries*, 438 (April 10, 1972). See also Kimball, *Nixon's Vietnam War*, 304; and Kimball, *Vietnam War Files*, 205–209.

6 *Haldeman Diaries*, 440, 441 (April 15–17, 1972); Kimball, *Nixon's Vietnam War*, 307.

7 Qiang Zhai, *China and the Vietnam War*, 203; Garthoff, *Détente and Confrontation*, 290; Kimball, *Nixon's Vietnam War*, 306.

8 Zhou Enlai and Nguyen Tien, April 12, 1972, in *77 Conversations*, 179.

9 Qiang Zhai, *China and the Vietnam War*, 203.

10 Memcons: Kissinger and Dobrynin, April 9, 12 and 15, 1972; Telcons: Kissinger and Dobrynin, Kissinger and Nixon, April 12, 1972, Dobrynin/Kissinger, 1972, vol. 10, box 493, PTF, NSC, NPMP; Dobrynin, *In Confidence*, 243–245.

11 Dobrynin, *In Confidence*, 245; Kissinger, *White House Years*, 1124–1126. In a swipe at the Soviets, Kissinger writes that Moscow "had pressed for months for a clandestine visit, almost certainly for the simple reason that Peking had had a secret trip and they were entitled to equality!" Such pettiness may have played a role, but ultimately it was Nixon and Kissinger's insistence that kept the trip secret. Kissinger cited in *White House Years*, 1124.

12 Kissinger to Nixon, April 18, 1972, USSR XXI, box 718, NSC, NPMP.

13 Kissinger, *White House Years*, 1135–1136; Kimball, *Nixon's Vietnam War*, 308. Telcon: Kissinger–Nixon, April 15, 1972, NSecA webpage.

14 Nixon to Kissinger, April 20, 1972, "Hak/President Memos 1971–," box 341, NSC, NPMP. See also Kimball, *Nixon's Vietnam War*, 308.

15 *Haldeman Diaries*, 443 (April 20, 1972).

16 Memcon: Kissinger, Brezhnev, et al., April 21, 1972, "HAK Moscow Trip—April 1972 Memcons," box 72, HAKOF, NSC, NPMP; Kissinger to Haig, April 21, 1972 (HAKTO 5), box 21, HAKOF, NPMP.

17 Memcon: Kissinger, Brezhnev, et al., April 22, 1972, "HAK Moscow Trip—April 1972 Memcons," box 72, HAKOF, NSC, NPMP. Summarized by Kissinger in *White House Years*, 1146–1147. See also Kimball, *Nixon's Vietnam War*, 308–309; Gaiduk, *Soviet Union and the Vietnam War*, 236–237.

18 Kissinger to Nixon, April 24, 1972, "HAK Moscow Trip—April 1972 Memcons," box 72, HAKOF, NSC, NPMP.

19 Telcon: Nixon and Haig, April 21, 1972, 9:35 P.M., box 999, Haig Chronological File, Haig Telcons 1972 [2 of 2], NSC, NPMP ("bullshit"); *Haldeman Diaries*, 445 (April 23, 1972). The following paragraphs are partly based on Kimball, *Nixon's Vietnam War*, 308–309; Kissinger, *White House Years*, 1144–1154; Garthoff, *Détente and Confrontation*, 290; Gaiduk, *Soviet Union and the Vietnam War*, 236. Dobrynin offers little on the Moscow meetings in his memoirs. Dobrynin, *In Confidence*, 245.

20 Kissinger to Haig, April 22, 1972 (HAKTO 8 and 10), box 21, HAKOF, NSC, NPMP.

21 Haig to Kissinger (TOHAK 32, 32, 36) April 22, 1972, box 21 HAKOF, NSC, NPMP.

22 Kissinger to Haig (HAKTO 12, 14), April 23, 1972, box 21 HAKOF, NSC, NPMP.

23 Kissinger to Haig (HAKTO 15, 19), April 24, 1972, box 21 HAKOF, NSC, NPMP. Eventually Kissinger did get most of the credit for SALT I. At a NSC meeting on May 1, Nixon approved the agreement Kissinger had reached with the Soviets on SLBM figures. He did so over the objections of Gerard Smith and William Rogers, who argued that the figures (656 for the United States and 950 for the Soviets), combined with the agreed ICBM freeze that favored the Soviets, was bound to leave Moscow with a numerical advantage in both categories of offensive weapons. Bundy, *Tangled Web*, 311–312. See also Kissinger, *White House Years*; Smith, *Doubletalk*, 370–378.

24 Kissinger to Nixon, April 24, 1972, "HAK Moscow Trip—April 1972 Memcons," box 72, HAKOF, NSC, NPMP. See also Kimball, Vietnam War Files, 211–214.

25   *Haldeman Diaries*, 543–544 (April 24, 1972).

26   Ibid., 545–546 (April 26, 1972). Nixon's speech in *American Foreign Relations, 1972: A Documentary Record*, 252–256. "It was a tough speech," Nixon writes in his memoirs, "and afterward I wished I had made it even tougher." Nixon, *RN*, 593.

27   Nixon to Kissinger, April 30, 1972, "HAK/President Memos 1971–," box 341, NSC, NPMP. See also Kimball, *Nixon's Vietnam War*, 312; Kissinger, *White House Years*, 1168.

28   *Haldeman Diaries*, 450 (May 1, 1972); Kimball, *Nixon's Vietnam War*, 312.

29   Kissinger, *White House Years*, 1169–1174; Kimball, *Nixon's Vietnam War*, 312–313; Loi and Vu, *Le Duc Tho–Kissinger Negotiations in Paris*, 220–227; Berman, *No Peace, No Honor*, 126–129. In fact, Kissinger had suggested, perhaps partly in jest, that the two sides publicize the record of their meetings. The North Vietnamese refused.

30   Kissinger to Haig (HAKTO 2) and Haig to Kissinger (TOHAK 2), May 2, 1972, box 22, HAKOF, NPMP.

31   This was one of the four occasions when, Nixon later recalled, he considered the use of nuclear weapons. The previous Vietnam-related case had been in October 1969, when Nixon ordered a secret nuclear alert. See William Burr and Jeffrey Kimball, "Nixon's Secret Nuclear Alert: Vietnam War Diplomacy and the Joint Chiefs of Staff Readiness Test, October 1969," *Cold War History* 3, no. 2 (January 2003): 113–156.

32   The basic options are outlined in Kissinger to Nixon, May 2, 1972, Lord Files, box 335. See also Kissinger, *White House Years*, 1174–1176; Kimball, *Nixon's Vietnam War*, 313; Berman, *No Peace, No Honor*, 130.

33   Dobrynin, *In Confidence*, 245–246; Kissinger, *White House Years*, 1176–1177.

34   *Haldeman Diaries*, 452–453 (May 3, 1972).

35   The longtime FBI director had died on May 2, prompting Nixon to write in his diaries: "I am glad I did not force him out." Ambrose, *Nixon: Ruin and Recovery*, 543

36   *Haldeman Diaries*, 453 (May 4, 1972).

37   Ambrose, *Nixon: Ruin and Recovery*, 538.

38   Kissinger, *White House Years*, 1184–1185; Nixon, *RN*, 603–604; Berman, *No Peace, No Honor*, 130; Kimball, *Nixon's Vietnam War*, 315.

39   *Haldeman Diaries*, 456 (May 8, 1972). Kissinger tells a different story. According to *White House Years*, when he arrived at Nixon's EOB office, Haldeman, with Nixon's consent, started raising a number of questions about the negative domestic impact that was likely to follow and could cost Nixon his reelection. Kissinger writes that he "passionately defended the decision" to go ahead with the mining. But, he writes, that this was evidently a way for Nixon to trick Kissinger into defending the decision and have it recorded on tape so that "the hated 'Georgetown social set'" could not argue that a difference of opinion between Kissinger and Nixon existed. It is, of course, entirely possible that both Kissinger and Haldeman recorded the events accurately, but the conspiratorial motive Kissinger ascribes to Nixon seems far-fetched. After all, Kissinger had little choice but to support the decision and Nixon showed no inclination to bring the tape to anybody's attention. Kissinger, *White House Years*, 1185–1186. See also Kimball, *Vietnam War Files*, 220–228.

40   Memcon: Kissinger and Dobrynin, May 8, 1972, Dobrynin/Kissinger, 1972, vol. 11, box 494, PTF, NSC, NPMP; Kissinger, *White House Years*, 1187–1189; Dobrynin, *In Confidence*, 246–247.

41   Cited in Kissinger, *White House Years*, 1190.

42   Kissinger to Nixon, May 17, 1972, box 328, Lord Files, PPS, RG 59, NA.

43   Memcons: Kissinger and Dobrynin, May 10, 12, 14 17 and 18, 1972, Dobrynin/Kissinger, 1972, vol. 11, box 494, PTF, NSC, NPMP.

44   Dobrynin, *In Confidence*, 248. The main opponents of the summit in the Politburo were Marshall Grechko and President Podgorny, while the chief ideologist, Suslov, was undecided.

45   Nixon to Haig, May 20, 1972, NSC Subject Files, "HAK/President Memos 1971–," box 341, NSC, NPMP; Kimball, *Nixon's Vietnam War*, 316.

46   Kissinger, *White House Years*, 1201.

47   Memcons: Nixon and Brezhnev, May 22, 1972 and Nixon, Brezhnev, Rogers, Podgorny, et al., May 23, 1972, "Mr. Kissinger's Conversations in Moscow May 1972," box 73, HAKOF, NSC, NPMP.

48   Kissinger, *White House Years*, 1210.

49   Memcons: Nixon, Brezhnev, Kissinger, Aleksander-Agentov, May 23, 1972 (4:00–6:00 P.M. and 7:20–9:55 P.M.), "Mr. Kissinger's Conversations in Moscow May 1972," box 73, HAKOF, NSC, NPMP.

50   Memcons: Kissinger, Gromyko et al., May 25 (3) and May 26, 1972, "Mr. Kissinger's Conversations in Moscow May 1972," box 73, HAKOF, NSC, NPMP.

51   Garthoff, *Journey Through the Cold War*, 269–270. The arrival of the SALT delegation had its own comic features: for example, no car had been arranged to transport Smith's principal aides, Paul H. Nitze and Raymond Garthoff, to the Kremlin and the two were forced to find their own way as best they could. Ibid.

52   Cited in Hersh, *Price of Power*, 550.

53   On the agreements and criticism, see Bundy, *Tangled Web*, 323–327, 345–347; Garthoff, *Détente and Confrontation*, 188–198, 298–301. Hyland in Isaacson, *Kissinger*, 436.

54   Garthoff, *Détente and Confrontation*, 290.

55   Cited in ibid., 292.

56   Memcon: Nixon, Brezhnev, Kissinger, Kosygin, et al., May 26, 1972, "Mr. Kissinger's Conversations in Moscow May 1972," box 73, HAKOF, NSC, NPMP.

57   Memcons: Kissinger, Gromyko, et al., May 28, 1972, Nixon, Brezhnev, Kissinger, and Aleksandrov-Agentov, May 29, 1972, "Mr. Kissinger's Conversations in Moscow May 1972," box 73, HAKOF, NSC, NPMP.

58   Kissinger recounts this story in *White House Years*, 1223–1224. See also Nixon, *RN*, 612–613. The experience reminded Nixon of his visit to the Soviet Union thirteen years earlier, when Khrushchev had pulled off a similar surprise.

59   Memcon: Nixon, Kissinger, Brezhnev, Kosygin, Podgorny, et al., May 24, 1972, "Mr. Kissinger's Conversations in Moscow May 1972," box 73, HAKOF, NSC, NPMP. See also, Kissinger, *White House Years*, 1227–1229.

60   Kissinger, *White House Years*, 1225–1229; Nixon, *RN*, 613–615. Winston Lord made this point as well. Winston Lord interview by the author. Memcon: Brezhnev, Nixon, Kissinger, Aleksander-Agentov, May 29, 1972, "Mr. Kissinger's Conversations in Moscow May 1972," box 73, HAKOF, NSC, NPMP.

61   Gaiduk, *Soviet Union and the Vietnam War*, 240; Kimball, *Nixon's Vietnam War*, 318.

62   Memcon: Kissinger, Gromyko, et al., May 27, 1972, "Mr. Kissinger's conversations in Moscow May 1972," box 21, NSC, HAKOF, NPMP.

63   *PPP: Richard Nixon, 1972*, 660–666.

64   Schulzinger, *Henry Kissinger*, 101.

Chapter 11

1   *Haldeman Diaries*, 517 (October 10, 1972).

2   Ibid., 515–517 (October 12 and 13, 1972); Kissinger, *White House Years*, 1360–1361; Nixon, *RN*, 691–692; Kimball, *Nixon's Vietnam War*, 340. Not surprisingly, neither Kissinger nor Nixon mentions the plans to deceive Rogers in their memoirs.

3   *Haldeman Diaries*, 658 (November 21, 1972).

4   Kimball, *Nixon's Vietnam War*, 319–320; Berman, *No Peace, No Honor*, 136; Kissinger, *White House Years*, 1303–1304; Gaiduk, *Soviet Union and the Vietnam War*, 240–241. See also Dobrynin, *In Confidence*, 257. The point about the hostile reaction that Podgorny faced in Hanoi should hardly be a surprise given the proximity of the Moscow summit and the Soviets' timid reaction to Linebacker I. But this hardly precludes the possibility that the Vietnamese were also ready to learn about any American proposals and willing to engage in peace talks. In other words, they were angry at the Soviets but realistic about the situation.

5   In a fascinating contrast to his other forays to the Middle Kingdom, this four-day trip is described in one vague paragraph. Kissinger, *White House Years*, 1304. Dobrynin briefly comments that Kissinger simply told him that "he had failed to reach an agreement with the Chinese on Vietnam." Dobrynin, *In Confidence*, 257.

6   Memcon: Kissinger, Zhou, et al., June 19, 1972, "China, Dr. Kissinger's Visit June 1972," box 97, HAKOF, NSC, NPMP.

7   Memcon: Kissinger and Zhou, June 20, 1971, "China, Dr. Kissinger's Visit June 1972," box 97, HAKOF, NSC, NPMP.

8   Memcon: Kissinger and Zhou, June 20, 1972, "China, Dr. Kissinger's Visit June 1972," box 97, HAKOF, NSC, NPMP.

9   Ibid. Emphasis added.

10   Memcon: Kissinger and Dobrynin, June 26, 1972, Dobrynin/Kissinger, 1972, vol. 12, part 2, box 494, PTF, NSC, NPMP. A few weeks later, just prior to Kissinger's return to the negotiation table in Paris, Dobrynin was invited to visit Nixon's Western White House in San Clemente, California. The president, once again, stressed the significance of ending the war in Vietnam. Yet most of the meeting was spent on other issues. Memcon: Nixon, Kissinger and Dobrynin, July 12, 1972, Dobrynin/Kissinger, 1972, vol. 12, part 1, box 494, PTF, NSC, NPMP.

11   Kissinger, *White House Years*, 1304; Small, *Presidency of Richard Nixon*, 90.

12   Zhou Enlai and Le Duc Tho, July 12, 1972, *77 Conversations*, 179–182.

13   The debate about the causes and timing of the breakdown of the Sino-Vietnamese alliance is still on. It seems fairly clear, though, that the cooperation between the two countries remained close, if increasingly tense, at least until early 1973 and that the significant tensions began to set in only after the unification of Vietnam in the spring of 1975. See Gilks, *Breakdown of the Sino-Vietnamese Alliance*, esp. chapters 5–6; Morris, *Why Vietnam Invaded Cambodia*, esp. chapter 6; essays by Westad, Chen and Tonneson in *77 Conversations*.

14   Kimball, *Nixon's Vietnam War*, 320–321; Kimball, *Vietnam War Files*, 240–246; Berman, *No Peace, No Honor*, 136–138; Kissinger, *White House Years*, 1312–1313; Loi and Vu, *Le Duc Tho–Kissinger Negotiations in Paris*, 244–254.

15   On July 20 Dobrynin—obviously well briefed—actually asked why Kissinger had not mentioned the political proposals during the Paris meetings. "Because we did not want to have it refused," Kissinger responded. "You are a good chess player," volunteered Dobrynin, perhaps in jest. Dobrynin/Kissinger, 1972, vol. 12, part 1, box 494, PTF, NSC, NPMP.

16   Kissinger to Bunker (WHS 2088), July 20, 1972, "Washington to Saigon, 2/21/72–7/23/72"; Bunker to Kissinger (Saigon 0114), July 20, 1972, "Saigon to Washington, 2/21/72–7/23/72," box 1, NSC Convenience Files, GFL.

17   Kimball, *Nixon's Vietnam War*, 321–322; Berman, *No Peace, No Honor*, 138–139; Kissinger, *White House Years*, 1315–1317; Loi and Vu, *Le Duc Tho–Kissinger Negotiations in Paris*, 259–265. Kissinger to Bunker, (WHS 2100), August 3, 1972, "Washington to Saigon, 7/25/72–9/13/72," box 1, NSC Convenience Files, GFL. Dobrynin also raised Kissinger's hopes by volunteering that "if the President was still far ahead [in the polls] in late September a break [in the negotiations] might come." Dobrynin/Kissinger, 1972, vol. 13, box 495, PTF, NSC, NPMP.

18   Kissinger, *White House Years*, 1318; Kimball, *Nixon's Vietnam War*, 322; Loi and Vu, *Le Duc Tho–Kissinger Negotiations in Paris*, 268–272.

19   Kimball, *Nixon's Vietnam War*, 329–332; Berman, *No Peace, No Honor*, 141–144; Kissinger, *White House Years*, 1321–1325; Hung and Schecter, *Palace File*, 65–67.

20   Kissinger to Haig, September 13, 1972, and Haig to Kissinger, September 14, 1972, box 23, HAKOF, NSC, NPMP. See also Kimball, *Nixon's Vietnam War*, 332–333; Kimball, *Vietnam War Files*, 246–253; Berman, *No Peace, No Honor*, 143–144; Kissinger, *White House Years*, 1326–1331. Nixon had signed the August 31 letter while conferring with Ambassador Bunker and Kissinger in Hawaii, a meeting that Thieu had declined to attend. The letter is reprinted in Hung and Schecter, *Palace File*, 68.

21   Kissinger to Bunker (WHS 2165), September 17, 1972, "Washington to Saigon, 9/16/72–10/17/72," box 2, NSC Convenience Files, GFL.

22   Haig to Kissinger, September 14, 1972, box 23, HAKOF, NSC, NPMP.

23   Kimball, *Nixon's Vietnam War*, 333–334; Berman, *No Peace, No Honor*, 146–147; Kissinger, *White House Years*, 1332–1334; *Haldeman Diaries*, 504–505 (September 16, 1972); Loi and Vu, *Le Duc Tho–Kissinger Negotiations in Paris*, 284–290.

24   Kissinger to Bunker, September 16 (WHS 2162) and September 17 (WHS 2165), 1972, both in "Washington to Saigon, 9/16/72–10/17/72," box 2, NSC Convenience Files, GFL.

25   Kissinger to Bunker, September 21 (WHS 2166) and September 22 (WHS 2168), 1972, "Washington to Saigon, 9/16/72–10/17/72"; Bunker to Kissinger, September 23, 1972 (Saigon 0164), "Saigon to Washington, 9/16/72–10/17/72," box 2, NSC Convenience Files, GFL. The September 22 letter is printed partly in Kissinger, *White House Years*, 1335; and Hung and Schecter, *Palace File*, 71.

26   Kimball, *Nixon's Vietnam War*, 327–329; Kissinger, *White House Years*, 1319; Haig to Kissinger, August 15, 1972, box 23, HAKOF, NSC, NPMP. In the telegram Haig wrote: "My personal view is that the problem is not with the principal (ie. Nixon) but with a very strong minded former cabinet member (ie. Connally) who seems to feel compelled to delve into our business."

27   Kimball, *Nixon's Vietnam War*, 334–335; Berman, *No Peace, No Honor*, 148–149; Kissinger, *White House Years*, 1335–1337; Loi and Vu, *Le Duc Tho–Kissinger Negotiations in Paris*, 292–299.

28   *Haldeman Diaries*, 510 (September 28, 1972). See also Kimball, *Nixon's Vietnam War*, 336.

29   Kissinger to Bunker, September 28, 1972 (WHS 2171), "Washington to Saigon, 9/16/72–10/17/72," box 2, NSC Convenience Files, GFL. Thieu's September 26 message is reprinted in Hung and Schecter, *Palace File*, Appendix B. Thieu's concerns may have been furthered when Bunker, upon Kissinger's instructions, told him to instruct his commanders to seize "maximum amount of critical territory" because of indications that the North Vietnamese "may surface a ceasefire proposal." Kissinger to Bunker, September 26, 1972 (WHS 2212), "Washington to Saigon, 9/16/72–10/17/72," box 2, NSC Convenience Files, GFL.

30   Memcon: Thieu, Haig et al., October 4, 1972, "Memos, speeches, correspondence, 9/26/72–11/11/72 (1)," box 6, NSC Convenience Files, GFL. See also Hung and Schecter, *Palace File*, 72–73, Appendix C (Thieu's letter).

31   Kimball, *Nixon's Vietnam War*, 336–337.

32   Memcon: Nixon, Gromyko, Kissinger, and Dobrynin, October 2, 1972, Dobrynin/Kissinger, 1972, vol. 13, box 495, PTF, NSC, NPMP; Memcon: Kissinger and Hua, October 3, 1972, PPS, Lord Files, box 328, RG 59, NA. See also Kissinger, *White House Years*, 1339; Kimball, *Nixon's Vietnam War*, 336.

33   Cited in Hung and Schecter, *Palace File*, Appendix A. See also Kimball, *Nixon's Vietnam War*, 337; Kissinger, *White House Years*, 1338–1339. Kissinger's talking points to Nixon for the president's meeting with Gromyko do not mention Vietnam but focus on Brezhnev's planned 1973 visit to Washington, the Conference on Security and Cooperation in Europe (CSCE) and the next round of SALT talks. Kissinger to Nixon, October 2, 1972, USSR XXVI, box 721, NSC Country Files, NPMP.

34   Kissinger, *White House Years*, 1345. After listening to Tho's proposal, Kissinger immediately asked for a break. The half-hour was spent mostly in shaking hands and exchanging congratulations. The one member of the group that was less than euphoric—correctly as it turned out—was John Negroponte. On this round of negotiations, see also Kimball, *Nixon's Vietnam War*, 338–339; Loi and Vu, *Le Duc Tho–Kissinger Negotiations in Paris*, 308–335.

35   Kissinger to Bunker, October 11 (WHS 2215), "Washington to Saigon, 9/16/72–10/17/72," box 2, NSC Convenience Files, GFL.

36   Kissinger, *White House Years*, 1351; Nixon, *RN*, 691; *Haldeman Diaries*, 514 (October 10, 1972).

37   *Haldeman Diaries*, 515–517 (October 12 and 13, 1972); Kissinger, *White House Years*, 1360–1361; Nixon, *RN*, 691–692; Kimball, *Nixon's Vietnam War*, 340.

38   Instead of the agreed-upon term *administrative structure* when referring to the Council of National Reconciliation and Concord, the North Vietnamese version still used the potentially more far-reaching term *political structure*. It is important to note, though, that there is a potentially significant difference in the manner by which Dobrynin and Kissinger indicate the Soviets received a copy of the draft agreement. While Kissinger writes that Dobrynin had

"received the text of the draft agreement from Hanoi," the Soviet ambassador maintains that "the Vietnamese had not even informed us of its existence" and he got the draft from Kissinger. Dobrynin, *In Confidence*, 260–261; Kissinger, *White House Years*, 1363–1364.

39 Kissinger to Haig (HAKTO 5), October 17, 1972. The decision to share more information with Rogers followed a heated Haig–Rogers meeting on October 17 that boiled down to the secretary of state (accurately) accusing Kissinger's deputy of lying when he, rather implausibly, denied having a copy of the political draft agreements. Haig to Kissinger (HAKTO 16 and 17), October 17, 1972. These and other telegrams relating to the trip in box 25, HAKOF, NSC, NPMP. See also Kissinger, *White House Years*, 1365; Kimball, *Nixon's Vietnam War*, 340–341; Berman, *No Peace, No Honor*, 160–162.

40 *Haldeman Diaries*, 521–522 (October 17, 1972).

41 The presence of a contingent of South Korean troops in Vietnam was part of the reason why Habib was invited to Saigon; his conviction was that Seoul would consider the agreement a victory.

42 Hung and Schecter, *Palace File*, 83–85.

43 Several messages between Haig and Kissinger on October 18–23 that summarize each meeting's developments can be found in box 25, HAKOF, NSC, NPMP. A particularly poignant one is Kissinger to Haig (HAKTO 26 and 28), October 21, 1972, in which Kissinger still pleads that he should go to Hanoi to finalize the agreement despite Thieu's obvious objections. Other messages, which repeat much of the same information but were written by Ambassador Bunker, are in "Saigon to Washington, 10/22/72–11/6/72," box 2, NSC Convenience Files, GFL. The accusation about conniving with the Chinese and the Soviets as well as being sold out are from Bunker to Haig (Saigon 0223), October 22, 1972. Kissinger, *White House Years*, 1380–1391 (citation 1380). For a slightly different version of the meetings, see Hung and Schecter, *Palace File*, 84–106. See also Kimball, *Vietnam War Files*, 254–256.

44 Kissinger, *White House Years*, 1388, 1391–1392.

45 Memcon: Kissinger, Huang Hua, et al., October 24, 1972, box 328, Lord Files, PPS, RG 59, NA. Emphasis added.

46 Dobrynin, *In Confidence*, 261; Kissinger, *White House Years*, 1393.

47 *Haldeman Diaries*, 523 (October 26, 1972). The key points of the agreements as well as a brief history of the negotiations and the timetable for signing the agreement were broadcasted over Radio Hanoi on October 25, Hanoi time. Kimball, *Nixon's Vietnam War*, 345. A complete text that was released a day later and printed, among other places, in *Beijing Review* the following week can be found in *American Foreign Relations, 1972: A Documentary Record* (New York, 1976).

48 Kissinger's account in *White House Years*, 1398–1405 (McGovern cited on 1404). His version of the Fallaci interview—which he calls a case of "skillful editing" and puts down to his own "naivete" (an astonishing statement from someone as adept at dealing with the press as Kissinger) in ibid., 1409–1410. The October 26 statement can be found in *American Foreign Relations, 1972*, 285–292. On punditry and the Fallaci interview: Schulzinger, *Henry Kissinger*, 113–115; Isaacson, *Kissinger*, 475–479; and Bundy, *Tangled Web*, 358. Bundy mistakenly asserts that Kissinger "wound up" with the dramatic "peace is at hand" statement; in fact, he virtually opened with it. Nevertheless, that was the sound bite that all observers seized upon. Nixon, while making much of the pressure that the statement put him under, does not mention the Fallaci interview in his memoirs.

49 Kissinger, *White House Years*, 1401.

50 Memcon: Kissinger, Huang Hua, et al., November 3, 1972, box 328, Lord Files, PPS, RG 59, NA. Emphasis added.

51 *Haldeman Diaries*, 537 (November 17, 1972).

52 Nixon, *RN*, 731.

53 For these developments, see Kimball, *Nixon's Vietnam War*, 350–367; Berman, *No Peace, No Honor*, 180–206; Loi and Vu, *Le Duc Tho–Kissinger Negotiations in Paris*, 357–422; Brigham, *Guerrilla Diplomacy*, 110–111; Kissinger, *White House Years*, 1395–1445. Kissinger in Nixon, *RN*, 733.

54   Memcons between Kissinger and Huang Chen, November 24 and December 7–8, 1972. See also Kimball, *Vietnam War Files*, 257–272.

55   Cited in Kimball, *Nixon's Vietnam War*, 363.

56   *Haldeman Diaries*, 679 (December 18, 1972).

57   Reston in Schulzinger, *Time for War*, 302. On the Christmas bombings and the domestic and international reactions, see Kimball, *Nixon's Vietnam War*, 365–366; Berman, *No Peace, No Honor*, 207–220; Small, *Presidency of Richard Nixon*, 91–92; Kissinger, *White House Years*, 1446–1457; Nixon, *RN*, 734–741.

58   Gaiduk, *Soviet Union and the Vietnam War*, 244–245; Dobrynin, *In Confidence*, 262–263. Brezhnev quoted in Brigham, *Guerrilla Diplomacy*, 111.

59   Mao Zedong and Nguyen Thi Binh, December 29, 1972; Zhou En-lai and Truong Chinh, December 31, 1972; Zhou En-lai and Le Duc Tho, January 3, 1973, in *77 Conversations*, 182–183.

60   Memcon: Kissinger and Huang Hua, January 3, 1973, box 328, Lord Files, PPS, RG 59, NA.

61   For more detailed accounts, see Kimball, *Nixon's Vietnam War*, 367; Berman, *No Peace, No Honor*, 221–239; Loi and Vu, *Le Duc Tho–Kissinger Negotiations in Paris*, 425–442; Kissinger, *White House Years*, 1457–1473. For a succinct analysis of the peace terms, see Bundy, *Tangled Web*, 365–368.

62   Kissinger to Bunker, December 13, 1972 (WHS 2271), "Washington to Saigon, 11/26/72–12/23/72," box 2, NSC Convenience Files, GFL.

63   Bunker to Kissinger, January 21, 1973 (Saigon 0348), "Saigon to Washington, 1/18/73–1/23/73"; Kissinger to Bunker, January 23, 1973, "Washington to Saigon, 1/18/73–1/23/73," box 3, NSC Convenience Files, GFL. The same folders include messages relating to Haig's trip to Saigon; more of Nixon's and Kissinger's messages are found in the same box in "Washington to Saigon, 12/27/72–1/15/73." Thieu's agony is well captured in Hung and Schecter, *Palace File*, 130–158. In one of the letters, from January 17, 1973, Nixon summed up Thieu's choices as follows: "you have two essential choices: to continue a course, which would be dramatic but short-sighted, of seeking to block the agreement; or use the Agreement constructively as a means of establishing a new basis for American-South Vietnamese relations."

64   Isaacson, *Kissinger*, 471–472.

65   For a brief and incisive analysis of public opinion and the end of the Vietnam War, see John Mueller, "Reflections on the Vietnam Antiwar Movement and on the Curious Calm at the War's End," in *Vietnam as History*, ed. Peter Baestrup (Lanham, MD, 1984), 151–157.

66   According to Schulzinger, *Time for War*, 306.

67   The debate about the causes and timing of the breakdown of the Sino-Vietnamese alliance is still on. It seems fairly clear, though, that the cooperation between the two countries remained close, if increasingly tense, at least until early 1973 and that the significant tensions began to set in only after the unification of Vietnam in the spring of 1975. See Gilks, *Breakdown of the Sino-Vietnamese Alliance*, esp. chapters 5–6; Morris, *Why Vietnam Invaded Cambodia*, esp. chapter 6; essays by Westad, Chen and Tønneson in *77 Conversations*.

68   Telcon: Kissinger and McNamara, January 3, 1973, NsecA website.

Chapter 12

1   Nixon, *RN*, 786–787; *Haldeman Diaries*, 574–575 (February 6, 1973). Haldeman and, in particular, Nixon were increasingly worried at the time that Kissinger was not doing a proper selling job on the Paris Agreements. Haldeman to Kissinger, January 25, 1973, "HAK/President Memos 1971," box 341, NSC, NPMP.

2   Cited in Kissinger, *Years of Upheaval*, 70.

3   Ibid., 23–43; Kissinger, *Ending the Vietnam War*, 435–438.

4   Zhou Enlai, Ngo Thuyen, and Nguyen Van Quang, January 24, 1973; Mao and Le Duc Tho, February 2, 1973, *77 Conversations*, 183–185; Qiang Zhai, *China and the Vietnam War*, 206–207.

5   Cited in Morris, *Why Vietnam Invaded Cambodia*, 66.

6   Kissinger, *Years of Upheaval*, 30.

7   Memcon: Kissinger, Le Duc Tho, et al., February 10, 1972, Hanoi Memcons February 10–13, 1973 [1 of 3], box 113, HAKOF, NSC, NPMP.

8   Memcon: Kissinger, Pham Van Dong, et al., February 10, 1972, Hanoi Memcons February
        10–13, 1973 [1 of 3], box 113, HAKOF, NSC, NPMP.
9   Memcon: Kissinger, Pham Van Dong, et al., February 11 (A.M. and P.M.), 1972, Hanoi Mem-
        cons February 10–13, 1973 [1 of 3], box 113, HAKOF, NSC, NPMP.
10   Memcon: Kissinger, Le Duc Tho, et al., February 12, 1972, Hanoi Memcons February 10–13,
        1973 [1 of 3], box 113, HAKOF, NSC, NPMP.
11   Kissinger, Years of Upheaval, 41.
12   Memcon: Kissinger, Pham Van Dong, Le Duc Tho, et al., February 12, 1972, Hanoi Memcons
        February 10–13, 1973 [1 of 3], box 113, HAKOF, NSC, NPMP.
13   Kissinger, Years of Upheaval, 43.
14   On the Nixon letters, Agnew trip, and postponement of Thieu's visit, see Hung and Schecter,
        Palace File, 159–161.
15   Bunker, "Cease Fire at 30 days," March 30, 1973, "Saigon to Washington, 2/26/73–3/30/73," box
        3, NSC Convenience File, GFL.
16   On Thieu's visit to San Clemente: Hung and Schecter, Palace File, 162–171.
17   Lord interview; Kissinger, Years of Upheaval, 44–71. On the February 1973 trip, see Mann,
        About Face, 60–63; Tyler, Great Wall, 149–151.
18   Memcon: Kissinger, Mao, Zhou, Lord, et al., February 17, 1973, in Kissinger Transcripts, 100.
19   Ibid., 101.
20   Kissinger, Years of Upheaval, 53–54.
21   Kissinger to Nixon, March 2, 1973. In Kissinger Transcripts, 112, 114, 116; Mann, About Face, 60.
        Emphasis added.
22   Zhou Enlai to CCP, March 1973, printed in Barnouin and Yu, Chinese Foreign Policy During
        the Cultural Revolution, 196–205. The sense that the February 1973 trip was a highpoint in
        Sino-American relations was shared by a number of Kissinger's aides, including Winston
        Lord. Lord interview.
23   Memcon: Kissinger and Zhou, February 18, 1973, in Kissinger Transcripts, 109. Also Kissinger,
        Years of Upheaval, 59–60.
24   Memcons: Kissinger and Zhou, February 16 and 18, 1973, in Kissinger Transcripts, 103–111.
25   See Shawcross, Sideshow, chapter 19.
26   Cited in Kissinger Transcripts, 114. It is worth noting that Kissinger does not mention such a
        statement in his memoirs.
27   Lankford, Last American Aristocrat, 198–202.
28   Interview with Brent Scowcroft, December 16, 2002.
29   Kissinger to Nixon, March 2, 1973, Kissinger Transcripts, 116–117.
30   Kissinger had written about such challenges in the 1960s in Troubled Partnership and in
        American Foreign Policy. The following paragraphs are largely based on Bundy, Tangled Web,
        413–419.
31   "The USSR and the Changing Scene in Europe," NIE 12–72, NIE's, 1951–83, box 5, CIA, RG
        263, NA.
32   The speech can be found in Mayall and Navari, End of the Post-War Era, 360–367.
33   See Stanley I. Kutler, Abuse of Power and Wars of Watergate, as well as Kissinger, Years of
        Upheaval, 152–155.
34   Costigliola, France and the United States, 174; Brandt, My Life in Politics, 175; Heath, Course
        of My Life, 493.
35   Kissinger, Years of Upheaval, 192.
36   For an elaborate description of the atmosphere at Zavidovo, see ibid., 229–235.
37   Kissinger to Nixon, May 11, 1973, "Kissinger Conversations at Zavidovo May 5–8, 1973," box
        75, NSC, NPMP.
38   For example: Elliot to Kissinger, March 29, 1973, USSR XXVIII, box 721, NSC, NPMP.
39   Memcon: Kissinger, Brezhnev, et al., May 7, 1973, "Kissinger Conversations at Zavidovo May
        5–8, 1973," box 75, NSC, NPMP.
40   Memcons: Kissinger, Brezhnev, et al., May 5, 6 and 7, 1973; Kissinger to Nixon, May 11, 1973,
        "Kissinger Conversations at Zavidovo May 5–8, 1973," box 75, NSC, NPMP.

41   Memcon: Kissinger, Gromyko, et al., May 8, 1973, "Kissinger Conversations at Zavidovo May 5–8, 1973," box 75, NSC, NPMP.

42   Kissinger to Nixon, May 11, 1973, "Kissinger Conversations at Zavidovo May 5–8, 1973," box 75, NSC, NPMP.

43   Kissinger, *Years of Upheaval*, 300.

44   Memcon: Kissinger, Gromyko, Dobrynin, and Saunders, June 23, 1973, Brezhnev visit, June 18–25, 1973, Memcons, box 75, NSC, NPMP. See also Kissinger, *Years of Upheaval*, 295–296.

45   Memcon: Nixon, Brezhnev, et al., June 23, 1973, Brezhnev visit, June 18–25, 1973, Memcons, box 75, NSC, NPMP.

46   Memcon: Nixon, Brezhnev, et al., June 18, 1973, Brezhnev visit, June 18–25, 1973, Memcons, box 75, NSC, NPMP.

47   Iliya Gaiduk, "Developing an Alliance: The Soviet Union and Vietnam, 1954–1975," in *The Vietnam War*, ed. Peter Lowe (Manchester: University of Manchester Press, 1998), 149–150.

48   Memcon: Nixon, Brezhnev et al., June 23, 1973, Brezhnev visit, June 18–25, 1973, Memcons, box 75, NSC, NPMP.

49   Kissinger and Huang Chen, June 19, 1973, box 328, Lord Files, PPS, RG 59, NA.

50   Zhou's comments to Bruce in Bruce to Kissinger, June 26, 1973 (Peking 005), box 328, Lord Files, PPS, RG 59, NA. Zhou had used Mao's imagery about the United States "stepping on China's shoulders to reach the USSR."

51   Memcon: Kissinger, Huang Hua, Bruce, et al., April 16, 1973, box 328, Lord Files, PPS, RG 59, NA.

52   Brigham, *Guerrilla Diplomacy*, 113–118.

53   See ibid., 118–120.

54   Memcons: Zhou Enlai, Pham Van Dong, Le Duan, and Le Thanh Nghi, June 5 and 6, *77 Conversations*, 187–191; Qiang Zhai, *China and the Vietnam War*, 207.

55   Kissinger to Bunker (WH 30984, undated), "Washington to Saigon, 4/16/73 to 5/22/73," box 3, NSC Convenience Files, GFL.

56   Memcons: Kissinger and Le Duc Tho, May 17 and 19, 1973, Paris Memcons May 17–23, 1973, box 114, HAKOF, NPMP.

57   Kissinger's account of the meetings in Kissinger, *Years of Upheaval*, 327–335.

58   Nixon to Thieu, May 30, 1973, "Saigon to Washington, 5/23/73 to 6/4/73," box 4, NSC Convenience Files, GFL.

59   Nixon to Thieu, June 10, 1973, "Saigon to Washington, 6/5/73 to 6/11/73," box 4, NSC Convenience Files, GFL. This particular folder carries a series of letters between Nixon and Thieu that essentially repeat the same points.

60   Whitehouse to Kissinger, June 8, 1973, "Saigon to Washington, 6/5/73 to 6/11/73," box 4, NSC Convenience Files, GFL.

61   Memcon: Kissinger and Huang Hua, May 27, 1973, "China Exchanges May 16–June 13, 1973," box 94, HAKOF, NPMP.

62   Memcon: Kissinger and Huang Hua, June 4, 1973, "China Exchanges May 16–June 13, 1973," box 94, HAKOF, NPMP; Memcon: Kissinger, Hua Chen, et al., June 14 and June 19, 1973, box 328, Lord Files, PPS, RG 59, NA.

63   Memcon: Kissinger and Huang Chen, July 6, 1973, "China Exchanges June 14–July 9, 1973," box 95, HAKOF, NPMP; Kissinger to Bruce, July 18, 1973, box 328, Lord Files, PPS, RG 59, NA. The War Powers Resolution went through several further revisions until a Joint House-Senate Resolution was approved in October. Finally, on November 7, the Senate and house overrode Nixon's veto. See Bundy, *Tangled Web*, 369–399.

64   Memcon: Kissinger, Scowcroft, Lord, Eagleburger, Howe, Solomon, and Lord, July 19, 1973, *Kissinger Transcripts*, 147–152.

65   Memcon: Kissinger and Dobrynin, July 10, 1973, Dobrynin/Kissinger, vol. 18, box 68, HAKOF, NPMP.

Chapter 13

1   *PPP: Richard Nixon, 1973* (Washington, DC: GPO, 1974), 815–817; Kissinger, *Years of Upheaval*, 431–432; *Gallup Poll, 1972–1975*, 183, 187.

2   Isaacson, *Kissinger*, 502–504; Schulzinger, *Henry Kissinger*, 129. See also Bundy, *Tangled Web*, 419–420. It is worth noting that Nixon has little to say about his reason for appointing Kissinger. Nixon, *RN*, 907. For Kissinger's much more elaborate version, see *Years of Upheaval*, 3–4, 414–423.

3   Isaacson, *Kissinger*, 503.

4   The account is based on ibid., 497–504.

5   *Public Papers of the President, Nixon, 1973*, 710–725; Schulzinger, *Henry Kissinger*, 126–127.

6   Isaacson, *Kissinger*, 497–500; Bob Woodward and Carl Bernstein, *All the President's Men* (New York: Simon & Schuster, 1974), 314–315; Hersh, *Price of Power*, 83–97 (for a detailed accounting of the wiretaps); Hersh, "Kissinger Said to Have Asked for Taps," *New York Times*, May 17, 1973; Evans and Novak, "The Innocence of Dr. Kissinger," *Washington Post*, May 24, 1973.

7   Kissinger, *Years of Upheaval*, 426.

8   See *American Foreign Policy 1973: A Documentary Record*, 349–353.

9   Isaacson, *Kissinger*, 584–586. See Kissinger, *Years of Upheaval*, 1111–1123. Telcon: Kissinger–Dobrynin, July 12, 1974, NSecA webpage.

10   Kissinger, *Years of Upheaval*, 433.

11   Ibid., 432–446; Isaacson, *Kissinger*, 505–507.

12   Chiefs of mission meeting on November 15, 1973. Executive Secretariat, Briefing Books, 1958–76, Lot 74D416, box 179, RG 59, NA.

13   Memcon: Kissinger, Rush, Donaldson, Sonnenfeldt, McCloskey, et al., February 14, 1974, box 369, Lord Files, PPS, RG 59, NA.

14   Kennan to Kissinger, September 19, 1973; Kissinger to Kennan (drafted by Eagleburger), October 11, 1973, USSR XXIX, box 722, NSC Country Files, NPMP.

15   Gallup poll cited in Schulzinger, *Henry Kissinger*, 2.

Chapter 14

1   Kissinger, *Years of Upheaval*, 450–459; idem, *Crisis*, 13–35; Dobrynin, *In Confidence*, 289–290. For more complete discussions of the October War (used as the basis for this chapter): Garthoff, *Détente and Confrontation*, 405–412; Quandt, *Peace Process*, 148–182; Lebow and Stein, *We All Lost the Cold War* (Princeton: Princeton University Press, 1994), 149–288.

2   Kissinger, *Years of Upheaval*; idem, *Crisis*, 421.

3   Cited in David A. Korn, "US-Soviet Negotiations of 1969 and the Rogers Plan," *Middle East Journal* 44, no. 1 (Winter 1990): 38.

4   See Quandt, *Peace Process*, chapters 2–4.

5   Kissinger to Haig (HAKTO 013), April 23, 1972, box 21, HAKOF, NSC, NPMP; Bundy, *Tangled Web*, 338.

6   Kissinger to Nixon, February 28, 1973; Saunders to Kissinger, March 1, 1973, box 922, VIP Visits, NSC, NPMP.

7   See Bundy, *Tangled Web*, 431–433; Quandt, *Peace Process*, 116–153; Yergin, *Prize*, 589–599.

8   Kissinger, *Years of Upheaval*, 459.

9   Memcon: Nixon, Gromyko, Kissinger, and Dobrynin, September 28, 1973, Dobrynin/Kissinger, vol. 19, box 68, HAKOF, NPMP.

10   Kissinger, *Crisis*, 16, 70.

11   Ibid., 68.

12   These developments and the paragraphs that follow are based largely on Bundy, *Tangled Web*, 434–444; Isaacson, *Kissinger*, 511–545; Garthoff, *Détente and Confrontation*, 413–434; Quandt, *Peace Process*, 152–169. For the accounts by Kissinger and Dobrynin: Kissinger, *Years of Upheaval*, 450–613, and *Crisis*; Dobrynin, *In Confidence*, 287–301.

13   Kissinger and Huang Chen, October 6 and 15, 1973, box 328, Lord Files, PPS, RG 59, NA.

14   Memcon: Kissinger, Schlesinger, Colby, Moorer, and Scowcroft, October 19, 1973, "Memcons April–Nov 1973 HAK + Presidential [2 of 5]," box 1027, NSC, NPMP.

15   Kissinger, *Years of Upheaval*, 548–550. For an assessment by a Kremlin insider, see Victor Israelyan, "The October 1973 War: Kissinger in Moscow," *Middle East Journal* 49, no. 2 (Spring 1995): 19–41.

16   Memcon: Kissinger, Brezhnev, Gromyko, et al., October 20, 1973, "Kissinger Trip to Moscow, Tel Aviv and London," box 76, NSC Country Files, NPMP.

17   Kissinger, *Years of Upheaval,* 551–552. For further details on these well-known events, see Olson, *Watergate;* and Kutler, *Wars of Watergate.*

18   Israelyan, "Kissinger in Moscow."

19   Memcon: Kissinger, Brezhnev, et al., October 21, 1973, "Kissinger Trip to Moscow, Tel Aviv and London," box 76, NSC, NPMP.

20   Kissinger, *Years of Upheaval,* 556–558. The memorandum of Kissinger's meeting with the three ambassadors is in "Kissinger Trip to Moscow, Tel Aviv and London," box 76, NSC, NPMP.

21   Memcon: Kissinger, Gromyko, et al., October 22, 1973, "Kissinger Trip to Moscow, Tel Aviv and London," box 76, NSC, NPMP.

22   For Kissinger's description of Meir, see Kissinger, *Years of Upheaval,* 220–222. Garment, *Crazy Rhythm,* 188. On Golda Meir, see Anna Claybourne, *Golda Meir* (Chicago: Heinemann, 2003); Richard Amdur, *Golda Meir: A Leader in Peace and War* (New York: Ballantine, 1990); Deborah Hitzeroth, *Golda Meir* (San Diego: Lucent Books, 1998); and Meir, *My Life.* (London: Weidenfeld and Nicholson, 1975).

23   Memcon: Kissinger, Meir, Mordechai Gazit, and Peter Rodman, October 22, 1973, "Kissinger Trip to Moscow, Tel Aviv and London," box 76, NSC, NPMP.

24   Memcons: Kissinger and Golda Meir; Kissinger, Meir, et al., October 22, 1973, "Kissinger Trip to Moscow, Tel Aviv and London," box 76, NSC, NPMP.

25   Kissinger, *Years of Upheaval,* 568–569. See also Garthoff, *Détente and Confrontation,* 420.

26   Brezhnev to Nixon, October 23, 1973, Box 70, NSC, NPMP. The following paragraphs are based mainly on Kissinger, *Years of Upheaval,* 568–575; idem, *Crisis,* 308–325; Garthoff, *Détente and Confrontation,* 420–423.

27   Telcon: Kissinger–Dobrynin, October 24, 1973, NSecA web page. Scowcroft interview with the author.

28   On this particular point, see Nixon, *RN,* 936–941; Haig, *Inner Circles,* 417. See also Kutler, *Wars of Watergate,* 411.

29   Garthoff, *Détente and Confrontation,* 430.

30   Memcon: Nixon, Kissinger, Dobrynin, and Haig, October 30, 1973, Dobrynin/Kissinger, vol. 20, box 69, HAKOF, NSC, NPMP.

31   Memcon: Kissinger, Mao, Zhou, et al., November 12, 1973, *Kissinger Transcripts,* 180.

32   Kissinger, *Years of Upheaval,* 646. On Sadat, see Kirk J. Beattie, *Egypt During the Sadat Years* (New York: Macmillan, 2000) and Arthur Diamond, *Anwar Sadat* (San Diego: Lucent Books, 1994); and Sadat, *In Search of Identity.*

33   Kissinger to Nixon, November 21, 1973, Dobrynin/Kissinger, vol. 20, box 69, HAKOF, NSC, NPMP.

34   Kissinger to Nixon (via Scowcroft), December 14, 16, 17, 1973, box 43, HAKOF, NSC, NPMP.

35   Kissinger to Nixon (via Scowcroft), December 19 and 21, 1973, box 43, HAKOF, NSC, NPMP.

36   Kissinger to Nixon (via Scowcroft), December 21, 1973, box 43, HAKOF, NSC, NPMP.

37   Memcon: Kissinger, Gromyko, Rodman, and Sukhodrev, December 22, 1973, Dobrynin/Kissinger, vol. 21, box 69, HAKOF, NSC, NPMP.

38   Memcon: Nixon, Kissinger, and Dobrynin, December 26, 1973, Dobrynin/Kissinger, vol. 21, box 69, HAKOF, NSC, NPMP.

39   Kissinger, *Years of Upheaval,* 792.

40   Memcon: Kissinger, Le Duc Tho, et al., December 20, 1973, box 369, Lord Files, PPS, RG 59, NA. Kissinger's only comment about the meeting is that Tho "was growing more unbearably insolent as America's divisions gradually opened up new and decisive opportunities for Hanoi." Kissinger, *Years of Upheaval,* 792.

41   Kissinger to Nixon (via Scowcroft), December 21, 1973, box 369, Lord Files, PPS, RG 59, NA.

42   Brigham, *Guerrilla Diplomacy,* 119–121; Nho Tang Trong, Doan Van Toai, and David Chanoff, *A Vietcong Memoir* (New York: Vintage, 1985), 229–231.

43   Memcon: Clements, Khiem, and Martin, October 2, 1974, "Saigon to Washington, 1/7/74–12/3/74," box 5, NSC Convenience Files, GFL.

44 See Bundy, *Tangled Web*, 484–487.

45 Kissinger's and Tho's messages in Scowcroft to Martin, January 18, February 6, February 19, March 20, and May 12, 1974, "Washington to Saigon 1/12/74–11/21/74," box 5, NSC Convenience Files, GFL.

46 The China trip is discussed in the following chapter.

47 Kissinger, *Years of Upheaval*, 799–804; Bundy, *Tangled Web*, 450–451.

48 Kissinger, *Years of Upheaval*, 846–850.

49 Brezhnev to Nixon, January 17, 1974, Dobrynin/Kissinger, vol. 21, box 69, HAKOF, NSC, NPMP.

50 Memcon: Kissinger and Dobrynin, February 1, 1974, Dobrynin/Kissinger, vol. 22, box 69, HAKOF, NSC, NPMP.

51 Memcon: Nixon, Kissinger, Gromyko, Dobrynin, Sonnenfeldt, and Stoessel, February 4, 1974, "US/USSR Presidential Exchanges," box 72, HAKOF, NSC, NPMP.

52 Cited in Schulzinger, *Henry Kissinger*, 164, 260.

53 Kissinger to Nixon (via Scowcroft), February 28, March 1, 2, and 3, 1974, box 48, HAKOF, NSC, NPMP (Nixon's handwritten comments on the March 1 report). See Kissinger, *Years of Upheaval*, 935–978.

54 Memcon: Cabinet meeting, March 8, 1974, "Memcons 1 March 1974–8 May 1974 [3 of 4]," box 1027, NSC, NPMP.

55 Kissinger, *Years of Upheaval*, 1022. For more on the decline of détente, see the following chapter.

56 Kissinger to Nixon, March 29, 1974, box 48, HAKOF, NSC, NPMP; Memcon: Kissinger, Brezhnev et al., March 27, 1974, *Kissinger Transcripts*, 259. Comment to Callaghan in ibid., 260.

57 Memcon: Kissinger, Brezhnev, Gromyko, et al., March 26 and 27, 1974, "Secretary Kissinger's pre-summit trip to Moscow, March 24–28, 1974, Memcons and Reports," box 76, NSC, NPMP. Analysis of some of the other issues discussed during these meetings can be found in the following chapter.

58 See Jussi M. Hanhimäki, "'They Can Write it in Swahili': Kissinger, the Soviets, and the Helsinki Accords, 1973–75," *Journal of Transatlantic Studies* 1:1 (Spring 2003): 37–58.

59 Memcons: Nixon, Kissinger, Gromyko, et al., and Kissinger, Waldheim, et al., April 15, 1974, "Memcons March 1–May 8 1974 HAK + Presidential [2 of 4]," box 1028, NSC, NPMP; Kissinger to Nixon (via Scowcroft), April 30, 1974, Dobrynin/Kissinger, vol. 22, box 69, HAKOF, NSC, NPMP.

60 Kissinger to Nixon (via Scowcroft), May 8, 1974, Dobrynin/Kissinger, vol. 22, box 69, HAKOF, NSC, NPMP.

61 Cited in Isaacson, *Kissinger*, 570.

62 Ibid., 572.

63 Ibid., 630–635.

Chapter 15

1 Sadat's remarks on signing the "Principles of Relations and Cooperation Between Egypt and the United States," June 14, 1974, *PPP: Richard Nixon, 1974*, (Washington, DC: GPO, 1975), 502.

2 Kutler, *Wars of Watergate*, 488; *New York Times*, June 1, 1974.

3 Cited in "Anatomy of Crisis," *Newsweek*, August 11, 2003.

4 East Asian Chiefs of Mission Conference, November 15, 1973 (Tokyo), Briefing Books, 1958–76, lot 74d 416, box 179, RG 59, NA.

5 Cited in Kutler, *Wars of Watergate*, 596–597.

6 See Bundy, *Tangled Web*, 484–487.

7 Kissinger, *Ending the Vietnam War*, 492.

8 Martin to Kissinger (Saigon 0618), June 22, 1974, "Saigon to Washington, 1/12/74 to 11/21/74," box 4, NSC Convenience Files, GFL.

9 Qiang Zhai, *China and the Vietnam War*, 136 (table of Chinese aid to Vietnam), 212.

10 Kissinger interview with the author.

11 Eagleburger to Kissinger, July 18, 1973, box 328, Lord Files, PPS, RG 59, NA.

12   Cited in *77 Conversations*, 192 n. 256. Emphasis added. On the CCP Party Congress, see Barnouin and Yu, *Ten Years of Turbulence*.

13   Bruce to Kissinger, October 23, 1973, State Department Records, RG 59, Briefing Books, 1958–76, lot 74D 416, box 192, NA.

14   Memcon: Kissinger, Zhou Enlai, et al., November 10, 1973, *Kissinger Transcripts*, 170–171. See also Kissinger, *Years of Upheaval*, 683–688. See also Tyler, *Great Wall*, 166–174.

15   Memcon: Kissinger, Mao, Zhou, et al., November 12, 1973, *Kissinger Transcripts*, 182.

16   Cited in Tyler, *Great Wall*, 168.

17   Kissinger to Nixon, November 19, 1973, box 330, Lord Files, PPS, RG 59, NA.

18   Chiefs of Missions meeting, November 15, 1973, East Asian Chiefs of Mission Conference, November 15, 1973 (Tokyo), Briefing Books, 1958–76, lot 74d 416, box 179, RG 59, NA.

19   Based on Isaacson, *Kissinger*, 611–621; Kaufman, *Henry M. Jackson*, 266–268; Bundy, *Tangled Web*, 348–350.

20   See *Haldeman Diaries*, 784–790 (April 17, 1973); Bundy, *Tangled Web*; Reeves, *President Nixon*; Garthoff, *Détente and Confrontation*, 367–369; Dobrynin, *In Confidence*, 266–270; Nixon, *RN*, 830–852; Kutler, *Wars of Watergate*, 309–320. Nixon's April 30 statement announcing the resignations of Haldeman and Ehrlichman can be found in Stanley Kutler (ed.), *Watergate: The Fall of Richard Nixon* (St. James, NY: Brandywine Press, 1996), 109–111. Kissinger's version of events in *Years of Upheaval*, 252–255 (the text drafted by Kissinger and Dobrynin in ibid., 1234, n. 10). Memcons: Kissinger and Dobrynin, April 10 and 16, 1973, Dobrynin/Kissinger, vol. 16, part 1, box 496, PTF, NSC, NPMP.

21   Dobrynin, *In Confidence*, 274.

22   Kissinger to Nixon, May 5, 1973, USSR XXIX, box 722, NSC Country Files, NPMP.

23   Memcon: Kissinger, Brezhnev, et al., May 8, 1973, "Kissinger Conversations at Zavidovo May 5–8, 1973," box 75, NSC, NPMP.

24   Memcon: Nixon, Brezhnev, et al., June 18 and 19, 1973, "Brezhnev visit, June 18–25, 1973, Memcons," box 75, NSC, NPMP.

25   Memcon: Kissinger, Sonnenfeldt, Hartman, et al., March 18, 1974, *Kissinger Transcripts*, 222–228. On March 6 and 15 Kissinger had met with Jackson but the senator persisted in his demand for an explicit Soviet guarantee of 100,000 annual exit visas. This, in part, explains Kissinger's anger at the March 18 meeting. Kissinger, *Years of Upheaval*, 991–994; Kaufman, *Henry M. Jackson*, 268–278.

26   Gladys Engel Lang and Kuert Lang, *The Battle for Public Opinion: The President, the Press, and the Polls During Watergate* (New York: Columbia University Press, 1983), 62–121; Olson, *Watergate*, chapters 4 and 5.

27   Memcon: Kissinger, Brezhnev, et al., March 26, 1974, "Secretary Kissinger's Pre-summit trip to Moscow, March 24–28, 1974, Memcons and Reports," box 76, NSC, NPMP. See Garthoff, *Détente and Confrontation*, 465–475.

28   See Tyler, *Great Wall*, 174. On Zhou, see Kuo-kang Shao, *Zhou Enlai and the Foundations of Chinese Foreign Policy*.

29   Solomon to Kissinger, January 25, 1974, and March 19, 1974, box 330, Lord Files, PPS, RG 59, NA. Winston Lord and Arthur Hummel also expressed their concern that a stalemate over the Taiwan normalization issue was going to make further progress in Sino-American relations a virtual impossibility. Hummel and Lord to Kissinger, January 29, 1974, box 330, Lord Files, PPS, RG 59, NA.

30   Solomon to Kissinger, January 25, 1974, and March 19, 1974, box 330, Lord Files, PPS, RG 59, NA. On Deng: David S. Goodman, *Deng Xiaoping and the Chinese Revolution: A Political Biography* (London: Routledge, 1994); Richard Evans, *Deng Xiaoping and the Making of Modern China* (New York: Penguin, 1997).

31   Kissinger, *Years of Renewal*, 868.

32   Ibid., 163.

33   Memcon: Kissinger and Deng, et al., April 14, 1974, in *Kissinger Transcripts*, 270–285.

34   Cited in Tyler, *Great Wall*, 175, 445 n. 186.

35   Yergin, *Prize*, 588–612.

36 Memorandum of meeting, November 15, 1973, Executive Secretariat Briefing Books, 1958–76, lot 74d 416, box 179, RG 59, NA.
37 Kissinger to Scowcroft and Nixon, December 11, 1973, box 43, HAKOF, NSC, NPMP.
38 Ibid. Kissinger to Nixon, December 22, 1973, box 43, HAKOF, NSC, NPMP.
39 For Kissinger's version of the Washington Energy Conference, see Kissinger, *Years of Upheaval*, 896–934.
40 Kissinger to RN/Scowcroft, March 29, 1974, box 48, HAKOF, NSC, NPMP. On Heath and Wilson: Stuart Ball and Anthony Sheldon, *The Heath Government, 1970–1974: A Reappraisal* (London: Longman, 1996); John Campbell, *Edward Heath: A Biography* (London: Jonathan Cape, 1993); Anthony Hornett, *The Fall of Mr. Heath's Government, 1973–1974* (St. Albans: A. Hornett, 1991); Ben Pimlott, *Harold Wilson* (London: Harper & Collins, 1993). See also the two prime ministers' memoirs: Heath, *Course of My Life*; Harold Wilson, *Final Term: The Labour Government, 1974–1976* (London: Weidenfeld and Nicolson, 1979).
41 Kissinger, *Years of Renewal*, 614. On the transfer of power and the crisis preceding it, see Anthony J. Nicholls, *The Bonn Republic: West German Democracy, 1945–1990* (London, 1997); Wolfram F. Hanrieder, *Germany, America, Europe: Forty Years of German Foreign Policy* (New Haven: Yale University Press, 1989); Jonathan Carr, *Helmut Schmidt: Helmsman of Germany* (London: Weidenfeld and Nicolson, 1985). See also the Chancellors' memoirs: Brandt, *My Life in Politics*; Helmut Schmidt, *Men and Powers: A Political Retrospective* (New York: Random House, 1989).
42 Kissinger, *Years of Renewal*, 621. On Pompidou and Giscard: Eric Roussel, *Georges Pompidou, 1911–1974* (Paris: J. C. Lattes, 1994); Serge Bernstein and Jean-Pierre Rioux, *The Pompidou Years, 1969–1974* (Cambridge: Cambridge University Press, 2000); J. R. Frears, *France in the Giscard Presidency* (London: Allen & Unwin, 1981); Samy Cohen and Marie-Claude Smouts, *La Politique exterieure de Valery Giscard d'Estaing* (Paris: Presses de la Fondation national des sciences politiques, 1985).
43 Kissinger to Nixon, June 26, 1974, box 950, VIP Visits, NSC, NPMP; Kissinger, *Years of Upheaval*, 934.
44 Garthoff, *Détente and Confrontation*, 474–475.
45 Kissinger to Nixon, June 19, 1974, Dobrynin/Kissinger, vol. 23, box 69, HAKOF, NSC, NPMP.
46 Memcon: Nixon, Brezhnev, Kissinger, Gromyko, et al., June 28, 1974, "Memcons Moscow Summit June 27–July 3, 1974," box 77, NSC, NPMP.
47 Dobrynin, *In Confidence*, 310–313.
48 Nixon, *RN*, 1027–1028; Kissinger, *Years of Upheaval*, 1161, 1170–1171. Memcon: Kissinger, Brezhnev, Gromyko, and Sonnenfeldt, October 26, 1974, "USSR Briefing Books, October 24–27, 1974," Box A1, TPF, NSC, GFL.
49 For a brief account of these agreements, see Garthoff, *Détente and Confrontation*, 475–481. Nixon's account is in *RN*, 1027–1039; Kissinger's in *Years of Upheaval*, 1151–1178.
50 Kissinger, *Years of Upheaval*, 1171.
51 Kissinger to Mission Chiefs, July 5, 1974, Briefing Books, 1958–76, lot 75D 91, Box 189, RG 59, NA.
52 *New York Times*, June 1, 1974.
53 Nixon cited in Kutler, *Wars of Watergate*, 505. See also Olson, *Watergate*.
54 Nixon, "Address to the Nation," August 8, 1974, *PPP: Richard Nixon, 1974*, 626–629.
55 As recalled by Kissinger in *Years of Upheaval*, 1207–1209.
56 Dobrynin, *In Confidence*, 315–316.

Chapter 16

1 Memcon: Kissinger, Brezhnev, et al., October 26, 1974, "USSR Briefing Books, October 24–27, 1974," box A1, TPF, NSC, GFL.
2 Dobrynin, *In Confidence*, 337.
3 Kissinger to Scowcroft, March 29, 1974, box 48, HAKOF, NSC, NPMP.
4 Isaacson, *Kissinger*, 601–602.
5 For a brief account on Ford's background, see Greene, *Presidency of Gerald R. Ford*, 1–6.

6   See ibid., 25–27. For Kissinger's comments on Rumsfeld, see Kissinger, *Years of Renewal*, 175–177.

7   Kissinger, *Years of Renewal*, 173–174.

8   James R. Schlesinger, *The Political Economy of National Security: A Study of the Economic Aspects of the Contemporary Power Struggle* (New York: Praeger, 1960).

9   Cited in Isaacson, *Kissinger*, 622.

10 On the October 1973 disagreements, see ibid., 518–523. On Schlesinger and Jackson: Kaufman, *Henry M. Jackson*, 287–289.

11 Greene, *Presidency of Gerald R. Ford*, 29–31.

12 Telcon: Nixon and Kissinger, 8:16 P.M., April 27, 1971, WHT: 2–52, NPMP.

13 Kissinger, *Years of Renewal*, 184, 187.

14 Ibid., 837. Brent Scowcroft, in an interview in December 2002, effectively concurred. Scowcroft interview, December 13, 2002.

15 Kutler, *Wars of Watergate*, 553–566; Greene, *Presidency of Gerald R. Ford*, 46–52. Ford's aides, especially his press secretary Philip Buchen, repeatedly but unsuccessfully argued that Nixon's acceptance of the pardon implied that he accepted guilt.

16 Kutler, *Wars of Watergate*, 569–571; Greene, *Presidency of Gerald R. Ford*, 56–58.

17 Dobrynin, *In Confidence*, 334–335; Kissinger, *Years of Renewal*, 255–257; Isaacson, *Kissinger*, 616–617; Greene, *Presidency of Gerald R. Ford*, 122–123. Kissinger to Ford, August 13 and 13, 1974, "USSR (1)," box 16, NSC Country Files, GFL.

18 Cited in Garthoff, *Détente and Confrontation*, 507. The discussion in the next two paragraphs is heavily based on ibid., 505–509; Greene, *Presidency of Gerald R. Ford*, 122–123; Isaacson, *Kissinger*, 614–621; Kaufman, *Henry M. Jackson*, 278–279; and Kissinger, *Years of Renewal* 255–260.

19 Kissinger, *Years of Renewal*, 259.

20 Kaufman, *Henry M. Jackson*, 439.

21 Kissinger, *Years of Renewal*, 257.

22 Memcon: Kissinger, Brezhnev, et al., October 24, 1974, *Kissinger Transcripts*, 327–344.

23 Ibid.

24 Memcon: Kissinger, Brezhnev et al., October 25 and 26, 1974, "USSR Briefing Books, October 24–27, 1974," box A1, TPF, NSC, GFL. At the October 18, 1974 NSC meeting Schlesinger had stressed the need for equal aggregates while Kissinger, despite his stance in Moscow, thought that an "asymmetric" approach was possible. NSC Meeting, October 18, 1974, box 1, NSC Meeting Minutes, GFL.

25 Kissinger to Ford (via Scowcroft), October 26, 1974, "10/20–11/9/74 HAK to (2)", box A10, TPF, NSC, GFL.

26 Memcon: Ford, Kissinger, Brezhnev, Gromyko, et al., November 23, 1974, "USSR 11/23–24/74 Vladivostok Summit," box A1, NSC, GFL. "Ford was not a man with a high sense of humor," Dobrynin would later write. Dobrynin, *In Confidence*, 330.

27 Ibid.

28 Kissinger, *Years of Renewal*, 294–295. This low impression of the Soviet leader may have been partly a result of the fact that after the welcome toasts that followed, Brezhnev had suffered a seizure. Despite advice from his doctors, however, he refused to miss any of the meetings.

29 This was discussed briefly in the afternoon of November 24. Memcon: Ford, Kissinger, Brezhnev, Gromyko, et al., November 24, 1974, "USSR 11/23–24, 1974, Vladivostok Summit," box A1, TPF, NSC, GFL.

30 Dobrynin, *In Confidence*, 329.

31 On May 7, 1975, for example, British Prime Minister Harold Wilson had told Kissinger and Ford that "he had been impressed by the fact that Brezhnev gave the appearance of an old man in a hurry," during Wilson's visit to Moscow in February 1975. *Documents on British Policy Overseas*, Series III, Volume II, *The Conference on Security and Cooperation in Europe, 1972–1975*, ed. By G. Bennett and K.A. Hamilton (London: The Stationery Office, 1997), 415 n. 6.

32 Memcons: Ford, Kissinger, Brezhnev, Gromyko, et al., November 23 and 24, 1974, "USSR 11/23–24/74 Vladivostok Summit," box A1, TPF, NSC, GFL. For the principals' accounts of the Vladivostok discussions, see Kissinger, *Years of Renewal*, 291–296; Ford, *Time to Heal*, 213–219;

Dobrynin, *In Confidence*, 327–332. A good overview can also be found in Garthoff, *Détente and Confrontation*, 494–500.

33   Dobrynin, *In Confidence*, 329; Kissinger, *Years of Renewal*, 302. On the post-Vladivostok technical difficulties, see Garthoff, *Détente and Confrontation*, 501–505.

34   Kaufman, *Henry M. Jackson*, 283–285. Solomon to Kissinger, August 18, 1974, box 331, Lord Files, PPS, RG 59, NA.

35   Solomon to Scowcroft, September 25, 1974, and Kissinger to Ford, October 15, 1974, "PRC (1)," box 13, NSC Country Files, GFL. Memcon: Kissinger, Huang Chen, et al., November 11, 1974, box 331, Lord Files, PPS, RG 59, NA. "Bored" in Lankford, *Last American Aristocrat*, 384. In 1974, Bruce took over as the U.S. ambassador to NATO, a post left vacant by the selection of Donald Rumsfeld as Ford's chief of staff.

36   The trip is described in some detail in Tyler, *Great Wall*, 193–200. For the atmosphere, see Kissinger, *Years of Renewal*, 869–874. Kissinger does not dwell on the details of this visit, perhaps in part because of its lackluster results.

37   Kissinger, *Years of Renewal*, 161, 871; Tyler, *Great Wall*, 194 ("nasty little man").

38   Cited in *Kissinger Transcripts*, 288, 289. On Mao's health problems, see Tyler, *Great Wall*, 191–193.

39   Memcon: Kissinger and Deng, November 26 and 27, 1974, *Kissinger Transcripts*, 294–298, 299–315.

40   Ibid. Kissinger to Ford (via Scowcroft), November 27, 28, and 29, 1974, "Kissinger Reports, China 11/25–29/74 Kissinger Trip (3)," box A1, TPF, NSC, GFL.

41   Kissinger to Ford (via Scowcroft), November 27, 28, and 29, 1974, "Kissinger Reports, China 11/25–29/74 Kissinger Trip (3)," box A1, TPF, NSC, GFL. Kissinger, *Years of Renewal*, 870. On the invitation see memcon: Kissinger, Deng, et al., November 27, 1974, *Kissinger Transcripts*, 300.

42   Kissinger to Ford, November 29, 1974, box 372, Lord Files, PPS, RG 59, NA.

43   NSC Meeting, December 2, 1974, box 1, NSC Meeting Minutes, GFL.

44   See sources cited in note 32.

45   Cited in Kaufman, *Henry M. Jackson*, 288.

46   Cited in Garthoff, *Détente and Confrontation*, 512. For a general overview of the Trade Act debacle: ibid., 505–516; Stern, *Water's Edge*, 173–190. Kissinger's perspective in *Years of Renewal*, 302–309.

47   Garthoff, *Détente and Confrontation*, 508, 510–512; Dobrynin, *In Confidence*, 336–337; Kissinger, *Years of Renewal*, 304–309; Paul Miltich to Ford, "National Security: Salt Treaties," December 12, 1974, box 32, Presidential Handwriting File, GFL.

48   Cabinet meeting minutes, January 8, 1975, box 3, James E. Connor Files, GFL.

49   Kissinger, *Years of Renewal*, 307.

50   Greene, *Presidency of Gerald R. Ford*, 101.

51   Memcon: Ford, Kissinger, Scowcroft, January 8, 1975, box 8, Memoranda of Conversations, NSC, GFL.

Chapter 17

1   Kissinger, *Ending the Vietnam War*, 493.

2   Communiqué, August 8, 1974 ("handed to Vorontsov at 7:45 pm"), Dobrynin/Kissinger, vol. 24, box 70, HAKOF, NSC, NPMP.

3   Memcon: Ford, Kissinger, Scowcroft, Phuong, August 9, 1974, box 4, Memoranda of Conversations, 1974–77, NSC, GFL; Greene, *Presidency of Gerald R. Ford*, 132.

4   Memcon: Ford, Kissinger, Scowcroft, September 10, 1974, box 5, Memoranda of Conversations, 1974–77, NSC, GFL.

5   Memcon: Clements, Martin, and Thieu, October 2, 1974, "Saigon to Washington, 1/7/74–12/3/74," box 5, NSC Convenience File, GFL.

6   Greene, *Presidency of Gerald R. Ford*, 133–135.

7   This correspondence as attachments from Scowcroft to Martin, August 13, 19, and 25, 1974, "Washington to Saigon, 1/12/74–11/21/74," NSC Convenience File, box 5, GFL.

8   Memcon: Brezhnev, Kissinger, Gromyko, et al., October 24, 1974, "Trip Briefing Books and Cables 11/74," box A1, TPF, NSC, GFL.

9   Memcons: Kissinger, Deng, et al., November 27 and 28, 1974; Scowcroft to Ford, November 29, 1974, box 372, Lord Files, PPS, RG 59, NA.

10   Memcon: WSAG, January 7, 1975, box 24, East Asian and Pacific Affairs Staff Files, NSC, GFL.

11   Memcon: Ford, Kissinger, Scowcroft, January 8, 1975, box 8, Memoranda of Conversations, 1974–77, NSC, GFL.

12   Memcon: Ford, Kissinger, Scowcroft, Rockefeller, Schlesinger, Brown, Congressional Leadership, January 28, 1975, box 8, Memoranda of Conversations, 1974–77, NSC, GFL Ford's request in *PPP: Gerald Ford, 1975*, vol. 1 (Washington, DC: GPO, 1976), 119–123.

13   Cabinet meeting, January 29, 1975, Cabinet Meeting Minutes, James E. Connor Files, box 4, GFL.

14   Memcons: Ford, Martin, and Scowcroft, February 15, 1974; Ford, Kissinger, and Scowcroft, February 25, 1975, box 9, Memoranda of Conversations, 1973–77, NSC, GFL.

15   Memcons: Ford, Kissinger, Scowcroft, Martin, and Weyand; and Ford, Scowcroft, Tran Kim Phuong, and South Vietnamese delegation, March 25, 1975, box 10, Memoranda of Conversations, 1974–77, NSC, GFL; Greene, *Presidency of Gerald R. Ford*, 136–137 (Thieu's letter).

16   Memcon: Ford, Kissinger, Scowcroft, March 27, 1975, box 10, Memoranda of Conversations, 1974–77, NSC, GFL.

17   NSC meeting, March 28, 1975, box 1, NSC Meeting Minutes, GFL.

18   WSAG meeting, April 2, 1975, box 25, East Asian and Pacific Affairs Staff Files, NSC, GFL.

19   Memcon: Ford, Kissinger, Scowcroft, April 3, 1975, box 10, Memoranda of Conversations, 1974–77, NSC, GFL; interview with Olav Njolstad.

20   Memcon: Ford, Kissinger, Schlesinger, Brown, Rumsfeld, Buchen, Marsh, and Scowcroft, April 11, 1975, box 10, Memoranda of Conversations, 1974–77, NSC, GFL.

21   Isaacson, *Kissinger*, 635–640; Kissinger, *Ending the Vietnam War*, 525–530.

22   Weyand to Ford, April 4, 1975, "Vietnam (13)," box 19, National Security Adviser. Presidential Country Files for East Asia and the Pacific, GFL.

23   Memcon: Ford, Kissinger, Scowcroft, April 11, 1975, box 10, Memoranda of Conversations, 1974–77, NSC, GFL.

24   Memcon: Ford, Kissinger, Schlesinger, Scowcroft, Senate Foreign Relations Committee, April 14, 1975, box 10, Memoranda of Conversations, 1974–77, NSC, GFL.

25   Cabinet meeting, April 16, 1975, box 4, James E. Connor Files, GFL.

26   Greene, *Presidency of Gerald R. Ford*, 139–140; Bundy, *Tangled Web*, 495–497. Ford's Tulane University speech can be found in *Public Papers of the President, Gerald Ford, 1975*, vol. 1, 568–573.

27   WSAG meeting, April 28, 1975, box A1, TPF, NSC, GFL.

28   WSAG meeting, April 29, 1975, box A1, TPF; NSC meeting, April 28, 1975, Box 1, NSC Meetings File, GFL.

29   Robert Tucker, "Vietnam: The Final Reckoning," *Commentary* 59, no. 5 (May 1975), cited in Jonathan Haslam, *No Virtue Like Necessity* (New Haven: Yale University Press, 2002), 98. *Time* article cited in Isaacson, *Kissinger*, 642.

30   See T. Christopher Jespersen, "The Bitter End and the Lost Chance in Vietnam: Congress, the Ford Administration, and the Battle Over Vietnam, 1975–76," *Diplomatic History* 24, no. 2 (Spring 2000): 265–293.

31   On the rescue, see Isaacson, *Kissinger*, 648–652; Schulzinger, *Henry Kissinger*, 203–205. Kissinger gives a thirty-page account of the rescue, but also concedes at the end that even with that, somewhat questionable, show of force, the reality remained that "we had entered Indochina to save a country, and we had ended by rescuing a ship." Kissinger, *Years of Renewal*, 575 (the crisis is analyzed on pages 547–575).

Chapter 18

1   Memcon: Kissinger, Huang Chen, et al., May 9, 1975, box 331, Lord Files, PPS, RG 59, NA.

2   Memcon: Kissinger, Huang Chen, et al., May 29, 1975, box 332, Lord Files, PPS, RG 59, NA.

3   On the Portuguese revolution, see Garthoff, *Détente and Confrontation*, 538–539; Arthur Jay Klinghoffer, *The Angolan War: A Study in Soviet Policy in the Third World* (Boulder, CO: Westview, 1980), chapters 1–3; Gleijeses, *Conflicting Missions*, 230–232; Hans Binnendijk, *Authoritarian Regimes in Transition* (Washington, DC: Foreign Service Institute, 1987); Peter Rodman, *More Precious Than Peace: The Cold War and the Struggle for the Third World* (New York: Scribners, 1994). Guinea-Bissau, Mozambique, and Cape Verde all became formally independent between September 1974 and July 1975. See also Kissinger, *Years of Renewal*, 629–630.

4   Kissinger, *Years of Renewal*, 630.

5   See Garthoff, *Détente and Confrontation*, 537–542. Kissinger's concerns elucidated in *Years of Renewal*, 626–634.

6   In fact, Kissinger justified the additional aid package in October 1975 as necessary for the resettlement of refugees from Angola.

7   Memcon: Ford, Suharto, Scowcroft, Kissinger (who joined at the very end of the conversation), July 5, 1975, box 13, NSC, Memoranda of Conversations, 1973–77, GFL. For more documents and a background essay on East Timor, see www.gwu.edu/%7Ensarchiv/NSAEBB/NSAEBB62/

8   For good discussions on East Timor, see Benedict R. Andersen, "East Timor and Indonesia: Some Implications," in *East Timor at the Crossroads: The Forging of a Nation*, ed. Peter Carey and G. Carter Bentley (Honolulu: University of Hawaii Press, 1995), 138–140; Adam Schwarz, *A Nation in Waiting: Indonesia's Search for Stability* (Boulder: Westview Press, 2000), 198–204. See also Theodore Friend, *Indonesian Destinies* (Cambridge, MA: Belknap Press, 2003).

9   Telegram from Jakarta Embassy to State Department, December 6, 1975, Country File, Far East-Indonesia, State Department Telegrams 4/1/75–9/22/76, GFL.

10   Kissinger to Ford, November 21, 1975, www.gwu.edu/%7Ensarchiv/NSAEBB/NSAEBB62/

11   In 2001 the green light to Suharto reemerged as one of the charges in Hitchens's *Trial of Henry Kissinger*, 90–107.

12   Klinghoffer, *Angolan War*, 9–14; Garthoff, *Détente and Confrontation*, 557–558; Gleijeses, *Conflicting Missions*, 235–242; John Marcum, *The Angolan Revolution*. vol. 2: *Exile Politics and Guerilla Warfare, 1962–1976* (Cambridge, MA: MIT Press, 1978), 194–202. For a very brief summary of the movements, see Isaacson, *Kissinger*, 675.

13   Carlucci to Kissinger, March 28, 1975, "Portugal (4)," NSC Country Files for Europe and Canada, box 10, GFL; Gleijeses, *Conflicting Missions*, 283–284. On U.S. policy, see also George Wright, *U.S. Policy Towards Angola: The Kissinger Years, 1974–1976* (Leeds: University of Leeds, 1990).

14   See Westad, "Moscow and the Angolan Crisis, 1974–1976: A New Pattern of Intervention," *CWIHP Bulletin* 8–9 (Winter 1996–97): 21–37.

15   CPSU CC Report: "About the Status of Soviet-Chinese Relations," February 12, 1971, in *CWIHP Bulletin* 6–7 (Winter 1995–96): 199–201.

16   Excerpts from Mao's talks with Kaunda, February 22, 1974. Cited in Barnouin and Yu, *Chinese Foreign Policy During the Cultural Revolution*, 153.

17   Garthoff, *Détente and Confrontation*, 560.

18   Ibid., 564–567; Westad, "New Pattern"; Gleijeses, *Conflicting Missions*, 246–272.

19   Cited in Gleijeses, *Conflicting Missions*, 284.

20   Ibid., 285. See also Kissinger's account of the meeting in Kissinger, *Years of Renewal*, 791–797.

21   On Chinese aid and involvement, see Klinghoffer, *Angolan War*, 101–108.

22   Edward Mulcahy to Kissinger (via Sisco), May 13, 1975, box 368, Lord Files, PPS, RG 59, NA; Gleijeses, *Conflicting Missions*, 285. The Church Committee and the intelligence investigations are described in the following chapter.

23   NSSM 224, May 26, 1975, box 2, NSSMs, NSC, GFL; Kissinger, *Years of Renewal*, 796–807.

24   Memcon: Kissinger, Huang Chen, et al., May 29, 1975, box 332, Lord Files, PPS, RG 59, NA.

25 Kissinger, *Years of Renewal*, 796–807; Nathaniel Davis, "The Angola Decision of 1975: A Personal Memoire," *Foreign Affairs* 57 (Fall 1978): 112; Garthoff, *Détente and Confrontation*, 563; Gleijeses, *Conflicting Missions*, 286–287.

26 Kissinger, *Years of Renewal*, 800–801, 806.

27 Gleijeses, *Conflicting Missions*, 286–289.

28 "DCI Briefing: Angola," NSC Meeting June 27, 1975, box 2, NSC Meeting Minutes, GFL.

29 Kissinger to Ford, June 26, 1975, box 2, NSC Meeting Minutes, GFL.

30 See Gleijeses, *Conflicting Missions*, 347–351.

31 NSC meeting minutes, June 27, 1975, box 2, NSC Meeting Minutes, GFL; Kissinger's talking points in "Africa—General (1)," box 1, Presidential Country Files for Africa, 1974–77, NSC, GFL.

32 Garthoff, *Détente and Confrontation*, 564–565; Greene, *Presidency of Gerald R. Ford*, 113–115; Kissinger, *Years of Renewal*, 807–809.

33 Memcon: Ford, Kissinger, Scowcroft, October 16, 1975, box 16, NSC Memcons, 1973–77, GFL. Caxito is located about sixty miles northeast of Luanda.

34 Garthoff, *Détente and Confrontation*, 564–567; Greene, *Presidency of Gerald R. Ford*, 113–114; John Stockwell, *In Search of Enemies: A CIA Story* (New York: W.W. Norton, 1978); Gleijeses, *Conflicting Missions*, 312–321.

35 Gleijeses, *Conflicting Missions*, 304–308, 347–352.

36 Kissinger, *Years of Renewal*, 815.

37 Gleijeses, *Conflicting Missions*, 238–239, 242–243; Garthoff, *Détente and Confrontation*, 569–571. Mao cited in Barnouin and Changgen, *Chinese Foreign Policy During the Cultural Revolution*, 153.

38 Memcon: Kissinger, Ch'iao Kuan-hua, et al., September 28, 1975, box 332, Lord Files, PPS, RG 59, NA.

39 Excerpts from these meetings in *Kissinger Transcripts*, 383–385.

40 Garthoff, *Détente and Confrontation*, 577–578; Dobrynin, *In Confidence*, 360–362; Kissinger, *Years of Renewal*, 818–825.

41 Kissinger, *Years of Renewal*, 826.

42 Memcon: Ford, Mao, Kissinger, et al., December 2, 1975 in *Kissinger Transcripts*, 402. See also Kissinger, *Years of Renewal*, 892; and Tyler, *Great Wall*, 215–219.

43 Memcon: Ford, Deng, Kissinger, et al., December 3, 1975, box 373, Lord Files, PPS, RG 59, NA.

44 In a conversation with his aides the following summer about the sale of CDC computers to China—computers that were meant for oil exploration but could be used for testing rockets—Kissinger wanted to work out an arrangement that "looks like safeguards," and go about it informally and quietly. He did not, he told Philip Habib and others, want the issue to end up in "Evans and Novak." Memcon: Kissinger, Habib, et al., July 12, 1976, box 332, Lord Files, PPS, Rg 59, NA.

45 Memcon: Ford, Kissinger, Deng, Huang Chen, et al. December 4, 1975, box 373, Lord Files, PPS, RG 59, NA. See Kissinger, *Years of Renewal*, 888–890.

46 On Ford's visit, see Tyler, *Great Wall*, 215–219.

47 Memcon: Kissinger, Ford, Scowcroft, and congressional leaders, December 10, 1975, Memcons 12/10/75, box A1, TPF, NSC, GFL.

48 A more detailed discussion on the intelligence investigations is in the following chapter.

49 Kissinger, *Years of Renewal*, 825–833; Gleijeses, *Conflicting Missions*, 331–332; Garthoff, *Détente and Confrontation*, 570.

50 Garthoff, *Détente and Confrontation*, 577–578, 587–588; Gleijeses, *Conflicting Missions*, 330, 366; Kissinger, *Years of Renewal*, 818–825.

51 Gleijeses, *Conflicting Missions*, 339–346.

52 Kissinger, *Years of Renewal*, 825.

53 See Gleijeses, *Conflicting Missions*, 333–334, 351–362.

54 Memcon: Brezhnev, Kissinger, et al., January 21, 1976, in *Kissinger Transcripts*, 438–441.

55 Memcon: Brezhnev, Kissinger, Gromyko, et al., January 22, 1976, *Kissinger Transcripts*, 453–455.

56 Memcon: Kissinger, Gromyko, et al., January 23, 1976, *Kissinger Transcripts*, 460–464.

57   See Jussi M. Hanhimäki, "Ironies and Turning Points: Détente in Perspective," in *Reviewing the Cold War: Approaches, Interpretations, Theory*, ed. by Odd Arne Westad (London: Frank Cass, 2000), 330–334; Westad, "New Pattern"; Garthoff, *Détente and Confrontation*, 582–588.

58   The war after November 11, 1975, is discussed in great detail in Gleijeses, *Conflicting Missions*, chapters 14–15.

59   Isaacson, *Kissinger*, 684.

60   See ibid., 688–692.

61   Minutes of NSC meeting, May 11, 1976, box 2, NSC Meeting Minutes, GFL. See also Gleijeses, *Conflicting Missions*, 390.

62   Cited in Westad, "Moscow and the Angolan Crisis," 21.

63   Citations in Garthoff, *Détente and Confrontation*, 580–581.

64   NSC meeting, December 17, 1975, box 2, NSC Meeting Minutes, GFL.

65   Isaacson, *Kissinger*, 685.

Chapter 19

1   For an account of the political costs of the Halloween Massacre, see Greene, *Presidency of Gerald R. Ford*, 158–162. For Ford's explanation of these changes and a heated exchange with Schlesinger, see Ford, *Time to Heal*, 323–332. Kissinger describes the Halloween Massacre from his perspective in *Years of Renewal*, 834–844. At the time the shake-up, particularly the firing of Schlesinger, was mistakenly interpreted as a boost to Kissinger's powers.

2   Ford, *Time to Heal*, 30.

3   Robert Teeter and Stuart Spencer to Richard Cheney, November 12, 1975, "Theme Speeches," box 5, James Reichley Files, GFL.

4   Memcon: Ford, Kissinger, Rumsfeld, Scowcroft, Bush, Ikle, March 18, 1976; Memcon: GF, HAK, Rumsfeld, BS, Cheney, April 15, 1976, both in box 18, Memoranda of Conversations, 1973–77, NSC, GFL.

5   The "McGovernite Congress" appears repeatedly in Kissinger, *Years of Renewal*. Citation in Kissinger's foreword to Richard Helms with William Hood, *Look Over My Shoulder*, xi.

6   Memcon: Ford, Kissinger, and Scowcroft, January 4, 1975, box 8, NSC Memoranda of Conversations, 1973–77, GFL.

7   This and the following paragraphs are based on Greene, *Presidency of Gerald R. Ford*, 102–103; Prados, *Lost Crusader*, 292–296; Cahn, *Killing Détente*, 78–81.

8   Memcon: Ford, Kissinger, Scowcroft, et al., January 4, 1975, box 8, Memoranda of Conversations, 1973–77, NSC, GFL. See Kissinger, *Years of Renewal*, 310.

9   For an analysis of the effectiveness of the Blue Ribbon Committee, see Kenneth Kitts, "Commission Politics and National Security: Gerald Ford's Response to the CIA Controversy of 1975," *Presidential Quarterly* 26, no. 4 (Fall 1996): 1081–1098; Cahn, *Killing Détente*; Greene, *Presidency of Gerald R. Ford*, 107–109. The so-called Pike Committee in the House of Representatives conducted its own investigation in 1975–76.

10   Memcon: Ford, Kissinger, Scowcroft, et al., January 4, 1975, box 8, Memoranda of Conversations, 1973–77, NSC, GFL.

11   Minutes of NSC meeting, May 15, 1975, box 1, NSC Meetings, GFL.

12   Memcon: Ford, Kissinger, Schlesinger, Rumsfeld, Scowcroft, et al., October 13, 1975, box 16, Memoranda of Conversations, 1973–77, NSC, GFL.

13   Hersh went after Kissinger in numerous articles that appeared in the *New York Times* before publishing the best-selling "anti-memoirs" in 1983: Hersh, *Price of Power*; Christopher Hitchens, *The Trial of Henry Kissinger*.

14   For a detailed account of Kissinger's role, see Jussi M. Hanhimäki, "'They Can Write it in Swahili': Kissinger, the Soviets, and the Helsinki Accords, 1973–1975." *Journal of Transatlantic Studies* 1, no. 1 (Spring 2003): 37–58.

15   Cahn, *Killing Détente*, 32–33.

16   Greene, *Presidency of Gerald R. Ford*, 151–152; Isaacson, *Kissinger*, 657–658.

17   "Building an Enduring Foreign Policy," address by Secretary of State Kissinger in Detroit, November 24, 1975, *Department of State Bulletin* (December 15, 1975), 848–849.

18 "The Moral Foundations of Foreign Policy," address by Secretary of State Kissinger, July 15, 1975, *Department of State Bulletin* (August 4, 1975), 166–167.

19 Kissinger's Press Conference, July 16, 1975, *Department of State Bulletin* (August 4, 1975), 181.

20 Kaufman, *Henry M. Jackson*, 292, 293.

21 Dobrynin, *In Confidence*, 346.

22 Cited in Greene, *Presidency of Gerald R. Ford*, 153; Ford, *Time to Heal*, 305.

23 Cabinet meeting, August 8, 1975, box 14, National Security Adviser, Memoranda of Conversations, GFL. For an analysis of the long-term impact of the CSCE, see Daniel Thomas, *The Helsinki Effect: International Norms, Human Rights and the Demise of Communism* (Princeton, NJ: Princeton University Press, 2001) and Hanhimäki, "Ironies and Turning Points: Détente in Perspective," in *Reviewing the Cold War: Approaches, Interpretations, Theory*, ed. Odd Arne Westad (London: Frank Cass, 2000), 326–342.

24 Reagan in Greene, *Presidency of Gerald R. Ford*, 153.

25 *The Gallup Poll, 1972–1975*, 595.

26 Kaufman, *Henry M. Jackson*, 287–290; Garthoff, *Détente and Confrontation*, 501–504.

27 Garthoff, *Détente and Confrontation*, 500. See Isaacson, *Kissinger*, 628.

28 NSC meeting, January 29, 1975, box 1, NSC Meeting Minutes, GFL.

29 NSC meeting, March 5, 1975, box 1, NSC Meeting Minutes, GFL.

30 NSC meeting, July 25, 1975, box 1, NSC Meeting Minutes, GFL.

31 Memcon: Ford, Brezhnev, Kissinger, Gromyko, et al., August 2, 1975, "USSR July 30–August 2, 1975: Ford/Brezhnev Meetings in Helsinki," box A1, TPF, NSC, GFL.

32 See Garthoff, *Détente and Confrontation*, 501–503; Dobrynin, *In Confidence*, 349–350.

33 Dobrynin, *In Confidence*, 351.

34 Cited in Kissinger, *Years of Renewal*, 1115.

35 Memcon: Brezhnev, Kissinger, et al., January 22, 1976, *Kissinger Transcripts*, 451.

36 See Garyhoff, *Détente and Confrontation*, 599–606; Hyland, *Mortal Rivals*, 162; Burr, *Kissinger Transcripts*, 469–470.

37 *The Gallup Poll, 1972–1975*, 601, 606–607. Henry Jackson's campaign was faltering, while Jimmy Carter hardly registered in late 1975 (52 percent of those interviewed said they "knew too little about him to judge"). Ibid., 598.

38 Robert Teeter to Richard Cheney, December 24, 1975, "Memoranda and Polling Data— Teeter (3)," box 4, Foster Chanock Files, GFL.

39 Greene, *Presidency of Gerald R. Ford*, 162–164; Isaacson, *Kissinger*, 693–694.

40 Memcon: Ford, Kissinger, Rumsfeld, Scowcroft, March 29, 1976, box 18, Memoranda of Conversations, 1973–77, NSC, GFL; Isaacson, *Kissinger*; 695–697; Kissinger, *Years of Renewal*, 862–866; Schulzinger, *Henry Kissinger*, 228–229.

41 Bruce Wagner to Rogers Morton, April 7, 1976, "DeBolt Subject File—Advertising," box A11, President Ford Committee Records, GFL.

42 Memcon: Ford, Kissinger, Rumsfeld, Scowcroft, Cheney, April 15, 1976, Memoranda of Conversations, 1973–77, NSC, GFL.

43 Memcon: Ford, Kissinger, Scowcroft, March 19, 1976, box 17, Memoranda of Conversations, 1973–77, NSC, GFL.

44 Isaacson, *Kissinger*, 688. For Kissinger's account, see *Years of Renewal*, 958–1016.

45 Greene, *Presidency of Gerald R. Ford*, 166–168.

46 Ambrose, *Nixon: Ruin and Recovery*, 489–493; Tyler, *Great Wall*, 220.

47 Memcon: Ford, Kissinger, Thomas S. Gates, Scowcroft, March 19, 1976, *Kissinger Transcripts*, 406.

48 The 1976 Republican Platform can be found at the Ford library's web site: www.ford.utexas.edu/library/document/platform/platform.htm

49 Cited in *Kissinger Transcripts*, 408.

50 Ford's acceptance speech: www.ford.utexas.edu/library/document/platform/platform.htm

51 Memcon: Ford, Kissinger, Scowcroft, August 30, 1976, box 20, Memoranda of Conversations, 1973–77, NSC, GFL.

52 *The Gallup Poll, 1976–1977*, 815, 851.

53   On Carter and his quest for the presidency: Burton I. Kaufman, *The Presidency of James Earl Carter* (Lawrence: University Press of Kansas, 1993); Kenneth E. Morris, *Jimmy Carter, American Moralist* (Athens: University of Georgia Press, 1996); Jules Witcover, *Marathon: The Pursuit of the Presidency, 1972–1976* (New York: Viking Press, 1977), 229–258. See also essays in Gary M. Fink and Hugh Davis Graham, eds., *The Carter Presidency: Policy Choices in the Post-New Deal Era* (Lawrence: University of Kansas Press, 2001).

54   Greene, *Presidency of Gerald R. Ford*, 175–176.

55   Ibid.; Isaacson, *Kissinger*, 699–701; Schulzinger, *Henry Kissinger*, 230–232.

56   Henry Keys memo, October 1976, "Second Debate: Henry Kissinger as an Issue," box 2, White House Staff Secretary, Special Files, GFL.

57   Isaacson, *Kissinger*, 700–703; Greene, *Presidency of Gerald R. Ford*, 185–187; Witcover, *Marathon*, 598–608; Ford, *Time to Heal*, 422; Hartmann, *Palace Politics*, 412–414. Mike Duval to Ford, October 18, 1976, "Debate Preparation," box 25, Michael Raoul-Duval Papers, GFL.

58   "Secretary Kissinger's News Conference at Hartford, Connecticut," October 27, 1976, *Department of State Bulletin*, vol. 75, no. 1952, 640–647.

59   The text of the interview can be found in *Department of State Bulletin* 76 (February 7, 1977): 102–107.

60   *The Gallup Poll, 1976–1977*, 893.

Chapter 20

1   "Kissinger to Lead 9/11 Panel," *Washington Post*, November 28, 2002, A1, A40.

2   Isaacson, *Kissinger*, 716–726.

3   *New York Times*, November 13, 1979, II, 8:2.

4   Isaacson, *Kissinger*, 706–711. James Reston in *New York Times*, October 28, 1979, IV, 19:1; William Safire in *New York Times*, November 29, 1979, 27:1, *White House Years* and *Years of Upheaval* were both published by Little, Brown; *Years of Renewal*—as all of Kissinger's books since the early 1990s—by Simon & Schuster.

5   For Haig's account of his time as secretary of state, see Alexander M. Haig Jr., *Caveat: Realism, Reagan, and Foreign Policy* (New York: Macmillan, 1984).

6   On these, see Isaacson, *Kissinger*, 715–716. On U.S.-Iranian relations, see Mark J. Gasiorowski, *U.S. Foreign Policy and the Shah: Building a Client State in Iran* (Ithaca: Cornell University Press, 1991); and James A. Bill, *The Eagle and the Lion: The Tragedy of American-Iranian Relations* (New Haven: Yale University Press, 1989).

7   Details of the Kissinger Commission in www.uscubacommission.org/htm/kisscom.htm. See also Isaacson, *Kissinger*, 724–726; and George P. Shultz, *Turmoil and Triumph: Diplomacy, Power, and the Victory of the American Ideal* (New York: Simon & Schuster, 1993), 403–404.

8   Kissinger, "Reversing Yalta," *Washington Post*, April 16, 1989; Isaacson, *Kissinger*, 727–729; Michael R. Beschloss and Strobe Talbott, *At the Highest Levels: The Inside Story of the End of the Cold War* (Boston: Little, Brown, 1993), 13–17; Raymond Garthoff, *The Great Transition: American-Soviet Relations and the End of the Cold War* (Washington, DC: Brookings, 1994), 376–377; James A. Baker III, *The Politics of Diplomacy: Revolution, War & Peace, 1989–1992* (New York: Putnam, 1995), 39–40; George H. W. Bush and Brent Scowcroft, *A World Transformed* (New York: Knopf, 1998), 25–28.

9   Cited in Isaacson, *Kissinger*, 748.

10   Baker, *Politics of Diplomacy*, 114. On the Eagleburger–Scowcroft trip and U.S reaction to Tiananmen Square, see Bush and Scowcroft, *World Transformed*, 105–111; Tyler, *Great Wall*, 343–379; Foot, *Practice of Power*, 246–253; and, in particular, Mann, *About Face*, 194–225.

11   Mann, *About Face*, 52.

12   Nigel Farndale, "Regarding Henry," *The Jerusalem Post*, February 12, 1999.

13   For an accounting of Kissinger Associates, see elitewatch.netfirms.com/Kissinger_Associates.html (hereafter elitewatch).

14   Leslie Gelb, *New York Times Magazine*, April 20, 1986; "The Big Business of Being Henry Kissinger," *Business Week*, December 2, 1985, 76; Rod McQueen, "Universal Contacts Turn Dr. Diplomacy into Dr. Bigbucks," *Financial Post*, April 30, 1990.

15   Cited in "Universal Contacts Turn Dr. Diplomacy into Dr. Bigbucks."

16   "The BCCI Affair: A Report to the Committee on Foreign Relations of the United States Sen-
      ate," by Senator John Kerry and Senator Hank Brown, December 1992, 102d Congress,
      2d Session, Senate, http://www.fas.org/irp/congress/1992_rpt/bcci/ See also elitewatch;
      "Kissinger Gave BCCI Advice," *Boston Globe*, November 11, 1991; "Rogue Bank Cast Its Net
      Worldwide," *Christian Science Monitor*, November 12, 1991; "Kissinger Firm Denies Reports
      of BCCI Link," *New York Times*, November 13, 1991.

17   On the BNL affair: Rep. Henry R. Gonzalez, "Kissinger Associates, BNL, and Iraq," Report
      to the House of Representatives, May 2, 1991, *Congressional Record*, H2762–2765; Alan Fried-
      man and Lionel Barber, "Congressional Inquiry: Kissinger's Firm Linked to BNL," *Financial
      Times*, April 26, 1991.

18   McLarty had served as Clinton's special envoy to the Americas. Bob Donahue, the CEO of
      GlobalNet, commented on his firm's relationship with Kissinger McLarty as follows: "as we
      quickly continue to build our network and customer base in Latin America, Kissinger
      McLarty Associates, with its political savvy and contacts, will help us establish rela-
      tionships and avoid pitfalls as we enter new markets." Cited in elitewatch.netfirms.com/
      Kissinger_Associates.html

19   Jeff Gerth and Sarah Bartlett, "Kissinger and Friends and Revolving Doors," *New York Times*,
      April 30, 1989, 1:1. See also "Kissinger: the Art of the Deal," *Harper's Magazine* (March 2001).

20   Henry Kissinger, "Tribute to Former President Richard M. Nixon," *Vital Speeches of the Day*,
      60: 16 (1994), 484.

21   For example, Kissinger, *Diplomacy*, 704–705.

22   Kissinger, *Years of Renewal*, 13.

23   John Lewis Gaddis, "The Old World Order," *New York Times Book Review*, March 21, 1999.

24   A sample of Kissinger's titles include: "Why We Can't Withdraw from Asia," *Washington Post*,
      June 15, 1993; "Turning a Fairy Tale Into Reality," *Newsweek*, September 27, 1993; "Outrage Is
      Not a Policy," *Newsweek*, November 1, 1997; "New World Disorder," *Newsweek*, May 31, 1999;
      "Our Nearsighted World Vision," *Washington Post*, January 10, 2000.

25   Henry A. Kissinger, *Does America Need a Foreign Policy? Toward a Diplomacy for the 21st* Cen-
      tury (New York: Simon & Schuster, 2001), 286.

26   Thomas Friedman even argues that Kissinger's book "has an audience of one: President
      George W. Bush." Friedman, "How to Run the World in Seven Chapters," *New York Times
      Book Review*, June 17, 2001.

27   Kissinger, *Ending the Vietnam War*. This book is essentially a combination of the Vietnam
      sections in Kissinger's memoirs with a few additional citations from documents. Its publi-
      cation coincided, almost exactly, with the thirty-year anniversary of the Paris Agreements of
      January 1973.

28   Hersh, *Price of Power*, 296.

29   Ibid., 640. Hersh's other publications include *"The Target Is Destroyed": What Really Hap-
      pened to Flight 007 and What America Knew About It* (New York: Random House, 1987); *The
      Samson Option: Israel's Nuclear Arsenal and American Foreign Policy* (New York: Random
      House, 1991); and *The Dark Side of Camelot* (Boston: Little, Brown, 1997).

30   Burr, *Kissinger Transcripts*.

31   Hitchens, *Trial of Henry Kissinger*, xi. For critiques of Hitchens, see Conrad Black, "A Parody
      of Justice: What's Hitchens Got Against Kissinger?" *Ottawa Citizen*, June 3, 2001; Midge
      Decter, "World Class," *National Review*, June 25, 2001; Peter McKenna, "Accusing Finger
      Pointed at Kissinger," *Montreal Gazette*, May 26, 2001. See also Jack F. Matlock Jr., "Read Their
      Lips," *New York Times*, August 12, 2001; Alfred P. Rubin, "Henry Kissinger and Christopher
      Hitchens," *The Times Literary Supplement*, July 19, 2001; Harvey Blume, "Kissinger, In Deed,"
      The American Prospect, July 30, 2001; Warren I. Cohen, "Is This Man Guilty of Crimes Against
      Humanity," *Los Angeles Times*, June 30, 2001; "Oh Henry," *The Economist*, April 19, 2001.

32   Hitchens, *Trial of Henry Kissinger*, 30.

33   Ibid., 100–105.

34   "Manhattan's Milosevic," *The Village Voice*, August 21, 2001. On the ICC, see http://www.un.org/law/icc/index.html.

35   For example: "Pinochet Judge Asks to Question Kissinger," *The Guardian*, April 17, 2002; "Kissinger on Trial," *San Francisco Chronicle*, April 21, 2002; "Kissinger May Face Extradition to Chile," *The Guardian*, June 12, 2002.

36   http://edition.cnn.com/2001/US/09/17/gen.kissinger.cnna/

37   Isaacson, "History Student: Henry Kissinger might just surprise you," *The New Republic* (December 16, 2002), 18; Lee Hamilton interview; Berger cited in *The Guardian*, November 29, 2002, 4.

38   William Safire, "Well, Hello Henry," *New York Times*, December 2, 2002; Fraser Nelson, *The Scotsman*, November 30, 2002.

39   Safire, "Well, Hello Henry," *New York Times*, December 2, 2002, A21; "Kissinger Needs to Prove It," *The Seattle Post-Intelligencer*, December 4, 2002, B6.

40   Cited in *Washington Post*, December 2, 2002, A6.

41   Maureen Dowd, "He's Ba-a-ack!" *New York Times*, December 1, 2002, Section 4, 9; "Kissinger Commission," *New York Times*, November 29, 2002, A38, Column 1 Mary McGrory, "Kissinger for Christmas," *Washington Post*, December 5, 2002, A35; "Kissinger," *Los Angeles Times*, December 3, 2002.

42   Helen Thomas, "Kissinger Unlikely Seeker of 9/11 Truth," *Seattle Post-Intelligencer*, December 8, 2002, G2; Tim Rutton, "Kissinger Kiss-Up," *Los Angeles Times*, December 5, 2002; Molly Ivins, "Kissinger Back at His Game," *Chicago Tribune*, December 12, 2002.

43   Kissinger, *Ending the Vietnam War*; and idem, *Crisis*.

Conclusion

1   Henry Kissinger, *Does America Need a Foreign Policy?*, 286.

2   Leslie H. Gelb and Justine A. Rosenthal, "The Rise of Ethics in Foreign Policy: Reaching a Values Consensus," *Foreign Affairs* (May–June 2003), 7.

Selected Bibliography

This book is heavily based on recently declassified archival materials in the Nixon Presidential Materials Project (particularly in the National Security Council Files), the State Department Files in the U.S. National Archives, and the Gerald R. Ford Library. In addition, the book utilizes several interviews (including Kissinger and such former members of his staff as Brent Scowcroft, Winston Lord, Helmut Sonnenfeldt, William Rogers, Peter Rodman, and Richard Solomon), oral histories, newspaper articles, periodical literature, and web site materials. Of the latter, the most important was unquestionably the National Security Archives web site, which includes excellent document collections for anyone interested in American foreign policy during the Kissinger years. The specific sources used are indicated in the relevant endnotes.

The list below includes a selection of those books that were most helpful for my research. It is not even close to being exhaustive, the numerous articles used in writing this book, for example, have been excluded. Readers interested in more detailed information are advised to check the following essay: Jussi M. Hanhimäki, "'Dr. Kissinger' or 'Mr. Henry'? Kissingerology, Thirty Years and Counting," *Diplomatic History* 27, no. 5 (November 2003): 637–676.

Books by Henry Kissinger
American Foreign Policy. New York: Norton, 1969.
Crisis: An Anatomy of Two Major Foreign Policy Crises. New York: Simon & Schuster, 2003.
Diplomacy. New York: Simon & Schuster, 1994.
Does America Need a Foreign Policy? Toward A Diplomacy for the 21st Century. New York: Simon & Schuster, 2001.
Ending the Vietnam War: A History of America's Involvement in and Extrication from the Vietnam War. New York: Simon & Schuster, 2003.
The Necessity for Choice: Prospects for American Foreign Policy. New York: Harper & Row, 1961.
Nuclear Weapons and Foreign Policy. New York: Harper & Row, 1957.
Observations. London: Michael Joseph Ltd., 1985.
White House Years. Boston: Little, Brown, 1979.
A World Restored: Metternich, Castlereagh, and the Problems of Peace, 1812–22. Boston: Houghton Mifflin, 1957.
Years of Upheaval. Boston: Little. Brown, 1982.
Years of Renewal. New York: Simon & Schuster, 1999.

Memoirs and Diaries
Arbatov, Georgi. *The System: An Insider's Life in Soviet Politics.* With an introduction by Strobe Talbott. New York: Times Books, 1992.
Bahr, Egon. *Zu Meiner Zeit.* Munich: Karl Blessing Verlag, 1996.
Brandt, Willy. *My Life in Politics.* New York: Viking, 1992.
Chennault, Anna. *The Education of Anna.* New York: Times Books, 1980.
Colby, William, with James McCargar. *Lost Victory: A Firsthand Account of America's Sixteen-Year Involvement in Vietnam.* Chicago: Contemporary Books, 1989.
Dobrynin, Anatoly. *In Confidence: Moscow's Ambassador to America's Six Cold War Presidents.* New York: Times Books, 1995.

Ehrlichman, John. *Witness to Power: The Nixon Years*. New York: Pocket Books, 1982.

Ellsberg, Daniel. *Secrets: A Memoir of Vietnam and the Pentagon Papers*. New York: Viking, 2002.

Ford, Gerald R. *A Time to Heal*. New York: Harper & Row, 1979.

Garment, Leonard. *Crazy Rhythm: From Brooklyn and Jazz to Nixon's White House, Watergate, and Beyond*. New York: DeCapo Press, 2001.

Garthoff, Raymond L. *A Journey Through the Cold War: A Memoir of Containment and Coexistence*. Washington, DC: Brookings, 2001.

Gates, Robert M. *From the Shadows: The Ultimate Insider's Story of Five Presidents and How They Won the Cold War*. New York: Simon & Schuster, 1997.

Green, Marshall, John H. Holdridge, and William N. Stokes. *War and Peace with China: First-Hand Experiences in the Foreign Service of the United States*. Bethesda, MD: Dacor Press, 1994.

Haig, Alexander. *Inner Circles*. New York: Warner Books, 1992.

Haldeman, H. R. *The Haldeman Diaries: Inside the Nixon White House*. New York: Berkley Books, 1994.

———. *The Ends of Power*. New York: Times Books, 1978.

Heath, Edward. *The Course of My Life*. London: Hodder and Stoughton, 1998.

Helms, Richard. With William Hood. *A Look Over My Shoulder: A Life in the Central Intelligence Agency*. Foreword by Henry A. Kissinger. New York: Random House, 2003.

Holdridge, John H. *Crossing the Divide*. Lanham, MD: Rowman & Littlefield, 1997.

Li Zhisui. *The Private Life of Chairman Mao*. New York: Random House, 1996.

Loi, Luu Van, and Nguyen Anh Vu. *Le Duc Tho–Kissinger Negotiations in Paris*. Hanoi: The Gioi Publishers, 1995.

Meir, Golda. *My Life*. London: Weidenfeld & Nicolson, 1975.

Nitze, Paul, *From Hiroshima to Glasnost: At the Center of Decision*. New York: Grove Weidenfeld, 1989.

Nixon, Richard. *RN: The Memoirs of Richard Nixon*. New York: Grosset & Dunlap, 1978.

Sadat, Anwar. *In Search of Identity: An Autobiography*. New York: Harper & Row, 1977.

Safire, William. *Before the Fall: An Inside View of the Pre-Watergate White House*. New York: Doubleday, 1975.

Walters, Vernon A. *Silent Missions*. New York: Doubleday, 1978.

Zhisui, Li. *The Private Life of Chairman Mao*. New York: Random House, 1994.

Zumwalt, Elmo R., Jr. *On Watch: A Memoir*. New York: Quadrangle, 1976.

Books

Aijazuddin, F. S. *From a Head, Through a Head, to a Head: The Secret Channel between the U.S. and China Through Pakistan*. Karachi: Oxford University Press, 2000.

———, ed. *The White House and Pakistan: Secret Declassified Documents, 1969–1974*. Karachi: Oxford University Press, 2002.

Ambrose, Stephen. *Nixon: The Triumph of a Politician, 1962–1972*. New York: Simon & Schuster, 1989.

———. *Nixon: Ruin and Recovery*. New York: Simon & Schuster, 1992.

Andrew, Christopher. *For the President's Eyes Only: Secret Intelligence and the American Presidency from Washington to Bush*. New York: HarperCollins, 1995.

Andrianopoulos, Gerry A. *Kissinger and Brzezinski: The NSC and the Struggle for Control of U.S. National Security Policy*. London: Macmillan, 1991.

Asselin, Pierre. *A Bitter Peace: Washington, Hanoi, and the Making of the Paris Agreement*. Chapel Hill: University of North Carolina Press, 2002.

Barnouin, Barbara, and Yu Changgen. *Ten Years of Turbulence: The Chinese Cultural Revolution*. London: Kegan Paul International, 1993.

———. *Chinese Foreign Policy During the Cultural Revolution*. New York: Kegan Paul International, 1998.

Bell, Coral. *The Diplomacy of Détente: The Kissinger Era*. New York: St. Martin's, 1977.

Berman, Larry. *No Honor, No Peace: Nixon, Kissinger, and Betrayal in Vietnam*. New York: Free Press, 2001.

Brigham, Robert K. *Guerrilla Diplomacy: The NLF's Foreign Relations and the Vietnam War*. Ithaca, NY: Cornell University Press, 1999.

Bundy, William. *A Tangled Web: The Making of Foreign Policy in the Nixon Presidency.* New York: Hill & Wang, 1998.

Burr, William, ed. *The Kissinger Transcripts: The Top Secret Talks with Beijing and Moscow.* New York: The New Press, 1999.

Cahn, Anne Hessing. *Killing Détente: The Right Attacks the CIA.* University Park: Pennsylvania State University Press, 1998.

Castle, Timothy N. *At War in the Shadow of Vietnam: U.S. Military Aid to the Royal Lao Government, 1955–1975.* New York: Columbia University Press, 1993.

Chang, Gordon. *Friends and Enemies: The United States, China and the Soviet Union, 1948–1972.* Stanford: Stanford University Press, 1990.

Chen Jian. *Mao's China and the Cold War.* Chapel Hill, NC: University of North Carolina Press, 2002.

Costigliola, Frank. *France and the United States: The Cold Alliance.* New York: Twayne, 1992.

Craig, Gordon, and Francis Loewenheim, eds. *The Diplomats, 1939–1979.* Princeton, NJ: Princeton University Press, 1994.

Davis, Nathaniel. *The Last Two Years of Salvador Allende.* Ithaca: Cornell University Press, 1985.

Evans, Richard. *Deng Xiaoping and the Making of Modern China.* New York: Penguin, 1997.

Foot, Rosemary. *The Practice of Power: U.S. Relations with China since 1949.* Oxford: Oxford University Press, 1995.

Fosdick, Dorothy, ed. *Staying the Course: Henry M. Jackson and National Security.* Seattle: University of Washington Press, 1987.

Friend, Theodore. *Indonesian Destinies.* Cambridge, MA: Harvard University Press, 2003.

Gaan, Narottam. *Indira Gandhi and Foreign Policy Making: The Bangladesh Crisis.* New Delhi: Patriot Publishers, 1992.

Gaddis, John. *Strategies of Containment: A Critical Appraisal of Postwar American National Security Policy.* New York: Oxford University Press, 1982.

Gaiduk, Iliya. *The Soviet Union and the Vietnam War.* Chicago: Ivan R. Dee, 1996.

Garthoff, Raymond. *Détente and Confrontation: American Soviet Relations from Nixon to Reagan.* 2nd ed. Washington, DC: Brookings, 1994.

Gilks, Anne. *The Breakdown of the Sino-Vietnamese Alliance, 1970–1979.* Berkeley: Institute of East Asian Studies, 1992.

Gleijeses, Piero. *Conflicting Missions: Havana, Washington, and Africa, 1959–1976.* Chapel Hill: University of North Carolina Press, 2002.

Golan, Galia. *Soviet Policies in the Middle East from World War II to Gorbachev.* New York: Cambridge University Press, 1990.

Golan, Matti. *The Secret Conversations of Henry Kissinger.* New York: Bantam, 1976.

Graubard, Stephen R. *Kissinger: Portrait of a Mind.* New York: Norton, 1974.

Greene, John Robert. *The Presidency of Gerald R. Ford.* Lawrence: University of Kansas Press, 1995.

———. *The Limits of Power: The Nixon and Ford Administrations.* Bloomington: Indiana University Press, 1992.

Hersh, Seymour. *The Price of Power: Kissinger in the Nixon White House.* New York: Summit Books, 1983.

Hitchens, Christopher. *The Trial of Henry Kissinger.* London: Verso, 2001.

Hoff, Joan. *Nixon Reconsidered.* New York: Basic Books, 1994.

Hung, Nguyen Tien, and Jerold L. Scheter. *The Palace File.* New York: HarperCollins, 1986.

Hyland, William G. *Mortal Rivals: Superpower Relations from Nixon to Reagan.* New York: Random House, 1987.

Isaacs, Arnold. *Without Honor: Defeat in Vietnam and Cambodia.* Baltimore: Johns Hopkins University Press, 1983.

Isaacson, Walter. *Kissinger.* New York: Simon & Schuster, 1992.

Kalb, Marvin, and Bernard Kalb. *Kissinger.* Boston: Little, Brown, 1974.

Kaufman, Robert G. *Henry M. Jackson: A Life in Politics.* Seattle: University of Washington Press, 2000.

Keith, Ronald C. *The Diplomacy of Zhou Enlai.* London: Macmillan, 1989.

Kimball, Jeffrey. *Nixon's Vietnam War.* Lawrence: University Press of Kansas, 1998.

———, ed. *The Vietnam War Files: Uncovering the Secret History of Nixon-Era Strategy*. Lawrence: University of Kansas Press, 2003.

Kornbluh, Peter, ed. *The Pinochet File: A Declassified Dossier on Atrocity and Accountability*. New York: The New Press, 2003.

Kutler, Stanley I., ed. *Abuse of Power: The New Nixon Tapes*. New York: Free Press, 1997.

Kutler, Stanley I. *The Wars of Watergate*. New York: Norton, 1990.

Kux, Dennis. *India and the United States: Estranged Democracies, 1941–1991*. Washington, DC: National Defense University Press, 1993.

———. *The United States and Pakistan, 1947–2000*. Baltimore: Johns Hopkins University Press, 2001.

Landau, David. *Kissinger: The Uses of Power*. Boston: Houghton Mifflin, 1972.

Lankford, Nelson D. *The Last American Aristocrat: The Biography of Ambassador David K.E. Bruce*. New York: Little, Brown, 1996.

Litwak, Robert S. *Détente and the Nixon Doctrine: Foreign Policy and the Pursuit of Stability*. Cambridge: Cambridge University Press, 1984.

Mann, James. *About Face: A History of America's Curious Relationship with China, from Nixon to Clinton*. New York: Vintage, 1998.

Maresca, John. *To Helsinki: The Conference on Security and Cooperation in Europe, 1973–1975*. Durham, NC: Duke University Press, 1985.

Mazlish, Bruce. *Kissinger: The European Mind in American Policy*. New York: Basic Books, 1976.

Mayall, James and Cornelia Navari, eds. *The End of the Post-War Era: Documents on Great-Power Relations, 1968–1975*. Cambridge, UK: Cambridge University Press, 1980.

Morris, Roger. *Uncertain Greatness: Henry Kissinger and American Foreign Policy*. New York: Harper & Row, 1977.

Morris, Stephen. *Why Vietnam Invaded Cambodia: Political Culture and the Causes of War*. Stanford: Stanford University Press, 1999.

Nelson, Keith L. *The Making of Détente: Soviet-American Relations in the Shadow of Vietnam*. Baltimore: Johns Hopkins University Press, 1995.

Olson, Keith W. *Watergate: The Presidential Scandal That Shook America*. Lawrence: University of Kansas Press, 2003.

Ouimet, Matthew J. *The Rise and Fall of the Brezhnev Doctrine in Soviet Foreign Policy*. Chapel Hill: University of North Carolina Press, 2003.

Prados, John. *Keepers of the Keys: A History of the National Security Council from Truman to Bush*. New York: Morrow, 1991.

———. *Lost Crusader: The Secret Wars of CIA Director William Colby*. New York: Oxford University Press, 2003.

Quandt, William B. *Peace Process: American Policy Toward the Arab-Israeli Conflict*. Berkeley: University of California Press, 1984.

Raza, Rafi. *Zufikar Ali Bhutto and Pakistan 1967–1977*. Karachi: Oxford University Press, 1997.

Reeves, Richard. *President Nixon: Alone in the White House*. New York: Touchstone, 2001.

Rubin, Barry, and Judith Colp Rubin. *Arafat: A Political Biography*. New York: Oxford University Press, 2003.

Schaffer, Harold B. *Ellsworth Bunker: Global Troubleshooter, Vietnam Hawk*. Chapel Hill: University of North Carolina Press, 2003.

Schulzinger, Robert D. *Henry Kissinger: Doctor of Diplomacy*. New York: Columbia University Press, 1989.

———. *A Time for War: The United States and Vietnam, 1941–1975*. New York: Oxford University Press, 1997.

Shao, Kuo-kang. *Zhou Enlai and the Foundations of Chinese Foreign Policy*. New York: St. Martin's Press, 1996.

Shawcross, William. *Sideshow: Kissinger, Nixon, and the Destruction of Cambodia*. New York: Simon & Schuster, 1979.

Sigmund, Paul E. *The United States and Democracy in Chile*. Baltimore: Johns Hopkins University Press, 1993.

Sisson, Richard, and Leo E. Rose. *War and Secession: Pakistan, India, and the Creation of Bangladesh.* Berkeley: University of California Press, 1990.

Small, Melvin. *Covering Dissent: The Media and the Anti-Vietnam War Movement.* New Brunswick, NJ: Rutgers University Press, 1994.

———. *Johnson, Nixon, and the Doves.* New Brunswick, NJ: Rutgers University Press, 1988.

———. *The Presidency of Richard Nixon.* Lawrence: University of Kansas Press, 1999.

Smith, Gerard C. *Doubletalk: The Story of the First Strategic Arms Limitation Talks.* Garden City, NY: Doubleday, 1980.

Snepp, Frank. *Decent Interval.* New York: Vintage, 1977.

Stern, Paula. *Water's Edge: Domestic Politics and the Making of American Foreign Policy.* Westport, CT: Greenwood Press, 1979.

Taylor, John G. *East Timor: The Price of Freedom.* London: Zeil Books, 1999.

Teiwes, Frederick C., and Warren Sun. *The Tragedy of Lin Biao.* Honolulu: University of Hawaii Press, 1996. *The Nixon–Kissinger Years: Reshaping America's Foreign Policy.* New York: Paragon House, 1989.

Todd, Olivier. *Cruel April: The Fall of Saigon.* New York: Norton, 1990.

Tucker, Nancy Bernkopf. *China Confidential: American Diplomats and Sino-American Relations, 1945–1996.* New York: Columbia University Press, 2001.

Tyler, Patrick. *A Great Wall: Six Presidents and China: An Investigative History.* New York: Century Foundation, 1999.

Westad, Odd Arne, Chen Jian, Stein Tonnesson, Nguyen Vu Thung, and James G. Hershberg, eds. *77 Conversations between Chinese and Foreign Leaders on the Wars in Indochina, 1964–1977.* Working Paper No. 22, Cold War International History Project, Washington, DC: Woodrow Wilson International Center for Scholars, 1998.

Yergin, Daniel. *The Prize: The Epic Quest for Oil, Money, and Power.* New York: Simon & Schuster, 1991.

Zhai, Qiang. *China and the Vietnam War, 1950–1975.* Chapel Hill: University of North Carolina Press, 2000.

Index